The Meaning of Folklore

Alan Dundes.

Photo by Simon Bronner

The Meaning of Folklore

The Analytical Essays of
Alan Dundes

Edited and Introduced by
Simon J. Bronner

Utah State University Press
Logan, Utah

© 2007 by University Press of Colorado

Published by Utah State University Press
An imprint of University Press of Colorado
245 Century Circle, Suite 202
Louisville, Colorado 80027

The University Press of Colorado is a proud member of
the Association of University Presses.

The University Press of Colorado is a cooperative publishing enterprise supported, in part, by Adams State University, Colorado State University, Fort Lewis College, Metropolitan State University of Denver, Regis University, University of Colorado, University of Northern Colorado, University of Wyoming, Utah State University, and Western Colorado University.

ISBN: 978-0-87421-683-7 (cloth)
ISBN: 978-1-64642-069-8 (paperback)
ISBN: 978-0-87421-684-4 (e-book)

Library of Congress Cataloging-in-Publication Data

Dundes, Alan.
   The meaning of folklore : the analytical essays of Alan Dundes / edited and introduced by Simon J. Bronner.
      p. cm.
   Includes bibliographical references and index.
   ISBN 978-0-87421-683-7 (cloth : alk. paper) — ISBN 978-1-64642-069-8 (pbk : alk. paper) — ISBN 978-0-87421-684-4 (ebook)
   1. Folklore. 2. Dundes, Alan. I. Bronner, Simon J. II. Title.
   GR71.D88 2007
   398.2—dc22

                              2007033333

CONTENTS

Preface to the Paperback Edition

Simon J. Bronner

ALAN DUNDES WAS ARGUABLY THE most globally renowned and influential folklorist of the twentieth century. Preparing *The Meaning of Folklore* early in the twenty-first century, I had to wonder if his ideas, his theories, and indeed his spirit would still resonate into the new millennium and whether new directions in folkloristics would depart from, or be inspired by, his example. That query about the afterlife of the "Lord of Lores," the lofty title that a journalist bestowed upon Alan (McDonald 2014), led me to listen extra attentively at American Folklore Society and Western States Folklore Society annual meetings for retrospectives on his career in addition to citations and applications of his work. I closely read reviews of *Meaning* not only for the response to my selection of, and commentaries on, Dundes's essays, but also for assessments of the lasting impact, and evolution, of his vision for the study of folklore. Valuing oral sources, I gathered Dundesiana from folklorists in casual surroundings (see Bendix 1995; Zumwalt 2013, 2018a). More formally, I scoured reference lists in academic journals and databases to check the number of times he was listed as an authority.

Given the honor of delivering the 2020 Alan Dundes Lecture at the University of California, Berkeley, at the invitation of the Alan Dundes Distinguished Professor of Folklore, I retraced the steps Alan took to his office and archives at the Anthropology Department in Kroeber Hall, to look for material signs of his legacy (Briggs 2020). Beyond noting the obvious onomastic tributes to Alan, I visited the offices of the Berkeley Folklore Archive, which Alan had established as part of what Wolfgang Mieder called the "Mecca of Folklore Studies" for international, comparative cultural analysis (Mieder 2011, 410; see also Zumwalt 2017). Mieder knew firsthand that going to Berkeley meant visiting Alan, and he witnessed Alan seemingly always being at the head of the academic pack. Alan stood out and drew attention wherever he went. His fervid mentoring of students—and colleagues—implied that Alan in death had gained status as an intellectual prophet. And like prophets, he was capable of stirring controversy and attracting doubters. Was his a prophetic "voice calling in the wilderness" (Matthew 3:1–3) or a man of the moment who changed his age? By way of reflecting on this new edition of Alan's writings more than fifteen years after his death, let me report what I found on his "good name" in scholarly and public discourse.

The new edition of *The Meaning of Folklore* three decades into the twenty-first century is manifest evidence that Alan Dundes's influence on theory and method remains not only in folkloristics but across many disciplines concerned with the study of society, arts, and culture. A decade after Dundes's death, the editors of *Theory in Social and Cultural Anthropology* (2014) featured his biography as a major theorist of anthropology with relevance to the latest trends (Bronner 2014), and *SAGE Research Methods* (2019), which claimed to be the largest encyclopedia of social science research ever published, highlighted his biography under the heading of "pioneers" alongside an impressive pantheon of scholarly giants in the twentieth century such as Franz Boas, Michel Foucault, Erving Goffman, and C. Wright Mills (Bronner 2019a). Absorbed as Alan was by the forms and symbolism of folklore, I would guess that he would actually have preferred the original categorization of the honorees as "game changers." He was, with Linda Dégh and Vladimir Propp, one of three folklorists listed and the only one who was born in the Americas. Although his intellectual reach extended to many disciplines and most of his teaching career was in an anthropology department, he remained throughout his life an advocate for thinking of folkloristics as a distinct discipline. Indeed, more than an advocate, he led the charge for the study of folklore wherever he went, and he was invited to speak far and wide.

Many folklorists active in the first quarter of the twenty-first century trace their interest to a transformative moment after meeting him or upon reading his work. Observing a cadre of adherents drawn to Alan, one visiting professor at Berkeley, in awe of his charisma and pronounced sense of mission, declared him "the Pied Piper of Folklore" and another called him "Folklore's Guru" (Mieder 2006, 217; Narayan 2018; see also Bronner 2018). Folklore historian Rosemary Lévy Zumwalt (2020) identified Alan with friendly rivals Richard M. Dorson and Roger Abrahams as among a select group of academic leaders that she dubbed the "Great Team of American Folklorists" during the last third of the twentieth century as each in his own way stared down naysayers. Of the three, though, Alan was the only one inducted into the prestigious American Academy of Arts and Sciences (2001) that gathers scholars at the forefront of all knowledge. Reflecting on the strides made by this "Great Team" devoted to growing folklore studies as a discipline, Zumwalt questioned whether their positions as program and audience builders for folklore would, or could, be repeated in the twenty-first century.

Despite Alan's denial of having ardent "followers" (Hansen 2005, 246), I can personally attest to meeting fervent admirers all over the world who mythologized him (Bronner 2018; Zumwalt 2013). His loyal students (estimated at over 20,000 by Wolfgang Mieder [2011, 410]) fanned out into teaching positions across academe and made his books and articles required reading for new generations of academic movers and shakers. He also had a popular influence, conspicuous during the coronavirus pandemic of 2019–2020 when pundits invoked his name to discuss apparently "sick" humor in response to tragedy (Deutsch 2020) and rumor-mongering evident in Jewish scapegoating (Conspiracy Watch 2020; Topor 2020). Triggered by toilet-paper shortages at the time, Dundes's controversial claims in the 1980s about German national character based upon anxiety over feces, and by extension the question of a cultural personality, drew commentary anew in the European popular press (Maesel 2020; Schmidbauer 2020; see also Bronner 2011a). As Wolfgang Mieder points out, Dundes wrote plainly and profoundly for a wide audience, for he was "an exemplary educator, an innovative scholar, and a humanist whose knowledge is that of a Renaissance person" (2006, 219). Mieder went on to declare that if a Nobel Prize existed for folklore, Alan would be everyone's first choice. Mieder proposed that Alan's search for fundamental, structural concepts of expressive forms that constitute the social and textual basis of folklore and their theoretical implications is modeled in his studies of the proverb, which Alan would reexamine in other more narrative genres. I also see an analytical foundation in his work on belief, related of course to the wisdom of the proverb, as a cognitive concept underlying the urge, indeed the need, to express oneself traditionally and ritually (see Dundes 1961). In this volume I have made the case that besides the interrelated issues

of communicative form and structure, symbolism and groups are additional key components of his overarching framework of folklore as a projective tool humans need as well as
a marker of cultural difference and identity.

If much of Alan's theory centered on the projective function of folklore, his insistence
in numerous lectures on "getting the folk and lore together," as an essay title included in
Meaning suggests, constitutes his main methodological contribution. By that he meant
that textual (and structural components), contextual (group and tradition-bearer), and textural (stylistic-performative) information should all be recorded, and analyzed, together, to
arrive at the meaning of expressive culture. And he cajoled various stripes of academics
that even if they did not identify as folklorists, they should give attention to the evidence
of folklore in material as well as social and oral forms, because it is symbolic material that
often expresses what people have difficulty expressing otherwise, and that ultimately gives
voice to the voiceless. He also had a message of applying this knowledge, often about material that was disturbing, because by knowing the ways that people speak their mind through
the psychological license given in folklore, society could better address issues of injustice
and inequality (Bell 2019; see also the opening paragraph of Dundes's essay in this volume
"The Ritual Murder or Blood Libel Legend"). He railed passionately against the miscon-
ception that folklore constituted error or backwardness and therefore should be eradicated.
He expounded on folklore's critical value to reveal human beliefs and attitudes and pointed
out that folklorists' findings should be essential to community leaders as well as to teachers
(see the opening paragraphs of "Folklore as a Mirror of Culture" in this volume). To make
the study of folklore more socially relevant, he often pleaded with folklorists to be less preoccupied with old collectanea and more with interpreting texts and explaining contemporary, traditionalized human thought and action. In that process he conceptualized folkloristics as a set of tools for unlocking timely puzzles rather than a salvage project of capturing
inert, extinct specimens to lock away (see especially his essay in this volume "The Study of
Folklore in Literature and Culture: Identification and Interpretation").

The need for interpretation in folkloristics is well accepted now but disputes naturally
arise in the discipline about the most appropriate interpretative approach. In the introduction to the first edition, I underscored the point that it is misleading to narrow Alan's
approach solely to psychoanalysis, although he was certainly a leading voice for incorporating, and revising, Freudian perspectives in folkloristics. I viewed Alan's interpretative message as connected more broadly to a view of humans as distinctive symbol-making, social
beings who rely on traditions to express themselves—in joy and anguish—in the frames
or situations of culture (this point especially comes through in "Folklore as a Mirror of
Culture"). In the tradition of folklore as an overarching label for interconnected traditions, Alan, "more than anybody else in folklore studies," according to Wolfgang Mieder,
"knew how to make sense out of incomprehensible or seemingly nonsensical folkloric traditions, from toys to symbols, from folk narratives to myths, from riddles to proverbs, from
art to mass lore, from tradition to innovation, from ethnics slurs to national character,
from belief to worldview" (2011, 411). He made sense of them by treating them as forms
in which the present and past question and sometimes come into conflict with each other.
He approached the panoply of examples as symbolic, cultural reactions of groups to surrounding conditions that often placed psychological, social, and political pressure on people, and he sought to know the sources and motivations for those responses.

Alan did not produce a definitive magnum opus on this theory as much as he sowed
seeds of multiple research projects and hypothesis-testing in his teaching, presentations,

and many essays. He often challenged audiences to understand his interpretations as original proposals that spur further research, and with that in mind, I subjectively selected his most provocative as well as foundational articles. Reviewers of the volume sometimes complained that my commentaries were either too critical or praising; my goal, however, was not to evaluate but rather to expose, and explain, the underlying logic of his propositions and the personal and intellectual backgrounds out of which they grew. Especially important to make this book a living document is to discern directions that future work could take from Alan's central examples and their interpretations.

In conference papers and publications that I perused as part of my ongoing project of the historiography of folklore studies (see Bronner 1987, 1998, 2019b), ideas that can be credited to Alan often go uncited, an indication of his sway on the discipline. For example, the distinction between "emic" and "etic" classification systems is commonplace in folkloristic discourse and have as a source Alan's essay, reproduced in this volume, "From Etic to Emic Units in the Structural Study of Folktales." His conceptualization of the folk group as two or more persons who share a trait in common and use folklore to gain a sense of identity is, I daresay, part of every introductory class on modern folklore. Use of "allomotif" is widespread in structuralist narrative studies, often without recognizing Alan's reasons for proposing the term. Another popular term, "metafolklore," even if not footnoted, owes to Alan's "Metafolklore and Oral Literary Criticism," also in this book. Although "worldview" is not of Alan's coinage, his usage of it being composed of folk ideas based on an understanding of beliefs underlying folk speech is fundamental and conspicuous in the titles of three essays in this volume (see also Dundes 1969; 1989, 83–91. Indeed, the basic modern concept of "context" as an analytical tool can be traced to Alan's analysis of the components of folklore as texture, context, and text (Dundes 1964).

Alan believed that scholarship was a cumulative enterprise and he highly valued bibliography. One indication is the Alan Dundes Folkloristic Collection of 9,000 books donated to the University of Southern California's Libraries Special Collections. It is notable not just for the rare individual titles but for bookshelves that integrate psychology and ethnography with genre studies of folktales, legends, jokes, proverbs, speech, and games, which suggest ultimately a movement toward a folkloristic theory of mind and structuralist inquiry (see Dundes's essays "Structuralism and Folklore" and "On Game Morphology" in this book). Delivering the keynote for the unveiling of the books to the public in 2011, Wolfgang Mieder gushed that the books "are proof and testimony of the work of a world-class folklorist, a book lover through and through, and a bookish philologist unequaled in modern times. This personal collection of books will keep the work and memory of Alan Dundes alive, and it will inspire future generations of folklorists to carry on Alan Dundes' conviction that 'Folklore Matters'!" (Mieder 2011, 416). The declaration, drawing from the title of an early compilation of his essays featuring the relation of folklore to the formation of social identity (Dundes 1989), is conspicuous on a huge poster designed for the introduction of his papers at the Bancroft Library. The poster had multiple images of Alan with the message "Folklore Matters" repeated in red and white, as if to invite a subliminal psychological command to engage folklore research. Speaking to journalists covering the opening, Alan's son and executor of his estate David Dundes reminded the audience that they should look ahead rather than dwell on his past, and his father's famous essay on future orientation came to mind (Dundes 1969). He asserted that his father "didn't want a memorial. He felt his scholarship was his legacy" (quoted in McDonald 2014). Alan's daughter Alison Dundes Renteln, professor of political science, anthropology, public policy, and law at the University of Southern California, reflected that her own teaching and scholarship, for example, was "inspired by [her] father." She continued, "I encourage students to reconsider their tacit assumptions, appreciate different points of view, and empower them to use their research to make the world a better place" (quoted in Bell 2019).

Alan coedited with Alison a two-volume work *Folk Law: Essays in the Theory and Practice of Lex Non Scripta* (1994) and maintained an interest in politics and the law through his life. His father was a lawyer who taught comparative politics in the evening in New York City. An intersection of his studies of humor and politics/law comes through in a number of essays on political humor, such as those about American politicians Gary Hart (1989) and Bill Clinton (1999), and restrictions in the former Soviet bloc (with C. Banc 1986, 1990), some of which were posthumously published in *"The Kushmaker" and Other Essays on Folk Speech and Folk Humor*, edited by Wolfgang Mieder (Dundes 2008). This intersection of topics and processes is evident into the new millennium in the work of Marc Galanter, Professor of Law Emeritus at the University of Wisconsin Law School, who dedicated his book *Lowering the Bar: Lawyer Jokes and Legal Culture* (2006) to Alan and who wrote the foreword to *Cracking Jokes: Studies of Sick Humor Cycles and Stereotypes* (1987), reprinted in 2017.

With much of the attention after Alan's death to his library and personal papers, and his campaign to expand interpretation, his collections and fieldwork might be overlooked, and I probably did not mention them enough in my previous introduction. Certainly the massive Berkeley archives is testament to his pushing students to experience folklore in situ and document the components, and meta-information, of folklore. In "The Study of Folklore and Literature: Identification and Interpretation" in this volume, Alan made a point of using "a fine example of folklore in culture from William Mzechteno, a 74-year-old Prairie Band Potawatomi in Lawrence, Kansas." Showing his sensitivity to the agency of the narrator, Alan recounts the questions about changes that Mzechteno makes to the narrative and his understanding of their symbolic meanings. His more extensive work in the field is most conspicuous in *La Terra in Piazza: An Interpretation of the Palio of Siena* (1975, winner of the Chicago Folklore Prize in 1976), which he coauthored with Alessandro Falassi of the University of Siena. His interest began during summer 1972 spent immersed in Siena and, as occurred with other projects, was sparked by apparent paradoxes of local customs, which he sought to resolve. (A similar inquiry while in Israel sparked the writing of *The Shabbat Elevator and other Sabbath Subterfuges: An Unorthodox Essay on Circumventing Custom and Jewish Character* [2002], and the idea of his often-reprinted essay "The Number Three in American Culture" [1968] was sparked by the birth of his third child, David.)

With Alan's devotion to the success of Berkeley's graduate students, he certainly would be heartened by the establishment of the Alan Dundes Graduate Fellowship Fund at the institution where he taught for forty-three years, in addition to the teaching chair and lecture in his honor (Briggs 2019). A noticeable omission of his name, however, is in American Folklore Society honorifics, probably a sign of a long-standing ambivalence of society leaders, who were sensitive to his outspoken criticism of the organization and the Indiana University home of the society. (Alan's name was proposed as a fitting title for the society's lifetime scholarly achievement award, but the proposal did not move forward; Alan was president of the society in 1980.) A manifestation of this tension was the publication in 2016 of *Grand Theory in Folkloristics*, edited by Lee Haring, following an earlier special issue of the *Journal of Folklore Research* in 2008. It leads with Dundes's 2004 plenary address to the society criticizing current trends of society folklorists (2005), followed by a number of responses. What this sequence epitomized was that even if Alan is gone, he is still leading the debates. Not muted even in death, his voice is front and center into the third decade of the twenty-first century. Eminent sociologist Gary Alan Fine noted in his chapter Alan Dundes's lead in advancing the view that "folkloristics must self-consciously incorporate large-scale, overarching theories of self, society, or narrative, such as those propounded by Freud, Lévi-Strauss, Marx, Propp, or Bakhtin. Dundes tried to move folklore away from its allergy to theory and its preoccupation with the presentation of texts and description of action, remarking on 'the continued lack of innovation in what we might term 'grand theory'" (Fine 2008, 12). For Lee Haring (2008), that allergy was a symptom of anti-theoretical attitudes of American scholars from which Alan departed. Offering a global perspective, Kirin Narayan, one of Alan's former students, added a defense that Alan's projective theory offers "broad applicability and capacity to deliver otherwise hidden insights" (2008, 84).

Charles Briggs in "Disciplining Folkloristics" attributes resistance to Alan's vision for folkloristics because of the narrow characterization of his work as psychoanalysis and argues that "Dundes' difficulties in generating more interest in theory emerges from his persistent efforts to press boundary-work as the sine qua non for discipline-building—or, increasingly, discipline-preservation—strategies for folkloristics" (2008, 95; see also Briggs 2015; Bronner 2019c). That is, Dundes, in the defensive posture of the Great Team of American Folklorists identified by Zumwalt, concentrated on defining and constructing borders between folklore and non-folklore (Briggs 2008, 100). I do not share that view of Alan's legacy. While attentive to the special characteristics, and meaning, of folklore as cultural expression and idea, Alan applied the tools of folkloristics to various topics that others considered popular, and even nonfolkloric, such as photocopied broadsides (1978), toys (1989, 83–91), and American football (1980). To be sure, my argument in *Meaning* was that a reading of Dundes's interpretations revealed more of an innovative post-Freudian thinker rather than a strict adaptation of psychoanalytic premises. Among his papers that have come to light is, in fact, a letter he wrote to psychoanalyst Anna Freud, Sigmund's daughter, in which he introduces himself as "a folklorist whose primary research interest lies in the application of psychoanalytic theory to the materials of folklore" (April 11, 1979). She responded promptly that his arguments were "very persuasive," and "above all," she "was very interested in your description of the difference between fact-finding and interpretation, and work on folklore in the way you outline it seems to me a fascinating task" (May 31, 1979). Alan undoubtedly was overjoyed to read her closing statement that "my father would have been very glad to read your paper [on King Lear]" (Renteln 2020). But I am not so sure Sigmund Freud would have approved of his use of "projective inversion" or emphasis on adolescent development in later psychological interpretations included in Part III of this book.

Indeed, Alan's major contribution to psychology in addition to folkloristics was to revise the Freudian concept of projection and point out the importance of situating symbolic interpretations within cultural contexts rather than presume universal bases of thought. He advanced the move from structural to projective and symbolic concepts for explaining traditionalized or repetitive behavior framed as folkloric (see his provocative reference to framing in "Folklore as a Mirror of Culture"; see also Dundes 2003; Silverman 2016). So influential was Dundes's emphasis on interpretation, according to folklorist Elliott Oring that by the early twenty-first century, "[f]olklorists would take up this injunction with a vengeance. We now publish interpretation after interpretation as we once published text after text" (2019, 144). He gives special praise for Alan's psychological interpretation using comparative data on the cockfight ("Gallus as Phallus," reproduced in this volume) for demonstrating the fallacy of anthropologist Clifford Geertz's localized interpretation based on social structure, which became the basis for many ethnographers' use of "thick description." With that essay Alan threw down a gauntlet for the next generation of scholars to make the next step from interpretation to explanation based upon not only depth psychology but more generally on symbolic and frame analysis (Bronner 2010, 2019c).

Giving Alan more tribute than the American Folklore Society in North America was the Western States Folklore Society, which published a special issue "Dundes Matters," whose title is a variation of Alan's book *Folklore Matters* (1993) (Gürel and Zumwalt 2014; see also Gürel 2005). Composed of essays by Alan's former students, the issue might be most notable for the essays by Stephanie Malia Hom (2014), which identifies a "Dundesian Reading" of the Festival of St. Agatha in eastern Sicily, and by Anthony Bak Buccitelli (2014), who applies the master's ideas on the mass-mediation of folklore (originally presented by Alan for the facsimile machine; see Dundes and Pagter 1978) to digital media (for more of a psychoanalytic reading, see Bronner 2011b). Observing the way that the festival with the central saint figure stirs "up male passions," Hom applies Alan's precepts that such framed events represent broadly an analysis of folklore as a "much-needed outlet for the expression of inner tensions and anxieties that cannot be stated otherwise in socio-cultural milieux" and "one can say and do in folkloric form things otherwise interdicted in everyday life" (Hom 2014, 147). So as not to repeat the Geertzian fallacy of attributing meaning to a single location, she examines, as her mentor would have insisted, comparative examples to venerate St. Agatha in Italy and other venues so as to determine the distinctive meanings that are generated.

Beyond Hom's methodological reflection for twenty-first-century work in folklore, Buccitelli reminds readers of a Dundesian concern for the compatibility of new forms of technology with the production of folklore, imagined as a variable, repeated forms that can be visual (Dundes 1978). Often non-Dundesian readings of folkloric phenomenon, Wolfgang Mieder points out, forget the multiplicity and mediation of folklore (Mieder 2006, 219). The designation of Dundesian analysis carries an irony because of the frequent use in anthropology of a "Boasian reading." Both intellectual "pioneers" Franz Boas and Alan Dundes were known not only for groundbreaking ideas that cut against the grain of prevalent ideas of their time but also for impassioned support of their students. In an analysis that could be called Dundesian, Zumwalt noted the metaphor of "giants" in the way they were characterized by their students and admirers (Zumwalt 2013, 163). Alan's actual height was 71.5 inches, but as the title of Richard A. Reuss's well-known article declared in reference to the awe of many a conference attendee, "That Can't Be Alan Dundes! Alan Dundes Is Taller than That!" (Reuss 1974, 308).

Far beyond his American home, Alan's name resounded loudly in international settings. In 2014, the Institute of Studies of Traditional Literature in the New University of Lisbon, Portugal, organized a conference on the occasion of what would have been Alan's eightieth birthday to continue the global conversation that Alan sparked into the new millennium. Titled "We Are the Folk: Rethinking Folklore in the Twenty-First Century," the conference sought to evaluate the multiplicity of folklore's meanings and "its capacity to integrate interactions between traditional and contemporary expressions and appropriations in particular social, cultural, and historical contexts," according to its organizers (Ermacora 2014). It invoked in its main title Alan's replacement of the evolutionist relegation of folklore to the sole possession of primitive folk as a lower stratum of society with the modernist recognition of folklore as part of everyday behavior and cognition. Speakers took Dundes's cue dramatized many years earlier to reconsider anew folklore as emergent traditions and folkloristics as a modern subject amid rapid technological and social changes in twenty-first-century societies (see Ribeiro 2017).

On another continent, the tribute to Alan was in the form of an oversized two-volume publication titled *Psycho-Cultural Analysis of Folklore: In Memory of Prof. Alan Dundes*, edited by P. Chenna Reddy and M. Sarat Babu (2018b), a dean and professor, respectively, at Telugu University and Rayalaseema University in India. They describe themselves as "disciples" of Alan who they called "a versatile genius" (Reddy and Babu 2018a, x). Alan would have been thrilled because he was especially fascinated with India as a diverse source of world mythology and folktale, and at the same time he was disturbed by the oppression of the caste system and prevalent notions of untouchability. He proudly displayed his book *Two Tales of Crow and Sparrow: A Freudian Folkloristic Essay on Caste and Untouchability* (1997), in which he used the symbolism of folklore and its connections to social historical traditions of toilet training to explain the puzzling, and to him "devastating," caste system. A large proportion of the forty-five participants in the volume edited by Reddy and Babu came from south Asia, but in keeping with the often-repeated Dundesian adage that "folklore is nothing if it is not international" (Zumwalt 2018b, v), an impressive array of writers emanated from almost every continent in the world. The south Asian editors were more sanguine about the potential for psychoanalytic analysis in folklore studies than their American colleagues, and they pointed to a general direction in the years ahead inspired by Alan toward an understanding of mind in the constant generation of, and reliance on, folklore for humans navigating through their many worlds from the self to the family, group, neighborhood, region, nation, and globe.

Going by some quantifiable indicators, Alan's articles according to the Web of Science have been cited 465 times between 2005 and 2019. That is more than any other members of the "Great Team" of American folklorists or the other folklorists designated as "pioneers" by *SAGE Research Methods*. If you go to JSTOR or Project Muse and enter "Alan Dundes" in that same period, you will receive over 1,200 choices. Or if you want to view his popularity on internet sites, a Google search will produce over 17,000 hits in that period, compared to 1,490 before then. So it is safe to say that even if one does not agree with many of Alan's interpretations, his ideas and name circulate widely. His writings continue to stimulate and invite questions—and debate. Each essay is a gem that should be examined closely for the time in which it was produced and its applicability to today's conditions. My hope for the years ahead is that the essays and various postscripts will also be engaged as a whole for their cumulative vision of an innovative intellectual giant. He still speaks to us. More than ever, he inspires—and provokes.

References

Banc, C., and Alan Dundes. 1986. *First Prize: Fifteen Years! An Annotated Collection of Romanian Political Jokes*. Rutherford, NJ: Fairleigh Dickinson University Press.

Banc, C., and Alan Dundes. 1990. *You Call This Living? A Collection of East European Political Jokes*. Athens: University of Georgia Press.

Bell, Alison. 2019. "How Dad Inspired Me: Professors Reflect on Their Fathers' Influence." *USC News*, June 14. https://news.usc.edu/102617/how-dad-inspired-me-professors-reflect-on-their-fathers-influence/. Accessed June 7, 2020.

Bendix, Regina. 1995. "Dundesiana: Teacher and Mentor in Campuslore, Anecdote, and Memorate." In *Folklore Interpreted: Essays in Honor of Alan Dundes*, ed. Regina Bendix and Rosemary Lévy Zumwalt, 49–66. New York: Garland.

Bendix, Regina, and Rosemary Lévy Zumwalt, eds. 1995. *Folklore Interpreted: Essays in Honor of Alan Dundes*. New York: Garland.

Briggs, Charles L. 2008. "Disciplining Folkloristics." *Journal of Folklore Research* 45: 91–105.

Briggs, Charles L. 2015. "Rethinking Psychoanalysis, Poetics, and Performance." *Western Folklore* 74: 245–74.

Briggs, Charles L. 2020. "Toward a Multigenealogical Folkloristics: The Berkeley Experiment." In *Folklore in the United States and Canada: An Institutional History*, ed. Patricia Sawin and Rosemary Lévy Zumwalt, 119–28. Bloomington: Indiana University Press.

Bronner, Simon J. 1987. *American Folklore Studies: An Intellectual History*. Lawrence: University Press of Kansas.

Bronner, Simon J. 1998. *Following Tradition: Folklore in the Discourse of American Culture*. Logan: Utah State University Press.

Bronner, Simon J. 2010. "Framing Folklore: An Introduction." *Western Folklore* 69: 275–97.

Bronner, Simon J. 2011a. "Symbolizing Tradition: On the Scatology of an Ethnic Identity." In *Explaining Traditions: Folk Behavior in Modern Culture*, by Simon J. Bronner, 319–49. Lexington: University Press of Kentucky.

Bronner, Simon J. 2011b. "Virtual Tradition: On the Internet as a Folk System." In *Explaining Traditions: Folk Behavior in Modern Culture*, by Simon J. Bronner, 398–450. Lexington: University Press of Kentucky.

Bronner, Simon J. 2014. "Dundes, Alan." In *Theory in Social and Cultural Anthropology: An Encyclopedia*, ed. R. Jon McGee and Richard L. Warms, 210–14. Los Angeles: SAGE.

Bronner, Simon J. 2018. "From Warrior Prince to Religious Prophet: The Mythologization of Alan Dundes." In *Psycho-Cultural Analysis of Folklore: In Memory of Prof. Alan Dundes*, ed. P. Chenna Reddy and M. Sarat Babu, 69–90. Delhi: B. R. Publishing.

Bronner, Simon J. 2019a. "Dundes, Alan." In *SAGE Research Methods*, ed. Paul Atkinson, Alexandru Cernat, Joseph W. Sakshaug, and Richard A. Williams. London: SAGE. http://dx.doi.org/10.4135/9781526421036745817. Accessed June 6, 2020.

Bronner, Simon J. 2019b. "Folkloristic Practices in a Converging Hyper Era." In *The Practice of Folklore: Essays Toward a Theory of Tradition*, by Simon J. Bronner, 272–96. Jackson: University Press of Mississippi.

Bronner, Simon J. 2019c. *The Practice of Folklore: Essays Toward a Theory of Tradition*. Jackson: University Press of Mississippi.

Conspiracy Watch. 2020. "Covid-19: Le retour du 'Juif empoisonneur.'" https://www.conspiracy-watch.info/covid-19-le-retour-du-juif-empoisonneur.html. Accessed June 6, 2020.

Buccitelli, Anthony Bak. 2014. "Paying to Play: Digital Media, Commercialization, and the Scholarship of Alan Dundes." *Western Folklore* 73: 235–56.

Deutsch, James. 2020. "How to Detect the Age-Old Traditions of Folklore in Today's COVID-19 Misinformation." *Smithsonian Magazine* (April 14). https://www.smithsonianmag.com/smithsonian-institution/how-detect-age-old-traditions-folklore-todays-covid-19-misinformation-180974656/. Accessed June 6, 2020.

Dundes, Alan. 1961. "Brown County Superstitions: The Structure of Superstitions." *Midwest Folklore* 11: 25–56.

Dundes, Alan. 1964. "Texture, Text, and Context." *Southern Folklore Quarterly* 28: 251–65.

Dundes, Alan. 1968. "The Number Three in American Culture." In *Every Man His Way: Readings in Cultural Anthropology*, ed. Alan Dundes, 401–24. Englewood Cliffs, NJ: Prentice-Hall.

Dundes, Alan. 1969. "Thinking Ahead: A Folkloristic Reflection of the Future Orientation in American Worldview." *Anthropological Quarterly* 42: 53–72.

Dundes, Alan. 1978. *Work Hard and You Shall Be Rewarded: Urban Folklore from the Paperwork Empire*. Bloomington: Indiana University Press.

Dundes, Alan. 1980. "Into the Endzone for a Touchdown: A Psychoanalytic Consideration of American Football." In *Interpreting Folklore*, by Alan Dundes, 199–210. Bloomington: Indiana University Press.

Dundes, Alan. 1989. "Six Inches from the Presidency: The Gary Hart Jokes as Public Opinion." *Western Folklore* 48: 43–51.

Dundes, Alan. 1993. *Folklore Matters*. Knoxville: University of Tennessee Press.

Dundes, Alan. 1997. *Two Tales of Crow and Sparrow: A Freudian Folkloristic Essay on Caste and Untouchability*. Lanham, MD: Rowman & Littlefield.

Dundes, Alan. 1999. "The Clinton Joke: Not Over Till the Punchline." *Zyzzyva* 15: 71–78.

Dundes, Alan. 2002. *The Shabbat Elevator and Other Sabbath Subterfuges: An Unorthodox Essay on Circumventing Custom and Jewish Character*. Lanham, MD: Rowman & Littlefield.

Dundes, Alan. 2003. "Better Late than Never: The Case for Psychoanalytic Folkloristics." *Journal of Folklore Research* 40: 95–99.

Dundes, Alan. 2005. "Folkloristics in the Twenty-First Century" (AFS Invited Presidential Plenary Address, 2004). *Journal of American Folklore* 118: 384–408.

Dundes, Alan. 2008. *"The Kushmaker" and Other Essays on Folk Speech and Folk Humor*, ed. Wolfgang Mieder. Burlington: University of Vermont.

Dundes, Alan. 2017 [1987]. *Cracking Jokes: Studies of Sick Humor Cycles and Stereotypes*. New Orleans: Quid Pro Books.

Dundes, Alan, and Alessandro Falassi. 1975. *La Terra in Piazza: An Interpretation of the Palio of Siena*. Berkeley: University of California Press.

Dundes, Alan, and Carl R. Pagter. 1978. *Work Hard and You Shall Be Rewarded: Urban Folklore from the Paperwork Empire*. Bloomington: Indiana University Press.

Ermacora, Davide. 2014. "CFP: We Are the Folk: Rethinking Folklore in the Twenty-First Century" (Lisbon, 22, 23, and 24 October 2014). H-Folk (April 24). https://networks.h-net .org/node/3128/discussions/24280/cfp-we-are-folk-rethinking-folklore-twenty-first-century -lisbon-22. Accessed June 7, 2020.

Fine, Gary Alan. 2008. "The Sweep of Knowledge: The Politics of Grand and Local Theory in Folkloristics." *Journal of Folklore Research* 45: 11–18.

Galanter, Marc. 2006. *Lowering the Bar: Lawyer Jokes and Legal Culture*. Madison: University of Wisconsin Press.

Gürel, Perin. 2005. "Folklore Matters: The Folklore Scholarship of Alan Dundes and the New American Studies." *Columbia Journal of American Studies* 7: 120–35.

Gürel, Perin, and Rosemary Lévy Zumwalt. 2014. "Introduction: Dundes Matters." *Western Folklore* 73: 139–45.

Hansen, William. 2005. "In Memoriam: Alan Dundes, 1934–2005." *Journal of Folklore Research* 42: 245–50.

Haring, Lee. 2008. "America's Antitheoretical Folkloristics." *Journal of Folklore Research* 45: 1–9.

Haring, Lee, ed. 2016. *Grand Theory in Folkloristics*. Bloomington: Indiana University Press.

Hom, Stephanie Malia. 2014. "La Terra in Sicilia: A Dundesian Reading of the Festival of St. Agatha." *Western Folklore* 73: 146–72.

Maesel, Markus. 2020. "Kopapier als Spiegel der deutschen Seele." *Weltgeflüster* (March 28). http://www.weltgefluester.de/index.php/2020/03/28/klopapier-als-spiegel-der-deutschen-seele/. Accessed June 7, 2020.

McDonald, Coby. 2014. "Lord of Lores: Papers of Famed Folklorist Alan Dundes Open to the Public." *California Magazine* (December 10). https://alumni.berkeley.edu/california-magazine /just-in/2016-05-02/lord-lores-papers-famed-folklorist-alan-dundes-open-public. Accessed June 6, 2020.

Mieder, Wolfgang. 2006. "'The Proof of the Proverb Is in the Probing': Alan Dundes as a Pioneering Paremiologist." *Western Folklore* 65: 217–62.

Mieder, Wolfgang. 2011. "Alan Dundes as Book Collector." *Proverbium* 28: 409–416.

Narayan, Kirin. 2008. "'Or in Other Words': Recasting Grand Theory." *Journal of Folklore Research* 45: 83–90.

Narayan, Kirin. 2018. "Folklore Gurus." In *Psycho-Cultural Analysis of Folklore: In Memory of Prof. Alan Dundes*, ed. P. Chenna Reddy and M. Sarat Babu, 105–14. Delhi: B. R. Publishing.

Oring, Elliott. 2019. "Back to the Future: Questions for Theory in the Twenty-First Century." *Journal of American Folklore* 132: 137–56.

Reddy, P. Chenna, and M. Sarat Babu. 2018a. "From the Editors Desk." In *Psycho-Cultural Analysis of Folklore: In Memory of Prof. Alan Dundes*, ed. P. Chenna Reddy and M. Sarat Babu, vii–xii. Delhi: B. R. Publishing.

Reddy, P. Chenna, and M. Sarat Babu, eds. 2018b. *Psycho-Cultural Analysis of Folklore: In Memory of Prof. Alan Dundes*. Delhi: B. R. Publishing.

Renteln, Alison Dundes. 2020. Letter to Simon J. Bronner, May 31.

Renteln, Alison Dundes, and Alan Dundes. 1994. *Folk Law: Essays in the Theory and Practice of Lex Non Scripta*. 2 vols. New York: Garland.

Reuss, Richard A. 1974. "'That Can't Be Alan Dundes! Alan Dundes Is Taller than That!': The Folklore of Folklorists." *Journal of American Folklore* 87: 303–17.

Ribeiro, Carlos Augusto. 2017. "Dualities, Intersections, and Convergences: Contemporary Art and (POP)ular Cultures." *Memoriamedia Review* 2, article 6. https://memoriamedia.net/pdfarticles/EN_MEMORIAMEDIA_REVIEW_Dualities.pdf. Accessed June 30, 2020.

Schmidbauer, Wolfgang. 2020. "Psychologie des Klopapierkaufs." *Psychologie Heute* (March 24). https://www.psychologie-heute.de/gesellschaft/40439-psychologie-des-klopapierkaufs.html. Accessed June 7, 2020.

Silverman, Eric K. 2016. "The Waters of Mendangumeli: A Masculine Psychoanalytic Interpretation of a New Guinea Flood Myth—and Women's Laughter." *Journal of American Folklore* 129: 171–202.

Topor, Lev. 2020. "COVID-19: Blaming the Jews for the Plague, Again." *fathom* (March). https://fathomjournal.org/covid-19-blaming-the-jews-for-the-plague-again/. Accessed June 6, 2020.

Zumwalt, Rosemary Lévy. 2013. "The Shaping of Intellectual Identity and Discipline through Charismatic Leaders: Franz Boas and Alan Dundes." *Western Folklore* 72: 131–79.

Zumwalt, Rosemary Lévy. 2017. "'Here Is Our Man': Dundes Discovered, The Development of the Folklore Program at the University of California, Berkeley." *Journal of American Folklore* 130: 3–33.

Zumwalt, Rosemary Lévy. 2018a. "Alan Dundes as a Persistent Presence: The Human Value in Personal Narrative." In *Psycho-Cultural Analysis of Folklore: In Memory of Prof. Alan Dundes*, ed. P. Chenna Reddy and M. Sarat Babu, 53–68. Delhi: B. R. Publishing.

Zumwalt, Rosemary Lévy. 2018b. "Foreword." In *Psycho-Cultural Analysis of Folklore* (In Memory of Prof. Alan Dundes), ed. P. Chenna Reddy and M. Sarat Babu, v–vi. Delhi: B. R. Publishing.

Zumwalt, Rosemary Lévy. 2020. "'The Great Team' of American Folklorists: Characters Large in Life and Grand in Plans." In *Folklore in the United States and Canada: An Institutional History*, ed. Patricia Sawin and Rosemary Lévy Zumwalt, 63–75. Bloomington: Indiana University Press.

Preface and Acknowledgments

THIS IS A BOOK THAT Alan Dundes should have put together, or so I told him. He probably would have done it, had not death in March 2005 put a halt to his tremendous production. The project came about after I read his proposal for a new compilation of his essays following *Bloody Mary in the Mirror* (2002a). I wanted him to do something different from what he planned. Rather than adding another capsule of writing, I cheekily told him it was time to reflect on the body of his major work covering more than forty years. He appreciated my suggestion that he should thematize his studies under analytical headings and produce a critical, retrospective work twenty-five years after his monumental essay collection, *Interpreting Folklore* (1980b). Still a vital voice in cultural inquiry, Dundes accepted the challenge and was ready to plunge into the project with his characteristic ebullience. He even invited me to write the foreword.

Dundes did not foresee that his life would suddenly be cut short. Or maybe he did. He predicted on several occasions that heredity was not in his favor because of the premature death of his father, and he opined, often with humor, that his diet did not fit into the "healthy fare" category. Still, with his giving barely a hint of slowing down, news of his heart attack came as a shock. When the University of California press office called me on the day he died, asking me for a quote to put in the public announcement, I quickly responded, "Alan Dundes will undoubtedly go down in history as one of the most influential folklorists, indeed one of the most influential minds, the world has known. That mind had an incredible range, reaching into cultures around the globe, and all manner of material including literature, narratives, art, customs, speech, and games. His specialty was not in a single genre, but in the provocative interpretation." It fit his devotion to learning that his final context when he was struck down was a Berkeley seminar room, as he was about to instruct and inspire another eager flock of students. This book, in part, elaborates on my soundbite, with the hope of reaching new generations of students with Dundes's insights.

Even if he had not died, I thought that a project to elucidate, and evaluate, Dundes's contributions to folkloristics was imperative. The season before he died, he had touched off a lively debate with an address to the American Folklore Society on the role of psychological perspectives and what he called "grand theory" in the future of folklore studies (2005c). Outside of the meetings, Dundes's ears must have been ringing with invocations of his name and work in global Internet discussions, symposia (including one in the Netherlands in which I was a participant), and classrooms. With his correspondence and essays stacked high on my desk, I put my words of advice into action. I checked with several of Dundes's confidants, and I consulted his widow, Carolyn Dundes, on the project. She sagely encouraged me to organize it as my book, rather than his, but commented that he would have liked the title and sections I had mapped out. The result of my effort testifies to his lasting legacy, offers products of his most fertile mind, and reflects on his contributions to the study of culture that he pursued vigorously through the materials of folklore and encapsulated as an analytic endeavor of folkloristics.

Why "meaning" as an organizing theme? It comes from Dundes's frequent reference to finding "patterns of meaning" as the goal of folkloristics. Meaning for Dundes was often hidden, frequently elusive, but uncoverable through folkloristic analysis. He saw meaning as the thinking underlying, and explaining, puzzling images, fantasies, and actions that pervade cultural life, often outside the awareness of participants in it. Rather than being random creations, the expressive texts of folklore—brought together in aggregate, traced historically and socially, identified and compared textually, understood in their cultural context, appreciated for their texture or performance, and mined for structure, belief, and symbol—showed patterns that the folklorist was trained to discern, and indeed *analyze*.

In Dundes's view, the scholar's role was more than reporting native exegesis or performance, but rather that of broad-based analysis involving scholarly organization and interpretation of folkloric materials. If ethnography reported culture on the natives' own terms, his folkloristics defined the terms, and expressions (and "projections"), by which natives could be understood. It should be emphasized that for Dundes, his "natives" were frequently "ourselves" rather than exotic others, attested to by his studies of children, students, musicians, scientists, and folklorists, in his family as well as his classroom and country. Frequently relying on the collections of others (his Berkeley folklore archives is one of the world's largest), his strength was to set up in the library and archives a kind of folkloristic operating table where he laid out his "corpus of data," as he liked to say, and surgically probed it, thereby revealing its inner workings to an anxious audience. Once the material was put back together, the analysis led to ideas on its *meaning*—with social and psychological implications—that would not be evident from a surface inspection. In fact, I could continue the metaphor by saying that he had a reputation akin to a famed master surgeon, bearing the aura of risk-taking ability that surrounds an authoritative figure who develops novel procedures and ingenious, if controversial, solutions. Elliott Oring (1975a) recognized this persona when he referred to folklorists informed by his incisive "operations" and taking on the role of "surgical interns." Noteworthy in this regard are Dundes's groundbreaking essays on the folklore of the medical profession (Dundes and George 1978; Dundes, L. Dundes, and Streiff 1999; also see chapter 13 in the present volume).

The body of material that Dundes worked on was, broadly stated, culture. Dundes pointed out that culture worked in strange, sometimes disturbing ways, and he sought to explain and even remedy it. Folklore is prime evidence of culture, indeed of humanity, he declared, and he came up with memorable phrases to drive the point home—folklore is a people's "symbolic autobiography," folklore gives an "inside out" view of society. Folklore, he affirmed in keywords of essay titles, was a *mirror* of culture, a *lens* for society, a *key* to behavior, a *projection* of mind. "Folklore is as old as humanity," he wrote for a definitive entry in the *World Book Encyclopedia* (1970). Negating the elitist view of folklore as an irrational relic of the past, however, he pointed out that folklore is alive and well today. He emphasized that folklore is always created anew, because people need it—for their identity, indeed for their existence. The paradox, and intriguing quality, of folklore was that it was always changing, and yet ever the same. It was local and universal; it was old and new. As for his resolution of this paradox, he spent his career showing that folklore is a product of mind that responds to and constructs culture.

Simon Bronner and Alan Dundes at the American Folklore Society's annual meeting, 1984.

I should explain my relationship to Dundes to contextualize my "analytics." After all, I was not one of his students, but I have made frequent use of his ideas in my work. Nonetheless, I have been known to dispute some of his cherished interpretations. We were friendly, and I held him in high esteem, but I hardly call myself one of his disciples. Then again, he claimed he did not have any (from my vantage, he certainly had devotees and followers), although one might say that all folklorists and psychological anthropologists owe him an intellectual debt. I know he appreciated my endeavor to integrate psychological theory and critical inquiry into folkloristics, and we shared a common mentor in Richard M. Dorson at Indiana University (and instruction from professors Felix Oinas and Warren Roberts). We talked about our common ethnic roots, and I provided him with sources for his studies of German and Jewish customs. We had a strong bond in a shared desire to promote a discipline of folkloristics, and he encouraged my research on its history and sociology (see *Following Tradition* [1998], also published by Utah State University Press, and *American Folklore Studies: An Intellectual History* [1986a] for the University Press of Kansas, for which he wrote an endorsement on the back cover). He wrote an afterword (2005a) for my volume *Manly Traditions*, we shared many a podium together, and he invited me to Berkeley to teach. In fact, after I edited his afterword, he told me I should edit more of his work. I was taken aback, since he had a reputation for maintaining tight control over it. At the time, I did not fathom how prophetic his words would be.

In my selection of his essays, I endeavored to show connections among data in the terms Dundes helped to define for the field—expressions of group, identity, worldview, and mind. He laid out the basic questions to be addressed: "Why does a particular item of folklore exist? And what does it mean to those who transmit and receive it?" Like a coach explaining his game plan, he wrote, in an unpublished manuscript, "It is precisely these questions which constitute the principal challenge to all of us in the field of folkloristics, the academic study of folklore, and which we need to address if this field is ever to achieve its rightful place in the academy." With these questions in mind, I created a sequence of essays to tell a story of his quest for meaning, beginning with what he would call structurally a "lack" (the absence of analysis in folklore classification and collection) to a "lack

liquidated" (meaning revealed through analytic means). I included essays that I thought
had stood the test of time and will be useful to students and scholars working with folklore
today and in the future; since some essays do go back a way, I updated some of the prose in
the text and made corrections where necessary.

I once asked Dundes to explain his preference for the intellectual platform of the essay.
He acknowledged that he was "inclined to use the shorter medium of the article or note"
rather than the "monograph or book format to report research findings," but he did not
elaborate on the folkloristic essay as a literary form, for which he was recognized as a master. Like the short story writer, Dundes used the essay to explore a variety of themes, situations, and settings. Always one to see layers of meaning, he often compressed his pointed
messages into memorable *double entendre* titles and themes (e.g., "Getting to the *Bottom*"
of "Sweet Bugger All," "*Second String* Humor," and my favorite, "Gallus as Phallus: A
Psychoanalytic Cross-Cultural Consideration of the Cockfight as *Fowl* Play"). The pedes-
trian view of his productivity is his curiosity about all manner of cultural expression—in
his familiar American home and abroad in exotic locales, in historical and contemporary
events, and in material as well as oral forms. To be sure, he was naturally inquisitive and,
some would say, obsessive. His wife was among those making the latter observation; when
asked about his hobbies, she said that he did not have any—his work was his life. He was
always pressing for answers to the "why" questions that others had not asked, and he was
amazingly well-read in a wide range of disciplines. His book collecting in any number of
languages was legendary. His long reach did not necessarily translate into a lack of concentration or specialization, since he had a special attraction to evidence present in speech and
narrative, based on the presumptions that people "speak their mind," and language constitutes a cognitive as well as a structural system.

It became quickly evident, from the first time I met him more than thirty-five years ago,
that the essay was his strongest vehicle for the driving idea. Each essay set forth a core idea
that he often presented as a proposal, supported by evidence drawn from an array of library,
ethnographic, and archival sources. He then invited commentary, critique, and application
in extensive tomes by others (sometimes allowing for collaboration), but upon forming the
thesis, he was ready, as he said to me at one shared podium, to "move on to the next idea."
He hinted at self-analysis of this tendency in "On the Psychology of Collecting Folklore"
(1975f), where he referred to the anal-ejective personality who prefers to "spread" his output in many outlets rather than "holding on" to his stuff. Most of all, what has distinguished Dundes as a writer is not just his prolific output, but the admirable accomplishment of having so many of his core ideas ripple widely into cultural scholarship.

As my introduction will show, he was often misunderstood or dismissed as preoccupied with sexual symbols in folklore, but he saw these, in Freudian terms, as among the
sensory layers of meaning, and also trenchantly interpreted the ideological and sociological ramifications of cultural expression. I summarize this approach as perceiving cultural
response (or adaptation) to anxiety and ambiguity (particularly evident in the critical concept of projection), *reflection* of belief and worldview (hence his rhetoric of mirror), and
intention (or consequence) in identity formation and communicative strategy (often represented by the idea of folklore as a key). He called himself a Freudian folklorist (his book
Parsing Through Customs [1987h] was subtitled "Essays by a Freudian Folklorist"), but I
find the appellation of "adaptive" or "post-Freudian" more fitting, considering the systemic
shift which occurred once he displaced Freud's emphasis on penis envy with male birth or
womb envy and its anal implications. Dundes's citations, in fact, make frequent reference

to the post-Freudian, symbolist works of Otto Rank, Ernest Jones, Sandor Ferenczi, Karen Horney, and Bruno Bettleheim, not only because of their consideration of folkloric evidence, but also because he carried the importance of feminine development and culturally relative context further than Freud. Moreover, Dundes distinctively adapted, and revised, selective aspects of Freudian theory—particularly the concepts of dream symbolism, anal eroticism, and repression—while rejecting notions of evolutionary origins and collective unconscious; and emphasized, *as a folklorist*, variation, text, and style, rather than pursuing the clinical interests of a psychologist.

Dundes was hardly a Freudian "one trick pony," however. He underscored this in an unpublished manuscript written before he died: "Unlike most academics that have a life-long specialization in a particular time period or individual, e.g., nineteenth-century Russian novels or William Faulkner, I have been fascinated by a wide variety of subject matters in my forty-year career as a professional folklorist. Each topic presents its own challenge to someone who seeks to understand it." As the essays in this volume demonstrate, he pursued cultural enigmas with a variety of methods, including linguistic, historical, cross-cultural comparative, ethnographic, feminist, and structural tools. To be sure, he was attracted to psychoanalytic theory for its exploration of mental and developmental processes that could explain folkloric fantasy, taboo, and ritual, but he also proposed corrections and alterations, such as his development of the themes of male cultural display, procreation, and aggression.

Folklore Matters, he proclaimed in a title of a previous book (1989d) as well as many presentations, to underscore both the range of materials in the subject and the significance of the expressive tradition, not coincidentally showing how speech takes on multiple meanings. The heart of the matter for him, I daresay, was the analysis that the compelling symbolic texts of folklore invite, and indeed demand. As the main platform for this inquiry, his essays had a lively, often polemical format—the problem statement or intellectual complaint, followed by his detailed exposition of folkloristic identification with a discerning eye for underlying structures, and reasoned, if provocative, interpretation. The scholarly audiences he addressed were prepared to be surprised, aroused, or offended. "Scholarship is not a popularity contest or about feeling good, it's a search for truth, which can be painful," he was wont to announce when an objection arose. He reached beyond academe, on television talk shows and in popular magazines, to get the significance of folklore as a subject and a field across to the public. His studies often had a reformist agenda, so that by making the "unconscious conscious" through cultural inquiry, social problems—including racism, sexism, anti-Semitism, homophobia, and the human proclivity for war—could be addressed at their fundamental sources.

Dundes did not claim that his analytic approach was embraced by all folklorists. Anything but. Still, he encouraged, and indeed wanted to provoke with his essays, a healthy theorizing about the existence and emergence of folklore in everyday life, past and modern. "Without symbolist perspectives or other grand theories," he told the American Folklore Society in 2004, "folklore texts will forever remain as mere collectanea with little or no substantive content analysis" (2005c). His concern was that folklore be more than a subject of descriptive inquiry; he declared often that its study should form a body of knowledge and analysis constituting a discipline. Accordingly, he unswervingly promoted the folkloristic enterprise, especially in the academic settings of folklore programs. He also was a missionary among psychologists, anthropologists, sociologists, literary scholars, historians, and linguists, urging them to become enlightened by the use of folkloric evidence, and the intellectual heritage of folkloristics.

Besides applying grand theories, Dundes advanced the identification of folklore genres and categories. Wide acceptance of what he called the "modern" idea of folklore (as expressive items enjoying multiple, variant existence, rather than restricted by the criteria of time and orality), and of the definition of folk groups as two or more people with a trait in common (removing the association of folk with a level of culture or class of society), greatly expanded the type of material considered as traditional, or "cultural." Dundes had a gift of discerning patterns and connections—among global cultures, across genres, and certainly between texts—based on an extraordinary recall for everything he read and experienced. His knowledge was encyclopedic; in fact, he wrote many high-profile encyclopedia entries defining folklore and the work of folklorists. He was elected president of the American Folklore Society and was a worldwide leader of the field, starting early in his career. Nonetheless, he often mentioned that his interpretations met resistance among a dominant stream of literal-minded colleagues who seemed timid or unable to propose "deep" meanings outside the awareness of informants. Having said this, he delighted in cutting against the intellectual grain (his critique in this volume of the "standard" tools of the motif and tale-type index in the essay on "emic" units is an example [1962]) to suggest meanings that had not been proposed before for well-known items, or to draw attention to overlooked or avoided material as folklore. Examples in his work are risque jokes, photocopied lore, and the speech of scientists and medical professionals. He relished debates with skeptics (evident in his plaint in "How Indic Parallels to the Ballad of the 'Walled-Up Wife' Reveal the Pitfalls of Parochial Nationalistic Folkloristics," [1995a], also reproduced here), and frequently even brought his friends and students to task.

Dundes brought into his arguments a world of knowledge compassed by folklore and an astounding bibliographic breadth. His importance as a folklorist, as well as a public intellectual, is significant for defining what he called the "modern" terms by which tradition is identified, and framing the questions in, and of, the field. Doubters of his symbolic readings still acknowledged that Dundes's definitions and methods had become standard equipment in the field's intellectual package, and he had a loyal legion of students and colleagues who absorbed, if not exactly replicated, his approach.

It is a formidable challenge to find all of Dundes's writing and take in his work as a whole. Besides being prolific, he issued his prose in far-flung publications. Part of the reason was that he was a peripatetic scholar. Accepting many invitations to speak around the world, he often gave the texts of his presentations to a local host publication, and tended not to retread his material. Although lodged in the disciplinary confines of the anthropology department at the University of California at Berkeley, he had an agenda of showing the applicability of folklore study to any number of fields, writing for psychological, linguistic, literary, scientific, philosophical, and historical journals in addition to anthropological publications. He acknowledged this tendency when he wrote on the manuscript I had that "one problem with that style of presentation [the essay] is that one's findings are often scattered in a variety of outlets, so much so that even the most dedicated student cannot locate all the writings of a particular scholar. My writings on folk speech and folk humor (including jokes) have appeared in such forums as *Zyzzyva*, a prominent West Coast literary magazine, *American Speech*, *Notices of the American Mathematical Society*, and in several festschrifts (volumes honoring scholars on the occasion of their retirement or birthday) in addition to regional folklore journals such as *Western Folklore* and *Midwestern Folklore*."

I therefore predict that there will be selections in this book that will be unfamiliar to even the most devoted of Dundes's followers. My goal, though, was not so much to unearth buried treasure (although there is some of that) as it was to feature notable statements of Dundes's core ideas, so as to inspire new analyses of "patterns of meaning." With the agenda of a sequel to *Interpreting Folklore* (1980b) in mind, I made an effort not to duplicate its contents, and avoided selections placed in recently published anthologies. Several seminal essays included here have not been generally available because they appeared in foreign, localized, or specialized publications. Folklorists may be familiar with the crux of the idea, but have not had the benefit of studying its original exposition. And for those new to his approach, there are classic statements of the method and theory of using folklore to address various cultural issues.

The selections show a range of analytical work, stretching from the beginnings of his career in the 1960s ("Folklore of Wishing Wells" from 1962 is the earliest) into the twenty-first century ("As the Crow Flies" was first published in 2004). In several places, I attached notes he penned to serve as postscripts to groundbreaking essays. The guiding principle for inclusion was his call in his last public address to folklorists in 2004, to show ways "to understand data that would otherwise remain enigmatic, if not indecipherable." The data include not only what folklorists study, but folklorists themselves (as the concluding essays "On the Psychology of Collecting Folklore" [1975] and "The Chain Letter" [1966] demonstrate). I have added headnotes to the essays to place these texts in an intellectual context, with attention especially to ways that Dundes's ideas have been applied or challenged in other studies.

The selections proceed generally from identification (with statements of definition and method) to interpretation (with special emphasis on sources of expression in the realm of the mind). The first section, entitled "Structure and Analysis," sets the stage for theoretical inquiry with explications of folklore as a concept and type of expression; definitions of basic terms such as "folk group," "folk idea," "folkloristics," and "metafolklore"; and demonstrations of comparative, historical, and structural approaches that were essential tools on Dundes's operating table. The section opens with the keynote (a term which Dundes, as a musician, approved) for the entire volume, looking at "Folklore as a Mirror of Culture," (1969a) and closes, in the controversial "Devolutionary Premise in Folklore Theory" (1975c), with a contemplation on the way that folklorists make, and skew, their subjects. Essays in the second section on "Worldview and Identity" explore the social functions of folklore in expressing the identities of people interacting within multiple, small groups; and the broader worldviews inculcated through national and often transnational beliefs and narratives. Dundes especially defied expectations of "the folk" being characterized as a lower sort by showing the high-context lore of the learned elite; as an illustration, part 2 includes discussions of folklore's meanings among scientists, musicians, and medical professionals. Religious and national identities are treated with analyses of narratives and trans-Atlantic folk speech.

Part 3 gets at the psychological and symbolist analysis, based on Freudian theory. At this point, Dundes would probably mention the predominant cognitive patterning of tripartite division in academic disciplines, as well as in Western civilization. The section includes his distinctive contributions to modern psychoanalytical interpretation of projective inversion and womb envy, relations of masculine play to combat, and the symbolist approaches of using allomotifs and symbolic equivalence. The signification of part 3 for the entire book is located in the emphatic opening that "folklore *means* something," in answer to the anti-intellectual popularization of folklore as ephemeral material or "mere" entertainment, and that what it means is critical to understanding how and why people express themselves. The closing words of this section, "there will always be folklore," are also a resounding reminder of the pervasive theme of the book, that folklore exists for a reason: it is a social and psychological necessity.

I am grateful to Carolyn Dundes for her cooperation in this project, critical reading of the manuscript, and kindness toward me. I also benefited from the sage counsel of Alan's beloved colleagues Wolfgang Mieder, Jay Mechling, Elliott Oring, Ronald L. Baker, Gary Alan Fine, and Haya Bar-Itzhak, and from the reflections of his former students Rachel Lewis, Perin Gürel, Rosemary Lévy Zumwalt, and Maria Teresa Agozzino. I also benefited from time with his daughter, Alison Dundes Renteln, who also was a collaborator with her father on several publications. Of the many dinners I shared with Dundes filled with his wit and wisdom, and commands of what to do with my life, one that stands out is a reunion of fellow travelers in Salt Lake City at the American Folklore Society in 2004, where he revealed much of himself in the company of Jan Harold Brunvand, Linda Dégh, and Patricia Turner, in addition to the usual collegial suspects I previously mentioned. Jay Mechling gave me the occasion to drop in on Alan's classroom at Berkeley, and we gained much from the experience. Marjolein Efting Dijkstra, Peter Jan Margry, and the wonderful staff at the Meertens Institute in Amsterdam, where I was in residence in 2005, were tremendously helpful in tracking down Dundes's European material and sharing their perceptions from what he would have undoubtedly called a European worldview. I should also recognize the many conversations I had with the late Sue Samuelson, a deep font of Dundesiana and one of his devotees, who became my colleague at Penn State. After Dundes's death, two special occasions filled with reminiscences of and tributes to Alan by numerous participants helped me outline the impact of his work: the Western States Folklore Society meeting held at the University of California at Berkeley in April 2006, and a symposium on folklore and American studies at Columbia University in New York City in March 2006.

At Penn State, School of Humanities staff member Sue Etter graciously helped with permissions and much more, and my colleague Michael Barton, Professor of American Studies and Social Science, suggested the title of the introduction and kindly passed along material on Dundes that he had accumulated. John Alley, executive editor at Utah State University Press, deserves special recognition for ushering the work along and deftly steering the project through various daunting channels. John Bealle enhanced this book by bringing a sharp folkloristic sensibility to his masterful crafting of the index. At home, my wife Sally Jo Bronner understood the need to complete this work and tell Dundes's stories.

I acknowledge the following organizations and publications for their kind permission to reprint essays in this volume:

American Anthropological Association for "Earth Diver: Creation of the Mythopoeic Male," *American Anthropologist* 64 (1962): 1032–51.

American Folklore Society for "From Etic to Emic Units in the Structural Study of Folktales" (75 [1962]: 95–105), "Study of Folklore in Literature and Culture: Identification and Interpretation" (78 [1965]: 136–42), "Folk Ideas as Units of Worldview" (84 [1971]: 93–103), (with Victoria George) "The Gomer: A Figure of Hospital Folk Speech" (91 [1978]: 568–81), and "How Indic Parallels to the Ballad of the 'Walled-Up Wife' Reveal the Pitfalls of Parochial Nationalistic Folkloristics" (108 [1995]: 38–53), all from the *Journal of American Folklore*.

Analytic Press for "Gallus as Phallus: A Psychoanalytyic Cross-Cultural Consideration of the Cockfight as Fowl Play," in *Essays in Honor of Alan Dundes*, ed. L. B. Boyer, R. Boyer, and Sonnenberg, 23–65 (Hillsdale, NJ, 1993).

Centre national de la recherche scientifique for "The Symbolic Equivalence of Allomotifs: Towards a Method of Analyzing Folktales" in *Le Conte: Pourquoi? Comment?*, 187–97 (Paris, 1984).

Finnish Literary Society for "Structuralism and Folklore," *Studia Fennica* 20 (1976): 75–93.

Finnish Society for the Study of Religion for "The Ritual Murder or Blood Libel Legend: A Study of Anti-Semitic Victimization through Projective Inversion" in *Temenos: Nordic Journal of Comparative Religion* 25 (1989): 7–32.

Folklore Society (England) for "Much Ado about 'Sweet Bugger All': Getting to the Bottom of a Puzzle in British Speech Play," *Folklore* 113 (2002): 35–49.

Hoosier Folklore Society for "Viola Jokes: A Study of Second String Humor" (with Meegan Brown), *Midwestern Folklore* 28 (2002): 5–17.

Indiana University Press for "Devolutionary Premise in Folklore Theory," *Journal of the Folklore Institute* 6 (1969): 5–19, and "The Motif-Index and Tale Type Index: A Critique," *Journal of Folklore Research* 34 (1997): 195–202.

Johns Hopkins Magazine for "Getting the Folk and the Lore Together," *Johns Hopkins Magazine* (January 1976), 23–31.

Johns Hopkins University Press for "The Folklore of Wishing Wells," from *American Imago* 19 (1962): 27–34.

Kroeber Anthropological Society for "Here I Sit—A Study of American Latrinalia," *Papers of the Kroeber Anthropological Society* 34 (1966): 91–105.

The Monist: An International Quarterly Journal of General Philosophical Inquiry for "Metafolklore and Oral Literary Criticism," 50 (1966): 505–16.

National Council of Teachers of English for "Folklore as Mirror of Culture," *Elementary English* 46 (1969): 471–82.

New York Folklore Society for "On Game Morphology: A Study of the Structure of Non-Verbal Folklore," *New York Folklore Quarterly* 20 (1964): 276–88.

New Scientist for "Science in Folklore? Folklore in Science?" 76 (1977): 774–76.

Proverbium for "'When You Hear Hoofbeats, Think Horses, Not Zebras': A Folk Medical Diagnostic Proverb" (with Lauren Dundes and Michael B. Streiff), 16 (1999): 95–103.

Tennessee Folklore Society for "On the Psychology of Collecting Folklore," *Tennessee Folklore Society Bulletin* 28 (1962): 65–74.

Trickster Press for "The Kushmaker," in *Folklore on Two Continents: Essays in Honor of Linda Dégh*, ed. Nikolai Burlakoff and Carl Lindahl, 210–16 (Bloomington, IN, 1980).

University of Virginia Press for "Madness in Method Plus a Plea for Projective Inversion in Myth," in *Myth and Method*, ed. Laurie L. Patton and Wendy Doniger, 147–59 (Charlottesville, VA, 1996).

University of Washington, Department of Scandinavian Studies, for "Chain Letter: A Folk Geometric Progression," *Northwest Folklore* 1 (1966): 14–19.

Utah State University Press for "As the Crow Flies: A Straightforward Study of Lineal Worldview in American Folk Speech," in *What Goes Around Comes Around: The Circulation of Proverbs in Contemporary Life*, ed. Kimberly J. Lau, Peter Tokofsky, and Stephen D. Winick, 171–87 (Logan, UT, 2004).

Western States Folklore Society for "Worldview in Folk Narrative" (54 [1995]: 229–32); and "Binary Opposition in Myth: The Propp/Lévi-Struass Debate in Retrospect" (56 [1997]: 39–50), both from *Western Folklore*.

Introduction

THE ANALYTICS OF ALAN DUNDES

IN A REFLECTIVE MOMENT UPON reaching forty years of age, Alan Dundes introduced his first collection of essays with the declaration, "My principal research interests focus upon the analysis of folklore" (1975g, xi). His emphasis of analysis signaled an unusual take on intellectual purpose. Most scholars respond to the question of interests with a genre, period, or location. Dundes, however, committed himself to the broad mission of uncovering and understanding meaning. Folklore is crucial to a knowledge of human experience, he observed, because "as autobiographical ethnography," it permits a view "from the inside-out rather than from the outside-in." That is, the advantage of folklore is that it conveys what people think in their own words and actions, and what they say or sing in folklore expresses what they might not be able to in everyday conversation. Dundes argued that in folklore, more than in other forms of human evidence, "one finds a people's own unselfconscious picture of themselves" (xi). That picture is not always pretty, as Dundes exposed in studies of anti-Semitic folklore, ethnic slurs, and abusive initiations. He insisted that uncensored, untethered scholarship was necessary to get beyond the popular urge to romanticize lore. His cause was to confront the harsh realities in expressive traditions, toward the twin goals of knowing ourselves internally (that is, psychologically) and externally (or socially and politically), and of righting wrongs in the world.

Dundes did not think of traditions as a relic of the past, and often took to the lectern to show that folklore was very much part of the modern technological world. When asked to speak, he gave a generic title of "Folklore in the Modern World" to cover contemporary joke fads, customs, and speech that reflected current issues and conditions. In this concern for the emergent nature of folklore, Dundes was a champion of the modern view that folklore is an artistic process rather than a dusty artifact, since, in his words, it is "something alive and dynamic" rather than "dead and static." It is not something relegated to primitivized others—historically or socially—but rather a behavioral pattern that everyone exhibits. Lashing out at the Victorian elitist characterization of folklore as "meaningless survivals," he emphasized that "folklore is a rich and meaningful source for the study of cognition and values" (1975g, xi–xii). Rhetorically, he then linked analysis to the uncovering of that which people cannot see—mind and belief—so as to find a *meaningful* understanding of "ourselves." Stated succinctly in his first collection of essays, his goal was to "bring unconscious content into consciousness" (xi).

Thirty years later, he was still promoting analysis and raising consciousness. During that time he gained a horde of students, colleagues, and followers—and a good number of detractors. But one thing for sure, he could not be ignored. His provocative analyses forced scholars from a wide spectrum of fields to think *with* as well as *about* folklore. That is, Dundes time and again pointed out that in addition to folklore being distinctive

1

as evidence, its study critically engaged issues of the day. To comprehend folklore, he preached, one needed to not only know the materials of tradition, but also to grasp the long distinguished intellectual heritage of international folklore scholarship. For his effort, he held the distinction of attracting an astounding number of festschriften, or volumes by associates honoring him (Boyer, Boyer, and Sonnenberg 1993; Mieder 1994b; Bendix and Zumwalt 1995; Lawless 2005; Gürel, 2007). In those heartfelt tributes, one inevitably finds assessments of his career and contributions to genre (proverb, humor, custom, legend, and myth), method (structuralism and psychoanalysis), and group studies (American, Native American, South Asian, African American, Jewish, and German).

This introduction contains its share of biographical assessment, but I propose to go beyond recounting his accolades to explicating his ideas in the context of folklorists' intellectual heritage and the issues of his day. I am therefore concerned not only for a reading of his work, but also for covering responses to his ideas as signs of a longstanding intellectual discourse on tradition and modernity. As an overview for the essays in this volume, I give attention to his distinctive rhetoric—drawing on psychological and anthropological theories, communication of structural and symbolic concepts, philosophical foundations, and, to borrow one of his favorite terms, his worldview. My narrative is guided chronologically from his first contributions during the 1960s to his final projects at the time of his death in 2005. I begin with the early development of his binary rhetoric, which I see as the hallmark of the "Dundesian perspective" on finding hidden or deep meanings through structural and symbolic analysis. I follow this section, in "That Can't Be Alan Dundes!," with the question of why Dundes, while still a young scholar, came to be mythologized, celebrated, and at times demonized for this perspective. In the section on "Folk and Folklorist," I turn to Dundes's lasting contribution of a "modern" definition of folk and his influential conception of the folklorist's significance in cultural work. Inspired by emergent lore of WWDS (What Would Dundes Say?) circulating about Dundes late in his career, I reflect on the culmination of his hermeneutic mission and the religious devotion he aroused. In sum, I analyze Dundes's sense of analysis to illuminate his, and our, quest for meaning in folklore.

Binarism and Deep Meaning

One way Dundes designated his analytical goal was to differentiate between folklore as the materials of folklore, and folkloristics as its theoretical study. Historically, he pointed to precedents in this usage in nineteenth-century folklore scholarship, and rhetorically, to the dichotomy between language as the material and linguistics as its study (2002a, vii; 2005c, 385–86). The appeal of folkloristics, which he had to insist was not another of his neologisms, was its analytical bent (1965d, 3; 1970, 324; 2005c, 385–86).

Dichotomies between inside and outside, material and its study, folk and lore, and conscious and unconscious pervade Dundes's work, to the point that binarism merits recognition as a Dundesian perspective. Introducing his first collection of essays, Dundes's mentor Richard Dorson sketched this intellectual framework, but did not signify it. He wrote, "To the lexicon of the folklorist he has added linguistic terms such as 'etic' and 'emic' unit, morphological concepts such as 'lack' and 'lack liquidated,' typologies of collectors such as 'anal retentive' and 'anal ejective.' In one scintillating article after another he has shown, or suggested, the ways in which folklore reflects our conscious and unconscious thoughts" (Dorson 1975, vii). To this list I would add "identification and interpretation" (in "The Study of Folklore in Literature and Culture" [1965c]), "deep and shallow play" (in "Gallus as Phallus" [1994]), "folklore and metafolklore" (in "Metafolklore and Oral Literary Criticism" [1966c]), "oral and literary" (in "Folklore as a Mirror of Culture" [1969a]), and "literal and symbolic" (in "Getting the Folk and the Lore Together" [1976a]), which are highlighted in the present volume to exemplify his dichotomous rhetoric. Often one oppositional category is in tension with the other, although unity or resolution may be possible. Dundes's ultimate example was folkloristics, which he described as a unity that arose out of the nineteenth-century struggle between anthropological and literary folklore "camps" (1975a, 10; 1988b, ix).

Dundes explained his preoccupation with analysis as necessary to overcome the "tendency to treat 'lore' as though it were totally separate from 'folk,'" which could be resolved by emphasizing the "fact that it is told by one human being to another" (1980e, viii). He contended that "getting the folk and the lore together," a phrase he used in the title of an article in this volume, meant a linkage of the behavioral act and social setting (folk) of the telling to content (lore). Thus in his view, deriving the meaning of folklore requires more than a literal reading of the text; it calls for contextualizing the expression in behavioral and social conditions. He emphasized this by referring to folklore as a form of sublimation: "Folklore offers a socially sanctioned outlet for the expression of taboo and anxiety-provoking behavior. One can do or say in folkloric form things otherwise interdicted in everyday life" (2005a, 359). To grasp why folklore is needed as an expressive outlet, one therefore needs to know the cultural values, taboos, anxieties, and beliefs of the society in which individual tradition-bearers operate in everyday life.

"By analyzing folklore," Dundes wrote, the scholar discovers "general patterns of culture" and raises "levels of consciousness" (2005a, 359). The assumption in this statement is not just that folklore can be ordered according to form, but that it is cognitively patterned (for example, through linear, circular, or binary thinking). Another presupposition is the existence of an unconscious—a part of the mind containing repressed instincts and their representative wishes, ideas, and images which are not accessible to direct examination. Although some critics would posit that mental activity can only be conscious, Freudian theory holds that unconscious ideas can be recognized when resistance and repression, processes of internalizing disturbing thoughts, are overcome, so that the ideas become conscious, that is, externalized.

Folklore holds psychological and cultural significance because, as an often momentary and a socially sanctioned outlet of expression, it uses symbols in elaborated narratives and in rituals to encapsulate (or intensify) experience and provide a release from reality. Folkloric evidence is different from historical documentation because it often constitutes fantasy, but that does not detract from its truthfulness or significance. "The apparent irrationality of much folklore," Dundes pointed out, "poses problems for literal-minded, historically oriented folklorists. It is not easy to find a rationale for the irrational, to make sense of 'nonsense,' but that is what folklorists seriously interested in interpretation must try to do" (1980e, viii). This statement smacks of a Hegelian process of contradiction and negation leading to rational unity, and one might go further to see a connection between Dundes's construction of symbols in the mind as the ultimate source of expression and Hegel's emphasis on the binary in mental operations to represent the mind's process of comprehension. Although scholars have made comparisons between Hegel's and Freud's conceptions of consciousness and human development, Dundes invoked Freud rather than Hegel because of the central concern in Freud's work—a folkloristic concern, Dundes said—for explaining the irrational and fantastic in expressive behavior (Dundes 1987i, 4–5; Butler 1976; Eecke 2006).

Freud extended the concept of negation to a connection between verbalized expression and consciousness (Freud 1961; Eecke 2006). In this view, the danger of repressed material becoming conscious through talk is mitigated by the talker's denial. Tension exists, then, between the unconscious and conscious, and between repressed and verbalized thought. Analysis resolves the conflict, and may be confirmed to the analyst by the teller's response of "I never thought of that." Folklore is especially important in making the unconscious conscious, Dundes affirmed, because it appears to be a "safe" fictive or ritual space in which to symbolize, and thereby control, anxiety or ambiguity, but if the realistic basis of the symbolism is exposed, repression recurs in another form. This transformation accounts for Dundes's emphasizing the observer's "analytical" rather than native posture in assessing meaning, although he urged analysts to collect "metafolklore," tradition-bearers' comments on their own traditions. These comments are in themselves part of belief, he observed, or else rationalizations for the need for expression (1966c,1975d). The analyst is essential in the Dundesian process of deriving meaning; an outside eye is necessary to discern the inside, or hidden, codes of meaning. Some folklorists, Dundes understood, would have the tradition-bearers' explanation of an event be sufficient, viewing the role of the folklorist as facilitating self-reflection by natives. But in a Dundesian perspective, the analyst needs to maintain a detached vantage rather than a position of advocacy, precisely because folk material involves personal and societal anxieties that are repressed or avoided and, when expressed, typically disguised. Discussing photocopy lore full of scatological and sexual references, for example, Dundes found that "humor is a *veil* barely concealing an expression of most of the major problems facing contemporary American society" (Dundes and Pagter 1978, xviii, emphasis added). Therefore, meaning lodges outside the awareness of the self, requiring an analyst to recognize it. That is not to say that folklorists, even more than other kinds of analysts, cannot rely on experience or participation to gain an "inside-out" view of the material. Dundes, for instance, referred to his specific Navy duty, home-ported in Italy in 1955, when he analyzed the taboo on sailors whistling on ship. Using the principle of "like produces like" from James Frazer's law of homeopathic magic, he concluded that whistling represented a "windstorm." And he drew on his participation in all-male groups for his interpretation of the roots of war in competitive phallocentric display that feminizes an opponent (2005c, 389; 1997e, 27). He also referred to his experience as a folklorist, and analyzed folklorists' folklore, as demonstrated in the last chapter of this volume, in which he finds a relation between collecting items and anal retention.

Despite the desire to be objective observers, folklorists are subject to the biases of the society in which they work and their traditions as a subgroup, Dundes iterated (1966a, 227, 245). For example, he pointed out the devolutionary thinking underlying Dorson's comment that "the idea that folklore is dying out is itself a kind of folklore" (Dundes 2005c, 406). The negation of the related pronouncement by Barbara Kirshenblatt-Gimblett that the discipline of folklore is "predicated on a vanishing subject" is that folklore is constantly emerging, which Dundes averred in the statement, "folklore continues to be alive and well in the modern world, due in part to increased transmission via e-mail and the Internet" (Kirshenblatt-Gimblett 1996, 249; Dundes 2005c, 406). Belief in a vanishing subject results in an obsession with collection and classification as an end in itself, a recovery project that justifies rushing into the field to gather folklore before lore and field both disappear. Dundes decried, in natural history terms, the antiquarian "quest for the quaint or... curious" as "butterfly collecting": "Items of folklore are treated as rare exotica, metaphorically speaking, to have a pin stuck through them and mounted in a display archival case such that it is almost impossible to imagine the folklore items were ever alive (that is, performed). Context is typically ignored, and it is the text only that is prized by the local collector" (2005c, 388).

A connotation of the devolutionary impulse to "get the lore before it disappears" is the need to witness lore for oneself, an empiricist assumption that leads to the glorification of knowledge *discovery* via the recording of lore rather than to the interpretation of aggregate data or individual texts/contexts. The implication is that a struggling or declining discipline may project its fear into a collecting praxis and the observation of a "devolving" subject. Denying folklore's persistence as a natural process of culture affirms the anxiety of "falling." Or the devolutionary belief may disguise a deeper fear involving the folklorist's motivation for interest in the material, linked, according to Dundes, with anal retention in the obsessive behavior of gathering, ordering, and piling (1975c; 1975e). The inference is that a way to deal with a problem of self is to attribute the problem to someone else or to something outside the self.

An alternative to devolution and the collecting obsession, one promoted by Dundes so as to "modernize" the subject, is recognizing that the study of folklore is itself emergent in nineteenth-century Europe, arising out of the perceived conflicts between rural life and industrialization, culture-based nationalism and imperial monarchies, and colonialism and cultural relativism (1965c, 1982b). For Dundes, folklore demanded an analytical project to explain its emergence and ubiquity. The binary matters to be resolved derive from its definitive characteristics of multiplicity and variation, leading to its quality of constantly changing yet staying the same, being specifically situated and universal, old and yet new (Dundes 1989c, 193–94). Rather than being dragged down by a narrow insistence on oral tradition, in the twenty-first century the science of tradition flourishes, expands, and spreads because it has to, if sense is to be made of mass-mediated culture and, further, so that this knowledge may be applied to address social problems in the world (1965c, 1980h).

Dundes linked dualism (particularly the importance of "double meaning") in psychoanalysis with the binary basis of structuralism. The pivotal structuralist approaches of Vladimir Propp (syntagmatic, relating to a sequential pattern of plot functions) and Claude Lévi-Strauss (paradigmatic, relating to a thematic set of contrasting relations), while often set in opposition to one another in surveys of structuralist approaches, are unified by Dundes to reveal mental processes underlying the structural patterns of fantastical expressions. For example, in the article "Binary Opposition in Myth," reproduced in this volume, Dundes concluded, "To the extent that the debate between Propp and Lévi-Strauss itself constitutes a kind of academic binary opposition, we earnestly trust that this essay will be understood as a form of constructive mediation" (1997a, 48). The point is that binary structure is basic, whether as the basis of a story (lack to lack liquidated), method (identification and interpretation), formation of a group (requiring at least two persons), authenticity of an item (confirmed by two or more versions), or indeed in the concept of folklore (uniting the social "folk" and the expressive "lore"). The binary is significant in this perspective not just as a framework, but as a representation of the way the mind works—as a psychological concept—and also as the social basis of transmitting, or sharing, folklore. Therefore, dualism constitutes the cognitive grammar of the expression itself, and the binary construction of a story or event comprises the drama or tension that draws attention to the expression, as apart from other forms of communication. Analysis is thus a discernment of this source—in the mind, group, and expression.

Binarism as a philosophy, even more than a method, that is connected to structural analysis is often attributed to Ferdinand de Saussure, a Swiss-born contemporary of Freud. The tie between the two is their shared interest in mental processes that are revealed in language. Saussure was concerned less with the laws of a particular language than with the rules governing all languages, which get at how humans cognitively order reality and create culture. Saussure's structuralism, which was adopted by notable scholars concerned with folklore such as Lévi-Strauss, Roman Jakobson, Petr Bogatyrev, and Dell Hymes, is the distinction of *parole* (translated from the French as both "word" and "speech") and *langue* ("language" or "tongue"; summarized by folklorists following Noam Chomsky as "competence") wherein the former represents the utterances of members of a language community (in speech acts, or "performance"), which manifest an underlying structure, and the latter is the generative structure (Hymes 1972, 47). Of importance to Dundes's semiotic theory of meaning was the resulting conclusion that words do not necessarily possess an intrinsic or a historically emergent significance. If *langue* is the totality of language, then parts of that structure have relationships to one another that can be independent of utterances with natural associations in the external world. Such relationships are ones of difference, because they refer to, indeed create, categories that distinguish signs from others, such as a dog not being a cat, horse, or pig. Dundes's scorn for literal-minded folklorists was rooted in their tendency to treat the utterances as reality, rather than analyzing the relationships that *underlie and generate* those utterances and order reality. In this model, language is always changing, but it is dependent on the social conventions established in a community of speakers as opposed to individual speakers' wills.

In "Proverbs and the Ethnography of Speaking," Dundes used the distinction between *parole* and *langue* to assert that an ethnographic goal of folklore research is geared toward communication or context. According to Dundes, folkloristics "is not simply the delineation of the structure of language as an isolated symbolic system or code, but rather the attempt to discover exactly how language is used in specific situations. . . . In this type of study, one is interested in not only the rules of a language, but also the rules for the use of the language" (Arewa and Dundes 1964, 71; see also Dundes 1966a. 242; 1976b, 1504; Ben-Amos 1972). This methodological statement led to his assertion of the importance of the social or contextual basis of folklore at the end of the essay: "Let's put the folk back in folklore!" (adapted linguistically from the structure of "Let's put the Christ back in Christmas," he said). Separating himself from other contextualists, however, Dundes warned against confusing surface *use* and disguised *meaning*. He inferred meaning from symbolic clues that might be outside the awareness of the speaker, and not apparent from the context. "Use is observed or collected from natives, while the interpretation" of meaning, he mused, is inevitably made from the analyst's viewpoint (Dundes 1975c, 52).

If Dundes implied that Saussure's dualism, which foregrounds the analytical use of cultural context and communication, is liberating, many post-structuralists have been uncomfortable with the "value hierarchy" in the binary constructions of either/or statements. The unavoidable domination of one pole over another, critics claim, results from the assumption that one side of the dichotomy, as linguist Katharina Barbe has written, "is seen as purer, more positive, and more basic than the other side" (2001, 89). Judging from his disapproval of elitism and his mediation of the objective/subjective dichotomy, Dundes might have agreed to an extent, but his interpretations suggest that he remained committed to the idea that the binary is fundamental because it represents the cognitive process. Saussure's semiotic distinction between "signifier" (an acoustic image) and "signified" (a concept) is evident in the Dundesian difference between use and meaning. In Dundes's writing, I do not find the post-structuralist view that binary distinctions are necessarily motivated by a desire to dominate, although Dundes, in his exposure of the construction of "othering" and "chauvinism" in narrative and speech, was well aware of the logic of imperialism in the intellectual constructions of West/East, civilized/primitive, white/black, mainstream/ethnic, men/women, and indeed scientific/folk (Dundes 1980h, 2; Dundes 1980a; Ashcroft, Griffiths, and Tiffin 2000, 24–25). Dundes brought into consciousness the unconscious predilection for binaries to comment on unequal power relations.

Dundes is often credited with pointing out the predominant cognitive pattern of trichotomy in American culture, which raises the question of the more universal role of the binary. His oft-cited essay, "The Number Three in American Culture" [1980d], drew meaning from a pattern that is prevalent but is not recognized; indeed, his lead-in is a quotation from Bronislaw Malinowski's *A Scientific Theory of Culture* (1944): "Nothing is as difficult to see as the obvious" (Dundes 1980d, 134). "Folklore," Dundes asserted in this essay, "is prime data for investigations of cognitive patterning" (137). As was his style, Dundes gave a broad array of evidence, such as: "In folk speech, one can give three cheers for someone, but not two or four. (And each cheer may consist of 'Hip, Hip, Hooray.') The starter for a race will say 'One, two, three, go.' He will not count to two or four. (Cf. The three commands 'On your mark, get set, go.') The alphabet is referred to as the ABCs and in the common folk simile, something is as easy as ABC; one does not speak of learning his ABs or his ABCDs" (136). His essential point was that three appears to be culture-specific, especially when compared to the "obsessive character" of the Native American use of four as a ritual or sacred number (135).

Although Dundes went no further in explaining the contrastive use of four in many Native American groups, I propose following this analytical approach to demonstrate that the significance of four in relation to the cosmology of space is natural; four represents a sacred circle, or the state of being symbolically complete, because it represents the four cardinal points forming the diameter and radius of circular space. Four stands for *everywhere*, that is, as far as the eye can see. From this standpoint, the Asian use of five as a pattern number in rituals and narratives adds the inner self, or center, as a point where the directions cross in the circle, suggesting the importance of introspection. Trichotomy, in my analysis, implies a bodily representation, apart from the binary mind, especially in the triangular importance of the head (as a source of wisdom and humanness) and shoulders (representing bodily support and strength) (Bronner 1986b, 15–16; see also Lease 1919, 72). Exploring the variety of possible meanings, Dundes suggested that trichotomy relates to the union that is the basis of society—the mother, father, and resulting child—before giving a psychoanalytic interpretation. Dundes used Freud in drawing the symbolic equivalence of three as "a masculine symbol, the *phallus cum testiculis*" and provocatively added that its prevalence in male-dominated Western civilization signifies "compensatory activity for not being able to give birth to children as females do." "This type of explanation," he mused, "would also make clear why aspects of American culture which are exclusively masculine, e.g., the military, the Boy Scouts, baseball, are especially three-ridden. (Note also that the Christian Trinity is all masculine. This would be further evidence that three is male creativity denying or replacing female creativity.)" (1980d, 158).

Dualism, Dundes observed, "is probably worldwide" and "assumed to have objective universal validity" (1965a, 186). Common "polarities," he philosophized, "include: life/death, body/soul, and male/female." He pointed out that the social extension of cognitive dichotomy was indicated by the concepts of "self/other" and "us/them," suggesting that the singular requires a pair for a sense of identity, to not only affirm what one is, but also what one is not (Dundes 1980d, 135). He also maintained the dyad as the basic unit of "sharing" and "transmitting" folklore. As linguistic evidence, he could have mentioned the colloquial expression of the base concept of the social in the folk saying, "Two is company and three's a crowd." Although Dundes did not go further with this line of reasoning, it is possible to extend the relation of the binary to the singular. Related to the "two is company" folk saying is the symbolic equating of one with emptiness in sayings such as "One is none, two is some, three is a sort, four is a mort," "One body is no body," and "One's as good as none" (Stevenson 1948, 1717–18). To be alone is to be *anti*-social, or unethical, since "only caring for oneself" implies an extreme egotism or selfishness (as in "looking out for number one"). To be single is to be unattached—marginally a "loner," or odd (which is implied in "being reclusive" or "a hermit"), or jocularly in the wellerism, "Every one to his own taste, said the old woman as she kissed her cow";—and *nontraditional,* anti-social, or unique, expressed in the phrase "going it alone." Dundes connected an exclusive scientific or elitist way of thinking with the singular notion of monolithism when he wrote, "inasmuch as folklorists, despite the fact that they are accustomed to thinking of variation in the texts of folklore, often wrongly assume that there is only one correct meaning or interpretation. There is no one right interpretation of an item of folklore any more than there is but one right version of a game or song. (We must overcome our penchant for monolithic perspectives as exemplified in monotheism, monogamy, and the like)" (1975d, 51–52).

The self, I would add, is a reference point from which historical as well as social connections are made, especially in references to someone being "original" (first), in the sense of being responsible for a creation (with Adamic overtones of Genesis) that is unprecedented and was copied thereafter. This cognitive association with the creative *"ur*-form" carries over into the frequent assumption that a single source of creation can be found for folklore, rather than a trans-cultural or psychological explanation of traditional expressions as "responses." Dundes was not unconcerned about origins, but he tended to locate expressions cross-culturally, often in far-flung environments, and suggested psychological responses rather than diffusion to explain the similarities.

Binary segmentation of the self (such as in the psychoanalytic concepts of id and ego), is shown in the dichotomous vernacular expressions of "being alone with one's thoughts" or "talking to oneself," which sociolinguistically implies an agent and a receiver of the message, and suggests a conversation between an "outer" and an "inner voice" (see Mechling 2006). A binary structure differs from other structural concepts in that it tends to signify psychological and social processes, while singularism and trichotomy typically have corporeal associations.[1]

Taking a cue from the dualism between manifest and latent meanings in "depth" psychology, Dundesian analysis uncovers "deep" meaning in the sense of something being about something that turns out to be something else. This point is probably the greatest barrier to acceptance of Dundes's interpretations, since there is frequently an assumption in his interpretations that the message the folklorist hears or sees is a disguise or distortion of meaning rather than truth taken at face value (see Dundes 1976b; Cohen 1980, 47–50; Oring 1975b; Oring 2003; Koven 2005). Even the rhetoric of "informant," used in collecting, suggests that something is revealed rather than in need of "interpretation" (i.e., as if the message was coded). The way to get to the "underlying" structure, the "hidden" meaning, or the "unstated" reason—to cite some rhetoric of depth analysis—is through identification and comparison of ciphers. Rather than being revealed in observable behavior (what Dundes called "descriptive data") in the field, symbolic meaning is discerned "beneath" the surface and traced to the mind. A critical question in this approach is whether the meaning can be "proven." Dundes addressed this issue by underscoring the value of interpretation, which presupposes that the subject or text of analysis is polysemous, rather than being misconstrued as having a singularly correct meaning that is, in his words, "monolithic" (1975d, 52; 1980e, ix).

Dundes used "interpretation" much as Freud used it in *Interpretation of Dreams* ([1900] 1999), to denote the results of an analytical process, that is, possibilities suggested by the analyst from attention to talked texts, and which are outside the awareness of the patient. Freud studied both dreams and folklore, and in fact related the two (Freud and Oppenheim 1958). Both are often viewed as "unintelligible and absurd," and as carrying little significance, although Freud ventured to show that they are important psychologically (Freud [1900] 1999, 128). In his essay "The Method of Interpreting Dreams: An Analysis of a Specimen Dream," Freud called for a "scientific treatment of the subject" involving the materialization of the content of a dream into comparable texts (132). Freud warned that "the object of our attention is not the dream as a whole but the separate portions of its content" (136). He described the analysis of the portions as a "decoding method, since it treats dreams as a kind of cryptography in which each sign can be translated into another sign" (130). The interpretation posits "hidden" meanings that the actor is not aware of. They are deduced from general principles, such as "a dream is the fulfilment of a wish" (154). Freud outlined a manifest content (*manifester Trauminhalt*), or "objects, actions, settings, and words that appear in the dream and are retained in memory," and latent content (*latenter Trauminhalt*), the "unconscious referents of the manifest content" (Oring 1993, 279). Tests can be applied to validate the symbolic conclusion about the unconscious thoughts, motivations, or patterns (*Traumgedanken*)—through corroboration in other "cases," and a reading of the analyzed texts for consistency (see Sherwood 1969, 196–202; Fine 1992; Oring 2003, 58–70).

But what if the patient or tradition-bearer denies the analytical meaning, even if the goal of making the unconscious content conscious is to "gain insight" and, ultimately, the reintegration of (or rationale for) personality or culture? Dundes took negation as confirmation, for, as he wrote, "if the participants consciously realized what they were doing, they would in all probability not be willing to participate. It is precisely the symbolic facade that makes it possible for people to participate in an activity without consciously understanding the significance of that participation" (2005a, 357). In other words, if the tradition-bearers were aware of the "deep" meaning, then they would not need the tradition.

Dundesian analysis identifies basic patterns or concepts, and consequently arrives at interpretations of their associations through symbolic equivalences (allomotifs) and social outlooks (worldviews). My thesis regarding Dundes's analytics is that his project to uncover "meaning" depended structurally on binary presumptions, and contextually on the "modern" reconstruction of folkloristics to "interpret." His goals were to centralize folklore studies as an academic discipline, and disrupt social hierarchy by conceptualizing tradition as human necessity. Meaning and interpretation in Dundesian analysis are typically doubled. Meaning divides into literal (manifest) and figurative (latent) layers, while interpretation has literary (textual/contextual) and religious (hermeneutic/mythological) as well as psychological and social connotations. With this in mind, in the sections that follow I will examine examples of his analysis to answer the doubled question of what folklore means, and what Dundes meant.

"That Can't Be Alan Dundes!"

In 1974, Richard Reuss drew attention to the "folklore of folklorists" by titling his article "That Can't Be Alan Dundes! Alan Dundes Is Taller Than That!" The exclamatory phrase was suggested by students at an American Folklore Society meeting, who traded narratives of their special awe for Dundes among the giants of the field. Reuss noted the "niagara of Alan Dundes lore washing over American academe," but in a bait-and-switch tactic, informed the reader that the essay was not about Dundes at all. The phrase signified, though, that even before Dundes turned forty, he had achieved mythological status and had come to represent folklore study as a disciplinary enterprise. The point of the exclamation, according to Reuss, was that "Alan Dundes in reality is taller than average, five feet eleven and one-half inches to be precise. Even so, it seems fair to say that were he seven feet tall he still would be hard put to measure up physically to the larger-than-life image of Alan Dundes created in the minds of many students through reading and discussion of his wide-ranging and prolific publications, his expansive writing style, and the constant references made to him and his work in the classroom of a local university" (1974, 308). This negation of reality by expectation and image raises the question of the real life of Alan Dundes, and how he came to be mythologized. If this is how others view Dundes, then how has he narrated himself in symbolic autobiography?

At the time that Reuss wrote his essay, much about the rising star was ambiguous. He revealed little of himself, although Richard Dorson (1975) gave a heroic cast to Dundes's character when he introduced *Analytic Essays in Folklore*, describing the author as a "brilliant" prodigy with an uncanny mental "gift," because he obtained his doctorate in folklore at Indiana University while still in his twenties and rose precociously to full professor by the age of thirty-three at the highly regarded University of California at Berkeley. Dorson told the following story: "While in my classes in folklore I insisted on the student documenting each textual item of folklore with informant data. Dundes, once a student in those classes, went one better on becoming the instructor and required that his student collectors in addition interpret the meaning of the recorded text. His quest for meanings has led him to seek context along with text, metafolklore as well as folklore, and thereby to reorient the conception of fieldwork; interpretations of tradition bearers should carry at least as much weight as those of investigators" (1975, vii). The junior Dundes, Dorson intimated, had bested the doctoral father and risen triumphantly to take his place among the pantheon of the discipline's gods (perhaps to replace the father). While proud of his boy, Dorson, like a disapproving dad, had questioned the rebellious spirit of his gang of "young Turks," and took junior to task for embracing a "school of interpretation most abhorrent to orthodox folklorists" (1972a, 25, 45). Perhaps that was the reference that motivated Dundes to subtitle a work on Jewish folklore "an unorthodox essay," playing on the double meaning of orthodox with respect to religion and convention as he applied a psychoanalytic approach to modern-day customs of circumventing restrictive Sabbath rules (2002c; see also Koven 2005).

Psychoanalytic inquiry into folklore was hardly new during the 1960s, when Dundes raised its banner as a "grand theory" for folkloristics (Dundes 1987i). Freud, beginning in the late nineteenth century, devoted much of his symbolist theory to the analysis of jokes, taboos, and myths, and among his followers and critics—Ernest Jones, Géza Róheim, Bruno Bettelheim, Karl Abraham, Otto Rank, Carl Jung, and Theodor Reik—extended the query of folklore as a form of fantasy and projection that related to human development and mental processes. Yet it was unusual for folklorists to apply psychoanalytic theory; both Freud and psychoanalysis were absent from the major mid-twentieth-century reference work of the field, *Funk and Wagnalls Standard Dictionary of Folklore, Mythology and Legend*, although "anthropological school" and "historic-geographic method" (literary) were featured entries (Leach 1949; see also Boas 1920, 318–21; Taylor 1940, 17). Despite psychiatrists' ubiquitous attention to folklore for inquiries into the human psyche, the main intellectual project of folklorists in the mid-twentieth-century was to trace the origin and distribution of folk material. Some of their concern was for showing folklore as an ancient source of literature, and for Dundes, that was driven by a devolutionary premise. The landmark works of the *Motif-Index of Folk-Literature* ([1932–36] 1975) and *The Types of the Folktale* (commonly referred to as the tale-type index [1928] 1961), prepared by Stith Thompson at Indiana University, and other classificatory compendia for riddles, ballads, proverbs, and songs influenced by the Finnish "historic-geographic" school, served notice, in Dundes's words, that "folklorists as a group tend to be biased in favor of literal, not symbolic, interpretations of folklore. They seek historical rather than psychological explanations of folkloristic phenomena" (1972, 9). Even among his fellow "young Turks," who were developing ethnographies of performance and communication during the 1960s, Dundes stood out. He complained that they had a reductionist tendency to treat folklore as "situated events" representing social relations, rather than as symbolic texts of psychological signification. He derided the favor of his colleagues for Clifford Geertz's influential performative concept of reading events as texts of "deep play" (1972, 1994), which Dundes slighted as "shallow play" because it did not posit psychological motivations for enacting the play, and remained at the level of social "reflection" (1994). He accused his seniors of dehumanizing folklore "by treating *lore* as though it had nothing whatever to do with *folk*," and of prudishly suppressing or ignoring the obscene materials that flourish in oral tradition and resound with sexual symbolism. Dundes liked to point out that Thompson left out material under "X" in the *Motif-Index* that he felt was obscene, even though it was this content that was most vibrantly oral in culture (Dundes 1972, 9–10). Dundes argued that humanizing folklore, or emphasizing the folk, would lead to psychological and social interpretations of people rather than a superficial "literal" (and therefore literary/historical) emphasis on lore.

From what mysterious roots had Dundes come out of the horizon, as either heretic or prophet? I cannot document a miraculous birth, but by his account, there were formative experiences (usually described in pairs of events and characters) and a moment of conversion that led him to take a career path of folklore study. His early life was filled with both city and country. He was born on September 8, 1934, in New York City, to a lawyer father and musician mother. When Dundes was still an infant, the couple moved the family sixty-five miles north of the city to a farm located near Patterson, New York, and there, in 1936, a sibling was added—his sister Marna. Being close in age, she was likely a factor in his later observations about the significance of sibling rivalry in the content of children's folklore. His father died in 1952, leaving the teenager in difficult emotional and financial straits as he pursued his education. Dundes recalled, many years later, "I lost my father when I was a sophomore, in 1952, and I have never completely gotten over it. . . . I have a picture of him on my dresser in the little room off our bedroom and so I see him every morning of my life" (Mieder 2006, 215). He recollected his father as an influence on his folklore interest because of his talents as a raconteur, and his early exit from Dundes's life may have influenced the folklorist's thinking about the father figure, as well his reputation for taking a paternalistic role toward students (Dundes 1962c; Dundes 1976d; Dundes and Edmunds 1995; Dundes 1987c; see also Bendix 1995, 58–62).

Reflecting on his family's ethnic background, Dundes acknowledged that while his parents were both Jewish, he was raised in a secular environment. In fact, he attributed their move to the farm as an escape from religious piety. He recalled, "I gathered from numerous conversations that both my parents had felt somewhat suffocated by the close Jewish atmosphere in which they lived in New York City and so when I was just one year old, they fled to a rural area near Patterson, New York, about sixty miles north of the city. . . . Although almost all of our family friends were Jewish, I did not have much exposure to formal religious practices. As a result, although I was always proud of my heritage, I felt quite ignorant of the religious elements in Judaism" (xii). Still, he absorbed reformist values expressed in *tikkun olam*, literally translated as "repairing the world," which is often invoked to connote a Jewish commitment to social justice, with the implication that learning can effect change. He said that he certainly related to Freud so strongly later because of the power of his ideas, but also because Freud, as a secular Jew, was seeking to explain issues of identity and anti-Semitism, which connected with what Dundes faced in life.[2] In his own analytics, Dundes considered Freud's use of exemplary Jewish jokes in the light of the Vienna's scholar's secular Jewish background. Dundes also recognized the linkage of cultural relativity espoused by another influential scholar with a Jewish background, Franz Boas, the father of modern anthropology (Dundes 1987i, 23–24).

Reflective of his ambivalent feelings about his ethnicity, Dundes's analytics tended to emphasize gender, rather than religious difference, as primary (1997c, 155–57). Dundes's experience with anti-Semitism and his emotional response to the horrors of the Holocaust were nonetheless significant factors in his later writing on German national character, ethnic slurs, blood libel and wandering Jew legends, and JAP (Jewish-American Princess) and Auschwitz jokes (Dundes 1984a, Dundes and Hauschild 1987, 1987e).[3] He held misgivings about regulation in organized religion, perhaps as a result of his parents' conversations about the "suffocation" of the synagogue, and he knew that some of his writing on religion was taken as irreverent, if not sacrilegious (2005c, 405). Nonetheless, in his book *Holy Writ as Oral Lit*, Dundes avowed that he held "a lifelong love of the Bible"; his "family Bible," he wrote, was the King James version (1999, vii). Rather than being a believer in one creed, however, he claimed to be interested in the nature of religion, especially to test Freud's comment that "a large portion of the mythological conception of the world which reaches far into the most modern religions is *nothing but psychology projected to the outer world*" (Dundes 1976b, 1505, emphasis in original).[4]

I see a connection between the ambiguity of his religious affiliation and his later assertion that a crucial consequence of folkloric transmission was a person holding simultaneous identities (1980h, 9; see also 1989c). He did not want to be essentialized into one monolithic stereotype; he had many other traits by which he socially identified himself at different times (folklorist, musician, father, professor). Although his father had been the president of a Jewish fraternity at City College of New York, the son did not associate with Jewish communal organizations in the same way. He reflected that when he became a folklorist, it was not to find his roots, although there are hints of a concern for social justice. He was preoccupied with groups outside his heritage that had suffered discrimination or colonialism: "Native Americans, African Americans, and the peoples of India, among others," according to his memoirs. It was not until a fateful trip to Israel in 1999, he acknowledged, that he "set about learning about Jewish religious ritual in earnest," although he did not become

Alan Dundes's library in his home, with cultural artifacts.

Photo by Simon Bronner

religious (2002c, xii). Even when he began writing on Jewish customs, he wanted to show that they were not exclusive, and he identified trans-cultural sources, a strategy that he also applied to the Christian Bible and Muslim Qur'an (1999, 2002c, 2003a). He also raised eyebrows by explaining customs of kashrut and Sabbath laws in relation to an anal-erotic cultural personality, and finding homoeroticism in Islam's position of prayer (2002c; 2004c).

When Dundes "set about learning," he read everything he could get his hands on, and at times referred to himself as more of a "library scholar" than a fieldworker. His voracious appetite for reading owed to a childhood regimen. His parents gave him an incentive to read as a young boy; they offered him a dollar for every hundred books he read, and he was free to choose the subjects. To earn the money, he had to keep a record of the books he finished. Standing out in number and memory in his accounting were anthologies of fairy tales. His parents' home was filled with books, and he remembered that "there was a multi-volume series called *Journeys Through Bookland* . . . [in which] were interspersed fairy tales, and I recall thumbing through the pages of the various volumes in search of these tales" (2002a, xi). If his eyes were already set on folk literature, his ears perked up for orally told jokes, and he developed a lively repertoire of his own. He recalled, "from grade school on, I became avidly interested in jokes, frequently repeating favorites to anyone who would listen to me. I recall with nostalgia how my father, despite his fatigue after a day of work sixty miles from home, would often share a 'new' joke he had heard during the day." As would occur so often later in life, an interest in oral material led him to scour the library. He added: "During my high school years, I eagerly devoured the few compilations of published jokes available in local libraries. . . . In college, as an English major, I learned to appreciate humor in more literary terms" (1987c, v).

A childhood passion for music, often overlooked in intellectual biographies of Dundes, deserves mention (Zumwalt 1995; Georges 2004; Mieder 2004; Hansen 2005; Gürel 2006; Nader and Brandes 2006). Influenced by his piano-playing mother, he was accomplished in music, studying the clarinet for many years and attending the Manhattan School of Music to take up music theory. Dundes recognized musical notation as a structural and symbolic system. He had a trained eye and ear for rendering performances in readable form, and seeing the relations of multiple parts. In "The Number Three in American Culture," he offered musical systems as a prime example of the principle that trichotomy consists of positions located in reference to some initial point. "In music," he authoritatively wrote, "the point of reference may be 'middle C,' which serves, for example as a midpoint between the [bass] and treble clefs in addition to functioning as a point of reference from which to describe voice ranges (e.g., 'two octaves above middle C')" (1980d, 136). He used music, too, to contrast Western and "primitive" music, in which "ternary time is not common . . . and thus its presence in Western and American music is all the more striking" (148). He also criticized ballad scholars for excising music from discussions of the text, and pointed out the nominal connection of the ballad to linguistic roots of "dance." If scholars made this connection, Dundes opined, they would realize that the ballad was not universal, as it tended to appear when they equated it with the folk-narrative text, but was culturally limited to Indo-European areas (1996b, ix–x).

When Dundes entered Yale, he declared music as his major. But a job in the library, working with the fiction collection, piqued his interest in literary classics, and he switched to English literature, to his mother's chagrin. His entrée into psychoanalytic theory occurred in a Yale classroom, through the reading of Otto Rank's *The Myth of the Birth of the Hero* ([1909] 2004) during his sophomore year. Rank had been a student of Freud's, and Dundes was mesmerized by his interpretation of the structural similarity in the hero cycles of different cultures. It provided a stark contrast to the dehumanized rhetoric of stimuli and reinforcement he heard in an elective course on behavioral psychology the previous semester. He recalled feeling disappointed in the material on behavioral psychology, because "it dealt only with explaining how homing pigeons managed to find their way and how white mice succeeded in running through mazes" (2002a, xii). Thus, Dundes's later equation of psychology with psychoanalysis was not out of a lack of awareness of other approaches; his conversion experience came from viewing the mind, rather than the body, as source (Dundes 1991a). Reflecting on what he called his "Aha!" response, he wrote, "perhaps it was my early attraction to fairy tales that made me check out the book, but in any event, I can still recall the thrill of discovery as I read Rank's remarkable essay" (2002a, xii). Even before he encountered the professional study of folklore, he had immersed himself in reading Freud. The later influence of Rank's analysis of traditional narrative can be discerned specifically in Dundes's writing on the hero cycle, and more generally in a concern for the psychological impact of birth and the mother's role in development, matters that forced a parting of the ways between Rank and Freud (Dundes 1990). Rank challenged Freud's assertion that myth and religion were rooted in the Oedipal complex by positing a pre-Oedipal phase, involving a separation anxiety ([1924] 1993; [1909] 2004; see also Lieberman 1998). Dundes referred to this phase, absent from Freud's theories, in his interpretations of flood and creation myths as male fantasies of female birth (1987b; 1988a).

Dundes's Yale classroom experience was one of two events that he called life-changing. He connected Rank's and Freud's studies of myths and jokes with his literary studies when he asked Paul Pickrel, his instructor for a course on the nineteenth-century English novel, whether he could investigate allusions to rural customs in the novels of Thomas Hardy. Uncertain of his ability to guide the young Dundes down this route, Pickrel referred him to faculty who could at Indiana University. Dundes completed his master of arts in teaching of English at Yale, and prepared for doctoral study at Indiana that would allow him, he said, "to combine my earlier interest in Freud with my chosen field of study: folklore" (2002a, xiii). In light of his writings—on the representation of the Civil Rights movement in folklore, and on conditions in the Soviet bloc—I believe that his attraction to folklore was also driven by what he perceived as its social relevance at a time of rising racial conflict nationally and Cold War political tension internationally. This is evident in pleas early in his writing career for cross-cultural attention to folklore as a way to bridge social and political differences (1969a; 1971b; 1973; Dundes and Abrahams 1969).

Another factor in his turn to folklore study was his talent as a joke teller. Psychoanalytic literature broached jokes together with folk and fairy tales because of their apparent symbolism of anxiety and aggression, but folklore studies, oriented toward literary and anthropological concerns for the purity of ancient texts and the sanctity of pre-modern cultures, respectively, rarely interpreted them psychologically. Dundes also was drawn to psychoanalysts' consideration of folk narrative, finding meaning in his childhood immersion in fairy tales as an alternative to the political uses of *Märchen* in the cause of romantic nationalism, including the Grimm Brothers in the nineteenth century and the Nazis and Soviets in the twentieth century (1966a, 233–34; 1969a, 472–73; 1970, 337; Oinas 1978; Dow and Lixfeld 1994; Bronner 1998, 184–236).

Reacting negatively to romantic nationalism and the conventional division of folklore studies by nation, Dundes's philosophical inclination was toward a global view of culture as well as politics (Dundes 1969a, 472–73). He believed that a fuller international awareness of folklore taught tolerance and social unity. One can read this sentiment in his complaint, published in a *Britannica* yearbook, that "folklore has too long been the tool of regionalism and nationalism." Lamenting that "folklore has more often been a divisive than a unifying influence in the world," he philosophized that "surely it is difficult to consider as an enemy someone who shares the same folktales and customs," and gave as examples the common traditions of peoples of Europe, Arabs and Jews, and Turks and Greeks. "If the world is ever to be truly united," he mused, "then the world's peoples as a 'folk' must have a world folklore. Some of this may come from the identification of old traditions held in common and some from newly generated ones" (1970, 337).

Dundes spent a year in France before he ventured out to the Midwest for doctoral study, and the tutelage of eminent folklorists Richard Dorson (known for historical approaches to American folklore), Erminie Wheeler-Voegelin (a specialist on Native American lore), Felix Oinas (an Estonian scholar from whom he learned of Russian formalist Vladimir Propp), David Bidney (a philosophical scholar of mythology and humanistic anthropology who was also accused of bucking scholarly orthodoxy), and Warren Roberts (a disciple of folktale scholar Stith Thompson's historic-geographic school). He traveled there with his bride Carolyn M. Browne, a graduate student of playwrighting in Yale's Drama School, whom he married in September 1958. He taught conversational English and managed to collect folklore in French, resulting in his first publication on tongue twisters in the *French Review* of 1960. Even in this early note, he demonstrated his attention to structure by noting a discernible pattern in the prevalence of word sequences containing the /s/ and /š/ phonemes (giving the English example of "She sells sea shells by the sea shore"). After this identification, he offered a functional interpretation involving the psychological effect of "the sense of power" children feel upon mastering the twisters (1960, 604–5).

The following year, while still a graduate student, Dundes published a note in the top-rank *Journal of American Folklore*, brashly suggesting that contemporary folklorists move from "worldwide collecting" of texts to considerations of the ultimate origins of folklore in individual development. Dundes applied Freudian theory in asserting that with increased parental discipline, the infant suppressed desires, which came out in dreams. "With maturity, however," Dundes wrote, "comes the ability to express these dreams in the form of folktales dealing with fictitious characters who are able, unlike the raconteur, to gratify their obscene wishes, at least temporarily" (Dundes and Schmaier 1961, 142). An example he gave was the role of humor "as an intrinsic quality of civilized manifestations of socially obstructed scatologic tendencies," that is, the symbolic reference by adults in obscene jokes of the pleasure of excrement in childhood (143–44).

Dundes gave an idea of the negative reception of his teachers to the psychoanalytic interpretation of scatalogic tendencies in his reminiscence of Professor Wheeler-Voeglin's course on North American Indian folklore. A memorable class took up the creation myth of the Earth-Diver, in which an animal brings up a tiny bit of mud from floodwaters, and the mud consequently expands magically to form the earth. A classmate gave a presentation on the myth that drew the professor's extra attention, since she had published commentary on it (Dundes 2002a, xiii–xiv). Dundes remembered, "When I heard the oral report, I could see immediately that it was a classic case of male anal-erotic creativity (in which males attempt to compete with females by creating from a substance produced by their bodies). I said as much in the seminar and was ridiculed by all assembled for this seemingly bizarre interpretation. I was sufficiently annoyed by this total rejection of my idea that I was inspired to write a paper on the subject that was later published in the *American Anthropologist* in 1962 [and reproduced in this volume]" (xiv). Dundes did not get much support for psychoanalytic interpretation from his adviser Richard Dorson, either. Dundes had thought that Dorson might be an advocate when he requested sources from Dundes, on psychoanalytic theory, for a survey of current folkloristic theories he was preparing for publication (Dorson 1963). Dundes felt betrayed by the published result, and told a revealing coming-of-age story, with himself shifting roles from naive seeker to hero-warrior: "Dorson did ably summarize all the sources I had so carefully given him, but only for the purpose of making fun of them. Instead of helping my cause, I had unwittingly aided and abetted the enemy. I had foolishly thought my professor had an open mind and that he sincerely wanted to learn something about the approach. Far from contributing to a greater understanding of the psychoanalytic approach to folklore, I had provided much of the ammunition used by Dorson to demean and ridicule it" (2002a, xv).

David Bidney, according to Dundes, had a more open mind toward psychoanalytic approaches to myth and folklore, but he criticized them for being reductionist (Bidney 1967, 8). Contributing an essay giving a psychoanalytic consideration of American football for Bidney's *festschrift* in 1979, Dundes wrote, "It is a pleasure to dedicate this essay to Professor David Bidney who taught me that there is no cultural data which cannot be illuminated by a judicious application of theory" (1979b, 237). Bidney questioned Freudian claims for the universality of symbols, and was attracted to Géza Róheim's revision of Freud's notion of the innateness of the content of the unconscious (Bidney 1967, 6–7). Róheim posited a situational understanding of folklore in which the content of tradition in different cultures expresses various dispositions to react emotionally to a common human experience. Bidney gave the example of a snake as a symbol of the penis. He explained Róheim's position that the snake as penis "is articulated by some individuals in a wide variety of cultures and is then accepted by others, who in turn utilize this symbol in their dreams as a means of expressing their psychological conflicts" (7). From this discussion with Bidney, Dundes was moved to edit for publication a volume of Róheim's essays, which he introduced with the remark, "His bold and sometimes startling interpretations of folklore have been an inspiration in my own research in the psychoanalytic study of folklore" (Dundes 1992, xxii). Although Dundes disagreed with Róheim's theory that folk narratives have their origin in dreams, and that the roots of these dreams are necessarily found in infancy, a significant lesson Dundes drew from Róheim and Bidney was that "there are *no* universals in folklore; not one single myth or folktale is found among every single people on the face of the earth, past and present" (xxiii).

Dundes completed his dissertation on a structural approach more acceptable to his teachers than psychoanalytic theory (1964b). A class project on a local collection of beliefs turned into an exercise in definition; it would be followed by many others that showed the structural characteristics of folklore genres, often ordered around a fundamental binary (Dundes 1961; Dundes and Georges 1963; Dundes 1975f). Writing on "The Binary Structure of 'Unsuccessful Repetition,'" Dundes extended his application of Vladimir Propp's morphology to Native American tales that begin with a "lack" and end with a "lack liquidated" (1962a). In an early challenge to the literary foundation of the tale-type index (Thompson [1928] 1961), Dundes identified a common binary of folk tales with "two moves, 'one of which ends positively and the other negatively,'" crossing Aarne-Thompson lines. The basis of his proposal to replace Thompson's etic (from phonetic) to emic (from phonemic) units of analysis that same year derived from his observation that "form is transcultural, content monocultural" (38). Therefore, tale types tended to overemphasize literal details associated with a single culture, rather than the cognitive patterning indicated by underlying structures. He concluded boldly with the declaration of a "*new science* of folklore which includes the structural study of folk tales" (174; emphasis added).

For beliefs, Dundes proposed a fundamental duality of condition and result. This led him to think about the belief in wishing wells, consisting of the condition "if you drop a coin in the well and make a wish," and the result "your wish will come true." And he came up with a Freudian alternative to the "literal" reading of magic: "Essentially there are two material objects involved in the action of an individual engaging in the custom: the well and the offering, which is usually a penny. Part of the key to the puzzle is provided by the very materials of folklore. The well is a frequent womb or maternal symbol" (1962f, 29). He drew the significance of the penny from its symbolic equivalence with feces, and therefore the custom involved "a fecal offering in return for either the good will of the mother or the avoidance of punishment" (31).

Having announced that he would not be deterred by naysaying folklorists, he landed an enviable post in anthropology at the University of California at Berkeley in 1963, and two years later helped create, with William Bascom, the M.A. folklore program there. From anthropology, he added another concept to the theoretical package that composed a Dundesian perspective. It drew from anthropological roots in Franz Boas's use of folklore texts to find reflections of a culture's distinctiveness (Boas 1916, 1935, 1938; see also Bascom 1954, 337–41). Dundes noticed two levels at which folklore acts as a reflective "mirror" of culture (1969a). First is the social commentary that folklore provides when tellers adapt old forms to new conditions, such as relating elephant jokes to the Civil

Rights movement (the dark African elephant is ignored even though it is hard to miss) or
dead baby jokes to the abortion debate during the 1960s (Dundes and Abrahams 1969;
Dundes 1979a). At an ideational level, the aggregate of folk wisdom in speech, proverbs,
and riddles signifies "folk ideas" that constitute a "worldview," or cultural outlook (Dundes
1971a). Examples are future orientation and lineal thinking in the progressive American
worldview, which Dundes contrasted with past orientation and circular representation in
Chinese culture (1969b, 2004a).

Dundes worried that his demonstration of folklore's disquieting reflections of society
would be taken by some reformers as an invitation to quash folklore. He sounded defensive, for instance, when publishing his interpretation of German concentration camp jokes
as psychological mechanisms to "come to terms with the unimaginable and unthinkable
horrors that occurred at Auschwitz" (Dundes and Hauschild 1987, 28). He explained that
"we are reporting these jokes not because we think they are amusing or funny, but because
we believe that *all* aspects of the human experience must be documented, even those that
most reflect the darker side of humanity. Unless or until the causes and extent of prejudice
are recognized, that prejudice will persist." He asked, "If the mirror image is unattractive,
does it serve any purpose to break the mirror?" His answer was, "The ugly reality of society
is what needs to be altered, not the folklore that reflects that reality" (38).

Dundes used the mirror concept to emphasize that the distinctive social historical conditions of a group make cultures relative to one another, rather than being arranged in
evolutionary or universal hierarchies (1966a, 241–45). This cultural relativism was especially important to his adaptation of Freudian theory. He challenged the psychoanalytic
assumption that Freudian mechanisms are cross-culturally valid. He took psychoanalysts
to task for a "cavalier disregard of cultural relativism, the notion that each human culture
is to some extent a unique, noncomparable entity" (Dundes 1987i, 23). Yet he was also
critical of anthropologists who extended historical particularism to what he considered
an "absurd" extreme. He wrote, "In applying the concept of cultural relativism to Freudian
theory, one comes up with the still all too often heard comment that psychoanalytic theory
applies only to Viennese Jewish culture. Any theory of culture developed in any particular cultural context may or may not apply to other cultures. It should and must be tested
in other cultural contexts in order to determine whether or not it has cross-cultural validity" (23–24). In this critique of relativism, he was influenced by his teacher David Bidney's
comparativist plaint that cultural relativism had obviated the evils of national ethnocentrism by establishing another type of ethnocentrism, one he called "serial." By this term
he meant the parochial attitude of viewing each culture from its own perspective only
(Bidney 1967, 427). Dundes set up his Freudian folkloristics, then, as a new comparative
approach to finding the psychological sources of culture, resulting from the mediation of
the seemingly polar opposites of psychoanalysts' classical Freudianism and anthropologists' cultural relativism.

Whereas Boas's use of "reflection" emphasized the unique historical conditions which
are embedded as collective memory in texts, and therefore construct a "particular" culture,
Dundes often found representations of *trans*-cultural connections in texts, which called
for psychological as well as historical readings, such as his frequent reference to Western
ideological beliefs. Considering that expressions often distorted reality in the process of
reflecting culture, folklore, in Dundes's view, could be more accurately described as a *key*
to unlock puzzles (Dundes 1962e). The concept of worldview in this unlocking process is
structural, because worldview ideas are underlying themes that drive expression. It relates

to psychoanalytic perspectives by assuming that there is a projective mechanism by which values are symbolically embedded and encoded in folk material, often outside the awareness of tellers. With these reflective and projective concerns organized into the binary of identification and interpretation, the Dundesian perspective became generalized as method (Dundes 1989e, 194–95).

If the Dundesian quest for meaning became regularized, if not normalized, how did the leading proponent of folkloristic interpretation become *mythologized*? One answer is that, unlike many of his cohorts who were characterized as noble "seekers," Dundes came to be narrated as an adventurer/warrior. He had a brash style that in reviewers' rhetoric epitomized "heroic," "visionary," "ambitious," and "unparalleled" action (Oring 1983, 88). His uncanny ability drew recognition, characterized this way in one review: "Alan Dundes probably knows more about folklore and folklore studies than any other living human being," and his mythological pluck elicited the description, "no matter how much his critics try to muddy the waters or thunder and rail, Alan Dundes will always come from behind and win the Grail" (Oring 1998, 64; Carroll 1993, 20). Students knew him as "The Master," "God," and "Himself"; colleagues referred to him as "the giant, our hero, the truly big man" and "sacred guide" (Bendix 1995, 50–51; Mieder 2004, 290; Bendix 2005, 487). Regina Bendix, who studied under him, remembered, "The capitalized 'He' . . . remains most prominent, for to those studying folklore at Berkeley, he is indeed the high priest of what he makes appear the most desirable discipline to work in: folkloristics" (1995, 51).

His hero story took the form of the young "gifted" prophet denied; undeterred, he ventured out on a crusading mission in which he shared insight with any audience that would listen, and implied the corruption of the elders. His proselytizing orations were delivered with *extra*ordinary speed, giving him an aura of superhuman physical as well as cerebral ability (Bendix 1995, 51–52). Known for his polemics, Dundes read his essays like homiletic jeremiads, warning of the wrong path taken by the flock, stirring dedication to the cause, and impelling believers to "carry the torch" (see Bercovitch 1980; Bendix 2005, 488; Dow 2005, 335). He thus attracted admirers outside the temple, who assigned him a priestly or seer status (in the unconventional dream land of California), despite his depiction of himself as a "leader without followers" (Nader and Brandes 2006, 269). Even after becoming firmly established in academe, Dundes constructed a self-description in which he skirted the mainstream of his field, and reveled in doing battle as well as breaking ground. Untethered to a specialized area, genre, or group, the world was his domain, the sky the apparent limit of subjects open to investigation. His pronouncements toward the end of his life sounded like pleas as well as prophecies (when not heeded, he could invoke the proverbial wisdom that "a prophet is not without honor except in his own country and in his own house" [Matthew 13:57]). His death in the classroom, preceded by a surprising one-million-dollar gift to endow a chair for folklore studies in his honor, only added to his mystique (Hansen 2005, 247).

Although reminiscences focused internally on battles he had with foes in the realm, narratives about Dundes could also be read as a projection of desires to spread folkloristic inquiry externally. The intimation was that folklore study is a repressed or belittled field struggling to achieve a wide intellectual priority (Nader and Brandes 2006, 270). Dundes was fond of referring to the goal of academic respectability accorded by analysis, and legendary depictions of his pugnacity against the disciplinary dragons guarding the ivory tower suggest a transference from "us" (folklorists) to "them" (the power elite of the academy). Dundes's fight for mainstreaming "deep" interpretation became emblematic of the cause to instill a consciousness of folklore, and to establish the authority of the folklorist universally. The negation of "That can't be Alan Dundes" became confirmation, in his own words, that "the promise of . . . folkloristics may yet be fulfilled," a variation of "the wish (dream) of folklorists may yet be fulfilled" (2002a, xvii).

Folk and Folklorist

The irony in Dundes's self-description of marginalization is that many of his ideas about folklore in fact became integrally linked with central modern concepts of folklore. One foundational example is the definition of folklore most folklorists have used since the 1960s. As a result of his widely used textbook, *The Study of Folklore* (1965b), Dundes largely succeeded in undoing the prevalent view that folklore is restricted to oral transmission. First, he pointed out that some orally learned items, such as driving a tractor or brushing one's teeth, are not ordinarily considered folklore. An orally transmitted item may be folklore, but Dundes logically concluded that "*by itself* [oral transmission] is not sufficient to distinguish folklore from non-folklore" (Dundes 1965d, 1; emphasis in original). Arguing that many forms of folklore such as autograph-album verse, epitaphs, and chain letters are exclusively written, Dundes further insisted that the criterion of oral transmission does not apply to many expressions considered traditional. He gave a long list of folkloric forms to suggest that folklore can take material forms, as well as oral ones. Lore did not mean only the spoken word, he insisted. But as Elliott Oring complained in his later textbook, *Folk Groups and Folklore Genres*, Dundes did not state a principle that connects all of these genres under the heading of "folklore" (1986, 15).

Dundes's answer to Oring was to avow that folklore repeats and varies (1989e, 193; 1998, 160). This characterization allowed for visual humor produced by photocopiers and, later, word processors, to be viewed as folklore, along with other non-oral forms. In *Work Hard and You Shall Be Rewarded*, Dundes demonstrated that "the materials contained in this study are traditional: they manifest multiple existence in space and time, and they exist in variant forms" (Dundes and Pagter 1978, xvii). Lore is "authentic," he averred, if it contains two or more versions, and change leading to the creation of variants is inevitable. Using his logic, one could construct the syllogism, "folklore is tradition and tradition is variation, so therefore variation is folklore."

Dundes recognized that the above characterization put the burden of proof on the lore, and he sought to contextualize its production socially in "folk." This modern folk differed from the Eurocentric idea of folk as a lower stratum of society. In an expansive definition, a folk group was, according to Dundes, "*any group of people whatsoever* who share at least one common factor" (Dundes 1965d, 2; emphasis in original). The pre-modern representation of folklore, coming from the soil/soul of the peasantry, influenced the perception of lore as artistry of the unlettered and survivals of the remote past (Dundes 1980h, 1–6; Bronner 1998, 184–236). Taking away a connection to the land, or to a lack of learning, emphasized that all people, by the nature of social interaction, use folklore as an instrumental, communicative device.[5] It can therefore emerge anew, or adapt old forms with different social associations, whether in conventional ethnic, occupational, and regional categories, among a group of friends, or in an organization. Much as Dundes's elastic folk has now been adopted as a given, a potential problem for folkloristics as a field is that it takes away the need for "folk" as a special modifier, for if all groups are by definition folk, then folk as a social category is potentially unnecessary (Oring 1986, 4). Jay Mechling questioned, in fact, whether one needed two persons to generate folklore, since expressive culture can be produced between a person and a pet, an imaginary object, or even oneself (Mechling 1989a, 2006). From a Dundesian perspective, the binary social premise still holds, even in "solo folklore," since an entity outside the self is created to share a tradition (Mechling 2006).

Implicit in Dundes's apparently structural definition was a criterion of bonding that merits evaluation. Dundes collapsed hierarchies by asserting that the folk "are us" (suggesting that every group produces some folklore), but atomized folk as well in contending that "there are an infinitude of folk groups" (1980h, 10). By describing what folk is, Dundes invited contemplation on what it is not, even though he was more interested in demonstrating its "rich variety" (9). It is possible to think of a group sharing a factor, but which does not traditionalize, or bond, through folklore (people on a bus, shopping at a store, driving the same car). The key test for the "folk group" is whether folklore is produced out of the social experience. Often overlooked, therefore, as Dundes's definition became standardized within folkloristics, is his qualification that "what is important is that a group formed for whatever reason will have some traditions which it calls its own." Thus the unstated part of the definition is that two or more persons who share a linking factor use *traditions* to bond, so to gain, in Dundes's words, "a sense of group identity" (1965d, 2). In other words, folklore is produced by groups who use folklore for the purpose of creating groupness. Despite the circularity of this logic, it has an instrumental purpose. It extends and democratizes the concept of folklore by affirming what Dundes called a "flexible" notion of tradition, and thereby negates folk as "monolithic" and "homogeneous" (1980h, 8).

In large measure, Dundes's "modern" definition reflects an American worldview, and in fact, in an early presentation, Dundes called it a characteristically "American concept of folklore" because of its differences from European models, geared toward the study of peasants and primitives (1966a). Unlike European class-based hierarchy, his social heterogeneity and simultaneity were democratic, in the sense of allowing mobile, "code-switching" participants to "choose" rather than inherit their identities (see Bronner 1986a, 94–129). "Part-time folk," as Dundes called typical "code-switching" moderns, have multiple, overlapping identities and "locate" their lore variously in city and country, street and home, profession and trade (1980h, 8–9). Instead of isolating tradition-centered groups, he proposed that all people have access to traditions; everyone creates them. Appearing integrative by sketching a variegated social landscape with a multiplicity of groups, he avoided racializing lore, and removed the devolutionary criteria of historical lineage, isolation, or illiteracy. Dundes implied agency in the groups' production of folklore, rather than the groups passively following or blindly receiving tradition, which he criticized as a "superorganic" model of culture, referring to the neologism of early Berkeley anthropologist A. L. Kroeber (Kroeber 1917; Dundes 1962g, 97; Dundes 1989a, 71–72; Dundes 1991a, 100; see also the critique of the superorganic by his teacher, David Bidney, in Bidney 1967, 329–33). If extended too far, though, Dundes's "flexible" definition could render everything as folklore, raising the specter that nothing is categorically folklore. Dundes, though, maintained a binary interpretation that the construction of folklore depended on something that folklore is not, ultimately turning to structural rather than social characteristics.

An example is his comparison of games to narratives in "On Game Morphology," reproduced in this volume. Although games and narratives are typically separated into social and oral genres, respectively, Dundes found a similar binary pattern of "lack to lack liquidated" prevalent in both (1964a). The implication for Dundes, therefore, was that they could and should be studied together as related traditions. In a consideration of culture-specific examples of trichotomy, he compared a scholarly article with a tale type because they both expressed such cognitive patterning. He related organized football to backyard games, Disney movies with orally transmitted tales, and television commercials and old sayings. This relying on folklore for treatment of all things cultural again raised the question of authenticity, that is, how to differentiate folk from popular materials. Dundes's structural answer was that a production *based upon* a folk model can be compared with, but distinguished from, "the folk model itself" (1965d, 1–2). The folk model, unlike the popular production, is more variable; the production tends toward fixed form. Variations characterizing different groups and individuals invite analysis of folklore's sociopsychological uses to explain diversity. Dundes editorialized that in contrast, "Literature and mass culture seem hopelessly rigid. . . . In studying them one must either seek to reconstruct the intellectual Zeitgeist or governing world-view paradigm present when the literary effort or popular/mass cultural product was created, or else abandon such a historical approach in favor of 'new criticism' or its successors in an attempt to investigate how an old literary favorite is understood by yet one more set of readers" (1998, 193).

Variation could define both folklore and the folklorist. Thinking about what differentiated the folklorist from the anthropologist, historian, literary scholar, or linguist—all occupations concerned with expressive culture—Dundes underscored the ability of the folklorist to deal with variations and continuities. He did not spare psychoanalysts from his criticism, because he pointed out mistakes caused by ignorance of textual variations, generic differences, and cross-cultural examples. He was especially critical of psychoanalysts, who based interpretations of fairy tales on the corpus of the Grimm brothers; such tales were not typical of tradition, since they were "fixed" by the brothers as composites of different versions (Dundes 1989e, 195–97; Dundes 1989f, 117–22; see also Carroll 1993, 6–7). He also sharply criticized Joseph Campbell and his Jungian followers for the universalist assumption that "all peoples share the same stories," leading to an unfounded conclusion of psychic unity that confused myths and folktales, which have different functions and variant structures (2005c, 394–98).

Variation is not only a prime characteristic of folklore, according to Dundes, but it is also one of folkloristics, which allows for theoretical diversity. Pointing this out was a way to justify incorporating psychoanalytic perspectives into a range of theories. Discussing the ballad of the "Walled-Up Wife," for instance, Dundes insisted, "just as literary criticism reveals genuine and legitimate differences of opinion about the meaning(s) of a short story or novel, so folkloristics must similarly encourage diversity in seeking to understand some of the finest specimens of human creativity, namely folklore" (1996b, xi). Dundes explained the resistance of folklorists and other cultural workers to psychoanalytic approaches as an avoidance of the traumas and taboo subjects raised by "plumbing the depths to explore the latent (as opposed to the manifest) content of folklore." "Folklorists, like other academics," he observed, "often choose an intellectual speciality as a form of escape from neurotic tendencies," and finding unconscious meanings in others's traditions would expose personal problems in their own (1992, xxii).

What, then, were the essential issues Dundes proposed for folkloristics in a modern, untethered analysis of folklore? The answer is evident in Dundes's outline of *The Study of Folklore* (1965b), roughly proceeding from the oldest concerns to the newest: origin, form, transmission, and function. He thereby suggested a historical progression, from where folklore came from in the past to what it does in the present. He then boiled folkloristic inquiry down to dual issues when he stated that "the two traits of folklore which most troubled folklorists were (1) the multiple existence of folklore, and (2) its apparent irrationality" (1987i, 4). It is possible to unfold these two characteristics into four concerns after examining Dundes's body of work:

1. *Multiple Existence across Space.* It is one thing to say that folklore spreads because it is appealing, but why does it pop up in the places it does, sometimes not connected by a social link? With the assumption that variation is inevitable as a result of multiple existence, why do certain patterns of variation emerge?

2. *Persistence through Time.* Frequently folklore is epitomized as being passed from generation to generation, as if it mindlessly survives. But what gets selected and what does not in the transmission and learning process? Related to this question is the role of modernization, since it is assumed in many Western industrial countries that modernization displaces, rather than creates, folklore. Yet new technologies associated with modernization foster folkloric creation, typically using "traditional" forms.

3. *Poetics and Projections.* Folklore draws attention to itself through both its content and style. It contains symbols and metaphors that raise questions about their sources and effects. Considering the social basis of lore, how does this lore reflect, distort, or project the values, feelings, and ideas of the groups that possess and perform the material?

4. *Rationale of Fantasy.* Folklore is frequently described as being fantastical, odd, or bizarre. Is there a rationale for this behavior that is given license as play, narrative, drama, and tradition? This problem involves the role of context and situation in the perception of lore by asking why something is appropriate in one instance but not in another. How do members inside a group (esoteric function) symbolize a group and its lore in contrast to non-members (exoteric function)?

In addition to delineating the problems of folklore that drive analysis, Dundes outlined a method of interpretation. Although he wanted to differentiate folklorists from other scholars concerned with cultural expression, he saw continuity in some of their methods of inquiry. Dundes suggested that the basic underlying structure of folkloristic research is *identification and interpretation*. The terms came from Archer Taylor's comparison of mid-twentieth-century literary and folkloristic methods, but Dundes did not limit interpretation, as Taylor did, to manifest readings using historical and formalistic background as the source of meaning (Taylor [1948] 1965). Interpreted meaning, according to Dundes, involved "plumbing the depths to explore the latent (as opposed to the manifest) content of folklore" (Dundes 1992, xxii). Dundes's use of identification and interpretation normalized a folkloristic division between description and analysis, although he often complained that what was presented as interpretation was too "literal" to provide insight or render analytical meaning (Dundes 1976d; Dundes 1998; Zolkover 2006, 45–48). A closer look at Dundes's polemical essay style, however, reveals a more multi-phased method than he acknowledged in asserting this basic binary.

Before identification, he often had a *problem statement*, involving an extended survey of bibliographic sources on the subject and the variations of the material under consideration. This opening section established the significance of his query, and, on many occasions, his dispute. He strove to break new ground in each essay by either reconsidering a previous interpretation (for example, in essays in this volume on the cockfight and earth-diver myth); complaining of a monocultural limitation, which he addressed with cross-cultural comparison or contrast (as in his writing in this volume on the ballad of the "Walled-Up Wife," and phrases using "bugger"); pointing out an action that had not been considered as a subject for inquiry (such as collecting as a praxis by folklorists); showing that an unlikely, usually learned or elite group was folk (among them scientists, mathematicians, trained musicians, and medical professionals); noting the effects of changing units of analysis (for example, etic to emic units); or correcting a nonfolkloristic treatment of folkloric material (such as Lévi-Strauss or Campbell on myth).

Dundes followed with an *identification*, predicated on the description of an item and the genre or genres to which it belonged. For Dundes, identification often involved material that had been neglected in previous collections, especially the extent of an item's variations, its various cultural contexts, behaviors associated with it, or the available metafolklore. Dundes constantly pointed out that previous scholars stopped short of analyzing the descriptive data, or analyzed the wrong thing. He thus moved to the *analysis*, which he defined as operating on the data to signify cultural patterns. This involved exposing underlying structures, or extracting symbols from a text for closer examination ("read out of" rather than "in" the data, he insisted); presenting contextual descriptions of an item's use (as in the invocation of proverbs in child rearing within Nigerian culture); using cross-cultural examples to draw comparisons and contrasts (such as "bugger," found in British speech, not being used as a derisive term in the United States); finding significance in etymologies and names as signs (for example, noting "testes" is the root of "contest," or the double meaning of "bull" as male genitals and "blowing," or commenting on the selection of Apollo as a name for a space program, when Apollo's sister Diana, the moon, is associated with virginity); or constructing the developmental chronology of an item or culture (such as the sources—in historic German farm practices, where display of manure piles represented prosperity—of feces as status symbols).

To Dundes, interpretation provided the critical leap from identifying patterns to recognizing cognition. It typically involved discerning meaning by reference to grand theory, and deducing generalizations that can serve to solve intellectual enigmas, resolve apparent paradoxes, and uncover hidden motivations (Dundes 2005c, 387–91). Dundes frequently turned to psychoanalytic theory because of his special concern for symbolic and developmental questions, but he also used suppositions from feminism (Karen Horney's idea of "womb envy"), linguistics (the Sapir-Whorf hypothesis, Kenneth Pike's emic and etic units, and Saussure's *langue* and *parole*), comparative ethnology (James Frazer's idea of homeopathic magic and Arnold Van Gennep's *rites de passage*), and cognitive anthropology (Dorothy Lee's premise of a lineal worldview). In its attention to functional causes, his interpretation frequently took as a given, following Malinowski, that folklore persisted because it served social and psychological functions that benefit people as individuals and members of groups, often as a response to ambiguity or anxiety.

Dundes typically did not stop at the point of interpretation. Frequently his conclusion constituted a final phase of what I call *implication*, and there I find his most original, and controversial, contributions. As others have pointed out, he did not introduce new paradigms as much as adapt social and psychological theories, so as to present provocative possibilities of folkloristic meaning, many of which had not been previously considered (Oring 1983; Carroll 1993, 7–8; Georges 2004). In his conclusions, though, he extended his analysis in often novel ways. His implications differed from many folklorists' *application* (the basis of applied or public folklore), because he usually did not propose programming to edify the public or procedures for professionals (1962g; 1980e, x; 2005a, 359–61; for the praxis of application, see M. O. Jones 1994). Instead, Dundes used his analysis and interpretation to consider either the social and political significance of the outlooks he uncovered, or the symbolic relationships among apparently diverse forms and traditions. He was not the first, for example, to claim that a German obsession with cleanliness and order has an anal-erotic character. Besides using folklore as a mirror of culture, however, he pointed to the implication of political uses of "elaborate purges," including the Holocaust, by comparing enemies to feces, and suggested that such purges could happen again (1984a, 141).

An implication he particularly touted came out of his interpretation of male competitive traditions such as football, cockfighting, and verbal dueling. In those studies, he argued that the aggressive behavior in these games represented attempts to demonstrate masculinity by feminizing one's opponent. He contended that this pattern was a reaction to the "female-centered conditional experience from birth through early childhood until adolescence" (1997e, 42). His implication was that such a behavior pattern constituted a cause of war. Claiming this as a "new argument," he wrote: "Those who may be skeptical of my attempt to offer a plausible rationale underlying male behavior in such activities apparently as diverse as games, hunting, and warfare will probably be pleased to hear that in none of the vast literature devoted to the psychology or sociology of sport—or for that matter in the even vaster scholarship devoted to seeking to articulate the causes of war—will they find anything like the theoretical argument I have proposed in this essay" (1997e, 42).

In making the argument for the sources of war, religion, male chauvinism, or folktales, Dundes used two key concepts that deserve discussion. The first was the idea of "projection," and the second was that of "symbolic equivalence." Both built on previous scholarship, psychoanalytic and linguistic, respectively, but Dundes revised them to apply his own stamp. Both also involved binary relationships between characters and representations, categorically referred to as A and B within the frame of a narrative or ritual.

The term *projection* has entered popular discourse through Freud. Dundes cited Freud's idea of projection from a 1911 paper, "Psycho-Analytic Notes upon an Autobiographical Account of a Case of Paranoia," in which Freud posited that the repression of "I hate him" becomes transposed to "He hates me" (Dundes 1987i, 37). It was Otto Rank, however, who in *The Myth of the Birth of the Hero* ([1909] 2004) described the transposition in folktales using Oedipal wish-fulfillment. Dundes argued that the label "projective inversion" is more appropriate than "transposition," since desires are not only inverted, but externalized. In a Dundesian perspective, Freud's projection can be read as symbolizing "I hate him," using slurs or stories in which the object of hate is victimized. Dundes defined projective inversion this way: "a psychological process in which A accuses B of carrying out an action which A really wishes to carry out him or herself" (1991b, 353). Dundes distinguished this kind of transposition from the transference of feelings onto an external object, which he called "projection." Dundes's projection is a way to deal with anxieties or pent-up emotions, and involves disguising the object in the external expression. Dundes especially discussed examples of projection in rituals and jokes such as "dead baby jokes," which expressed anxiety over abortion; "light bulb jokes," which showed the importance of social organization through the double entendre of technology and sex expressed by "screwing in a light bulb"; Jewish-American Princess jokes, which projected unease over the independence of women generally through the stereotype of the self-centered Jewish daughter; and "Bloody Mary rituals," with representations of blood both in the name of the girl and the act of drawing blood, expressing fear of menstruation among pre-adolescent girls (1987c, 2002a).

Dundes found that projective inversion is especially prevalent in folktales and legends, suggesting that their narrative elaboration signifies a heightened level of taboo. Examples include the themes of incest and infanticide, evident in a classic Oedipal plot in which a father-king attempts to kill his newborn son, a projective inversion of the son's wish to kill his father. Dundes's contribution was to view such a tale according to female projection, and take early psychoanalysts to task for their male-centeredness because they missed the significance of a father-king's act of locking up his daughter to protect her. Dundes proclaimed that early Freudians were mistaken in assuming that this merely reflected a father's wish to marry his own daughter. He asserted instead that the daughter would like to marry her own father. Examining the folktale plot underlying Shakerspeare's *King Lear*, Dundes concluded that "the daughter's wish to marry her father is transformed through projective inversion into the father's wish to marry his daughter, just as the son's wish to kill his father is similarly transformed into the father's wish to kill his own son. Both transformations leave sons and daughters guilt free. Fairy tales, after all, are always told from the child's point of view, not the parents'. I concluded that King Lear was essentially a girl's fairy tale told from the father's point of view" (1987i, 37; see also 1976d).

Dundes frequently presented projective inversion as a way to explain enigmatic features of the world's best-known traditions and themes. He was concerned, for instance, that approaches to the widely (but not universally) known vampire legend focused on either the repulsion or seduction of the figure. Building on the folkloric variations of the legend featuring attacks on younger family members and efforts of the vampire to drink milk rather than blood, Dundes hypothesized that the vampire is an incarnate expression of a child's ambivalence toward his or her parent of the opposite sex. The inversion is that instead of infants sucking from adult breasts, adults thrive on children's bodies. The life-giving liquid can be water, blood, or milk. Vampires according to this theory are bloodthirsty because death is debirth, represented by sucking, but as the dead are angry, they suck their victims to death (Dundes 1998).

Another of Dundes's provocative reinterpretations used projective inversion to analyze the "blood libel" or "ritual murder" legend, a source of European anti-Semitism. In the legend, a Christian child is killed to furnish blood for consumption during Jewish rites (Aarne-Thompson motif V361). The story has been recognized as one of the most persistent anti-Semitic narratives among European Christians since the twelfth century. As a legend, it is frequently told as a true event, in spite of its implausibility, since the consumption of blood by humans is forbidden in Jewish law (Genesis 9:4; Leviticus 3:17, 17:12). Dundes purports to solve this puzzle, noting especially its coincidence with the Easter/Passover season, by pointing out the *projection* of guilt to another group through the *projective inversion* of Christians committing murder.

> For the commission of an aggressively cannibalistic act, participants in the Eucharist would normally feel guilt, but so far as I am aware, no one has ever suggested that a Catholic should ever feel any guilt for partaking of the Host. Where

is the guilt for such an act displaced? I submit it is projected wholesale to another group, an ideal group for scapegoating. By means of this projective inversion, it is not we Christians who are guilty of murdering an individual in order to use his blood for ritual religious purposes (the Eucharist), but rather it is you Jews who are guilty of murdering an individual in order to use his or her blood for ritual religious purposes, making matzah. The fact that Jesus was Jewish makes the projective inversion all the more appropriate. It is a perfect transformation: Instead of Christians killing a Jew, we have Jews killing a Christian!" (1991b, 354).

As the above example demonstrates, Dundesian interpretations were derived from content analysis, conceptualized as a "systematic, objective description of the content of communication" (Dundes 1962h, 32; see also Pool 1959). Dundes's approach was heavily dependent on the assumption that wishes and feelings were disguised in the form of textual symbols, and expressed through the "safe" outlet of narrative.

Aware of the criticism that symbolist interpretations of texts are difficult to empirically verify, Dundes responded with the concept of "symbolic equivalence," using units of analysis he called allomotifs and motifemes. Dundes asked, "How do we know, in short, that A is a symbol of B (or B of A)? Is it only a matter of accepting a proposed symbolic equation on faith, or is there in fact a methodology which would permit a measure of certitude in determining the meaning(s) of symbols?" (1987j, 167). Heading off the objection that the discernment of symbols is impressionistic, he arranged functions within a structural system that could replace the prevalent non-structural classification of motifs as minimal units in narrative. His structural system was the sequence of functions for dramatis personae outlined by Vladimir Propp's "morphology" (Dundes 1968b; Propp [1928] 1968). The motif is based on plot features which Propp asserted were "vague and diffuse," while the function relies on "exact structural features" (Dundes 1962g, 101; see also Ben-Amos 1980). Dundes highlighted the distinction between functions and motifs by applying linguist Kenneth Pike's distinction between etic units, constructs created by the analyst to handle comparative cross-cultural data, and emic ones that deal with particular events as parts of larger wholes, to which they are related and from which they obtain their ultimate significance (1962g, 101–2). A function is an emic unit because, in Dundes's words, it stays "closer to the tale as it exists when told by a raconteur to an audience" (1987j, 168). Dundes proposed that Propp's function in Pike's scheme of analysis would be called a "motifeme," while "allomotif" would designate a motif that occurs in any given motifemic context. Applying a linguistic analogy, Dundes offered that allomotifs are to motifemes as allophones (any of various acoustically different forms of the same phoneme) are to phonemes (speech sounds designated by speakers of a particular language), and allomorphs (variant phonological representations of a morpheme) are to morphemes (minimal meaningful language units) (1962g, 101).

Dundes's goal in establishing this structural system was to gain access to implicit native formulations of symbolic equivalences (Dundes 1984c; Dundes 1987j; Carroll 1992b). This could be done, he asserted, by "empirically reviewing the content of field-collected versions of a tale type." The explanatory logic, Dundes pointed out, was, "If A and B both fulfill the same motifeme, then in some sense is it not reasonable to assume that the folk are equating A and B. In other words, allomotifs are both functionally and symbolically equivalent." Thus he disavowed that the interpretation came from "some biased folklorist wrongly imbued with a particular mindset belonging to one symbolic school or another" (1987j,

168). Dundes insisted that instead of an analyst "reading in" an idea to the text, the symbolic equation is "read out" of it. Thus, Dundes concluded his controversial interpretation of German national character with the disclaimer, "It is not I who is claiming that the German love of order may stem from a love of ordure—it is in the folklore" (Dundes 1984a, 153).

To make the case for the symbolic equivalence of nose and phallus, for instance, Dundes cited field-recorded texts from apparently different traditions: one is an anti-Jewish joke, while the other is a Texas blason populaire.

> Two Jews were walking beside a lake. One of them struck his finger in the water and said, "Wow, the water's cold!" The other one stuck his nose in and said, "Yes, and deep, too."

> Two Texans are walking across the Golden Gate Bridge in San Francisco. In the middle of the bridge, they decide to take a leak [to urinate]. One says, "Boy, this water's cold"; the other comments, "But not very deep." (1987j, 169)

Dundes realized that the placement of the nose and phallus within the telling of the text had similar "functions," but that did not conclusively prove symbolic equivalence. He explained, "It is perfectly true that examining the allomotific gamut within a particular motifemic slot shows only functional equivalence. We can tell that A and B are functional or symbolic equivalents, but not necessarily that A is a symbol of B or that B is a symbol of A. On the other hand, if we find evidence in a given culture that either A or B is a tabooed subject, then we might well expect that the non-tabooed subject might be substituted for the tabooed subject rather than vice versa" (1987j, 170). Dundes corroborated the nose/phallus equation by finding additional instances in a variety of genres, or by establishing the cultural contexts in which it occurred. He modified the frequent psychoanalytic assumption that symbolism is universal, though, with cultural relativism, and echoed the "sometimes a cigar is just a cigar" quote attributed to Freud: "Please keep in mind that I am not arguing that a nose always stands for a phallus—even just within Western cultures, the provenience of the above-mentioned materials. Sometimes a nose is a nose!" (171). In the other examples I cited of traditions symbolically involving blood, for instance, the liquid has culturally based meanings. Dundes found evidence in the vampire legend of a parental link in the equivalence of blood and milk in a motifemic slot. In the religious context of the European-Christian blood-libel legend, Dundes saw evidence of blood's representation of the Eucharist, but in the American context, in which rituals for menarche are rare, blood as expressed by pre-adolescent girls symbolized menses.

Dundes's method of using emic units raises a number of questions about identifying symbols in one context with references to symbols in another. Besides the nose/phallus connection, one should ask about the substitution of Texans for Jews, *if* the Jewish joke indeed preceded the Texan narrative; and its concluding negation of "deep," if in fact that is a representative ending. Dundes warned that several variants need to be examined, since he is himself a critic of choosing one form of the text as emblematic of a type. Elliott Oring, a frequent reviewer of Dundes's work, called the methodology of symbolic equivalence "the surrogate symbolic nexus syndrome," and worried that "the soundness of this operation should to some extent prove inversely proportional to the 'distance' the interpreter must travel from his primary symbolic context to establish the symbol-referent nexus." Although purportedly an objective process, allomotif analysis, according to Oring, still appears subjective because the selection of symbol-referent nexes may exclude "a number of possible and perhaps contradictory nexes for a single symbol." In considerations of cultural relativism, one needs to ask why a trait in society A informs the meaning of an item in societies B and C. The question remains, then, as Oring put it, "Why should the key to the meaning of folklore in one cultural and geographical context be found only in another?" (1983, 86).

One answer from Dundes was to separate, as levels of analysis, the transcultural structural interpretation and the culturally specific textual one. In Dundes's approach, formal analysis precedes content analysis. On this formal level, the structure survived translation, independent of language. Dundes gave the proverb, which he formally defined as combining a topic and a comment, as an example of this (1962h, 37). The simplest form of proverb could be rendered in English with the example "money talks"; it can be extended by filling structural slots, as in the examples "Barking dogs seldom bite" or "Still waters run deep." But the structure presumably could be identified in any language, Dundes proposed (36–37). The content tended to be variable, as opposed to the constancy of the form. One can also identify a linguistic level dependent on the particular language in question. Borrowing the term "textural" from linguist Thomas Sebeok, Dundes pointed out that textural elements, or stylistic features, ordinarily cannot survive translation. In the proverb, equational forms (A = B) such as "Time is money" or "Seeing is believing" are independent of language or code. But "A friend in need is a friend indeed" has the textural feature of rhyme, which "reinforces the structural pattern in that the two sides of the equation rhyme" (1962h, 37; see also Sebeok 1962; Dundes 1975f; Dundes 1980g; Sein and Dundes 1964).

When Dundes interpreted the content of the "A = B" proverbial form "seeing is believing" as *meaning*, he found the American context of dependence on sight for judgments to be symbolically equivalent to the active eye taking precedence over the passive agent of the ear (1980f, 90). The source of action in the mind is even expressed visually in the phrase "the mind's eye." The priority of seeing over touch also established an expansive, outer-directed worldview ("looking as far as the eye can see"), in contrast to the inner or tradition-directed outlook of an intimate community (expressed by "stay in touch") (89; see also Bronner 1982; Bronner 1986b, 1–4). The American hierarchy of senses he identified also suggested, for him, the priority of written language that must be seen in a future-oriented society. The *implication*, according to Dundes, was that "much of the study of 'natural history' often turns out to be 'cultural history' in disguise. Theories and ideas about the natural world are invariably couched in terms of a specific human language and are based upon data obtained from human observation. With human observation expressed in human language, one simply cannot avoid cultural bias." This insight allowed him to comment, too, on why so many social theorists fail to notice folklore, to their detriment, despite the fact that it can reveal so much: "We do not see the lens through which we look" (1980f, 92). Dundes held up folklore as crucial evidence of human thought and action, but pointed out that many scholars miss it because it is too close to their own experience. It is viewed as ordinary, although for Dundes that made it especially important to reflect everyday life, or to serve as an outlet for anxieties not communicated by other means.

WWDS

A simple lapel button crafted with Dundes in mind, and containing several layers of significance, encapsulates some of his impact on the intellectual heritage of folkloristics. One of Dundes's students placed it in my hand at a folklorists' conference in 2005, and beamed with the message, "I guess I don't have to explain to you what it means." I looked down and

WWDS button.

Photo by Simon Bronner

saw the crisp black letters WWDS against a plain white background. Her comment made me think that she must have received some puzzled reactions to the initialism, but the process of figuring it out forced the viewer to engage in a Dundesian enterprise of digging beneath the textual surface for meaning. It was an invitation to talk, and break into folklore. The initialism, as verbal lore, had floated around Berkeley for years before the button commodified the message for a wider audience.[6]

WWDS immediately signals it is an initialism not only because of the succession of capital letters, but also because of the two Ws in a row, not found in English. The capitalization indicates that the combination of letters is important, a signifier for something larger and longer. The four letters recall the popular initialism WWJS used in Christian circles. It stands for "What Would Jesus Say?" and reminds listeners of an ethical message amid today's hectic, acronym-filled, modern world.[7] Its form is reinforced by the popularity of text-messaging initialisms (such as WTMI for Way Too Much Information), and indeed WWJS circulates widely in electronic communication.[8] By recognizing the initialism, religious believers created a social bond through esoteric knowledge. Among some Christian believers, such initialisms are common as mottos or devotional meeting starters. For instance, one can also hear or see the initialisms JCLU (Jesus Christ Loves You) and CTR (Choose the Right, popular among Mormons), or acronyms such as ACTS (Adoration, Contrition, Thanksgiving, Supplication), FROG (Fully Rely on God), and PUSH (Pray Until Something Happens). One might even get variations of WWJS as WWJD (Walking With Jesus Daily or What Would Jesus Do?) and WWYD (What Would You Do?).[9] Folklore collections from Catholic school students include the practice of inscribing initialisms on examinations to summon aid: JPFM (Jesus Pray For Me) or SJOC (Saint Joseph of Cupertino, colloquially known as the patron saint of the stupid) (Huguenin 1962). Some Christian initialisms use negation by substituting new meanings to worldly initials, such as turning TGIF, "Thank God It's Friday," to "Thank God I'm Forgiven" or "Thank God I'm Free." Rather than the proverbial topic and comment, these phrases have an interrogative structure of an agent/sender, and action with an implied receiver. In other words, the ritual of figuring out the button's message implies a communication model in which the message draws attention to itself, and meaning is produced or perceived.

The ubiquity, or righteousness, of WWJS has also led to many parodies in talk and written prose, suggesting the repression or resentment of the sentiment or commenting on the modern irreligious/existential state of the world:

WWJS—Who would Jesus shoot?
WWJS—What would Jesus smoke?
WWJS—Who would Jesus spank?
WWJS—Where would Jesus surf?
WWJS—Where would Jesus shop?
WWJB—Who would Jesus bomb?
WWJD—Who wants jelly donuts?
WWJD—What would Jesus drive?
WWJD—What would Jerry [Garcia] do?
WWJD—What would [Michael] Jordan do?

Low approval ratings for WWJCD (What would Jackie Chan do?) and WWSWJS (What Web site would Jesus surf?), in online discussion threads with the metafolkloristic online feature of ranking variants, suggest the importance of the four-letter form. I suspect that Dundes might have commented on the double-binary form and the Western cultural bias for four, signifying an abundant quantity (four corners of the world, four seasons, four quarters in sports) (see Dundes 1980d; Brandes 1985).[10] He also might have pointed to the nominal suggestion of double meaning in the linguistic clue of WW, spoken as "double-u, double-u," which also denotes "world wide" (e.g., World War, World Watch, World Wide Web, and indeed WWDS for World Wide Day in Science) and trouble (as in WWW for What Went Wrong and Wet, Wild, and Wicked).

Dundes might have compared analysis of this form to his exegesis of light bulb jokes ("Many Hands Make Light Work" [1987g]) that feature the question "How many *x* does it take to screw in a light bulb?" The answers are based on social stereotypes: Californians—ten, one to screw it in and nine others to share the experience; New Yorkers—three, one to screw it in and two to criticize; psychiatrists—only one, but the light bulb has to really want to change; Iranians—one hundred, one to screw it in and ninety-nine to hold the house hostage; Jewish mothers—I would rather sit in the dark. There he read, out of the many variant forms, a future-oriented worldview in which groups, not individuals, were agents of change. That orientation created anxiety in individuals to keep up with change, from a fear of falling behind. The joke, with all its variants assigned for different groups, grades and mocks social inadequacy, as demonstrated by technological failure. The symbolic significance of technological energy (a light bulb) is heightened by an implied meaning of sex, as in the alternative answer for Californians: "they don't screw in light bulbs, they screw in hot tubs." Therefore, in the American context where the jokes arose, the acutely felt, repressed fear of sexual inadequacy is wrapped up with constant striving for social success, political power, and national progress. Dundes concluded that "when we joke about the impotence of others, we are joking about our own potential lack of power" (1987g, 149).

Following the line of reasoning in "Many Hands Make Light Work," WWDS might imply spiritual failure, coupled with the anxiety over intellectual inadequacy. The symbolic action in WWDS of putting Dundes on an iconic pedestal is to turn the question "Is

Dundes smarter than us all?" into "Am I smart enough?" Yet the acronym is also ambiguous enough to create the possibility of distance; it can be perceived as meaning he is not holier or smarter but marginal or different, indeed *far*-fetched and *outland*ish. If there is a double meaning, it is an extension from the self to the folklorist group that turns "What would Dundes say about us or our world?" into "Are we significant/spirited/global enough?" The text connotes a binary opposition of Dundes's *meaning* to our *meaningless* scholarship. This opposition has a value hierarchy according superiority to the Dundesian first pole, shown in couplets such as deep/surface, latent/manifest, emergent/vanishing, symbolic/literal, and mind/body. Rather than finding strength in the support of a mainstream majority, the text glorifies the defiant, pietistic few who follow the introspective, interpretative path.

At a structural level, the multiplicity of the form WWJS reflects the essentializing of folklore as textual repetition and variation, but perhaps less obvious is the contextual idea of folklore as creation—emerging constantly in modern settings and with new media (Dundes 1980h, 17–19; see also Jakobson and Bogatyrev 1980; Abrahams 1977; Ben-Amos 1977). Pursuing the esoteric Dundes connection to the button further, one can detect biographical references to Dundes's scholarly investment in folk speech, including his first publications on mnemonic devices and interrogative replies; belief and religion, especially his study of the Jesus hero cycle, suggesting a transference from subject to author; and of course the communicative frame of humor and play (including the initialisms and acronyms in Dundes 1980d, 140–41). One might argue that the legitimacy of WWDS as a variant comes from both the maintenance of the four-letter form with WW as the first function, and the inclusion of both D and S from the tradition of asking what Jesus would *do* as well as *say*.

As a representation of a community of believers, the button obviously equates Dundes with Jesus. However, the frame of play that usually accompanies the presentation of the button denies a genuine sacrilegious intention. But there is clearly an assignment of savior/prophet status to Dundes, and the implication that he, too, had a gospel to spread. I can imagine Dundes might recognize a response to anxiety as well, since here folklore emerges from the impulse to explain his prodigious output as somehow supernatural, and to express a fear of inadequacy in those unable to match his standards. Produced in Dundes's end days and coming from students known for devotion to his causes as well as pursuit of his support, the button also represents the fear of losing Dundes as a father figure and mentor (see Bendix 1995, 50–51). Personal fear of loss is projected to a disciplinary "lack." The message is, at another level, a reminder of the power of communication generally and words specifically. In concluding with "say," the button highlights the significance of speech, and perhaps equates the D of what Jesus would *do* with the D of Dundes as a hero figure. Dundes is singled out, not just as a Freudian folklorist, structuralist, or functionalist preaching to the masses to change their ways, but as *Dundes*, a unique persona who cast a long, if often not fully appreciated, shadow. Most of all, it suggests the distinctiveness of Dundes's structural and psychoanalytic commentary on what scholars do, imparting that they might be enlightened by taking his perspective into account. There is also a jeremiad implicit in the question of what he would say, since his rhetoric often carried polemical disapproval of the worldly or disciplinary state of things. In sum, Dundes has been mythologized because his representation offers revelation, and thereby serves a redemptive function for those on a cultural quest for meaning. Even if one does not agree with his interpretations, his confidence in having found the truth gives hope that the goal can be reached.

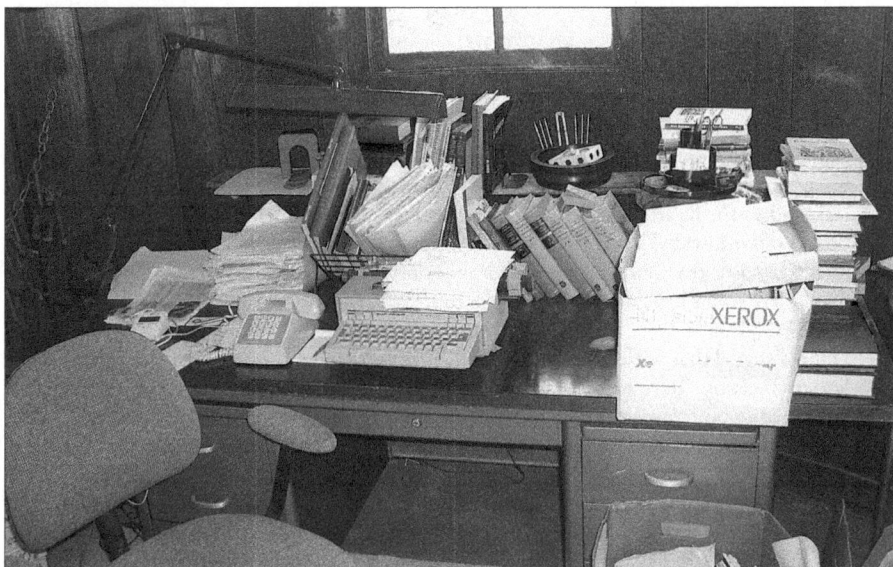

Photo by Simon Bronner

Alan Dundes's desk in his basement workroom.

Set in hermeneutic terms, Dundes's analytics was about finding *sources*—in mind, in society, in the past, in scholarship. Folklore is itself a source for genesis and for modern existence, from culture, tradition, and belief. Folklore is the scripture, Dundes suggested, that can be read for meaning here (within the local) and there (out in the world). Folklore can be parsed for both the immediate and the ultimate, for the particular and the universal, and the innovative and the traditional (Dundes 1987b). Dundes indeed referred to the metaphor of folklore as cultural scripture when he pointed out that those documents known as scripture, such as the Hebrew and Christian Bibles and the Qur'an, incorporate folklore. To show his logic in connecting the sacredness of religion with the spirituality of tradition, he provided the following syllogism in *Holy Writ as Oral Lit*:

1.   Folklore is characterized by multiple existence and variation.
2.   The Bible is permeated by multiple existence and variation.
3.   The Bible is folklore! (1999, 111)

He then stated that Jesus would have understood his argument, because when asked for a sign from heaven, Jesus cited a belief from tradition, a variant of the widely known saying "Red sky in the morning, sailors (shepherds) take warning." (Matthew 16:2–3; Dundes 1999, 112). Dundes saw himself finding meaning, as Jesus did, out of the signs of folklore, "the signs of the times." I am not suggesting that Dundes's essays are holy chapter and verse. But they arguably can be read as scholarly homilies that seek folkloristic meaning. He addressed fundamental questions of existence by pointing to folklore as an expression of the human condition. He asked, historically, how and why our ideas of culture got started; socially, how and why they are transmitted and shared; and psychologically, how and why they are conceived and perceived. In his analytics, Dundes collapsed the social/artistic binary of folk and lore to locate cultural identity, comprehend thought, and capture the human spirit.

Notes

1. Dundes was not consistent in connecting mind to the binary and body to the trinary. In "The Number Three in American Culture," he cited the precedent of Emory Lease who proposed that "the primary divisions of the human arm and leg, not to mention the finger, tend to support trichotomic thinking," but reflected that "anatomical datum would appear to reinforce 'two' rather than 'three.'" He argued, "There are two sexes, two ears, eyes, nostrils, arms, legs, and so forth. These universally recognized pairs would help to explain why dualism is probably worldwide." Yet he then goes on to present dualism as a cognitively based concept by referring to the fundamental dichotomies of "self/other" and "us/them" to underscore that "there seems little doubt that 'two' is more widely distributed in the world than 'three'" (1980e, 135).

2. Dundes shared these reflections with me when we were invited guests at the Hoosier Folklore Society meeting, Terre Haute, Indiana, in 1997. Dundes was hardly alone in his attraction, attributed to both Jewish and scholarly background, to Freud's subversion of biological determinism, which was used to justify racist attitudes toward Jews (Gilman 1993a, 6–10; Gilman 1993b, 3–48). Yet as Elliott Oring points out in *The Jokes of Sigmund Freud*,, there is also an implied ambivalence toward Jewish identity in Freud's analysis of Jewish jokes, and the thesis could be extended to Dundes (Oring 1984, 102–18). Indeed, Oring's book is dedicated to Dundes. Indicative of Dundes's concern for drawing more attention to Freud's Jewish background is the first English translation of Isidor Sadger's *Recollecting Freud* ([1930] 2005), edited and introduced by Dundes, with a chapter on "Freud and Judaism" (90–100).

3. His "strong outrage" at the Holocaust was related to me by Carolyn Dundes at the Western States Folklore Society meeting in Berkeley, April 2006. Another indication is Dundes's correspondence to Wolfgang Mieder (July 3, 2001), in which he singled out the Holocaust as "a great human tragedy" (see Mieder 2006a, 174).

4. The way his wife, Carolyn Dundes, expressed his attitude toward religion to me was that "he was interested in *all* religions" (conversation, Western States Folklore Society meeting, Berkeley, California, April 2005).

5. Gary Alan Fine has pointed out the precedent of what he calls a "sociological" view in Joseph Jacobs's "The Folk" (Jacobs 1893; Fine 1987). Dundes was aware of Jacobs's view, since he reprinted his essay in *Folklore: Critical Concepts in Literary and Cultural Studies*, edited by Dundes (2005b). My discussion of the influence of Jacobs's Jewish background and consciousness of diasporization on his view, in 1893, of folklore created in contemporary situations, could be applied to Dundes's situation when he proposed his "modern" concept of folklore in 1962 (Bronner 1998, 135–37). Although Jacobs (1854–1916) was a diffusionist, while Dundes called himself a structuralist and psychoanalytic folklorist, they arguably also shared a protest against prevalent trends promoted by the senior guard of their fields. For Jacobs, evolutionary doctrine was his target, whereas for Dundes it was historic-geographic methodology. For Jacobs's contrary position in British folklore studies, see Dorson (1968, 266–73). Dorson did not give Dundes the same kind of biographical treatment, but he did write the foreword to Dundes's *Analytic Essays*, in which he compared him more to another British folklorist, Andrew Lang, for "the gift" of an "inquiring mind" (1975).

6. September 17, 2006 correspondence from folklorist Maria Teresa Aggozino, a long-time associate of Dundes at Berkeley. "WWDS" also shows up in a discussion thread on the Hebrew song *Had Gadya* (Little Goat) at the website LiveJournal (http://rymenhild.livejournal.com/42896. html, accessed September 22, 2006). Shuduri_sour posted a message labeled "WWDS" on April 14, 2005, and wrote, "after seven classes with the late Professor Alan Dundes, I can confidently say that this song is indicative of some oral aggressive tendencies." Charles Clay Doyle, in his 2006 Archer Taylor Lecture, "Is the Pope Catholic? Some Unfinished Business about Proverbs," at the Western States Folklore Society meeting, Berkeley, California, April 21, 2006, prefaced the lecture with a reminiscence of hearing WWDS at Berkeley.

7. A Google search of the Internet on September 22, 2006, revealed other meanings of WWDS, including World Wide Day in Science, What Would Dad Say, Watson Wyatt Data Services, and What Would the Democrats be Screaming. But for most receivers of the button, there is an awareness of WWDS as an adaptation of WWJS for "What Would Jesus Say?" It uses the form of the initialism to replace the usual association of such worldly signifiers as corporate or media representations (e.g., WWDS in Muncie, Indiana, for a radio station or WWE for World Wrestling Entertainment) and self-actualization messages (e.g., SALT for Self Actualization for Leadership Training).

8. WWJS is listed on the online Urban Dictionary, a reference list for contemporary slang, at http://www.urbandictionary.com/define.php?term=wwjs, accessed September 22, 2006. It lists an example of conversational usage as, "Hey, should I abort this baby? WWJS?"

9. Lists of variations can be found at a webpage for "Christian Acronyms" at the website managed by the Creative Ladies Ministry, http://www.creativeladiesministry.com/acronyms.html, accessed September 22, 2006.

10. Dundes discussed acronyms as expressions of cognitive patterns in "The Number Three in American Culture" (1980d, 140). Although he emphasized the ubiquity of three names for organizational names, he implied that four is a symbol of "more than enough" when he delineated "general statements about the nature of trichotomy." His second statement was, "If there are more than three terms, the additional ones will not infrequently be defined primarily in terms of one of the extremes. For example, in shirt sizes, one finds small, medium, and large. The size 'extra-large' is certainly linguistically and very probably conceptually derived from 'large,' rather than possessing separate individual status" (136). The symbolic meaning of four as a quantity of abundance was explored more by Dundes's Berkeley colleague, Stanley Brandes, in *Forty* (1985).

REFERENCES

Aarne, Antti. 1910. *Verzeichnis der Märchentypen, mit Hülfe von Fachgenossen Ausgearbeitet*. FFC [Folklore Fellows Communications] 3. Helsinki: Suomalainen Tiedeakalernian Toimituksia.

Abrahams, Roger D. 1977. Toward an Enactment-Centered Theory of Folklore. In Bascom 1977, 79–120.

———. 1979. Folklore in Culture: Notes Toward an Analytic Method. In Brunvand 1979, 390–403.

Adler, Thomas A. 1982. The Uses of Humor by Bluegrass Musicians. *Mid-America Folklore* 10:17–26.

Arewa, E. Ojo, and Alan Dundes. 1964. Proverbs and the Ethnography of Speaking Folklore. *American Anthropologist* 66:70–85.

Ashcroft, Bill, Gareth Griffiths, and Helen Tiffin. 2000. *Post-Colonial Studies: The Key Concepts*. New York: Routledge.

Avedon, Elliott M. 1979. The Structural Elements of Games. In *The Study of Games: A Source Book*, ed. Elliott M. Avedon and Brian Sutton-Smith, 419–26. Huntington, NY: Robert E. Krieger.

Azuonye, Chukwuma. 1990. Morphology of the Igbo Folktale: Ethnographic, Historiographic and Aesthetic Implications. *Folklore* (1990): 36–46.

Azzolina, David S. 1978. *Tale Type- and Motif-Indexes: An Annotated Bibliography*. New York: Garland.

Banc, C., and Alan Dundes. [1986] 1990. Always the Jews. In *You Call This Living? A Collection of East European Political Jokes,* 160–68. Athens: Univ. of Georgia Press. Orig. pub. as *First Prize: Fifteen Years!; An Annotated Collection of Romanian Political Jokes* (London: Associated Univ. Presses, 1986).

Barbe, Katharina. 2001. The Dilemma with Dichotomies. *Language and Communication* 2:89–103.

Bar-Itzhak, Haya. 2005. *Israeli Folk Narratives: Settlement, Immigration, Ethnicity*. Detroit: Wayne State Univ. Press.

Bascom, William R. 1954. Four Functions of Folklore. *Journal of American Folklore* 67:333–49.

———, ed. 1977. *Frontiers of Folklore*. Boulder, CO: Westview Press.

Bauman, Richard, and Charles L. Briggs. 2003. *Voices of Modernity: Language Ideologies and the Politics of Inequality*. Cambridge: Cambridge Univ. Press.

Ben-Amos, Dan. 1972. Toward a Definition of Folklore in Context. In Paredes and Bauman 1972, 3–15.

———, ed. 1976. *Folklore Genres*. Austin: Univ. of Texas Press.

———. 1977. The Context of Folklore: Implications and Prospects. In Bascom 1977, 36–53.

———. 1980. The Concept of Motif in Folklore. In *Folklore Studies in the Twentieth Century*, ed. Venetia J. Newall, 17–36. Totowa, NJ: Rowman & Littlefield.

Bendix, Regina. 1995. Dundesiana: Teacher and Mentor in Campuslore, Anecdote, and Memorate. In Bendix and Zumwalt 1995, 49–66.

———. 2005. Alan Dundes (1934–2005). *Journal of American Folklore* 118:485–88.

Bendix, Regina, and Rosemary Lévy Zumwalt, eds. 1995. *Folklore Interpreted: Essays in Honor of Alan Dundes*. New York: Garland.

Bercovitch, Sacvan. 1980. *American Jeremiad*. Madison: Univ. of Wisconsin Press.

Berkman, Susan C. J. 1978. "She's Writing Antidotes": An Examination of Hospital Employees' Use of Stories about Personal Experiences. *Folklore Forum* 11:48–54.

Bidney, David. 1967. *Theoretical Anthropology*. 2nd. augm. ed. New York: Schocken.

Birney, Adrian. 1973. Crack Puns: Text and Context in an Item of Latrinalia. *Western Folklore* 32:137–40.

Bishop, Julia C., and Mavis Curtis, eds. 2001. *Play Today in the Primary School Playground*. Philadelphia: Open University Press.

Boas, Franz. 1916. Tsimshian Mythology. In *Thirty-first Annual Report of the U.S. Bureau of American Ethnology*, Smithsonian Institution, 29–1037. Washington, DC: Government Printing Office.

———. 1920. The Methods of Ethnology. *American Anthropologist* 22:311–21.

———. 1935. *Kwakiutl Culture as Reflected in Mythology*. Memoirs of the American Folklore Society 28. New York: G. E. Stechert.

———. 1938. Mythology and Folklore. In *General Anthropology*, ed. Franz Boas, 609–26. Boston: D. C. Heath.

Boles, Jacqueline, and Lyn Myers. 1988. Chain Letters: Players and Their Accounts. *Deviant Behavior* 9:241–57.

Botkin, Benjamin A. 1944. *A Treasury of American Folklore: Stories, Ballads, and Traditions of the People*. New York: Crown Publishers.

Bourke, John G. 1891. *Scatologic Rites of All Nations: A Dissertation upon the Employment of Excrementitious Remedial Agents in Religion, Therapeutics, Divination, Witchcraft, Love-Philters, etc., in all Parts of the Globe*. Washington, DC: W. H. Lowdermilk.

Boyer, L. Bryce, Ruth M. Boyer, and Stephen M. Sonnenberg, eds. 1993. *Essays in Honor of Alan Dundes*. Vol. 18 of *The Psychoanalytic Study of Society*. Hillsdale, NJ: Analytic Press.

Brandes, Stanley. 1985. *Forty: The Age and the Symbol*. Knoxville: Univ. of Tennessee Press.

Bremond, Claude. 1977. The Morphology of the French Fairy Tale: The Ethical Model. In Jason and Segal 1977, 49–76.

Brewster, Paul G. 1971. The Foundation Sacrifice Motif in Legend, Folksong, Game, and Dance. *Zeitschrift für Ethnologie* 96:71–89.

Bronner, Simon J. 1982. . . . Feeling's the Truth. *Tennessee Folklore Society Bulletin* 48:117–24.

———. 1986a. *American Folklore Studies: An Intellectual History*. Lawrence: Univ. Press of Kansas.

———. 1986b. *Grasping Things: Folk Material Culture and Mass Society in America*. Lexington: Univ. Press of Kentucky.

———. 1988. *American Children's Folklore*. Little Rock, AK: August House.

———. 1990. "Left to Their Own Devices": Interpreting American Children's Folklore as an Adaptation to Aging. *Southern Folklore* 47:101–15.

———. 1995. *Piled Higher and Deeper: The Folklore of Student Life*. Little Rock, AR: August House.

———. 1992. Elaborating Tradition: A Pennsylvania-German Folk Artist Ministers to His Community. In *Creativity and Tradition in Folklore,* ed. Simon J. Bronner, 277–325. Logan: Utah State Univ. Press.

———. 1998. *Following Tradition: Folklore in the Discourse of American Culture*. Logan: Utah State Univ. Press.

———. 2004. "This is Why We Hunt": Social-Psychological Meanings of the Traditions and Rituals of Deer Camp. *Western Folklore* 63:11–50.

———. 2005a. Contesting Tradition: The Deep Play and Protest of Pigeon Shoots. *Journal of American Folklore* 118:409–52.

———. 2005b. "Gombo" Folkloristics: Lafcadio Hearn's Creolization and Hybridization in the Formative Period of Folklore Studies. *Journal of Folklore Research* 42:141–84.

———. 2005c. Plain Folk and Folk Society: John A. Hostetler's Legacy of the Little Community. In *Writing the Amish: The Worlds of John A. Hostetler*, ed. David Weaver-Zercher, 56–97. University Park: Pennsylvania State Univ. Press.

———. 2005d. Secret Erections and Sexual Fabrications: Old Men Crafting Manliness. In *Manly Traditions: The Folk Roots of American Masculinities*, ed. Simon J. Bronner, 274–314. Bloomington: Indiana Univ. Press.

———. 2006a. *Crossing the Line: Violence, Play, and Drama in Naval Equator Traditions.* Amsterdam: Amsterdam Univ. Press.

———, ed. 2006b. *Encyclopedia of American Folklife*, 4 vols. Armonk, NY: M. E. Sharpe.

———. 2006c. Folk Logic: Interpretation and Explanation in Folkloristics. *Western Folklore* 65:401–34

———. 2007. Analyzing the Ethnic Self: The *Hinkel Dreck* Theme in Pennsylvania-German Folk Narrative. *Columbia Journal of American Studies* 8:19–53.

Brunvard, Jan Harold. 1977. F. A. R. K. [Folklore Article Reconstitution Kit]. *Journal of American Folklore* 90:199–202.

———, ed. 1979. *Readings on American Folklore*. New York: W. W. Norton.

———, ed. 1996. *American Folklore: An Encyclopedia*. New York: Garland.

Burson, Anne C. 1982. Pomp and Circumcision: A Parodic Skit in a Medical Community. *Keystone Folklore* 1:28–40.

Burson-Tolpin, Anne. 1989. Fracturing the Language of Biomedicine: The Speech Play of U.S. Physicians. *Medical Anthropology Quarterly* 3:285–93.

Butler, Clark. 1976. Hegel and Freud: A Comparison. *Philosophy and Phenomenological Research* 36:506–22.

Campion-Vincent, Véronique. 2005. *Organ Theft Legends*. Jackson: Univ. Press of Mississippi.

Carroll, Michael P. 1987. Praying the Rosary: The Anal-Erotic Origin of a Popular Catholic Devotion. *Journal for the Scientific Study of Religion* 26:486–98.

———1992a. Allomotifs and the Psychoanalytic Study of Folk Narratives: Another Look at "The Roommate's Death." *Folklore* 103:225–34.

———. 1992b. Folklore and Psychoanalysis: The Swallowing Monster and Open-Brains Allomotifs in Plains Indian Mythology. *Ethos* 20:289–303.

———. 1993. Alan Dundes: An Introduction. In L. B. Boyer, R. M. Boyer, and Sonnenberg 1993, 1–22. Hillsdale, NJ: Analytic Press.

Clements, William M. 1986. The Ethnic Joke as Mirror of Culture. *New York Folklore* 12:87–98.

Clifford, James, and George E. Marcus, eds. 1986. *Writing Culture: The Poetics and Politics of Ethnography*. Berkeley: Univ. of California Press.

Cohen, Perry S. Psychoanalysis and Cultural Symbolization. 1980, 47–60. In *Symbol as Sense: New Approaches to the Analysis of Meaning*, ed. Mary LeCron Foster and Stanley H. Brandes, 45–68. New York: Academic Press.

Constantinescu, Nicolae. 2003. Contexts and Interpretations: The Walled-Up Wife Ballad and Other Related Texts. In *The Flowering Thorn: International Ballad Studies*, ed. Thomas A. McKean, 161–67. Logan: Utah State Univ. Press.

Davies, Christie. 1998. *Jokes and Their Relation to Society*. Berlin: Mouton de Gruyter.

De Caro, Francis A. 1976. Concepts of the Past in Folkloristics. *Western Folklore* 35:3–22.

Dégh, Linda. 1968. The Negro in the Concrete. *Indiana Folklore* 1:61–67.

———. 1994. The Approach to Worldview in Folk Narrative Study. *Western Folklore* 53:243–52.

Demos, John. 2004. *Circles and Lines: The Shape of Life in Early America*. Cambridge, MA: Harvard Univ. Press.

Dorson, Richard M. [1952] 1972. *Bloodstoppers and Bearwalkers: Folk Traditions of the Upper Peninsula*. Cambridge, MA: Harvard Univ. Press. Repr. 1972.

———. 1957. Standards for Collecting and Publishing American Folktales. *Journal of American Folklore* 70:53–57.

———. 1963. Current Folklore Theories. *Current Anthropology* 4:93–112.

———. 1964. Collecting Oral Folklore in the United States. In *Buying the Wind: Regional Folklore in the United States*, ed. Richard M. Dorson, 1–20. Chicago: Univ. of Chicago Press.

———. 1968. *The British Folklorists: A History*. Chicago: Univ. of Chicago Press.

———. 1972a. Concepts of Folklore and Folklife Studies. In *Folklore and Folklife: An Introduction*, ed. Richard M. Dorson, 1–50. Chicago: Univ. of Chicago Press.

———. 1972b. *Folklore: Selected Essays*. Bloomington: Indiana Univ. Press.

———. 1972c. Techniques of the Folklorist. In Dorson 1972b, 11–32.

———. 1973. *America in Legend*. New York: Pantheon.

———. 1975. Foreword to *Analytic Essays in Folklore*, by Alan Dundes, vii. The Hague: Mouton.

———, ed. 1983. *Handbook of American Folklore*. Bloomington: Indiana Univ. Press.

Dow, James R. 2005. Alan Dundes (1934–2005). *Fabula* 46:331–35.

Dow, James R., and Hannjost Lixfeld, eds. 1994. *The Nazification of an Academic Discipline: Folklore*. Bloomington: Indiana Univ. Press.

Dresser, Norine. 1994. The Case of the Missing Gerbil. *Western Folklore* 53:229–42.

Duncan, Robert J. 1976. Chain Letters: A Twentieth Century Folk Practice. In *What's Going On? (In Modern Texas Folklore)*, ed. Francis E. Abernethy, 47–58. Austin, TX: Encino Press.

Dundes, Alan. 1960. French Tongue Twisters. *French Review* 33:604–5.

———. 1961. Brown County Superstitions. *Midwest Folklore* 11:25–56.

———. 1962a. The Binary Structure of 'Unsuccessful Repetition' in Lithuanian Folk Tales. *Western Folklore* 21:165–74.

———. 1962b. Earth-Diver: Creation of the Mythopoeic Male. *American Anthropologist* 64:1032–51.

———. 1962c. The Father, the Son, and the Holy Grail. *Literature and Psychology* 12:101–12.

———. 1962e. Folklore: A Key to Culture. *Overseas: The Magazine of Education Exchange* 2:8–14.

———. 1962f. The Folklore of Wishing Wells. *American Imago* 19:27–34.

———. 1962g. From Etic to Emic Units in the Structural Study of Folktales. *Journal of American Folklore* 75:95–105.

———. 1962h. Trends in Content Analysis: A Review Article. *Midwest Folklore* 12:31–38.

———. 1962i. Re: Joyce—No In at the Womb. *Modern Fiction Studies* 8:137–47.

———. 1963. Rejoinder to Parker's Comments on Dundes' Article. *American Anthropologist* 65:915–18.

———. 1964a. On Game Morphology: A Study of the Structure of Non-Verbal Folklore. *New York Folklore Quarterly* 20:276–288.

———. 1964b. *The Morphology of North American Indian Folktales*. FFC [Folklore Fellows Communications] 195. Helsinki: Suomalainen Tiedeakatemia [Academia Scientiarum Fennica].

———. 1965a. On Computers and Folk Tales. *Western Folklore* 24:184–89.

———, ed. 1965b. *The Study of Folklore*. Englewood Cliffs, NJ: Prentice-Hall.

———. 1965c. The Study of Folklore in Literature and Culture: Identification and Interpretation. *Journal of American Folklore* 78:136–43.

———. 1965d. What is Folklore? In Dundes 1965b, 1–3.

———. 1966a. The American Concept of Folklore. *Journal of the Folklore Institute* 3:226–49.

———. 1966b. Here I Sit—A Study of American Latrinalia. *Papers of the Koreber Anthropoligical Society* 34:91–105.

———. 1966c. Metafolklore and Oral Literary Criticism. *Monist* 50:505–16.

———, ed. 1968a. *Every Man His Way: Readings in Cultural Anthropology*. Englewood Cliffs, NJ: Prentice-Hall.

———. 1968b. Introd. to *Morphology of the Folktale*, by Vladimir Propp [1928] 1968, xi–xvii.

———. 1968c. Ways of Studying Folklore. In *Our Living Traditions: An Introduction to American Folklore*, ed. Tristram Potter Coffin, 37–47. New York: Basic Books.

———. 1969a. Folklore as a Mirror of Culture. *Elementary English* 46:471–82.

———. 1969b. Thinking Ahead: A Folkloristic Reflection of the Future Orientation in American Worldview. *Anthropological Quarterly* 42:53–71.

———. 1970. Myths, Tales, and Games: What Do They Really Mean? In *1971 Britannica Yearbook of Science and the Future*, ed. Richard G. Young, 324–37. Chicago: Encyclopedia Britannica.

———. 1971a. Folk Ideas as Units of Worldview. *Journal of American Folklore* 84:93–103.

———. 1971b. Laughter Behind the Iron Curtain: A Sample of Rumanian Political Jokes. *Ukrainian Quarterly* 27:50–59.

———. 1971c. The Making and Breaking of Friendship as a Structural Frame in African Folk Tales. In *Structural Analysis of Oral Tradition*, ed. Pierre Maranda and Elli Köngäs Maranda, 171–85. Philadelphia: Univ. of Pennsylvania Press.

———. 1972. Foreword to *Folklore and Psychoanalysis*, by Paulo de Carvalho-Neto, 9–12. Miami: Univ. of Miami Press.

———, ed. [1973] 1990. *Mother Wit from the Laughing Barrel: Readings in the Interpretation of Afro-American Folklore*. Englewood Cliffs, NJ: Prentice-Hall. Repr. Jackson: Univ. Press of Mississippi, 1990.

———. 1975a. The American Concept of Folklore. In Dundes 1975b, 3–16.

———. 1975b. *Analytic Essays in Folklore*. The Hague: Mouton.

———. 1975c. The Devolutionary Premise in Folklore Theory. In Dundes 1975b, 17–27. Orig. pub. 1969 in *Journal of the Folklore Institute* 6:5–19.

———. 1975d. Metafolklore and Oral Literary Criticism. In Dundes 1975b, 50–60.

———. 1975e. On the Psychology of Collecting Folklore. In Dundes 1975b, 121–29. Orig. pub. 1962 in *Tennessee Folklore Society Bulletin* 28:65–74.

———. 1975f. On the Structure of the Proverb. *Proverbium* 25:961–73.

———. 1975g. Preface to *Analytic Essays in Folklore*, Dundes 1975b, xi–xii.

———. 1975h. Slurs International: Folk Comparisons of Ethnicity and National Character. *Southern Folklore Quarterly* 39:15–38.

———. 1976a. Getting the Folk and the Lore Together. *Johns Hopkins Magazine* (January): 23–31

———. 1976b. Projection in Folklore: A Plea for Psychoanalytic Semiotics. *MLN* 91:1500–33. Repr. in Dundes 1980b.

———. 1976c. Structuralism and Folklore. *Studia Fennica* 20:75–93.

———. 1976d. "To Love My Father All": A Psychoanalytic Study of the Folktale Source of *King Lear. Southern Folklore Quarterly* 40:53–66. Repr. in Dundes 1980b.

———. 1977. Science in Folklore? Folklore in Science? *New Scientist* 76:774–76.

———. 1978a. The Hero Pattern and the Life of Jesus. In *Essays in Folkloristics*, by Alan Dundes, 223–62. Meerut: Folklore Institute.

———. 1978b. Mairymaking in *Ulysses:* A Legendary Source for a Lost Pin. *Cahiers du Centre d'Études Irlandaises* 3:69–73.

———. 1978c. A Potawatomi Version of Aarne-Thompson Tale Type 297A, Turtle's War Party. *Norveg* 21:47–57.

———. 1979a. The Dead Baby Joke Cycle. *Western Folklore* 38:145–57.

———. 1979b. Into the Endzone for a Touchdown: A Psychoanalytic Consideration of American Football. In *Essays in Humanistic Anthropology: A Festschrift in Honor of David Bidney*, ed. Bruce T. Grindal and Dennis M. Warren, 237–51. Washington, DC: Univ. Press of America. Repr. in Dundes 1980b.

———. 1980a. The Crowing Hen and the Easter Bunny: Male Chauvinism in American Folklore. In Dundes 1980b, 160–75.

———. 1980b. *Interpreting Folklore*. Bloomington: Indiana Univ. Press.

———. 1980c. The Kushmaker. In *Folklore on Two Continents: Essays in Honor of Linda Dégh*, ed. Nikolai Burlakoff and Card Lindahl, 210–16. Bloomington, IN: Trickster Press.

———. 1980d. The Number Three in American Culture. In Dundes 1980b, 134–59.

———. 1980e. Preface to *Interpreting Folklore*, Dundes 1980b, vii–xi.

———. 1980f. Seeing is Believing. In Dundes 1980b, 86–92.

———. 1980g. Texture, Text, and Context. In Dundes 1980b, 20–32.

———. 1980h. Who are the Folk? In Dundes 1980b, 1–19.

———. 1982a. Misunderstanding Humor: An American Stereotype of the Englishman. *International Folklore Review* 2:10–15. Repr. in Dundes 1987c.

———. 1982b. Volkskunde, Völkerkunde, and the Study of German National Character. In *Europäische Ethnologie*, ed. Heide Nixdroff and Thomas Hauschild, 257–65. Berlin: Dietrich Reimer Verlag.

———. 1984a. *Life is Like a Chicken Coop Ladder: A Study of German National Character Through Folklore.* New York: Columbia Univ. Press.

———, ed. 1984b. *Sacred Narrative: Readings in the Theory of Myth.* Berkeley: Univ. of California Press.

———. 1984c. The Symbolic Equivalence of Allomotifs: Towards A Method of Analyzing Folktales. In *Le Conte: Pourquoi? Comment?*, ed. Geneviève Calame-Griaule, Veronika Görög-Karady, and Michèle Chiche, 187–97. Paris: Centre national de la recherche scientifique.

———. 1986. Comment (Colloquy on National Character). *Focaal: Tydschrift voor Anthropologie* (April): 33–37.

———. 1987a. The American Game of 'Smear the Queer' and the Homosexual Component of Male Competitive Sport and Warfare. In Dundes 1987h,178–94.

———. 1987b. Couvade in Genesis. In Dundes 1987h, 145–66.

———. 1987c. *Cracking Jokes: Studies of Sick Humor Cycles and Stereotypes.* Berkeley, CA: Ten Speed Press.

———. 1987d. The Curious Case of the Wide-Mouth Frog: Jokes and Covert Language Attitudes. In Dundes 1987c, 55–61.

———. 1987e. The Jew and the Polack in the United States: A Study of Ethnic Slurs. In Dundes 1987c, 115–38.

———. 1987f. The Jewish American Princess and the Jewish American Mother in American Jokelore. In Dundes 1987c, 62–81.

———. 1987g. Many Hands Make Light Work, or Caught in the Act of Screwing in Light Bulbs. In Dundes 1987c, 143–49.

———. 1987h. *Parsing Through Customs: Essays by a Freudian Folklorist.* Madison: Univ. of Wisconsin Press.

———. 1987i. The Psychoanalytic Study of Folklore. In Dundes 1987h, 3–46.

———. 1987j. The Symbolic Equivalence of Allomotifs in the Rabbit-Herd (AT 570). In Dundes 1987h, 167–77.

———, ed. 1988a. *The Flood Myth.* Berkeley: Univ. of California Press.

———. 1988b. Foreword to *American Folklore Scholarship: A Dialogue of Dissent*, by Rosemary Lévy Zumwalt, ix–x. Bloomington: Indiana Univ. Press.

———. 1989a. The Anthropologist and the Comparative Method in Folklore. In Dundes 1989d, 57–82.

———. 1989b. The Building of Skadar: The Measure of Meaning of a Ballad of the Balkans. In Dundes 1989d, 151–68

———. 1989c. Defining Identity through Folklore. In Dundes 1989d, 1–39.

———. 1989d. *Folklore Matters.* Knoxville: Univ. of Tennessee Press.

———. 1989e. Interpreting "Little Red Riding Hood" Psychoanalytically. In *Little Red Riding Hood: A Casebook,* ed. Alan Dundes, 192–238. Madison: Univ. of Wisconsin Press.

———. 1989f. The Psychoanalytic Study of the Grimms' Tales: "The Maiden Without Hands" (AT 706). In Dundes 1989d, 112–50.

———. 1990. The Hero Pattern and the Life of Jesus. In *In Quest of the Hero*, 179–223. Princeton, NJ: Princeton Univ. Press.

———. 1991a . The Psychological Study of Folklore in the United States. *Southern Folklore* 48:97–120.

———.1991b. The Ritual Murder or Blood Libel Legend: A Study of Anti-Semitic Victimization through Projective Inversion. In *The Blood Libel Legend: A Casebook in Anti-Semitic Folklore,* ed. Alan Dundes, 336–78. Madison: Univ. of Wisconsin Press. Orig. pub. 1989 in *Temenos: Nordic Journal of Comparative Religion* 25:7–32.

———. 1992. Introd. to *Fire in the Dragon and Other Psychoanalytic Essays on Folklore*, by Géza Róheim, ed. Alan Dundes, ix–xxvi. Princeton, NJ: Princeton Univ. Press.

———. 1994. Gallus as Phallus: A Psychoanalytic Cross-Cultural Consideration of the Cockfight as Fowl Play. In *The Cockfight: A Casebook*, ed. Alan Dundes, 241–84. Madison: Univ. of Wisconsin Press. Orig. pub. in L. B. Boyer, R. M. Boyer, and Sonnenberg 1993, 23–65.

———. 1995a. How Indic Parallels to the Ballad of the "Walled-Up Wife" Reveal the Pitfalls of Parochial Nationalistic Folkloristics. *Journal of American Folklore* 108:38–53.

———. 1995b. Worldview in Folk Narrative. *Western Folklore* 54:229–32.

———. 1996a. Madness in Method Plus a Plea for Projective Inversion in Myth. In *Myth and Method*, ed. Laurie L. Patton and Wendy Doniger, 147–59. Charlottesville: Univ. Press of Virginia.

———. 1996b. Preface. In *The Walled-Up Wife: A Casebook*, ed. Alan Dundes, ix–xi. Madison: Univ. of Wisconsin Press.

———. 1997a. Binary Opposition in Myth: The Propp/Lévi-Strauss Debate in Retrospect. *Western Folklore* 56:39–50.

———. 1997b. *From Game to War, and Other Psychoanalytic Essays on Folklore*. Lexington: Univ. Press of Kentucky.

———. 1997c. The Motif-Index and Tale Type Index: A Critique. *Journal of Folklore Researh* 34:195–202.

———. 1997d. *Two Tales of Crow and Sparrow: A Freudian Folkloristic Essay on Caste and Untouchability*. Lanham, MD: Rowman & Littlefield.

———. 1997e. Traditional Male Combat: From Game to War. In Dundes 1997b, 25–45.

———. 1997f. Why is the Jew 'Dirty'? A Psychoanalytic Study of Anti-Semitic Folklore. In Dundes 1997b, 92–120.

———. 1998. The Vampire as Bloodthirsty Reverant: A Psychonalytic Post Mortem. In *The Vampire: A Casebook,* ed. Alan Dundes, 159–75. Madison: Univ. of Wisconsin Press.

———. 1999. *Holy Writ as Oral Lit: The Bible as Folklore*. Lanham, MD: Rowman & Littlefield.

———. 2002a. *Bloody Mary in the Mirror: Essays in Psychoanalytic Folkloristics*. Jackson: Univ. Press of Mississippi.

———. 2002b.The Greek Game of *Makria Yaidoura* [Long Donkey]. In Dundes 2002a, 122–36.

———. 2002c. *The Shabbat Elevator and Other Sabbath Subterfuges: An Unorthodox Essay on Circumventing Custom and Jewish Character*. Lanham, MD: Rowman & Littlefield.

———. 2003a. *Fables of the Ancients? Folklore in the Qur'an*. Lanham, MD: Rowman & Littlefield.

———. 2004a. As the Crow Flies: A Straightforward Study of Lineal Worldview in American Folk Speech. In *What Goes Around Comes Around: The Circulation of Proverbs in Contemporary Life*, ed. Kimberly J. Lau, Peter Tokofsky, and Stephen D. Winick, 171–87. Logan: Utah State Univ. Press.

———. 2004b. "How Far Does the Apple Fall from the Tree?": Pieter Brueghel the Younger's *Netherlandish Proverbs*. In *The Netherlandish Proverbs: An International Symposium on the Pieter Brueg(h)els*, ed. Wolfgang Mieder, 15–45. Burlington: Proverbium / Univ. of Vermont.

———. 2004c. "What If Mahomet Won't Go for the Mountin'?": An Analysis of an Arabic-Islamic Joke. *Midwestern Folklore* 30:5–14.

———. 2005a. Afterword: Many Manly Traditions—A Folkloristic Maelstrom. In *Manly Traditions: The Folk Roots of American Masculinities*, ed. Simon J. Bronner, 351–63. Bloomington: Indiana Univ. Press.

———, ed. 2005b. *Folklore: Critical Concepts in Literary and Cultural Studies*. 4 vols. London: Routledge.

———. 2005c. Folkloristics in the Twenty-First Century (AFS Invited Presidential Plenary Address, 2004). *Journal of American Folklore* 118:385–408.

Dundes, Alan, and Roger Abrahams. 1969. On Elephantasy and Elephanticide. *Psychoanalytic Review* 56:225–41.

————. 1987. On Elephantasy and Elphanticide: The Effect of Time and Place. In Dundes 1987c, 41–54.

Dundes, Alan, and E. Ojo Arewa. 1964. Proverbs and the Ethnography of Speaking Folklore, *American Anthropologist* 66:70–85.

Dundes, Alan, and Meegan Brown. 2002. Viola Jokes: A Study of Second String Humor. *Midwestern Folklore* 28:5–17.

Dundes, Alan, and Lauren Dundes. 2002. The Elephant Walk and Other Amazing Hazing: Male Fraternity Initiation through Infantilization and Feminization. In Dundes 2002a, 95–121.

Dundes, Alan, Lauren Dundes, and Michael B. Streiff. 1999. "When You Hear Hoofbeats, Think Horses, Not Zebras": A Folk Medical Diagnostic Proverb. *Proverbium* 16:95–103.

Dundes, Alan, and Lowell Edmunds, eds. 1995. *Oedipus: A Folklore Casebook.* Madison: Univ. of Wisconsin Press.

Dundes, Alan, and Alessandro Falassi. 1975. *La Terra in Piazza: An Interpretation of the Palio of Siena.* Berkeley: Univ. of California Press.

Dundes, Alan, and Victoria George. 1978. The 'Gomer': A Figure of Hospital Folk Speech. *Journal of American Folklore* 91:568–81.

Dundes, Alan, and Robert Georges. 1962. Some Minor Genres of Obscene Folklore. *Journal of American Folklore* 75:221–26.

————. 1963. Toward a Structural Definition of the Riddle. *Journal of American Folklore* 76:111–18.

Dundes, Alan, and Thomas Hauschild. 1987. Auschwitz Jokes. In Dundes 1987c, 19–40.

Dundes, Alan, Jerry W. Leach, and Bora Özkök. The Strategy of Turkish Boys' Verbal Dueling Rhymes. *Journal of American Folklore* 83:325–349.

Dundes, Alan, and Carl R. Pagter. 1978. *Work Hard and You Shall Be Rewarded: Urban Folklore from the Paperwork Empire.* Bloomington: Indiana Univ. Press.

————. 1991. The Mobile SCUD Missile Launcher and Other Persian Gulf Warlore: An American Folk Image of Saddam Hussein's Iraq. *Western Folklore* 50:303–22.

Dundes, Alan, and Paul Renteln. 2005. Foolproof: A Sampling of Mathematical Folk Humor. *Notices of the American Mathematical Society* 52:24–34.

Dundes, Alan, and Maurice Schmaier. 1961. Parallel Paths. *Journal of American Folklore* 74:142–45.

Easterlin, Nancy. 2005. Making Knowledge: Bioepistemology and the Foundations of Literary Theory. In *Theory's Empire: An Anthology of Dissent,* ed. Daphne Patai and Will H. Corral, 621–35. New York: Columbia Univ. Press.

Eecke, Wilfried Ver. 2006. *Denial, Negation and the Forces of the Negative: Freud, Hegel, Lacan, Spitz, and Sophocles.* Albany: State Univ. of New York Press.

Ellis, Bill. 2000. *Raising the Devil: Satanism, New Religions, and the Media.* Lexington: Univ. Press of Kentucky.

El-Shamy, Hasan M. 2004. *Types of the Folktale in the Arab World: A Demographically Oriented Tale-Type Index.* Bloomington: Indiana Univ. Press.

Factor, June. 1989. *Captain Cook Chased a Chook: Children's Folklore in Australia.* New York: Penguin.

Fenton, Alexander. 1967. An Approach to Folk Life Studies. *Keystone Folklore Quarterly* 12:5–21.

Fine, Gary Alan. 1987. Joseph Jacobs: A Sociological Folklorist. *Folklore* 98:18–93.

————. 1992. Evaluating Psychoanalytic Folklore: Are Freudians Ever Right? In *Manufacturing Tales: Sex and Money in Contemporary Legends,* 45–58. Knoxville: Univ. of Tennessee Press.

Fine, Gary Alan, and Jacqueline Boles. 2006. Chain Letters. In Bronner 2006b, 166–70.

Fleisher, Mark Stewart. 1981. The Potlatch: A Symbolic and Psychoanalytic View. *Current Anthropology* 22: 69–71.

Foster, George. 1953. What is Folk Culture? *American Anthropologist* 55:159–73.

Freud, Sigmund. [1900] 1999. *The Interpretation of Dreams.* Oxford: Oxford Univ. Press. Orig. pub. as *Der Traumdeutung* (Leipzig and Vienna: F. Deuticke, 1900).

———. [1905] 1995. Infantile Sexuality. In *The Basic Writings of Sigmund Freud*, ed. Abraham A. Brill. Modern Library ed. New York: Modern Library. Orig. pub. as *Drei Abhandlungen zur Sexualtheorie* (Leipzig: F. Deuticke, 1905); orig. Modern Library ed. pub. 1938.

———. 1913. Foreword to John G. Bourke's *Scatologic Rites of All Nations*. In *Der Unrat in Sitte, Brauch, Glauben und Gewohnheitrecht der Völker*. Trans. Hans Ihm. Leipzig: Ethnologischer Verlag.

———. 1961. Negation. In *The Standard Edition of the Complete Psychological Works of Sigmund Freud*, ed. James Strachey, 19:237–39. London: Hogarth Press.

Freud, Sigmund, and D. E. Oppenheim. 1958. *Dreams in Folklore*. New York: International Universities Press.

Garry, Jane, and Hasan El-Shamy, eds. 2005. *Archetypes and Motifs in Folklore and Literature*. Armonk, NY: M. E. Sharpe.

Geertz, Clifford. 1972. Deep Play: Notes on the Balinese Cockfight. *Daedalus* 101:1–37.

———. 1973. *The Interpretation of Cultures*. New York: Basic Books.

———. 1994. Deep Play: Notes on the Balinese Cockfight. In *The Cockfight: A Casebook*, ed. Alan Dundes, 94–132. Madison: Univ. of Wisconsin Press.

Georges, Robert A. 1972. Recreations and Games. In *Folklore and Folklife: An Introduction*, ed. Richard M. Dorson, 173–89. Chicago: Univ. of Chicago Press.

———. 1983. The Universality of the Tale-Type as Concept and Construct. *Western Folklore* 42:21–28.

———. 2004. Alan Dundes (1934–2005): A Remembrance and an Appreciation. *Western Folklore* 63:279–85.

Georges, Robert A., and Michael Owen Jones. 1980. *People Studying People: The Human Element in Fieldwork*. Berkeley: Univ. of California Press.

———. 1995a. Folklore as Genre and Type. In Georges and M. O. Jones 1995c, chapter 4.

———. 1995b. Folklore in Cultural Contexts. In Georges and M. O. Jones 1995c, chapter 6.

———. 1995c. *Folkloristics: An Introduction*. Bloomington: Indiana Univ. Press.

Gilkey, Carolyn F. 1990. The Physicist, the Mathematician and the Engineer: Scientists and the Professional Slur. *Western Folklore* 49:215–20.

Gilman, Sander L. 1993a. *The Case of Sigmund Freud: Medicine and Identity at the Fin de Siècle*. Baltimore: Johns Hopkins Univ. Press.

———. 1993b. *Freud, Race, and Gender*. Princeton, NJ: Princeton Univ. Press.

Girsch-Bock, Mary. 2006. *Carcinoid Cancers, Zebras and Stardust*. Bloomington, IN: Unlimited Publishing.

Glassie, Henry. 1975. *Folk Housing in Middle Virginia: A Structural Analysis of Historic Artifacts*. Knoxville: Univ. of Tennessee Press.

Goldberg, Christine. 1973. The Historic-Geographic Method: Past and Future. *Journal of Folklore Research* 21:1–18.

Goldberg, Harriet. 2000. *Motif-Index of Folk Narratives in the Pan-Hispanic Romancero*. Tempe: Arizona Center for Medieval and Renaissance Studies.

Goldstein, Kenneth S. 1964. *A Guide for Field Workers in Folklore*. Hatboro, PA: Folklore Associates.

Gonos, George, Virginia Mulkern, and Nicholas Poushinsky. 1976. Anonymous Expression: A Structural View of Graffiti. *Journal of American Folklore* 89:40–48.

Gordon, Beverly. 2003. Embodiment, Community Building, and Aesthetic Saturation in 'Restroom World,' a Backstage Women's Space. *Journal of American Folklore* 116:444–64.

Groce, Nancy. 1996. Knowing the Score: The Transmission of Musician Jokes Among Professional and Semi-Professional Musicians. *New York Folklore* 22:37–47.

Gürel, Perin. 2006. Folklore Matters: The Folklore Scholarship of Alan Dundes and the New American Studies. *Columbia Journal of American Studies* 7:120–36.

———, ed. 2007. Folklore Matters. Special Section in *Columbia Journal of American Studies* 8:6–172.

Hand, Wayland, ed. 1971. *American Folk Legend: A Symposium*. Berkeley: Univ. of California Press.

Hansen, William. 2005. In Memoriam: Alan Dundes, 1934–2005. *Journal of Folklore Research* 42:245–50.

Harris-Lopez, Trudier. 2003. Genre. In *Eight Words for the Study of Expressive Culture*, ed. Burt Feintuch, 99–120. Urbana: Univ. of Illinois Press.

Hasan-Rokem, Galit, and Alan Dundes, eds. 1986. *The Wandering Jew: Essays in the Interpretation of a Christian Legend*. Bloomington: Indiana Univ. Press.

Hill, Jane H., and Bruce Mannheim. 1992. Language and World View. *Annual Review of Anthropology* 21:381–406.

Holbek, Bengt. 1990. Variation and Tale Type. In *From One Tale . . . to the Other: Variability in Oral Literature*, ed. Veronika Görög-Karady and Michèle Chiche, 471–85. Paris: Centre national de la recherche scientifique.

———. 1993. Interpretation by Allomotifs. In L. B. Boyer, R. M. Boyer, and Sonnenberg 1993, 235–54.

Honko, Lauri. 1989. Folkloristic Theories of Genre. In *Studies in Oral Narrative*, ed. Anna-Leena Siikala, 13–28. Helsinki: Finnish Literature Society.

Hufford, David. 1989. Customary Observances in Modern Medicine. *Western Folklore* 48:129–43.

Huguenin, Charles A. 1962. A Prayer for Examinations. *New York Folklore Quarterly* 18:145–48.

Hultkrantz, Åke. 1960. *General Ethnological Concepts*. Copenhagen: Rosenkilde and Bagger.

Hymes, Dell. 1972. The Contribution of Folklore to Sociolinguistic Research. In Paredes and Bauman, 42–50.

Isaac-Edersheim, E. 1986. Ahasver: A Mythic Image of the Jew. In Hasan-Rokem and Dundes 1986, 195–210.

Israeli, Raphael. 2002. *Poison: Modern Manifestations of the Blood Libel*. Lanham, MD: Lexington Books.

———. 2003. *Islamikaze: Manifestations of Islamic Martyrology*. London: Frank Cass.

Jackson, Bruce. 1972. "The Greatest Mathematician in the World": Norbert Wiener Stories. *Western Folklore* 31:1–22.

———. 1987. *Fieldwork*. Urbana: Univ. of Illinois Press.

Jackson, Bruce, and Edward D. Ives, eds. 1996. *The World Observed: Reflections on the Fieldwork Process*. Urbana: Univ. of Illinois Press.

Jacobs, Joseph. 1893. The Folk. *Folklore* 4:233–38.

Jakobson, Roman, and Petr Bogatyrev. 1980. Folklore as a Special Form of Creation. Trans. John M. O'Hara. *Folklore Forum* 13:1–21.

Jansen, William Hugh. 1965. The Esoteric–Exoteric Factor in Folklore. In Dundes 1965b, 43–51.

Jason, Heda. 2000. *Motif, Type and Genre: A Manual for Compiling of Indices and a Bibliography of Indices and Indexing*. FFC [Folklore Fellows Communications] 273. Helsinki: Suomalainen Tiedeakatemia [Academia Scientiarum Fennica].

Jason, Heda, and Dimitri Segal, eds. 1977. *Patterns in Oral Literature*. The Hague: Mouton.

Jauhiainen, Marjatta. 1998. *The Type and Motif Index of Finnish Belief Legends and Memorates*. FFC [Folklore Fellows Communications] 267. Helsinki: Suomalainen Tiedeakatemia [Academia Scientiarum Fennica].

Jones, Michael Owen, ed. 1994. *Putting Folklore to Use*. Lexington: Univ. Press of Kentucky.

Jones, Steven Swann. 1990. *The New Comparative Method: Structural and Symbolic Analysis of the Allomotifs of Snow White*. FFC [Folklore Fellows Communications] 247. Helsinki: Suomalainen Tiedeakatmeia [Academia Scientiarum Fennica].

Journal of Folklore Research. 1997. Special issue, *Journal of Folklore Research* 34, no. 3 (September–December). Contains commentaries by Uther, Dundes, and other folklorists on classification by motif and type.

Kammen, Michael G. 1972. *People of Paradox*. New York: Knopf.

Karsh, Efraim. 2006. The Long Trail of Islamic Anti-Semitism. *Israel Affairs* 12:1–12.

Kearney, Michael. 1972. World View Theory and Study. *Annual Review of Anthropology* 4:247–70.

———. 1984. *World View*. Novato, CA: Chandler & Sharp.

Ketner, Kenneth. The Role of Hypotheses in Folkloristics. *Journal of American Folklore* 86:114–30.

Kirshenblatt-Gimblett, Barbara. 1996. Topic Drift: Negotiating the Gap between the Field and Our Name. *Journal of Folklore Research* 33:245–54.

Klein, Cecilia F. 1993. Teocuitlatl, "Divine Excrement": The Significance of "Holy Shit" in Ancient Mexico. *Art Journal* 52:20–27.

Knapp, Mary, and Herbert Knapp. 1976. *One Potato, Two Potato: The Folklore of American Children.* New York: W. W. Norton.

Koven, Mikel J. 2005. Review of *The Shabbat Elevator and Other Sabbath Subterfuges: An Unorthodox Essay on Circumventing Custom and Jewish Character,* by Alan Dundes. *Journal of American Folklore* 118:501–2.

Kroeber, A.L. 1917. The Superorganic. *American Anthropologist* 9:163–213.

Krohn, Kaarle. 1971. *Folklore Methodology.* Trans. Roger L. Welsch. Austin: Univ. of Texas Press.

Lawless, Elaine, ed. 2005. Special issue, dedicated to the memory of Alan Dundes. *Journal of American Folklore* 118, no. 470 (Fall 2005).

Leach, Maria, ed. 1949. *Funk & Wagnalls Standard Dictionary of Folklore, Mythology and Legend.* 2 vols. New York: Funk & Wagnalls.

Lease, Emory B. 1919. The Number Three: Mysterious, Mystic, Magic. *Classical Philology* 14:56–73.

Lechte, John. 1994. *Fifty Key Contemporary Thinkers: From Structuralism to Postmodernity.* New York: Routledge.

Lee, Dorothy. [1959] 1968. Codifications of Reality: Lineal and Nonlineal. In *Every Man His Way: Readings in Cultural Anthropology,* ed. Alan Dundes, 329–43. Englewood Cliffs, NJ: Prentice-Hall. Orig. pub. in *Freedom and Culture,* by Dorothy Lee (Englewood Cliffs, NJ: Prentice-Hall, 1959).

Legman, Gershon. [1968] 1975. *Rationale of the Dirty Joke: An Analysis of Sexual Humor.* 2nd ser. New York: Breaking Point. Orig. pub. 1968.

Lichman, Simon. 1982. The Gardener's Story: The Metafolklore of a Mumming Tradition. *Folklore* 93:105–11.

Lieberman, E. James. 1998. *Acts of Will: The Life and Work of Otto Rank.* New York: Free Press.

Limón, José E. 1982. Legendry, Metafolklore, and Performance: A Mexican-American Example. *Western Folklore* 42:191–208.

Longenecker, Gregory J. 1977. Sequential Parody Graffiti. *Western Folklore* 36:354–64.

Lovell-Smith, Rose. 1996. Dundes' Allomotifs and Female Audiences: A Reading of Perrault's *Les Fées. Fabula* 37:241–47.

Maccoby, Hyam. 1982. *The Sacred Executioner: Human Sacrifice and the Legacy of Guilt.* London: Thames & Hudson.

MacDonald, Margaret Read. 2006. *Ten Traditional Tellers.* Urbana: Univ. of Illinois Press.

Malinowski, Bronislaw. 1944. *A Scientific Theory of Culture.* Chapel Hill: Univ. of North Carolina Press.

McClearn, Duane. 2004. Interest in Sports and Belief in Sports Superstitions. *Psychological Reports* 94:1043–47.

McDowell, John Holmes. 1979. *Children's Riddling.* Bloomington: Indiana Univ. Press.

Mechling, Jay. 1980. The Magic of the Boy Scout Campfire. *Journal of American Folklore* 93:35–56.

———. 1984a. High Kybo Floater: Food and Feces in the Speech Play at a Boy Scout Camp. *Journal of Psychoanalytic Anthropology* 7:256–68.

———. 1984b. Patois and Paradox in a Boy Scout Treasure Hunt. *Journal of American Folklore* 97:34–42.

———. 1989a. "Banana Cannon" and Other Folk Traditions between Human and Nonhuman Animals. *Western Folklore* 48:312–23.

———. 1989b. Richard M. Dorson and the Emergence of the New Class in American Folk Studies. *Journal of Folklore Research* 26:11–26.

———. 2001. *On My Honor: Boy Scouts and the Making of American Youth.* Chicago: Univ. of Chicago Press.

———. 2006. Solo Folklore. *Western Folklore* 65:435–54.

Meehan, Susan E., and Simon J. Bronner. 2006. Hospitals. In Bronner 2006b, 592–96.

Megas, Georgios A. 1976. *Die Ballade von der Arta-Burcke: Eine Vergleichende Untersuchung.* Thessaloniki: Institute for Balkan Studies.

Mieder, Wolfgang. 1978. The Use of Proverbs in Psychological Testing. *Journal of the Folklore Institute* 15:45–56.

———, ed. 1994a. Alan Dundes: Master Folklorist and Paremiologist. *Proverbium* 11:1–14.

———. 1994b. *Festschrift for Alan Dundes on the Occasion of His Sixtieth Birthday, September 8, 1994.* Burlington: Univ. of Vermont.

———. 2004. Alan Dundes (1934–2005): In Memoriam. *Western Folklore* 63:287–90.

———, ed. 2006a. *Best of All Possible Friends: Three Decades of Correspondence Between the Folklorists Alan Dundes and Wolfgang Mieder.* Burlington: Univ. of Vermont.

———. 2006b. "The Proof of the Proverb is in the Probing": Alan Dundes as Pioneering Paremiologist. *Western Folklore* 65:217–62.

Mullen, Patrick. 1978. The Folk Idea of Unlimited Good in American Buried Treasure Legends. *Journal of the Folklore Institute* 15:209–20.

Nader, Laura, and Stanley Brandes. 2006. Alan Dundes (1934–2005). *American Anthropologist* 108:268–70.

Nakamura, Hejime. 1964. *Ways of Thinking of Eastern Peoples: India-China-Tibet-Japan.* Honolulu: Univ. of Hawaii Press.

Naugle, David K. 2002. *Worldview: The History of a Concept.* Grand Rapids, MI: Wm. B. Eerdmans.

Neugaard, Edward J. 1993. *Motif-Index of Medieval Catalan Folktales.* Binghamton, NY: Medieval and Renaissance Texts and Studies.

Newall, Venetia J. 1986. Folklore and Male Homosexuality. *Folklore* 97:123–47.

Oinas, Felix, ed. 1978. *Folklore, Nationalism, and Politics.* Columbus, OH: Slavica Press.

Oliver, Paul. 1960. *The Meaning of the Blues.* New York: Collier Books.

Opie, Iona, and Peter Opie. 1959 *The Lore and Language of Schoolchildren.* New York: Oxford Univ. Press.

———. 1969. *Children's Games in Street and Playground.* New York: Oxford Univ. Press.

Oring, Elliott. 1975a. The Devolutionary Premise: A Definitional Delusion? *Western Folklore* 34:36–44.

———. 1975b. Everything is a Shade of Elephant: An Alternative to a Psychoanalysis of Humor. *New York Folklore* 1:149–59.

———. 1983. Review of *Interpreting Folklore*, by Alan Dundes. *Journal of American Folklore* 96:84–88.

———. 1984a. Dyadic Traditions. *Journal of Folklore Research* 21:19–28.

———, ed. 1984b. *Humor and the Individual.* Los Angeles: California Folklore Society.

———. 1984c. *The Jokes of Sigmund Freud: A Study in Humor and Jewish Identity.* Philadelphia: Univ. of Pennsylvania Press.

———. 1986. On the Concepts of Folklore. In *Folk Groups and Folklore Genres: An Introduction*, ed. Elliott Oring, 1–22. Logan: Utah State Univ. Press.

———. 1988. Folklore Methodology and American Humor Research. In *Humor in America: A Research Guide to Genres and Topics*, ed. Lawrence E. Mintz, 213–30. Westport, CT: Greenwood.

———. 1992. *Jokes and Their Relations.* Lexington: Univ. Press of Kentucky.

———. 1993. Victor Turner, Sigmund Freud, and the Return of the Repressed. *Ethos* 21:273–94.

———. 1998. Review of *From Game to War and Other Psychoanalytic Essays on Folklore*, by Alan Dundes. *Western Folklore* 57:63–64.

———. 2003. *Engaging Humor.* Urbana: Univ. of Illinois Press.

Paredes, Américo, and Richard Bauman, eds. 1972. *Toward New Perspectives in Folklore.* Austin: Univ. of Texas Press.

Parker, Seymour. 1983. Concerning Dundes' "Earth-Diver": Creation of the Mythopoeic Male. *American Anthropologist* 65:913–15.

Pool, Ithiel de Sola, ed. 1959. *Trends in Content Analysis.* Urbana: Univ. of Illinois Press.

Powell, Timothy B. 1999. Re-Thinking Cultural Identity. In *Beyond the Binary: Reconstructing Cultural Identity in a Multicultural Context*, ed. Timothy B. Powell, 1–13. New Brunswick, NJ: Rutgers Univ. Press.

Pronin, Emily, Daniel Wegner, Kimberly McCarthy, and Sylvia Rodriguez. 2006. Everyday Magical Powers: The Role of Apparent Mental Causation in the Overestimation of Personal Influence. *Journal of Personality and Social Psychology* 91:218–31.

Propp, Vladimir. [1928] 1968. *Morphology of the Folktale.* Rev. and ed. Louis A. Wagner, trans. Laurence Scott. 2nd ed. Austin: Univ. of Texas Press. Orig. pub. as *Morfologiia Skazki* (Leningrad [St. Petersburg]: Academia, 1928).

———. 1984. *Theory and History of Folklore.* Ed. Anatoly Liberman, trans. Ariadna Y. Martin, Richard P. Martin, and others. *Theory and History of Literature* 5. Minneapolis: Univ. of Minnesota Press.

Rahkonen, Carl. 2000. No Laughing Matter: The Viola Joke Cycle as Musicians' Folklore. *Western Folklore* 59:49–63.

Rank, Otto. [1909] 2004. *The Myth of the Birth of the Hero: A Psychological Exploration of Myth.* Trans. Gregory C. Richter and E. James Lieberman. Baltimore: Johns Hopkins Univ. Press. Orig. pub. as *Der Mythus von der Geburt des Helden: Versuch einer Psychologoischen Mythendeutung* (Leipzig: [F.] Deuticke, 1909).

———. [1924] 1993. *The Trauma of Birth.* New York: Dover. Orig. pub. as *Das Trauma der Geburt und Seine Bedeutung für die Psychoanalyse* (Leipzig: Internationaler Psychoanalytischer Verlga, 1924); orig. English trans. pub. London: Kegan Paul, Trench, Trubner (1929).

Rappaport, Ernest A. 1975. The Ritual Murder Accusation: The Persistence of Doubt and the Repetition Compulsion. In *Anti-Judaism: A Psychohistory.* Chicago: Perspective Press. Repr. in *The Blood Libel Legend: A Casebook in Anti-Semitic Folklore*, ed. Alan Dundes, 304–35. Madison: Univ. of Wisconsin Press, 1991.

Reuss, Richard A. 1974. "That Can't Be Alan Dundes! Alan Dundes is Taller than That!": The Folklore of Folklorists. *Journal of American Folklore* 87:303–17.

Rey-Henningsen, Marisa. 1994. *The World of the Ploughwoman. Folklore and Reality in Matriarchal Northwest Spain.* FFC [Folklore Fellows' Communications] 254. Helsinki: Suomalainen Tiedeakatemia [Academia Scientiarum Fennica].

Roberts, John M., Malcolm J. Arth, and Robert R. Bush. 1959. Games in Culture. *American Anthropologist* 61:597–605.

Rotton, James, and I.W. Kelly. 1985. A Scale for Assessing Belief in Lunar Effects: Reliability and Concurrent Validity. *Psychological Reports* 57:239–45.

Sadger, Isidor. [1930] 2005. *Recollecting Freud.* Ed. Alan Dundes. Madison: Univ. of Wisconsin Press. Orig. pub. as *Sigmund Freud: Persönliche Erinnerungen* (Vienna: E. Wengraf, 1930).

Schmaier, Maurice D., and Alan Dundes. 1961. Parallel Paths. *Journal of American Folklore* 74:142–45.

Schmidt, Sigrid. 1995. The Worker Immured in the Oker Dam in Germany. *Fabula* 36:205–16.

Sebeok, Thomas A. 1962. The Texture of a Ceremis Incantation. *Mémoires de la Société Finno-Ougrienne* 125:523–37.

Segal, Robert, ed. 1996. *Structuralism in Myth: Lévi-Strauss, Barthes, Dumézil, and Propp.* New York: Routledge.

Sein, Maung Than, and Alan Dundes. 1964. Twenty-Three Riddles from Central Burma. *Journal of American Folklore* 77:72–73.

Shai, Donna. 1976. A Kurdish Jewish Variant of the Ballad of "The Bridge of Arta." *AJS Review* 1:303–10.

Shapiro, Fred R. 1987. Etymology of the Computer Bug: History and Folklore. *American Speech* 62:376–78.

Shenhar, Aliza. 1987. Metafolkloristic Additions to Stories by the Artistic Narrator. *Folklore* 98:53–56.

Sherwood, Michael. 1969. *The Logic of Explanation in Psychoanalysis*. New York: Academic Press.

Sire, James W. 2004. *Naming the Elephant: Worldview as a Concept*. Downers Grove, IL: InterVarsity Press.

Skeels, Dell. 1967. Two Psychological Patterns Underlying the Morphologies of Propp and Dundes. *Southern Folklore Quarterly* 31:244–61.

Smith, Henry Nash. [1950] 2005. *Virgin Land: The American West as Symbol and Myth*. Cambridge: Harvard Univ. Press. Orig. pub. 1950.

Stern, Stephen, and Simon J. Bronner. 1980. American Folklore vs. Folklore in America: A Fixed Fight? *Journal of the Folklore Institute* 17:76–84.

Stocker, Terrance L., Linda W. Dutcher, Stephen M. Hargrove, and Edwin A. Cook. 1972. Social Analysis of Graffiti. *Journal of American Folklore* 85:356–66.

Stevenson, Burton, ed. 1948. *The Macmillan Book of Proverbs, Maxims, and Famous Phrases*. New York: Macmillan.

Stitt, Michael J., and Robert K. Dodge. 1991. *A Tale and Motif Index of Early U.S. Almanacs*. New York: Greenwood Press.

Strack, Hermann L. 1909. *The Jew and Human Sacrifice: Human Blood and Jewish Ritual; An Historical and Sociological Inquiry*. New York: Bloch.

Suárez-Orozco, Marcelo M. 1993. A Psychoanalytic Study of Argentine Soccer. In L. B. Boyer, R. M. Boyer, and Sonnenberg 1993, 211–34.

Sutton-Smith, Brian. 1972a. *The Folkgames of Children*. Austin: Univ. of Texas Press.

———. 1972b. Strategy in Games and Folk Tales. In Sutton-Smith 1972, 341–57.

Sutton-Smith, Brian, and P. V. Gump. 1972. The 'It' Role in Children's Games, In Sutton-Smith 1972, 433–41.

Sutton-Smith, Brian, Jay Mechling, Thomas W. Johnson, and Felicia R. McMahon, eds. 1999. *Children's Folklore: A Source Book*. Logan: Utah State Univ. Press.

Taloş, Ion. 1997. *Meşterul Manole*. Vol. 2 of *Contribuție la studiul unei teme de folclor european*. Bucureşti: Editura Grai şi Suflet-Cultura Naţională.

Tangherlini, Timothy R. 1998. *Talking Trauma: Paramedics and Their Stories*. Jackson: Univ. Press of Mississippi.

Tappe, Eric. 1984. A Rumanian Ballad and its English Adaptation. *Folklore* 95:113–19.

Tatum, James C. 2000. *A Motif-Index of Luis Rosado Verga's Mayan Legends*. FFC [Folklore Fellows Communications] 271. Helsinki: Suomalainen Tiedeakatemia [Academia Scientiarum Fennica].

Taylor, Archer. 1940. Some Trends and Problems in Studies of the Folk-Tale. *Studies in Philology* 37:1–25.

———. [1948] 1965. Folklore and the Student of Literature. In *The Study of Folklore*, ed. Alan Dundes, 34–42. Englewood Cliffs, NJ: Prentice-Hall. Orig. pub. 1948 in *Pacific Spectator* 2:216–23.

Thompson, Stith, trans. and ed. [1928] 1961. *The Types of the Folktale: A Classification and Bibliography*. FFC [Folklore Fellows Communications] 74. Helsinki: Suomalainen Tiedeakatemia [Academia Scientarum Fennica]. Orig. pub. 1928.

———. [1932–36] 1975. *Motif-Index of Folk-Literature: A Classification of Narrative Elements in Folk-Tales, Ballads, Myths, Fables, Mediaeval Romances, Exempla, Flabiaux, Just-Books, and Local Legends.*. Rev. and enl. ed. 6 vols. Bloomington, Indiana Univ. Press. Orig. pub. as FFC [Folklore Fellows Communications] 106–9 (Helsinki: Suomalainen Tiedeakatemai [Academia Scientarium Fennica], 1932–36).

Tobacyk, Jerome, and Gary Milford. 1983. Belief in Paranormal Phenomena: Assessment of Instrument Development and Implications for Personality Functioning. *Journal of Personality and Social Psychology* 44:1029–37.

Toelken, Barre. 1996. *The Dynamics of Folklore*. Logan: Utah State Univ. Press.

Turner, Judith W. 1972. A Morphology of the 'True Love' Ballad. *Journal of American Folklore* 85:21–31.

Uther, Hans-Jörg. 2004 *The Types of International Folktales*. 3 vols. FFC [Folklore Fellows Communications] 286. Helsinki: Suomalainen Tiedeakatemia [Academia Scientiarum Fennica].

Weigle, Marta. 1987. Creation and Procreation, Cosmogony and Childbirth: Reflections on *Ex Nihilo*, Earth Diver, and Emergence Mythology. *Journal of American Folklore* 100:426–35.

Widdowson, John. 1977. *If You Don't Be Good: Verbal Social Control in Newfoundland*. St. Johns, NF: Institute of Social and Economic Research.

Wilson, William A. 1976. The Evolutionary Premise in Folklore Theory and the 'Finnish Method.' *Western Folklore* 35:241–49.

———. 1986. Documenting Folklore. In *Folk Groups and Folklore Genres*, ed. Elliott Oring, 225–54. Logan: Utah State Univ. Press.

———. 1995. Folklore, a Mirror for What? Reflections of a Mormon Folklorist. *Western Folklore* 54:13–21.

———. 2005. Fieldwork and Ethnography. In *Living Folklore: An Introduction to the Study of People and Their Traditions*, ed. Martha C. Sims and Martine Stephens, chapter 7. Logan: Utah State Univ. Press.

———. 2006. The Study of Mormon Folklore: An Uncertain Mirror for Truth. In *The Marrow of Human Experiences: Essays on Folklore*, 182–200. Logan: Utah State Univ. Press.

Winick, Stephen D. 2004. "You Can't Kill Shit": Occupational Proverb and Metaphorical System Among Young Medical Professionals. In *What Goes Around Comes Around: The Circulation of Proverbs in Contemporary Life*, ed. Kimberly J. Lau, Peter Tokofsky, and Stephen D. Winick, 86–106. Logan: Utah State Univ. Press.

Wolfenstein, Martha. 1978. *Children's Humor: A Psychological Analysis*. Bloomington: Indiana Univ. Press, 1978.

Wistrich, Robert S. 2002. *Muslim Anti-Semitism: A Clear and Present Danger*. New York: American Jewish Committee.

Würzbach, Natascha. 1995. *Motif Index of the Child Corpus: The English and Scottish Popular Ballad*. Berlin: W. de Gruyter.

Zolkover, Adam. 2006. Dorson, Discipline Building, and "The Identification of Folklore in American Literature. *Folklore Historian* 23:45—59.

Zumwalt, Rosemary Lévy. 1995. Alan Dundes: Folklorist and Mentor. In Bendix and Zumwalt 1995, 1–32.

Part I

Structure and Analysis

1

FOLKLORE AS A MIRROR OF CULTURE

Introduction

Alan Dundes was considered a master teacher as well as a scholar. His study of folklore offers insight into instruction, since folklore is an essential way that cultural knowledge and wisdom is passed down from generation to generation and from peer to peer. He practiced what he preached, for in 1994 he received a distinguished teaching award from the University of California at Berkeley, an accolade he greatly cherished. In his own education, he received a graduate degree in teaching of English from Yale University in 1955. In this 1969 essay, originally appearing in an English education journal, he urged K–12 teachers to use folklore as an instructional tool to develop tolerance, and to use the students' own cultural traditions to enhance learning. Unlike many educational approaches encouraging adults to concoct, and often sanitize, literary materials for children to digest, he called on teachers to rely on raw oral lore "performed by children for other children." He was famous, in fact, for requiring his own college students to collect fifty items of folklore that they would then describe and interpret. In this essay, he provided sociopsychological perspectives that can be used to decipher folk material.

Dundes pointed to children's folklore, not as something to be repressed, but rather to be brought out into the open. As he showed, it reflects, as only folklore can, issues of sibling rivalry, puberty, and parent/child relations. He distinguished folklore—as evidence—from the use of other materials, because it is "autobiographical ethnography, a people's own description of themselves." He evaluated what children typically relate in folklore to "areas of special concern," or anxieties that are expressed more readily in folklore than in everyday conversation.

Dundes's concern for the plight of African Americans and Vietnamese was voiced in his writings during the Civil Rights movement and the Vietnam War. He referred to the presence of the Cold War in relating alternative answers to the riddle joke of "what's black and white and red all over?" Other conflicts mentioned in the essay have outlasted the Cold War, such as ethnic and international tension grounded in cultural misunderstanding. Folklore, as a mirror of culture, reveals differences and similarities in ways of thinking, and he hoped that its study could therefore be a tool for teaching cultural understanding.

This essay encapsulates, at an early stage in Dundes's career, many of the principles of a "modern" concept of folklore that became influential in folkloristics. He distanced himself from the Grimm brothers' legacy of romantic nationalism, and advocated folklore as an adaptive strategy of modern life. He also expanded the scope of folk materials from oral to written and material items. His advocacy of the idea that folklore is constantly being created anew in contemporary life was especially important. It is not a relic of the past, as many people believe, but an expression of present-day issues.

Dundes's title invokes the "mirror" concept of Franz Boas, considered the father of modern anthropology, that folklore is invaluable as a reflection of a particular culture's conditions and values. He expanded Boas's inquiry by suggesting that the interpretation of symbols lodged within folkloric performances were a result of folklore serving the function of a socially sanctioned outlet for suppressed wishes and anxieties. He also inferred the strategic use of folklore to upset power relations, as his examples of child/parent communication demonstrate. Characteristically—given his fondness throughout his writing career for reflexively turning the analyst's cultural mirror back on the analyst as a way to disrupt the hierarchies of observer and observed—he examined the folklore that teachers possess, after spending time showing the value of understanding children's folklore. In the process, he identified the common cognitive pattern of trichotomy as a Western scholarly, as well as cultural, bias, a point he later expanded in "The Number Three in American Culture" in *Interpreting Folklore* (1980b). This essay is also significant for separating the hierarchical view of folk as a lower stratum, which he associated with the nineteenth-century approach of the Brothers Grimm, from the *modern* concept, which contains the key social definition of folk as "any group of people whatsoever who share at least one linking factor." Thus, he concluded that "we all are folk"—whether urban or rural, young or old, religious or secular.

In folkloristic writing, the "mirror" concept is still applied to relate historical and cultural information about a group, with the presumption that it is also a marker of a particularistic social identity. (See, for instance, Clements 1996; Rey-Henningsen 1994; Wilson 1995, 2006; and Georges and Jones 1995.) It is also referenced when the details of folklore appear *not* to reflect culture, suggesting the psychological possibility of folklore distorting or inverting reality (see chapter 14, "Getting the Folk and the Lore Together"). In Dundes's words, "It was not understood [in Boas's mirror concept] that an item of folklore can serve as a vehicle which *requires* an individual to do what he may not be permitted to do in everyday reality (e.g., in courtship games, complete strangers may kiss, in games of chase, acts of physical aggression are mandatory)" (Dundes 1966a, 243; see also chapters 15 and 17 in this volume).

Alan Dundes continued his interest in children's folklore throughout his career, connecting folklore to human development and infantile anxieties. He also drew on children's humor, such as dead baby jokes, to underscore the emergent nature of folk humor, which he typically analyzed psychoanalytically (1987c). He wrote the foreword to Martha Wolfenstein's *Children's Humor* (1978), and the title essays of his anthologies *From Game to War* (1997b) and *Bloody Mary in the Mirror* (2002a) delve into children's rituals and games. For more interpretative sources on the folklore of children and their teachers, see Bishop and Curtis 2001; Bronner 1988, 1995; Factor 1989; Knapp and Knapp 1976; McDowell 1979; Opie and Opie 1969, 1972; Sutton-Smith 1972; and Sutton-Smith et al. 1999.

Folklore as a Mirror of Culture

THE VARIOUS FORMS OF FOLKLORE: myths, folktales, legends, folksongs, proverbs, riddles, games, dances and many others can provide a vital resource for a teacher who seriously wishes to (1) understand his students better, and (2) teach those students more effectively about the world and about the human condition. For folklore is autobiographical ethnography—that is, it is a people's own description of themselves. This is in contrast to other descriptions of that people, descriptions made by social workers, sociologists, political scientists or anthropologists. It may be that there is distortion in a people's self image as it is expressed in that people's songs, proverbs, and the like, but one must admit that there is often as much, if not more, distortion in the supposedly objective descriptions made by professional social scientists who in fact see the culture under study through the culturally relative and culturally determined categories of their own culture. Moreover, even the distortion in a people's self image can tell the trained observer something about that people's values. Out of all the elements of culture, which ones are singled out for distortion, for special emphasis?

Folklore as a mirror of culture frequently reveals the areas of special concern. It is for this reason that analyses of collections of folklore can provide the individual who takes advantage of the opportunities afforded by the study of folklore a way of seeing another culture *from the inside out* instead of *from the outside in*, the usual position of a social scientist or teacher. Whether the "other culture" is far from the borders of our country or whether the "other culture" is lodged within these borders, a world shrunk by modern technological advances in transportation and communications demands that education keep pace. We need to know more about Vietnamese worldview; we need to know more about African American values.

One or the greatest obstacles impeding a better understanding of Vietnamese, African American or any other culture is what anthropologists term "ethnocentrism." This is the notion, apparently held in some form by all the peoples of the earth, that the way *we* do things is "natural" and "right" whereas the way *others* do them is "strange," perhaps "unnatural" and maybe even "wrong." The Greek historian Herodotus described ethnocentrism, without, of course, using the term, as follows:

> If one were to offer men to choose out of all the customs in the world such as seemed to them the best, they would examine the whole number, and end by preferring their own; so convinced are they that their own usages surpass those of all others.

One of the purposes of studying folklore is to realize the hypothetical premise. Man cannot choose out of all the customs in the world until he knows what these customs are. Traditional customs are part of folklore. Obviously the point in collecting, classifying, and analyzing the customs and other forms of folklore is not necessarily to allow the investigator to choose a way of life other than his own. Rather by identifying the similarities, the actual historical cognates such as hundreds of versions of Cinderella, a tale which folklorists label as Aarne-Thompson tale type 510 in the internationally known index of Indo-European folktales first published in 1910, or by identifying the near-similarities, the probably noncognate folkloristic parallels which seem to depend upon universal or quasi-universal human experiences (such as the introduction of death into the world because of some unthinking or foolish action on the part of a culture hero or trickster figure), one has convincing data which can effectively be used to promote international understanding. If only the Turks and Greeks realized that they had the same folktales and the same lovable wise fool of a Hodja figure in many of these tales. The same holds for the Arabs and the Jews. In this light, it is sad to think that folklore, instead of being used as a constructive force for internationalism, has all too frequently been the tool of excessive nationalism.

The history of folklore studies reveals that folklorists in many different countries have often been inspired by the desire to preserve their national heritage. The Grimms, for example, at the beginning of the nineteenth century, imbued with nationalism and romanticism, and armed with the fashionable methodology of historical reconstruction, collected folktales and legends with the hope of rescuing something ur-German, that is, something truly Teutonic, before it faded from the scene altogether. The Grimms were surprised and probably more than a little disappointed when they discovered that many of their "Teutonic" tales had almost exact analogues in other European countries. The Grimms incidentally, like most nineteenth century collectors, rewrote the folklore they collected. This retouching of oral tales continues today in the children's literature field where reconstructed, reconstituted stories written in accordance with *written not oral conventions* are palmed off as genuine folktales.

One can see that the basic mistrust of folk materials is part of a general ambivalence about the materials of oral tradition, the materials of the folk. On the one hand, the folk and their products were celebrated as a national treasure of the past; on the other hand, the folk were wrongly identified with the illiterate in a literate society and thus the folk as a concept was identified exclusively with the vulgar and the uneducated. (The folk to a modern folklorist is any group of people whatsoever who share at least one common linking factor, e.g., religion, occupation, ethnicity, geographical location, etc., which leads to: Jewish folklore, lumberjack folklore, African American folklore, and California folklore. As an American I know American folklore; as a professor I know campus folklore; as a member of a family, I know my own family folklore.) The equation of folklore with ignorance has continued. The word folklore itself considered as an item of folk speech means fallacy, untruth, error. Think of the phrase "That's folklore." It is similar to the meaning of "myth in such phrases as "the myth of race." This is *not,* however, what folklore and myth mean to the professional folklorist. A myth is but one form or genre of folklore, a form which consists of a sacred narrative explaining how the world and man came to be in their present form. Folklore consists of a variety of genres most of which are found among all peoples of the earth. Nevertheless, the association of folklore with error (consider "folk" medicine as opposed to "scientific" medicine) has made it difficult for the study of folklore as a discipline to gain academic respectability and has generally discouraged the use and study of folklore by educators.

It is still mistakenly thought that the only people who study folklore are antiquarian types, devotees of ballads which are no longer sung and collectors of quaint customs which are no longer practiced. Folklore in this false view is equated with survivals from an age past, survivals which are doomed not to survive. Folklore is gradually dying out, we are told. Moreover, since folklore is defined as error, it is thought by some educators to be a good thing that folklore is dying out. In fact, it has been argued that one of the purposes of education is to help stamp out folklore. As humans evolve, they leave folklore behind such that the truly civilized human is conceived to be folkloreless. From this kind of thinking, one can understand why education and folklore have been on opposite sides and also why when well meaning educators move into other cultures, e. g., in Africa or in a ghetto school, they actually believe they are doing their students a service by helping to suppress local customs, superstitions, folk speech, and other folkloristic traditions. So it is that African students are taught Shakespeare and Chaucer as great literature while their own superb oral literature is not deemed worthy of classroom treatment, assuming that the western educated teacher even knows of its existence. How many teachers of literature, of the epic in particular, are aware of the fact that the epic is a living oral form and that epics up to 13,000 lines are now being sung in Yugoslavia, among other places? How many teachers of African American children have ever heard of the "dozens" (or "rapping and capping" or "sounding" etc.) or of the "toast," an important African American folklore genre in rhyme reminiscent of epic form? Yet, the technique of verbal dueling known as the "dozens" and the epic toast are extremely viable forms of African American folklore and they encapsulate the critical points and problems in African American family structure and in black-white relations. One could teach both literature and social studies from such folkloristic texts (were they not "obscene" by our standards) with the advantage that these texts would be known by the students from their own lives and experience.

Why not teach children about the nature of poetry by examining their own folk poetry: nursery rhymes, jump rope rhymes, hand clap rhymes, ball bouncing rhymes, dandling rhymes, and autograph book verse among others? There is almost no method or approach found in the study of literature which could not also be applied to folk materials. One could discuss formal features such as metrics, rhyme, alliteration; one could discuss content features such as characterization, motivation, themes. By using the materials of folklore as a point of departure, the educational process may be comprehended as dealing with the real world rather than with a world apart from the world in which the students live. With folklore, the classroom becomes a laboratory or forum for a consideration of "real life" as it is experienced and perceived by those being educated. Let me briefly provide just a few examples of folklore and try to illustrate how they might be used to enliven and stimulate classroom discussions.

One technique which can immediately show children something important about the nature of oral tradition is to select one item of folklore and ask each child to tell the other members of the class his or her *version* of the item. It doesn't matter what the item is: when Christmas presents are opened (Christmas Eve, Christmas morning, one on Christmas Eve and the rest on Christmas day, etc.) or what one says near the end of *Hide and Seek* to summon all the other players: Olly, olly oxen free, Olly Olly Ocean free, (All ye, all ye "outs" in free?????), Home free all, etc. After a number of versions have been elicited, the students should be able to see that although there is considerable diversity, there is also considerable uniformity. If there are differences—such as how many candles are placed on the birthday cake (some have the number of candles equal to the number of years old while others have that number plus one with the extra grow on, etc.), even these differences are traditional. How many children believe that the number of candles left burning after the attempt to blow them out signifies the number of children one will have? How many believe the number left burning signifies the number of years to pass before one's wish (made right before the blowing attempt) comes true? Through such devices, the children can learn that there are frequently subtraditions within traditions. Then the teacher may ask the children "Which version is correct?" "Which version is the right one?" Normally, there will be extended debate on this, individual students championing their own individual versions, perhaps pointing to the statistical evidence available within the classroom to support one version over another. Gradually, the children will come to realize that in folklore as in life, there is often no one correct or right version. One traditional version is just as traditional as another version. A's way of observing Christmas or birthday rituals is no better and no worse than B's. Isn't this a marvelous way of showing what ethnocentrism is: people insisting that the way they know is best and proper while the strange unfamiliar way is wrong? And isn't this a marvelous way of teaching tolerance? If children can learn that their fellows' ways are not "wrong" but "alternative, equally traditional" ways of doing things, this could be one of the most important lessons they are ever likely to learn.

Having illustrated the nature of variation in folklore, the teacher might wish to discuss why there is variation. Here the difference between oral and written (or printed) traditions is crucial. Folklore is passed on by means of person to person contact. And an item of folklore may be changed by different individuals in accordance with their own individual needs, the demands of a particular social context—the make-up of the audience—is it boys and girls, just boys, children and grown-ups, etc. or the requirements of a new age. So it is that each item of folklore is passed on through time, sometimes remaining the same, sometimes changing. This is why the task of collecting and analyzing folklore can never be completed. Tomorrow's version of a folksong may or may not be the same as the one we know today which in turn may or may not be the same as the one which was known in the past. This is in marked contrast to the products of written tradition. If one reads a play of Shakespeare or a novel of James Joyce today, one can be reasonably sure that one hundred years from now, the identical text will be read by others.

There is a tendency to underestimate the differences between a visual/written record and an aural/oral record. It has only recently been suggested that the mass media, radio, television, motion pictures, etc. have, by discouraging or impinging upon time formerly spent in reading, made us an oral rather than a written culture. Actually, one should say, has made us an oral culture *again*. In evolutionary terms, pre-literate society which was orally oriented became literate, but now we have "post-literate" man who is influenced by oral communication once more. Yet the education system has not always kept pace. The traditional emphasis has been upon "reading and writing." What about "speaking?" Oratory, valued so much by oral cultures around the world, has become almost a lost art in literate societies. Interestingly enough, in African American culture there is tremendous value placed upon rhetoric as one aspect of style. The "man of words" is highly esteemed and anyone who has heard African American preachers use their voices surely recognizes the eloquent power of that oral style.

It is a pity that our educational philosophy continues to worship the written word. Note that "literacy" is still thought by some to be a *sine qua non* for an individual to be able to vote. The fact that intelligent peoples all over the world are capable of reaching decisions without anything more than oral communication seems to be overlooked. We tend to trust what is "down in black and white." "Put it in writing" we say; we tend to distrust oral testimony, regarding it as unreliable. We forget that much of what is written down—in newspapers, in books, circulated as oral communication first. Even the Bible was in oral tradition before it was committed to written form! With such bias in favor of written tradition, it is easy to see why there has been relatively little interest in the study of oral tradition. But by failing to recognize the differences between oral and written traditions, we do a disservice to ourselves as well as our students. Who has never heard someone give orally an address which was written out in advance? Yet relatively few written works read well aloud. Similarly, students taking written notes from an instructor's free-flowing oral classroom delivery are often dismayed by the sentence fragments, the agreement errors, etc. There are major lexical and stylistic differences between oral and written tradition. "Indeed, Moreover, One cannot escape the conclusion . . ." are acceptable written conventions, when *seen* on a printed page, but they may *sound* stilted when heard in speech. A word or phrase may *look* right, but *sound* wrong. But by the same token, a word or phrase which sounds fine, may look terrible in print. In oral speech, one can use slang, folk similes (as cool as a cucumber) and folk metaphors (to fly off the handle). In written tradition, these are branded as "clichés" by diligent teachers of English composition. Such teachers are wont to warn their students to "avoid clichés." The folklorist would urge that children *not* be told never to use clichés but rather that they be taught the difference between oral and written traditions and *not* to confuse the conventions of each. In oral tradition, originality is neither desired or expected. The more traditional (= unoriginal) the better. However, in our written tradition, originality is essential. But children can not avoid clichés. Do they not learn to speak before they learn to read and write? The point is simply that children should not be taught to write as they speak and they should not be taught to speak as they write. The unfortunate confusion of oral and written conventions is one reason why most printed collections of folklore are spurious. They have been edited and rewritten to conform to written rather than oral style. The expletives, meaningful pauses, the stammers, not to mention the eye expressions, the hand movements and all the other body gestural signals are totally lost in the translation from oral to written tradition. This is why it is impossible to learn what folklore is by reading books. If one is interested in learning about folklore, one must elicit oral tradition. A useful class exercise might be to have a child tell a joke or legend to his classmates whose task it becomes to write it down. One could then discuss at length just what was "left out" in the written version that had been in the oral version.

In order to more fully understand and utilize folklore, one must have some idea of the functions of folklore. Folklore reflects (and thereby reinforces) the value configurations of the folk, but at the same time folklore provides a sanctioned form of escape from these very same values. In fairy tales, the hero or heroine is inevitably told not to do something; don't look in the secret chamber, don't answer the door, etc. Of course, the protagonist violates the interdiction. He may be punished for his disobedience, but usually he comes out ahead in the end. For example, the hero marries the princess. The escape mechanism is equally obvious in traditional games. On the one hand, educators urge that games be played to teach "teamwork," "cooperation," and "fair play." On the other hand, once in the game, children can compete and they can compete aggressively. One can "steal" the bacon or "capture" the flag of the opposing team. In "King of the Mountain," boys can push rivals off the raft. In adolescent games such as "Spin the Bottle," "Post Office," or "Padiddle," the rules *require* the participants to do that which they would very much like to do but which they might not otherwise do. Folklore provides socially sanctioned forms of behavior in which a person may do what can't be done in "real life." One is not supposed to push anyone around in real life—at least if one believes the "Golden Rule," but in games one is supposed to take a chair and leave someone else without one to sit on (in "Musical Chairs"). As a young adolescent, one cannot kiss a casual acquaintance without feelings of guilt or hearing cries of derision. Yet in kissing games, one must do so. The folkloristic frame not only permits, but *requires* the taboo action and it also thereby relieves the individual from assuming the responsibility (and guilt) for his or her actions. The individual has no choice; it is a mere spin of the bottle or some other act of chance (such as seeing a car with only one headlight working) which dictates the sexual behavior. In children's games, the drama of real (adult) life is often enacted, Yet neither teacher nor student may be fully aware of just what is involved in a particular game. In much the same way, folk—and social—dances allow for heterosexual body contact in a society which true to its Puritan heritage has consistently condemned the body and its domain. The fact that boys can dance with girls, girls can dance with girls, but boys cannot dance with boys in American culture reflects our great fear of homosexuality. This is striking when one recalls that most societies even have men's dances from which women are excluded. Americans remain slaves to a tradition in which the body is seen as dirty, as something to be denied or repressed. Note that we still insist on *physical* (corporal) punishments for intellectual/mental lapses. The body is punished, not the mind, every time a child is struck or spanked!

As a specific example of how folklore functions, let me cite one riddle text. A child comes home from school and at the dinner table asks his parents: "What is black and white and red all over?" The parent, if he or she is alert and has a good memory, replies: "A newspaper" which in fact is one of the older traditional answers to this riddle. But there are other modern traditional answers. Some of these are: a sunburned zebra, an embarrassed zebra, a zebra with measles, a wounded nun, a bloody integration march, and for the sophistocate: *Pravda,* the *Daily Worker,* or the *New York Times* which involves an interesting play on the original "newspaper" answer. Now what precisely is going on? What function, if any, does this riddle or the hundreds like it serve? I believe that this kind of riddle provides an effective mechanism for reversing the normal adult-child relationship in our society. In our society, it is the parent or teacher who knows all the answers and who insists upon proposing difficult if not "impossible" questions to children. However, in the riddle context, either the parent doesn't know the answer to the elephant or little moron joking question—in which case the child can have the great pleasure of telling him or her what the answer is *or* the parent gives the "wrong" answer (e.g., "newspaper" would be considered "wrong" by the child who has *another* answer in mind—and aren't there plenty of instances where the child answers an adult's question perfectly well but fails because his answer was not the particular answer the adult desired'? This is also what happens whenever an unthinking adult asks the kind of questions which can be labeled as being "Guess what's in my mind" questions. In this instance where the parent has given the "wrong" answer, the child has the even more exquisite pleasure of *correcting* rather than merely informing the parent.) Children also use riddles with their peers where a similar function is evident. A child goes one up if he or she has a riddle which stumps a friend. I should perhaps mention that riddles or joking questions are by no means confined to children's usage. Many adults use such devices in daily interpersonal rituals. Some of these riddling questions provide serious reflections of our culture. Do you remember the "knock-knock" cycle? Well, have you heard the World War II knock-knock joke? No? Okay, "Knock-knock" (audience): "Who's there?"—(long silent pause—signifying that no one would be left to answer in the event of total nuclear world war).

Literature for Children or Literature of Children

The analysis of the content of children's folklore could help anyone seriously interested in understanding children. I refer specifically to that portion of children's folklore which is performed by children for other children. This is distinct from that portion of children's folklore which consists of materials imposed upon children by parents and teachers. The analysis of the latter kind of children's folklore would probably give more of an insight into parents and teachers' worldview than the worldview of children. I suspect that in courses dealing with children's literature, it is this latter category which receives most of the attention. In other words, the emphasis is on "literature for children" rather than "literature of children"! (By "literature of children" I mean their oral literature, their folklore, their traditions, not their little individual written compositions or poems.) This is, in my opinion, the same kind of thinking that makes Peace Corps teachers teach Shakespeare and Chaucer to African students instead of utilizing African folktales and proverbs, that is, using some of the "native" literature as the basis for an understanding of the nature of prose and poetry. Educational, as well as foreign, policy is invariably made in accordance with the value system of us, the teacher or the American. Such decisions may be rational from our point of view; they may even prove to be "correct," but in the majority of cases, these decisions are probably all too often made without sufficient knowledge of the groups we honestly want to help. We tend to think of the "other" people be they inhabitants of villages in Asia or children in our classroom as poor little sponges who need to soak up as much of our material as they possibly can.

The phrase "culturally deprived" is a prime example of this faulty kind of thinking. From an anthropological perspective, of course, there can be no such thing as culturally deprived. Culture in anthropological usage refers to the total way of life of a people, and not to a very select group of elitist materials such as opera, the great books, etc. All human beings have culture in general; some people share one culture rather than another. Hopi culture is different from Vietnamese culture. So it is impossible in this sense for any individual to be "culturally deprived"; our minority groups have just as much culture as anybody else. The point is simply that it is another culture, a different culture. To call a minority group "culturally deprived" is a kind of survival of nineteenth century "white man's burden" thinking. The real question is: Do we want "them"—and "them' could be African Americans, South Vietnamese, children in our classrooms, etc.—to give up their culture and accept our culture in its place or do we not insist on a melting pot metaphor with the pot to take on the consistency of the dominant ethos? In my opinion, the "unmelting pot" might be a more apt metaphor. If so, then perhaps we should allow or better yet, encourage "them" to enjoy, understand, and take pride in their own culture. Obviously, the culture of our children is closer to our adult culture than the culture of a distinct ethnic minority or some foreign population to our culture in general. Nevertheless, the principle in terms of educational philosophy is the same.

What kinds of things do we see in our children's own folklore?

> Teacher, teacher, I declare
> I see so and so's underwear.

> Charlie Chaplin went to France
> To see the ladies' underpants . . .

> I see London; I see France
> I see so and so's underpants.

We see the child's curiosity about the body and the immediate body covering. The child finds it difficult to accept the adult's apparent rejection of the body and its natural functions. Consider the following jump rope rhyme:

> Cinderella, dressed in yellow
> Went downtown to see her fellow.
> On the way her girdle busted.
> How many people were disgusted? 1, 2, 3, etc.

Clearly, children, in this instance little girls, are fascinated by a particular undergarment, the girdle. Note that the girdle busts while Cinderella is on the way to see, or in some versions to kiss, her fellow. Do children really know what they are saying?

Folklore and Sibling Rivalry

Less symbolic, but equally important are the sentiments underlying these familiar jump rope verses:

> Fudge, fudge, tell the judge
> Mama's got a new born baby.
> It ain't no girl, it ain't no boy
> Just a newborn (or "common" or "plain ol'" or "ordinary") baby
> Wrap it up in tissue paper
> Throw (send) it down the elevator.
> First floor, miss
> Second floor, miss, etc. (until the jumper misses)

This is really an extraordinarily revealing rhyme. First of all, why is the judge informed about the newborn baby? Is the judge the person who can take away children from parents or the person who has the power to punish parents for mistreating children? In any case, here is explicit sibling rivalry. What child does not resent the arrival upon the scene of the new born child who threatens the previously existing relationship between the older children and the mother? Notice how the poor baby is demeaned. It is sexless. It's not a girl, not a boy, in other words, it's *nothing*. It's just—and that word "just" tells all—an ordinary baby, nothing exceptional, nothing to make a fuss about. And what does the jumper-reciter recommend should be done with the baby? *Throw* it down the elevator. The jumper then jumps as many floors as she can without missing. Thus by being a skillful jumper, a girl can send her baby sibling far away. The more jumps without misses, the further the baby is sent away. Thus through jumping rope, a young girl is able to do something "constructive" about getting rid of her inevitable aggression against the new sibling rival. This inter-sibling hostility, I submit, is an integral part of American children's world-view. Look at the following jump rope rhyme:

> I had a baby brother
> His name was Tiny Tim.
> I put him in the bathtub
> To teach him how to swim.

> He drank up all the water;
> He ate up all the soap.
> He tried to eat the bathtub
> But it wouldn't go down his throat.
> He died last night
> With a bubble in his throat.

This is an equally blatant example of an expression of sibling rivalry. Note the tense of the verb in the first line. I *"had"* a baby brother. Here is wishful thinking, a common element in all folklore. The baby rival is gone, and before the rhyme really gets started. What of the rest of the rhyme's content? Precisely where is it that the newborn baby gets so much obvious physical attention? In American culture, it is the bath. It is during and after bathing that the baby is fondled, powdered, played with, etc. So the older child takes things into his own hands. He puts the baby into the tub pretending to teach him how to swim. What does the baby do in the tub? He tries to eat everything. Babies are in fact orally inclined as it is this body zone which provides the initial point of contact with the world, a body zone which operates by incorporating what is needed, i.e., mother's milk. From the older child's point of view, the baby is always being fed—hence it appears to have an insatiable appetite. What then is more appropriate from the older child's perspective than to have his baby brother choke to death from eating something he shouldn't be eating, from trying to eat too much, that is, symbolically speaking, from trying to take too much, more than his share of their common parent's bounty. Of course, children hate their parents too:

> Step on a crack (line)
> Break your mother's back (spine)

Symbolism in Folklore

No doubt many people who are unsympathetic to psychology and symbolism may doubt the validity of the above interpretations of children's folklore. Such interpretations, they would argue, are being *read into* innocent folklore rather than being *read out* of the folklore. Yet the astonishing thing is that much the same symbolism is contained in the folklore for children as communicated by parents and teachers. It has long been wrongly assumed that folktales—e.g., Grimms' *Kinder und Hausmärchen* and nursery rhymes are strictly children's fac e. This is not true. These materials were related by adults to other adults as well as children. If adult males have Oedipus complexes, then it is clear why it is they who relate the story of Jack and the Beanstalk. A boy lives alone with his mother, throws beans out of a window at his mother's request, climbs a tall magic beanstalk, hides from the threatening giant in the friendly giant's wife's oven, kills the giant by cutting the giant stalk with an axe which is often helpfully provided by his mother waiting at the foot of the stalk, and finally lives happily ever after with his mother! (Parents, of course, to the infant's eye view or the world appear to be giants!) For women with Electra complexes, it is normally a girl versus a wicked stepmother or witch. Whereas the donor figure in male folktales may be a female (cf. Jack's mother, the giant's wife), in female folktales, the helper may be a male (cf. the woodsman in "Little Red Riding Hood"), although to be sure sometimes kind father figures help boys and kind mother figures (e.g., fairy god-mothers) help girls. In Hansel and Gretel, the children are tempted orally and they nibble at the witch's house. (The children were not given food by their parents.) The witch, like so many cannibalistic villains in fairy tales, intends to employ the infant's first weapon (eating, sucking, biting) by devouring the children. In this tale, the heroine, Gretel, succeeds in duping the witch into being burned up in her own oven. The female-oven symbolism is consistent. In Jack and the Beanstalk, the boy hides in the giant's wife's oven to escape the giant; in Hansel and Gretel, a tale featuring a girl's point of view, the heroine eliminates the female villain by making her enter her own hot oven! And what of Cinderella who we noticed in jump rope rhymes? What is the significance of the story of a girl who marries a prince because of a perfect fit between a foot and a glass slipper? What has the ideal marriage to do with a foot fitting into a slipper? And why do we still tie old shoes on the bumpers of cars carrying newlyweds off on their honeymoon?

One clue to the symbolism of slippers and shoes comes right from Mother Goose. One of the rhymes which parents read to children is:

> There was an old woman who lived in a shoe.
> She had so many children she didn't know what to do.

A literal, historical interpretation would have to locate a place where women once lived in actual shoes, But how would one explain the stated connection between "living in a shoe" and "having lots of children." Fortunately, another verse to this rhyme reported in the Ozarks in the 1890's makes the symbolism even more overt:

> There was another old woman who lived in a shoe.
> She didn't have any children; she knew what to do.

With symbolic systems, it is never a matter of one isolated instance. Within a given culture, there are whole consistent patterns of symbolism. The symbolism of a culture will be manifested in the folklore of that culture. So we should not be surprised to find other nursery rhymes:

> Cock a doodle doo
> My dame has lost her shoe
> Her master's lost his fiddling stick
> They don't know what to do.

Remember these are part of the children's folklore which is transmitted to children by parents and teachers. I do not necessarily believe that parents are aware of the symbolic content of folklore any more than I believe that children are consciously aware of all the symbolism. Clearly, folklore could not function successfully as an outlet if there were conscious awareness of its being so used. Folklore is collective fantasy and as fantasy, it depends upon the symbolic system of a given culture. I should be remiss if I did not state my conviction that the communication of collective fantasy and symbols is a healthy thing and I would strongly oppose those educators who advocate placing Mother Goose and fairy tales on a high shelf or locked case in the library. Folklore is one way for both adults and children to deal with the crucial problems in their lives. If our folklore sometimes deals with sexuality and the interrelationships between members of a family, then this is obviously something of a problem area in our daily lives. We know that folklore in all cultures tends to cluster around the critical points in the life cycle of the individual (e.g., birth, initiation, marriage, death) and the calendrical cycle of the community (e.g., sowing, harvesting, etc.) In fact, if one collects the folklore of a people and then does a content analysis of that folklore, one is very likely to be able to delineate the principal topics of crisis and anxiety among that people. So if American folklore, both adult and children's folklore, has a sexual element, then we must face the problem which is reflected in the folklore. Squelching folklore as if such a thing were really possible—it is impossible to censor oral tradition as opposed to print—would not help in solving the original problems which generated the collective fantasies in the first place.

Folklore About Teachers

There can be no doubt that folklore reflects culture and as a final example, I will briefly mention teacher folklore. The folklore of and about teachers reflects both teachers' attitudes about themselves and students' attitudes about teachers. There is the resentment of administrators as illustrated in the numerous dean stories, e.g., "Old deans never die; they just lose their faculties." There are the parodies of teaching methods. An English teacher is explaining to her class how to write a short story: It should have religion, high society, sex, and mystery. Within a few moments, a little boy says, "OK. I'm finished." The teacher, surprised at the speed of the boy's composition, asks him to read his short story aloud to the class. "My God," said the duchess, "I'm pregnant! Who did it?" There are also commentaries on teachers who run their classes without any regard for what their students might like or think. A professor gives an advanced seminar in algebraic functions. Only one student shows up. However, he strides to the lectern and reads his hour-long lecture. Each day, the professor does the same thing. He sets up his notes and reads his lecture. One day, while at the blackboard writing a long series of equations and formulas, the professor sees the one student's hand raised. "Excuse me, professor, but I don't see why x cubed equals y cubed. Why wouldn't x cubed equal y cubed plus z cubed?" The professor replied, "That's a very interesting question but I don't want to take up valuable class time with it. See me at the end of the hour." In a variant of this joke, it is a professor of art history who offers a seminar in advanced Burmese vase painting. Again there is one student and again the professor reads his lecture. This time, the professor is at the faculty club talking to his colleagues. When they discover that he has only one student for the seminar, they ask him what he is doing in the class. He tells them that he reads his lecture just as he always has. "Good heavens," one colleague exclaims, "with just one student why don't you run the class as a discussion?" whereupon the professor replied, "What is there to discuss?" Of course, I don't have to say how distasteful modern students find this philosophy of education.

The folklore of teaching includes elementary school teachers too. For example, there's the story of the elementary school teacher who taught look-say reading. One day in backing her car out of a parking place on the street, she banged into the car parked behind her. She immediately got out to survey the possible damage and looking at her rear fender she said, "Oh, oh, oh, look, look, look, Damn, Damn, Damn!" Notice the threefold repetition in the punchline. There are three words each of which is repeated three times. Is this unusual? Certainly not. Three is the ritual number in American folklore. Whether it's three brothers in folktales, three wishes, a minister, a priest, and a rabbi, or the fact that there are frequently three action sequences in jokes and three repetitions of lines in folksongs: John Brown's body lies a moulderin' in the grave, Polly put the kettle on, Lost my partner what'll I do? etc., the pattern is the same. This pattern is *not* universal; most American Indian peoples have the ritual number *four*. Here is yet another illustration of how by analyzing the folklore we gain insight into the culture which it mirrors. Three is a ritual number not just in American folklore, but in all aspects of American culture: time—past, present, future; space—length, width, depth; and language—good, better, best, etc.

This is why we have the three R's (Reading, 'Riting and 'Rithmetic), Primary, Secondary, and Higher Education, the latter with its three degrees B.A., M. A., and PhD., the first of which can be cum laude, magna cum laude, and summa cum laude. This is why we have such pedagogical principles as: "Preview, Teach, and Review" which retains its tripartite form in the folk translation: tell 'em what you're going to tell 'em, tell 'em, and tell 'em what you told 'em.

Folklore as a subject of study can be a most rewarding one. It does serve as a mirror of culture and it is a mirror well worth looking into. The teacher who encourages his or her class to examine their own folklore or better yet sends them out with collecting projects, such as collecting the folklore of a group from another "culture" can give students as well as him or herself an educational experience of immeasurable value. We need to use every available means to better understand ourselves and our fellow men and women. Folklore is one such means, one available for the asking. We are all folk. All one needs to begin such work is people, people to ask and people to listen. Whether individuals ask about their own folklore or ask others about their folklore, if they listen, they will learn.

2

The Study of Folklore in Literature and Culture: Identification and Interpretation

Introduction

At the time Dundes wrote this essay, during the 1960s, most scholars concerned with the study of folklore aligned with either literary or anthropological camps, a result of their educational background or organizational affiliation in a humanities or social science department. Dundes observed that what he called the "binary division" in the field had literary scholars, on one side, stressing the text and anthropologists, on the other, emphasizing context. In this seminal essay, Dundes proposed a folkloristic method that combined the pursuit of texts and contexts, and provided a foundation for a distinctive modern discipline of folkloristics.

To be sure, scholars had a methodological toolkit at their disposal, but it was often divided into approaches for specific genres, such as the historical-geographic literary method for finding the origin and distribution of folktales, or the ethnographic field observation of customs. While being an advocate of comparative approaches, Dundes recoiled at the comparative method associated with Victorian anthropologists, which treated folklore as "meaningless" survivals or relics of an evolutionary lower rung of a cultural ladder amidst humanity's upward climb toward "civilization." This natural history model adapted nineteenth-century evolutionary doctrine to propose a universal psychic unity, and a unilinear model of culture that all societies pass through (i.e., stages of savagery, barbarism, and civilization). The question that Dundes asked was whether an integrative approach could be established that connected various genres of folklore, and that had a culturally relative perspective which accounted for the emergent quality of folklore.

The folklorist, to Dundes, was a scholarly identity that signaled an overarching concern for the study of tradition, and emphasized the study of "text within context," past and present. In a rhetoric reminiscent of a homiletic jeremiad, Dundes bemoaned folklorists' literary-oriented collecting of texts as an end in itself. At the same time, he was critical of anthropological studies that did not account for textual evidence, or were narrowly focused on a single culture. While identification sounds straightforward, it is a demanding task to account for contextual and textual (or performance) information, in addition to recording texts. Dundes recognized that folklore research depends largely on field-collected texts, so as to know the circumstances and communication of an item in folklore, but he also included working with historical and literary sources as a legitimate part of the identification stage. In this essay, the text was annotated using standard references, such as the tale-type index prepared first by Finnish scholar Antti Aarne (1910) and later revised by American folktale specialist Stith Thompson ([1928] 1961) and German literary academician Hans-Jörg Uther (2004). The annotation checked the item's provenance and distribution, and allowed Dundes to make statements to the effect that the tale uttered by his informant was European, probably French. Interpretation was necessary, he asserted, to draw meaning out of the material, and to gain academic respectability for the folkloristic enterprise. The interpretation he demonstrated here uses psychoanalytic and sociological theory, preceded by an analysis of aspects of the tradition: the nominal (e.g., the significance of French names in the Native American text), the symbolic (e.g., the equivalence of mother to sweetheart in *Ulysses*), and the functional (e.g., the action whereby Stephen's character kills the mother).

There is a narrative structure underpinning this method, suggesting that it has connections to a quest of discovery for hidden meaning. Dundes posited that a story basically proceeds from a lack (something missing) to liquidation of that lack (something found or rescued). Similarly, a folkloristic method, in the very least, comprises identification and interpretation in search of buried or disguised meaning that is not apparent from a literal reading. In addition, a narrative may contain other functions, such as an interdiction and violation, to extend the plot. So too, did Dundes imply that "analysis," an operation upon the data—and especially formal and content analyses—led to an interpretation that proposed a meaning.

Dundes's methodological purpose in this essay was to show the way that proper identification, folkloristically derived, was crucial to a convincing interpretation. By calling the conclusion "interpretation" rather than "explanation," Dundes suggested a possibility of meaning, instead of positing causation (such as a chronology of events). Dundes's interpreted meanings are frequently "latent," hidden beneath the literal surface details of the text, and are corroborated by reference to the context. Theoretically, Dundes's social and psychoanalytic meanings are not the only ones that could be posited, although he advocated for these kinds of inquiries because of their connections to cognitive patterning, which he hypothesized was a source for expressive culture.

Dundes's terms of "identification" and "interpretation" had a precedent in eminent folklorist Archer Taylor's essay "Folklore and the Student of Literature" ([1948] 1965), which Dundes reprinted in his textbook *The Study of Folklore* (1965b). In his essay, Taylor observed that a fundamental problem connecting folklore and literature "concerns the identification and interpretation of popular elements in a piece of literature." Taylor, however, was, to Dundes's way of thinking, stuck on literal aspects of texts rather than on uncovering the deeper psychological meanings and ethnographic considerations of context. For Taylor, "the description of gestures, the determination of the times and places in which they have been used, and their interpretation—such are the tasks in folklore."

In addition to constructing a folkloristic methodology, Dundes's research contributed to Joyce (1978b, 1962i), Oedipal myth (Dundes and Edmunds 1995), and Native American folklore studies (1964b, 1978c).

Dundes's methodological concerns are evident in "Metafolklore and Oral Literary Criticism" (1966c) and "The Symbolic Equivalence of Allomotifs: Towards a Method of Analyzing Folktales" (1984c), reprinted in this volume. Dundes gave an overview of folkloristic study in "The American Concept of Folklore" (1966a) and "Ways of Studying Folklore" (1968c). For other statements on the formation of a distinctive folkloristic method, see Bronner 2006c; Abrahams 1979; Dorson 1972c, 1983; Fenton 1967; Georges and Jones 1995c; Goldberg 1984; Ketner 1973; Krohn 1971; Oring 1988, 1986; and Toelken 1996.

The Study of Folklore in Literature and Culture: Identification and Interpretation

MANY OF THOSE OUTSIDE THE discipline of folklore and even some of those within tend to divide folklorists into literary or anthropological categories. With this binary division comes a related notion that each group of folklorists has its own methodology appropriate for its special interests; hence there is thought to be a method for studying folklore in literature and another method for studying folklore in culture. Looking at this dichotomy from the viewpoint of a professional folklorist, one can see that it is false; moreover it is a dichotomy whose unfortunate persistence has tended to divide unnecessarily scholars working on similar if not identical problems. The basic methodology of studying folklore in literature and studying folklore in culture is almost exactly the same; in other words, the discipline of folklore has its own methodology applying equally well to literary and cultural problems.

There are only two basic steps in the study of folklore in literature and in culture. The first step is objective and empirical; the second is subjective and speculative. The first might be termed identification and the second interpretation. Identification essentially consists of a search for similarities; interpretation depends upon the delineation of differences. The first task in studying an item is to show how it is like previously reported items, whereas the second is to show how it differs from previously reported items—and, hopefully, why it differs.

Professional folklorists who are usually skilled in the mechanics of identification are apt to criticize literary critics and cultural anthropologists for failing to properly identify folkloristic materials before commenting upon their use. And folklorists are quite right to do so. Naive analyses can result from inadequate or inaccurate identification. Plots of traditional tale types might be falsely attributed to individual writers; European themes in a European tale told by American Indians might be mistakenly considered to be aboriginal elements. However, folklorists themselves might be criticized for doing no more than identifying. Too many studies of folklore in literature consist of little more than reading novels for the motifs or the proverbs, and no attempt is made to evaluate how an author has used folkloristic elements and more specifically, how these folklore elements function in the particular literary work as a whole. Similarly, listing the European tales among the North American Indians does not in itself explain how the borrowed tale functions in its new environment. The concern of folklorists with identification has resulted in sterile study of folklore for folklore's sake and it is precisely this emphasis on text and neglect of context which estranged so many literary critics and cultural anthropologists. The text-without-context orientation is exemplified by both anthropological and literary folklore scholarship. Folklorists go into the field to return with texts collected without their cultural context; folklorists plunge into literary sources and emerge with dry lists of motifs or proverbs lifted from their literary context. The problem is that for many folklorists identification has become an end in itself instead of a means to the end of interpretation. Identification is only the beginning, only the first step. Folklorists who limit their analysis to identification have stopped before asking any of the really important questions about their material. Until folklorists are prepared to address themselves to some of these questions, they must be resigned to living on the academic fringe in a peripheral discipline. As illustrations of how interpretation must follow initial identification in the study of folklore in context, the following brief discussion of a folktale found in James Joyce's *Ulysses* and a European tale found among the Prairie Band Potawatomi is offered.

In Joyce's *Ulysses,* one finds many different kinds of folklore, including tale types, nursery rhymes, tonguetwisters, folksongs, mnemonics, palindromes, and children's games.[1] Joyce's keen interest in folklore is further attested by his use of one of the minor characters, Haines, as an English folklorist come to Ireland to collect Irish folklore. Of all the examples of folklore in *Ulysses,* I have selected the riddle Stephen Dedalus asks his class to demonstrate the techniques of identification and interpretation. After reciting the opening formula and first line of a well known riddle for writing, Stephen asks his class this riddle:

> The cock crew
> The sky was blue:
> The bells in heaven
> Were striking eleven.
> 'Tis time for this poor soul
> To go to heaven.

The first riddle that Stephen recites in this situation—"Riddle me, riddle me, randy ro / My father gave me seeds to sow"—has been identified by scholars as the first part of riddle number 1063 in Archer Taylor's great compendium, *English Riddles from Oral Tradition,* and also has received interpretive examination (Weldon Thornton says, for example, that Stephen's suppression of the last part of the riddle may be an admission of his failure as a writer[2])—but so far as I know, no one has correctly identified the riddle Stephen puts to his class. Stephen's students are as much in the dark as the literary critics, though he gives them the answer, "the fox burying his grandmother under a hollybush." Work has been done on the problem of identification, since because of Joyce's frequent allusions to it throughout the book it is obviously of some importance to the interpretation of the book itself.[3] Several scholars have pointed out the similarity of Joyce's riddle with one in P. W. Joyce's *English as We Speak It in Ireland:*[4]

> Riddle me, riddle me right
> What did I see last night?
> The wind blew
> The cock crew,
> The bells of heaven
> Struck eleven.
> 'Tis time for my poor *sowl* to go to heaven.
> Answer: the fox burying his mother under a holly tree.

P. W. Joyce did not identify the riddle and he even commented upon what he called "the delightful inconsequences of riddle and answer." Yet a trained folklorist knows immediately that the riddle is closely related to a subtype of an international tale type, Aarne-Thompson 955, The Robber Bridegroom. In this subtype, which is very popular in Anglo-American oral tradition, the villainous suitor is frequently named Mr. Fox. Mr. Fox plans to do away with his betrothed and often the frightened girl, hidden in a tree, actually watches Mr. Fox digging her grave-to-be. Later at a large gathering the girl recites the riddle describing the villain's actions and thus unmasks the villain and reveals his nefarious plot. The folklorist can tell from the riddle text alone that there is a reference to the whole folktale, but there is additional evidence that Joyce himself knew the tale. In the memorable Circe chapter, the mob shouts derisively at Bloom as a disgrace to Christian men, a vile hypocrite, and the like: "Lynch him! Roast him! He's as bad as Parnell was. Mr. Fox!" [5] This very last allusion is what T. S. Eliot calls an objective correlative in that the mob scene in the folktale is evoked, a scene in which all those present cry out at the evil designs of the wicked Mr. Fox. So much for the identification of Stephen's riddle. What about the interpretation?

All previous interpretations of the significance of the riddle and fox imagery have been made without the benefit of a correct initial identification. William M. Schutte, for example, suggests that Stephen thinks of himself as a fox in that the fox as the wily foe of the hounds employs the weapons of silence, exile, and cunning. Schutte also says that the fox must be Stephen who killed his mother without mercy and who cannot stop scratching at the ground where she is buried.[6] However, in terms of the folktale the fox only plans to kill his sweetheart; he does not actually commit the crime. The fox is judged by his thought rather than by his act. In the novel Stephen did not kill his mother, but he judges himself in thought: "I could not save her"; earlier Buck Mulligan had spoken of Stephen killing his mother.[7] Of even more interest is the fact that in most versions of the tale Mr. Fox's victim is his bride-to-be, whereas in the Joyce variant the fox's victim is a mother. If the mother is equivalent to a sweetheart, then this would be part of the extensive Oedipal aspect of Stephen's character which I have discussed elsewhere.[8] In this light, Stephen the fox kills his mother instead of marrying her as she expected. If the P. W. Joyce text of the riddle was the source for James Joyce, then Stephen's changing the mother of the original to grandmother in the answer he gives the class also points to Stephen's Oedipal problem, for it is clear that in Stephen's own mind the fox's victim is a mother, not a grandmother.

The folktale source also clarifies the puzzling association of the fox and Christ. "Christfox" is described as a "runaway in blighted treeforks."[9] The latter description suggests not only a crucifixion but also the striking scene in the tale when the girl victim, hiding in a tree, looks down upon Mr. Fox digging her grave. The accompanying phrase "women he won to him" could allude to the Bluebeard Mr. Fox plot as well as to Christ and His faithful females. Stephen as "Christfox" is both victim and villain, both innocent and guilty. The point is, however, that unless the reader understands Joyce's skillful use of the riddle from the tale type as an objective correlative, he cannot appreciate the paradox.

One could proceed in similar fashion to identify and interpret other folkloristic elements in *Ulysses*. For example, one might examine Joyce's ingenious adaption of the riddling question "Where was Moses when the light went out ?"[10]—or the impact of Stephen's singing the anti-Semitic ballad "Sir Hugh" or "The Jew's Daughter" (Child 155) at that point in the novel when the Gentile Stephen has been invited to stay the night at the home of the Jew Bloom, who has a marriageable daughter;[11] but these and other examples would only demonstrate the point made here in the exegesis of the Fox riddle.

So the literary critic without proper knowledge of folklore can go wrong in identification and consequently in interpretation—but so can the anthropologist who knows only the basic tools of his discipline's trade. In April of 1963 I collected a fine example of folklore in culture from William Mzechteno, a 74-year-old Prairie Band Potawatomi in Lawrence, Kansas. Here is the raw story as I transcribed it, with myself identified by the initial D and my informant with the initial M.

M. Well there was once, there was a little boy. There was always a little boy, you know, and he had a name, his name was ah—[pause of six seconds' duration]—P'teejah. His name is P'teejah, and ah—

D. P'teejah?

M. Yeah. And he, he had a little, let's see now—[pause of three seconds' duration]—oh, he had a little tablecloth, you know. He can eat, you know, there's food every time he spreads that tablecloth on the ground or anywheres; he name many food, any kinda food he wants. It'd just appear on the, right on the tablecloth and was eaten. Well, all he had to do to clean up, you know, is just shake; everything was disappear, you know, into thin air. And he was goin' long the road one time, he met a soldier, he had a cap on. Uniform caps, you know, those soldiers wear. And the soldier was hungry. [The boy asked] "You got anything to eat?" [The soldier answered] "Oh, I got this hard bread." It's all he had. [The boy said] "Let's see that bread," he told him, "oh, that's hard, that's no good, not fit to cat," he told him. He throw it away. [The soldier said] "Mustn't do that, it's all I got to eat." (The boy said] "I'll give you something better," he told him. He pull out his tablecloth, and spread it on there, on the ground. "You name anything you want, ANYTHING! So he, ah, he named all he wanted to eat, Soldier, he was real hungry. "So, if you want any of that red water, you can have that too," he told him, whiskey.

D. Red water?

M. Yeah, they call it red water [laughing].

D. Who called it red water?

M. The Indian boy. They called it red water.

D. Yeah?

M. Yeah, 'cause it's red, you know. He didn't call it fire water.

D. This is an Indian boy?

M. Yeah, yeah, And, oh the soldier enjoyed his meal; he filled up, you know, and "Well, I got something to show you," he told me. He [the soldier] took his cap off, you know, and he throwed it on the ground and said, "I want four soldiers." And sure enough, four soldiers, there, well armed, stood there at attention. "It's pretty good," he [the boy] told him, "but you can go hungry with those four soldiers," he told him [laughing]. So, he put on his cap, you know. Course the soldiers disappeared, and he start to go and then the soldier said, "Say, little boy, how you like to trade? I'll give you this cap for that cloth." Naw, he wouldn't trade. "I'd go hungry without it." Oh, he got to thinking, you know. He said, "Well soldiers could get me something to eat," he thought, I guess. So, he traded, fair trade. He kept looking back, the little boy, you know. He had that little cap on. He thought about his tablecloth. He sure hated to lose it. So he, come to his mind, you know, "I'll get it." He took off [laughing] that cap and throwed it on the ground. "Four soldiers," he told 'em. Soldiers come up, you know, stood up right there and [he] says, "See that man goin' over there. He took my tablecloth away from me," he told 'em, "you go and git it [giggling laugh]." So they went [laughing] after that man; he fought 'em like every-thin'. "You belong to me," he said, "No [laughing] we belong to him over there," they said. So then he got his table-cloth and the boy got it back. And he had the cap too. That's where.

D. The boy was, you say, an Indian boy?

M. Yeah.

D. But the soldier was a white man.

M.   Yeah.

D.   So the Indian boy was fooling the white man.

M.   Yeah, [laughing] he put it on him.

D.   In a trade, too.

M.   Yeah, it was a fair trade but he was using his noodle [laughing].

D.   That's very nice. I didn't know it was an Indian boy.

M.   Yeah.

D.   I see.

M.   Yeah.

D.   Well, that's good, that's a fine story.

In order to analyze this tale in terms of Potawatomi culture, one must first identify the tale not as an indigenous Indian story, but as a European tale type. From the detail of the magic food-providing tablecloth (Motif D 1472.1.8), the professional folklorist can easily identify the tale as a version of tale type 569, The Knapsack, the Hat, and the Horn. Moreover, from internal evidence one can without difficulty demonstrate that the tale was borrowed originally from a French source. The Indian boy's name is P'teejah and the long pause before the utterance of the name shows the narrator's praiseworthy concern with getting the name right. P'teejah is a recognizable corruption of the French folktale character of Petit-Jean. As a matter of fact, Franz Boas in his essay "Romance Folk-Lore among American Indians" observed that the name of this French figure had been taken over by a number of American Indian groups.[12] Another trace of French culture is the allusion to "red water" which is probably wine although the narrator interpreted it as whiskey. So the tale has been identified: It is a borrowing from a French version of Aarne-Thompson tale type 569 and certainly not an aboriginal tale type. But the statement that it is a European tale does not answer such questions as what have the Potawatomi done with the tale?—how have they changed it and how do these changes tell us something about present-day Potawatomi culture? As a general rule European tales among American Indian groups can be used as indexes of acculturation. If the European tale is little changed, then it is probable that the borrowing Indian culture is waning if not defunct. If on the other hand the European tale is reworked and adapted to fit American Indian rather than European values, then it is more than likely that the American Indian culture in question is still a going concern. What about this Potawatomi tale?

First of all, the hero has been changed from a French character to an Indian boy. The narrator was questioned repeatedly about the identity of P'teejah and each time he insisted that P'teejah was an Indian boy. Secondly, the magic cap which belonged to the white soldier worked magic in American Indian symbolic terms rather than in European. Four soldiers were produced, not three; four is the ritual number of the Potawatomi as of most American Indian groups. Thus the magic soldier-producing hat (Motif D 1475.4) operates in American Indian terms and this in a sense is precisely what the whole tale does. In the tale the soldier offers to make a trade—protection in exchange for food, an exchange not unusual in the light of American colonial history. One senses that the exchange is unfair and that the adult European soldier is tricking the young Indian boy into giving up his only source of food. But in this folktale the Indian boy gets the best of the trade, the "fair trade" proposed by the white man. Although the hero does not appear to have planned his actions in advance, the narrator commented after telling the tale that the boy had "used his noodle," that is, he had out-thought the white man. In this tale of wish fulfillment, the

Indian boy has sufficient force to overpower the European soldier antagonist and to regain his original abundance of food.

In the cultural phenomenon which anthropologists term nativistic movements, it is common for the borrowing, dominated culture to dream of taking over the dominating culture's artifacts without the presence of members of that culture.[13] In this tale the Potawatomi has control of European artifacts; it is the Indian boy who is able to offer the soldier "red water" rather than soldier offering the Indian liquor—it is the Indian boy who uses the white man's object to defeat the white man. One can see even from these few comments why this particular European tale could easily have been accepted by Potawatomi raconteurs and audiences. A few deft changes made it a tale with considerable appeal for most Potawatomi. One can see from a "mistake" made by the narrator that he identified with the Indian boy. After the soldier finished eating, be told the boy he had something to show him. At this point, Mr. Mzechteno said "Well, I got something to show you," he told *me*. This use of "me" instead of "him" strongly suggests that the story was in some sense about Mr. Mzechteno and perhaps other Potawatomi. This detail plus the informant's frequent laughter demonstrate his enjoyment of and involvement with the tale.

The study of Joyce's use of a riddle and the study of a Potawatomi adaptation of a European tale appear to be distinct, but the methodology employed in both studies was the same. Identification was equally necessary. Failure to identify the Mr. Fox riddle in *Ulysses* could result in one's being unable to appreciate fully Joyce's use of this folkloristic element and accordingly limiting in a small way one's comprehension of the novel; failure to identify the Potawatomi tale as a standard European folktale might have made it difficult to determine just what changes the Potawatomi had introduced. One might have assumed, for example, that it was a Potawatomi idea to cast the dupe as a soldier, but in fact the soldier is frequently the dupe in European versions of the tale. But identification though necessary was only the first step, a prerequisite for interpretation. If it is true that folklorists too often identify without going on to interpret whereas literary critics and anthropologists interpret without first properly identifying folklore, then it seems obvious that some changes are needed. Either folklorists are going to have to educate their literary and anthropological colleagues in the mechanics of identifying folklore or they will have to undertake some of the problems of interpretation themselves. Ideally, both alternatives might be effected so that the study of folklore could become something more than a scholarly series of shreds and patches or a motley medley of beginnings without ends and ends without proper beginnings.

Notes

1. Page references to *Ulysses* are from the Modern Library edition. For a sample of Joyce's use of folksongs see Mabel P. Worthington, "Irish Folk Songs in Joyce's *Ulysses.*" *PMLA*, LXXI, 3 (June, 1956), 321–339.
2. Weldon Thornton, "An Allusion List for James Joyce's *Ulysses,* Part 2, 'Nestor,'" *James Joyce Quarterly*, I, 2 (Winter, 1964), 3.
3. *Ulysses*, 47, 60, 191, 288, 480, 544, 545, 557.
4. Scholars who have noted this source include Joseph Prescott, "Notes on Joyce's *Ulysses,*" *Modern Language Quarterly*, XIII, (1952), 149, and William M. Schutte, *Joyce and Shakespeare: A Study in the Meaning of* Ulysses (New Haven, 1957), 102, note 4.
5. *Ulysses*, 482.
6. Schutte, 103. W. Y. Tindall also remarks on Stephen's identification with the cunning fox,

but he equates the buried grandmother with Stephen's mother, the Church, and the Poor
Old Woman (Ireland) in his *James Joyce: His Way of Interpreting the Modern World* (New
York, 1950), 23.

7.   *Ulysses*, 46.

8.   Alan Dundes, "Re: Joyce—No in at the Womb," *Modern Fiction Studies*, VIII, 2 (Summer,
1962), 137–147.

9.   *Ulysses*, 191.

10. *Ulysses*, 754.

11. *Ulysses*, 674–676.

12. Franz Boas, *Race, Language and Culture* (New York, 1940), 517. See also Alanson
Skinner, *The Mascoutens or Prairie Potawatomi Indians, Part III—Mythology and Folklore*,
Bulletin of the Public Museum of the City of Milwaukee, VI, 3 (January, 1927), 400–402.

13. Sometimes the dominating culture's artifacts may be used as weapons against it. In this
instance the Potawatomi have borrowed a European folktale and successfully employed
it to attack Europeans. For another example of Potawatomi borrowing of European folktales in which the tales are used as vehicles for Indian superiority over whites, see Gary H.
Gossen, "A Version of the Potawatomi Coon-Wolf Cycle: A Traditional Projection Screen
for Acculturative Stress," *Search: Selected Studies by Undergraduate Honors Students at the
University of Kansas*, IV (Spring, 1964), 8–54.

3

METAFOLKLORE AND
ORAL LITERARY CRITICISM

Introduction

Dundes combines the linguistic concept of "metalanguage" (a language used to make statements about other languages) with literary criticism (usually associated with thematic readings of expressive language in novels and poetry) to propose an "oral literary criticism" using the evidence of "metafolklore." Dundes defined oral literary criticism as tradition-bearers' comments on their traditions, and metafolklore as stories or sayings about folklore. For folkloristics, the significance of this kind of material is what it reveals about attitudes toward, and perceptions of, folklore from a native viewpoint. It can provide contextual information for folklorists assessing the role of folklore in a society or situation.

Dundes's complaint was that long lists of beliefs, proverbs, games, and tales compiled by collectors typically left out the tradition-bearers' commentaries that accompanied their rendition of the material. He pointed out that the information tradition-bearers provided often signaled meanings perceived by performers and audiences of folklore. The commentaries may describe something about the telling, but they may also be a type of folklore that makes statements about folklore. For instance, I have frequently heard from my Pennsylvania neighbors, who eat pork and sauerkraut on New Year's Day to insure good luck, that the reason for this is expressed in a traditional saying: "Pigs root forward and chickens scratch backwards." They thus view eating pork as leaving the past behind and pushing ahead to the new year. Folklorists have asked the question, however, about the combination of pork with sauerkraut, to which residents often respond, "It's a tradition," suggesting a link to German heritage in the region, or to the now routine annual family gathering on New Year's. Comparing that tradition to other New Year's food traditions involving items which expand (such as black-eyed peas and rice in the South), and using the principle of like actions producing like results, I interpreted my neighbors' tradition as being based on the idea that both pigs and cabbage symbolize tremendous growth in a year. Pork also has a cultural context, since, for many residents, it raises images of Pennsylvania German farm life, but the tradition is not restricted today to residents of German background, and commercial supermarkets promote the consumption of the folk dish by advertising it before the New Year.

Since Dundes's essay was originally published in 1966, soliciting commentary about collected material has now become standard fieldwork procedure. See, for example,

William Wilson's "Documenting Folklore" (1986), and Martha Sims's and Martine Stephens's chapter on "Fieldwork and Ethnography" in *Living Folklore* (2005). Yet as Jan Harold Brunvand noted, in introducing Dundes's essay in his *Readings on American Folklore*, while folklorists give more attention to the meanings tradition-bearers provide for their expressions in various situations, as a result of Dundes's concept, "many folklorists stop, however, with symbolic interpretations where no final proof can be found for the suggested meanings" (1979, 405). That is, the analyst collecting the oral literary criticism might hesitate to propose "symbolic interpretations" that are outside the awareness of the tradition-bearer. Dundes pointed out that the "deep meanings" of the material may be repressed, because they are disturbing, or disguised within the metafolklore. An example is Dundes's interpretation of a popular American girls' ritual of summoning a ghost out of a mirror in a darkened bathroom by repeating "Mary Worth," "Mary Whales," or "Bloody Mary" multiple times. The metafolkloric commentary on the ritual, in a birthday or pajama party event, as "Bloody Mary" was significant, according to Dundes, connecting it with bleeding as a sign of maturation. Its oral literary description as a tradition restricted to girls suggested a meaning to Dundes that the girls did not directly acknowledge: a projection of anxieties about menarche. The cultural context is the definition of menstruation, in a male-dominated society, as something unpleasant and disgusting. Dundes concluded, "Rather than being persuaded by their culture to feel shame and embarrassment about menstruation, the ritual might be construed as an attempt to celebrate the onset of menses" (2002a).

Of note in the essay is Dundes's call for a "Thematic Apperception Test" for folklore. Folklorist Wolfgang Mieder reported that proverbs, especially, have been used in various psychological tests as measures of intellectual functioning and verbal comprehension (1978). Psychologists have also come up with tests to assess "superstitious behavior" and "paranormal belief" that relate to folklorists' collections of beliefs. A danger is that such tests pathologize faith and belief as abnormal, and do not take into account the cultural contexts and social situations in which beliefs are expressed. Further, oral literary criticism may reveal attitudes that tests miss. Many people may conversationally express the traditional phrase "knock on wood" to insure that a string of luck continues, for instance, but would not say they are superstitious. Folklorists tend to relativize belief according to the traditions from which people come, rather than for personal functionality. In sum, oral literary criticism and metafolklore can be especially important tools in assessing individual, as well as social, differences in attitudes toward tradition. For psychological literature on tests to assess belief, see Tobacyk and Milford 1983; Pronin et al. 2006; Rotton and Kelly 1985; and McClearn 2004.

Dundes demonstrated the use of oral literary criticism in a later essay, also reprinted in this volume, on the anti-Semitic blood libel legend. There, he analyzed as a kind of lore the frequently expressed commentary that the story is either true or not. Another location in which oral literary criticism and metafolklore are analyzed, expanding the present essay's discussion of Yoruba folklore and the metafolkloric saying "A proverb is like a horse," is in "Proverbs and the Ethnography of Speaking Folklore" (Dundes and Arewa 1964). In it, Dundes underscored the use of folklore as a means of communication, and offered examples not only of how particular Yoruba proverbs were performed in a particular setting, but also of how their meanings were perceived, based on the commentary of the tradition-bearer, Arewa. Especially evident throughout his essays on the concept of folklore found in this volume, Dundes frequently referred to the popular comment, "That's just folklore," as a kind of folklore in itself, revealing ambivalent modern attitudes toward tradition. He often used it to launch a discussion of the disconnection between the objectively viewed centrality of folklore in modern everyday life, and people's subjective popular perceptions of it. For him, it underscored the dire need for the serious study of folklore, and its challenge of achieving academic respectability.

A number of titles by other authors feature Dundes's idea of metafolklore, including Limón (1982); Lichman (1982); and Shenhar (1987).

Metafolklore and
Oral Literary Criticism

THE THEORETICAL ASSUMPTION THAT FOLKLORE was limited to a survival
and reflection of the past was a crippling one for the study of folklore in context. For if in
fact folklore did reflect only the far distant past, then clearly there was no point in bothering to attempt to collect the present context of folklore. A past-oriented folklore collector
would tend to regard his or her informants as relatively unimportant carriers of precious
vestigial fragments, fragments which might prove useful in the central task of historically
reconstructing the past. For the execution of historico-comparative studies, one needed
only minimal information concerning the place and date of collection. It is clear that for
the kinds of theoretical and methodological questions that nineteenth century folklorists were asking, e.g., "what was the original form of an item of folklore and what were the
genetic relationships between various forms or subtypes of that item of folklore?" place
and date of recording were sufficient.

In the twentieth century with the increasing amount of ethnographic fieldwork, it
became glaringly apparent that folklore reflected the present as well as the past and that
there was certainly a context in which folklore was used. Nevertheless, custom is strong
even among scholars and the "butterfly" or "object-curio-collecting" philosophy has continued. Long lists of proverbs are published in folklore journals accompanied by no explanation of either use or meaning. Anthropologists append to their ethnographies a token
section consisting of folktales and myths but with little or no comment on their relationship to other aspects of the culture. The "object-collecting" philosophy is itself a survival
of the antiquarian days of folklore studies. Folklore texts without contexts are essentially
analogous to the large numbers of exotic musical instruments which adorn the walls of
anthropological or folk museums and grace the homes of private individuals. The instrument is authentic as is the folklore text, but the range of the instrument, the tuning of the
instrument, the function of the instrument, and the intricacies of performing with the
instrument are rarely known.

It was Malinowski who was most vociferous in calling for context. In his important
1926 essay "Myth in Primitive Psychology," he repeatedly pointed out the fallacy of collecting mere texts, calling them mutilated bits of reality. Here again is the notion of folklore as fragments, but not fragments of the past, fragments of the present. In one formulation, Malinowski observed, "The text, of course, is extremely important, but without
the context it remains lifeless."[1] More recently, Bascom has continued the call for context. Auguring well for future folklore field research is Goldstein's praiseworthy concern
for context in his valuable *Guide for Field Workers in Folklore.* He specifically lists "folklore processes" as one of the principal kinds of folklore data to be obtained in the field.[2]
In another recent development in the study of folklore context, it has been suggested that
the ways and means of using folklore are just as highly patterned as the materials of folklore themselves. The identification of the rules for the use of an item of folklore, or the

"ethnography of speaking folklore" as it has been termed, suggests that to the "laws" of form (Olrik) and the "laws" of change (Aarne) may be added the "law" of use.[3] The discovery of such laws or rules opens a new area of folklore research.

The current interest in the collection of context, however, has partially obscured the equally necessary and important task of collecting the meaning(s) of folklore. One must distinguish between *use* and *meaning*. The collection of context and preferably a number of different contexts for the same item of folklore is certainly helpful in ascertaining the meaning or meanings of an item of folklore. But it cannot be assumed that the collection of context per se automatically ensures the collection of meaning. Suppose a folklorist collected the following Yoruba proverb:

A proverb is like a horse: when the truth is missing, we use a proverb to find it.[4]

Let us assume that he or she also collected the typical context of this proverb in which it is employed in an introductory capacity prior to uttering another proverb which was designed to settle a particular dispute, The introductory proverb announces to the audience that the arbitrator is planning to use a proverb and reminds them of the great power and prestige of proverbs in such situations. But from this text and context, does the collector know precisely what the proverb means? What exactly is meant by comparing a proverb to a horse? While the meaning(s) of a proverb are unquestionably involved in an individual's decision whether or not the quotation of that particular proverb is appropriate in a given context, the folklore collector may miss the meaning(s) even though he or she has faithfully recorded text and context. One cannot always guess the meaning from context. For this reason, *folklorists must actively seek to elicit the meaning of folklore from the folk.*

As a terminological aid for the collection of meaning, I have proposed "oral literary criticism."[5] The term is obviously derived from "literary criticism," which refers to a host of methods of analyzing and interpreting works of written literature. Even a beginner in literary criticism soon discovers that there are alternative and rival interpretations of one and the same work of art. The identical phenomenon occurs in the case of folklore which for the sake of the discussion we may call "oral literature" (although this unfortunately tends to exclude nonverbal folklore). For each item of oral literature, there is a variety of oral literary criticism. This is an important point inasmuch as folklorists, despite the fact that they are accustomed to thinking of variation in the texts of folklore, often wrongly assume that there is only one correct meaning or interpretation. There is no one right interpretation of an item of folklore any more than there is but one right version of a game or song. (We must overcome our penchant for monolithic perspectives as exemplified in monotheism, monogamy, and the like.) There are multiple meanings and interpretations and they all ought to be collected. One could ask ten different informants what each thought a given joke meant and one might obtain ten different answers. It is difficult to determine the gamut of interpretation because there has been comparatively little collection of oral literary criticism.

The interpretation which is made is inevitably from the collector's point of view. There is nothing wrong with analytic as opposed to native interpretations, but the one does not eliminate the need for the other. Unfortunately, in a few instances, the analyst-collector suggests that this interpretation is really the natives' own interpretation. Melville Jacobs, for example, tries to "see the literature as it appeared to Chinooks,"[6] but one wonders if the Chinooks would have agreed with Jacobs' interpretations. Jacobs has reconstructed oral literary criticism but this may not be the same as the oral literary criticism he might have collected. The nature of his criticism is revealed in his discussion of Clackamas Chinook humor when he speaks of his methodology. ". . . I enumerated 130 instances in the Clackamas collection *where I was certain* that an audience at a folkloristic recital responded with smiles or laughter" or ". . . I took each of the 130 fun situations and attempted to pinpoint each fun generating factor or stimulus to humor *which I believe* to have been present in them" make the analytic bias clear.[7] Jacobs was not present at a Clackamas Chinook tale-telling session—he collected the tales from a highly acculturated informant in relative isolation—and he can give little more than educated guesses. Even in our own culture, it would be difficult to guess whether or not a "funny" story got a laugh and more particularly to know just at what points in the joke laughs were stimulated. One must not only record laughter (distinguishing types of laughter—a giggle, a bellylaugh), but one must try to find out what was funny and why the audience members laughed or did not laugh.

It is not easy to collect oral literary criticism. Much of it has probably never been consciously formulated. Yet the meanings and traditional interpretations of folkloristic materials are transmitted from individual to individual and from generation to generation just as is folklore itself. But some types of oral literary criticism are easier to collect than others and it might be well to mention them first.

One source of oral literary criticism comes from folklore itself rather than directly from the folk. There are a limited number of folkloristic commentaries on folklore. As there is a term "metalanguage" to refer to linguistic statements about language, so we may suggest "metafolklore" to refer to folkloristic statements about folklore. Examples of metafolklore or the "folklore of folklore" would be proverbs about proverbs, jokes about joke cycles, folksongs about folksongs and the like. Metafolklore is not necessarily intragenre. There are proverbs about myths, for example. The previously cited Yoruba proverb would be an instance of metafolklore. It is a folkloristic commentary about a folklore genre, namely, the proverb: "A proverb is like a horse: when the truth is missing, we use a proverb to find it." This clearly indicates an attitude towards a key function of proverbs in Yoruba culture, the function being the determination of truth in problem situations or disputes. Of course, since metafolklore is still, after all, folklore, it is necessary to elicit oral literary criticism of the metafolkloristic texts themselves. The meaning of the Yoruba proverb, according to one informant, is that by mounting a horse, as opposed to goats, sheep, dogs, and other animals found among the Yoruba, one can quickly obtain a superior perspective. From the back of a horse, one can see further than one can from the ground and the immediate local problem may be seen in a new and better light. A proverb is like the horse inasmuch as it also provides a speedy and efficacious means of getting above the immediate problem-situation and of placing it in a perspective which is more likely to result in finding a just and proper solution.

An example of a metafolkloristic joke is the following: It was a dark and stormy night and this guy goes up to this old farm house. He's a salesman and he says to the farmer, "I'm a salesman, my car broke down, and I need a place to stay." And the farmer says, "That's all right, but there's just one thing, we have no extra rooms to spare so you'll have to sleep with my son." And the salesman says, "Oh my God, I must be in the wrong joke." Here is a folk comment on the nature of the traveling salesman joke cycle. Invariably the jokes involve the seduction of the farmer's daughter and/or wife. In most jokes in the cycle, as you may know, the farmer explains to the salesman that he can stay but that the only available space is in his daughter's room. This is thus a joke about a joke cycle and it draws attention to one of the critical content features of the cycle. Once again, one could elicit oral literary criticism of this bit of metafolklore. One might find, for example, that the substitution of homosexuality for heterosexuality is particularly significant in the light of our culture's taboo against homosexual activities. The mere suggestion of such activities to a traveling salesman, the epitome of unrestrained heterosexual impulse, is so shocking as to call a halt to the story. In other words, at the very mention of homosexuality, the American male wants out because this activity is "wrong": the salesman is in the *wrong* joke. (The breaking out of the joke is analogous to the breaking of the "fourth wall" in theatrical parlance.) Actors normally regard the proscenium as the fourth wall of a room. Occasionally, an actor will break the convention and will speak directly to the audience. Some plays, like this traveling salesman joke, specifically call for the breaking of the conventional vehicle.

Sometimes the metafolklore may comment on the formal features rather than on the content of folklore. For example, consider the following melafolkloristic joke based upon the "knock, knock" cycle.

Knock!
Who's there?
Opportunity.

Here attention is drawn to the distinct characteristic reduplicative opening formula of jokes in this cycle: knock, knock. The use of just one "knock" is incorrect but is rationalized by reference to a proverb: "opportunity only knocks once." Such parodies of and plays on folkloristic forms can be useful sources of the folk's own attitudes towards their folklore.

Another source of overt literary criticism besides metafolkloristic texts consists of the asides or explanatory commentary made by raconteurs as they tell tales or sing songs. These asides are sometimes unwisely eliminated by the overscrupulous editor but they should not be. Two examples from a Potawatomi informant may illustrate the nature of these asides. At the beginning of one tale, my informant said, "Well there was once, there was a little boy. There was always a little boy, you know, and . . . "[8] The line "There was always a little boy" is a folk confirmation of one of the important characteristics of certain folktales, namely that the protagonist is a little boy. Such a comment might be particularly valuable if the folklorist-collector did not know in advance what kinds of tales were in his informant's repertoire. The comment indicates that there are a great many tales with little boys in them and it also serves to authenticate the particular tale he is recounting. It is as if to say that traditional tales must have little boys in them as protagonists and so in this traditional tale I am about to tell there is this required stereotyped character.

Another self-critical aside made by my informant came in a version of *Big Turtle's War Party*. In the mock plea (Motif K 581.1, drowning punishment for turtle) episode, the villagers are devising ways to kill the captured turtle. First they discuss throwing him into a kettle of boiling water, but the turtle threatens to splash the water and scald their children. Next, the villagers suggest tying him to a tree and shooting him with buckshot—at which point the narrator observed "I don't know whether they had any buckshot in those days or not" before concluding with the final throwing of the turtle into a river à la the tarbaby rabbit into the briarpatch. This commentary challenges the historical accuracy of the tale. Given the time setting of this American Indian tale—when animals were like people, the occurrence of such an obvious acculturated element of material culture as buckshot upset the sensibilities of my sensitive story-teller. However, he did not deny or alter the traditional tale as he knew it. He merely inserted a partial disclaimer, thereby expressing his own parenthetical doubts.

The problem with metafolklore and with the raconteur's asides is that they provide at best only an incomplete picture of the folk's evaluation of their folklore. For some folklore, no metafolklore has been recorded; for some genres few asides have been published. What is needed is the rigorous and systematic elicitation of oral literary criticism. A tale or song might be treated by the folklorist-collector much as a modern psychiatrist treats a dream. As the psychiatrist asks his dreamer-patient to "free associate" and to comment on the various elements in the dream, so the folklorist-collector should ask his informant to "free associate" in the same manner, attempting to explain or comment on each element in the tale. Too often the text-hungry folklorist immediately after the recitation of a tale or song will say, "That's fine, do you know any more like that . . ." and he will not patiently seek to have the informant provide a folk exegesis of the tale just told. Perhaps the collector should consider the item of folklore collected as a projective test or should we say "projective text" and in that event he should ask the informant to make up a story about the story.

Even more desirable would be to elicit the oral literary criticisms of both raconteur and audience. The meaning for the tale teller is not necessarily the same as the meaning for the audience or rather the different meanings for different members of the audience. It is incredible that folklorists speak of *the* meaning of a folktale. Moreover, the existence of multiple meanings suggests communication blocks. One might assume that if A and B, members of the same culture, both know a given folklore text that this text serves as a strong bond linking A and B. However, if A and B interpret the text differently, then A's addressing it to B might result in misunderstanding rather than understanding. The following may serve to illustrate multiple meanings.

There is a folk metaphor (proverbial phrase) "to have an axe to grind" and to me it means to have a bias as a lobbyist might have. If I said, "Watch out for so and so, he has an axe to grind," I would be warning against accepting what that individual said at face value inasmuch as his words or actions would be influenced by what I considered to be a vested interest. Archer Taylor told me that he thought the metaphor connoted the asking of a favor inasmuch as it takes two men to grind an axe, one to spin the whet-stone and the other to hold the axe. Thus if one individual came to another and announced that he had an axe to grind, he would be asking the other person to stop what he was doing and help him grind the axe. The dictionary supports this interpretation by saying "to have an object of one's own to gain or promote."[9] However, there is another traditional meaning of this metaphor, the meaning of "grudge." According to informants, "to have an axe to grind" is similar to having a "bone to pick" with someone. One informant related that if he had neglected to do one of his assigned household chores, say taking out the garbage at the end of the day, the next morning his mother would say to him "I've got an axe to grind with you, you didn't take the garbage out last night." The informant explained that "I've got an axe to grind with you" meant "There's going to be friction, sparks were going to fly, just as sparks fly when an axe is ground." I discovered that my wife also uses this meaning. Our neighbor's dog occasionally knocks over and rifles our garbage can. My wife indicated that she would think it appropriate to call up our neighbor and say, "I have an axe to grind with you," meaning there was something she was angry about. Here then are two distinct interpretations of the same folk metaphor.

In some instances the meaning may be fairly constant, but the evaluation of the common meaning may vary. For example, the proverb "A rolling stone gathers no moss" means that a person who moves around from place to place, not staying in any one place for very long, will never belong to a place, or look as though he belongs to that place. The oral literary critical difference concerns whether this is good or bad. In the older tradition, it was bad and the proverb might be cited to keep someone from roaming too far and wide, to urge him to stay at one place. But in modern usage, at least in some quarters, the accumulation of moss is considered to be a negative characteristic and the "rolling stone" is conceived of as the ideal unencumbered life. Admittedly these differences could be gleaned from printed contextual instances of the proverb in novels and newspapers, but the point is that folklore collectors ought to obtain direct oral interpretations of the proverb at the time of collection.

As has been noted, it is not always easy to elicit oral literary criticism. The folk know and use folklore without bothering to articulate their aesthetic evaluations. For some types of oral literary criticism, e.g., symbolism, an indirect method of eliciting might be recommended. The problem in symbolism is that the folk may not be completely conscious of the one or more symbolic meanings of an element of folklore. This is understandable in view of the fact that it is often the taboo activities and ideas which find expression outlets in symbolic form. If the folk consciously recognized the symbolic significance of the joke or folksong element, this element might not be able to continue to serve as a safe, socially sanctioned outlet. (Cf. the popular belief that analysis of a work of art interferes with or ruins ones enjoyment of it.) Fortunately, much of the symbolism in folklore is baldly stated and may be obvious enough to some of the members of the culture concerned. But the study of symbolism would surely be greatly advanced if symbolic interpretations of folklore were obtained from the folk rather than from Freudian folklorists. No one likes to accept an *ex cathedra* pronouncement that a shoe can symbolize female genitalia. Even the folkloristic "evidence" such as is provided by nursery rhymes among other genres leaves the issue in some doubt.

> There was an old woman who lived in a shoe
> She had so many children she didn't know what to do.

People don't live in shoes and the possible connection between a woman's living in a shoe and having lots of children requires explanation. The sequel verse: "There was another old woman who lived in a shoe, she didn't have any children, she knew what to do" suggests the sexual nature of the symbolism with the implicit statement that a knowledge of contraceptive measures can allow a woman to live in a shoe and not have children. One might also consider the possible symbolism in:

> Cock a doodle doo!
> My dame has lost her shoe
> My master's lost his fiddling stick
> And doesn't know what to do.[10]

Maybe there isn't a reference to a woman who has lost her vagina matched by a man who has lost his phallus, but if not, the logical connection between a shoeless dame and fiddle stick-less master remains to be seen. But the point is that one should not guess at such interpretations; one should go to the primary sources and ask the folk. Let field data prove or disprove armchair guesswork. What does the shoe suggest to the informant? Can the informant draw a picture of the old woman and her shoe? Perhaps a modified Thematic Apperception Test based upon the nursery rhyme (or other folklore) can be devised and administered. While it may be true that not all informants will be equally facile in articulating oral literary criticism, some will be able to do so. Even a passive bearer of tradition (as opposed to the active bearer who tells the tale or sings the song) may he able to contribute an interpretation. Folklorists should be just as anxious to collect variant interpretations of a folksong's meaning as they are to collect variants of the folksong's text![11]

As a final argument for the collection of oral literary criticism, I would note the interpretation of the word folklore itself, especially among the folk. The meaning of "folklore" in the phrase 'That's just folklore' is similar to one of the meanings of myth, namely falsehood, error, and the like. I suspect that it is this pejorative connotation which has encouraged some folklorists to consciously avoid the term substituting instead "verbal or spoken art," "oral or folk literature," and many others. More serious is the fact that this "folk" interpretation of the word "folklore" makes it difficult for the discipline of folklore and its practitioners to gain academic status. If folklore is error, then a Ph.D. in folklore is the height of folly, and the notion of a whole discipline devoted to error is unthinkable in the academic context of the search for truth. To use the term folklore without an awareness of the folk interpretation of the term is unwise.

One final point concerns the necessity for the continued and repeated attempts to elicit oral literary criticism. It is a commonplace that each generation reinterprets anew its folklore, but do we have records of these interpretations and reinterpretations? Sometimes the text is altered to fit new needs, but probably it is the interpretation of texts which changes more. The task of collecting oral literary criticism from a folk can never be completed any more than the task of collecting folklore from that folk can be. Even if both texts and interpretations remained almost exactly the same over a long period of time, this would still be well worth knowing. It might be an important index of the overall stability of that folk. Here also is an opportunity to use the scores of texts without commentary which line library shelves and archives. These texts may be taken *back into the field* and folk *explication de texte's* sought. Our goal for future folklore collection should be fewer texts and more contexts, with accompanying detailed oral literary criticisms.

Notes

1.   Bronislaw Malinowski, *Magic, Science and Religion* (Garden City: Doubleday 1954), p.104.
2.   William R. Bascom, "Four Functions of Folklore," *Journal of American Folklore* 7 (1954), 333–349; Kenneth S. Goldstein, *A Guide for Field Workers in Folklore* (Hatboro, Pa: Folklore Associates, 1964), p. 23.
3.   See E. Ojo Arewa and Alan Dundes, "Proverbs and the Ethnography of Speaking Folklore," *American Anthropologist*, 66:6, Part 2 (1964), 70–85. For the laws of folklore form, see Axel Olrik's classic paper "Epic Laws of Folk Narrative," in *The Study of Folklore*, ed. Alan Dundes (Englewood Cliffs, N.J.: Prentice-Hall, Inc., 1965), pp. 129–41. For the laws of folkloristic change, see Antti Aarne, *Leitfaden der Vergleichenden Marchenforschung*, Folklore Fellows Communications No. 13 (Harnina, 1913), pp. 23–29.
4.   In Yoruba, the proverb is;

Owe	l'esin	òrò;	bi	òrò	bá	sonù
proverb	is horse	word	if	word	got	lost
òwe	l'a	fi	ńwá	a		
proverb	is we	use	finding	it		

For the proverb and its explanation, I am indebted to E. Ojo Arewa.
5.   Alan Dundes, "Texture, Text, and Context," *Southern Folklore Quarterly*, 28 (1964), 263; Arewa and Dundes, op. cit., p. 73.
6.   Melville Jacobs, *The Content and Style of an Oral Literature* (Chicago, 1959), p. 3.
7.   Ibid, pp. 178–179. Italics mine.

8. This first example was published, see Alan Dundes, "The Study of Folklore in Literature and Culture: Identification and Interpretation." *Journal of American Folklore*, 78 (1965), 139. The second example was published as "A Potawatomi Version of Aarne-Thompson Tale Type 297A, Turtle's War Party," *Norveg* 21 (1978), 47–57.

9. *Webster's New World Dictionary of the American Language,* College Edition (Cleveland and New York, 1960). This is the meaning found in *The Oxford Dictionary of English Proverbs* (2d ed.; Oxford, 1948), p. 17; Archer Taylor and Bartlett Jere Whiting, *A Dictionary of American Proverbs and Proverbial Phrases 1820–1880* (Cambridge, 1858), pp. 10–11.

10. The rhyme of the old woman who lived in a shoe is number 546 in the canonical *Oxford Dictionary of Nursery Rhymes,* ed. Iona and Peter Opie (Oxford, 1951). The Opies suggest (p. 435) that "the shoe has long been symbolic of what is personal to a woman until marriage." The Opies do not mention the sequel verse which dates from the 1890's in American Ozark tradition. See Joseph C. Hickerson and Alan Dundes, "Mother Goose Vice Verse," *Journal of American Folklore*, 75 (1962), 256. As for the "Cock a doodle-doo" rhyme, number 108 in the Opies' collection, one finds not even an oblique circumlocutory hint of any symbolic interpretation. Nursery rhymes should really be studied further. One wonders, for example, why the three blind mice (Opies' number 348) tried to run after the farmer's wife. If it were an Oedipal theme, then the cutting off of the presumptuous mice's tails would be appropriate symbolic castration.

11. It should be mentioned that recently a number of folklorists have observed that the meaning of the folklore to the folk must be investigated. For typical statements see G. Legman, *The Horn Book: Studies in Erotic Folklore and Bibliography* (New Hyde Park, N.Y.: University Books, 1964), p. 285; Goldstein, op. cit.,(Hatboro, 1964), pp. 23, 106, 140. Linda Dégh, in description of the future tasks of folklore collectors (written in Hungarian) urges folklorists to leave the explanations to the storyteller and the members of his or her audience, see *Ethnographia*, 74 (1963), 1–12.

4

From Etic to Emic Units in the Structural Study of Folktales

(*Postscript*) The Motif-Index and the Tale Type Index: A Critique

Introduction

Dundes opened this essay on folk material with a binary division of diachronic and synchronic perspectives of time. Diachronic approached the development of material historically, whereas synchronic analysis examined items contemporaneously. Dundes observed that diachronic approaches had dominated thinking about folklore, leading, he argued, to analyses of lore without the folk, that is, without the social basis of the material. One result, he claimed, was the identification of original forms without questioning how those forms came into being in the first place. A move toward synchronic approaches raised the issue of the basic unit of analysis, especially if comparative work was to be carried out. Pointing out problems with the literary "motif" as a comparative unit of narrative, Dundes proposed the use of structural units such as motifeme and allomotif. These were drawn from the formalist theories of Vladimir Propp, who conceived of predictable "functions" or actions that occur in certain places within the sequence of the story.

The advantage of the structural units of motifeme and allomotifs, according to Dundes, was that they represented the elements of a story as they were told by a narrator. In this way, they composed "emic" units (applying a term proposed by linguist Kenneth Pike). Drawn from "phonemic," a sound used in a language community, emic generally refers to native categories. Etic is comparable to "phonetic," a system devised by the analyst's rendering of speech sounds, thus forming what is thought of as an "analytic" category.

The rhetoric of "type" and "motif" came from literary study, in which key incidents and objects were used to categorize the composition of stories and to suggest subjects for imaginative treatment. Applied to oral literature, type referred to recognizable unified plots that tended to remain intact in collected stories around the world, and could be organized into various themes, such as "animal tales" (types 1–299), "tales of magic" (300–749), and "formula tales" (2000–2399). Motifs were components of stories that drew attention to themselves, such as the object "glass shoes" (F823.2) or the incident of "Slipper test. Identification by fitting of slipper" (H36.1) in Cinderella. The letters before the numbers range from A (mythological motifs) to Z (miscellaneous groups of motifs). Their arrangement suggests a hierarchy of narrative, giving primary place to the oldest or most developed myths, and secondary position to folktales, going from "Animals" (B) to "Traits of Character" (W). Humor, presumably more contemporary and concise, is relegated to the end in the famous "X" slot ("Humor concerning sex" was X700–799). The classification system of the motif-index has been likened to the Dewey decimal system of library classification, because decimal points allow for expansion as the corpus of known folktales grows.

The tale-type and motif indexes, now standard reference works identifying folk narrative building blocks, were conceived of in the early twentieth century as a way to globalize the study of folktale, with the intent of finding the origins and distribution of its elements. Even before the landmark original volumes on tale types by Antti Aarne (1910) and Stith Thompson ([1928] 1961), there had been classifications of songs and stories that attempted to identify units of narrative so as to facilitate international comparison. Although recognizing Dundes's criticisms, folkloristic advocates of motif and type indexes, such as Hasan El-Shamy, have noted that Thompson's motif-index was the first reference to go beyond "mere alphabetical lists of terms" and differentiate between motifs and folktale types. Thompson also incorporated more folk material than Aarne, since Thompson included ballads, fables, local legends, and jokes. Aarne's tale-type index systemized mostly European wonder tales into a numerical list, and identified subtypes. It implied that all versions of a type had a genetic relationship, but Thompson's motif index did not ([1932–1936] 1975). The extent of classificatory work, according to the principles established by Aarne and Thompson, is indicated by 186 entries in David S. Azzolina's *Tale Type- and Motif-Indexes* (1987). It is a list that has continued to grow (see El-Shamy 2004; Jason 2000; Goldberg 2000; Tatum 2000; Jauhiainen 1998; Würzbach 1995; Neugaard 1993; and Stitt and Dodge 1991).

Attached to Dundes's original 1962 polemic against the tale-type and motif indexes is a postscript with a more temperate tone, published thirty-five years later. He pointed out additional problems of the indices, based on etic units, but announced that they still provided "two of the most valuable tools in the professional folklorist's arsenal of aids for analysis." Some of Dundes's concerns for expanding the coverage of the indices were addressed in the three volumes of Hans-Jörg Uther's *The Types of International Folktales* (2004). The commentaries on classification by motif and type by Uther, Dundes, and other folklorists can be read in a special issue of the *Journal of Folklore Research* (1997), and in *Archetypes and Motifs in Folklore and Literature* (Garry and El-Shamy 2005). See also Ben-Amos 1980; Georges 1983; and Holbek 1990.

The structural analysis of motifemes and allomotifs, as it turns out, has not displaced the identification of motifs and types in folkloristics. However, for the purposes of comparison and interpretation, Dundes's oft-cited essay signaled more attention paid to alternative, emic systems of representing narratives as they are learned and communicated. Dundes demonstrated the symbolic equivalence of allomotifs for a single tale type in "The Symbolic Equivalence of Allomotifs in the Rabbit-Herd (AT 570)," reprinted in *Parsing Through Customs* (1987j). He also used a Proppian classificatory approach in his doctoral dissertation, published as *The Morphology of North American Indian Folktales* (1964b). Dundes's influence is apparent in the essays in *Patterns in Oral Literature*, edited by Heda Jason and Dimitri Segal (1977), which took up the challenge of structural models for oral literature. Other studies using allomotifs include S. S. Jones 1990; Lovell-Smith 1996; Holbek 1993; and Carroll 1992a, 1992b.

From Etic to Emic Units in the
Structural Study of Folktales

TRADITIONALLY, THE STUDY OF FOLKLORE in general and folktales in particular has tended to be diachronic rather than synchronic. The emphasis has clearly been
upon the genesis and development of folkloristic materials rather than upon the structure
of these materials. Folklorists of the late nineteenth century were much more concerned
with how folklore came into being than with what folklore was. Genetic explanations were
considered sufficient to define the nature of folklore. Thus the solar mythologists claimed
that the bulk of folkloristic materials was primitive man's poetic translation of celestial
phenomena such as the rising and setting of the sun. After the "eclipse of solar mythology" as Richard M. Dorson has so felicitously phrased it,[1] there came the Anthropological
School. The members of this group were convinced that folklore evolved from historical
facts and primordial customs. In the course of the unilinear evolution of all cultures, there
were preserved vestigial remains of the archaic origins. These remains were termed survivals in culture, and the study of these survivals was called folklore. The modern version of
this form of diachronic study is fostered by the advocates of the myth-ritual theory who
claim that all myth evolves from ritual. Since no attempt is made to explain the ultimate
origin of the ritual, one can see that the question of genesis has been dropped in favor of
the question of evolutionary development. Similarly, in the most modern method of folklore study, the so-called Finnish historical-geographical method, questions of ultimate origin are eschewed. The aim of this method is the delineation of the "complete life history of
a particular tale."[2] The users of the historical-geographical method attempt to determine
the paths of dissemination and the process of development of folkloristic materials. By
assembling all the known versions of a particular tale, the folklorist seeks to reconstruct
the hypothetical original form of the tale. There is, however, no attempt to explain how
this original form may have come into being in the first place. Thus there has been a movement away from the early interest in genesis and cause towards an interest in the process
of transmission and evolutionary development. But in any case, the study of folklore has
remained diachronic.

All three approaches to folklore—the mythological, the anthropological, and the historical-geographical—are alike not only in that they are diachronic, but also in that they
are comparative. All three utilize materials from many cultures. This was why it became
apparent to folklorists, no matter which of these approaches they favored, that for comparative studies there had to be some convenient means of referring to individual parts
or pieces of folkloristic items as well as to these items as wholes. In the second place, in
order to have trustworthy comparison, one needed to operate with comparable units. This
was particularly important to the members of the Finnish school inasmuch as it was precisely the differences of some of the smaller units of a given folktale upon which the conclusions of a historical-geographical study were often based. Unfortunately, the system of
units which was developed was primarily intended to answer only the first need, that is, of

supplying a means of referring to individual parts and pieces of folklore as well as to larger chunks of folklore. The criterion of having genuine comparable units did not enter into the construction of either the motif-index or the Aarne-Thompson tale-type index. Thus however useful the motif-index and tale-type index may be as bibliographical aids or as means of symbol shorthand, their basic units, namely the motif and tale type, do not provide an adequate basis for comparative studies.

In order to see the inadequacy of the motif and tale type as units to be used in the comparative study of the folktale, one must have some idea of what any kind of a basic unit should consist of. Units are utilitarian logical constructs of measure which, though admittedly relativistic and arbitrary, permit greater facility in the examination and comparison of the materials studied in the natural and social sciences. It is important that units be standards of one kind of quantity (e.g., units of heat, length, and so forth). Units can be conceived as being abstractions of distinct entities which may be combined to form larger units or broken down into smaller units. There is an infinitude of units since they are man-made categorical attempts to describe the nature of objective reality. With a relativistic perspective, one can see that no matter what unit one considers, other smaller subunits may be postulated. Historically, this is what has happened in the development of the neutron from the atom which in turn developed from the molecule. A minimal unit may thus be defined as the smallest unit useful for a given analysis with the implicit understanding that although a minimal unit could be subdivided, it would serve no useful purpose to do so.

Folklorists are not alone with regard to encountering difficulties in defining appropriate units. As Kluckhohn points out: "Most anthropologists would agree that no constant elemental units like atoms, cells, or genes have as yet been satisfactorily established with culture in general."[3] On the other hand, in one area of anthropology, namely linguistics, such units as the phoneme and the morpheme have been delimited. Roman Jakobson remarks in connection with the phoneme that "Linguistic analysis with its concept of ultimate phonemic entities signally converges with modern physics which revealed the granular structure of matter as composed of elementary particles." However, most anthropologists and linguists seem to feel that the units of linguistics, although extremely useful in the study of language, are of little or no use outside the linguistic area.[5] One notable exception is Kenneth Pike, who has even tried to employ linguistics-like units in an analysis of all human behavior. In his ambitious *Language in Relation to a Unified Theory of the Structure of Human Behavior,* Pike makes a number of stimulating theoretical statements which appear to be applicable to folklore. Although Pike makes no mention of folklore by name, he begins his study with an analysis of a party game which falls, of course, in the realm of folklore. If one examines Pike's theoretical presentation, one can see that it may well be that folklorists can profit from the model provided by linguists. True, it is always dangerous to use ready-made patterns since there is the inevitable risk of forcing material into the prefabricated Procrustean pattern. However, this technique is justified if it aids in solving a problem, in this instance, namely the determination of units in folklore. It therefore remains to be demonstrated that first, the motif and tale type are nonstructural, or to use Pike's apt term, etic units, and second that there are empirically observable structural or emic units in folktales which may be discovered through the application of quasi-linguistic techniques.

One cannot criticize the motif on the basis of its not being monomial or indecomposable. As has already been stated, any unit can be subdivided into smaller units. However, the motif is open to criticism as a unit in that it is not a standard of one kind of quantity.

Thompson's discussion of the motif makes this clear. According to Thompson, a motif is "the smallest element in a tale having a power to persist in tradition."[6] It is noteworthy that in this definition, the crucial differentia is what the element does (i.e., persists in tradition) rather than what the element is. The definition is thus diachronic rather than synchronic. Thompson speaks of three classes of motifs. First there are actors; second are "items in the background of the action—magic objects, unusual customs, strange beliefs and the like"; and third there are "single incidents" which, according to Thompson, "comprise the great majority of motifs." Exactly what an incident is is never stated. If motifs can be actors, items, and incidents, then they are hardly units. They are not measures of a single quantity. There are, after all, no classes of inch or ounce. In addition, the classes of motifs are not even mutually exclusive. Can one conceive of an incident which does not include either an actor or an item, if not both? It is reiterated that without rigorously defined units, true comparison is well-nigh impossible. Can an actor be compared with an item?

Perhaps the most important theoretical consequence of the use of the motif as a minimal unit has been the tendency to regard motifs as totally free entities which are independent of contextual environments. Moreover, the superorganic abstraction is often given a life of its own. When Thompson in speaking of motifs asks: "Do some combine freely everywhere?" the wording is no accident. The abstract units are the subject of the verb and the question is whether they do the combining. This is made clear by Thompson's following question: "Are some isolated, *living* an independent life as a single-motif tale-type?"[7] But the most critical consequence of chopping up folklore into motifs is that mentioned above, namely that the motif is considered to be a completely isolable unit. Furthermore, such a unit is often assumed to be able to enter freely into limitless combinations. Lowie, for example, speaks of a "perfectly free" element of folklore which could appear in various combinations.[8]

Yet if motifs are truly free to combine, then the larger unit, the tale type, appears to be on somewhat shaky ground. A type, according to Thompson, is "a traditional tale that has an independent existence." Once again, it may be seen that the tale type is not defined in terms of morphological characteristics. Instead, just as in the case of the motif, the criterion of existence through time is employed. Thompson notes that a complete tale or type is "made up of a number of motifs in a relatively fixed order and combination." If the motifs are in a relatively fixed order, then it appears to be unlikely that they "combine freely everywhere." However, if one presumed from the description of a tale type that a tale type was simply a unit made up of smaller units called motifs, one would have to take account of the fact that one class of motifs, namely incidents, may serve as "true tale-types," and, in fact, according to Thompson, "By far the largest number of traditional types consist of these single motifs."[9] If this is so, then the distinction between motif and tale type seems somewhat blurred.

The Hungarian folklorist Hans Honti has given probably the best description of the tale type as a unit.[10] He observes that there are three possible ways of looking at the tale type as a unit. First, the tale type is a binding together of a number of motifs; second, the tale type stands as an individual entity in contrast with other tale types; and third, the tale type is, so to speak, a substance which is manifested in multiple appearances called variants. Honti then points out that in purely morphological terms, a tale type is only a formal unit when contrasted with other tale types. He rejects the other two types of unity after making a comparison with botanical classification. He notes that plants are composed of similar morphological elements: roots, stalks, leaves, and so on. However much these elements may differ in different types, they are uniform within individual types. Thus one can put plants into a structurally based classification system according to the constitution of their roots, stalks, leaves, and so on. But, in the case of folktales, the type is either made up of a variable combination of motifs or a great number of variants. In other words, the constituent elements of folktales, according to Honti, are not constant, but rather extremely variable. This makes strictly morphological classification difficult. It should be noted here that folklorists have somehow sensed that there is something of a fixed pattern in the arrangement of motifs in a folktale, but at the same time they have realized that the motifs may vary considerably. The very heart of the matter of folktale analysis is to ascertain what is constant and what is variable. This may well involve the distinction between form and content.[11] Form would be the constant while content would be the variable. In this light, one can see that the Aarne-Thompson tale typology is based upon the content, that is, the variable.

Aarne has three major divisions of folktales: Animal Tales, Ordinary Folktales, and Jokes and Anecdotes. The second division, which is the largest, has numerous subdivisions including: A. Tales of Magic, B. Religious Tales, C. Novelle or Romantic Tales, and D. Tales of the Stupid Ogre. Moreover, subdivision A., Tales of Magic, is further subdivided into: Supernatural Adversaries, Supernatural or Enchanted Husband (Wife) or Other Relatives, Superhuman Tasks, Supernatural Helpers, Magic Objects, Supernatural Power or Knowledge, and Other Tales of the Supernatural. Aarne then groups his tales, which by the way were restricted to collections from northern and western Europe, under these subjective headings. Only the Formula Tales category, which is listed under Jokes and Anecdotes, may be said to be based upon structural criteria.

One can see from even a cursory examination that this classification is not based upon the structure of the tales themselves so much as the subjective evaluation of the classifier. And yet this is all that folklorists have in the way of tale typology. If a tale involves a stupid ogre and a magic object, it is truly an arbitrary decision whether the tale is placed under II A, Tales of Magic (Magic Objects), or II D, Tales of the Stupid Ogre. With regard to the subdivisions of Tales of Magic, where would one classify a folktale in which a superhuman task is resolved by a supernatural helper who possesses supernatural power? Perhaps the best illustration of the fact that Aarne-Thompson typology is based upon the variable and not upon the constant may be found by examining tale types which differ only with respect to the dramatis personae. In the Animal Tale (Type 9), The Unjust Partner, there is a version listed in which in the division of the crop, the fox takes the corn while the benighted bear takes the more bulky chaff. Under the Tales of the Stupid Ogre, one finds Tale Type 1030, The Crop Division. It is the same story except that the dramatis personae are a man and an ogre. Under the Stupid Ogre listing, Aarne notes that the tale sometimes appears with a fox and a bear as the principals, and in fact he even comments in his preface to the type index upon this duplication of materials: "This narrative has been listed among the ogre tales, to which apparently it originally belonged; but it is also found with a note as to its proper place, among the animal tales as a transaction between fox and bear or man and bear." This example is by no means unique. One may see the same kind of distinction with regard to differences in the dramatis personae by comparing such tale types as 4 and 72; 43 and 1097; 123 and 333; 153 and 1133; 250 and 275; and 38, 151, and 1159; to name just a few.[12]

Another serious difficulty with the tale type as a unit is the fact that often one or more tale types are included in another tale type. This is analogous to the occurrence of actor and item motifs in incident motifs. Thus in some versions of Tale Type 1685, The Foolish

Bridegroom, there appears the incident in which the fool, when told to cast "good eyes" at the bride, throws ox-eyes and sheep-eyes on the plate. This "incident" also appears as Tale Type 1006, Casting Eyes, listed under Tales of the Stupid Ogre. This blending and incorporation of tale types is indicated by the fact that in the case of a complex tale such as Type 300, Dragon Slayer, there are no less than eight other tale types which the classifiers recognized were sometimes commingled. One can see that even Honti's claim, that tale types were morphological units in that one tale type contrasted with other tale types, is not demonstrable. Actually, any professional folklorist engaged in folktale research knows very well that folktales, as collected from informants, very often are combinations of two or more Aarne-Thompson tale types. The point is that no matter how useful the Aarne-Thompson index may be in locating critical studies and variants, the Aarne-Thompson tale type as a structural unit of folklore leaves much to be desired. In fairness, it should be stated that neither Aarne nor Thompson ever intended the index to be any more than a reference aid. "It is, of course, clear that the main purpose of the classification of traditional narrative, whether by type or motif, is to furnish an exact style of reference, whether it be for analytical study or for the making of accurate inventories of large bodies of material. If the two indexes can in this way promote accuracy of terminology and can act as keys to unlock large inaccessible stores of traditional fiction, they will have fulfilled their purpose."[13]

However, what has happened is that this laudable index terminology has begun to be thought of as a kind of typology. Some folklorists tend to regard Tale Type 1030, The Crop Division, as a generic kind of unit. What is more, because the Aarne-Thompson tale typology has achieved international currency and has done a great deal to facilitate international folktale research, folklorists are afraid to introduce an entirely new system. For example, Honti notes that if tales could be arranged according to a theoretically appropriate morphological system instead of a theoretically inadmissible logical system, it might be somewhat easier to work through folktale material. Nevertheless, he states his conviction that this does not constitute enough reason to replace the well-established Aarne-Thompson system. He comments on the inconvenience which would result from putting the catalogs of the various national folklore archives under a new system.[14] This kind of thinking is very dangerous and leads to intellectual stagnation, which the field of folklore can ill afford. In any field of learning, particularly in the natural or social sciences, if something is faulty or inadequate and recognized as such, it should be changed. Folklorists are supposed to study tradition, not be bound by it. Tradition and convenience are hardly sufficient reasons for scholars to perpetuate an acknowledged error. Comparative studies in folklore require carefully defined units, and if the motif and Aarne-Thompson tale type do not meet these needs, then new units must be devised.

New units have been suggested through the application of something like linguistic methodology to folkloristic materials. In particular, a Russian folklorist, Vladimir Propp, in 1928 published *Morphology of the Folktale.* In this work Propp pays tribute to Joseph Béier for being the first to recognize that folktales contained invariant and variable elements. However, Bedier, whose key work, *Les Fabliaux,* was published in 1893, despite an attempt to express these related elements schematically, failed to determine the exact nature of the invariable units. Propp, borrowing the schematic technique, set himself the task of defining the invariable units of folktales.

Propp's aim was to delineate a morphology of fairy tales, and by fairy tales, he meant those tales classified by Aarne between 300 and 749, which Aarne termed "Tales of Magic."

Propp's study was synchronic, which was in marked contrast to the rest of folklore scholarship. Propp hoped to describe the fairy tale according to its component parts and to indicate the relationship of these components to each other and to the whole. He begins by defining a new minimal unit, the function. He did this because he noticed that the names of the dramatis personae as well as their attributes changed but that the actions or functions of the dramatis personae did not change. In other words, to use an example mentioned previously, on a functional level, the tale of Tale Type 1030, Crop Division, is the same whether the dramatis personae are animals or humans. Hence Propp states that "The functions of a folktale's dramatis personae must be considered as its basic components; and we must first of all extract them as such."[15] To illustrate how the minimal constituent unit of the function may be extracted from the dramatis personae, Propp, drawing material from four separate fairy tales, gives the following example:

1.   A king gives an eagle to a hero. The eagle carries the hero (the recipient) away to another kingdom.

2.   An old man gives Súčenko a horse. The horse carries Suenko away to another kingdom.

3.   A sorcerer gives Ivan a little boat. The boat takes him to another kingdom.

4.   The princess gives Ivan a ring. Young men appearing from out of the ring carry him away into another kingdom and so forth.

Clearly, though the dramatis personae vary, the function is the same. Structurally speaking, it does not matter whether the object which carries the hero to another kingdom is an eagle, a horse, a boat, or men. Propp then proceeds to further define the function, and his further definition of the function is one of the most revolutionary and important contributions to folklore theory in decades.[16] Propp states that "an action cannot be defined apart from its place in the process of narration."[17] This single statement reveals the unmistakable fallacy of thinking of folklore in terms of isolated motifs. The action or function can only be defined in its place in the process of narration. Honti, who was not familiar with Propp's work, had said that it was difficult to conceive of a motif other than as part of a type,[18] but Propp went much further. Not only is the minimal unit to be considered as part of a type, but it must also be considered with respect to where it occurs in that type.

Propp does succeed in distinguishing between the constant and the variable in folktales. He notes: "Functions serve as stable, constant elements in folktales, independent of who performs them, and how they are fulfilled by the dramatis personae."[19] After analyzing a randomly selected sample of 100 Russian fairy tales, Propp was able to draw the following startling conclusions. First, the number of functions known in the fairy tale is limited. In fact, Propp discovered that there are thirty-one possible functions. Furthermore, the sequence of functions is always identical. This does not mean that all thirty-one functions are in every fairy tale, but only that "the absence of several functions does not change the order of those remaining." As a result of his analysis, Propp is able to suggest a new unit to replace the Aarne-Thompson tale type. "Tales evidencing identical functions can be considered as belonging to one type. On this basis, an index of types can be created not relying upon plot features which are essentially vague and diffuse but, rather, upon exact structural features." Propp finds that every one of the 100 tales in his sample will fit into one formula and he concludes that "All fairy tales, by their structure, belong to one and the same type."[20]

The distinction between the old minimal unit, the motif, and the new minimal unit, the function, may be seen very well in terms of Kenneth Pike's valuable distinction between the etic and the emic. The etic approach is nonstructural but classificatory in that the analyst devises logical categories of systems, classes and units without attempting to make them reflect actual structure in particular data. For Pike, etic units are created by the analyst as constructs for the handling of comparative cross-cultural data.[21] In contrast, the emic approach is a mono-contextual, structural one. "An emic approach must deal with particular events as parts of larger wholes to which they are related and from which they obtain their ultimate significance, whereas an etic approach may abstract events, for particular purposes, from their context or local system of events, in order to group them on a world-wide scale without essential reference to the structure of any one language or culture." ". . . emic units within this theory are not absolutes in a vacuum, but rather are points in a system, and these points are defined RELATIVE to the system. A unit must be studied, not in isolation, but as a part of a total functioning componential system within a total culture. It is this problem which ultimately forms the basis for the necessity of handling emics as different from etics. . . ."[22] Pike believes that the emic structure is a part of the pattern of objective reality and is not merely the construct of the analyst. Whether one follows Pike on this point or whether one considers that emic units are like beauty in being solely in the eyes of the beholder, one can see that the distinction between structural and nonstructural units is sound. For a complete discussion of the distinction between etic and emic (coined by using the last portions of the words phonetic and phonemic), one should consult Pike's work.

Pike's delineation of the simultaneous trimodal structuring of emic units is of considerable importance for folktale analysis. Pike's three modes are the feature mode, the manifestation mode and the distribution mode. At the risk of oversimplifying Pike's elaborate scheme, one might translate the modes into Propp's analysis by seeing the feature mode as exemplified by the function, the manifestation mode by the various elements which can fulfill a function, and the distribution mode by the positional characteristics of a particular function, that is, where among the thirty-one possible functions it occurs. One reason for bothering to put Propp's analysis in Pike's terminology is an extraordinary verbal coincidence. Pike's minimum unit of the feature mode is the EMIC MOTIF or MOTIFEME.[23] In other words, Propp's function in Pike's scheme of analysis would be called a MOTIFEME. Since the term function has not yet achieved any amount of currency among folklorists, it is here proposed that MOTIFEME be used instead.

With the establishment of the structural unit, MOTIFEME, one can see the usefulness of the term ALLOMOTIF for those motifs which occur in any given motifemic context. Allomotifs would bear the same relationship to motifeme as do allophones to phonemes and allomorphs to morphemes. The term MOTIF would continue to be used, but only as an etic unit like the phone or morph. The difference between etic and emic analysis of folktales, that is the difference between analysis by motif and analysis by motifeme, is considerable. For example, Propp's twelfth function or motifeme refers to the hero's being tested, interrogated, or attacked in preparation for his receiving either a magical agent or helper. For instance, a prospective donor may test the hero by assigning him difficult tasks. On the other hand, the twenty-fifth motifeme involves the assignment of a difficult task, usually by the villain. In other words, etically, or in terms of motifs, the same motif may be used in different motifemes. This means that the mere analyzing of folktales into motifs may be misleading. Folklorists are accustomed to treat all occurrences of a particular motif as being of equal or identical significance. This is, in Pike's theory, tantamount to treating homophonous or homomorphic forms as identical in meaning.[24] However, one might legitimately ask how one recognizes the appropriate motifeme for a particular motif. If one observes a specific motif, how can one ascertain which motifeme it subserves? Propp addresses himself to this very question. Again, it is the notion of a function or motifeme in the frame of sequential context, i.e., *in situ*. It is always possible to define a function or motifeme according to its consequences. Accordingly, if the receiving of a magical agent follows the solution of a task, then the motif belongs to the twelfth motifeme and it is clearly a case of the donor testing the hero. If, on the other hand, the receipt of a bride and a marriage follow, then the motif belongs to the twenty-fifth motifeme, the imposition of a difficult task.

It is not only important to realize that the same motif may be used in different motifemes, but it is equally important to realize that different motifs may be used in the same motifeme. Thus the helpful animal could be a cow, cat, bird, fish, and so on. Recalling that motifs are actors and items, it is obvious that for a given function or motifeme, there may be literally hundreds of motifs which would he appropriate. (Of course, not all "appropriate" motifs would necessarily be traditional, i.e., actually found in folktales.) An example of the alternation of motifs is provided by the different versions of the Potiphar's wife story. This is the story of a son-figure whom a mother-figure tries to seduce. When the son-figure refuses, the mother-figure accuses the son of attempting to violate her, whereupon a father-figure metes out punishment to the son-figure. In many versions the punishment is blindness. In other versions, the hero's feet are cut off. In probably the oldest known version of the tale, that of "The Story of the Two Brothers," dating from the fourteenth or thirteenth century B.C., the son-figure, Baîti, castrates himself.[25] One could say that the consequences of the seduction attempt include the cutting off of the hero's leg or phallus and blindness. Since these consequences are distributionally similar, they would appear to be part of the same motifeme, that is, they would appear to be allomotifs. Castration and blindness do not seem to be in complementary distribution but rather appear to be in free variation. In fact, it is probable that one element could be substituted for the other without changing the plot structure. In this light, a curious Greek version of the Potiphar's wife story becomes a little more intelligible. Phoenix, the son of Amyntor, was accused by Phthia, Amyntor's concubine, of having violated her. The father, on the strength of the concubine's false accusation of seduction, blinded his son and cursed him with childlessness.[26] If blindness and castration are allomotifs, then the connection between blindness and childlessness is not so remote.

An example of allomotifs in the folklore of a primitive culture may be found in the North American Indian test tales. In Boas's important study of the Tsimshian versions of the test theme, a jealous uncle or brother subjects the hero to tests.[27] In order to obtain a wife, the hero must survive any one of the following elements: a snapping door, caves which open and close, a closing tree cleft or canoe, a clam with crushing shells, dangerous animals guarding a door, or a vagina dentata. All these elements appear to be allomotifs of the same motifeme, which, incidentally, looks very much like Propp's twenty-fifth motifeme, "A difficult task is proposed to the hero."

The notion of allomotifs has important theoretical implications for the Finnish historical-geographical method. In this method, considerable significance is placed upon the differences occurring in the variants of a given tale. By plotting the time (historic) and place (geographic) of a given story element, one attempts in this method to reconstruct the original form of the tale and its mode of development and dissemination. If, however, the arsenal of a storyteller included allomotifs, that is, if there are two or more traditional motifs any of which would fulfill a particular motifeme, then the analyst would have to be extremely cautious in evaluating such alternations. This would also explain why a given storyteller might tell the same tale differently upon different occasions. The choice of a specific allomotif (e.g., an obscene one) might be culturally conditioned by the type of audience. Furthermore, what folklorists have hitherto considered as two separate tale types or blends of tale types might be rather a case of the alternation of allomotifs or allomotif clusters. As Propp points out, although the storyteller apparently creates within a definite sequence of motifemes, he is "absolutely free in his choice of the nomenclature and attributes of the dramatis personae."[28]

The phenomenon of the limiting nature of a sequential formula of motifemes merits study. It would be of interest, for example, to ascertain whether there is an absolute minimum number of motifemes necessary for the construction of a folktale. Propp speaks only of an upper limit. It would also be interesting to know if the sequence corresponded in any way with the structure of other cultural elements, such as ritual. In addition, a psychological study of the motifemic sequence might help to elucidate the etiology of the pattern. It should be noted that as yet no attempt has been made to see if there is motifemic patterning in folktales other than fairy tales, to say nothing of the other genres of folklore. Moreover, it has not yet been determined whether motifemic patterning varies from culture area to culture area. It is not even known whether or not there is such patterning in the folktales of primitive cultures. Motifemic analysis of all types of folktales in all types of cultures must be accomplished before any reliable comparative work may be attempted. Just as comparative linguistics is based upon emic analysis,[29] so ultimately must comparative folklore and mythology. In other words, solid synchronic analysis is needed to define adequately the formal structural characteristics of folkloristic genres before truly meaningful diachronic, i.e., historical, studies may be undertaken.

It seems safe to say that the emic unit of the motifeme (Propp's function) marks a tremendous theoretical advance over the etic unit of the motif. With regard to larger units, such as tale types, Propp was quite right when he said that "Types do exist, not on the level outlined by Aarne, but on the level of the structural properties of folk-tales. . . ."[30] However, the use of the emic unit should not he construed as in any way replacing the need for the etic units. The emic unit replaces the etic unit as a structural unit to be used as the basis for comparative studies; but with respect to the practical matters of classification and cataloging, there is certainly a definite place for etic units. As Propp himself observed, his basic task was "clearly the extraction of the 'genera.'"[31] Claude Lévi-Strauss, in a lengthy commentary on Propp's work, notes that before such formalistic studies, folklorists tended to ignore what folktales had in common, but that after formalistic analysis, folklorists are deprived of the means of seeing how folktales differ.[32] If Propp has found, so to speak, a "generative grammar" for Aarne-Thompson tale types 300 to 749, how can individual variants of the same structural tale type be distinguished? The point is that a structurally based tale typology does not in any way eliminate the need for a practical index such as Thompson's. As Honti suggested, synthetic and morphological typology should not be used instead of analytical indices and systems, but in addition to them. Assuming that there may be different formulaic sequences of motifemes for different kinds of folktales or for folktales in different culture areas, there could well be a tale-type index based upon morphological criteria. But this index would be in addition to the Aarne-Thompson type index and would be cross-referenced so that a folktale scholar could tell at a glance what Aarne-Thompson tale types belonged to which morphological tale types. As Pike notes, etic analysis must precede emic analysis. It is therefore obvious that folklorists need both and further that they should not mistake the one for the other.

The structural study of folklore has really just begun. Except for a few scattered studies such as Sebeok's study of charms,[33] there has been very little work of this kind. With the aid of the rigorous definition of structural units, the future of structural studies in folklore looks promising indeed.

Notes

1. Richard M. Dorson, "The Eclipse of Solar Mythology," *Journal of American Folklore*, LXVIII (1955), 393–416.
2. Stith Thompson, *The Folktale* (New York, 1951), p. 430.
3. Clyde Kluckhohn, "Universal Categories of Culture," in *Anthropology Today,* ed. A. L. Kroeber (Chicago, 1953), p. 517.
4. Ibid., p. 517, n. 24.
5. C. F. Voegelin and Z. S. Harris, "Training in Anthropological Linguistics," *American Anthropologist,* n.s. LIV (1952), 324–325; Kluckhohn, p. 517.
6. For Thompson's discussion of the motif, see *The Folktale,* pp. 415–416.
7. Ibid., p. 426. Italics mine.
8. Robert Lowie, "The Test-Theme in North American Mythology," *JAF,* XXI (1908), p. 109.
9. Thompson, pp. 415–416.
10. Hans Honti, "Märchenmorphologie and Märchentypologie," *Folk-Liv,* III (1939), pp. 307–8.
11. Form is not here considered as separate from meaning. There is wisdom in Pike's notion of a form-meaning composite in contrast to form without meaning or meaning without form. See Kenneth L. Pike, *Language in Relation to a Unified Theory of the Structure of Human Behavior,* Part I (Glendale, 1954), pp. 74, 99, 150.
12. This discussion is based upon Stith Thompson's revision of Antti Aarne's *Verzeichnis der Märchentypen, The Types of the Folk-Tale,* FF Communications, No. 74 (Helsinki, 1928). However, none of the duplication has been eliminated in Thompson's 1961 revision of the tale-type index.
13. Thompson, *The Folktale,* p. 427.
14. Honti, p. 317.
15. Vladimir Propp, *Morphology of the Folktale,* ed. Svatava Pirkova-Jakobson, trans. Laurence Scott, Publication Ten of the Indiana University Research Center in Anthropology, Folklore, and Linguistics (Bloomington, 1958), 19. Propp's study was also issued as Part III of the *International Journal of American Linguistics,* XXIV, No. 4 (1958), and as Volume 9 of the Bibliographical and Special Series of the American Folklore Society.
16. The importance of this particular theoretical point was not noted by either Archer Taylor or Melville Jacobs in their respective reviews of Propp's work. See *The Slavic and East European Journal,* XVII (1959), pp.187–189; *JAF,* LXXII (1959), pp. 195–396.
17. Propp, p. 19.
18. Honti, p. 308.
19. Propp, p. 20.
20. Ibid., pp. 21, 95.
21. Pike, pp. 9–10, 20.
22. Ibid., pp. 10, 93.
23. Ibid., p. 75.
24. Ibid., p. 48.

25. The various versions of the Potiphar's wife story may be found in Maurice Bloomfield, "Joseph and Potiphar in Hindu Fiction," *Transactions and Proceedings of the American Philological Association*, LIV (1923), pp. 141–167, and Norman M. Penzer, *The Ocean of Story: Being C. H. Tawney's Translation of Somadeva's Kathā Sarit Sāgara* (London, 1923 ff.); II, pp. 120–121; III, pp. 109–110. The story of the Two Brothers may be found in G. Maspero, *Popular Stories of Ancient Egypt*, trans. C. H. W. Johns (New York, 1915).

26. *Apollodorus The Library*, trans. J. G. Frazer, The Loeb Classical Library (London, 1921), II, p. 75. It is interesting that psychoanalysts consider that blindness may, in certain situations, be a symbolic equivalent of castration. This suggests that an examination of the allomotifs or different culturally determined localizations in the motifemes of borrowed international tales may provide insight into the system of symbolic equivalents employed in a given culture.

27. Franz Boas, *Tsimshian Mythology, Annual Report of the Bureau of American Ethnology*, XXXI (Washington, 1916), pp. 794–810.

28. Propp, p. 102.

29. Pike, pp. 8, 18. See also Robert Lado, *Linguistics Across Cultures* (Ann Arbor, 1957), p. 10.

30. Propp, p. 10.

31. Ibid., p. 24.

32. Claude Lévi-Strauss, "L'analyse morphologique de contes russes," *International Journal of Slavic Linguistics and Poetics*, III (1960), pp. 122–149.

33. Thomas A. Sebeok, "The Structure and Content of Cheremis Charms, Part I," *Anthropos*, XLVIII (1953), pp. 369–388. Unfortunately, most linguists err in treating linguistic units such as the morpheme as structural units of the folktale. This was recently pointed out by J. L. Fischer in his "Sequence and Structure in Folktales" in *Men and Cultures*, ed. Anthony F. C. Wallace (Philadelphia, 1960), pp. 442–446, when he observed that if a folktale were translated from one language to another, the structure of the folktale might well remain the same though the linguistic structure would obviously change.

Postscript

The Motif-Index and the Tale Type Index: A Critique

IT MUST BE SAID AT the outset that the six-volume *Motif-Index of Folk-Literature* and the Aarne-Thompson tale type index constitute two of the most valuable tools in the professional folklorist's arsenal of aids for analysis. This is so regardless of any legitimate criticisms of these two remarkable indices, the use of which serves to distinguish scholarly studies of folk narrative from those carried out by a host of amateurs and dilettantes. The identification of folk narratives through motif and/or tale type numbers has become an international sine qua non among bona fide folklorists. For this reason, the academic folklore community has reason to remain eternally grateful to Antti Aarne (1867–1925) and Stith Thompson (1885–1976) who twice revised Aarne's original 1910 *Verzeichnis der Märchentypen*—in 1928 and in 1961—and who compiled two editions of the *Motif-Index* (1922–1936; 1955–1958).

There has been considerable discussion of the concepts of motif and tale type. Highlights of the motif literature include Bodker 1965:201–202; Meletinski 1977; Ben-Amos 1980; Courtes 1982; Bremond 1982; and Warzbach 1993. Representative views of the tale type may be found in Honti 1939; Greverus 1964; Jason 1972; and Georges 1983. Thompson defined the motif as "the smallest element in a tale having a power to persist in tradition" (1946:415; 1950b:1137).

Perhaps the most lucid delineation of the concept of tale type was made by the brilliant Hungarian folklorist János Honti. In his 1937 essay in *Folk-liv,* Honti proposed three different ways of considering a tale type as a viable unit of analysis. First, it consisted of a specific binding together of motifs; second, any one tale type could stand as a unique entity in contrast with other tale types, e.g., Cinderella is not the same story-plot as Little Red Riding Hood; and third, a tale type could be perceived as a kind of cookie-cutter Platonic form or model which manifested itself through multiple existence (such multiple instances being termed versions or variants). In an extended essay on "The Tale—Its World," Honti makes it perfectly clear that he understands that "the concept of 'type' is merely an ideal construction." But by the same token, Honti does not recognize the genuine utility of the concept: ". . . for the researcher, behind all these variants, only one 'type' exists . . . and therefore scholarship is entitled to construct a conceptual unity, considering the variants as constantly changing phenomena of an unchanging process" (1975:35). Although Honti employs the term "variants," his definition of type seems eminently sane. It should be kept in mind, however, that a tale type is a *composite* plot synopsis corresponding in exact verbatim detail to no one individual version but at the same time encompassing to some extent *all* of the extant versions of that folktale.

There have been at least two major criticisms of the concepts of motif and tale type to date. The first, articulated most effectively by Scandinavian folklorists, concerns the alleged "independence" of the units. Anna Birgitta Rooth in a "Digression" entitled "The

Tale as Composition," appended to her classic dissertation on Cinderella (1951:237–40), suggested that individual motifs were more often than not found to be interdependent upon other motifs in a given tale, and she proposed the notion of "motif-complex" to describe such tradition collocations of motifs. Similarly, Bengt Holbek argued that standard Aarne-Thompson tale typology "does violence" to the actual material collected in the field insofar as so-called types were often combined (1964:160). Yet despite his lifelong reservations about the concept of tale type—"It is not very clear"—Holbek did reluctantly admit that "types *do* exist to some extent" (1987:157, 158). It is certainly true that inasmuch as the magic tale (AT 300–749) typically ends with marriage—according to Propp's *Morphology of the Folktale* (1988:63–64)—AT 480, The Spinning-Women by the Spring. The Kind and the Unkind Girls, which does *not* end with a marriage, frequently serves as the introduction to another tale type that *does* end with a marriage, e.g. AT 510A Cinderella (Roberts 1994:102).

The second criticism has to do with the alleged Eurocentrism of the concepts of motif and tale type. The argument in a nutshell is that these concepts were developed from a European data corpus and hence may not be applicable to nonwestern material, e.g., African folk narrative (Finnegan 1970:327–28). The idea in part stems from the correct observation that African storytellers in general favor improvisation more than do European storytellers and that this penchant for improvisation makes the notions of fixed motifs and tale types superfluous and irrelevant. The empirical evidence, however, would disprove this largely anti-European, anti-colonist ideological position insofar as there do seem to be identifiable African narrative motifs and stable traditional tale types (cf. Dundes 1977 and especially Bascom 1992).

Three other criticisms of the motif and the tale type might conveniently be grouped under the rubrics of 1) Overlapping, 2) Censorship, and 3) Ghost Entries. Thompson recognized the fuzziness and vagueness of his definitions of motif and tale type, but he actually went so far as to defend such definitions because supposedly they avoided "long debates" (cf. Dundes 1964:54). Thompson admitted that "somewhat more than half of the types" in the tale type index "consist of a single narrative motif" (1946:417, 439). This means that to a large extent the motif and tale type systems are overlapping. The vast majority of animal tales (AT 1–299) are *both* single tale type numbers and single motif numbers. The same holds true for "Tales of the Stupid Ogre" (AT 2009–2430) among others. So then what is the essential difference, if any, between a motif and a tale type? In these instances, virtually none. The distinction becomes more meaningful in more complex tales, e.g., "Tales of Magic" (AT 300–729) which consist of sequences of numerous motifs rather than just one. One of the key differences between a motif and a tale type is that all versions of a tale type are assumed to be genetically related, that is, they are assumed to be cognate, whereas all narratives listed under a motif heading may or may not be related. Any account of the origin of the sun, for example, could be listed under motif A710, Creation of the Sun. To be fair, Thompson himself was well aware of this distinction (1946:415–16; 1950a:753).

The problem of "overlapping" goes far beyond the confusion of motif and tale type in so many narratives. It occurs within *both* the conceptualization of motifs and tale types. In defining motifs, Thompson claims they fall in to three classes: actors, items, and incidents (1946:415–16). (It is the latter category of "incidents" that overlaps with tale types.) The obvious difficulty is: how can there possibly be an "incident" motif that does not include either an "actor" motif or an "item" motif? The categories of motifs delineated by Thompson are thus not at all mutually exclusive and in fact are unavoidably overlapping.

Tale types are also overlapping although this problem was caused by Aarne's original classification scheme and cannot be blamed on Thompson. Aarne elected—in retrospect unwisely—to classify folktales partly on the basis of dramatis personae. Thus his first section consisted of animal tales (AT 1–299) in which the principal actors in the tales were animal characters. (For the inconsistencies even within Aarne's animal categories, see von Sydow 1948.) Aarne's mistake was not classifying tales on the basis of narrative plot rather than the dramatis personae. The reality of folktales, for example, demonstrates that the same tale can be told with either animal or human characters. As a result of Aarne's mistake, we often find the very same tale, that is, tale type in the true genetic sense, listed twice in the Aarne-Thompson index under two separate numbers. Thompson tried his best to alleviate the problem through a system of cross-referencing, but the fundamental theoretical issue was not really resolved. A substantial number of animal tales, for example, are clearly also tales involving ogres or numskulls. AT 9B In the Division of the Crop the Fox Takes the Corn = AT 1030 The Crop Division. Russian folklorist Vladimir Propp pointed out this obvious overlap in 1928 (1968:5–6). In similar fashion, AT 43 = AT 1097; AT 121 = AT 1250; AT 123 = AT 333; AT 126 = AT 1149, etc. The point is that the same tale should not have two or more different tale type numbers! So we can see that in some instances, motifs overlap with tale types, and in others, tale types overlap with other tale types. Such overlapping surely suggests that both the current motif and tale type systems are flawed.

Another serious problem with both the motif and tale type indices involves the recurring issue of censorship. Thompson indulged in what can only be described as absurd and excessive prudery. To the extent that folkloristics is a science, albeit a social science, it cannot or should not be victimized by self-imposed censorship. This is especially grievous in the case of folkloristic data because so much of folklore deals with unabashedly taboo topics. In that context, a decision by a scholar to omit "obscene" data from standard collections and indices is inexcusable. Thompson states his philosophy with respect to such motifs in an obscure footnote in the *Motif-Index* (1957:514, n. 1): "Thousands of obscene motifs in which there is no point except the obscenity itself might logically come at this point, but they are entirely beyond the scope of this present work. . . . In view of the possibility that it might become desirable to classify these motifs and place them within the present index, space has been left from X700 to X749 for such motifs." One cannot possibly help but wonder at Thompson's skewed logic in leaving only fifty numerical slots for "thousands of obscene motifs." (For an incisive critique of Thompson's prudery, see Legman's 1962 essay "Toward A Motif-Index of Erotic Humor.") So obscene folklore motifs were simply intentionally omitted by Thompson in the *Motif-Index*. A slightly different strategy was employed in the tale type index. In this index, Thompson does assign numbers to some obscene tales, but his accompanying verbal synopsis is either too brief to be of much use or is absent altogether. Two examples should suffice. AT 1420G Anser Venalis (Goose as Gift) is followed by the following oblique sentence: "The lover regains his gift by a ruse (obscene)." This is not a very informative synopsis. What is the ruse? (For a version of this tale, see Afanasyev 1966:56–57, 268–69). Even worse is Thompson's listing of AT 1355*. Here the number is followed only by "(obscene)," which tells us absolutely nothing whatsoever about the content of the tale. Why even bother to include such a useless entry? (For a possible version of this tale, see Afanasyev 1966:183–84.) This sort of conscious omission of "obscene" folklore from the tale type and motif indices surely impairs the utility of these otherwise helpful scholarly aids.

Finally, a problem which is more of an annoyance is what might by termed "ghost entries." Now it must be understood that in a mammoth compilation of the scope of the indices under discussion, it is quite understandable that typographical errors or occasional omissions are bound to occur. Thompson did, after all, carry out his enormous labors in the pre-computer era. Still, such errors can be frustrating to would-be users of the indices. There is no point in listing all such errata, but several examples may illustrate the problem. Thompson's bibliographical code of signalling monographic studies of a particular tale type with a double asterisk prefix as opposed to mere lists of versions by a single asterisk is employed throughout the Aarne-Thompson tale type index, but is never explained. The explanation is, however, to be found in the introduction to the *Motif-Index* (1955:23) where the same system is utilized.

Many of the errors are minor. For instance, under motif B31.1 Roc. A giant bird which carries men off in its claws, we find a cross-reference to K186.1.1, Hero sewed up in an animal hide so as to be carried to height by bird. But inspection reveals that there is no such motif as K186.1.1! There is, however, motif K1861.1 which is the correct motif. It is just a typographical error involving a mere decimal point, but it could prove terribly frustrating to even an experienced user of the *Motif-Index*. In volume 6, the index volume of the *Motif-Index*, under the entry "Book" we find the last reference to be "value to b. depends on appreciation of it through J1061.5." In the relevant J section, we find J1061.1 through J 1061.4, but no J1061.5.! In the same volume 6 under the entry "Shadow," we find "undesired lover asked not to step on s. K1277.6." A quick check shows that there is no motif K1277 at all. Similar discrepancies occur in the tale type index. Under AT 74C Rabbit Throws Coconut, we find "Cf. Type 22." But there is no tale type 22! After AT 1510 The Matron of Ephesus, we find "Cf. Type 1752" but there is no such tale type listed. These sorts of errors could be corrected in future editions of these indices.

Less easy to correct is one last basic theoretical deficiency to be found in the tale type index. Whereas the *Motif-Index* offers worldwide coverage of folk narrative, the tale type index does not. According to Thompson's introduction, "the folktales of all the world" are *not* considered in the index. Rather, it is only the Indo-European folktale which is the acknowledged delimited corpus covered. In Thompson's own words, "Strictly then, this work might by called 'The Types of The Folk-Tale of Europe, West Asia, and the Lands Settled by These Peoples'" (Aarne and Thompson 1961:7). By definition, then, native American tale types and African tale types, among other nonwestern narratives, are intentionally excluded. The problem is that some of the tales presently included in the tale type index are *not* Indo-European tales at all, but rather are incontrovertibly native American or African tale types! Two examples may suffice to illustrate this claim. AT 297A, Turtle's War Party, is a classic native American tale type (cf. Dundes 1978). It is *not* found in the Indo-European narrative tradition at all. Its occurrence in Japan alone was apparently the basis for its inclusion in the AT index. Taking Thompson's introduction to the index at face value, an unwary index user might wrongly assume that the native Americans borrowed it from the Indo-European corpus, but this is not the case. AT tale type 291 Deceptive Tug-of-war, is an equally classic *African* tale type. It is *not* found in the Indo-European corpus except for one lone text reported in Peru. Again, it is evidently this single Peruvian text that convinced Thompson to include it in his 1961 revision of the Aarne index. (For references to sixty-one African versions of this tale, see Paulme and Bremond 1980.) Again, the naive user of the index might wrongly conclude that all of the many versions in Africa and in the African diaspora had been borrowed from the Indo-European tradition, but this is not the case. One day when there are comprehensive published tale type indices for *all* African tale types and for *all* native (North and South) American tale types, such errors will be easier to correct.

The overlapping difficulties of the motif and tale type indices aside, the unfortunate omission of obscene folk narrative notwithstanding, and overlooking or ignoring the ghost references and the misleading inclusion of native American and African tale types in the AT index, the fact remains that the motif and tale type indices with all their faults remain indispensable for the identification of traditional folk narratives. Since identification is a necessary prerequisite for interpretation, we folklorists simply cannot do without these standard indices. Moreover, the individual tale type indices for particular cultures or countries (cf. Assolina 1987) can serve as field guides or "finding lists" for prospective fieldworkers. Imperfect though they may be, they represent the keystones for the comparative method in folkloristics, a method which despite postmodernist naysayers and other prophets of gloom continues to be the hallmark of international folkloristics.

References

Aarne, Antti. 1910. *Verzeichnis der Märchentypen.* FF Communications No. 3. Helsinki: Suomalaisen Tiedakateniian Toimituksia.

Aarne, Alan, and Stith Thompson. 1961. *The Types of the Folktale.* FF Communications No. 184. Helsinki: Academia Scientarium Fennica.

Afanasyev, Aleksandr N. 1966. *Russian Secret Tales.* New York: Brussel and Brussel.

Azzolina, David S. 1987. *Tale Type- and Motif- Indexes: An Annotated Bibliography.* New York: Garland.

Bascom, William.1992. *African Folktales in the New World.* Bloomington: Indiana University Press

Ben-Amos, Dan. 1980. "The Concept of Motif in Folklore." In *Folklore Studies in the 20th Century,* ed. Venetia Newall, 17–36. Totawa, NJ: Rowman and Littlefield.

Bødker, Laurits. 1965. *Folk Literature (Germanic).* Copenhagen: Rosenkilde and Bagger.

Bremond, Claude. 1982. "A Critique of the Motif." In *French Literary Theory Today: A Reader,* ed. Tsvetan Todorov, 125–46. Cambridge: Cambridge UniversityPress.

Courtés, Joseph. 1982. "Motif et type dans la tradition folklorique. Problèmes de typologie." *Littérature* 45:114–27.

Dundes, Alan.1964. *The Morphology of North American Indian Folktales.* FF Communications No. 195. Helsinki: Academia Scientarium Fennica.

———.1977. "African and Afro-American Tales. In *African Folklore in the New World,* ed. Daniel J. Crowley, 35–53. Austin: University of Texas Press.

———. 1978. "A Potawatomi Version of Aarne-Thompson Tale Type 297A, Turtle's War Party." *Norveg* 21:47–57.

Finnegan, Ruth. 1970. *Oral Literature in Africa.* Oxford: Clarendon Press.

Georges, Robert A. 1983. "The Universality of the Tale-Type as Concept and Construct." *Western Folklore* 42:21–28.

Greverus, Ina-Maria. 1964. "Thelma, Typus und Motiv: Zur Determination in her Erzählforschung." In *IV International Congress for Folk-Narrative Research in Athens,* ed. Georgios A. Megas, 130–39. Athens: Laographia.

Holbek, Bengt. 1964. "On the Classification of Folktales." In *IV International Congress for Folk Narrative in Athens,* ed. Georgios A. Megas, 158–61. Athens: Laogiaphia.

———. 1987. *Interpretation of Fairy Tales.* FF Communications No. 239. Helsinki: Academia Scientarium Fennica.

Honti, János. 1939. "Märchenmorphologie und Märchentypologie." *Folk-Liv* 3:307–18.

———. 1975. *Studies in Oral Epic Tradition,* Budapest: Akadémiai Kiadó.

106   The Meaning of Folklore

Jason, Heda. 1972. "Structual Analysis and the Concept of the 'Tale Type.'"*Arv* 28:35– 54.
Legman, G. 1962. 'Toward a Motif-Index of Erotic Humor." *Journal of American Folklore*
    75:227–48.
Meletinski, Eleasar. 1977". Principes sémantiques d'un nouvel index des motifs etdes sujets." *Cahiers*
    de Littérature Orale 2:15–24.
Paulme, Denise, and Claude Bremond. 1980. "Le conte de 'Jeu de la corte' et la ruse de la 'peau
    pourrie' en Afrique." *Cahiers de Littérature Orale* 8:49–77.
Propp, Vladimir. 1968. *Morphology of the Folktale.* Austin: University of Texas Press.
Roberts, Warren E. 1994. *The Tale of the Kind and Unkind Girls.* Detroit: Wayne State University
    Press.
Rooth, Anna Birgitta. 1951. *The Cinderella Cycle.* Lund: C. W. K Gleerup.
Thompson, Stith. 1964. *The Folktale.* New York: The Dryden Press.
———. 1950a. "Motif." in *Standard Dictionary of Folklore Mythology and Legend,* ed.Maria Leach,
    753. New York: Funk & Wagnalls.
———. 1950b. "Type." In *Standard Dictionary of Folklore Mythology and Legend,* ed. Maria Leach,
    1137–38. New York: Funk & Wagnalls.
———. 1955–1958. *Motif-Index of Folk-Literature.* 6 vols. Bloomington: Indiana University Press.
Von Sydow, C. W. 1948. "Popular Prose Traditions and Their Classification." In *Selected Papers on*
    Folklore, ed. Laurits Bødker, 127–45. Copenhagen: Rosenkilde and Bagger.
Würzbach, Natasha. 1993. "Theorie and Praxis des Motiv-Begriffs." *Jahlbuch für Volksliedforschung*
    38:64–89.

5

How Indic Parallels to the Ballad of the "Walled-Up Wife" Reveal the Pitfalls of Parochial Nationalistic Folkloristics

Introduction

Dundes frequently emphasized the need for cross-cultural research, with the goal of forming an international folkloristics. He complained of a tendency among scholars to divide folklore into national categories, which might lead to problematic claims that traditions belong to a unique location. In cross-cultural comparisons, Dundes identified key features that remain consistent across cultures, as well as those distinctive details that are part of "oicotypes" (also called ecotypes), a term he borrowed from Swedish folklorist Carl von Sydow, to describe differences in narratives owing to the cultural and geographical environment in which they are told. In the ballad of the "Walled-Up Wife," for instance, the feature that makes it distinctive among foundation sacrifice narratives is the position of a woman as the sacrificed victim. Dundes noted, however, that in contrast to European versions of the ballad, where the wife has to be duped into entering the partly built construction, in India "the young bride knows ahead of time that she is the intended victim to be sacrificed." Another difference is that the structure being built in India is a well or water tank, while in Europe it is typically a bridge, castle, or monastery. Dundes attributed these differences to diverging worldviews and value systems, but saw an important continuity in the woman's role as sacrifice so the structure will remain erect. The family connection is in the detail of an adversely affected child being left behind, or an infant seeking to nurse from the immured woman's breast. Within European versions, Greeks predominantly place the sacrifice in a bridge, while Romanians refer primarily to the construction of a monastery. The consistent motif is that despite the best efforts of a group of men to construct the magnificent structure by day, it falls at night (Thompson motif D2192, Work of Day Magically Overthrown At Night). The sacrifice insures that the structure will stand, but at a tremendous human price for the male builder.

Dundes turned his attention to the ballad and legend of the "Walled-Up Wife" because in over two hundred years of scholarship, it has gained status as one of the most famous poetic texts in the world. It gained renown in 1824, when Jacob Grimm translated into German a version sent to him by Serbian folklorist Vuk Karadžić, and then sent it to the

107

revered writer Johann Wolfgang von Goethe. As a result of public interest in southeast-ern Europe in the wake of the Crimean War (1854–1856), with the British allied with the Ottoman Empire against the Russians in southeastern Europe, versions of the ballad, as an example of Balkan tradition, appeared widely in English publications. It also inspired literary adaptations, such as English poet W. M. W. Call's "Manoli: A Moldo-Wallachian Legend" in 1862 (see Tappe 1984).

Emphasizing the key symbolic role of the woman in this narrative, Dundes typified the narrative as the "Walled-Up Wife," but it is known in different countries by a host of different names. Serbian folklorists have concentrated on "The Building of Skadar," while Hungarians have been primarily concerned with "Clement Mason." In Romania, "Meşterul Manole" holds sway (280 variants in the study by Ion Taloş [1997]), and Greek folklorists have given attention to "The Bridge of Arta" (328 variants, according to Georgios A. Megas [1976]). Dundes pointed out that even for comparativists, the ballad had been associated with the Balkans, and was often presumed to originate there, although he found evidence for an Indic origin because of the relation of "A Feast for the Well" (*Keregehara*) to the foundation sacrifice motif. Other theories of origin hold that it has a classical source, in Greek myths of the passage over a bridge from life to death, or a Biblical connection to the story of Jephthah's sacrifice of his daughter for victory in battle (Judges 11:30–40).

The most common origin theory applied to the widespread ballad was that it had roots in an ancient custom whereby female victims were ritually killed as a form of foundation sacrifice. It advanced the thesis that details of the ritual were preserved, in the expressive forms of song and story, after the ritual was no longer practiced. Dundes objected that the myth-ritual theory was not an "ultimate origins explanation." Although it posited a his-torical connection as a source for the text, it did not answer the questions of why the ritual was practiced or where it came from. It was also frequently at a loss to explain why particu-lar rituals persisted in folklore and others did not. Dundes criticized the theory for its fal-lacious assumption of a causal link between a ritual that occurred in the distant past, and the performance of the ballad.

Another issue in the history of scholarship on the ballad was, how did it diffuse across borders if it was not the sole creation of a single country? Dundes pointed to the influence of mobile Gypsies as a conduit of the tradition, and others have also considered a Jewish diasporic possibility (see Shai 1976). Folklorist Paul Brewster has suggested that the bal-lad reached American playgrounds in the form of the well-known rhyme "London Bridge is Falling Down," with its lines about a falling bridge and a trapped "fair lady" (1971). A narrative connection with motifs of the ballad are also apparent in American legends of haunted bridges, such as material collected by folklorist Linda Dégh about a "big, mod-ern bridge" with a woman or child in the foundation (1968). The feature that suggests a link is the action of the woman/child unwittingly becoming entombed when going to retrieve a metal object (in the ballad it is often a ring). Other cognates have been identi-fied in Germany and Africa (see Schmidt 1995). Dundes resisted the historic-geographic idea that the feature of the bridge or dam is blindly inserted into the story because it was heard that way along its path of diffusion. For instance, in this essay, he asked why the edi-fice that fell was so often a dam, bridge, castle, or well. He discerned symbolism in these objects, related to womb enclosures by shape or water content. In material culture, they are also visible technological achievements, often associated with male occupations, that defy feminine nature or stand out on the landscape and invite narrative commentary. Dundes discussed further the psychoanalytic idea of a tomb/womb equation in relation to the vampire legend (1998).

Plot similarities of ballad texts of the "Walled-Up Wife" in a number of countries raises the question of symbolic meanings that could apply *across* cultures, and might therefore explain the appeal of the ballad through time and across space. (For another example in which Dundes found that adding texts to the Eurocentric data used to analyze a narrative suggested an interpretation differing from previous scholarship, see his discussion of "Little Red Riding Hood" [1989e].) In the present essay, Dundes pointed out that these meanings varied according to the perspective taken—in this case, whether male or female. The text could have multiple meanings, and the folklorist could also evaluate whether some meanings arose more prominently than others because the story was told more frequently from a particular perspective. Dundes applied a feminist psychoanalytic interpretation from symbolic evidence in the ballad, at least from a woman's perspective, of entrapment in married life. He adapted Freud's male-oriented "Oedipus complex" into what he called the "male edifice complex" in the story, a working out of guilt by a man prioritizing career over family. The male "erection" by day, according to Dundes, was contrasted to family time at night, when the structure falls. Male hubris brings death in the story, he observed. Dundes predicted that as attitudes toward non-egalitarian marriage and the suppression of women change, the ballad will likely not be needed psychologically.

After the "Walled-Up Wife" essay appeared, Romanian folklorist Nicolae Constantinescu took up Dundes's challenge to observe the meanings that derive from different-gendered perspectives. He noticed that performances of the Romanian *colind*, or Christmas carol, containing the walled-up wife motif were usually plaintive songs that were sung by women to other women. According to Constantinescu, its apparent "funeral function," bemoaning the death of female freedom upon marriage in Balkan social organization, supported Dundes's contention. But he observed a complication in that ballad versions were performed by male professional singers for a male audience in designated settings, such as wedding parties and coffee shops. Constantinescu accounted for this masculine appropriation of what appears to be a feminist symbolic song by noting that the central themes changed according to the gender of the performer and the associated genre. In the carol, women altered the emphasis from the master mason's deeds, in the men's ballad, to the wife's acts: her determination to bring her husband's lunch against all obstacles, and her responsibility to the infant left behind (2003).

Dundes devoted a volume to different collections and interpretations of the ballad in *The Walled-Up Wife*. In light of the themes of sacrifice and marriage that he considered in the present essay, readers may want to know that he "lovingly dedicated" his book to his "wife, Carolyn, whose many sacrifices made my career as a folklorist possible" (1996b). Dundes implied that his interest in the ballad was not just because of its long history of scholarship and its lessons about comparativist work, but also as a result of his relating to the theme he identified in this essay, the "difficulties of balancing career and marriage for males." This is a viewpoint he did not include in a prior study of the ballad, "The Building of Skadar (1989b).

How Indic Parallels to the Ballad of the "Walled-Up Wife" Reveal the Pitfalls of Parochial Nationalistic Folkloristics

THE GOVERNING INTELLECTUAL PARADIGM IN 19th-century folkloristics was the historical reconstruction of the past, modeled in part on the parallel disciplines of archaeology and philology. There were, to be sure, competing forms of diachronic searches for origins, but most involved some type of historical-comparative-diffusionistic bias. Synchronic concerns with structure, function, context, performance, and the like would not emerge until the next, that is, the 20th, century.

Among the most prominent 19th-century folklore theories of origins was the so-called Indianist hypothesis. One of the acknowledged starting points of the argument that much of European folklore had originated in India was Theodor Benfey's (1809–1881) introduction to the first German translation of the *Panchatantra* in 1859. Champions of the "Indianist" school of folkloristics included William Clouston (1843–1896), Joseph Jacobs (1854–1916), and Emmanuel Cosquin (1841–1919), among others. The influence of Max Müller (1823–1900), a leading Indologist (despite the fact that he never once set foot in India) and the Aryan-migration notions that he espoused gave further credence to the Indianist school inasmuch as it was believed that "the Aryan peoples emigrated from India and carried their language and myths with them" (Dorson 1968:178). The Indianist theory has gone the way of most 19th-century folklore theories. In other words, it has been relegated to a long footnote in the history of 19th-century folkloristics. It is not my purpose here to attempt to resuscitate the Indianist theory, but I cannot forbear noting that the theory was primarily applied to folk narrative with special emphasis on myths and folktales. The ballad genre seems to have been pretty much ignored by those advocating Indic origins.

The Walled-Up Wife

One of the most famous ballads in the world in terms of the amount of scholarship devoted to it is surely "The Walled-Up Wife." Found widely reported throughout the Balkans, it has intrigued and bedeviled East European folklorists for more than one hundred and fifty years. Romanian folklorist Ion Taloş, who has devoted a book-length monograph to the ballad (1973), has this to say about it: "The song about the mason's wife is a ballad of rare beauty, perhaps the most impressive in world folklore" (1987:400). This echoes the sentiment of Jacob Grimm, who called the ballad "one of the most outstanding songs of all peoples and all times" (Dundes 1989:156).

The basic plot involves a group of men who seek to construct a castle, monastery, or bridge. Through supernatural means, whatever is constructed during the day is undone at night. A dream revelation or some other extraordinary means of communication informs the would-be builders that the only way to break the negative magic spell is to sacrifice the first woman (wife or sister) who comes to the building site the next day. When the chief architect's own young wife arrives, she is duly immured. Often the process is thought to

110

be a joke or game by the female victim until a poignant moment in the ballad when she suddenly realizes that she is being sacrificed by her husband and his colleagues. In some versions, she begs for an aperture to be left so that she can continue to nurse her baby. Sometimes a milky spring marks the site of the alleged event, a site where infertile women or mothers suffering from a lack of lactation later come in the hope of obtaining a folk medical cure. This brief synopsis does not by any means do justice to this powerful ballad (and legend), but it should be sufficient to identify it for those not familiar with it. Since the ballad is apparently not in the English and Scottish canon and does not appear in Western Europe generally, it is not particularly well known among folklorists in Western Europe and the United States.

In Eastern Europe, in contrast, however, it is extremely common and well known. In Serbia, it has the title of "The Building of Skadar"; in Hungary, it is often called "Clement Mason"; in Romania, it is "Master Manole"; in Greece, it is "The Bridge of Arta"; and so on. The numbers of collected texts of this ballad are truly staggering. Greek folklorist Georgios Megas based his study of the ballad on 333 Greek versions (Megas 1976:5) for example. Bulgarian folklorist Lyubomira Parpulova analyzed 180 Bulgarian versions of the ballad (Parpulova 1984:425). When one adds the numerous Hungarian, Romanian, Serbian, and Albanian versions to the Greek and Bulgarian texts, we are dealing with a ballad for which we have more than seven hundred texts available.

The ballad of the walled-up wife has fascinated some of the leading folklorists of the 19th and 20th centuries. One of the earliest versions was a Serbian text of "The Building of Skadar" collected by Vuk Karadžić's (1784–1864), the founder of Serbian folkloristics. He began publishing his *Narodne srpske pjesme* in Vienna in 1814. At that time, Jacob Grimm (1785–1863) was serving as a delegate to the Vienna Congress (from October 1814 to June 1815), and he eventually wrote a review of Karadžić's first volume of folksongs (Wilson 1986:112). In 1824, Karadžić's sent a new edition of the folksongs to Grimm, who was so delighted with "The Building of Skadar" that he began to translate it. He sent his translation to Goethe in May of the same year, but Goethe was appalled by what he considered to be the heathen-barbarity of the ballad (Dundes 1989:156; Milović 1941:51). Grimm would later discuss the ballad as a prime example of "foundation sacrifice" in his *Teutonic Mythology* (1966:III, 1143). But that was just the beginning of the enormous mass of scholarship devoted to the ballad. Among the dozens—note the use of the plural—of monographs on the topic, there are major studies by such distinguished scholars as Cocchiara, Eliade, Megas, Taloş, and Vargyas. Much of the earlier scholarship has been ably surveyed by Vargyas in his magisterial essay "The Origin of the Walled-up Wife," which is chapter III of his excellent *Researches into the Medieval History of Folk Ballad* (1967:173–233). Vargyas, arguably one of the leading ballad authorities of the 20th century, continued his detailed and meticulous investigation of the ballad in his *Hungarian Ballads and the European Tradition II* (1983:18–57). Vargyas considers virtually all texts available in print and reviews their contents, not to mention summarizing the incredible number of essays and monographs on the ballad written, I might add, in a bewildering variety of languages.

If one wished to describe the bulk of scholarship treating the ballad, one could say that two principal features characterize the literature. From Jacob Grimm on, there has been a host of essays using the ballad to illustrate a conventional myth-ritual thesis that the story represented a survival from an actual practice of the past of offering a human sacrifice in order to appease supernatural spirits who were believed to be involved in or threatened by the proposal to build some kind of structure, for example, a bridge. An example of the logic adduced: the river goddess will be deprived of "food" by a bridge that will permit all passengers to cross the stream safely. Hence a human sacrifice must be offered to appease the goddess (Mitra 1927:41). Famed comparativist Reinhold Köhler's 1894 paper (first published in 1873) is representative, but one could easily cite many others including Gittée 1886–1887, Krauss 1887, Feilberg 1892, Sartori 1898, Sainean 1902, De Vries 1927, O'Sullivan 1945, Cocchiara 1950, and Brewster 1971 (see also Taloş 1973:25). The second observable trend in the scholarship is the persistent attempt to establish a national origin for the ballad. Through a modified form of the comparative method, folklorists have sought to "prove" that the ballad originated in one locale rather than another. Zihni Sako ends his discussion of Albanian versions with the unequivocal statement: "it seems to us that the original source of the ballad is Illyria, that is, Albania" (1984:165). Similarly, Georgios Megas ended one of his several essays on the ballad this way: "I hope that it is clearly demonstrated from the publication of my full-fledged investigation that Greece must be considered as the cradle and homeland of our ballad" (1969:54, my translation). Megas reiterated this position at the very end of his 1976 monograph on the ballad when he (rightly) rejected the idea that polygenesis could be responsible for the different versions of the ballad found throughout the Balkans, and (wrongly) concluded that the single origin of the ballad *must* have been the Greek territory in early Byzantine times (1976:179). It is not difficult to see a high correlation between the hypothetical country of origin and the nationality of the researcher! (For a convenient chronological summary of the long-standing origins debate, see Vargyas 1967:178–179 and its continuation 1983:55–57; for other comprehensive accounts of previous scholarship devoted to the ballad, see Dundes 1989:153–155, Megas 1976:125–179, and Taloş 1973.) I am by no means the first to underscore the extreme nationalistic bias in ballad origin scholarship. Ballad specialist David Buchan, in his essay "British Balladry: Medieval Chronology and Relations," has this to say about Child 73, "Lord Thomas and Fair Annet": "Grundtvig thought its origin Danish, Gerould thought its origin British, Doncieux thought it French, which perhaps tells us more about the ethnocentricity of ballad scholars than about 'Lord Thomas'" (Buchan 1978:104). As to why the ballad as opposed to other genres of folklore should have been the focus of nationalistic proprietary "wars," one can only speculate that the ballad's hallowed status vis-à-vis other folklore genres—either as the detritus of glorious epics of the past or alternatively as a relatively late medieval elitist creation, not related to any primitive origins—might account for why ardent nationalistic scholars were so anxious to claim exclusive "ownership" of such treasures. Also since two or more neighboring nations appeared to have the "same" ballad, it was perhaps almost inevitable that it would become a natural bone of contention.

For more than a century, there has been a brisk many-sided debate among Balkans folklorists as to which country had the right to claim "credit" for originating the walled-up wife ballad. It may be difficult for some modern folklorists to appreciate just how heated the debate was over which of the numerous nationalistic competing claims was "correct." One illustrative example may suffice to indicate the intensity of the furor. In 1863 the noted Hungarian collector of folksongs, János Kriza (1811–1875), a Unitarian minister from Transylvania influenced in part by Herder and Percy, published a collection of folksongs. He called the songs "the collection of the flowers of the mind of the Székeley people—its wild roses, if I may so describe them" (as quoted in Ortutay 1973:498). In that collection, entitled *Vadrózsák* (Wild Roses), Kriza included a Hungarian version of the walled-up wife ballad: Kömives Kelemennë. Almost immediately upon publication of the collection, one Julian Grozescu (whose name clearly suggests Romanian origin) accused Kriza of having plagiarized this ballad and one other from a Romanian source. These accusations became the basis of a famous court trial in Budapest. Although Kriza was not guilty of plagiarism, the *Vadrózsák* lawsuit saddened him for the rest of his life. Ortutay's comment on the matter is of interest in the present context: "It has come to light on the basis of more recent collections and European comparative ethnographic research that the charges of plagiarism brought against Kriza were unfounded, and that the two ballads in question, like the others, constitute an integral part of both Hungarian and European folk-poetry, including the Romanian. It is obvious today that the accusations were groundless; they were inspired by the awakening Rumanian nationalism, Hungarian nationalism defended itself against them" (Ortutay 1973:501).

An Indianist Origin via the Gypsies

None of the many scholars involved in the dispute over the origin of the walled-up wife were aware of the fact that the ballad was extremely popular in India as well. (For references to published texts in Telegu and Kannada, see Dundes 1989:165, n. 25.) The first hint of a possible Indic origin of the ballad came from Francis Hindes Groome (1851–1902), who included the "Story of the Bridge" in his 1899 *Gypsy Folk-Tales*. Groome had translated into English a somewhat-garbled Gypsy version reported by Alexandre G. Paspati (1870:620–623). Of particular interest is Groome's endnote, which begins with an apology: "I hesitated whether to give this story; it is so hopelessly corrupt, it seems such absolute nonsense. Yet it enshrines beyond question, however confusedly, the widespread and ancient belief that to ensure one's foundation one should wall up a human victim" (Groome 1899:13). Later in the same note, Groome makes the following observation: "The Gypsy story is probably of high antiquity, for two at least of the words in it were quite or almost meaningless to the nomade [sic] Gypsy who told it" (cf. Paspati 1870:190–191). Groome continues: "The masons of southeastern Europe are, it should be noticed, largely Gypsies; and a striking Indian parallel may be pointed out in the Santal story of 'Seven Brothers and Their Sister' (Campbell 1891:106–110). Here seven brothers set to work to dig a tank but find no water, and so, by the advice of a yogi, give their only sister to the spirit of the tank. 'The tank was soon full to the brim, and the girl was drowned.' And then comes a curious mention of a Dom, or Indian vagrant musician, whose name is probably identical with Doum, Loin, or Rom, the Gypsy of Syria, Asia Minor, and Europe" (Groome 1899:13). To my knowledge, this is the only suggestion in print that there might be a connection between the Balkans ballad of the walled-up wife and a cognate story in India.

In 1925, B. J. Gilliat-Smith published another Gypsy version of "The Song of the Bridge" in the *Journal of the Gypsy Lore Society*. The text was accompanied by a learned comparative note by W. R. Halliday. Halliday summarily dismisses Groome's suggestion of a possible Indic parallel: "Actually the parallel does not extend further than the building of a tank by seven brothers and the drowning of their sister (not the wife of one of them), in order that the tank may fill with water. The similarity, in fact, is derived merely from the common origin of the two stories in the belief in the necessity for Foundation Sacrifice, which we have noted to be world-wide. *I have personally no doubt whatsoever* that the *Song of the Bridge* is a localized form of story arising out of this wide-spread custom and *belongs properly to the Balkan area*" (1925:111, emphasis added). Halliday was dead wrong in failing to see that the Indic narratives were cognate with the Balkans ballad. But then again, every scholar who has written on the ballad has also failed to consider the many Indic versions of the narrative. (Vargyas too dismissed the two Gypsy texts [1967:194] as being of little or no consequence.)

Objective readers who take the time to read through the hundreds of Balkans texts and the Indic versions can easily see for themselves that they are unquestionably part of a common Indo-European tradition, although the ballad apparently never became popular in Western Europe. (It is worth noting that folklorist A. H. Krappe (1894–1947) posited an Indic origin for a legend involving the foundation sacrifice of a child (rather than a wife-bride), a legend that may or may not be cognate with the walled-up wife (Krappe 1927:165–180). Given the possible/probable Indic origin of the ballad, the Gypsy texts, garbled though they may be, support this hypothesis inasmuch as the origin of the Gypsies is presumed to be India. A Bulgarian Gypsy text of the ballad reported in 1962 (Čerenkov 1962) tends to confirm the traditionality of the narrative among Gypsy groups. If this is so, then all of the petty arguments between Balkans folklorists about which country's versions are the earliest become more or less beside the point. The moral of this exemplum is that the comparative method can be effective only when *all* available versions of a ballad or folktale are taken into account.

Consider one of the issues raised in Halliday's dismissal of a possible Indic parallel. The Indic text involves the drowning of a "sister" of the water-tank builders rather than "the wife of one of them." But as Vargyas observes, "The victim is not always a wife: in the Serbian, Albanian, and Roumanian she may be the sister of the builder. This appears to be a secondary element" (1967:202). It should also be noted that in many modern Indic texts the victim is a daughter-in-law, that is, a wife. So both the wife and sister appear as victims in the Indic texts. The "sister instead of wife" argument therefore cannot constitute a legitimate objection to the cognation hypothesis.

Formulaic Evidence

Not only are the Balkans ballad and Indic song-tale plots cognate, but there are formulaic features that provide indisputable evidence of the genetic relationship between the two sets of texts. In the Balkans, the entombment of the female victim is often described in a moving series of lines in which the poor girl is ever so gradually covered, typically from the lower body to the upper body, from toe to head so to speak. The girl speaks of being walled up to the knees, to her breast, to her throat; or knees, breast, eyes; or knees, waist, breast, and throat (Vargyas 1983:46–48). In the Rumanian text analyzed in such depth by Mircea Eliade (1907–1986), "the wall rose over higher, burying her, up to the ankles, up to the calves, up to the ribs, up to the breasts . . . up to the eyes" (Eliade 1972:168).

Let us briefly consider three Santal folktales. In the first, "The Magic Fiddle" (Campbell 1891:52–56), the sister is sent to get water, but the water vanishes when she tries to scoop some up in her pitcher. Gradually the water "reaches to my ankles . . . to my knee, to my waist, to my breast, to my neck . . . to a man's height" and the girl drowns. In a second tale (Campbell 1891:106–110), the girl goes to fill her pitcher "but she could not do so, as the water rose so rapidly. The tank was soon full to the brim, and the girl was drowned." In a third Santal tale, entitled "How Sabai Grass Grew" (Bompas 1909:102–106), the sister is sent to the tank to draw water. "Directly the girl drew near to the bank the water began to bubble from the bottom; and when she went down to the water's edge, it rose to her instep." Gradually the water rises to her ankle, knees, waist, and neck. "At last it flowed over her head and the water-pot was filled, but the girl was drowned." In a modern Kannada text published in 1989, the water touches the daughter-in-law's feet, knee, and waist:

> She climbed a step and the water came up
> She climbed two steps and the water touched her feet
> She climbed three steps and the water touched her knee
> She climbed four steps and the water touched her waist
> She climbed five steps and the water drowned her
> The youngest daughter-in-law Bhagirathi
> She became a feast for the well [*Aniketana* 1989:371]

In an unpublished version from northern India collected in 1991 (Kirin Narayan, personal communication, 1994), the beleaguered female victim begs her brothers: "Don't brick up my feet . . . my midriff . . . breasts . . . neck . . . mouth . . . eyes . . . head." This version is even closer to the southeastern European texts inasmuch as the woman in this instance is bricked up into the foundation of a waterway under construction.

The demonstration of this formulaic parallel alone—even without the obvious plot similarity—would obviously offer strong support for the proposed Indic origin of the Balkans ballad.

What is especially fascinating in the light of the likely Indic source for the ballad is the fact that a number of the Balkans texts end with the formation of a magical spring that contains either pure water or nourishing milk (Vargyas 1967:203). In the Romanian version cited by Eliade, Manole, the master builder, is so saddened by the sacrificial death of his beloved young wife that he killed himself: "and from the woodwork high on the roof, he fell, dead; and where he was shattered a clear fountain sprang up, a trickle of water, salt with his tears" (Eliade 1972:169). The "spring" motif could well be an instance of what folklorists call peripheral distribution or marginal survival. Certainly the "spring" motif is reminiscent of the water-tank image so common in the Indic versions. For that matter, even the suicidal jump may not be a Romanian innovation. In a Kannada text, for example, the bereaved husband wept and "jumped into the well" (*Aniketana* 1989:38).

The Pitfalls of Parochial Nationalism

It is truly sad to think of so many eminent folklorists writing lengthy essays and learned monographs on this ballad in total ignorance of the Indic texts. It is especially distressing for those scholars who tried so hard to find the "origin" of the ballad and were misled by (1) wrongly limiting the areas of their comparative efforts—that is, failing to consult available Indic texts in print, and (2) by yielding to an excessively emotional and ideological nationalistic bias. The methodological lesson to be learned seems simple enough. The comparative method cannot possibly succeed if whole sets of cognate versions of an item of folklore are ignored. Folklorists who insist upon working in narrow parochial nationalistic mindsets are no better than unsophisticated anthropologists who are utterly convinced that a tale or song they collect from "their" people or "their" village is absolutely unique when in fact it is but one version of a narrative to be found among many peoples. The impressive veneer of comparativism found in the numerous monographic treatments of the walled-up wife ballad cannot cover the egregious error of having failed to take Indic cognate texts into account.

To be sure, Indian folklorists are no less parochial. They are just as unaware of the massive Balkans scholarship on the ballad as Balkanologists are unaware of the ballad's existence in India. Accordingly, Indian scholars analyze "their" local version of the ballad (see Govindaraja 1989; Srikantaiah 1989) without reference to any other versions just as, say, Romanian scholars, analyze only the Romanian text of the ballad (see Anghelescu 1984; Filiti 1972).

Another instructive illustration of the consequences stemming from excessive nationalistic zeal concerns aesthetics. Invariably, investigators claim that their "national" version of the ballad is the most beautiful. Romanian scholar L. Sainean contended, for example, "From the point of view of beauty and comparative originality, the Serbian and Romanian versions take first place; the Bulgarian songs, because of their loose form, give the impression of being detached fragments; the Albanian traditions are pale imitations of the Greek or Serbian ballads . . . the Hungarian variants seem to echo the Romanian ballad" (1902:360–361, as translated in Eliade 1972:174). Not surprisingly, Hungarian scholars disagreed with this assessment. Vargyas notes, "I think the examples shown make it clear on the uniform evidence of several details that the Hungarian formulation shows the purest form," although to be sure, he does suggest a Bulgarian rather than a Hungarian origin (1967:222, 228; 1983:37). Of course, it is the height of ethnocentric subjectivity to claim that one national version of a cross-culturally distributed folksong is more "beautiful" or "aesthetically pleasing" than that of another nation. The texts from India are surely every bit as poignant and eloquent as those from the Balkans—and remember, these were not even known to the myriad of Balkanologists making aesthetic assessments of the relative merit of ballad versions. Again, it can hardly be coincidence that the national version adjudged best or purest just happens to come from the same nation of which the scholar making the judgment is a citizen!

Parochial nationalism also turns out to be a critical factor in the few attempts to interpret the ballad. Greek scholars, seizing upon the "bridge" motif in "The Bridge of Arta," have suggested that the ballad may have originated from the mythological hair bridge over which the souls of the dead are required to pass on their way to the afterlife (Beaton 1980:122–124; Megas 1976:72). The problem here is that other versions of the ballad involve a castle, monastery, or water tank, rather than a bridge. So while the mythological "hair bridge" may appear plausible to those who know only the Greek "Bridge of Arta" tradition, it is highly implausible in the light of the total range of ballad variants. (It would also require that the Bridge of Arta be the original form of the ballad, which seems unlikely given the many versions from India.)

Another striking instance of a nationalistic interpretation of the ballad is Zimmerman's suggestion that "The Founding of Skadar" with its "immurement" can "represent the subjugation of the Serbian peoples at the time" of the Turkish domination. Moreover, "the survival of the infant" would accordingly represent "the ultimate survival of the nation" (Zimmerman 1979:379). It is certainly possible that the ballad could have such allegorical significance to nationalistic-minded Serbs, but this reading could scarcely apply to the Albanian, Bulgarian, Greek, Hungarian, Romanian, and Indic versions of the ballad.

Cross-Cultural Interpretation

What is needed in international folkloristics—as opposed to nationalistic folkloristics—are interpretations of items of folklore which could in theory apply to most if not all of the versions of that item of folklore. This is not to deny the importance of identifying oico-types and analyzing those oicotypes in terms of national or regional personality character-istics. But it does stress the inevitable limitations of nationalistic readings of folklore items with cross-cultural distribution. (One can compare Geertz's classic reading of the cock-fight in Bali with a cross-cultural interpretation of the same event [Dundes 1994:94–132, 241–282].) Clearly the comparative method continues to be essential for establishing the distribution pattern of any particular item of folklore. But merely demonstrating historic-geographic trait distributions is no substitute for searches for the meaning(s) of folklore. It is one thing to note that the ruse of sending the wife-victim into the foundation to retrieve an intentionally dropped wedding ring is "encountered in the Bulgarian, Greek, Albanian and Serbian versions" (Vargyas 1983:37), but what is the significance, if any, of this motif? And how does it relate to the possible overall meaning(s) of the ballad?

Over the past one hundred and fifty years of thinking about this ballad, the only "cross-cultural" theory to be consistently applied is that of myth-ritual. Specifically, it has long been assumed that the ballad is a survival-reminiscence of human sacrifice, a ritual required to appease otherwise hostile supernatural spirits who for various reasons oppose the building of some ambitious construction. What this theory utterly fails to illuminate is why the vic-tim to be sacrificed must be *female*. In theory the supernatural spirit could just as well be appeased by the sacrifice of a male victim. In fact, the myth-ritual theory of foundation sac-rifice explains very few of the actual details of the ballad plot. How, for example, does the myth-ritual theory account for the ring-dropping device to induce the wife-victim to enter the foundation? The myth-ritual theory also suffers from being a *literal* one; that is, it is pred-icated upon the notion that the construction ritual is historical. This is why so many Balkans scholars have spent so much time trying to locate the actual monastery or bridge that sup-posedly inspired the story (see Sapkaliska 1988:170; Zimmerman 1979:374). If the ballad did originate in India as now seems probable, all those efforts would appear to be in vain. (They do, however, show how ballads and legends in their paths of diffusion tend to become localized in a particular place, tied to a particular topographic feature in the landscape.)

A few women scholars have sought to find metaphorical meaning in the bal-lad. Zimmerman proposes a Christian reading of the ballad in which "the traditional Christian beliefs in an ultimate reward for suffering and the triumph of good over evil" are emphasized (1979:379). It is not entirely clear how these values are reflected in the sacrifice of a woman in a wall. Zimmerman also refers to "guilt-ridden cultural memories about foundation sacrifices" indicating that she has not completely abandoned the stan-dard myth-ritual theory (1979:379). In her analysis of the Bridge of Arta, Mandel argues a Lévi-Straussian opposition of nature and culture. Specifically, uncreative male culture "relies on the appropriation of female nature" (Mandel 1983:180). Although Mandel identifies women with nature, she also insists that women are liminal "between nature and culture" and act "as the mediator[s] between the worlds of the living and the dead" (1983:182). It is not immediately apparent how women can be both nature and medi-ating figures *between* nature and culture. However, Mandel's suggestion that the ballad deals with the men's attempt to "exercise power and control over the woman's sexuality and fertility" has merit (1983:182). But when she speaks in similar terms of the "bridge" as a liminal construction—"contiguous to both banks of the river" but belonging to nei-ther (1983:181), she falls into the nationalistic parochial pitfall of thinking only in terms of the Greek versions of the ballad. The bridge may well be liminal, but what about a castle or a water tank? Once again we see the theoretical difficulties arising from inter-preting an item of folklore in terms of just one culture (or one set of versions), when that same item of folklore is found in many different cultures. It is noteworthy that Mandel, in typical anthropologist fashion, dismisses all of the many published studies of the song because they only address "questions of diffusion and origin" and hence are deemed "not relevant to the argument presented here" (1983:175, n. 4).

Another interesting interpretation is offered by Lyubomira Parpulova when she has recourse to Van Gennep's celebrated rites of passage. Parpulova gives the myth-ritual the-ory a new life when she argues that the ballad reflects a ritual of transition. But she, too, cannot escape the older theoretical bias. She suggests that, rather than looking for a rite that underlies the ballad, "why not assume . . . a myth lying at the root of both the rite and the ballad." And she speaks further of "the different forms of constructional human sac-rifice, probably practiced in the past and preserved as legend" (Parpulova 1984:427). She hints at a possible connection of ritual separation of girls (e.g., after childbirth) with the ballad, although she maintains that there may not necessarily be a direct link (1984:435). One serious problem with the linkage to childbirth is that not all of the ballad texts refer to either a pregnant victim or an infant to be nursed through the wall. Still, Parpulova does cite a Bulgarian song in which a prison "is decoded as married life" (1984:433), and she insightfully suggests that the walling up may express "the inevitability of a woman's fate: to be transformed into the foundations of a new construction, a new world, a new family" that "is not always very pleasant" (1984:434).

Toward Multiple Interpretations

As I have previously argued, we can view the walled-up wife ballad as a metaphor for mar-ried life in all those societies in which it is sung (Dundes 1989). By entering marriage, the woman is figuratively immured. She is kept behind walls—to protect her virtue and to keep her confined. The ring-dropping ruse—which none of the earlier critics have addressed—would certainly support this feminist metaphorical interpretation. The hus-band drops the ring into the foundation and persuades the faithful wife to go in after it. It is the act of searching for a wedding ring which seals her fate literally and figuratively. The fact that a man is willing to sacrifice his wife in order to build a bigger and better castle, bridge, water-tank shows the second-class status of women in such societies. In that male chauvinist world, women's role is to stay protected from the outside world and to concen-trate upon nurturing her infants (preferably sons)! The fact that women living near Skadar in modern times seek the chalky liquid from the walls to mix with drinking water in order "to restore milk to women who cannot nurse" continues to underscore women's nurturant role (Zimmerman 1979:380). The ideal wife nurtures males—either by bringing food to her husband working on a construction site or by giving suck to her newborn son.

Whereas myth-ritual totally fails to explain why it must be a female victim in the ballad, the present hypothesis would explain why it must be a woman who is sacrificed. Marriage is a trap—for women. That is the ballad's message. She must sacrifice everything, her mobil-ity—she is transfixed—and even her life. The only aperture—in some versions—is a tiny window through which she can continue to suckle her infant son.

I believe this is a plausible metaphorical reading of the ballad of the walled-up wife, but is it the only possible reading? Certainly not. And this brings us to a final issue in our brief consideration of the ballad's significance. Nineteenth-century folklorists, if they thought about the meaning of folklore at all, invariably proposed some monolithic hypothesis. While they understood perfectly well the multiple existence of folklore texts, they did not realize that meanings could also be multiple. As variation is a hallmark of folklore texts, so is it also to be found in folklore interpretations.

Ever since Propp delineated the various dramatis personae in the magic tale (Aarne-Thompson tale types 300–749) in 1928, folklorists have had the methodological tools to explore the possibility of investigating the crucial matter of perspective or point of view in folktales or ballads. Any given folktale or ballad may give priority to one of several vantage points. Perhaps the most obvious distinction concerns whether the tale is told from the perspective of the hero or the victim, assuming they are two different characters. (Propp made an important differentiation between hero-victims—who saved themselves—and hero-seekers who saved victims [1968:36].) Although, in theory, a tale could be told from the villain's point of view, this is more common in written literature than in oral tradition.

In my analysis of the folktale source of Shakespeare's *King Lear*, I tried to demonstrate that an originally girl-centered folktale was retold by Shakespeare from a male parent's point of view (1976). In the same way, A. K. Ramanujan revealed that the Indic Oedipus tale was told from the mother's viewpoint rather than the son's (1983). Similarly, Jack Zipes has brilliantly shown how the female-centered tale of Little Red Riding Hood was recast by male collectors, namely, Perrault and the Grimm brothers, so as to satisfy the agenda of male ideology. (In the original oral tale, the heroine saves herself through her own cleverness—an example of Propp's hero-victim—whereas in the Perrault and Grimm "rewrites," the heroine is either eaten up by the wolf or else saved by an intervening male woodsman [Zipes 1993:30–34, 375–378].) Finally, Jim Taggart in his splendid *Enchanted Maidens* (1990) proved from his own field materials from Spain that there were distinct male and female versions of the same tale type, a differentiation that could frequently be correlated with the gender of the tale-tellers. Bengt Holbek in his magnum opus devoted to the European fairy tale also sought to distinguish "Masculine" and "Feminine" tales (1987:161, 417).

What this suggests in terms of the ballad of the walled-up wife is that there are at the very least two distinct possible perspectives: one would be that of the victim, the wife who is immured, and the second would be that of the male builder. It is obviously a matter of opinion as to whose story the ballad tells. Is it the tragic fate of the female? Or the tragic grief of the builder-widower? Just as there is no one correct "text" of an item of folklore, there is no one correct "interpretation" of an item of folklore. Folklorists must accustom themselves to accepting multiple interpretations just as they have learned to accept the existence of multiple versions of texts.

As mentioned above, I have proposed a feminist reading of the ballad which argues that the plot provides a deadly metaphor for marriage from India to the Balkans in which a wife is forced to give up her freedom and mobility by the demands of her husband and his family (e.g., in patrilocal residence). But if we look at the ballad text from the builder's perspective, we may get quite a different reading. All versions of the ballad involve one or more males involved in some kind of construction enterprise. This is true whether the goal is the building of a bridge, a castle, a monastery, or a dam (to hold water). I have somewhat facetiously called this a male edifice complex (Dundes 1989:161). But the key motif is that whatever is constructed during the day is deconstructed at night. Folklorists know this as Motif D2192, Work of day magically overthrown at night. Now it is perfectly obvious that we are dealing with fantasy here inasmuch as buildings do not disappear night after night after repeated daily attempts to put them up. Thus if we consider the motif in metaphorical or symbolic terms, we must ask what could it mean to have something raised during the day to be razed at night? If we use the verb *erect* instead of *raise*, perhaps the symbology might be clearer. Men fear that they may not be able to sustain an *erect*ion, especially at night, a time for love-making. In terms of males versus females, males may try to express their masculinity by denying any dependence upon women. Boys become men by means of rites of passage (normally administered by males, not females) in which they formally repudiate any hint of maternal control. The most surprising feature of such rites of passage as Bettelheim (1962) and others have suggested is that the men frequently imitate or emulate female procreative behavior. In the ballad, men force a sacrificial woman to be enclosed in a man-made construction—just as men were originally enclosed in a female womb. That the male symbolism is not completely successful is hinted at by those versions of the ballad where the woman, though immured, is permitted to succor her *male* baby through an aperture. Still, the male message in the ballad concerns the importance of creating a *permanent erection*, and one that, in imitation of the female, can contain a human being within it. The fallacy of the "phallicy" is that the male womb results in the death of its occupant whereas female wombs—if all goes well—contain new life. In that sense, the ballad represents wishful thinking on the part of males, that they can create remarkable edifices just as women procreate, but the sad reality is that the male hubris brings only death to the female. Male death is opposed to female life, and the male insistence upon erecting his edifice complex or complex edifice means that his obedient, subordinate female must sacrifice her life for that male enterprise.

Keep in mind that one need not choose between the female or male interpretations of the walled-up wife. The ballad as sung in India more often reflects the female victim's point of view as opposed to the Balkans where the story is seemingly most frequently told from the male builder's perspective. In any event, perhaps neither the female nor the male interpretation may be deemed valid, but they are surely a welcome alternative to the simplistic, literal myth-ritual building sacrifice theory that has dominated the scholarship devoted to this extraordinary ballad up to the present time. Both these interpretations also are, unlike the earlier parochial nationalistic readings of the ballad, applicable to the ballad in *all* of its versions, not to just the versions found in Serbia, or Hungary, or Romania. Moreover, rather than tying the ballad to an unproven myth-ritual hypothesis of human sacrifice, these interpretations link the ballad to the ongoing traumatic relations prevailing in the battle of the sexes, which would help explain why the ballad continues to be a painful and poignant reminder of the difficulties of balancing a career and marriage for males, and of achieving freedom of movement and opportunity for females in India and in the Balkans.

The future of the ballad's popularity in India and the Balkans may be in question. The "liberation" of women—the very word liberation refers to the basic complex of ideas which generated the ballad in the first place, a complex that insisted that women were *not* free, *not* liberated—may in time make the ballad's message obsolete. As more and more women become builders of bridges, castles, and dams, perhaps it will be men who will be forced to become the "victims" of their wives' ambitions.

References

Anghelescu, Serban. 1984. The Wall and the Water. Marginalia to 'Master Manole'. *Cahiers Roumains d'études littéraires* 4:79–83.

Aniketana. 1989. Keregehara—A Feast for the Well. *Aniketana* 2(1):35–38.

Beaton, Roderick. 1980. *Folk Poetry of Modern Greece.* Cambridge: Cambridge University Press.

Bettelheim, Bruno. 1962. *Symbolic Wounds: Puberty Rites and the Envious Male.* New York: Collier Books.

Bompas, Cecil Henry. 1909. *Folklore of the Santal Parganas.* London: David Nutt.

Brewster, Paul G. 1971. The Foundation Sacrifice Motif in Legend, Folksong, Game, and Dance. *Zeitschrift für Ethnologie* 96:71–89.

Buchan, David. 1978. British Balladry: Medieval Chronology and Relations. In *The European Medieval Ballad: A Symposium,* ed. Otto Holzapfel, 98–106. Odense: Odense University Press.

Cammiade, L. A. 1923. Human Sacrifices to Water Spirits. *The Quarterly Journal of the Mythic Society* 13:693–694.

Campbell, A. 1891. *Santal Folk Tales.* Pokhuria: Santal Mission Press.

Čerenkov, L. N. 1962. A New Version of the Sons of the Bridge. *Journal of the Gypsy Lore Society* 41:124–133.

Cocchiara, Giuseppe. 1950. Il polite di Arta. I sacrifici nella letteratura popolare e nella storia del pensioro magico-religioso. *Annali del Museo Pitrè* 1:38–81.

De Vries, Jan. 1927. De sage van het ingemetselde kind. *Nederlandsch Tijdschrift voor Volkskunde* 32:1–13.

Dorson, Richard M. 1968. *The British Folklorists.* Chicago: University of Chicago Press.

Dundes, Alan. 1976. To Love My Father All: A Psychoanalytic Study of the Folktale Source of *King Lear. Southern Folklore Quarterly* 40:353–366.

———. 1989. The Building of Skadar: The Measure of Meaning of a Ballad of the Balkans. In *Folklore Matters,* ed. 151–168. Knoxville: University of Tennessee Press.

———. 1994. *The Cockfight: A Casebook.* Madison: University of Wisconsin Press.

Eliade, Mircea. 1972. Master Manole and the Monastery of Arges. In *Zalmoxis: The Vanishing God,* 164–190. Chicago: University of Chicago Press.

Feilberg, H. F. 1892. Levende begravet. *Aarbog for Dansk Kulturhistorie,* 1–60.

Filiti, Grégoire. 1972. Hypothèse historique sur la genèse de la ballade de Maître Manole. *Südos-Forschungen* 31:302–318.

Gilliat-Smith, B. J. 1925. The Song of the Bridge. *Journal of the Gypsy Lore Society,* 3rd series, 4:103–114.

Gittée, Aug. 1886–1887. Les rites de la construction. I. La victime enfermée. *Melusine* 3:497–498.

Govindaraja, Giraddi. 1989. The Awareness of Values in Folk Poetry. *Aniketana* 2(1):47–52.

Grimm, Jacob. 1966. *Teutonic Mythology.* 4 vols. New York: Dover.

Groome, Francis Hindes. 1899. *Gypsy Folk-Tales.* London: Hurst and Blackett.

Holbek, Bengt. 1987. *Interpretation of Fairy Tales: Danish Folklore in a European Perspective.* FF Communications No. 239. Helsinki: Academia Scientiarum Fennica.

Köhler, Reinhold. 1894. Eingemauerte Menschen. In *Aufsätze über Märchen und Volkslieder,* 36–47. Berlin: Weidmann.

Krappe, Alexander Haggerty. 1927. The Foundation and the Child's Last Words. In *Balor with the Evil Eye,* 165–180. New York: Institut des Études Françaises, Columbia University.

Krauss, Friedrich S. 1887. Das Bauopfer bei den Südslaven. *Mitteilungen der Anthropologischen Gesellschaft in Wien* 17:16–24.

Mandel, Ruth. 1983. Sacrifice at the Bridge of Arta: Sex Roles and the Manipulation of Power. *Journal of Modern Greek Studies* 1:173–183.

Megas, Georgios A. 1969–1970. Die Ballade von der Artas-Brücke. *Zeitschrift für Balkanologie* 7:43–54.

———. 1976. *Die Ballade von der Arta-Brücke: Eine vergleichende Untersuchung.* Thessanoniki: Institute for Balkan Studies.

Milović, Jevto M. 1941. *Goethe, seine Zeitgenossen und die serbokroatische Volkspoesie.* Leipzig: Harrassowitz.

Mitra, Sarat Chandra. 1922. On Some Vestiges of the Custom of Offering Human Sacrifices to Water-Spirits. *The Quarterly Journal of the Mythic Society* 12:397–405.

———. 1923. Further Note on the Custom of Offering Human Sacrifices to Water-Spirits. *The Quarterly Journal of the Mythic Society* 13:589–590.

———. 1927. On the Indian Folk-Belief about the Foundation-Sacrifice. *Man in India* 7:30–41.

O'Sullivan, Sean. 1945. Foundation Sacrifices. *Journal of the Royal Society of Antiquaries* 75:45–52.

Ortutay, Gyula. 1973. János Kriza. In *Festschrift für Robert Wildhaber,* ed. Walter Escher et al., 492–501. Basel: Verlag G. Krebs.

Parpulova, Lyubomira. 1984. The Ballad of the Walled-Up Wife: Notes about Its Structure and Semantics. *Balkan Studies* 25:425–439.

Paspati, Alexandre G. 1870. *Études sur les Tchinghianés.* Constantinople: Antoine Koromèla.

Propp, Vladimir. 1968. *The Morphology of the Folktale.* Austin: University of Texas Press.

Ramanujan, A. K. 1983. The Indian Oedipus. In *Oedipus: A Folklore Casebook,* ed. Lowell Edmunds and Alan Dundes, 234–261. New York: Garland.

Sako, Sihni. 1984. The Albanian Entombment Ballad and Other Common Balkan Different Versions. In *Questions of the Albanian Folklore,* 155–165. Tirana: 8 Nëntori.

Sainean, L. 1902. Les rites de construction d'apres la poesie populaire de l'Europe Orientale. *Revue de l'Histoire des Religions* 45:359–396.

Šapkaliska, Teodora. 1988. Die Einmauerung von Lebewesen in Bauwerken als Motiv in der Makedonischen Volksballade. In *Ballads and Other Genres,* 167–171. Zagreb: Zavod za istrazivanje folklora.

Sartori, Paul. 1898. Ober des Bauopfer. *Zeitschrift für Ethnologie* 30:1–54.

Srikantaiah, T. N. 1989. Kerege Haara—A Tribute. *Aniketana* 2(1):39–46.

Taggart, James M. 1990. *Enchanted Maidens: Gender Relations in Spanish Folktales of Courtship and Marriage.* Princeton: Princeton University Press.

Taloş, Ion. 1973. *Mesterul Manole: Contributie la studiul unei Teme de folclor european.* Bucuresti: Editura Minerva.

———. 1987. Foundation Rites. In *The Encyclopedia of Religion.* Vol. 5, ed. Mircea Eliade, 395–401. New York: Macmillan.

Vargyas, Lajos. 1967. *Researches into the Mediaeval History of Folk Ballad.* Budapest: Akadémiai Kiadó.

———. 1983. *Hungarian Ballads and the European Ballad Tradition.* Vol. II. Budapest: Akadémiai Kiadó.

Wilson, Duncan. 1986. *The Life and Times of Vuk Stefanovic Karadžić 1787–1864.* Ann Arbor: Michigan Slavic Publications.

Zimmerman, Zora Devrnja. 1979. Moral Vision in the Serbian Folk Epic: The Foundation Sacrifice of Skadar. *Slavic and East European Journal* 23:371–380.

Zipes, Jack. 1993. *The Trials & Tribulations of Little Red Riding Hood.* 2nd ed. New York: Routledge.

6

Structuralism and Folklore

(*Postscript*) Binary Opposition in Myth:
The Propp/Lévi-Strauss Debate in Retrospect

Introduction

Dundes used structuralism to define and compare folklore genres, and, methodologically, as the key element of an analytic step—deriving cultural meaning—in an objective science of folkloristics. He defined structuralism as the "study of the interrelationships or organization of the component parts of an item of folklore," and was especially drawn to Russian folklorist Vladimir Propp's morphology, which designated functions of dramatis personae within a linear plot sequence. He also was intrigued with French anthropologist Claude Lévi-Strauss's non-linear idea of binary opposition as a reflection of universal mental processes, and used it as a basis for his reflections on trichotomy as a primarily Western cognitive pattern. Dundes interacted with the French scholar when they were colleagues in anthropology at Berkeley in the fall of 1984. The kinds of questions they discussed, which drove the use of structural analysis, concerned thinking and learning processes revealed by folklore. An example is the issue of how folklore, like language, is acquired in childhood, and the ways in which structures are learned that allow the generation of variations. Dundes presented further goals for structural analysis: predicting culture change, examining cultural determination of content, and making cross-genre comparisons. As a philosophy, Dundes's version of structuralism allowed for human agency and cultural determinism, often denied in anti-humanistic structuralism, although Dundes adhered to the structuralist principle that meaning derives from causal relationships within a structure.

Dundes was introduced to Proppian theory and Russian formalism through two of his instructors at Indiana University, European folklorist Felix Oinas and Hungarian-born semiotician Thomas Sebeok, and he completed his dissertation, which he refers to in this essay, on the morphology of American Indian folktales. Dundes made a lasting contribution by revising Propp's long and rigid sequence of thirty-one functions in the folktale into a body of ten functions, grouped into five motifemic pairs. He discerned elementary sequences that are the basis of what people think of as "story": assignment of task to accomplishment of task, and lack to lack liquidated. The two sequences can combine to form a single, complex one: lack, to assignment of task, to accomplishment of task, to lack liquidated. Comparing Native American tales to European narratives, he found cultural differences in the way that the stories were separated by intervening pairs of lacks and liquidations of those lacks. He explained what he called the greater "motifemic depth" in European tales by their cultural context of deferred gratification or reward. Dundes's use of cultural psychology and functional revision has been instrumental in a number of structural analyses (including Bar-Itzhak 2005; Azuonye 1990; Bremond 1977; Turner 1972; and Skeels 1967). He also applied structural analysis to tales outside of North America (1971c).

Dundes was instrumental in expanding Proppian analysis to the English-speaking world by introducing a translation of Propp's *Morphology of the Folktale* ([1928] 1968). There, he iterated the distinction between Propp's "syntagmatic" analysis, borrowing from the notion of syntax in the study of language, and Lévi-Strauss's "paradigmatic" one, which seeks to describe a pattern or paradigm (usually based upon an a priori principle of binary opposition) underlying the folkloric text. Dundes praised paradigmatic work for relating the schematic structure to worldview and cultural context. He pointed out that Lévi-Strauss's approach facilitated the modern synchronic reconceptualization of myth (and other forms of folklore) as *models*, replacing the diachronic notion of myth as a charter set back in primeval time. Yet Dundes had methodological concerns, since, in contrast to syntagmatic approaches, paradigmatic analyses were "speculative and deductive, and they are not as easily replicated." Although praising Propp for developing a syntagmatic method that was empirical and inductive, he worried that the resultant analyses considered the text alone, in isolation from its social and cultural context. This observation led him to frequently write, in explanations of structuralism, that "structural analysis is not an end in itself." For Dundes, it was an analytical task, following identification, that led to interpretation.

The structural analytical step in Dundes's folkloristic method, occurring between identification and interpretation, typically comprised (1) discovery of a minimal unit, (2) investigation of the relationships between different minimal units in combination, and (3) cross-cultural comparisons to determine the spread or particularity of the structure. Interpretation typically discerned psychoanalytical or symbolist meanings (in this essay he mentioned examples of customs, such as bullfights and weddings, in addition to narratives and proverbs), and the determination of "worldview," that is, general outlooks, values, and beliefs that drive human action and inform ethical judgments. A structural analysis of these interpretations need not follow only Proppian or Lévi-Straussian lines. Under the category of structuralism, which Dundes identified as an evolving philosophy, he included widely known perspectives for the tripartite (syntagmatic) ordering of "rites of passage" introduced by French folklorist Arnold van Gennep, and British social anthropologist James George Frazer's paradigmatic division of homeopathic and contagious magic in the early twentieth century.

In this essay, Dundes criticized the idea of the "superorganic," which he finds pervasive both in many anthropological treatments of custom, and in literary searches for origins using the Finnish or "historic-geographic" method. This idea was introduced by evolutionist Herbert Spencer, and articulated by Berkeley anthropologist A. L. Kroeber (1917). It is a structural argument about the Western binary of social and organic forces, expressed, Kroeber stated, in other oppositions, such as body/soul, body/mind, and physical/mental. The superorganic idea implied that culture was above the level of the human organism and had a force of its own, rather than being constructed by social or individual forces. Dundes (in this essay), and others (such as his anthropological teacher David Bidney) railed against this idea, preferring the philosophy that culture involved human volition and emotion. Dundes's structuralist goal was to find minimal units of cultural expression to demonstrate this individual and social agency. Dundes criticized the historic-geographic reduction of narratives to tale types as representing a superorganic assumption, since they suggested that tales diffuse without human agency, and, as invented units, existed as ontological entities. Dundes delivered his criticism directly to the brain-center of the historic-geographic method, since he delivered this essay in Finland in 1976, home to the legacy of twentieth-century folklorist Antti Aarne and the "Aarne-Thompson" system of classification ("Thompson" refers to American folklorist Stith Thompson, who was greatly influenced by Finnish folkloristics).

In his postscript published thirty-one years later, Dundes reflected on the lasting influence of Propp and Lévi-Strauss on the structural analysis of narrative, and attempted to mediate what had been seen as opposition to their structural approaches. Dundes used the occasion to comment on the difference between how folkloristics and anthropology dealt with myth, since he took Lévi-Strauss to task for not being folkloristically aware of folklore genres. Similarly, he questioned the interpretations of psychoanalysts because of their lack of a folkloristic differentiation between tale and myth (see 2005c). In contrast, folkloristic analysis was privileged, because its structural assumptions were based upon a comparative, wide-ranging knowledge of the genres of folklore. Dundes also made other contributions to structural analysis, using it to define genres and apply cross-genre interpretation, such as in "The Structure of Superstition," "Toward a Structural Definition of the Riddle," and "On the Structure of the Proverb," included in *Analytic Essays in Folklore* (1975b), and "On Whether Weather 'Proverbs' Are Proverbs" and "April Fool and April Fish: Towards a Theory of Ritual Pranks" in *Folklore Matters* (1989d).

Structural analysis is not restricted to verbal genres; it has also been applied to non-verbal material (see, for example, Glassie 1975 and Bronner 1992, 2006a). Comparing games to narratives as an example of cross-genre analysis, Dundes structurally examined play in "On Game Morphology" (1963a; see the next chapter of the present volume). For further discussion of the structuralism of Propp and Lévi-Strauss, see Propp (1984) and Segal (1996).

By the time Dundes wrote his postscript, a "post-structuralist" movement held sway in folkloristics that was characterized by microanalyses of folkloric performances as distinct events. An open philosophical question is whether this big tent of post-structuralism runs counter to the principles established by structuralism, or if it is an outgrowth of it. Dundes's explication of modern terms of analysis in his essays "Texture, Text, and Context" and "From Etic to Emic Units in the Structural Study of Folktales" (see chapter 4) are often viewed in folkloristic historiographies as precursors of poststructuralist approaches (1980g, 1962g). Dundes's structuralist concern for the social and cultural context of lore, synchronic treatment of models (deriving from the distinction between signifier and signified), the creative generation of expressive variations, and the structure of native performance (which he called "emic" in contrast to previous, text-centered "etic" approaches) echoes through many contemporary post-structuralist analyses. Yet Dundes also expressed dismay at the lack of hypothesis building and symbolist generalization in the prevalent post-structuralist microanalysis, which implied the non-comparable uniqueness of each performance, and restricted meaning to the consciousness of the actor in a performance (see Dundes 2005c; Bronner 2006c). He adhered to uncovering underlying cognitive structures in folkloric texts, in order to explain the acquisition and generation of folklore as a renewable resource across cultures. He championed the view iterated in this essay that in revealing "patterns of metaphors," structuralist analysis "should provide unrivaled insights into the worldview and behavior of peoples everywhere."

Structuralism and Folklore

IN THE PAST SEVERAL DECADES, there is no theoretical trend which has had more impact upon both the humanities and the social sciences than structuralism. The scholarly discussions of structuralism in literature, in anthropology, and in general are part of a rapidly burgeoning bibliography.[1] There are even historical studies of the development of structuralism from Russian formalism among other intellectual precursors.[2]

The field of folkloristics is no exception and in fact the growth of structuralism in folklore scholarship has been so enormous competing schools or methods in carrying out structural analysis have emerged. Thus there are followers of Lévi-Strauss as opposed to followers of Propp to name two of the major contributors to the structural approach to folklore. Lévi-Strauss brand of structural analysis has been applied with equal fervor to the story The Three Bears[3] and to classical and Sumerian myths.[4] Propp's methodology has inspired analyses of American Indian tales,[5] African tales,[6] and Sicilian puppet plays.[7]

It is not my intention to survey all the structural studies in folklore which have been undertaken thus far. For one thing, the bibliography has become almost unmanageable. A case in point is the long list of surveys and critiques of Lévi-Strauss's narrative analysis.[8] For another, there are already useful, fairly comprehensive surveys of the folkloristic structural scholarship available in print.[9]

Nor shall I be concerned here with unraveling the influences of one structuralist upon another or with identifying early anticipations of structuralism in folklore. It is nevertheless interesting to see the suggestion in Jason's notes to her recent translation of Nikiforov's 1927 essay *On the Morphological Study of Folklore* that Propp may have borrowed several concepts central to his own morphological study from Nikiforov. Similarly, it would be interesting to know whether Lévi-Strauss was influenced directly or indirectly by French philosopher-sociologist Gabriel Tarde's ambitious attempt at the turn of the century to describe oppositional paradigms as one of the important organizing principles of both the natural world and human society. Though Tarde lacked Lévi-Strauss's cross-cultural anthropological sophistication, he does speak of such matters as the question of the reversibility or irreversibility of social facts[10] and he does suggest that the middle term of an oppositional pair can combine with one of the members of the pair to form a new opposition,[11] a proposal which seems strangely akin to Lévi-Strauss's statement about myth structure: "We need only to assume that the two opposite terms with no intermediary always tend to be replaced by two equivalent terms which allow a third one as a mediator; then one of the polar terms and the mediator becomes replaced by a new triad and so on."[12] However, questions of precursors and influences belong to the history of structuralism and this is really not my topic. Rather I should like to consider briefly some though by no means all of the theoretical issues of the application of structuralism to folklore.

First, it should be understood that structuralism, the study of the interrelationships or organization of the component parts of an item of folklore, is not limited to narrative analysis. Because of Lévi-Strauss's concern with myth and Propp's with Märchen, structural analysis is sometimes wrongly thought to be limited to folk narrative materials. This is definitely not the case. Structuralism can be applied to any genre of folklore. There are already a number of structural studies of such genres as proverb, riddle, and superstition.[13] One can argue that there is a decided advantage to applying the techniques of structural analysis to so-called minor genres. If structural analysis works at all, then it should work as well with minor genres as with major genres. As a matter of fact, the minor genres are obviously much easier to investigate inasmuch as the texts are relatively brief. Thus it would appear to be easier to attempt a structural analysis of curses or blessings or toasts than to seek to discern the structure of an epic consisting of thousands of lines.

The problems of structural analysis are approximately the same no matter what the genre. The problems include discovering or defining a minimal structural unit, and understanding how these minimal units combine into traditional patterns. Perhaps the most difficult task is the discovery of a minimal structural unit. What, if any, are the minimal units of proverbs or of riddles? Without a minimal unit, it is almost impossible to undertake structural analysis. It is true that structural analysis is more concerned with the relationships or organizational patterns of the units than with the units per se. But how can one discuss relationships intelligently without specific reference to the terms or units which are presumed to be related?

Let me give an example of a minimal structural unit from my investigations of proverbs. From an analysis of English proverbs, I have proposed the following tentative definition: "A proverb is a traditional propositional statement consisting of at least one descriptive element, a descriptive element consisting of a topic and a comment." The minimal unit is the descriptive element, although to be sure there are two component parts: the topic and the comment. It might be mentioned at this point that the critical question of precisely where to make one's "cuts," that is, where to subdivide what may well be a continuum, is not easy to settle and the answer as often as not is admittedly somewhat arbitrary. In theory, one can always divide any proposed minimal unit into still smaller units (just as molecules yield atoms which yield protons, neutrons, and electrons, etc.). My suggestion of the descriptive element as the basic minimal unit of proverbs[14] is thus not meant as necessarily being any ultimate or absolute unit. On the other hand, I believe it is a heuristic unit. For it can help to explain why there can be proverbs in English consisting of as few as two words. Examples include: Time flies; Money talks; and Opposites attract. In "Time flies," there is only one topic: time, and only one comment: flies. This proposed unit of analysis also explains why there cannot be any one-word proverbs. There may be plenty of traditional single words in slang and folk speech, but such items would not be considered proverbs if my basic unit were accepted as a valid definitional criterion. And this brings us to one of the important purposes of structural analysis in folklore: the definition of genres.

Inasmuch as structural analysis is essentially a form of rigorous descriptive ethnography, it is potentially of great interest to those folklorists concerned with genre theory. It is almost impossible to define an item of folklore in terms of origin (especially since origins are almost always unknown despite the centuries of speculative historical reconstruction efforts). It is equally unsatisfactory to try to define a genre in terms of function for it is not uncommon for different genres of folklore to fill the same functional slot. A traditional gesture may serve instead of a proverb, for example, in summing up a situation or recommending a course of action. Functionally, the gesture would be equivalent to a proverb, but not all gestures function as proverbs. So function (and context) alone are not always sufficient to determine genre. Since structural analysis is concerned with the item itself rather than factors external to the item (factors such as its origin or function), it is more likely to

be of assistance in determining the morphological characteristics of that item, characteristics which may be criteria to be used in defining a genre.

Once having proposed the descriptive element as the minimal structural unit of the
proverb, I was able to see proverbs with two or more descriptive elements in a new light.
Proverbs with two descriptive elements might have these elements in opposition (although
there are also nonoppositional proverbs). In oppositional proverbs, either the topics can
be in opposition, or the comments can be in opposition, or *both* topics and comments can
be in opposition. Examples of the latter case would be "Here today, gone tomorrow," "Last
hired, first fired," and "The spirit is willing but the flesh is weak."

Without recapitulating my entire analysis of proverb structure, I hope it is nevertheless
clear what the initial steps in structural analysis were, namely the discovery of a minimal
unit, followed by an investigation of the relationships prevailing between different minimal units in combination. Note that if a given instance of structural analysis is valid, then it
ought to be possible to replicate the analysis. Thus if my analysis of English proverb structure is sound, then other researchers ought to be able to duplicate my findings. If my analysis were applicable to non-English proverbs, then that too is testable. This is surely one
of the great advantages of structural analysis. To some extent, it is always empirically veri-
fiable. A structural analysis of a game or of a riddle can always be tested against the original data with which the analysis was made. So much of previous folklore research has been
totally unverifiable whether it was a matter of some supposed chronological or evolutionary (or devolutionary) sequence or whether it was a matter of "reading in" some interpretation albeit solar, historical, or psychoanalytic. It has always been difficult to verify interpretations of folklore and more often than not, it comes down to a matter of accepting one
interpretation rather than another on pure faith. In marked contrast, structural analysis, at
least in theory, offers the possibility of some objectivity rather than subjectivity. Of course,
it is perfectly true that there may well be subjectivity and more than a little interpretation
involved in the initial selection of a minimal unit (or even in the whole notion that there is
such a thing as a minimal constituent unit). Still, no matter how speculative the units may
be initially, they can be tested. One can take Propp's function or what I term motifeme and
check it against a corpus of folktales.

While on the subject of minimal units of analysis, I might mention the issue of whether
such units truly represent the nature of the compositional structure of the folkloristic item
under investigation or whether the units are nothing more than hypothetical though
heuristic constructs created by imaginative researchers. This theoretical issue has been
described previously as the God's truth position versus the hocus-pocus view. God's truth,
of course, implies that the units and patterning of these units actually are inherent in the
data whereas the more skeptical hocus-pocus alternative suggests that the proposed units
and unit patterns are only figments of an analyst's fertile imagination. In other words, a
God's truth folklorist might argue that folktales have structure; a hocus-pocus folklorist
might contend that the various structural schemes proposed by Bremond, Greimas, Propp,
Lévi-Strauss, etc. have been imposed upon folk narratives. The crucial question is then:
does a folklorist *discover/describe* the existent structure of folkloristic genres or does he
or she *invent/create* structural schema? Most practitioners of structural analysis assume
that they are discovering, not inventing, the patterns they discuss. Lévi-Strauss, in referring to the code he is studying in mythology, makes an unequivocal statement: "This code
. . . has neither been invented nor brought in from without. It is inherent in mythology
itself, where we simply discover its presence."[15] I too would agree generally with such a

God's truth position, that the materials of folklore really are highly structured, but I would also suggest that the various structural schemes proposed by analysts are only "manmade" approximations of God's truth. Although the structural schema almost invariably purport to be God's truth itself, it is probably much more intellectually honest to admit that structural analysis thus far has consisted largely of hocus-pocus. Ideally, each succeeding generation of structural folklorists will substitute a more accurate and refined version of structural analysis for any given genre, with each new analysis coming ever closer to describing the underlying structural pattern. On the other hand, if one assumes that there is such an underlying pattern, one must in theory admit the possibility of discerning that pattern at any point in time and consequently that any one particular analysis could be accurate enough so as not to require further refinement. In any event, the methodological implications are simply that each proposed hocus-pocus scheme must be tested and retested . . . against the empirical reality which is the subject of structural analysis. God's truth in this metaphorical sense is not necessarily unknowable.

The question of whether structure is "knowable" raises yet another important theoretical issue in structuralism. Structural analysts claim that they have identified structural patterns in myth, fairy tale, or some other genre. In short, they say they "know" what the underlying structural patterns are and that they can articulate them. But what about the informants who tell the tales? Do they "know" the structural patterns which underlie the tales they tell? Lévi-Strauss contends that as a rule they do not: "Although the possibility cannot be excluded that the speakers who create and transmit myths may become aware of their structure and mode of operation, this cannot occur as a normal thing, but only partially and intermittently. . . . In the particular example we are dealing with here, it is doubtful, to say the least, whether the natives fascinated by mythological stories, have any understanding of the systems of interrelations to which we reduce them."[16] It is true that speakers of a language are perfectly well able to speak that language without being able to articulate the rules or grammatical principles which linguists have described in considerable detail. Propp too suggests that storytellers are constrained insofar as he claims they cannot depart from the overall sequence of functions in fairytale structure,[17] which may imply that storytellers do not know the superorganic structural patterns which limit their creativity.

I wonder if it is not possible that storytellers in some sense do "know" the structural patterns which underlie their narratives. I suspect that children do in fact extrapolate folkloristic patterns such that they are well able to pass judgment as to whether a given folktale or riddle is being properly told. Even if individuals cannot articulate the patterns—and why, after all, should the creators of hocus-pocus schemes attach any significance to whether or not informants can articulate the analysts' particular brands of hocus-pocus—that does not necessarily mean that the informants are not aware of the underlying patterns. The incredible and brilliant *Conversations with Ogotemmêli* show pretty clearly that the blind hunter Ogotemmêli knew infinitely more about the structural patterns underlying Dogon culture than did professional ethnographer Marcel Griaule who had been searching for such patterns for more than fifteen years. One might here object that there is a distinction between native categories and analytic categories.[18] This is true. Native categories, from inside a culture, are always worth studying; but they may or may not constitute accurate empirical descriptions of data as sought by objective analysts from either inside or outside that culture. On the other hand, there is something unpleasantly patronizing and condescending about statements which deny natives any insight into the mechanics of their folklore. In this context, I might cite Lévi-Strauss's boast in which he states: "I therefore claim to show not how men think in myths, but how myths operate in men's minds without their being aware of the fact."[19] This view is strikingly similar to Jung's position as stated in his essay *The Psychology of the Child Archetype,* where he claims that "primitive" mentality differs from the civilized in that conscious thinking has not yet developed. In his words, "This shows itself in the circumstance that the primitive does not think *consciously,* but that thoughts *appear.* The primitive cannot assert that he thinks; it is rather that 'something thinks in him.'"[20] With this superorganic notion of abstractions operating independently in men's minds, one is not surprised to find Jung claim "The primitive mentality does not *invent* myths, it *experiences* them."[21] The human in this view is merely a passive unthinking vehicle through which archetypal myth material is transmitted. Frankly, it is extremely difficult to imagine any folklorist who had ever collected folklore in the field arguing along these lines. Informants certainly vary with respect to sensitivity and to the amount of insight they may have into the nature of their folklore, but it is surely an error to assume that folklore is learned and passed on in a totally mechanical, unreflective manner. By the same token, it is probably fair to say that, the majority of taletellers have not ever bothered to articulate the structural rules or epic laws governing the composition of their narratives. It is not so much that they could not do so, but more likely that they have little interest in doing so. It is enough to tell and enjoy a folktale without speculating at length about its compositional (and psychological) devices. Finally, since structural analysts are themselves humans and hence members of one or more folk groups, it is clear that humans are capable of selfconsciously examining the structure of their folkloristic creations.

The idea that myths and other genres of folklore can operate in men's minds without humans being aware of the fact is part of a much larger unfortunate tendency in folkloristics. I refer to the pervasiveness of superorganic thinking in folklore theory. In essence, this tendency divides folklore into folk and lore with the emphasis decidedly upon the lore. As a result, the folk are ignored. Folklore is studied as though it has little or nothing to do with people. Such notions as automigration in which tales (rather than people) migrate or the law of self-correction (that tales correct themselves), or the concept of *zersingen* according to which the very process of folklore performance is deemed destructive which is thought to result in the eventual degeneration of folklore over time, are all examples of superorganic principles or laws of folkloristics which are presumed to operate independently of human emotion and volition.

I am convinced that it is this unmitigated penchant for superorganic, "folk*less*" theory and methodology which has led to the great interest in structuralism in European folkloristic circles. With structuralism, folklorists are free to continue to concentrate upon text and text alone. Just as the comparative method treated texts wrenched from contexts, so structuralism could be applied to these same texts. Although old fashioned comparativists may have initially distrusted structuralism because of its synchronic bias (and its apparent cavalier disregard of diachronic factors), it soon became obvious to text-oriented folklorists that structuralism was a method which could be applied to the same kinds of archive materials previously utilized in comparative studies. Instead of determining subtypes and plotting charts of tale diffusion, researchers could begin to chop up texts into their supposed component parts. With structuralism as with the comparative method, it was not necessary to consider the storytelling process, or the relationship of tale content to the personalities of tale tellers and their audience.

If we think of the taletelling process as involving 1. a tale teller, 2. the tale text, and 3. the audience, we can see that both the comparative method and structuralism tend to disregard everything except the tale text. This is too bad inasmuch as it is clear that folk-lorists need to study the performance aspects of tale telling, the personal esthetics of the tale teller, and the nature of the understanding of the folktale by different members of the audience. There has been little concrete discussion in the folkloristics literature on pre-cisely what different members of an audience understand by a given item of folklore even though it is clear that the same item of folklore may mean very different things to differ-ent listeners. In terms of a simple communications model, the scholarship has been largely concerned with the encoding of the message so to speak by the sender or originator (e.g., the oral-formulaic theory) and the message itself (e.g., all the text-oriented theories and methods). Relatively little research has been devoted to the process of decoding the mes-sage, that is, the intricacies of the listener's perceptions and understandings of the mes-sage. One would think that the investigation of audiences and their different understand-ings (and misunderstandings) of folklore communication events is a likely area for future research. If Lévi-Strauss is correct when he says that myths (and by implication other folk-lore genres) operate in men's minds without their being aware of the fact, then it is obvious that the central question of what a tale-teller and his audience *consciously* understand when a tale is told could not possibly be answered by structural analysis.

A related theoretical issue in considering structuralism and folklore concerns uni-versalism. Are there universal structures? Or are structures limited to particular culture areas or individual cultures? Or are there structures peculiar to one particular folklore item? One finds studies labeled structural in which there is a single text analyzed. On the other hand, Lévi-Strauss speaks of mythical thought in general which he claims "always works from the awareness of oppositions towards their progressive mediation."[22] The implication is clearly that this alleged characteristic of mythic thought is as widespread as myth itself. Propp's morphological description of the fairy tale is based upon Russian materials, but since most if not all of the tales in the corpus are international tale types, one may well assume that Propp's analysis holds (with some variation) for at least all Indo-European Märchen. Part of the difficulty here is really a question in genre theory. Are folklore genres universal or at least cross-cultural? Is there a riddle structure which will be manifest wherever riddles exist? Or are there different riddle structures for different riddle traditions in different cultures?

This brings us to the role of structuralism with respect to identifying oicotypes. Either there will be locally popular structural patterns and thus structural oicotypes or the iden-tification of cross-cultural structural patterns will greatly assist researchers in concen-trating upon local oicotypical content differences within a common structural frame. In other words, there may be types of a structural nature or oicotypes of content. The point is that whether a folklorist employs the comparative method or structuralism, he or she is concerned with 1. defining similarities, and 2. delineating differences. I should like to stress that it is possible to discover hypothetical oicotypes through either the comparative method or structural analysis. Ideally, both methods should be employed. If one under-takes a full-fledged historic-geography study of a single tale type, one could well discover a subtype or form of the tale peculiar to a given cultural area. However, on the basis of a single local form of only one tale type, one would not really have sufficient evidence to support a claim of having isolated an oicotype. One would need to have historic-geo-graphic studies of other tale types which showed the same or similar local forms of those tales before one could comfortably assume that an oicotype had been discovered. The dif-ficulty is that not that many tales in the Aarne-Thompson canon have been subjected to a comprehensive historic-geographic monographic treatment. Thus a cautious scholar committed only to the comparative method in folktale studies might feel it was premature to search for potential oicotypes by making a "comparative study of comparative studies" of folktales. Here is where structural analysis can be of considerable assistance. If a folklorist undertakes a structural analysis of even a single text from a given culture, and if he or she is successful in articulating the structural pattern, he or she may in fact have isolated a pattern which is oicotypical. For a structural analysis, one does not need the thousands or at any rate hundreds of versions of a single tale type so essential for a historic-geographic study. So long as the one text were representative (and admittedly some additional texts of the tale would be necessary to determine this), the structural analysis might be useful. If a structural pattern were discerned, one would then seek to discover if the identical pattern were to be found in other tale types. This could be accomplished in a matter of days rather than the years it takes to complete even a single historic-geographic study. If a consistent structural pattern were identified in this way—as I believe I have demonstrated in the case of the Unsuccessful Repetition pattern in Lithuanian folktales—then an oicotype may have been discovered. If the delineation of a hypothetical oicotype is accurate, then it should be theoretically possible to predict in advance what will happen to tales which are borrowed by the culture in question. I have tried to show, for example, how European tales have been recast into American Indian structural patterns[23] and into African structural patterns.[24] Comparative studies and structural studies are thus hardly mutually exclusive. To the contrary, these often opposed methods are highly compatible and they may be mutually supportive. If one located a hypothetical oicotype, one might wish to see if the same or similar local form were found elsewhere. If it were, this would not necessarily destroy the value of the initially discovered oicotype. If there are other cultures with a penchant for unsuccessful repetition, that would not invalidate the discovery that Lithuanians have such an oicotype.[25] Admittedly, it is more likely that content rather than structure will be oicotypical. Structures appear to be cross-cultural (though not necessarily universal) whereas content seems to be more often than not culturally relative.

I should like to indicate my conviction that structures are not necessarily limited to single folklore genres. This is not to deny that structural analysis may be useful in defining genres. Rather it is a question of the possible arbitrariness of genre definitions as well as of the entire subject matter of folklore itself. If structural patterns are culture-wide phenomena (leaving aside the question of possible universality of such patterns for the moment), then it would be folly to assume that structural patterns are limited to single genres of folklore. In this sense, it is misleading for Olrik to claim that the "Law of Three" (das Gesetz der Dreizahl) is strictly an epic law peculiar to folk literature.[26] I have attempted to show that such a pattern is characteristic of American (and Indo-European) thought in general.[27] This in no way minimizes the value of undertaking structural analyses of folkloristic materials. It is precisely because general cultural patterns are so explicit in folkloristic materials that makes structural analysis of folklore so important. If we are successful in isolating and describing a structural pattern present in an item or genre of folklore, we may have provided a useful aid to understanding the nature of the culture at large as well as the cognitive categories, ideological commitments, and concrete behavior of the people sharing that culture. For surely one of the goals of structural analysis of folklore or any other variety of cultural materials (language, written literature, etc.) is to afford insight into worldview. It is difficult to gain access to the worldview of another culture (or even to one's own worldview). But if the identification of structural patterns in folklore can be of service in articulating the basic nature of one's own worldview and the worldviews of others, then the study of folklore would be absolutely indispensable to a better understanding of humanity.

In evaluating the achievements of Lévi-Strauss and Propp with respect to the above mentioned issues, we find that Lévi-Strauss is very much concerned with relating structural patterns to worldview. Propp in contrast, admittedly working at an earlier period and from more of a literary than an anthropological perspective, tended to study structural patterns as ends in themselves. To be sure, Lévi-Strauss and Propp are not concerned with the same types of structural patterns. Propp was primarily interested in identifying the sequential, continuous or syntagmatic structure of Russian fairy tales. Lévi-Strauss on the other hand wishes to identify oppositional patterns of discontinuities, or the paradigmatic structure of myth in general. Lévi-Strauss is perfectly well aware of the sequential structure of myth; he just doesn't consider it very important. It is the underlying "schemata" rather than the "sequences" of myth which interest him. In his words, "The sequences form the apparent content of the myth; the chronological order in which things happen."[28] As sociologists seek latent as opposed to manifest function and as psychoanalysts seek latent as opposed to manifest content, Lévi-Strauss seeks underlying paradigmatic patterns rather than what he considers to be the apparent, manifest sequential structure. Lévi-Strauss's goal is analogous to Chomsky's search for deep structure as opposed to superficial surface structure (and perhaps also to Jung's search for universal archetypes). In his early essay on "The Structural Study of Myth," Lévi-Strauss states (my emphasis), "The myth will be treated as would be an orchestra score *perversely* presented as a unilinear series and everywhere our task is to re-establish the correct disposition."[29] The "perverse" sequential or syntagmatic structure, that is, the narrative structure studied by Propp is clearly not the object of Lévi-Strauss's type of structural analysis.

In my opinion, Lévi-Strauss is not analyzing the structure of myth narrative, that is the compositional structure of myths as narrated, but rather he is analyzing the structure of the world described in myths. This is a perfectly legitimate intellectual enterprise. It is simply a different intellectual enterprise from Propp's attempt to analyze the sequential structure of Russian fairy tales. The difference is thus between the structure of myth as a narrative genre and the structure of the image of reality depicted in the world defined by the myth. Propp is concerned with the structure of a continuum, of continuities; Lévi-Strauss is concerned with the structural pattern of discontinuities. Since Lévi-Strauss is trying to identify oppositional paradigms in the world described in myth, he does not choose to be limited by the chronological order in which elements of the paradigm occur in a given narrative. If high/low, night/day, male/female, etc. instances occur anywhere in the narrative, Lévi-Strauss feels free to extrapolate them and re-order them in his delineations of the paradigm. Moreover, since it is the world described in myth rather than any one myth itself which is of interest, Lévi-Strauss is not limited to the data contained in a single myth (or even of myths of a single culture). Any data in any myth can be used *comparatively* to illuminate different exemplifications of the oppositional paradigm. In effect, Lévi-Strauss's methodology in *Mythologiques* is as much a tour de force of the comparative method (though not exactly the historic-geographic variety!) as it is of structuralism. In any event, whether one prefers Lévi-Strauss's paradigmatic brand of structural analysis to Propp's syntagmatic or not, one must applaud his attempt to relate the structural patterns he discerns to the society (and world) at large. For instance, Lévi-Strauss often tries to show how the pattern he finds in myth is isomorphic with kinship among other patterns in the culture.

For all Lévi-Strauss's interest in demonstrating the widespread nature of binary oppositional structures, he makes relatively little use of the total range of folklore genres. Here one must keep in mind that despite Lévi-Strauss's extended analyses of myth, he is really not a folklorist. Rather, he is like so many anthropologists and philosophers inasmuch as he tends to restrict his research with folkloristic materials to myth alone, or any rate to folk narrative since some of the items he treats are folk-tales rather than myths. It was Köngäs and Maranda in *Structural Models in Folklore* who first drew attention to the possible extension of Lévi-Strauss's analysis of myth to other genres of folklore. On the other hand, the notion of the centrality of opposition to folkloristic genres was quite clearly stated by Danish folklorist Axel Olrik as one of his epic laws, namely the Law of Contrast (*das Gesetz des Gegensatzes*) in the first decade of the twentieth century. The point is that it would appear that oppositions are just as important in the structure of riddles and proverbs as in the structure of myth. Oppositions are equally prominent in other genres.

In some cases, actual oppositions in nature or at least what is perceived as an opposition may be the subject of folklore. For example, Kuusi has masterfully demonstrated the vast distribution of traditional descriptions of what various peoples say on those occasions when sunshine and rain occur at the same time, e.g., the devil is beating his wife. The simultaneous occurrence of sunshine and rain is surely understood as an instance of opposition. Sometimes, oppositions in nature are imagined as is commonly the case in locutions for never such as "When water runs uphill."[30] Consider the following autograph book verse:

> When roses bloom in winter,
> And the snowflakes fall in June;
> When the sun shines at midnight,
> And the moon shines at noon;
> When the waters cease their flowing,
> And two times two are ten;
> When joy is sorrow and today is tomorrow,
> Maybe I'll forget you then.

There is surely no dearth of examples of opposition in folklore. Sometimes an opposition in nature, so to speak, is used as a model for a would-be opposition in culture. For example, the fact that hens occasionally crow like roosters has been used by the folk in the following way:

> A whistling maid and a crowing hen
> Are neither fit for gods nor men.

In this instance, we find male chauvinism making use of the opposition to recommend that women restrict themselves to socially defined women's roles and behavior. A maid who whistles (like a boy) is by analogy depicted as being as unnatural as a hen which crows (like a rooster). I might mention parenthetically that male chauvinism in folklore is not limited to denying women the right to assume male roles or practice activities normally associated with males. Male chauvinism also includes men usurping roles or activities normally associated with women. These oppositions are not challenged. The most obvious example concerns the ability to bear children. From the creation of Eve from Adam's rib and Noah's building his ark to float around for approximately nine months right down to modern folklore, we find countless instances of males denying female procreativity and in fact appropriating such activity for themselves. Patriarchal societies evidently needed male creation narratives to bolster their sense of male superiority. Modern examples might include a male rotund Santa Claus who delivers packages down the chimney, the male stork who explicitly delivers babies down the same chimney, and finally the male easter bunny who brings eggs—eggs being clearly associated with females. Whereas the would-be attempt of women to act like men (as in whistling) is singled out for scorn, there is no comparable conscious criticism of men's usurpation of the female childbearing role in either narrative or custom (e. g., couvade).

It is easy to think of hundreds of examples of the occurrence of oppositions in folklore for as Olrik observed such opposition constitutes a major rule of epic composition.[31] Hero-villain, trickster-dupe would be examples of individual characters in opposition, but sometimes the opposition is contained in a single character. Half-man/half-animal, e.g., a mermaid, or similar combinations of god and man or god and animal would be examples. The wise fool who commonly combines folly and wisdom and who may confuse the literal and the metaphorical would be another. Indeed, a wise fool of the Hodja variety is a veritable walking oxymoron. Perhaps the prime illustration of the centrality of opposition or paradox in folklore would be virgin birth.

In view of this, it is tempting to argue that all folklore, not just myth, consists of forming and attempting to resolve oppositions. The oppositions may concern life/ death, good/ evil, truth/falsehood, love/hate, innocence/guilt, male/female, man/god, large/small, child/adult, etc. If pleasure truly does depend upon the reduction of tension, then one of the reasons why folklore gives pleasure is because it reduces the tensions it creates by resolving oppositions. In folk-tales, the paradoxical tasks, e.g., carrying water in a sieve, are invariably solved by the hero or heroine. The apparent contradiction in oppositional riddles is always resolved by the answer to the riddle. In proverbs, the formation of the opposition may itself be an answer or response to a question posed in life, e.g., "The longest way round is the shortest way found" suggests that what appears to be the longer path may in fact be the most direct and efficient. This is analogous to the modest choice motif (L 211) in which the worst looking casket proves to be the best choice. The same opposition between appearance and reality is common in proverbs, e.g., "Good things come in small packages" or "Never judge a book by its cover."

A recognition of the oppositional structure of so much of folklore makes it easier to understand the different functional contexts of folklore. Van Gennep in his classic *The Rites of Passage* made one of the first structural studies of folklore. One does not always think of Van Gennep as a structuralist, but his own statement of purpose clearly identifies him as such. "The purpose of this book is altogether different. Our interest lies not in the particular rites but in their essential significance and their relative positions within ceremonial wholes—that is, their order." As all folklorists know, Van Gennep identified a syntagmatic structural pattern of separation, transition, and incorporation. In his words, "The underlying arrangement is always the same. Beneath a multiplicity of forms, either consciously expressed or merely implied, a typical pattern always recurs: *the pattern of the rites of passage.*"[32] This is unquestionably a structuralist perspective. I would add that changes of state or status imply transition between two opposed categories. Thus funerals are transitions from life to death; weddings are transitions from unmarried to married (and also resolutions of oppositions between two family units, one of the bride and one of the groom). Giving birth to a child makes one a parent. All these critical life crises are marked by folklore. Folklore tends to cluster around times of anxiety be it in the individual life cycle or the calendrical cycle of the entire community. (The transition from winter to spring of course involves another opposition, from death to life). In view of this one might go so far as to argue that it is in part the oppositional nature of much of folklore which makes it so appropriate for such critical times. For example, I have suggested that one reason why riddles might be told at wakes is that answering oppositional riddles might provide a microcosm of the desire to resolve the opposition between the living and the dead at a funeral rite.[33] Similarly, I have suggested that one reason why riddles are used so often in courtship rituals might be because of their oppositional structure.[34] In exogamous societies, the bride and groom must be unrelated. The marriage qua ritual essentially relates two individuals who were previously unrelated. Riddles, structurally speaking, may provide a model for this event. The descriptive elements in opposition make it appear that the elements are unrelated. The answer to the riddle succeeds in eliminating the apparent contradiction and unites the elements in harmony. If this explanation is at all valid, then structural analysis can be seen as a useful tool for anyone who wishes to explain *why* a given genre or item of folklore is used precisely when it is. If the structure of an item of folklore can be shown to be isomorphic with the structure of the specific context in which that item occurs, then we may have advanced considerably in our understanding of folkloristic phenomena and how such phenomena function.

The point which is crucial is that structural analysis is not an end in itself. It is only a means to an end, that end being a better understanding of the nature of human beings, or at least of a particular society of humans. The possible if not probable universality of binary opposition in folklore may suggest that structural analysis may not, after all, be very useful in defining genres or revealing cultural differences. That is a legitimate criticism of any universal principle. It is equally true of Frazer's laws or principles of sympathetic magic. If homeopathic magic is universal, then it cannot be used to differentiate one culture from another. However, by the same token, the existence of universal structural principles would in no way preclude culturally relative content analyses. The universal principle is one thing; its concrete manifestation in one or more specific cultural contexts may be another. For example, in American wedding ritual, the bride throws a bouquet of flowers to her bridesmaids. This can be understood as a homeopathic articulation of her willingness or wish to be deflowered. (The bridesmaid who catches the bouquet is said to be the next to marry which would be an exemplification of contagious magic.) The issue here is not necessarily the validity of this interpretation so much as the fact that it was the application of a universal principle, that of homeopathic magic, which provided the clue for a symbolic explanation of why a particular item of folklore, in this case, a custom, was appropriate in a given context. In the same way, the slipping of a circular ring over an outstretched finger provides a homeopathic model for the sexual consummation of the marriage. (The fact that it is the groom who places the ring on the bride's finger suggests that marriage provides sanctioned access to or control over the genitals of one's spouse.) Some conservative folklorists may object to such symbolic interpretations of wedding customs, but whether it is throwing rice (seed, semen) to wish homeopathically (and contagiously) the newlyweds a fertile union or whether in Jewish weddings it is the groom's breaking a glass (virginity) with his foot, the appropriateness of such ritual behavior in such a context seems clear enough. Again, the correctness or incorrectness of the interpretation is not the issue. Rather it is the possibility of utilizing a universal organizing principle, in this instance, homeopathic magic, to explain a particular piece of folkloristic behavior. (In this context, we can understand the outbreak of "streaking," running naked, that is, uncovered, in a public place as in part a symbolic statement of social protest against the "cover-up" of the Watergate political scandal of the early 1970's.)

Not all structural analysis claims universality. Propp's morphology used only Russian materials and there is no reason to assume universality without so much as testing a given structural formulation against materials from a large sampling of cultures. But even if Propp's morphology applies only to Russian culture (or to Indo-European cultures as it most probably does), the question of the meaning of Propp's analysis remains unanswered. Propp convincingly demonstrated the syntagmatic structure of European Märchen, but he did not say very much about the meaning of the pattern he delineated. Admittedly, structural analysis is objective or at least it is supposed to be whereas the interpretation of a structural pattern is subjective. Yet without interpretation, structural analysis can be just as trivial and sterile as motif and tale type identification. It is not enough to identify or describe, though description is a necessary first step. Structural analysis without interpretation is little more than a form of academic gamesmanship in which the construction of some more or less abstruse model is seen as the ultimate goal. What then is the significance of Propp's morphology? How does the pattern he described in such exemplary detail relate to Russian or European culture as a whole?

If we apply Van Gennep's structural pattern to Propp's morphology, we can see that functions 1–11 constitute a sequence of separation. Function 1, One of the members of a family absents himself from home, to function 11, The hero leaves home, seem to describe the break up or departure from one's natal family. Function 15, The hero is transferred, delivered, or led to the whereabouts of an object of search, to function 31, The hero is married and ascends the throne, might be said to constitute a sequence of incorporation. The incorporation involves the formation of a new family unit (through marriage). In terms of Van Gennep's scheme of analysis, the crucial transitional sequence would be Propp's functions 12 through 14, the donor sequence. It is the donor, often encountered in an area between the hero's homeland and the other land, who makes it possible for him to succeed in his quest. If the fairy tale is in part an account of a marriage quest, then the donor figure may be serving the role of a matchmaker.

The difficulty the hero or heroine has in leaving home may reflect the comparable difficulties one encounters in life in leaving home. Similarly, the even greater obstacles encountered in the other land from the eventual spouse's family may also be accurate in terms of the problems which need to be solved whenever an individual moves in to live with his or her in-laws. The transition from childhood to adulthood and its successful completion through marriage may thus be one of the primary subjects of fairytales. From tales, children may be expected to learn that one must leave the security of one's initial home to find a suitable spouse. Whether one brings a spouse home or stays on to live in the spouse's land would simply reflect the different possibilities of postnuptial residence, e.g., patrilocal or matrilocal.

I do not wish to be misconstrued as believing that fairytales reflect only normal everyday ordinary life. Fairytales are fantasy, one must remember. They are very much analogous to dreams. If being asleep and being awake are in opposition, then dreams are intermediate. One is asleep, but one imagines one is awake. So in a similar manner, the fairytale takes place once upon a time, outside of normal time and space, but it is told as though it were reality, in real time and space. (To the extent that dreams are inevitably narrated, they often take on the appearance of folktales. Whereas some scholars have argued that dreams are the source of folktales, I see no reason for assuming that any one clement of culture is necessarily logically prior to any other element of culture. It is equally possible that patterns of dream narrative are in fact derived from folktales. It would be interesting to apply Propp's morphology, for example, to dreams of individuals from Indo-European cultures to see the extent, if any, to which dream structure resembles fairytale structure.)

My own view of fairytales is that they express child-parent conflicts and also sibling rivalry. Boys conquer large male rivals (giants, dragons) while girls outwit large female rivals (stepmothers, witches) as well as evil brothers or sisters. Ambivalence towards parents is suggested by the fact that the donor figure and the villain may be the same sex. In Cinderella, the heroine may be helped by a cow or fairy godmother while she is hindered by a wicked stepmother. Similarly, in male centered fairytales, the donor figure and the villain may both be male, suggesting a son's ambivalence towards his father. To the extent that the so-called Freudian family romance may be reflected in fairytales, I believe it would be a mistake to think that fairytales were no more than fictionalized accounts from the old, natal family to the new, conjugal family. The point is simply that Propp's morphology makes it possible to speculate about the significance of fairytales in new ways.

It is precisely this possibility of seeing folklore in new ways which makes structural analysis worthwhile. Let me give another example. In comparing the morphology of North American Indian tales and European tales, I drew attention to the number of motifemes which intervened between the members of a motifeme pair such as Lack and Lack Liquidated.[35] Specifically, I suggested that American Indian folktales had a lesser *motifemic depth* than European tales. In Propp's morphology, there arc many functions which may occur between 8a and 19, Lack and Liquidation of the Lack. Cumulative tales[36] also reflect comparable motifemic depth insofar as the initial lack may be separated from final liquidation by a whole series of intervening pairs of lacks and liquidations of those lacks. I failed to say, however, that the greater motifemic depth of European tales might reflect an important principle of European culture and that is the whole notion of deferred gratification or reward. I have since analyzed the future orientation in American worldview in these terms and I even suggested that the popularity of the shaggy dog story in which an excessively long buildup to what is usually regarded as a disappointing punch line is essentially a metacultural parody of this worldview principle.[37] The practice of living for the future either the immediate future or for life in the next world is made fun of in the shaggy dog story insofar as it is implied that the reward is never worth the long wait. The shaggy dog story builds expectations only to deny them in contrast to fairytales and cumulative tales in which expectations are almost always fulfilled. What is important in the present context is that the structure of narrative is closely related to principles or elements of world-view.

We may hope that the rewards of structural analysis will not be long deferred. As more and more structural analyses of folklore genres and items are undertaken, we stand to gain more and more insight into both folklore and folk. It is not enough to collect and classify folklore. Nor is it sufficient to carry out structural analyses without interpretation. Structural studies, like comparative studies, should be the jumping off points for interpretation. For example, it is not enough to analyze the structure of the game of Chinese chess or even to compare its traits with European chess. What folklorists should be interested in is establishing the existence of oicotypes and the relationships of oicotypes to such matters as national character, ideology, and worldview. Thus in Chinese chess, it is such details as the lack of a queen among the chess pieces which is of particular interest. The male bias in Chinese social organization (where women are expected to be servile, obedient, and to stay out of men's way) is clearly reflected in Chinese chess. Actually, Chinese chess is almost certainly an older form than European chess. So the addition of the powerful queen and the presence of a relatively weak king in European chess should be of interest to students of European family structure, especially in view of the psychoanalytic interpretation of chess according to which the object of the game is to put the opposing king (father) in jeopardy/ check so that he cannot move (impotence?), often by using one's own queen (mother) effectively.[38] Regardless of whether or not the term "checkmate" does derive from the Persian words "shah" "mat" (the king is dead), it is curious that the English words strongly suggest suppressing a "mate," perhaps the mate of the opponent's queen. The relevance of checking a queen's mate in the light of the Oedipus complex according to which one wishes to eliminate the father in order to have one's mother to oneself ought to be obvious enough. It is probably no accident that the addition of the queen in chess occurred at approximately the same time in history (eleventh or twelfth century) as the emergence of the Madonna complex in southern Europe.

The interpretation of the structural features need not, of course, be psychoanalytic. That is simply my own personal bias. I believe that structural analysis can facilitate all kinds of different modes of interpretation. Again, in Chinese chess, the equivalent of pawns, that is, soldiers, can move to the eighth rank at the opposite end of the board. However, whereas pawns in European chess can be transformed into queens or other powerful pieces, the pawns in Chinese chess must remain pawns. The possible implications with respect to differences in patterns of social mobility are clear. The analogy for folktale study is simply that we must go beyond the comparative listing of motifs and traits in different cultural areas. We must not stop with structural descriptions of Russian fairytales. We must make attempts to interpret the meanings (and I use the plural advisedly) of folklore. It is not enough to say that folklore is a mirror of a culture. We must try to see what it is that folklore reflects.

I believe it is through structural analysis that we may best view the reflection afforded by folklore. First we need rigorous structural descriptions of the kind provided by Bouissac for the lion tamer's act in the circus, but we also need interpretative studies showing how the structural patterns provide metaphors for the culture at large, studies such as Geertz's brilliant analyses of Javanese shadow puppet plays[39] and the Balinese cockfight.[40] It would be possible, for example, to describe the structure of a Spanish or Mexican bull fight in a manner similar to Bouissac's superb account of circus acts, but if the analysis failed to relate the struggle between man and bull to Spanish and Mexican norms of masculinity, it would be insufficient. In the bullfight, there is a battle to see who penetrates whom. The matador tries to place his sword in the bull (after allowing the bull to make many passes) while the bull presumably is trying to gore the matador. The loser, the one penetrated, is emasculated or feminized. If the matador is particularly brilliant, he may be awarded various extremities of the bull, e.g., the ears, hooves, tail, etc. which suggests the complete humiliation of the bull. Whether the bull is a father symbol or simply another male, the battle represents the matador's attempt to demonstrate in public his masculine prowess at the expense of another male, a pattern which is also to be found in verbal dueling among adolescent males throughout the Mediterranean area.[41]

In sum, I would say that structural analysis is but one of the methodological techniques available to folklorists. In combination with the comparative method, it can be used to define genres and identify oicotypes. After rigorous structural descriptions, the folklorists may be better able to see how folklore contains and communicates the central metaphors of a society. The analysis and interpretation of these patterns of metaphors should provide unrivalled insights into the worldview and behavior of peoples everywhere.

Notes

1. Cf. Bastide 1962; Gardner 1972; Parain-Vial 1969; Piaget 1970; Scholes 1974; Viet 1965.
2. Cf. Ehrlich 1955, and especially Jameson 1972.
3. Hammel 1972.
4. Kirk 1970.
5. Dundes 1964b.
6. Paulme 1972.
7. Pasqualino 1970.
8. E.g. Boon 1972; Geertz 1967; Leach 1970; Scholte 1969.
9. Cf. Dundes 1964b; Hendricks 1970; Maranda 1972. Meletinsky 1970, 1971 and 1973; Pop 1967a, 1967b, and 1968; Teneze 1970; Voigt 1969 and 1972; Waugh 1969; for bibliography Breymayer 1972b.
10. Tarde 1902, 69.
11. Tarde 1897, 292–293.
12. Lévi-Strauss 1955, 40.
13. For proverb, see Dundes 1975; Greimas 1970, 309–314; Kuusi 1966 and 1972; Milner 1969a, 1969b and 1969c. For riddle, see Georges and Dundes 1963. Köngäs-Maranda 1971; Scott 1969; Todorov 1973. For superstition, see Dundes 1961.
14. and riddles, cf. Georges and Dundes 1963.
15. Lévi-Strauss 1969, 12.
16. Ibid., 11–12.
17. Propp 1968, 112.
18. Ben-Amos 1969.
19. Lévi-Strauss 1969, 12.
20. Jung 1963.
21. Ibid.
22. Lévi-Strauss 1955, 440.
23. Dundes 1964b, 99–100.
24. Dundes 1971, 179–180.
25. Dundes 1962.
26. Olrik 1965, 133–134.
27. Dundes 1968.
28. Lévi-Strauss 1967, 17.
29. Lévi-Strauss 1955, 432.
30. Cf. Taylor 1948/1949.
31. Olrik 1965, 135–136.
32. Van Gennep 1960, 191.
33. Dundes 1963, 217.
34. Dundes 1964b, 257.
35. Ibid., 94.
36. Cf. Propp 1973.
37. Dundes 1969.
38. Cf. Reider 1959.
39. Geertz 1957.
40. Geertz 1972.
41. Cf. Ingham 1964, Zurcher and Meadow 1967.

References

Anozie, Sunday O. (ed.) 1970. Structuralism and African Folklore. *The Conch* 2, no. 2.

Barnes, Daniel R. 1970. Folktale Morphology and the Structure of Beowulf. *Speculum* 45.

Bastide, Roger 1962. *Sens et usages du terme structure dans les sciences humaines et sociales*. The Hague.

Ben-Amos, Dan 1969. Analytical Categories and Ethnic Genres. *Genre* 2.

Boon, James A. 1972. *From Symbolism to Structuralism: Lévi-Strauss in a Literary Tradition*. New York.

Bouissac, Paul 1971. Poetics in the Lion's Den: The Circus Act as a Text. *Modern Language Notes* 86.

Bremond, Claude 1964. Le message narratif. *Communications* 4.

———— 1966. La logique des possibles narratifs. *Communications* 8.

———— 1970. Morphology of the French Folktale. *Semiotica* 2.

———— 1973. *Logique du recit*. Paris.

Breymayer, Reinhard 1972a. Vladimir Jakovlevič Propp (1896–1970). Leben, Wirken und Bedeutsamkeit. *Linguistica Biblica* 15/16.

———— 1972b. Bibliographic zum Werk Vladimir Jakovlevič Propps und zur strukturalen Erzählforschung. *Linguistica Biblica* 15 /16.

Calgeras, Roy C. 1973. Lévi-Strauss and Freud: Their "Structural " Approaches to Myths. *American Imago* 30.

Caws, Peter 1968. What is Structuralism? *Partisan Review* 35.

Chabrol, C. and L. Marin (eds.) 1971. Sémiotique narrative: récits bibliques. *Langages* 6, no. 23.

———— 1974. *Le récit évangelique*. Paris.

Colby, B. N. 1966a. The Analysis of Culture Content and the Pattering of Narrative Concern in Texts. *American Anthropologist* 75.

———— 1966b. Cultural Pattern in Narrative. *Science* 151.

———— 1973. A Partial Grammar of Eskimo Folktales. *American Anthropologist* 75.

Doležel, Lubomir 1972. From Motifemes to Motifs. *Poetics* 4.

Dorfles, Gillo 1965. Pour ou contre l'esthétique structuraliste. *Revue Internationale de Philosophic* 19.

Drobin, Ulf 1969. A Review of Structuralism. *Temenos* 5.

Dundes, Alan 1961. Brown County Superstitions. *Midwest Folklore* 11.

————1962. The Binary Structure of "Unsuccessful Repetition" in Lithuanian Folk Tales. *Western Folklore*.

———— 1964a. On Game Morphology: A Study of the Structure of Non-Verbal Folklore. *New York Folklore Quarterly* 20.

———— 1964b. *The Morphology of North American Indian Folktales*. FFC 195. Helsinki.

————1964c. Texture, Text and Context. *Southern Folklore Quarterly* 28.

———— 1968. The Number Three in American Culture. Alan Dundes (ed.), *Every Man His Way*. Englewood Cliffs.

———— 1969. Thinking Ahead: A Folkloristic Reflection of the Future Orientation in American Worldview. *Anthropological Quarterly* 42.

———— 1971. The Making and Breaking of Friendship as a Structural Frame in African Folktales. Pierre Maranda and Elli Köngäs-Maranda (eds.), *Structural Analysis of Oral Tradition*. Philadelphia.

———— 1975. On the Structure of the Proverb. *Proverbium* 25.

Ehrlich, Victor 1955. *Russian Formalism*. The Hague.

Fabre, Daniel 1969. Jean de L'Ours: Analyse formelle et thématique d'un conte populaire. *Travaux du Laboratoire d'Ethnographie et de Civilisation Occitanes* 2. Carcassonne.

Gardner, Howard 1972. *The Quest for Mind: Piaget, Lévi-Strauss and the Structuralist Movement*. New York.

Geertz, Clifford 1957. Ethos, World-View and the Analysis of Sacred Symbols. *The Antioch Review* 17.

———— 1967. The Cerebral Savage: On the Work of Claude Lévi-Strauss. *Encounter* 28.

———— 1972. Deep Play: Notes on the Balinese Cockfight. *Daedalus, Proceedings of the American Academy of Arts and Sciences* 101, no. 1.

Geninasca, Jacques and Catherine Geninasca 1972. Conte populaire et identité du cannibalisme. *Nouvelle Revue de Psychanalyse* 6.

Georges, Robert A. 1970. Structure in Folktales: A Generative-Transformational Approach. *The Conch* 2, no 2.

Georges, Robert A. and Alan Dundes 1963. Toward a Structural Definition of the Riddle. *Journal of American Folklore* 76.

Glassie, Henry 1973. Structure and Function, Folklore and the Artifact. *Semiotics* 7.

Greimas, Algirdas Julien 1965. Le conte populaire russe (Analyse functionelle). *International Journal of Slavic Linguistics and Poetics* 9.

———— 1966. *Sémantique structurale*. Paris.

———— 1970. *Du Sens: Essais sémiotiques*. Paris.

———— 1971. Narrative Grammar: Units and Labels. *Modern Language Notes* 86.

Griaule, Marcel 1965. *Conversations with Ogotemmêli: An Introduction to Dogon Religious Ideas.* London.

Hammel, Eugene A. 1972. *The Myth of Structural Analysis: Lévi-Strauss and the Three Bears.* Addison-Wesley Module in Anthropology 25.

Hansen, Barge 1971. *Folkeeventyr. Struktur og genre.* Copenhagen.

Hendricks, William O. 1970. Folklore and the Structural Analysis of Literary Texts. *Language and Style* 3.

———— 1973a. Linguistics and Folkloristics. *Current Trends in Linguistics* 12.

———— 1973b. Methodology of Narrative Structural Analysis. *Semiotica* 7.

———— 1973c. Verbal Art and the Structuralist Synthesis. *Semiotica* 7.

Holbek, Bengt 1972. *Structuralisme og folkloristik.* Folk og Kultur.

Ingham, John M. 1964. The Bullfighter: A Study in Sexual Dialectic. *American Imago* 21.

Jameson, Fredric 1972. *The Prison-House of Language: A Critical Account of Structuralism and Russian Formalism.* Princeton.

Jason, Ueda 1971. The Narrative Structure of Swindler Tales. *Arv* 27.

Jung, C. G. 1963. *The Psychology of the Child Archetype.*

———— C. G. Jung and C. Kerenyi. [1963] *Essays on a Science of Mythology.* New York.

Kermode, Frank 1969. The Structures of Fiction. *Modem Language Notes* 84.

Kirk, G. S. 1970. *Myth: Its Meaning and Functions in Ancient and Other Cultures.* Berkeley and Los Angeles.

Köngäs, Elli-Kaija and Pierre Maranda 1962. Structural Models in Folklore. *Midwest Folklore* 12.

Köngäs-Maranda, Elli 1969. Structure des énigmes. *L'Homme* 9.

———— 1971, The Logic of Riddles. Pierre Maranda and Elli Köngäs-Maranda (eds.), *Structural Analysis of Oral Tradition.* Philadelphia.

Kuusi, Matti 1957. *Regen bei Sonnenschein; zur Weltgeschichte eine Redensart.* FFC171. Helsinki.

———— 1966. Ein Vorschlag für die Terminologie der paromiologischen Strukturanalyse. *Proverbium* 5.

———— 1972. *Towards an International Type-System of Proverbs.* FFC 211. Helsinki.

Lane, Michael 1970. *Introduction to Structuralism.* New York.

Laubscher, Annemarie 1968. Betrachtungen zur Inhaltsanalyse von Erzählgut. *Paideuma* 14.

Leach, Edmund 1961. *Lévi-Strauss in the Garden of Eden: An Examination of Some Recent Developments in the Analysis of Myth.* Transactions of the New York Academy of Sciences 23.

———— 1967. *The Structural Study of Myth and Totemism.* London.

———— 1970. *Claude Lévi-Strauss.* New York.

Lévi-Strauss, Claude 1955. The Structural Study of Myth. *Journal of American Folklore* 78.

———— 1960. L'Ananyse morphologique des contes russes. *International Journal of Slavic Linguistics and Poetics* 3.

———— 1964. *Mythologiques I: Le Cru et le Cuit.* Paris.

———— 1966. *Mythologiques II: Du Miel aux cendres.* Paris.

———— 1967. The Story of Asdiwal. Edmund Leach (ed.). *The Structural Study of Myth and Totemism.* London.

———— 1968. *Mythologiques III: L'Origine des manières de table.* Paris.

———— 1969. *The Raw and the Cooked.* New York.

———— 1971. *Mythologiques IV: L'Homme Nu.* Paris.

Levin, Isidor 1967. Vladimir Propp: An Evaluation on his Seventieth Birthday. *Journal of the Folklore Institute* 4.

Macksey, Richard and Eugenio Donato (eds.) 1970. *The Languages of Criticism and the Sciences of Man: The Structuralist Controversy.* Baltimore.

Maranda, Pierre (ed.) 1972. *Mythology.* Baltimore.

Maranda, Pierre and Elli Köngäs-Maranda (eds.) 1971. *Structural Analysis of Oral Tradition.* Philadelphia.

Meletinsky, Eleasar M. 1970. Problème de la morphologic historique du conte populaire. *Semiotica* 2.

———— 1971. Structural-Typological Study of the Folktale. *Genre* 4.

———— 1973. Typological Analysis of the Paleo-Asiatic Raven Myths. *Acta Ethnographica* 22.

Meletinsky, E. M. and S. J. Nelkjudov, E. S. Novik, D. M. Segal 1973. La folclorica russa e I problemi del metodo strutturale. Jurij M. Lotman and Boris A. Uspenskij (eds.), *Richerche Semiotiche: Nuove Tendenze delle Scienze Umane nell'URSS.* Torino.

Meletinsky, E. and D. Segal 1971. Structuralism and Semiotics in the USSR. *Diogenes* 73.

Migeli, Silvana 1973. Struttura e Senso del Mito. *Quaderni del Circolo Semiologico Siciliano* 1. Palermo.

Milner, G. G. 1969a. What is a Proverb? *New Society* 332.

———— 1969b. Quadripartite Structures. *Proverbium* 14.

———— 1969c. De l'armature des locutions proverbiales: Essai de taxonomic sémantique. *L'Homme* 9.

Nathhorst, Bertel 1968. Genre, Form and Structure in Oral Tradition. *Temenos* 3.

———— 1969a. *Formal or Structural Studies of Traditional Tales.* Stockholm.

———— 1969b. Reply to Ulf Drobin's Criticism. *Temenos* 5.

Nikiforov, A. I. 1973. On the Morphological Study of Folklore. *Linguistica Biblica* 27/28.

Olrik, Axel 1965. Epic Laws of Folk Narrative. Alan Dundes (ed.), *The Study of Folklore.* Englewood Cliffs.

Parain-Vial, Jeanne 1969. *Analyses Structurales et Idéologies Structuralistes.* Toulouse.

Pasqualino, Antonio 1970. Per un'anailisi morfologica della letteretura cavalleresca: I reali diFrancia. *Uomo & Cultura* 3, no. 5/6.

Pauline, Denise 1972. Morphologic du conte africain. *Cahiers d'Etudes Africaines* 12.

Piaget, Jean 1970. *Structuralism.* New York.

Pop, Mihai 1967a. Metode noi in cercetarea structurii basmelor. *Folclor Literar* 1.

———— 1967b. Aspects actuels des recherches sur la structure des contes. *Fabula* 9.

———— 1968. Der formelhafte Charakter der Volksdichtung. *Deutsches Jahrbuch für Volkskunde* 14.

Propp, Vladimir 1968. *Morphology of the Folktale.* Austin.

———— 1971. Generic Structures in Russian Folklore. *Genre* 4.

———— 1972a. *Le Radici Storiche dei Racconti di Fate.* Torino.

———— 1972b. Transformations in Fairy Tales. Pierre Maranda (ed.), *Mythology.* Baltimore.

———— 1973. La fiaba cumulativa russa. Jurij M. Lotman and Boris A. Uspenskij (eds.), *Richerche Semiotiche: Nuove Tendenze delle Scienze Umane nell'URSS.* Torino.

Reider, Norman 1959. Chess, Oedipus and the Mater Dolorosa. *International Journal of Psycho-Analysis* 40.

Retel-Laurentin, Anne 1970. Structure and Symbolism: An Essay in Methodology for the Study of African Tales. *The Conch* 2, no. 2.

Roder, Viggo 1970. On Propp's "Morphology of the Folktale." *Poetik* 3.

Rohan-Csermak, Géza de 1965. *Structuralisme et folklore.* IV International Congress for Folk-Narrative Research. Athens.

Savard, Remi 1969. L'Hôte maladroit, essai d'analyse d'un conte Montagnais. *Interpretation* 3, no. 4.

Scholes, Robert 1974. *Structuralism in Literature.* New Haven.

Scholte, Bob 1969. Lévi-Strauss' Penelopean Effort: The Analysis of Myths. *Semiotica* 1.

Scott, Charles T. 1969. On Defining the Riddle: The Problem of a Structural Unit. *Genre* 2.

Tarde, G. 1897. *L'Opposition Universelle: Essai d'Une Théorie des Contraires.* Paris.

———— 1902. Opposition des Phénomènes. *Les Lois Sociales.* Paris.

Taylor, Archer 1948/1949. Locutions for Never. *Romance Philology* 2.

Tenèze, Marie-Louise 1970. Du conte merveilleux comme genre. *Arts et Traditions Populaires* 18.

Todorov, T. 1965. L'Heritage Méthodologique du Formalisme. *L'Homme* 5.

———— 1973. Analyse du Discours: L'Exemple des Devinettes. *Journal de Psychologie normale et pathologique* 70.

van Gennep, Arnold 1960. *The Rites of Passage.* London.

Viet, Jean 1965. *Les méthodes structuralistes dans les Sciences socialec.* Paris.

Voigt, Vilmos 1969. Toward Balancing of Folklore Structuralism. *Acta Ethnographica* 18.

———— 1972. Some Problems of Narrative Structure Universals in Folklore. *Acta Ethnographica* 21.

Waugh, Butler 1966. Structural Analysis in Literature and Folklore. *Western Folklore* 25.

Zurcher, Louis A. and Arnold Meadow 1967. On Bullfights and Baseball: An Example of Interaction of Social Institutions. *International Journal of Comparative Sociology* 8.

Postscript

Binary Opposition in Myth:
The Propp/Lévi-Strauss Debate in Retrospect

IN 1928, RUSSIAN FOLKLORIST VLADIMIR Propp published his pathbreaking *Morphology of the Folktale* in a limited printing of only 1600 copies (Bravo 1972:45). In his *Morphology*, Propp delineated a syntagmatic sequence of thirty-one functions which he claimed defined the Russian fairy tale (Aarne-Thompson tale types 300–749). Unfortunately, the few Western scholars who read Russian and Propp's important monograph had little impact upon the direction of folk narrative study. Only famed linguist Roman Jakobson in his 1945 folkloristic commentary for the Pantheon edition of Afanas'ev's *Russian Fairy Tales* referred to Propp's research in a brief summary of his findings (1945:640–641). It was not until Professor Thomas A. Sebeok of Indiana University arranged for an English translation of Propp's *Morphology* in 1958 that Propp's remarkable analysis became accessible to Western folklorists (cf. Breymayer 1972; Bremond and Verrier 1982; and Cardigos 1996:33–36, but see Chistov 1986:9).

Three years earlier, French anthropologist Claude Lévi-Strauss had responded favorably to an invitation issued by the same Professor Sebeok who was then the editor of the *Journal of American Folklore* to participate in a symposium on myth. (Among others in that symposium were David Bidney, Richard M. Dorson, Reidar Th. Christiansen, Lord Raglan, and Stith Thompson.) Lévi-Strauss's paper, entitled "The Structural Study of Myth" which initiated a veritable flood of "structural" enterprises, was written without any knowledge of Propp's *Morphology*. The 1955 JAF issue was published as a separate book under the title *Myth: A Symposium* in 1958, the same year Propp's *Morphology* appeared in English.

In his essay, Lévi-Strauss contended "that mythical thought always works from the awareness of oppositions towards their progressive mediation" and further that "the purpose of myth is to provide a logical model capable of overcoming a contradiction" (1955:440, 443). Lévi-Strauss has persisted in his "definition" of myth or mythical thought. In *The Naked Man,* the final volume of the four-volume *Mythologiques,* in a chapter entitled "Binary Operators," he has this to say of "mythemes," his neologism intended to refer to basic units of myth: "Of course, all mythemes of whatever kind, must, generally speaking, lend themselves to binary operations, since such operations are an inherent feature of the means invented by nature to make possible the functioning of language and thought" (1981:559). To be sure, Lévi-Strauss is well aware that he has been "accused" of "overusing" "the notion of binary opposition" (1995:185).

Like Propp, Lévi-Strauss had proposed a formula for the structure of narrative, but unlike Propp, his formula was totally algebraic involving "functions" and "terms" (1955:442; for a discussion of the formula, see Mosko 1991). Whereas Propp had extrapolated his thirty-one function sequence from the linear order of events recounted in his 100 fairy tale corpus, Lévi-Strauss sought to discover what he felt was the underlying paradigm (of oppositions). Lévi-Strauss did recognize the "order" of events as presented in narrative as told, but he elected to ignore that "order." In his terms, "The myth will be treated as would be an orchestra score *perversely* presented as a unilinear series and where our task is to re-establish the correct disposition" (1955:432, my emphasis). The use of the descriptive label "perversely" seemed to suggest that the linear sequential order (utilized by Propp) was an obstacle to be overcome by Lévi-Strauss in his efforts to arrive at the supposed underlying paradigm. As Champagne puts it, "Lévi-Strauss regards such linear, sequential forms as obvious and superficial" (1995:42).

Lévi-Strauss is certainly cognizant of the difference between syntagmatic and paradigmatic structure (1988:205). Moreover, throughout his four volume *Mythologiques* series, Lévi-Strauss repeatedly denigrates the sequential syntagmatic while at the same time praising the virtues of the paradigmatic. In *The Raw and the Cooked,* the first of the *Mythologiques* volumes, Lévi-Strauss claims that a detail of one myth which is "absurd on the syntagmatic level" becomes "coherent from the paradigmatic point of view" (1969:253). Again and again, the syntagmatic context is summarily dismissed. In speaking of another myth, Lévi-Strauss argues, "If we consider only the syntagmatic sequence—that is, the unfolding of the story—it appears incoherent and very arbitrary in construction" (1969:306), and he proceeds to generalize, "Considered purely in itself, every syntagmatic sequence must be looked upon as being without meaning," and the only solution involves "replacing a syntagmatic sequence by a paradigmatic sequence" (1969:307). Interestingly enough, although Lévi-Strauss's methodology wears the trappings of structuralism, his actual method is a form, an idiosyncratic form to be sure, of the *comparative method.* It is through comparison with one or more other myths (not always cognates!) that the elusive meaning of a myth text can be "revealed." Lévi-Strauss is explicit on this point: "Finally, one detail in the Bororo myth that remained incomprehensible when viewed from the angle of syntagmatical relations, becomes clear when *compared* to a corresponding detail in the Kayapo myth" (1969:210, my emphasis). In this case, it is a Kayapo text which purportedly illuminates a Bororo text, but the comparison can go either way: "The Kayapo-Kubenkranken version (M8) contains a detail that in itself is unintelligible and that can only he elucidated by means of the Bororo myth, M55" (1969:131). So although Lévi-Strauss is essentially known as a structuralist, the empirical fact is that he is much more of a comparativist than a structuralist.

Lévi-Strauss's methodology is consistent and explicit: "By dividing the myth into sequences not always clearly indicated by the plot, and by relating each sequence to paradigmatic sets capable of giving them a meaning, we eventually found ourselves in a position to define the fundamental characteristics of a myth . . ." (1979:199). Sometimes the comparative paradigm could come from within the same culture as the original myth; sometimes from without. "While the episode of Moon appears to be nonmotivated in the syntagmatic chain of the Thompson myth considered alone, it finds its place again in a paradigmatic ensemble as a permutation when related to other myths of these same Indians" (1955:140n) but alternatively the range of Lévi-Strauss's comparative method can be large, so large that he is willing to compare a South American Indian myth with possible cognates in North America to find meaning. Speaking of an episode in his "Tucuna reference myth," Lévi-Strauss has this to say: "This episode which cannot be interpreted according to the syntagmatic sequence, and on which South American mythology as a whole fails to shed any light, can only be elucidated by reference to a paradigmatic system drawn from North American mythology" (1979:17).

In 1959, Lévi-Strauss was appointed to the prestigious chair of Social Anthropology at the College de France and for his inaugural lecture, he chose a Tsimshian narrative reported by Franz Boas to analyze. His analysis of "La Geste d'Asdiwal" was a brilliant tour de force revealing four distinct levels of binary oppositions: geographic (e.g., east vs. west), cosmological (e.g., upper world vs. lower world), economic (land-hunting vs. sea-hunting), and sociological (e.g., patrilocal residence vs. matrilocal residence). Again, there is no reference to Propp in his Asdiwal essay which was published in the *Annuaire, 1958–1959, Ecole pratique des hautes études, Section des sciences religieuses.*

By 1960, Lévi-Strauss had definitely read Propp's *Morphology*. We know this because in that year, he published an extensive review of it. Appearing initially in the *Cahiers de l'institut des Sciences Economiques Appliquées* as "La structure et la forme. Rélexions sur un ouvrage de Vladimir Propp," it was also printed as "L'analyse morphologique des contes russes" in volume III of the *International Journal of Slavic Linguistics and Poetics*. In his review, Lévi-Strauss duly praised Propp for being an innovator ahead of his time, but he also criticized Propp's analysis. A sample of the praise reads: "The most striking aspect of Propp's work is the power with which it anticipated further developments. Those among us who first approached the structural analysis of oral literature around 1950, without direct knowledge of Propp's attempts a quarter of a century earlier, recognize there, to their amazement, formulae—sometimes even whole sentences—that they know well enough they have not borrowed from him. . . . [There] are so many intuitions, whose perspicacity and prophetic character arouse our admiration. They earn for Propp the devotion of all those who, unknown to themselves, were his followers" (Lévi-Strauss in Propp 1984:175). However, it is with one of the primary criticisms of Propp by Lévi-Strauss that we are presently concerned.

Lévi-Strauss faults Propp for analyzing wondertales. For, according to Lévi-Strauss, "Tales are constructed on weaker oppositions than those found in myths" (Propp 1984:176; cf. Cardigos 1996:34). In this context, Lévi-Strauss claims that "the tale lends itself imperfectly to structural analysis. . . . Should he [Propp] not rather have used myths" instead (1984:177)? Lévi-Strauss then goes on to give his guess as to why Propp did not use myths. "As he is not an ethnologist, one can suppose that he had no access to or control over mythological material collected by him and among peoples known to him" (1984:177).

The idea that a professional folklorist, a professor of folklore, did not know enough about myths to analyze them is, of course, preposterous, and it should come as no surprise to learn that Propp upon reading Lévi-Strauss's review was insulted by the insinuation that he knew nothing about myth. Stung by Lévi-Strauss's criticism, Propp wrote a strong rebuttal which appeared first in the 1966 Italian translation of his *Morphology* immediately following the Lévi-Strauss review. (Propp's *Morphology* has had an enormous impact in Italy [cf. de Meijer 1982].) Lévi-Strauss, however, was given the last word in the form of a brief postscript in which he expressed or perhaps feigned surprise at Propp's anger. He had meant, he averred, only to offer "a homage" to a pioneering effort—although it is noteworthy that Lévi-Strauss has continued to avoid making any mention of Propp in any of his many writings on myth and structure. Lévi-Strauss's original review, Propp's rebuttal, and Lévi-Strauss's postscript are available in English translation in Propp's *Theory and History of Folklore*, a selection of Propp's essays published by the University of Minnesota Press in 1984. (It is a pity that Propp's footnotes to his rebuttal did not appear in the

Minnesota Press translation, especially the one that referred to *The Morphology of North American Indian Folktales!*)

In his rebuttal, "The Structural and Historical Study of the Wondertale," Propp first thanks the Italian publisher Einaudi for inviting him to write a rejoinder to Lévi-Strauss's review. He then observed that Lévi-Strauss has an important advantage inasmuch as he is a philosopher whereas Propp is merely an empiricist (1984:68). Propp replies that he will not dwell on the logic of such an argument as "since the author does not know myths, he studies wondertales," but it is clear that he does not think much of it. "No scholar can be forbidden to do one thing and urged to do another," he comments. The interested reader should consult the full texts of the debate for all the nuances and facets of the arguments on both sides. Here one may note that Propp in turn critiqued Lévi-Strauss's "re-write" of Propp's thirty-one function scheme by saying, "My model corresponds to what was modeled and is based on a study of data, whereas the model Lévi-Strauss proposes does not correspond to reality and is based on logical operations not imposed by the data . . . Lévi-Strauss carries out his logical operations in total disregard of the material (he is not in the least interested in the wondertale, nor does he attempt to learn more about it) and removes the functions from their temporal sequence" (1984:76). As we have already noted in some detail, Lévi-Strauss would make no apology for "removing" functions from their temporal sequence. In part, we have the two scholars talking past one another: Propp is concerned with empirically observable sequential structure whereas Lévi-Strauss is interested in underlying paradigms, typically binary in nature. (My own view is that Lévi-Strauss is not so much describing the structure of myth as he is the structure of the world described in myth. That is a significant distinction.)

There is other evidence of Lévi-Strauss's rather Olympian posture with respect to his version of "structure" in myth. In the first volume of his magnum opus, *The Raw and the Cooked,* he doubts that the natives of central Brazil would have any understanding of "the systems of interrelations" he finds in their myths. Moreover, he adopts a truly superorganic position when he says, "I therefore claim to show not how men think in myths, but how myths operate in men's minds without their being aware of the fact" (1969:12), a statement strangely reminiscent of Jung's equally mystical claim in his "The Psychology of the Child Archetype" essay, ". . . the primitive cannot assert that he thinks; it is rather that something thinks in him! . . ." (1963:72). Lévi-Strauss appears to reject the Jungian universalistic "archetypal" approach to myth (1969:56; 1995:188), and most writers comparing Lévi-Strauss and Jung tend to see more differences than similarities (cf. Chang 1984 and Messer 1986). However, readers can judge the possible parallelism between the two statements cited above for themselves.

In any event, Lévi-Strauss never repudiated his superorganic statement. Indeed, he is well aware of the Anglo-American attitude towards it. In his 1977 Canadian CBC series of talks, published as *Myth and Meaning,* Lévi-Strauss begins by referring to this very statement: "You may remember that I have written that myths get thought in man unbeknownst to him. This has been much discussed and even criticized by my English-speaking colleagues, because their feeling is that, from an empirical point of view, it is an utterly meaningless sentence. But for me it describes a lived experience, because it says exactly how I perceive my own relationship to my work. That is, my work gets thought in me unbeknown to me" (1979:3). Were one to object that Lévi-Strauss's own thought should not be compared to myth, one would be obliged to recall Lévi-Strauss's unabashed comment about *The Raw and the Cooked* that ". . . this book on myths is itself a kind of myth" (1969:6) which upon reflection is entirely consistent with Lévi-Strauss's contention that the Freudian reading or interpretation of Oedipus "should be included among the recorded versions of the Oedipus myth on a par with earlier or seemingly more "authentic" versions" (1955:435).

But this inquiry is not intended to be a full-fledged discussion of either Lévi-Strauss's or Propp's methodologies. (For an initial entree into Lévi-Strauss's voluminous writings on myths and the criticism of them, see Lapointe and Lapointe [1977]; for Propp, see Breyrnayer 1972, Liberman 1984, and Ziel 1995). The aim is to consider only the issue of binary opposition in myth. Let us assume for the sake of argument that Lévi-Strauss is correct in his assumption that myths reveal binary oppositions more clearly than do folktales and that "Tales are constructed on weaker oppositions than those found in myths."

In his 1955 essay in JAF, what narrative does Lévi-Strauss choose to demonstrate his version of "structural analysis?" He chooses the story of Oedipus. Now since Lévi-Strauss is an anthropologist and not a folklorist, he is evidently not all that familiar with the standard genre definitions of myth, folktale, and legend, distinctions which have been observed for nearly two centuries ever since the times of the brothers Grimm who devoted separate major works to each of these three genres. (For definitions, see Bascom 1965 and Bødker 1965). Suffice it to say that if a myth is a sacred narrative explaining how the world and humankind came to be in their present form," then it is perfectly obvious that the story of Oedipus is NOT a myth. As folklorists very well know, it is in fact a standard folk-tale, namely, Aarne-Thompson tale type 931. (The number was assigned by Aarne in his original *Verzeichnis der Märchentypen,* FFC 3, published in 1910.) So it turns out that Lévi-Strauss, like Propp, began his analysis of "myth" with a folktale! In the same essay, after discussing one actual myth, that of the Zuni emergence, he proceeds to talk about "the trickster of (native) American mythology" and refers to "the mythology of the Plains" citing "Star Husband" and "Lodge-Boy and Thrown-Away" (1955:440). But these latter allusions are all to folktales, not myths. At least Lévi-Strauss is consistent, that is, consistently mistaken. In *The Origin of Table Manners,* the third volume in the *Mythologiques* series, he devotes no less than two chapters to the "Star Husband" myth (1979:199–272), this even though he had read Stith Thompson's classic study "The Star Husband *Tale*" (my emphasis). No serious folklorist would label the Star Husband story a myth, but then again Lévi-Strauss is no folklorist. He refers to Stith Thompson, by the way, as "the eminent *mythographer*" (1979:19) (again, my emphasis). The fact is that Stith Thompson wrote very little about myth, preferring instead to concentrate on his beloved folktale! One might well argue that if Lévi-Strauss insists upon calling folktales such as Star Husband "myths," he is perfectly justified in reclassifying Stith Thompson, an acknowledged specialist in the folktale, as a "mythographer" or "mythologist."

What about the subject of Lévi-Strauss's inaugural lecture, the story of Asdiwal (which he cautiously labelled "geste")? This is not a myth either. If it were believed to be historically "true" by the Tsimshian, then it would be a legend. If not, it would be a folktale, a fictional narrative not believed to be any more historical than such Western folktales as Cinderella or Little Red Riding Hood. In no way is the geste of Asdiwal an account of how the world or humankind came to be in their present form. It is not a myth by folkloristic standards.

And what about the texts, the hundreds of texts, analyzed in the four-volume *Mythologiques* and the two later sequels (1988, 1995)? Are they all myths? The initial narrative discussed, "The Macaws and their Nest" is a Bororo version of the "bird-nester," a narrative which Lévi-Strauss (arbitrarily) labels M1 (key myth). But the narrative is not a myth at all in the technical sense of the term. It is a straightforward folktale! This is not to say that Lévi-Strauss does not analyze some myths in *Mythologiques*. The important point is that he analyzes *both* myths and folktales indiscriminately.

If the Oedipus, Asdiwal, and bird-nester narratives are all folktales rather than myths, then we might pose to Lévi-Strauss the same question he addressed to Propp: if folktales are constructed on weaker oppositions than those found in myths, why did Lévi-Strauss choose folktales rather than myths to demonstrate his theory of binary oppositions? It seems to me that Lévi-Strauss is hoist by his own petard! The obvious answer is that binary oppositions are just as strong in folktales as they are in myth. Lévi-Strauss's own insightful analysis of Asdiwal is a perfect case in point. The fact that Lévi-Strauss, like the majority of anthropologists, doesn't know the difference between a myth and a folktale should not be a factor. Most anthropologists use the term "myth" when the narratives they discuss are unmistakably folktales or legends. The appalling ignorance among anthropologists and others concerning such standard folk narrative genre distinctions as myth and folktale might account for why despite a deluge of critical writing on Lévi-Strauss's *Mythologiques* and other studies of "myth" by anthropologists and sociologists (cf. Thomas et al. 1976; Carroll 1978, and Mandelbaum 1987), no one seems to have noticed that Lévi-Strauss was analyzing folktales more often than myths. Even those critics who have commented specifically on the Propp/Lévi-Strauss debate (e.g., Bravo 1972, de Meijer 1970, Janovic 1975) failed to remark on this matter.

So if Lévi-Strauss has analyzed folktales rather than myths, what happens to his notion that "mythical thought always works from the awareness of oppositions towards their progressive mediation," and "the purpose of myth is to provide a logical model capable of overcoming a contradiction?" Clearly, the notion needs to be amended. But there is more.

One could well argue that binary opposition is a universal. Presumably all human societies, past and present, made some kind of distinction between "Male and Female," "Life and Death," "Day and Night" (or Light and Dark), etc. Certainly we can find binary oppositions in genres of folklore other than myth and folktale. Take the proverb genre, for example. Some proverbs have both topics and comments in opposition: "United we stand; divided we fall" (united vs. divided; stand vs. fall); "Man proposes; but God disposes" (Man vs. God; proposes vs. disposes); "Last hired; first fired" (last vs. first; hired vs. fired) etc. (Dundes 1975). The same kinds of binary opposition also occur in traditional riddles (Georges and Dundes 1963). Examples of oppositional riddles include:

> I am rough, I am smooth
> I am wet, I am dry
> My station is low, my title high
> My king my lawful master is,
> I'm used by all, though only his. (highway)
> Large as a house
> Small as a mouse,
> Bitter as gall,
> And sweet after all. (pecan tree and nut)

And what about the curse genre? There are traditional Jewish-American curses which are clearly based on binary oppositions:

You should have lockjaw and seasickness at the same time.
May you eat like a horse and shit like a little bird.

Could we not assert on the basis of the above examples that a proverb (riddle, curse) can serve as " a logical model capable of overcoming a contradiction?"

If binary opposition is a universal—or even if it were confined to folklore genres as diverse as myth, folktale, proverb, riddle, and curse—the question is: how can binary opposition be used to define the nature of myth? This is not to deny that binary oppositions can be found in myth. The critical point is that binary opposition is in no way peculiar to myth. If this is so, then what Lévi-Strauss has isolated in his analysis of "myth" tells us precious little about the nature of myth in particular. To be fair, since Lévi-Strauss is actually interested in the nature of human thought (rather than myth per se), perhaps it doesn't matter that binary opposition as a distinctive feature is not confined to myth. Quite the contrary. If binary oppositional thought is a pan-human mental characteristic, that is well worth noting. But then we must not pretend that the presence of binary oppositions in a narrative necessarily identifies that narrative as a myth. Although Lévi-Strauss occasionally actually cites an Aarne-Thompson tale type number (1995:181), the truth is that for the most part he totally ignores the basic "myth-folktale-legend" genre categories. From a folkloristic vantage point, it is the height of hubris to write a four-volume (plus two sequel volumes) introduction to a science of mythology without even recognizing or knowing the difference between a myth and a folktale!

Finally, we are obliged to remind the reader that the presence of binary opposition in folklore is hardly a new idea. One of Axel Olrik's epic laws proposed in the first decade of the twentieth century was *Das Gesetz des Gegensatzes,* the Law of Contrast. "This very basic opposition is a major rule of epic composition: young and old, large and small, man and monster, good and evil" (Olrik 1965: 135; cf. 1992:50). Furthermore, the principle was beautifully illustrated by another Danish folklorist, the late Bengt Holbek in his three-dimensional paradigmatic model for Danish folk-tales: low vs. high, young vs. adult, and male vs. female (Holbek 1987:453), a conceptual model borrowed from Elli Köngäs Maranda (Maranda and Maranda 1971:23). The wheel may have been re-invented but it also comes full circle, inasmuch as Maranda was inspired by none other than Lévi-Strauss!

To the extent that the debate between Propp and Lévi-Strauss itself constitutes a kind of academic binary opposition, we earnestly trust that this essay will be understood as a form of constructive mediation.

References

Bascom, William. 1965. The Forms of Folklore: Prose Narratives. *Journal of American Folklore* 78:3–20.

Bødker, Laurits. 1965. *Folk Literature (Germanic).* Copenhagen: Rosenkilde and Bagger.

Bravo, Gian Luigi. 1972. Propp e la morfologia della fiaba. In *Folklore e Antropologia,* ed. Alberto Mario Cirese. Palermo: Palumbo Editore. Pp. 43–77.

Bremond, Claude and Jean Verrier. 1982. Afanassiev et Propp. *Littérature* 45 (février):61–78.

Breymayer, Reinhard. 1972. Vladimir Jakovlevič Propp (1895–1970)—Leben, Wirken and Bedeutsanikeit. *Linguistica Biblica* 15:36–66.

Cardigos, Isabel. 1996. *In and Out of Enchantment: Blood Symbolism and Gender in Portugese Fairytales.* FF Communications No. 260. Helsinki: Academia Scientiarum Fennica.

Carroll, Michael P. 1978. Lévi-Strauss on the Oedipus Myth: A Reconsideration. *American Anthropologist* 80:805–814.

Champagne, Roland A. 1992. *The Structuralists on Myth:* An *Introduction.* New York: Garland.
Chang, M. Joseph. 1984. Jung and Lévi-Strauss: Whose Unconscious? *Mankind Quarterly* 25:101–114.
Chistov, Krill. 1986. V.ᵞa. Propp—Legend and Fact. *International Folklore Review* 4:815.
De Meijer, Pieter. 1970. Eenvoudige Vertelstructuren: Propp en Lévi-Strauss. *Forum der Letteren* 11:145–159.
———. 1982. Propp in Italy. *Russian Literature* 12:1–10.
Dundes, Alan. 1975. On the Structure of the Proverb. *Proverbium* 25:961–973.
Georges, Robert A., and Alan Dundes. 1963. Toward A Structural Definition of the Riddle. *Journal of American Folklore* 76:111–118.
Holbek, Bengt. 1987. *Interpretation of Fairy Tales.* FF Communications No. 239. Helsinki Academia Scientiarum Fennica.
Jakobson, Roman. 1945. On Russian Fairy Tales. In *Russian Fairy Tales.* New York:Pantheon. Pp. 631–656.
Janovič, Clara Strada. 1975. Introduzione. Vladimir Ja. Propp, *Edipo alla Luce del Folclore.* Torino: Giulio Einaudi editore. vii-xviii. Translated into English in *Russian Literature* 12 (1982), 45–55.
Jung, C. G. 1963. The Psychology of the Child Archetype. In C. G. Jung and C. Kerenyi, *Essay on a Science of Mythology.* New York: Harper & Row. Pp. 70–100.
Lapointe, Francois H. and Claire C. Lapointe. 1977. *Claude Lévi-Strauss and His Critics: An International Bibliography of Criticism (1950–1976).* New York: Garland.
Lévi-Strauss, Claude. 1955. The Structural Study of Myth. *Journal of American Folklore* 68:428–444.
———. 1959. La Geste d'Asdiwal. *Annuaire, 1958–1959, Ecole pratique des hautes études* (Paris). Pp. 3–43.
———. 1960. L'Analyse morphologique des contes russes. *International Journal of Slavic Linguistics and Poetics* 3:122–149.
———. 1969. *The Raw and the Cooked, Introduction to a Science of Mythology*, Vol.1. New York: Harper & Row.
———. 1973. *From Honey to Ashes, Introduction to a Science of Mythology*, Vol. 1. New York: Harper & Row.
———. 1978. *Myth and Meaning.* New York: Schocken Books.
———. 1979. *The Origin of Table Manners, Introduction to a Science of Mythology*, Vol. 3. New York: Harper & Row.
———. 1981. *The Naked Man, Introduction to a Science of Mythology*, Vol. 4. New York: Harper & Row.
———. 1988. *The Jealous Potter.* Chicago: University of Chicago Press .
———. 1995. *The Story of Lynx.* Chicago: University of Chicago Press.
Liberman, Anatoly. 1984. Introduction. Vladimir Propp, *Theory and History of Folklore*, Minneapolis: University of Minnesota Press. Pp. ix-lxxxi.
Mandelbaum, David G. 1987. Myths and Myth Maker: Some Anthropological Appraisals of the Mythological Studies of Lévi-Strauss. *Ethnology* 26:31–36.
Maranda, Elli Köngäs, and Pierre Maranda. 1971. *Structural Models in Folklore and Transformational Essays.* The Hague: Mouton.
Messer, Ron. 1986. The Unconscious Mind: Do Jung and Lévi-Strauss Agree? *Journal of the Anthropological Society of Oxford* 17:1–26.
Mosko, Mark S. 1991. The Canonic Formula of Myth and Non-Myth. *American Ethnologist* 18:126–151.
Olrik, Axel. 1965. Epic Laws of Folk Narrative. In *The Study of Folklore,* ed. Alan Dundes. Englewood Cliffs: Prentice-Hall. Pp. 129–141.
———. 1992. *Principles for Oral Narrative Research.* Bloomington: Indiana University Press.
Propp, Vladimir. 1966. *Morfologia della Fiaba,* con un intervento di Claude Lévi-Strauss e una replica dell'autore. Torino: Giulio Einaudi Editore.

————. 1968. *Morphology of the Folktale.* Austin: University of Texas Press.

————. 1984. *Theory and History of Folklore.* Minneapolis: University of Minnesota Press.

Thomas, L. L., J. Z. Kronenfeld, and D. B. Kronenfeld. 1976. Asdiwal Crumbles: A Critique of Lévi-Straussian Myth Analysis. *American Ethnologist* 3:147–173.

Thompson, Stith. 1965. The Star Husband Tale. In *The Study of Folklore,* ed. Alan Dundes. Englewood Cliffs: Prentice-Hall. Pp. 424–474.

Ziel, Wulfhild. 1995. *Bibliographien zu 'Slawischfolkloristisches Schriftgut' aus Vorlesungsrepertoire von Vladimir Propp....* Frankfurt am Main: P. Lang.

7

ON GAME MORPHOLOGY:
A STUDY OF THE STRUCTURE OF
NON-VERBAL FOLKLORE

Introduction

This essay is included as a demonstration of Dundes's structural analysis, derived from methods introduced by Vladimir Propp and other Russian formalists. But its statement on the materials covered by folkloristic inquiry is even more significant. In 1964, when this essay was published, most folklore studies focused on what was called "oral literature." Dundes showed the domination of narrative in folkloristic thought by pointing out the binary of "verbal/non-verbal" dividing traditional genres. The negation of "non-verbal" assumes that "verbal" (that is, speech and narrative) is the central term by which "other" genres are evaluated.

Dundes set out to change that definitive preoccupation with oral literature as part of his general campaign to treat folklore as a type of knowledge in social lives, rather than a relic textual form. This is what he meant by an elastic "modern" concept of folklore, in which all cultural expressions that repeat and vary within groups constitute folklore. If games and dances can be shown to have comparable structures, then they are part of a whole called folklore, rather than divisible into central verbal and marginal non-verbal parts. The organic rhetoric of morphology is significant, because it refers to the holistic structure of an organism (such as a plant), which has observable essential parts enabling the organism to live. The linear structure analyzed in morphology differs from the presentation of non-sequential "elements" for games, such as rules governing action, and physical setting. See, for example, the ten elements in E. M. Avedon (1979). Robert A. Georges (1972) gave a folkloristic definition of games, i.e., behavioral models defined by competition and rules.

Dundes's intention here was to raise epistemological questions about the rationale for including different types of material under the rubric of folklore. His revelation that many forms of children's play, coming at a formative time in human development, composed a narrative plot involving a departure and return to home has stimulated other studies focusing on the sociopsychological meaning of this structure for children. I suggested that the structural function of the game narratives described by Dundes was to enact the tripartite structure of rites of passage (separation, transition, incorporation) on a daily basis, at a time of rapid physical and social changes, especially in American society, which is noted for encouraging the values of individualism and self-reliance in children (Bronner 1990). When children mature, they are discouraged from game playing, and the departure from home theme is not reinforced. An example is the interpretation of "Hide and Seek" in America, a game encouraging individualism because of the symbolic roles it assigns. In contrast to countries having games with a more authoritarian It role, in this American game a parental, low-power It searches for children who independently hide before returning to the "safe" home base. (See the experiments with high and low power Its in Sutton-Smith and Gump 1972). Although stating that folktales and games are "quite different media of expression," Brian Sutton-Smith observed that they are similar in being models that "represent behaviors occurring in other settings, both real and imaginary." His cross-cultural study of twenty-five societies found that those possessing games of strategy tended to have folktales in which the outcome is determined by strategy. He posited that games of strategy were associated with high obedience training in childhood, and that strategic outcomes in tales were culturally provided rewards for obedience in games. In contrast, the game of "Hare and Hounds" (and the related chasing games of "Tag" and "Hide and Seek") involved physical skills associated with achievement training (1972; also see Roberts, Arth, and Bush 1959).

Dundes's subsequent work in games shifted to the gendered nature of structural rules. Following his reference to the bullfight in the previous chapter on "Structuralism and Folklore," he found a male/female binary in the competitive structure of boys' games "Hare and Hounds," in fact, is typically described as a male game). He argued that the game begins as male to male combat, but ends in the victory of one male, who "feminizes" the opponent (see the chapter on "Gallus as Phallus" in this volume, as well as other essays by Dundes [1987a, 1997e]). Other issues of genre analysis in folkloristics that Dundes raised also remain (See Harris-Lopez 2003; Georges and Jones 1995a; Honko 1989; and Ben-Amos 1976).

On Game Morphology:
A Study of the Structure of Non-Verbal Folklore

ARE CHILDREN'S GAMES, A FORM of non-verbal folklore, and folktales, a form of verbal folklore, structurally similar? I am suggesting in the following article that they are and also that there are many other non-verbal analogues to verbal folklore forms. Consequently, the definition of folklore should not be limited to verbal materials.

Although structural analysis, as an effective means of descriptive ethnography, has been applied to a number of types of folklore expression, it has not been employed in the study of children's games. Yet games, in general, and competitive games, in particular, are obviously patterned. In competitive games, the participants are aware that play is governed by definite limiting rules. The application and the interrelationship of these rules result in an ordered sequence of actions by the players, and these action sequences constitute the essential structure of any particular game.

In order to delineate the structure of a game, or any other form of folklore, one must have a minimum structural unit. Only with such a unit can there be any precise segmentation of the continuum of game action. As a trial unit, I propose to use the *motifeme,* a unit of action which has been used in structural studies of folktales.[1] One obvious advantage of employing the motifeme is that if game action can, in fact, be broken down into motifemes, then it would be relatively easy to compare the structure of games with the structure of folktales.[2] Before examining the pronounced similarities in game and folktale structure, it is necessary to emphasize one important difference between the two forms. The difference is dimensionality. The folktale is concerned with conflict between protagonist and antagonist, but the sequence of plot actions is unidimensional. Either the hero's actions or the villain's actions are discussed at any one moment in time at any one point in the tale. Vladimir Propp, a Russian folklorist, made, in 1928, a thought-provoking examination of fairy tales and devised a distribution of functions (motifemes) among the *dramatis personae* of the tales.[3] He noted, for example, that functions VIII (villainy), XVI (struggle), and XXI (pursuit) belong to the villain's sphere of action. Certainly, functions IV (reconnaissance) and V (delivery) in Propp's analysis are villain and not hero actions. In games, however, one finds a contrast: there are at least two sequences of actions going on *simultaneously.* When A is playing against B, both A and B are operating at the same time, all the time. This is theoretically true in folktales, but only one side's activities (usually the hero's) are described at a given point in the tale. A folktale is, therefore, a two-dimensional series of actions displayed on a one-dimensional track, or, conversely, a game is, structurally speaking, a two-dimensional folktale.

In his notable discussion of folktale morphology, Propp drew particular attention to function VIII, villainy. In this function, a villain causes harm or injury to one member of a family by abducting a person or stealing an object, etc., thus creating the actual movement of the folktale.[4] At the same time, he astutely observed that a folktale could begin with the desire to have something or a deficiency or lack as a given ground-rule. In the analysis, Propp considered lack (function VIIIa) as morphologically equivalent to villainy (function VIII). If a folktale did not begin with a state of lack, then a state of lack could be created by an act of villainy. This same distinction can also be applied to the structure of many games.

A game can begin with an object which is missing, or the object may be hidden before play begins. In some games nothing is missing, but the initial portion of game action (corresponding to Propp's "initial" or "preparatory" section of the folktale, functions I–VII) brings about the requisite state of lack or insufficiency. In games of the first type, an individual may hide from the group (as in "Hare and Hounds") or the group may hide from an individual ("Hide and Seek"). In games of the second type, an individual or object may be abducted or captured, which also results in a lack. This happens, for example, in the child-stealing game of "The Witch." Other characteristics shared by both folktales and games will become apparent in the following discussion of several specific games.

In "Hare and Hounds,"[5] the boy chosen as the Hare (the choosing by counting out rhymes or other means may be construed as pre-game activity) runs away to hide. Usually a fixed time span, a specific number of minutes, or counting to some arbitrary number, marks the formal beginning of the chase, much as the iteration of an opening formula marks the passage from reality to fantasy in the beginning of a folktale. In fact, some games actually have opening formulas such as "Ready or not, here I come." The game, then, begins with a lack, the missing Hare. The quest, so popular in folktales, is equally popular in games. The Hounds attempt to find and catch the Hare, just as the hero in folktale seeks to liquidate the initial lack (function XIX).

Note, however that two sets of actions, or motifeme sequences, are involved in the game. One action is from the point of view of the Hounds, the other from the perspective of the Hare. The sequences include the following motifemes: lack, interdiction, violation, and consequence.[6] In one motifemic sequence, the Hounds want to catch the Hare (lack). They are required to catch him before he returns "home," a place agreed upon previously (interdiction). If the Hounds fail to do so (violation), they lose the game (consequence). In the second motifemic sequence taking place simultaneously with the first, the Hare wants to go "home" (lack), but he is required to arrive there without being caught by the Hounds (interdiction). If he fails to do so (violation), he loses the game (consequence). It is possible to win the game, by liquidating the lack, by either of two actions: catching the Hare or returning "home" safely. But it is impossible for both Hare and Hounds to win and also impossible for both Hare and Hounds to lose. Here is another point of contrast with folktales. In folktales, the hero always wins and the villain always loses. In games, however the outcome is not so regular or predictable: sometimes the Hare wins, and sometimes the Hounds win. As Caillois has pointed out, one characteristic of competitive games is that the opponents are equal and, in theory, each opponent stands the same chance of winning.[7]

The game of "Hare and Hounds" might be structured as follows:

	Lack	*Interdiction*	*Violation*	*Consequence*
Hare	wants to go home	without being caught by Hounds	is caught (isn't caught)	loses game (wins game)
Hounds	want to catch absent Hare	before he arrives back home	do not catch Hare (do catch Hare)	lose game (win game)

The double structure is also illuminated by comparison with analogous folktale structure. From the Hare's point of view, one could say there was a hero pursued (function XXI) and that the hero is rescued from pursuit (function XXII), assuming the Hare wins. The game-folktale analogy is even closer in those versions in which the Hare is required to leave signs, such as strips of paper, to mark his trail. In folktales, when the hero runs from his pursuer, he often places obstacles in the latter's path. These objects mark the trail, but also serve to delay the pursuer. From the point of view of the Hounds, i.e., with the Hounds as heroes, the Hare appears to serve as a donor figure, inasmuch as the dropped slips of paper are "magical agents" (identified as function XIV) which aid the hero-Hounds in liquidating the initial lack.[8] The donor sequence, then, is another point of similarity between games and folktales.

In a popular American children's game which Brewster calls "Steps,"[9] the leader, or "it," aids the others in reaching him (to tag him) by permitting various steps, such as baby steps, giant steps or umbrella steps. In this game, the donor figure grants the privilege of using certain "magical" steps. The fact that the magical aid is not granted until the hero is tested by the donor is also a striking parallel to folktale morphology. After the donor ("it") permits the number and type of steps, (e.g., four baby steps), the recipient ("hero") is required to say "May I?" If the latter passes the politeness test, he is permitted to take the steps which bring him closer to his goal. However, should he neglect to express the etiquette formula, the donor will penalize him by ordering him to step backwards, thus moving him away from the goal. More often than not in folktales, civility or politeness to the donor will provide the needed magical agents while discourtesy deprives the would-be hero of these same agents.

In some games, the presence of a donor sequence appears to be optional rather than obligatory, as is also true in folktales. In "Thimble in Sight"[10] an object, such as a thimble, is hidden. Actually, the object is supposed to be visible but not obvious. The children seek to discover or notice the object (lack). As each child does so (lack liquidated), he indicates his success by exclaiming a verbal formula such as "rorum torum corum," much as the successful player in "Hide and Seek" announces his return "home" with the phrase "Home free." (These verbal formulas would appear to be analogous to closing formulas in folktales.) In this form of "Thimble in Sight" there is no donor sequence but in some versions, the hider aids the thimble-seekers by giving helpful clues such as "You're freezing" or "You're cold," when the seeker is far away from the quest-object, and "You're warm" or "You're burning," when the seeker is close to the object. In such versions, the seeker could presumably request assistance from the donor by asking, "Am I getting warm?" Nevertheless, since the game can be played without the donor sequence, it is clear that the sequence is structurally not obligatory.

The frequency of the donor sequence in games and folktales also demands attention. One would suspect, for example, that since the donor sequence is comparatively rare in American Indian folktales, as compared with Indo-European folktales, the donor sequence would be infrequent in American Indian games. The presence or absence of such a sequence might even be correlated with magic and religion. If a person can make magic or seek a religious vision as an individual, then the need for a donor might be less than in those cultures in which experts or intermediaries supply magic or religion.

So far, mention has been made of a number of games in which the initial lack is part of the given. The game's action does not begin until an object or person is removed or secreted. "It" may absent himself or herself in order to produce the initial lack situation. However, in

"The Witch" the lack is the result of "its" abducting someone.[11] In this game, the parallel to folktale structure is also apparent. A mother leaves her seven children, named after the days of the week (Propp's function I, "One of the members of a family is absent from home"— still bearing in mind that Propp's morphological analysis was made of folktales and not games). Before leaving, the mother tells her children, "Take care the Old Witch does not catch you" (function II, "An interdiction is addressed to the hero"). The witch enters and the children do not take heed (function III, "The interdiction is violated"). The witch pretends that the children's mother has sent her to fetch a bonnet (function VI, "The villain attempts to deceive his victim in order to take possession of him or of his belongings"). The child goes to get the bonnet (function VII, "The victim submits to deception and thereby unwittingly helps his enemy"). The witch abducts one of the children (function VIII, "The villain causes harm or injury to one member of a family"). The mother returns, names her seven children, and thus discovers that one of her children is missing. The remaining children cry, "The Old Witch has got her" (function IX, "Misfortune or shortage is made known"). The sequence of motifemes is repeated until the witch has abducted all the children. This action is analogous to the repetition of entire moves in folktales, e.g., elder brothers setting out successively on identical quests.

The mother then goes out to find the children (function X, "The seeker agrees to or decides upon counteraction," and function XI, "The hero leaves home"). The mother encounters the witch and asks her for information about the whereabouts of her children. In the standard ritual dialogue, one finds possible traces of the standard donor sequence, as identified by functions XII–XIV. In this game, the witch functions as donor. The mother finally arrives at the place where her children are being held captive (function XV, "The hero is transferred, reaches, or is led to the whereabouts of an object of search"). This function or motifeme is of great significance to the structural analysis of both games and folktales. Propp remarks (page 46), "Generally the object of search is located in another or different kingdom." Anyone familiar with children's games will recall that many make mandatory the penetration of the opponent's territory. In "Capture the Flag" (Brewster, pages 69–70), the object of the search is the opponent's flag, clearly located in the "enemy's kingdom."

Now the mother discovers her lost children (function XIX, "The initial misfortune or lack is liquidated"), and mother and children pursue the witch. The one who catches the witch becomes the witch in the next playing of the game. In folktales, a pursuit often follows the liquidation of the initial lack, but more commonly the villain pursues the hero (function XXI, "The hero is pursued"). The hero inevitably escapes (function XXII, "The hero is rescued from pursuit"). Propp remarks that "a great many folktales end on the note of rescue from pursuit." The same might be said of games. In many games, "it," or the villain, is the one who pursues the "hero"-seekers after the latter have obtained the quest-object, such as the flag in "Capture the Flag." Of course, one reason why the game of "The Witch" is similar to folktales is the fixed nature of the outcome! The witch never wins, just as the villain in folk tales never wins.

Critics have been sceptical of Propp's morphological analysis on the grounds that he limited his material to Russian fairy tales. Competent students of the folktale, however, are aware that most, if not all, of the tales Propp analyzed can, in fact, be classified according to the Aarne-Thompson system as tale types. Others complain that Propp was too general and that his functions apply to literary as well as to folk materials. It is true that Propp's concept can be correlated to the plot structure of *Beowulf* and to most of the *Odyssey*

(Cf. his functions XXI to XXXI with the end of the *Odyssey*). Clearly, the game of "Old Witch" contains a number of Propp's functions and, in one sense, the game appears to be a dramatized folktale. Moreover the "Old Witch" game bears a superficial resemblance to the Aarne-Thompson tale type 123, "The Wolf and the Kids." But what is important here is that the morphological analysis of folktales appears to apply equally well to another genre of folklore—traditional games, thereby providing further confirmation of the validity of Propp's analysis.

When one perceives the similarity between the structure of games and folktales it is also possible to see parallels among special forms of the two genres. For example, one type of folktale is the cumulative take. In these tales (Aarne-Thompson types 2000–2199), one finds chains of actions or objects. Usually, there is repetition with continual additions. In ballads this stylistic feature is termed "incremental repetition." Stith Thompson, in his discussion of tales of this type, noted, but without further comment, that they had "something of the nature of a game."[12] This game-tale analogy is obvious in "Link Tag" in which "it" tags someone. The tagged person must take hold of the tagger's hand and help him or her tag others; the next one tagged joins the first two and so on.[13] (The same structure is obviously found in those folk dances in which couples or individuals form ever-lengthening chains.)

Another sub-genre analogy might be trickster tales (or jokes) and pranks. In trickster tales and in most pranks or practical jokes, the primary motifemes are fraud and deception (Propp functions VI and VII) so there can even be an exact identity of content as well as form in folktales and games.[14] For example, in some versions of tale type 1530, "Holding up the Rock," a dupe is gulled into believing that he is holding up a wall. But "Hold up the wall" is a hazing stunt at Texas Agricultural and Mechanical College, in which, according to one report, a student is required to squat with his back against a wall as if supporting it.[15] A more surprising example is the prank analogue of tale type 1528, "Holding Down the Hat," in which victims were fooled into grabbing feces concealed under a hat.[16] Perhaps the greatest similarity in trickster tale and prank morphology is their common parodying of standard folktale and game structure. Instead of liquidating an actual lack, a false lack is feigned. Thus the unsuspecting initiate is sent snipe-hunting, armed with a sack and a flashlight, or an apprentice is persuaded to seek some quest-object which, according to the occupation group, may be striped paint, a board-shortener, or a left-handed monkey wrench.

The morphological similarity between game and folktale suggests an important principle which may be applied to other forms of folklore. Basically, these different forms derive from the distinction between words and acts. Thus, there is verbal folklore and non-verbal folklore. The distinction is made most frequently with respect to myth and ritual. Myth is verbal folklore or, in Bascom's terms, verbal "art."[17] Ritual, in contrast, is non-verbal folklore or non-verbal art. Myth and ritual are both sacred; folktale and game are both secular. (Whether all games evolved from ritual is no more or less likely than the evolution, or rather devolution, of folktales from myths.) Whereas folklorists have, for some time, known of the similarities between myth and ritual, they have not recognized the equally common characteristics of folktale and game. Moreover, they have failed to see that the verbal/non-verbal dichotomy applies to most, if not all, of the standard genres of folklore. The proverb, clearly an example of verbal folklore, has for its non-verbal counterpart the gesture. They are functionally equivalent as both forms may sum up a situation or pass judgment on a situation. Riddles are structurally similar to proverbs in that both are based upon topic/comment constructions, but they are distinct from proverbs in that there is always a referent to be guessed.[18] Non-verbal equivalents include a variety of difficult tasks and puzzles. The distinction between proverbs and riddles applies equally to gestures and non-oral riddles. The referent of the gesture is known to both the employer of the gesture and his audience *before* the gesture is made; the referent of the non-oral riddles is presumably known initially only by the poser.[19]

Superstitions are also illuminated by this verbal/non-verbal distinction. Folklorists have long used terms such as "belief" and "custom" or "practice" in discussions of superstitions. In this analysis, practices or customs would be examples of non-verbal folklore since actual physical activity is involved. The distinction may even apply to folk music. If folk narrative, for example, is set to music, it would then be termed folksong; if a game were set to music, it would then be termed folk dance. (Note that the etymology of the term "ballad" supports this distinction.) I am *not* implying that folksong derives from folk narrative or that folk dance derives from game but only suggesting that these supposedly disparate genres have much in common. For example, the basic sequence of lack and lack liquidated found in folktales and games is also found in folk dance. In many dances, a couple is separated, or from the man's point of view, he has lost his partner (lack). The remainder of the dance consists of reuniting the separated partners (liquidating the lack).[20] Moreover, the leaving of home and returning home occurs in folktales, games, folk dances and folk music. Structurally speaking, it does not matter whether "home" is a house, a tree, a position on a dance floor or a note.

The techniques of structural analysis should be applied to genres of folklore other than games and folktales. These forms, from the design of quilt patterns to tongue-twisters, can be defined structurally. One would guess that such analyses will reveal a relatively small number of similar structural patterns underlying these apparently diverse forms.

Specifically, I have tried to demonstrate that at least one nonverbal form of folklore, children's games, is structurally similar to a verbal form, the folktale. If, then, there are non-verbal analogues (e.g., games) for verbal folklore forms (e.g., folktales), then folklore as a discipline cannot possibly be limited to the study of just verbal art, oral literature, or folk literature, or whatever smiliar term is employed. Kenneth Pike has observed that "Verbal and non-verbal activity is a unified whole, and theory and methodology should be organized or created to treat it as such."[21] It is time for folklorists to devote some of the energies given over to the study of verbal folklore to the study of folklore in its non-verbal forms. Compared to folk narrative and folksong, such forms as folk dance, games, and gestures have been grossly neglected.[22] Admittedly there are complex problems of transcription but surely they are not insuperable.

Notes

1. See the author's "From Etic to Emic Units in the Structural Study of Folktales," *Journal of American Folklore*, 75 (1962), 95–105; and "Structural Typology of North American Indian Folktales," *Southwestern Journal of Anthropology*, 19 (1963), 121–30.
2. A recent interesting study by John M. Roberts, Brian Sutton-Smith, and Adam Kendon, "Strategy in Games and Folk Tales," *Journal of Social Psychology*, 61 (1963), 185–199, demonstrates that folktales and games are strikingly similar models of competitive situations and that folktales with strategic outcomes are positively correlated with the occurrence of games of strategy in given cultural settings. However, the comparison of game and folktale content was limited to a generalized consideration of "outcomes." The delineation of game structure should facilitate this type of cross-cultural study.
3. Vladimir Propp, *Morphology of the Folktale,* edited by Svatava Pirkova-Jakobson, translated by

Laurence Scott, Publication Ten of the Indiana University Research Center in Anthropology, Folklore, and Linguistics (Bloomington, 1958), pp. 72–75. Propp's study was also issued as Part III of the *International Journal of American Linguistics*, XXIV, No. 4 (1958), and as Volume 9 of the Bibiliographical and Special Series of the American Folklore Society.

4. Propp, 29.

5. Alice Bertha Gomme, *The Traditional Games of England, Scotland, and Ireland,* vol. I (New York, 1964), 191.

6. . One should remember that an interdiction is a negative injunction. Compare, for example, "Don't open your eyes" with "Keep your eyes closed." It should also be kept in mind that one form of consequence can be lack, while another form can be liquidation of lack (Propp's functions VIIIa and XIX). Brian Sutton-Smith in "A Formal Analysis of Game Meaning," *Western Folklore*, 18 (1959), 13–24, lumps game action into a cover-all term, "The Game Challenge." While he does discuss the structure of game time and space, he does not really conceive of games as linear structural sequences of actions nor does he appear to be aware that there are two distinct sets of action sequences in the game he analyzes, "Bar the Door," one set for theperson who is "it," the central player, and one set for the children who attempt to run past "it" as they go from one base to the other.

7. Roger Caillois, *Man, Play, and Games,* translated by Meyer Barash (New York, 1961), 14. The double set of rules existing in games makes their analysis somewhat different from the analysis of folktales. Sometimes the two patterns are distinct in that there is no rapid change from one set of rules to the other for an individual player. In baseball, for example, the rules of "offense" apply for the team at bat until three men have been put out. Similarly, the rules of "defense" for the team in the field apply for the same period. At the end of the period, the teams exchange places (and rules). However, in other games, such as basketball or football, the rules can change at any time. In football, an intercepted pass or a recovered fumble by the team on defense immediately transforms the defense team into an offense team, and the same action immediately transforms the team previously on offense to a defense team. In "How many miles to Babylon?" described in Paul G. Brewster, *American Nonsinging Games* (Norman, 1953), 52–53, players who attempt to run from one end of a rectangular space to another may be caught by the player in the middle; they now belong to that player and aid him in catching others trying to cross the field.

8. It is quite likely that magical gestures such as touching a certain tree, crossing one's fingers, or assuming a certain "safe" position (such as squatting in "Squat Tag") are analogous to the host of magical agents which protect protagonists in folktales.

9. Brewster, op. cit.,164.

10. William Wells Newell, *Games and Songs of American Children* (New York, 1963), 152; Brewster, op. cit., 46.

11. Gomme, op. cit., Vol. II, 391–396. For a New York State version called "Old Witch," see Anne Gertrude Sneller, "Growing Up," *NYFQ,* Vol. XX, No. 2 (June 1964),89–90 (Editor).

12. *The Folktale* (New York, 1951), 230 and 234.

13. Brewster, op. cit., 67.

14. Ibid., 120–126.

15. Fred Eikel, Jr., "An Aggie Vocabulary of Slang," *American Speech*, 18 (1946), 34.

16. James R. Caldwell, "A Tale Actualized in a Game," *JAF*, 58 (1945), 50.

17. William R. Bascom, "Verbal Art," *JAF*, 68 (1955), 245–252.

18. Robert A. Georges and Alan Dundes, "Toward a Structural Definition of the Riddle," *JAF*, 76 (1963), 113 and 117.

19. For examples of non-oral riddles, see Jan Brunvand, "More Non-Oral Riddles," *Western Folklore*, 19 (1960), 132–133. Note that this form of folklore is defined negatively, in terms of the presumably primary verbal form: riddles. In the same way, the term "practical joke" represents a qualifying of the primary term "joke," which is also verbal. Even the term used here of "non-verbal folklore" continues the same bias in favor of the primacy of verbal forms. At least gestures are not called non-oral or non-verbal proverbs.

20. In the structure of folk dance, the same distinction is found of beginning either with a state of lack or causing a state of lack by an act of villainy. Some dances have an "it" who is without a partner (lack) and who seeks to obtain one (lack liquidated). Other dances begin with couples, but during the dance one or more couples become separated (lack) and reunite only at the end of the dance (lack liquidated). For an interesting study of dance morphology, see Olga Szentpal, "Versuch einer Formanalyse der Ungarischen Volkstanze," *Acta Ethnographica*, 7 (1958), 257–334; also Gyorgy Martin and Erno Pestovar, "A Structural Analysis of the Hungarian Folk Dance (A Methodological Sketch)," Ibid., 10 (1961), 1–40.

21. *Language in Relation to a Unified Theory of the Structure of Human Behavior,* Part I (Glendale, 1954), 2. These categories of "verbal" and "non-verbal" folklore are arbitrary distinctions which do not necessarily reflect objective reality. Obviously jump rope rhymes, counting out rhymes, and finger rhymes involve both words and actions.

22. Alexander Haggerty Krappe, for example, in his *The Science of Folklore* (New York, 1930), gives these forms short shrift. The unfortunate trend continues. One looks in vain for extended mention of these forms in annual folklore bibliographies, works in progress lists, and surveys of folklore research.

8

The Devolutionary Premise in Folklore Theory

Introduction

To encourage the "modern" or American break of folkloristics from its intellectual parent, nineteenth-century European folklore studies, thirty-three-year-old Dundes criticized his elders for holding a deep bias against progress. It was an extension of another historiographical argument in his earlier essay "From Etic to Emic Units in the Structural Study of Folktales" (1962g, and chapter 4 in this volume)—namely, that modern structural and contextual theories were refreshingly synchronic, while previous approaches were diachronic, mired in problematic historical-geographic searches for origin. Dundes sought to disrupt the binary underlying prevalent theories in the field—including survival, myth-ritual, and historic-geographic perspectives. He saw this binary as setting a superior elite civilization against a primitivized folk culture. This led to other oppositions, with one pole, assumed to be the later development, dominating or displacing the other, associated with the distant past or "folk": urban/rural, rhymes/myth, science/spirituality. Dundes wanted to underscore his social definition of folk as any group with a linking factor, and lore as a necessary element of life, past and present. Thus, he declared these as timeless criteria in stating that "there has always been folklore and in all likelihood there will always be folklore." Instead of viewing change to lore as bad or necessarily degenerative, he argued for a model in which folklore "actually improved or rather evolved in time." Folklore and its study then stood for something growing—in scope and importance. Only then, he concluded, can folkloristics make progress.

Dundes first presented this paper to professional folklorists at the American Folklore Society meeting in 1967, as part of a special session on the history of folklore scholarship. As with his studies of folklore, in his historiography Dundes sought to uncover structural patterns that revealed driving ideas, often outside the awareness of participants in a culture or discipline. Folklorist Elliott Oring recalled that when he gave the paper, Dundes ignited "a rather animated debate" about whether folklore in reality was indeed vanishing, rather than about whether folklorists unconsciously followed what Dundes called "the vise of devolutionary thought." Responding to the comment by famed songhunter Alan Lomax, that true folk songs were in danger of extinction, Dundes asserted if Lomax would consider the ever popular but often neglected genre of jokes, he would realize that folklore was growing and emerging. But the obsession with folk songs as a vanishing expression of a golden age was, Dundes observed, indicative of the devolutionary mindset. As the title of Oring's reminisce, "The Devolutionary Premise: A Definitional Delusion?" (1975a), suggests, Dundes preferred to turn the debate toward the question of whether there was, as Oring put it, "some unconscious sado-masochistic compulsion of folklorists to devolve the lore that they love." Readers can consider his criticism that Dundes sees a devolutionary bias because he (Dundes) worked with a different definition of folklore from those theorists he analyzed. Oring pointed out, for instance, that jokes were known in the nineteenth century, but they "weren't considered folklore." Therefore, Dundes has a presentist argument, including the criteria used for judging "progress," in discovering devolutionary premises in studies that do not have them. As Oring stated, "to impute a devolutionary premise to survivalist theory is to criticize antiquarians for studying antiques, or to suggest that antiques may be very new rather than very old." That is not to deny devolutionary tendencies in some folklore theories, but, rather, to question whether a binary exists between past and present theories of folklore, or, for that matter, between folklore studies as a practice and other disciplines considered more evolutionary.

Without diving into the debate of whether devolutionary belief as a cognitive pattern is an illusion or not, William A. Wilson has written that Dundes demonized the historic-geographic method as devolutionary, although some of its practitioners did in fact construct "a model in which folklore actually improved or rather evolved in time." Wilson pointed to Julius Krohn, a prominent figure associated with the "Finnish School" of historic-geographic folklore studies, who in the 1880s propounded a view that *Kalevala* poems were not fragmented survivals from a golden age of the past, but, because they had been imbued with a Finnish national spirit through centuries of oral transmission, were constantly re-created and improved (1976). This point of information raised a more general question, sparked by Dundes, about the varied concepts and categorizations of past (e.g., "golden age," "primitive," "ancient," "pre-industrial") and present ("industrial," "urban," "modern," "post-modern"), as well as their interrelationships (e.g., in the idea of folk practices, such as hunting, as an "escape" from modernity as well as an integral part of it; in slang and legend; and indeed in jokes). (See, for instance, De Caro 1976; Bronner 1998; and Bauman and Briggs 2003.) One suggestion that Oring made was to differentiate among the approaches to specific genres, so that Freud's jokes invited evolutionary consideration, while Lomax's ballads impelled devolutionary analysis.

Writing in the twenty-first century, Dundes doubted that folklorists had been able to undo devolutionary thinking. In a jeremiad-sounding address to the American Folklore Society, he cited references, after he published his "Devolutionary Premise" essay (1975c), to folkloristics as "predicated on a vanishing subject" (Kirshenblatt-Gimblett 1996) and to "the disappearance of its subject matter" (Ben-Amos 1972). His answer, one applauded by many folklorists, was that "folklore continues to be alive and well in the modern world, due in part to increased transmission via e-mail and the Internet." Adapting the famous epigrammatic phrase attributed to Mark Twain (a charter member of the American Folklore Society), Dundes quipped, "Reports of folkloristics' death have been greatly exaggerated" (2005c).

Annotations of two terms in this essay may be helpful to readers. "Ur-form" (also referred to as *Grundform* in German) refers to the original or archetypal form from which many variants emerged. Two of the scholars mentioned by Dundes are usually credited with spreading its use: Antti Aarne (1867–1925) from Finland, who developed the tale-type index, a standard international reference for folktales; and Walter Anderson

(1885–1962), who taught in Germany (born in Belarus and raised in Estonia). The use of Ur has a biblical reference to the Book of Genesis; it was the birthplace of the first patriarch Abraham (translated as "father of a multitude" or "leader of many"). Ur exemplifies the "many from one" philosophy in a holy scripture. The metaphor is meant to show the multiple trajectories of narrative offspring, since Abraham is viewed as the patriarch for Judaism, Islam, and Christianity, and, even within those, for a number of variations, such as the twelve tribes of Israel.

Gesunkenes Kulturgut is a German phrase, literally meaning sunken cultural materials. It was coined as a folkloristic term in 1902 by German folklorist and philologist Hans Naumann (1886–1951). He used it to describe the process by which expressions originating in the upper stratum of society "sink" to, or are adapted by, the lower stratum. It assumed a rigid class structure, arranged hierarchically by wealth and occupation, since it suggested interchange between an aristocracy and peasantry at the top and bottom, respectively. As the reference work *General Ethnological Concepts* by Åke Hultkrantz outlined, and Dundes averred, the concept is much older. Hultkrantz gave examples from the mid-nineteenth century, and claimed that among European scholars, it "has been widely accepted" (1960). Still, Hultkrantz recognized alternative theories of transmission; one suggested a reverse vertical direction from the bottom to the top, but nonetheless maintained the binary of simple folk and sophisticated aristocracy to which Dundes objected. Several ethnologists cited by Hultkrantz viewed culture as both an up and down flow, while others, such as Berkeley anthropologist George Foster (1914–2006) suggested a "circular relationship" in which folk culture "draws on and is continually replenished by contact with the products of intellectual and scientific social strata, but in which folk culture continually, though perhaps in a lesser degree, contributes to these non-folk societies" (1953). In one of Dundes's last publications, he was still complaining of the prevalence of *gesunkenes Kulturgut* theory in historical scholarship. Taking up the proverbs represented in the famous painting *Netherlandish Proverbs* by Pieter Bruegel, he found that the devolutionary thinking evident in *gesunkenes Kulturgut* had been prominent in preventing credit being given to the cultural creativity of ignorant, illiterate peasants in the painting. Rather than relying on "educated aristocratic individuals," Dundes proclaimed, Bruegel "favored folk material rather than elitist classical or biblical versions" of proverbs. Other examples he gave were that Polyphemus (AT 1137) began with Homer's *Odyssey*, and that the "Taming of the Shrew" (AT 901) originated with Shakespeare's play, although it was clear to Dundes that both authors borrowed the plots from oral tradition. "The point is," Dundes concluded, that "it is folklore which is the source of high culture, not the other way around" (2004b, 18).

The Devolutionary Premise in Folklore Theory

THERE HAS BEEN FAR TOO little progress observed in the development of folkloristics. But this lack of "progress" is not so surprising in view of the unmistakable and consistent bias against progress inherent in the majority of folklore theories. Even a cursory examination of the intellectual history of folklore scholarship reveals a definite unquestioned basic premise that the golden age of folklore occurred in the past, in most cases specifically the far distant past. As a result of the past-oriented Weltanschauung of most folklorists—and it is really with the worldview of folklorists that this essay is concerned —it has always appeared to be logically necessary and highly desirable to engage in historically reconstructing the golden age of folklore. The endless quest for the land of "ur" as in "ur-form," or "archetype" in Finnish Method parlance, continues unabated in conservative folkloristic circles. Inasmuch as the means and direction of folklore methodology are probably inescapably controlled by the nature of the theoretical premises, hitherto largely unexamined, held by professional folklorists, it is absolutely essential that these crucial underlying premises be held up to the light of reason if there is ever to be any appreciably significant change in methods of folklore analysis.

The bias against "progress" in folklore theory may be easily demonstrated by briefly considering some of the numerous examples of degeneration, decay, or devolution—the particular term is not the issue—which abound in so much of traditional folklore theory. Perhaps the most obvious instances are those underlying the various folklore transmission theories. Typically, surveys of such theories begin with a detailed consideration of degeneration, perhaps signaling its hallowed position.[1] The most common devolutionary notion is that folklore decays through time. Another notion is that folklore "runs down" by moving from "higher" to "lower" strata of society. These two notions are by no means mutually exclusive and in fact one can without difficulty imagine that if folklore really moved from "higher" to "lower" strata, it could easily undergo textual deterioration at the same time. Classic examples of these notions include Max Müller's "*disease* of language" according to which theory of semantic devolution the original names of Vedic and other gods became confused or forgotten as time passed, as well as Hans Naumann's "*gesunkenes Kulturgut*"[2] which held that cultural items originating in the upper stratum of society filtered down to the lower stratum which was wrongly thought to be synonymous with the "folk." A logical consequence of this "aristocratic" origin of folklore theory was that folklore consisted largely of reworked remnants which had managed somehow to survive the presumed downward transmission of culture.

It should be remarked that the *gesunkenes Kulturgut* notion is still very much with us. Folklorist Walter Anderson believed that folktales usually moved from "culturally higher" to "culturally lower" peoples, according to Stith Thompson,[3] who echoes the idea, pointing out that American Indians have borrowed European tale types whereas Europeans have not borrowed American Indian tales. Thompson even goes so far as to say that "If the principle is really valid we may ask whether tales must keep running down hill culturally until they are found only in the lower ranges," although he concedes this would be an overstatement of Anderson's position. Nevertheless, Thompson's own devolutionary bias may well have led him to misinterpret the available data regarding a hypothetical archetype for the "Star Husband" tale which he studied using the Finnish method. Like all devolutionary folklorists, he assumes that the original form of the tale must have been the fullest and most complete version. Later, shorter versions are thus assumed to be fragments. The devolutionist normally postulates a movement from complex to simple whereas an evolutionist might argue that the development from simple to complex is equally likely. In any case, Thompson is forced to label some of the shorter versions of Star Husband as confused or fragmentary despite the fact that his "fragmentary" versions demonstrate a common uniform pattern.[4]

There are many other striking illustrations of the devolutionary premise in folklore transmission theories. The Grimms argued that folktales were the detritus of myths[5] and just as folktales were assumed to be broken down myths, so it was held that ballads were the detritus of epics or romances.[6] But perhaps no more overt statement of the premise can be found than in the conception of "*zersingen*" in folksong theory. "*Zersingen*" refers to the "alterations of a *destructive* nature"[7] which occur as songs are sung. The very act of singing a folksong is thus construed to be a potentially destructive act endangering the continued stability of the song sung.[8] Moreover, just as singing songs is presumed to destroy them, so the telling of folktales is thought to run the risk of ruining them. Retelling a tale allows the forgetfulness of the raconteur to become a factor.[9] This is implicit in Walter Anderson's famous superorganic "law of self-correction" (*Gesetz der Selbstberichtigung*).[10] Anderson's idea was that folktale stability was not attributable to the remarkable memories of raconteurs, but was rather the result of an individual's hearing a given tale on many different occasions, perhaps from many different sources. Narratives essentially corrected themselves, argued Anderson, but the very term used indicates the devolutionary bias. Why is it assumed that folktales need to be *corrected*? Only the unquestioned assumption that folktales become "incorrect" through time can possibly justify the notion that folktales need to "correct themselves"— granting for the sake of argument that tales rather than people do the "correcting."

A critical correlative of the devolutionary premise is the assumption that the oldest, original version of an item of folklore was the best, fullest, or most complete one. A change of any kind automatically moved the item from perfection toward imperfection. Partly for this reason, one finds a deep resentment of change and an equally deep-seated resistance to the study of change in folklore. A similar situation prevailed until relatively recently in anthropology where even up to the first several decades of the twentieth century pioneer ethnographers sought to obtain "pure" precontact cultural data. Students of the American Indian, for example, would often write up their field data as if the Indians had never been exposed to or affected by acculturative European influences. Mooney, in collecting Cherokee tales, specifically commented that he did not bother to record what were obviously European borrowings. This made perfect sense in the light of a past-oriented Weltanschauung. If the forms of the past were more valuable, then it logically followed that changes of any kind were by definition potentially destructive in nature. Although anthropologists have learned to accept and study culture change, folklorists generally have tended to continue to look askance at change.

The Hungarian folklorist Ortutay, in probably the most detailed critique of folklore transmission theories, notes that, "Retelling nearly always involves a change" and although there may be an element of creativity involved in making any change, "in its later, final stages . . . oral transmission comes to be equivalent to deterioration, to a process of stuttering forgetfulness."[11] The same attitude towards change is expressed by Stith Thompson when in summarizing Walter Anderson's views he says, "The first time a change of detail is made in a story it is *undoubtedly* a *mistake*, an *error* of memory." [12] Deleterious changes could be caused by weakness of memory, unwelcome interpolations, or from contaminations of themes. Note the obvious pejorative connotation of the term "*contaminated* text," a term which once again reflects the ever present devolutionary premise.[13]

The generally negative attitude towards change has been clearly reflected in folklore methodology. Just as ethnographers carefully sifted through unavoidable details obviously only recently added through acculturative contact in an attempt to discover the pure unadulterated original native culture, so practitioners of the Finnish historic-geographic method sought to work backwards through the unfortunate changes (or, in Thompson's terms, the mistakes and errors) in order to find the pure unadulterated original ur-form. The difficulties of searching for the ur-form, too often presumed to be hopelessly hidden by the destructive, deteriorative effects of oral transmission were considerable, but not always insurmountable. Possibly one of the most ambitious and optimistic efforts was made by students of the Bible engaged in Form Criticism.

Form Criticism, according to Redlich,[14] is a method of study and investigation which deals with the preliterary stage of the Gospel tradition, when the material was handed down orally. It was assumed that Biblical materials before being set down in written tradition "were subject to the usual inevitable fate of oral tradition, such as adaptation, alteration, and addition." However, it was also assumed that there were definite, discernible laws governing the oral transmission process, laws which once discovered might be applied (in reverse) to the written Gospels. By thus working backwards, Form Critics hoped to be able to reconstruct "the narratives as they actually happened and the sayings as they were actually uttered by our Lord."[15]

A few folklorists have commented upon the consequences of the devolutionary premise. Von Sydow, for instance, challenged the hypothesis that the original form of a folktale was necessarily the most complete, most logical version,[16] although he confessed this had been his own view when he began his folktale research. Similarly, Gerould in *The Ballad of Tradition* deplores the "unfortunate tendency on the part of scholars to take it for granted that earlier ballads are likely to be better than later ones. . . ."[17] Yet Gerould argues that the process of deterioration is inevitable: "Degeneration of noble themes and captivating tunes must have gone on ever since ballads became current. . . ."[18] The implicit nature of the devolutionary premise is also revealed in the wording of Gerould's consideration of the American "Old Bangum" versions of "Sir Lionel" (Child #18) when he observes, "The interesting point about all these versions, it seems to me, is the evidence they give that changes and even abbreviations do not necessarily imply any structural degeneracy."[19] More recently, Ortutay has suggested that short elementary forms such as proverbs or jests are "most capable of resisting the corroding effect of degressive processes."[20]

Despite a few critical comments by folklorists, there does not appear to be much awareness of the enormous impact of devolutionary ideas upon folklore theory and methodology. At best, folklorists seem to accept the idea that the universe of folklore is running down. Even Olrik's so-called epic laws of folklore were presumed to weaken in time. Olrik suggested, for example, that the law of the number three "gradually succumbs to intellectual demands for greater realism." [21] One possible reason for the lack of awareness may be that folklore has often been associated with evolution rather than devolution. And the interesting question does arise, how folklorists could remain so utterly committed to a devolutionary worldview at a time when ideas of evolution and of progress were so much at the fore of European intellectual thought.

The intellectual history of the idea of progress is reasonably well documented[22] and there can be no doubt that this idea came into prominence at about the same time that the discipline of folklore began to emerge. Progress meant more than that the "moderns" were just as good as the "ancients" as had been argued in the late seventeenth century. Progress meant that the golden age was not behind us but ahead of us.[23] The positivistic ethic of the ultimate perfectibility of man and society had considerable influence upon the course of most academic disciplines. However, as we shall see, the effect of the evolutionary idea of progress on the treatment of folklore materials was largely a negative rather than a positive one.

To be sure, there were some attempts to borrow evolutionary ideas in folklore theory. One of the most striking instances is Hartland's suggestion that narratives all over the world followed a basic evolutionary general law.[24] Folktales, and specifically incidents in tales, changed with different stages of civilization in accordance with this law. Speaking of an incident in the Forbidden Chamber cycle of tales, Hartland observed, "The incident in this shape is specially characteristic of savage life. As with advancing civilization the reasoning which has moulded it thus becomes obsolete we may expect that the incident itself will undergo change into a form more appropriate to the higher stages of culture. . . ."[25] An item of folklore had to become fit in order to survive. Hartland spoke of the popular mind and how it "rendered by a process analogous with that of natural selection, which we may call traditional selection, the version that has reached us predominantly over all others."[26] Hartland even suggested that it was traditional selection which tended to "eliminate the ruder and coarser, preserving and refining, not necessarily the more credible, but the more artistic." The idea that traditional selection operated in such a way as to ensure esthetically superior products was of course entirely in keeping with the concept of evolution as progress.

In spite of this isolated example of a positive application of evolutionary "progress" oriented theory to folklore—and there are several others—it is quite evident that the concept of progress per se had a devastatingly negative effect upon folklore theory. The association of folklore with the past, glorious or not, continued. Progress meant leaving the past behind. From this perspective, the noble savage and the equally noble peasant—folkloristically speaking—were destined to lose their folklore as they marched ineluctably towards civilization. Thus it was not a matter of the evolution *of* folklore; it was more a matter of the evolution *out of* folklore. This may best be seen in the work of Tylor who in adamantly opposing rigid degenerative theories definitely championed unilinear cultural evolution. At the same time, he forcefully argued the *devolution* of folklore. There was no inconsistency in this. On the one hand, Tylor states that "notwithstanding the continual interference of degeneration, the main tendency of culture from primaeval up to modern times has been from savagery towards civilization."[27] On the other, Tylor conceived folklore, that is, "survivals," to be "transformed, shifted or *mutilated*" fragments of culture.[28] To put it succinctly, as humans evolved, so folklore devolved. Tylor's view of folklore is clear. For example, he suggested that it might be possible to trace the origins of games of chance from ancient divination rituals insofar as such games were "survivals from a branch of savage philosophy, once of high rank though now fallen into merited decay."[29] In an unequivocal statement, Tylor remarks, "The history of survival in cases like those of the folk-lore and occult arts which we have been considering, has for the most part been a history of dwindling and decay. As men's minds change in progressing culture, old customs and opinions fade gradually . . . ," although Tylor does admit that there are in fact occasional exceptions to this "law."[30] If survivals or folklore were truly dying or dead, then it made a good deal of sense for Tylor to argue that the folklorist's or ethnographer's course should be like that of the anatomist who carried on his studies if possible on dead rather than on living subjects.[31] Here we have the ultimate logical consequence of devolution: death. And this is why devolutionary-minded folklorists have devoted themselves by definition to dead materials. The view, still widely held, is that as all the peoples of the world achieve civilized status, there will be less and less folklore left until one day it will disappear altogether. Thus Ruth Benedict could write authoritatively in the *Encyclopaedia of Social Sciences* in 1931 that "in a strict sense folklore is a dead trait in the modern world."[32] Are folklorists doomed to study only the disappearing, the dying, and the dead?

Of course, the gloomy reports of the death of folklore are in part a result of the misguided and narrow concept of the folk as the illiterate in a literate society, that is, the folk as peasant, as *vulgus in populo*, as isolated rural community.[33] Since the majority of folklorists in Europe and Asia continue to restrict the concept of folk in this way, citing as a matter of fact the definitions of folk society offered by American anthropologists Redfield and Foster for authority,[34] it is easy for them to believe that gradually the folk are dying out. With the devolutionary demise of folk or peasant culture, the deterioration of folklore was a matter of course. Ortutay puts it in these terms: "We suggest that, as long as the oral tradition of the peasantry continued to exist as a uniform system . . . degressive and deteriorative processes played a secondary role in the dialectics of oral transmission."[35] Since unquestionably one of the reasons for the break-up of peasant culture is the advent of industrialization, Communist folklorist Ortutay is able to point the accusing finger of blame at capitalism for destroying peasant (= folk) culture and consequently for destroying folklore.[36] Of course, if folklorists were able to free themselves from so narrow and obsolescent a concept of folk, they could see that there are still numerous active functioning folk groups (e.g., ethnic, religious, occupational, etc.) and that the peasant community is just one of many different types of "folk." In fact, even as this one type of formerly rural homogeneous folk group becomes transformed into urban, heterogeneous, part-time folk groups, new types of folklore are emerging, some of which are actually caused by capitalism as in the creation of folklore from commercial advertisements.[37]

Yet even attempts to repudiate the idea that folklore is dying cannot fully escape the traditional devolutionary bias. Richard Dorson ends his book *American Folklore* with the statement that "The idea that folklore is dying out is itself a kind of folklore."[38] On the one hand, Dorson is indicating that this idea is a traditional one, but, in addition, since he obviously doesn't believe that folklore is dying out, the second use of the term folklore has a hint of the idea of folklore as falsehood or fallacy. In any event, the meaning of "folklore" in the phrase "That's folklore" in popular parlance refers to an error. This continued pejorative connotation of the word folklore[39] has a close connection with the devolutionary premise.

If folklore is conceived to be synonymous with ignorance, then it follows that it is a good thing for folklore to be eradicated. With this reasoning, educators and social reformers seek to stamp out superstitions encouraging folk medical practices on the grounds that such practices are either harmful in and of themselves or harmful to the extent that they delay or discourage consultation with practitioners of scientific medicine. In this light, it is not just that folklore is dying out, but rather it is a good thing that folklore is dying out. Moreover since it is regrettable that folklore isn't dying out at an even faster pace, the implication is that people should give the devolutionary process a helping hand.

The education versus folklore (or to put it in other terms: truth versus error) dichotomy is intimately related to the devolutionary premise. In essence, the idea is that the more education, especially the more literacy, the less the illiteracy and thus the less the number of folk and the less the folklore. It is wrongly assumed that literate people have no folklore.

This is really the evolutionary progress idea restated. As nonliterate and illiterate people become literate, they will tend to lose their folklore. Typical is Gerould's remark: "Not until the spread of primary education and the conversion of the general public from oral to visual habits, which took place in the nineteenth century, was folk-song marked for destruction."[40] Much sounder, of course, is Albert Lord's position: "While the presence of writing in a society *can* have an effect on oral tradition, it does not *necessarily* have an effect at all."[41] It is certainly doubtful whether increased literacy and education have seriously affected the quality and quantity of folk speech or jokes, at least in American culture. Moreover, if there is any validity to what has been termed the concept of "postliterate man" (as opposed to preliterate or nonliterate man), referring to the idea that the information communicated by such mass media as radio, television, and movies depends upon the oral-aural circuit rather than upon writing or print, then it becomes even more obvious that oral tradition in so-called civilized societies has not been snuffed out by literacy.

The difference between a future oriented worldview involving progressive evolution out of folklore and a past oriented worldview reveling romantically in the glorious folkloristic materials of nationalistic patrimonies seems to be clear cut. However, it is important to realize that not everyone shares the future oriented evolutionistic postulate. There are a number of devolutionary based philosophies of life, philosophies which decry the inroads made by civilization. In such philosophies of cultural primitivism[42] the golden age remains safely embedded in the past while the evils of civilization do their deadly work, destroying all that is deemed good and worthwhile. From this perspective, folklore and civilization are still antithetical—just as they were in Tylorian times, but the critical difference is that folklore is good and civilization is bad, rather than the other way around. The distinction can also be expressed in terms of utility. The nineteenth century doctrine of progress included a bias towards utilitarianism. Evolution and progress meant an increase of useful cultural items. In this light, folklore as a vestigial remain or relic was defined as essentially useless.[43] With the substitution of devolution for evolution in general worldview, there comes the possibility of transvaluing folklore into something use*ful* rather than use*less*. An example of this may be found in some of the psychological approaches to folklore.

Freud summarized the devolutionary philosophy of life in *Civilization and Its Discontents*—the title itself indicates the bias—when he stated that "our so-called civilization itself is to blame for a great part of our misery, and we should be much happier if we were to give it up and go back to primitive conditions."[44] Note also that the Freudian method consisted of clarifying or removing *present* neuroses by treating them as survivals from a fuller, more complete event in the individual's *past*. The historical reconstruction of the traumatic ur-form to explain apparently irrational and fragmentary phenomena is cut from the same methodological cloth as the majority of folklore reconstruction techniques, More revealing perhaps for folkloristics are the actual approaches to folklore found in the anthroposophical tradition of Rudolf Steiner and his followers as well as in the applications of analytical psychology by Carl Jung and his followers. For both Steiner and Jung, folklore represented an important vehicle by means of which individuals could travel backwards through time to gain vital spiritual benefit. In other words, one of the ways of getting back to nature, ideal human nature that is, and away from forward marching destructive civilization, was by regaining contact with folklore. Rudolf Steiner's influential lecture "The Interpretation of Fairy Tales," given on December 26, 1908, in Berlin, clearly illustrates the devolutionary nature of civilization as opposed to folklore. Fairy tales, according to Steiner, belong to time immemorial when people still had clairvoyant powers and when they had access to spiritual reality. In modern times, people have wrongly engaged in intellectual pursuits and have gotten out of touch with spiritual reality. Fortunately, by reading and understanding (anthroposophically, of course) fairy tales, moderns can attempt to rediscover their long lost spiritual heritage. In like fashion with only slightly less mystical language does Jung argue that myths and their archetypes "hark back to a prehistoric world with its own spiritual preconceptions."[45] Like Steiner, Jung assumes that the primeval spiritual reality is fundamentally a Christian one, and, like Steiner, he is unalterably opposed to intellectual and rational attempts to explain the content of myth. Perhaps the overt Christian cast of Steiner and Jung's approach to folklore accounts for the placement of the golden age in the past. Fallen from grace and tainted by civilization, people need to find balm for their injured souls by immersing themselves in myths and tales which are presumed to offer the possibility of at least partial spiritual salvation. In this view, it is not folklore but the spiritual person which is running the risk of dying out. It is curious how little notice the Steiner and Jung positions have obtained from folklorists, for in truth they are pioneers in the uncharted area of applied folklore. Folklore in their conceptual framework provides a unique source of therapy for the troubled if not sick mind of the modern person.

Having delineated the nature of the devolutionary premise, one can see the history of folklore scholarship in a new light. It would appear that each successive methodological innovation has consisted largely of a slightly different application of devolutionary theory. If it is accurate to say that Max Müller's solar mythology yielded to Andrew Lang and company's "anthropological folklore" approach, then one can see that the crucial notion of the "disease of language" was replaced by a notion that fully formed "rational" savage ideas devolved through time to become fragmentary, irrational mental survivals in civilization. Moreover, one might consider that one offshoot of the survival theory was the more specific myth-ritual approach in which games, folkdances, and popular rhymes were presumed to be degenerate derivatives of original myths or even earlier rituals. One thinks, for example, of Lewis Spence's contention that folk rhymes including some nursery rhymes are frequently survivals of myth and ritual, "that is, they represent in a *broken-down* or *corrupted* form, the spoken or verbal description of rite."[46] In addition, if it is accurate to say that the late nineteenth century unilinear cultural evolutionary based doctrine of survivals in turn lost its sway in folklore circles to make way for the Finnish version of the older comparative method, then one can similarly see that the degeneration oriented concept of mutilated, vestigial survivals has been succeeded by a technique whereby multitudinous versions of an item of folklore—versions which are said to suffer from the alleged ravages of performance—are amassed with the hope of reconstructing the perfect, albeit hypothetical, basic form from which these numerous partial realizations must have sprung. The question is thus not whether there is a devolutionary bias or premise in folklore theory and method. There can be no doubt that there is. The question is merely which devolutionary scheme is in vogue at any given point in time.[47]

In evaluating the significance of identifying a devolutionary premise in folklore theory, there are several possibilities. One of these is that folklore is in fact devolving and that the various expressions of the devolutionary premise simply attest to this. Another possibility, however, is that the devolutionary premise is a culture bound product of a larger nineteenth century European worldview, a worldview which favored romanticism and primitivism, and which encouraged scholars in many disciplines to look and work backwards, that is, toward the presumed perfect past. If this were the case, then it might be useful to suggest alternative a priori premises so that modern folklorists might be enabled to escape the vise of devolutionary thought. One could, for example, propose a cyclic scheme[48] in which it was assumed that folklore materials could rise phoenix-wise after a period of degeneration. Or one could construct a model in which folklore actually improved or rather evolved in time. Why must we assume, for example, that jokes told in any one age are necessarily inferior in any way to those told in ages past? Is it not within the realm of human possibility that a new version of an old joke might be a finer example of oral style and humor than its precursors? There should be recognition of the fact that change per se is not necessarily negative. Change is neutral; it is neither good nor bad. It may be either; it may be both. In this light, the unity, as Ortutay referred to it, of "one creation—innumerable variants"[49] need not depend upon the idea that the initial one creation is perfect and the innumerable variants which follow merely imperfect derivatives. The whole idea of one creation giving rise to multiple variants is very likely a manifestation of what the intellectual historian Lovejoy described under the framework of the great chain of being, a dominant intellectual concept in eighteenth and nineteenth century Europe.[50] The many deriving from the one may certainly be conceived as belonging not to a set in which perfection is necessarily assumed to be logically prior to imperfection, but rather to a set in which members may be ranked genealogically or hierarchically (e.g., in esthetic terms) or even as existential equals.

With a more eclectic theoretical framework, one might say that folklore in general is NOT devolving or dying out, but only that *some* genres or *some* examples of *some* genres are decreasing in popularity or usage, e.g., the true riddle or ballad in American urban society. By the same token, one might say that folklore in general is NOT evolving or being born, but only that *some* genres or *some* examples of *some* genres are increasing in popularity or usage and that occasionally new folklore forms are created. One need not, in other words, place the golden age either in the far distant past or in the far distant future. One may merely indicate that folklore is a universal: there has always been folklore and in all likelihood there will always be folklore. As long as humans interact and in the course of so doing employ traditional forms of communication, folklorists will continue to have golden opportunities to study folklore.

Notes

1. Gyula Ortutay, "Principles of Oral Transmission in Folk Culture," *Acta Ethnographica*, VIII(1959), 175–221, provides such a survey. See especially pp. 200–207. See also Douglas J. McMillan, "A Survey of Theories Concerning the Oral Transmission of the Traditional Ballad," *Southern Folklore Quarterly*, XXVIII (1964), 299–309.
2. For a convenient summary of Naumann's theory, see Adolf Bach, *Deutsche Volkskunde* (Heidelberg, 1960), pp. 64–69, 435–440; or Åke Hultkrantz, *General Ethnological Concepts* (= *International Dictionary of Regional European Ethnology and Folklore*, Vol. I) (Copenhagen, 1950), pp. 158–159.
3. Stith Thompson, *The Folktale* (New York, 1951), p. 438.
4. For some critical details which suggest that a devolutionary premise can bias hypotheses in historic-geographic studies, see Alan Dundes, ed., *The Study of Folklore* (Englewood Cliffs, N.J., 1965), pp. 449–450, n. 9.
5. Thompson, op. cit., p. 370.
6. Cf. Ortutay, op. cit., p. 202; D. K. Wilgus, *Anglo-American Folksong Scholarship Since 1898* (New Brunswick, N.J., 1959), p. 43.

7. The definition is from Laurits Bødker, *Folk Literature (Germanic)* (= *International Dictionary of Regional European Ethnology and Folklore*, Vol. II) (Copenhagen, 1965), p. 330. The emphasis is added.
8. For extended discussions of "*zersingen*," see Renata Dessauer, *Das Zersingen. Ein Beitrag zur Psychologie des deutschen Volkliedes* (= Germanische Studien, No. 61) (Berlin, 1928);Hermann Goja, "Das Zersingen der Volkslieder. Ein Beitrag zur Psychologie der Volksdichtung," *Imago*, VI (1920), 132–242, an abridged form of which appeared in translation as "The Alteration of Folksongs by Frequent Singing: A Contribution to the Psychology of Folk Poetry," *The Psychoanalytic Study of Society*, ed. Sidney Axelrad and Warner Muensterberger (New York, 1964), III, 111–170. "*Zersingen*" and related phenomena are also discussed by Bach, op. cit., pp. 509–510. Note that if folklorists truly believed in the reality of "*zersingen*," they might well exert an all out effort to prevent any further performances of folklore inasmuch as they have assumed that deterioration is an inevitable concomitant or result of performance. One can just imagine folklorists running around begging the folk not to sing folksongs, kindly explaining to them that singing them in time destroys them. This is perhaps analogous to librarians who are so concerned about injuries to and losses of books that they would almost prefer to keep all books safely locked up, away from all potential readers. The difference, of course, is that folklorists could not possibly stop the folk from using folklore—even if they wanted to. Nevertheless, in a way a modified version of "*zersingen*" philosophy does appear to prevail among those folklorists who express great anxiety about quickly collecting folklore before it disappears, dies out, or suffers *further* "loss" of meaning.
9. Kaarle Krohn, *Die Folkloristische Arbeitsmethode* (= Instituttet for Sammenlignende Kulturforskning, Series B, No. 5) (Oslo, 1926), pp. 59–65; Thompson, op. cit., p. 436.
10. Cf. Dieter Glade, "Zum Anderson'schen Gesetz der Selbstberichtingung," *Fabula*, VIII (1966), 224–236.
11. Ortutay, op. cit., p. 180.
12. Thompson, op. cit., p. 437. The emphasis is added.
13. Cf. Krohn, op. cit., pp. 84–85; Thompson, op. cit., p. 437; Ortutay, op. cit., p. 203; and Bach, op. cit., p. 519.
14. E. Basil Redlich, *Form Criticism: Its Value and Limitations* (London, 1939), p. 9.
15. Ibid., p. 11.
16. Dundes, op. cit., p. 233.
17. Gordon Hall Gerould, *The Ballad of Tradition* (New York, 1957), p. 214.
18. Ibid., p. 185.
19. Ibid., p. 174. The emphasis is added.
20. Ortutay, op. cit., p. 207.
21. Dundes, op. cit., p. 134.
22. Some of the standard sources include John Baillie, *The Belief in Progress* (London, 1950); J. B. Bury, *The Idea of Progress: An Inquiry into its Origin and Growth* (New York, 1955);Morris Ginsberg, *The Idea of Progress: A Revaluation* (London, 1963); and Charles van Doren, *The Idea of Progress* (New York, 1967).
23. Harry Elmer Barnes, *An Intellectual and Cultural History of the Western World*, 3rd rev. ed.(New York, 1965), II, p. 840.
24. Edwin Sidney Hartland, *The Science of Fairy Tales* (London, 1890), p. 350.
25. Edwin Sidney Hartland, "The Forbidden Chamber," *Folk-Lore Journal*, III (1885), p. 239. For a similar borrowing from evolutionary theory in folksong, see D. K. Wilgus, op. cit., p. 61.
26. Edwin Sidney Hartland, *The Legend of Perseus* (London, 1896), III, p. 156.
27. Edward B. Tylor, *The Origins of Culture*(= *Primitive Culture*, Part I) (New York, 1958), p. 21.
28. Ibid., p. 17. The emphasis is added.
29. Ibid., p. 78.
30. Ibid., p. 136.
31. Ibid., p. 158.

32. See Alan Dundes, "The American Concept of Folklore," *Journal of the Folklore Institute*, III (1966), p. 235.

33. For a useful survey of the various conceptualizations of "folk," see Hultkrantz, op. cit., pp. 26–129.

34. The point is that there is really no connection between the restricted "folk" of *folk* society in which "folk" is used simply as a synonym for peasant and the "folk" of *folk*lore. A folk or peasant society is but one example of a "folk" in the folkloristic sense. Any group of people sharing a common linking factor, e.g., an *urban* group such as a labor union, can and does have folklore. "Folk" is a flexible concept which can refer to a nation as in American folklore or to a single family. The critical issue in defining "folk" is: what groups in fact have traditions?

35. Ortutay, op. cit., p. 201.

36. Ibid., pp. 201, 206.

37. Alan Dundes, "Advertising and Folklore," *New York Folklore Quarterly*, XIX (1963), pp. 143–151.

38. Richard M. Dorson, *American Folklore* (Chicago, 1959), p. 278.

39. The negative connotation of "folklore" is by no means limited to the English-speaking world. See, for example, the final comments in Elisée Legros' valuable *Sur les noms et les tendances du folklore* (= *Collection d'études publiée par le Musée de la vie wallonne*, No.1) (Liege, 1962), p. 47.

40. Gerould, op. cit., p. 244.

41. Albert Lord, *The Singer of Tales* (New York, 1965), pp. 134–135.

42. For an extended discussion of this concept, see Arthur O. Lovejoy and George Boas, *Primitivism and Related Ideas in Antiquity* (Baltimore, 1935), p. 7. Also relevant are: Lois Whitney, "English Primitivistic Theories of Epic Origins," *Modern Philology*, XXI (1924), pp. 337–378; and John D. Scheffler, "The Idea of Decline in Literature and the Fine Arts in Eighteenth-Century England," *Modern Philology*, XXXIV (1936), pp. 155–78.

43. One of the best treatments of "survivals" is Margaret T. Hodgen, *The Doctrine of Survivals: A Chapter in the History of Scientific Method in the Study of Man* (London, 1936). See also Fred W. Voget, "Progress, Science, History and Evolution in Eighteenth- and Nineteenth-Century Anthropology," *Journal of the History of the Behavioral Sciences*, III (1967), pp. 132–155.

44. Sigmund Freud, *Civilization and Its Discontents*, translated from the German by Joan Riviere (Garden City, 1958), p. 29.

45. Carl G. Jung and Carl Kerenyi, *Essays on a Science of Mythology* (New York, 1963), p. 72. Judging from Carlos C. Drake's survey, "Jung and His Critics," *Journal of American Folklore*, LXXX (1967), pp. 321–333, there appears to have been little notice taken of Jung's pro-Christian and antirational approach to myth. Jung claims that Christ exemplifies the archetype of the self and that in general pure intellectual insight as opposed to "experience" is not enough, although he admits that he cannot pass on *his* experience to his public. See *Psyche & Symbol*, ed. Violet S. de Laszlo (Garden City, 1958), pp. 32–36. In any case, when Jung speaks of the "de-Christianization of our world" and "the Luciferian development of science and technology" (p. 35), it is an expression of devolutionary worldview. For Steiner's approach to folklore, see his *The Interpretation of Fairy Tales* (New York, 1929), or any of the works cited in Alan Dundes' review of Julius E. Heuscher, *A Psychiatric Study of Fairy Tales*, in *Journal of American Folklore*, LXXVIII (1965), pp. 370–371.

46. Lewis Spence, *Myth and Ritual in Dance, Game, and Rhyme* (London, 1947), p. 2. The emphasis is added.

47. Once the devolutionary premise has been pointed out, it is easy to find examples of it. For example, there is André Varagnac's "Les causes de la décadence du folklore dans les pays industriels," in *IV International Congress for Folk-Narrative Research in Athens: Lectures and Reports*, ed. Georgios A. Megas (Athens, 1965), pp. 600–605.

48. Some of the various cyclic schemes are summarized in Lovejoy and Boas, op. cit., pp. 1–7; see also van Doren, op. cit., pp. 117–121, 159–193.

49. Ortutay, op. cit., p. 182.

50. Arthur O. Lovejoy, *The Great Chain of Being* (Cambridge, Mass., 1957).

Part II

Worldview and Identity

9

FOLK IDEAS AS UNITS OF WORLDVIEW

(*Postscript*) Worldview in Folk Narrative

Introduction

The opening essay of this section is significant for its groundbreaking interpretation of worldview in folkloristic terms. Dundes was not the first to point to the interpretation of worldview as a valuable goal of cultural study, but he made a tremendous contribution by proposing that worldview—a concept often noted for its diffuseness and vagueness—could be clarified with reference to the fundamental units of analysis he called "folk ideas." Dundes thought of worldview generally as "the way a people perceive the world and its place in it," and sought to objectify this perception with the use of folklore as source material. An important distinction he made between folk ideas and expressive genres (such as beliefs or proverbs) was that the folk idea was not a genre, but rather was evident across genres. Folk ideas underlaid the thought and action of a given group of people, and, therefore, were markers of their identity. Yet, in Dundes's words, "they are not likely to appear consistently in any fixed-phrase form." They were not "myths," which folklorists thought of as a narrative form, and they could be popularly used to connote fallacy. The issue was not the veracity of these ideas, but rather that they were "underlying assumptions" affecting outlooks as well as expressions. Dundes also referred to folk ideas as "unstated premises," "existential postulates," "notions," "conceptions," or "cultural axioms" that could be discerned not only in folk culture, but also in popular movies and television, objects, advertising, and other commercial items. He thus called upon folklorists to broadly commit to the study of human thought, rather than follow a natural history model of the collection and classification of items somehow divorced from contemporary life.

Dundes applied a linguistic model, by likening folk ideas to generative principles of grammar that were difficult for natives to articulate. He argued that just as languages were governed by inducible principles, worldviews were equally highly patterned. The whole could be discerned from cultural expressions, "particles," as Dundes called them. Thus, folklore became especially significant as a comparable, empirical source that acted as a metaphor for the cultures in which it was found. Methodological problems still had to be addressed, such as whether the compared material, especially in different contexts, was in fact comparable; whether the texts were truly representative; and whether the quantity and variety of texts were sufficient. Still, Dundes emphasized that the pursuit of worldview was crucial to the overall objective of identifying cultural patterning in microcosms. These microcosms, he hypothesized, "may be isomorphically parallel to macrocosms," that is, they were minute expressions of overarching, culturally shared cognition and values.

Since Dundes had contributed to, and called for, the definition of genres, particularly with structural criteria, his criticisms of genre work in the "folk ideas" essay may seem surprising. He did not abandon the definitional project, but his concern was that collection and classification had become ends in themselves rather than steps in identification, leading toward interpretation. The renowned archives he amassed at Berkeley, arranged in fact by genre, are testimony to the utility of collection and classification in the folkloristic enterprise. He implied, though, that the obsession for ordering aggregate data was a disciplinary "folk idea," or at least a "habit of thinking" that "artificially" limited research; see his suggestion (in the essay on the psychology of collecting, later in this volume) for theorizing that collecting and classification were forms of anal retention by which material was held in, and therefore not worked with into expansive interpretations. A keystone of his comparative approach was to find symbolically equivalent images and texts across genres, cultures, and even transmitting media. In his scholarly jeremiad, he insisted that the goal of the folkloristic enterprise should not be the assignment of collected items to one genre or another, but, instead, the interpretation of their meaning.

Dundes was not alone in his plea and plaint. His "folk ideas" essay originally appeared as part of a paradigm-changing symposium called *Toward New Perspectives in Folklore*. Richard Bauman, in his introduction to this book, characterized Dundes as taking "a characteristic role [in the group], that of extender and rearranger of the conceptual boundaries of the field," and sharing with others a questioning of "the received canon" of folklore genres and diachronic methods. Unlike others in his cohort, who were oriented toward contextual and performance perspectives, and who, in the words of editor Paredes, were "less interested in defining a general concept of folklore than in delimiting folklore in specific situations" (1972), Dundes called for cutting an even wider conceptual swath with folklore. His objectives were more cognitive than behavioral, more global than situational, more macro than micro.

Subsequently, a number of studies picked up on Dundes's concept of folk ideas. For example, Patrick Mullen extended the comparison of Mexican and American worldviews. From fieldwork with the borderlands fishing community on the Texas Gulf Coast, he reported different patterns in the conclusion of buried treasure stories among Mexicans and Americans. With the former, tellers report finding treasure, while with the latter, treasure is not retrieved or the seeker is fatally cursed. Mullen concluded that the narrative evidence confirmed Dundes's contrast of limited good in Mexican society (as described by George Foster) and unlimited good in American society (1978). In the Mexican view, since wealth was limited and a rigid class system prevented mobility, the explanation given of a person's success was that he or she must have landed treasure. With "good" or wealth perceived as unlimited, and mobility accessible in the American worldview, the legends discouraged finding the treasure because work would be rewarded. America, according to Dundes, "remains a land of opportunity, that boundless wealth is still readily available to anyone with the energy and the initiative to dig for it."

Dundes pointed out that folk ideas were not only narrated, but also materialized. To demonstrate, he extended the analysis of how national societies perceive "good" via his study of folk toys that featured pecking chickens placed on a paddle. The beaks are attached to a weighted string, and when the paddle is moved, the beaks peck at the wooden surface on the paddle. He found that the American versions of the toy are the only ones to use edible food; each chicken has an individual portion of corn kernels, leading him to the conclusion that "only a country with an abundant food supply could waste food to construct or decorate a toy" (1989). Other countries vary in the space provided for pecking and in the extent of food depicted, which suggested to Dundes that makers constructed toys in accordance with the "unstated premises" of their society. He showed objects produced in India that "hint at a basic overpopulation problem," while Swedish versions have "an unbounded and near infinite amount of food." For an alternative interpretation of the toy in a situated event using a psychoanalytical perspective, see Bronner 2005d.

Dundes's concept of the folk idea did not go unchallenged. Stephen Stern and Simon J. Bronner criticized the ahistorical tendencies of worldview analysis, which often led to the false conclusion that the perception of limits remained constant through time, and extends uniformly to the whole society (1980). Methodologically, there was the temptation to be selective with the evidence, ignoring contradictory sources that did not fit the theme, either to give the appearance of an unequivocal pattern, or to begin with one's conclusion and find data to fit the theme. Aware of the methodological pitfalls, Dundes himself warned that "it is dangerous to speculate on the basis of too few texts or exemplars."

Another critical concern is the extension of identity to generalizations of national character. Dundes raised this worry in this essay, when he attempted to differentiate between stereotypes as false generalizations ("folk fallacies," he called them) and folk ideas. Seeking to show American folklore as a reflection of an American type or theme, folklorist Richard M. Dorson—coming out of an American Studies background—fused the concept of folk ideas to the approach of "image, symbol, and myth" (which he credited to the work of Henry Nash Smith; see Smith 1950). In this approach, distinctive expressions of Americanness, arising historically from unique American conditions, were held up as signs of national identity. See, for example, the "American Cultural Myths" ("The Noble and Ignoble Savage," "Rags to Riches," "Fables of Innocence," and "American Adam") described in the *Handbook of American Folklore*, which Dorson edited (1983), or his narrative study, *America in Legend* (1973). Methodologically, one examined the expressions of values (visible images and texts in art, literature, and folklore), evaluated them for their symbolism, and connected them to overarching non-narrative "myths" or ideas. The significance of this model was that it suggested that ideas drive action, thus setting up a causal connection between culture and historical events. But critics have also noted the reductionist tendency to equate societies to singular "characters" that stress exceptional traits or values; they bristle at the implications of a collective American mind or "group think." Dundes, for his part, acknowledged that sometimes prevalent ideas in a society can be oppositional, suggesting cultural tensions and paradoxes (for an American Studies demonstration of this notion, see Kammen 1972).

Dundes defined "national character" as a "cluster of specific personality traits which can be empirically identified" (1986). He added that as a folklorist, he examined these traits as expressed in folklore, and encouraged the comparative study of national character. Following from the folklorist's concern for how traditions diffuse, he hypothesized that people take their national character with them when they migrate. "Individuals may behave differently in a foreign setting," he wrote, "but it is not so easy to shed one's national character." He distinguished between national *stereotypes* and *character* as the difference between what people perceive they (or others) are like in the former, and what people actually are in the latter. Acknowledging regional, ethnic, and class differences with a nation's boundaries, he nonetheless advocated for an empirical approach to national character that shed its past associations with romantic nationalism and national socialism, and dealt with cultural patterning (and shared "folk ideas") in a society. Here is the source of the comment, cited above, which he offered to colloquy speakers in the Netherlands who were critical of national character. "There is a difference between New Englanders in the United States and residents of the so-called "Deep South," but there are also commonalities which *all* Americans share regardless of regionalism, class affiliation, or ethnic identity. For example, the delight in exaggeration (as opposed to the understatement of Englishmen) seems to be a general facet of American national character, a delight incidentally which probably masks a basic feeling of insecurity and inferiority vis-à-vis Europeans. Boasting and bragging (about being the biggest and best) is a sure sign of such feelings of cultural inferiority. In the same way, Prussians may be different from Bavarians, but both north and south Germans share a penchant for matters scatological." His last statement referred to his study of German national character (1984a). (He told the group that his publisher insisted on replacing his use of "national character" in the original title with "culture.") Regarding Dundes's thesis of migrating traits, see the use of his concept in Bronner 2007. For other statements on national character, see Dundes 1975h, 1969b.

Eminent folklorist Linda Dégh iterated the concept that worldview motivates any human action. She defined it as the "sum total of subjective interpretations of perceived and experienced reality of individuals," and noted that narratives, in particular, are "loaded with worldview expressions." Reviewing Dundes's call for worldview study, she argued that folklorists had an advantage in using the "specific" source material of folklore, rather than the "inconcrete" materials of other fields (1994). A year later, in the same journal, Dundes took her cue, and both encouraged renewed attention to the concept and elaborated on his use of worldview—more than twenty years after his initial publication. In his postscript, he constructed a binary between an "old" and "modern" notion of worldview. In his model, the old approach was synonymous with cosmology, the view of one's place in the world or cosmos. In contrast, the modern notion was more cognitive and structural. In his words, "it refers to the way in which people perceive the world through native categories and unstated premises or axioms." One difference between the two notions, he pointed out, was the level of conscious awareness. Cosmology was conscious, while the second kind of worldview was not. He mused that the modern concept was not a Freudian or Jungian unconscious, but a linguistic one in the sense that "speakers of a language are not 'conscious' of the grammatical laws governing their speech." Looking to the future, he urged folklorists to delineate the unconscious worldview postulates, which, he wrote, "are so artfully articulated in folk narrative and other forms of folklore."

For further discussion of worldview in cultural study, see Kearney 1972, 1984; Hill and Mannheim 1992; Naugle 2002; and Sire 2004.

Folk Ideas as Units of Worldview

FOR SOME TIME NOW, FOLKLORISTS have become increasingly annoyed at what they regard as a nonprofessional and indiscriminately extended use of the term "myth" to apply to a wide variety of materials. Accordingly, folklorists are wont to shudder when they read discussions about the "myth" of capitalism or the "myth" of race by different social scientists, who often use "myth" simply as a synonym for "error" or "fallacy." These definitely are not what the folklorist means by the term "myth," folklorists carefully explain to questioning students. To the folklorist, a myth is first of all a narrative and that alone rules out most of what modern social scientists refer to under the rubric of myth. Generally speaking, social scientists' use of the term "myth" has little or nothing to do with traditional narrative forms. Rather it has to do with a belief or a belief system. Moreover, their use of the term "myth" nearly always carries an explicit negative connotation as in Ashley Montagu's book in which race or racism is referred to as man's most dangerous myth.[1]

If folklorists wish to guard their own narrow definition of myth in the sense of a sacred oral narrative, explaining how the earth or man came to be in their present form, then they ought to offer some constructive terminological alternative to refer to those cultural phenomena that nonfolklorists persist in calling myths. The mere insistence by folklorists that such phenomena as political "myths" are not really true myths doesn't solve the problem. If these materials are not myths, then what are they? And should they, whatever they are, be studied by folklorists or not?

I believe that there are traditional notions or conceptions that properly belong in the province of the professional folklorist but which have never been fully recognized as being part of folklore because of the folklorist's obstinate tendency to be bound by traditional genres. There can be no question that genre theory has been instrumental in shaping the discipline of folkloristics. Once any corpus of folklore has been collected, it is to matters of genre classification that folklorists invariably turn. Obviously the exigencies of archiving have forced the folklorist to think in terms of classification and genres. "What do I call this?" and "Where do I file it?" are common questions in folklore archives around the world. Within conventional genres, for example, myth, folktales, and games, there are, of course, elaborate refinements of subclassification schemes created in order to facilitate "information retrieval." But despite the practical necessity of defining and refining genre categories, the fact remains that the folklorist's habit of thinking of his or her field almost exclusively in terms of traditional genres tends to be a limiting one. It is a habit which leads him or her to emphasize certain kinds of folkloristic materials and to totally ignore others.

The genre divisions often artificially limit research. For example, a scholar may write about themes in mythology or even in a single myth and pay no attention to the occurrence of the identical themes in other genres. Even course offerings in folklore, and occasionally whole research institutes, are organized by genre. Yet surveys or even partial surveys of various supposedly established genres reveal that there is frequently little agreement among folklorists as to precisely what a given genre is.[2] Are genres cross-cultural or not? Is what American folklorists consider under the genre label "proverb" the same as what a German folklorist calls a *Sprichwort* or what a Japanese folklorist calls *kotowaza*? We are aware of the fact that in any one culture there may be a difference between folk or native categories on the one hand and analytic categories on the other. What the folk in the United States might term "old sayings," the American folklorist might group under "superstition," "proverb," etc. But what are the criteria for the establishment of these various analytic categories? And to what extent are these criteria applicable to folkloristic materials from other cultures?

Let me illustrate some of the difficulty by citing a concrete example. Most American folklorists would probably agree that "Lightning never strikes twice in the same place" is a bona fide item of folklore. But to what genre does it belong? I believe that depending upon the specific context and use of this item in a particular situation, the item may be either a superstition *or* a proverb in terms of conventional genre distinctions. If the item is believed literally to be a fact of nature—an individual in the midst of a thunderstorm consciously standing on a place where lightning has previously struck to avoid being hit—then the item would normally be classified as a folk belief or superstition. If, on the other hand, it is taken metaphorically to mean simply that history is nonrepetitive and that an individual who has suffered one misfortune is unlikely to suffer an identical one, then the item would most probably be labelled as a proverb. Incidentally, this example demonstrates the fallacy of simply collecting folklore text items without regard to context and publishing long lists of raw data without accompanying full explanations.

There are many other perplexing problems having to do with genre assignment. To what genre does "All signs fail in dry weather" belong? I would be tempted to classify it as a metafolkloristic proverb commenting upon the lack of reliability of sign superstitions having to do with predicting rainfall. How would American folklorists classify the idea that when it thunders, God is moving his furniture, or that potato carts are rolling across the sky, or that two clouds are bumping their heads together, or that angels are rolling stones downhill? The variant which ascribes thunder to gnomes' bowling up in the sky is probably related to Washington Irving's story of Rip Van Winkle.[3] To say that such items are used to allay the fears of small children when they hear thunder is not to say to what genre of folklore they belong. Other weather phenomena are similarly described: "The old woman is picking her geese" means it's snowing, with the falling snow presumably being the plucked goose feathers, and the rain is "Angels crying." These are not proverbs and they are not superstitions. They are rarely if ever believed to be true and they are hardly traditional causal statements of the form "If A then B, unless C." Kuusi in his excellent study of "The Devil is Beating His Wife," said when rain falls but the sun continues to shine, uses the term circumlocution.[4] Of course, one might argue that it doesn't really matter to what genres such items belong. It is sufficient to collect and analyze the items without worrying about how to classify them. The practical question of where to file them in folklore archives still remains, however.

One could imagine that in time folklorists might agree as to the generic nature of fictive weather descriptions, but what about a notion found in American culture that everything or every person has its or his price? There are numerous traditional expressions concerning the measure of money, for example, "Money isn't everything but it helps," "Money talks," "What does it mean in dollars and cents?" In fact, Americans are suspicious of items priced too low. Bargains are desirable, but "something for nothing" may be of poor quality. The rule of thumb seems to be "You get what you pay for." This idea that any object can be measured in monetary terms seems to be a traditional one in American culture; but it is not always stated in fixed-phrase form, and therefore it is probably inappropriate to call it a proverb. Moreover, if it is not a traditional statement of cause and effect we folklorists would probably not feel comfortable in classifying it as a superstition—though possibly we might attempt to label it as a folk belief. In any event, I suggest that the idea that any thing or any person can be "bought"—whether or not it is ultimately true—is a part of American worldview. Furthermore, it is an important part of American worldview inasmuch as Americans may deal with peoples from other cultures who do not share such a materialistic, capitalistic view of the world. To the extent that such premises or ideas are traditional, I believe they are part of folklore and that they should be studied by folklorists. As a concession to our nominalizing penchant, I propose we term such notions "folk ideas."

By "folk ideas," I mean traditional notions that a group of people have about the nature of humanity, of the world, and of life in the world. Folk ideas would not constitute a genre of folklore but rather would be expressed in a great variety of different genres. Proverbs would almost certainly represent the expression of one or more folk ideas, but the same folk ideas might also appear in folktales, folksongs, and in fact almost every conventional genre of folklore, not to mention nonfolkloristic materials. However, insofar as folk ideas are the unstated premises which underlie the thought and action of a given group of people, they are not likely to appear consistently in any fixed-phrase form.

There may well be other terms that might be considered more appropriate than "folk ideas," for instance, "basic premises," "cultural axioms," or "existential postulates."[6] The particular term is really not the point. What is important is the task of identifying the various underlying assumptions held by members of a given culture. All cultures have underlying assumptions and it is these assumptions or folk ideas which are the building blocks of worldview. Any one worldview will be based upon many individual folk ideas and if one is seriously interested in studying worldview, one will need first to describe some of the folk ideas which contribute to the formation of that worldview. Sometimes, folk ideas may be articulated in a particular proverb or exemplum, but if folk ideas are normally expressed not in one but rather in a variety of genres, then it is imperative that the folklorist make the attempt to extrapolate such ideas from the folklore as a whole. To do this, the folklorist must of necessity escape the self-imposed bind of genres and categories. Once one has identified a number of folk ideas present in a culture, one may begin to perceive what the pattern, if any, of these ideas is and how each of the ideas is related to the total worldview of that culture.

It would be folly at this point even to speculate about the possible number of folk ideas in American culture, but it might be useful to discuss several tentative folk ideas as a means of illustrating the nature of such ideas and how they are manifested in folklore. Let us assume for the sake of argument that one American folk idea is that there is no real limit as to how much of any one commodity can be produced. The traditional phrase "There's (plenty) more where that came from" could refer to an invitation to eat heartily as there is an abundant supply in the kitchen or it could refer to a warning to a bully that there is more punishment in store for him if he doesn't keep his distance. If we wished to label this particular tentative folk idea, we might term it "the principle of unlimited good." One advantage of this label is the contrast it affords with the "principle of limited good" which anthropologist George Foster has suggested as a characteristic notion in Mexican (and other) peasant cultures.[6] This also raises the interesting question of how folk ideas as units of worldview of the "scientific" observer might influence what "folk ideas" the folklorist might discover in the other cultures he studies. The notion of "limited good" is obviously particularly striking to members of a culture who share a notion of unlimited good.

There seem to be numerous expressions of the folk idea of unlimited good in American society. "The sky's the limit" would be one expression while "shooting the moon" in the card game of hearts or "going for broke" might be others. The idea that "Any man can be President" (despite that fact that no woman and no African American has ever been President) suggests the lack of limit to opportunity. Politicians who promise "a car in every garage and a chicken in every pot" could only be convincing in a culture where there were a virtually limitless number of cars and chickens possible.

Another illustration of the principle of unlimited good is perhaps provided by American buried treasure legends. In this context, it may be significant that most accounts end with the treasure still not recovered. This suggests that Americans think that America remains a land of opportunity, that boundless wealth is still readily available to anyone with the energy and initiative to go dig for it. The fact that the legends are open ended—they do not end as some legends do—may indicate that they are standing invitations to Americans to dig and provide their own happy ending to the story. This may have to do with other American folk ideas such as: "Hard work will pay off," "Where there's a will, there's a way," and more precisely with the proviso that the "pay off" and "way" will consist of material reward, for instance, treasure or money. American buried treasure legends afford an interesting comparison with Mexican treasure tales insofar as the latter traditions include the finding of the treasure. In fact, as Foster observes, it is the finding of buried treasure that is used to explain the appearance of sudden wealth in a Mexican peasant community where the principle of limited good prevails.[7] Normally, with such a view, one could only obtain wealth at someone else's expense. The discovery of buried treasure may represent a form of supernatural aid for fortunate individuals. In contrast, in American worldview, the good fortune of one individual does not necessarily mean misfortune for another. With a notion of unlimited good, there can be good fortune for all.

The contrast between limited good and unlimited good is one which could be extended way beyond discussions of buried treasure legends. For instance, a comparison of Mexican (and for that matter, European) universities with American universities in the area of professorial appointments reveals the same contrast. In the hierarchical European system, there is usually only one professor in a subject at a particular university or at any rate only a few professors. There is thus "limited good" and one cannot obtain a "chair" unless it is vacated, for example, by the death of an incumbent. This is why young academicians are forced to wait expectantly—almost vulture-like—for an opening to occur. They must then fight each other for the post. In the American system, there are many professors in a subject at a university. In theory, there is room for all to be advanced and one need not wait or hope for a colleague's misfortune in order to be promoted.

Assuming that there is a folk idea in American culture having to do with the notion of unlimited good, we can see that it may be manifested in materials as diverse as proverbs and legends. But are there folk ideas which are without expression in traditional folklore genres? If so, then this would present special methodological problems for the folklorist who was anxious to identify folk ideas. Let us consider as a possible American folk idea the notion that if something is good for you, it must taste bad. If it doesn't have a bad taste, then it probably won't help you. This notion could apply to food; for example, to vegetables which children are asked to consume in the name of good health, or to bitter medicines. (One popular brand of mouthwash even features the bad taste of the product in its

1970 advertising as though its awful taste were somehow conclusive proof of its effectiveness.) This possible folk idea may or may not be related ultimately to the Puritan attitudes towards pleasure and pain to the effect that pleasure is sinful and that one must experience pain and the denial of pleasure to achieve salvation. (This association with the Puritan ethic is also suggested by the corollary idea that if something tastes good—like candy— it must be bad for your health.) In any case, the point here is simply that the folk idea of bad-tasting things being more likely to be good for one than good-tasting things is, in my opinion, a part of traditional American thought that is likely to be overlooked by folklorists whose powers of observation are limited by conventional genre categories.

Both ideas, that of unlimited good and that of salvation through suffering, share a commitment to progress. Tomorrow will be better than today, and today in turn is better than yesterday. The future orientation in American worldview is tied to a "bigger and better" principle![8] However, it is "achieving" rather than "achievement" that counts and the folk ideas lead ultimately to frustration. This may be seen by considering some of the many forms and symbols of success in American culture, for example, position in a rank-order scheme, as in football teams or automobile rental agencies vying to be "number one," the acquisition of sizable financial resources—the size often indicated by the number of figures in one's annual salary, the number of acres of one's estate, the number of rooms (especially bathrooms!) in one's home, and the number of cars that one owns. But it is not success per se that is worshipped. Rather it is the process of becoming a success that is admired. Once one has achieved success, one is established and it is time to look for a new achiever. There must always be new losers or underdogs to root for. Americans love upsets; they love to see favorites and front-runners get beaten. "Records were made to be broken."

These folk ideas produce frustration. On the one hand, there is a drive towards success, but on the other hand, attainment of success can, by definition, be but a temporary one in the context of a progressive continuum of change. Whatever the success is, it is bound to be surpassed by a new success, probably by someone else. This is noncyclic worldview. It is linear and it builds from successful climax to successful climax. This means that with an open system, one can never achieve the ultimate climax, one can never achieve perfection. With the principle of unlimited good, there are always more mountains to be scaled, problems to be solved, money to be made. This suggests a worldview which allows satisfactions, but only limited ones. In other words, the principle of unlimited good in and of itself implies frustration since one can in theory never acquire all the good however good is measured.

The linearity of American life so beautifully described by Dorothy Lee[9] and so evident in the American definitions of success and progress should not blind us to the possibility that two or more folk ideas in a single worldview system may be in opposition. One need not assume that all the folk ideas of a given culture are necessarily mutually reconcilable within a uniform, harmonious worldview matrix. For example, the line is one model of American thought. One respects directness and "straight" talk. One dislikes people who are "crooked" and one hopes they will eventually go "straight" and get "squared" away (for example, ex-con Square Johns) . People who get "out of line" need to be "straightened out." In business, one tries to get a "line" on something, a "line" of goods perhaps. One must be "sharp" and look for "angles." In general, the line is opposed to the circle. Circular reasoning is despised, as are most roundabout ways of speaking. "Going around in circles" is a traditional metaphor for ineffectiveness and futility. It is believed that people who are lost go in circles. One of the traditional goals of mathematicians is to "square the circle," a neat encapsulation of the "line conquering the circle."

Recently, the line versus the circle opposition has taken a new turn. It has been restated in terms of straight versus groovy. Curves mean "curvaceous" and sex; lines mean "straight" or "square" and the denial of sex. There is a movement away from the "straight and narrow" towards the "groovy and broad." It is possible that part of the shift has come from African American subculture. For decades, African Americans accepted the straight world of the dominant white culture, even to the extent of trying to "straighten" kinky, curly hair. But finally, African American culture has begun to stop denying cyclicity and circularity. In fact, middle class whites have even begun to imitate African American culture. This may be seen in folk and popular dance. The "square" dance and the standard popular dance step known as the "box step" have yielded to twisting, rotating round dance movements as the American white body has sought release from the restricting confines of Puritan strait-jackets. Professor Roger Abrahams has suggested to me that the circular worldview may stem from the cyclic nature of rural country life with its calendrical cycle as model. Following this reasoning, one is tempted to see urban life as insisting upon the more efficient line as in square city blocks and actual efforts to eliminate curves in well-travelled roads.

There are other examples of folk ideas in opposition. For instance, in American culture there is the folk idea that all individuals are or should he equal in terms of opportunity. We have already mentioned the "Any man can be President" philosophy. Through rugged individualism, any person can in theory move "from rags to riches" in a Horatio Alger-like pattern. This folk idea is supported by the Puritan ethic and capitalism. At the same time, there is the folk idea, intimately related to the notion of democracy, that political decisions should be made not on the basis of individual wishes, but on the basis of what is deemed best by and for the majority. Thus if social security and a welfare state are adjudged best for the majority, then individuals must turn over the fruits of free enterprise to the state for redistribution to the less fortunate. It is not easy to reconcile pure capitalism and pure socialism. It is just as difficult to reconcile pure rugged individualism with the idea that the individual must deny individualism in favor of what is best for the group. Both principles are taught to American children and the fundamental opposition is left unresolved. (In some sense, of course, all human societies have to wrestle with the problem of the rights of the individual versus the rights of the group to which that individual belongs.) This is why American children may become confused when they learn on the one hand that leadership is a good and necessary thing but then, on the other hand, that in an ideal democracy, everyone is equal and leaders are resented.

One solution to the leadership-democracy paradox is suggested by a children's game. It is variously titled "Patterns" or "Find the Leader." A group of children gather in a circle and send an individual who has been chosen "It" out of the room or away from the playing area. One child in the circle is then selected as "leader" and all the others have to imitate his or her actions, such as handclapping, jumping up and down, and whirling around in place. The leader changes the motions at intervals of his choice. "It" is summoned and given three guesses to identify who in the circle is the leader, that is, who is responsible for causing the various changes in the group's movements. Obviously, a successful leader is one who can artfully conceal the fact that it is he who is the first to start a new body movement. By the same token, the other members of the circle must be able to follow without revealing to "It" that they are following rather than leading. This children's game may thus be providing a model for an ideal leadership role in American society, namely, that one should lead without making it obvious that he is leading. Americans in positions of authority may be forced to give orders in a nonauthoritarian way in contrast to leaders in societies who do not share the folk idea of egalitarianism ("anybody is as good as anybody else") and who are free to lead in autocratic, authoritarian fashion. This may be why in American culture one may ask rather than order a subordinate to perform a certain task. Moreover, subordinate employees may be given some of the accouterments of higher status positions, for example, enlisted men wearing officer-style caps or janitors being rechristened custodians.

There are many other folk ideas in American culture which could be mentioned; an important one is the idea that science and technology can eventually solve any problem. Any problem which has not yet been solved could in theory be solved if enough money could be poured into appropriate research efforts. Here we see a combination of the folk idea concerning the infallibility of science and technology and the idea of the "everything having its price." (Also implied is the folk idea that humans can control their environment—rather than the environment controlling them.) However, the purpose of this essay is not to attempt even a partial itemization of American folk ideas but only to call attention to the possibility of the existence of folk ideas.

One problem arising from the discussion of folk ideas has to do with traditional stereotypes. The question is: are traditional stereotypes folk ideas or not? By traditional stereotypes, I refer to such notions as "The French are great lovers," "Blacks have a natural sense of rhythm," or "Jews have big noses." These might well be examples of what political scientists or sociologists would call "myths"; but folklorists would surely not call these myths. But just what would they call them? Are they folk beliefs? I am tempted to term such traditional statements "folk fallacies" rather than folk ideas. They would be folk fallacies because they are demonstrably false. Of course, there is always the matter of "proving" to everyone's (including bigots') satisfaction that folk fallacies are in fact fallacious. No doubt, if the distinction between folk fallacies and folk ideas were to be accepted, there might well be disputes about where individual items should be appropriately placed and in this way should be plunged once more into the hopeless quagmire of genre-type classificatory arguments. Yet I do think there is value in making a distinction between folk fallacies and folk ideas. One difference is that the folk are normally consciously aware of folk fallacies (though not necessarily that they are fallacies) and can articulate them without difficulty. Folk fallacies are part of the stated premises of a culture. In contrast, individuals may or may not be consciously aware of folk ideas and they may not be able to articulate them at all. In this sense, folk fallacies tend to be "native" or folk statements as opposed to "analytic" statements which are descriptions of reality made as a result of and only after analytic study. Folk ideas would be more a matter of basic unquestioned premises concerning the nature of man, of society, and of the world, and these premises although manifested in folklore proper might not be at all obvious to the folk in whose thinking they were central. Folk fallacies such as stereotypes would therefore be part of the conscious or self-conscious culture of a people whereas folk ideas would be part of the unconscious or unself-conscious culture of a people.

The distinction between conscious and unconscious culture is not always easy to draw. By unconscious culture, I do not mean repressed culture in any Freudian sense. Rather I refer to the fact that individual members of a culture are not able to consciously articulate all aspects of their culture. Fortunately, people with virtually no conscious idea of the nature of the grammar of their language are able to speak perfectly well and be understood by other members of their culture who likewise have no conscious awareness of the grammatical nature of their language. There have been many metaphors for this lack of consciousness (for example, a fish is not aware it is in water since it knows no other medium), but one of the most apt was used by Ruth Benedict when she remarked that "we do not see the lens through which we look."[11]

One of the essential tasks of anthropologists and folklorists is to make people aware, consciously aware, of their cultures. However, if people become conscious of what was formerly unconscious, will the cultural patterning change? In the present context, the question would be: if unstated folk ideas become stated folk ideas, will this have any effect upon the influence of these ideas? It is a moot point. On the one hand, one could argue that if more Americans were consciously aware of the folk idea that everything has its price, it would not necessarily alter this mode of perceiving reality in the slightest. On the other hand, if one wished to offer alternative measurement schemes, it would obviously be extremely helpful to know what measurement criteria were already being employed. Thus making the cultural unconscious conscious is the first step toward change—if that is what is desired—much as psychoanalytic therapy aims to help individuals by first making their unconscious conscious.

A final point should be made with respect to the relationship between folk ideas and folk values. In discussions of worldview, there is commonly a distinction made between worldview and ethos. Worldview refers to the cognitive, existential aspects of the way the world is structured. Ethos refers to the normative and evaluative (including esthetic and moral judgments) aspects of culture." Hoebel's terms are "existential postulates" as opposed to "normative postulates" or values, though he seems to include both types of postulates in the all encompassing term worldview." In my opinion, it is possible if not probable that there may be value judgments surrounding a folk idea, but the folk idea in one sense can be considered independent of such value judgments. Assuming there is an American folk idea that there is an unlimited amount of good, one can imagine that some individuals might feel that this situation was a desirable one while others might feel that it was undesirable. The folk idea per se would simply be an empirical description of the nature of reality (or at least a segment of reality as perceived in one particular culture). Folk ideas, then, are no more than descriptive constructs and as such they are neither good nor bad. The idea that everything has its price could be either good or bad or neither. In contrast, the proverb "Money is the root of all evil" takes a definite moral position.

Folklorists in deciding whether or not they wish to make use of a concept such as folk ideas should probably consider a number of factors. First of all, there is the question of the traditionality of unstated premises. It is one thing to call a tale type traditional and quite another to call the one or more folk ideas expressed in that tale type traditional. Moreover, if folk ideas are articulated only after analysis, isn't there a considerable risk in calling such ideas traditional? Might not one be in danger of labelling a particular analyst's idiosyncratic formulations as "traditional?" Although an analyst might claim that his formulations of "folk ideas" were extrapolated directly from folklore, they might perhaps be little more than figments of his fertile imagination.

Secondly, doesn't the proposed emphasis to be placed upon the search for folk ideas constitute a serious threat to the continued research on individual genres? Aren't folk ideas in fact a kind of glorified super-genre supposedly underlying all other folklore genres?

There is also the question of methodology. How precisely does a folklorist determine what the folk ideas of a given folk group are? How can one work inductively from folkloristic data to arrive at a delineation of one or more folk ideas?

There are certainly legitimate questions to be raised about the conceptualization of folk ideas and their utility and practicality for folklore research. Nevertheless, I believe the fundamental issue is the nature of the discipline of folkloristics. If folklorists are interested only in collecting and preserving the heirlooms of the past so as to produce a permanent, antiquarian "museum of the mind," then they need not concern themselves with the possibility of studying folk ideas. However, if folklorists view folklore as raw material for the study of human thought, then they might wish to seriously consider adopting this concept or an improved analogous one. Folk ideas are not limited to folklore and they can surely be found in movies, television, and the mass media generally. (In theory, a given folk idea might pervade nearly every aspect of a culture.) Anyone therefore truly interested in folk ideas—as opposed to being interested only in proverbs or in jokes—will have to cast his net widely enough to include popular or literary culture as well.

If one is intrigued by the possibilities of examining folklore as source material for the study of worldview, he or she might welcome a smaller unit of analysis. The concept of worldview is too vague and diffuse to be of obvious use to folklorists. However, folk ideas as units of worldview are much more manageable. Moreover, those writers who have long been accustomed to using the term "myth" in a loose sense might be encouraged to use "error" or "folk fallacy" where such is their meaning (as in the "myth" that blacks have a natural sense of rhythm) and to use "folk idea" where that is appropriate, such as, the "myth" of the frontier in American thought is clearly related to the folk idea of unlimited good (with good expressed in space and opportunity), among others.

Finally there is the matter of the relevance of folk ideas to comparative studies and applied folklore. It is perfectly conceivable that the identification of sets of folk ideas from different cultures will facilitate valuable comparative analyses. No doubt when two cultures come into contact, it is the conflict of folk ideas which causes the most difficulty. Yet inasmuch as these folk ideas are unconscious, unstated premises, it is almost impossible to place one's finger on the specific details of the conflict. If folklorists can aid in the task of identifying folk ideas, they may be able to assume a key role in improving communications between peoples (and subcultures) and reducing the number of misunderstandings which might otherwise arise. This would permit the study of folklore to take its proper place among the "applied" social sciences.

Notes

1. Ashley Montagu, *Man's Most Dangerous Myth: The Fallacy of Race* (New York, 1945)
2. For an excellent discussion of genre theory see Dan Ben-Amos, "Analytical Categories and Ethnic Genres," *Genre*, 2 (1969), 275–302. For samples of the extreme diversity and proliferation of genre and subgenre terminology, see Laurits Bødker, *The Nordic Riddle Terminology and Bibliography*, vol. II (Copenhagen, 1964) or Bødker, *Folk Literature (Germanic): International Dictionary of Regional European Ethnology and Folklore* (Copenhagen, 1965).
3. The story in which the hero bluffs the ogre by claiming that the thunder is the noise made by the rolling of his brother's wagon is classified as Aarne-Thompson tale type 1147.
4. Matti Kuusi, *Regen bei sonnenschein: zur Weltgeschichte einer Redensart*, FFC 171 (Helsinki, 1957). For a discussion of "jocular ficts," see C. W. von Sydow, *Selected Papers on Folklore* (Copenhagen, 1948), pp. 80, 372–373.
5. There is simply no agreement in the anthropological literature as to what to call what I am terming folk ideas. Clyde Kluckhohn, for example, was extremely interested in the "unstated assumptions" that a people take for granted. In his exemplary discussion of nine such assumptions among the Navaho, he referred to them as "Some Premises of Navaho Life and Thought." See Clyde Kluckhohn and Dorothea Leighton, *The Navaho*, rev. ed. (Garden City, NY, 1962), 303–314. E. Adamson Hoebel speaks of "cultural postulates" in his textbook *Anthropology:*

The Study of Man, 3rd ed. (New York, 1966), 23; and he has delineated sixteen major basic postulates underlying Cheyenne culture in *The Cheyennes: Indians of the Great Plains* (New York, 1960), 98–99. Hoebel does see postulates as providing the frame of reference for a people's worldview.

6. George M. Foster, "Peasant Society and the Image of Limited Good," *American Anthropologist*, 67 (1965), 293–315. See also Foster, *Tzintzuntzan: Mexican Peasants in a Changing World* (Boston, 1967), 122–152; "World View in Tzintzuntzan: Re-examination of a Concept," *Summa Anthropológica, en homenaje a Roberto J. Weitlaner* (Mexico, D.F., 1966), 385–393.

7. Foster, "Treasure Tales and the Image of the Static Economy in a Mexican Peasant Community," *Journal of American Folklore*, 77 (1964), 39–44. Compare Gerald T. Hurley, "Buried Treasure Tales in America," *Western Folklore*, 10 (1951), 197–216.

8. For an extended discussion, see Alan Dundes, "Thinking Ahead: A Folkloristic Reflection of the Future Orientation in American Worldview," *Anthropological Quarterly*, 42 (1969), 53–72.

9. Dorothy Lee, "Codifications of Reality: Lineal and Nonlineal," *Psychosomatic Medicine*, 12(1950), 89–97; reprinted in a collection of her essays, *Freedom and Culture* (Englewood Cliffs, N.J., 1959), 105–120, and in Alan Dundes, ed., *Every Man His Way: Readings in Cultural Anthropology* (Englewood Cliffs, N.J., 1968), 329–343.

10. Traditional stereotypes about other nations and cultures are normally grouped by folklorists under such labels as ethnic slurs or blason populaire. See Alan Dundes, ed., *The Study of Folklore* (Englewood Cliffs, NJ, 1965), 43–44.

11. Ruth Benedict, "The Science of Custom," *The Century Magazine*, 117 (1929), 641–649; reprinted in Dundes, *Every Man His Way*, 180–188.

12. This involves another thorny theoretical controversy. I follow Geertz's distinction between ethos and worldview. See Clifford Geertz, "Ethos, World-View and the Analysis of Sacred Symbols," *The Antioch Review*, 17 (1957), 421–437; reprinted in Dundes, *Every Man His Way*, 302–315.

13. E. Adamson Hoebel, *Anthropology*, 23, 500.

Postscript

Worldview in Folk Narrative

LINDA DÉGH'S ELOQUENT ADVOCACY OF an approach to the study of folk narrative which concentrates upon the extrapolation of worldview (1994) is most welcome. Dégh rightfully critiques the post-modern muddle which seems to result in either re-inventing the wheel or simply spinning wheels already in place (1994:246). As a folklorist who has long been concerned with analyzing worldview (Dundes 1969) utilizing folklore ranging from festivals (Dundes and Falassi 1975:185–240) to folk toys (Dundes 1986), I would like to echo and amplify Dégh's plea for more attention to worldview in folk narrative studies.

First of all, there is an abundant literature devoted to the concept of worldview including essays by anthropologists Redfield (1953), Geertz (1957), and Foster (1966). For representative surveys, see Kearney (1972, 1984). As for the more limited area of worldview as reflected in folk narrative, one might mention Melville Jacobs' all too brief chapter, "World View," in his now classic *The Content and Style of an Oral Literature* (1959:195–199), Blackburn's attempt to isolate worldview principles from Chumash oral narratives (1975), and Sparing's effort to identify worldview themes in Schleswig-Holstein folktales (1984). Perhaps the most inspirational in-depth treatments of the worldview of individual cultures involving some attention to folk narrative would be Marcel Griaule's *Conversations with Ogotemmêli* (1965) which should be required reading for every serious folklorist, and Gerardo Reichel-Dolmatoff's *Amazonian Cosmos* (1971).

Sometimes the folkloristic treatment of worldview is quite limited, if not completely idiosyncratic. Italian folklorist Cirese, for example, uses "world-view" to refer exclusively to the Marxist-Gramscian notion of the hegemony of the oppressors over the "subaltern" (1974). It is true that Gramsci's famous seven page "Osservationi sul folclore" (1971) did utilize the concept of worldview (cf. Byrne 1982), but only in the highly restricted Marxist class-conscious sense.

If I were asked to select the best single essay on worldview in folk narrative, it would be an easy choice to make. It is Sandor Erdész's remarkable essay, "The World Conception of Lajos Ami, Storyteller," which appeared in *Acta Ethnographica* in 1961. In this essay, we learn that an illiterate storyteller's worldview came largely from details contained in the vast repertoire of folktales that he told. Particular worldview premises are documented by Erdész when he cites parallels to Ami's interview responses, parallels from the actual folktales told by Ami. I shall not summarize this fascinating article further but rather urge folklore students to read it in its entirety.

However, the essay does afford an excellent opportunity to distinguish two different notions of worldview, both of which are discernible in folk narrative. I should like to briefly distinguish the two notions as a means of encouraging further research in worldview through folk narrative.

193

The older notion of worldview tended to consider the term synonymous with cosmology. Worldview in that sense meant people's view of their place in the world, in the cosmos. This is the sense employed by Erdész, who notes that Ami sees Budapest as the "center of the world," and that since Adam and Eve fell from the Garden of Eden to land "someplace between Vienna and Buda," the door or gate to Eden is located above that area. As there is an upper world, so there is also a lower world which one enters through the "Hole of the World" which Ami claimed was to be found somewhere in Russia.

A more modern notion of worldview tends to be more cognitive and structural. It refers to the way in which people perceive the world through native categories and unstated premises or axioms. Thus the cosmology itself (the older sort of worldview) could provide data from which one could extrapolate principles of the newer kind of worldview. Let me illustrate with a few details from the Erdész essay.

According to Ami, there is a firmament so thick that "no human being could cut through it." Even the famed mythical Sky-High tree was forced to curve "thirteen times under the firmament" because it could not break through to achieve its full height. Similarly, it is deemed impossible to reach the "edge of the world." People who tried to cross the North Pole with an airplane "got so frozen that they couldn't break through it." Where the firmament touched the earth, it was so low "that the swallow has to drink water kneeling on the black cottonweed." Moreover, the reason why the cottonweed is black is "because the sun couldn't shine under the angle of the sky" and therefore the cottonweed there "cannot become green."

These striking images (most of which are derived directly from the folktales told by Ami) clearly convey messages of limitation, of stunted growth and development. The Sky-High tree was forced to curve thirteen times since it was unable to break through the firmament; a swallow was forced to kneel—a physical impossibility since birds have no knees—in order to drink where the firmament touched the earth; cottonweed in such an enclosure must be black because even the powerful sun cannot reach it. The worldview principles here articulate the fatalistic acceptance of the impossibility of unlimited mobility. Even the sun is obliged to remain in its own orbit, Ami explains. A peasant must know his or her place in the world and remain in it. There are impenetrable walls everywhere— above with the firmament and also at the edge of the world. Even with modern technology, such as an airplane, one cannot break through the surrounding barriers. (Whether the plight of the Hungarian peasant with respect to social or spacial mobility is to be attributed to the bourgeois class system or to the socialist regime then in place is debatable. What is not debatable is the consistent worldview articulated by Ami.)

One important difference between the two kinds of worldview discussed above has to do with conscious awareness. The account of worldview as cosmology is clearly conscious. Most individuals in the West, for example, presumably could confirm the folk belief that "heaven" is located "above" the earth whereas "hell" is located "below" (despite the fact that what is "below" on one side of the earth is the same direction as "above" on the opposite side!) In contrast, it is by no means obvious that either Ami or the folklore-collector Erdész, for that matter, were fully aware of the many metaphors of stricture and boundedness. More than likely this second kind of worldview is not in consciousness. It is not like a Freudian or Jungian unconscious, but rather unconscious in the same way that speakers of a language are not "conscious" of the grammatical laws governing their speech.

It is my hope that future folklorists will seek to delineate the "unconscious" worldview postulates which are so artfully articulated in folk narrative and other forms of folklore.

References

Blackburn, Thomas C. 1975. *December's Child: A Book of Chumash Oral Narratives*. Berkeley: University of California Press.

Byrne, Moyra. 1982. Antonio Gramsci's Contribution to Italian Folklore Studies. *International Folklore Review* 2:70–75.

Cirese, Alberto M. 1974. Concezione del Mondo, Filosofia spontanea e folclore in Gramsci. In *Demologia e Folklore: Studi in Memoria de Giuseppe Cocchiara*, 105–142. Palermo: S. F. Flaccovio.

Dégh, Linda. 1994. The Approach to Worldview in Folk Narrative Study. *Western Folklore* 53:243–252.

Dundes, Alan. 1969. Thinking Ahead: A Folkloristic Reflection of the Future Orientation in American Worldview. *Anthropological Quarterly* 42:53–72.

———. 1986. Pickende Huhner: Thesen zum Weltbird im Spielzeug. In *Volkskultur in der Moderne: Probleme and Perspektiven empirischer Kulturforschung*, 323–331. Reinbek bei Hamburg: Rowohlt Taschenbuch Verlag. Reprinted in translation in *Folklore Matters*. 1989, 83–91. Knoxville: University of Tennessee Press.

Dundes, Alan, and Alessandro Falassi. 1975. *La Terra in Piazza: An Interpretation of the Palio of Siena*. Berkeley: University of California Press.

Erdész, Sandor. 1961. The World Conception of Lajos Ami, Storyteller. *Acta Ethnographica* 10:327–344.

Foster, George M. 1966. World View in Tzintzuntzan: Re-examination of a Concept. In *Summa Anthropologica, en homenaje a Roberto J. Weitlaner*, 385–393. Mexico, D.F.: Instituto Nacional de Antropologia e Historia.

Geertz, Clifford. 1957. Ethos, World-view and the Analysis of Sacred Symbols. *Antioch Review* 17:421–437.

Gramsci, Antonio. 1971. Osservazioni sul folclore. In *Letteratura e Vita Nazionale*, 265–274. Roma: Editori Riuniti.

Griaule, Marcel. 1965. *Conversations with Ogotemmêli: An Introduction to Dogon Ideas*. Oxford: Oxford University Press.

Jacobs, Melville. 1959. *The Content and Style of an Oral Literature*. Chicago: University of Chicago Press.

Kearney, Michael. 1972. World View Theory and Study. *Annual Review of Anthropology* 4:247–270.

———. 1984. *World View*. Novato: Chandler & Sharp.

Redfield, Robert. 1953. Primitive World View and Civilization. In *The Primitive World and Its Transformations*, 84–110. Cornell: Cornell University Press.

Reichel-Dolmatoff, Gerardo. 1971. *Amazonian Cosmos: The Sexual and Religious Symbolism of the Tukano Indians*. Chicago: University of Chicago Press.

Sparing, Martarethe Wilma. 1984. *The Perception of Reality in the Volksmärchen of Schleswig-Holstein: A Study in Interpersonal Relationships and World View*. Lanham: University Press of America.

10

AS THE CROW FLIES:
A STRAIGHTFORWARD STUDY OF LINEAL
WORLDVIEW IN AMERICAN FOLK SPEECH

Introduction

Dundes cited Dorothy Lee's "Codifications of Reality: Lineal and Nonlineal" ([1950] 1968) as the inspiration for his rhetorical analysis of American speech, in which he sought evidence of a lineal worldview. Introducing Lee's essay in his anthology *Every Man His Way*, Dundes praised it as a work in "comparative cognition," pointing out that "the perception and classification of 'objective reality' is not culture-free, no matter how ardently a scientist wishes it were. However, by studying the nature of individual cultural cognitive systems, we may be able to see the arbitrariness and the normally unperceived biases of such systems, including our own" (1968a).

Writing in 2004 to honor his close friend and colleague Wolfgang Mieder, a world-renowned specialist in proverb scholarship, Dundes expanded on his thesis of the "linearity of American life," outlined in two paragraphs of "Folk Ideas as Units of Worldview" (1971a, and reprinted in this volume). After Dundes's death, Mieder speculated on Dundes's reason for writing on linearity: "I do recall both of us as basically non-religious individuals speaking on occasion about life having a beginning and an end, progressing along with steps and mutations along the way. We both felt that as two 'odd birds' we could do no more than to move along with our scholarly work and teaching in a lineal fashion 'as the crow flies' before our short life span would straightforwardly come to its end forever" (2006b, 239).

In his focus on lineality, published a year before his death, Dundes especially brought out examples of folk speech to demonstrate the analytical method of extrapolating, from the rhetoric of folkloric examples, a common theme as an expression of an individual cultural cognitive system. It is important to remember his point, though, that such analyses should not be limited by conventional genre categories, because the theme cuts across genres; in Dundes's own rhetoric, it "underlies" expressions as "unstated postulates" or "cultural axioms." The resulting huge stack of examples of lineal references in American culture led him to question how distinctive the lineal cognitive system was in the world, and from where it may have arisen historically, socially, and psychologically. What set his analysis of linearity apart from other worldview principles—such as future-orientation (evident as a

196

faith in success and progress), abundance (also stated as "unlimited good"), and the infallibility of science—is the oppositional rhetorical position of linearity against circularity within the same society.

As with other cognitive binaries expressed rhetorically, Dundes found that one pole tended to dominate over the other, and argued that the American experience, especially, had a legacy of linearity. There were confrontational moments that drew attention to the tension of the binary. In 1971, he found significance in a countercultural protest of "groovy and broad" against a "straight" and "square" establishment. In the midst of the Civil Rights movement, he also pointed to racial implications of cognitive dissonance between "the straight world of the dominant white culture" and the cyclicity and angularity (a term used by black folklorist-writer Zora Neale Hurston) of African-American culture in dance, music, craft, and dress (hair). See, for example, the readings on African-American aesthetic forms in *Mother Wit from the Laughing Barrel: Readings in the Interpretation of Afro-American Folklore*, which he edited ([1973] 1990). Citing his friend and folklorist colleague Roger Abrahams, he also viewed the binary of city and country as representative of linear and circular worldviews, respectively. He commented on the domination of the city in the binary: "One is tempted to see urban life as insisting upon the more efficient line as in square city blocks and actual efforts to eliminate curves in well-travelled roads."

More balanced, in Dundes's view, was the unresolved tension between individualism (expressed as a single line) and groupness (often represented as a circle), which led to an especially American vacillation between wanting strong leadership and egalitarian democracy. Perhaps Dundes's view showed his folkloristic grounding in the social group as the basis of identity, since much of American Studies scholarship, based on popular sources, tends to emphasize American individualism as a dominant worldview. A folkloristic argument for a European-American "individual orientation" was made, however, by Barre Toelken (1996, 266–72). Another active binary, according to Dundes, was between a sight-oriented world, popularly associated with literacy and modernity, and the oral/aural channels of folk society. Using the visual worldview principle underlying sayings on the theme of "Seeing in Believing," emblematic of a "deep seated penchant for the visual sense" among Americans (in a title with the saying in *Interpreting Folklore* [1980b]), Dundes nonetheless wondered if electronic media created a postliterate society, which was once more primarily oral/aural because Americans heard their news more than they read it. This was one reason why the media had not displaced folklore, he mused, because the media enabled narrative communication. Reliance on "reading, 'riting, and 'rithmetic" was a sign of lineal thinking, because it privileged the plot line, signature line, and bottom line, respectively, in fixed, and therefore permanently certain, forms. Dundes *insightfully* remarked, "Americans still prefer to get agreements in writing rather than to trust a gentleman's handshake (a tactile sign) or take someone's word or say-so (oral sign) for a contract. Once an agreement is down in black and white, Americans watch out for, and read, the small print, with an 'eye' toward avoiding an unfavorable set of conditions" (1980h, 90).

In the present essay, more than in earlier essays, Dundes emphasized the gendered nature of line and circle as male and female representations, respectively. It is telling that of the many examples he gave in the essay, he chose "As the Crow Flies" for its title. Perhaps this was a self-reference to his argument for the prevalence of male chauvinism in American folklore, in an essay entitled "The Crowing Hen and the Easter Bunny" (1980a). This latter essay alluded to variations of the rhyme "Whistling maids and crowing hens, Never come to no good ends," in which crowing was rhetorically connected to male behavior. Besides the idea that a woman who whistled was acting like a man (i.e., the suggestion that whis-tling was intrusive, even an omen of storms, therefore going against the "expected passive, docile, sex-stereotyped behavior norm," according to Dundes), it was a rooster that was supposed to crow (see "Gallus as Phallus" in this volume for further symbolic associations of the rooster to hypermasculine display), and a crow that flew (flying being especially direct and pointed).

Dundes offered a sobering implication for worldview theory in the cognition of "nat-ural association," whereby violent actions were taken to remove a disruption of natural order. Reading the rhetoric of the English verse, "I know not which live more unnatu-ral lives, Obeying husbands or commanding wives," he warned of the resulting attitude: "By implication, a woman who acts like a man is unnatural and should be eliminated." Noting evidence of lore that Dundes neglected (from women particularly) which stig-matizes men, especially in the context of what historians have called the feminization or domestication of American culture, some folklorists countered that Dundes overstated his case, and should have analyzed more of the dialogic practices of everyday life in which male and female control are negotiated through expressive exchanges in mixed, as well as all-male, contexts. In some cases, such as adolescent male recitations and initiations, manly bravado may convey insecurity and stigmatization more than dominance and chauvinism. See, for example, various essays in Simon J. Bronner's *Manly Traditions*, with an afterword by Dundes (2005a).

Another gendered example related to linearity, according to Dundes, was the use of "end" in male games, based on crossing and penetrating lines. In "Into the Endzone for a Touchdown: A Psychoanalytic Consideration of American Football," Dundes stated: "Evidently there is a kind of structural isomorphism between the line (as opposed to the backfield) and the layout of the field of play. Each line has two ends (left end and right end) with a "center" in the middle. Similarly, each playing field has two ends (endzones) with a midfield line (the fifty-yard line). . . . The object of the game, simply stated, is to get into the opponent's endzone while preventing the opponent from getting into one's own endzone" (1979b; also in *Interpreting Folklore* [1980b]). He argued that manliness was demonstrated or "proven" in the frame of play by a linear (i.e., phallic) attack on a male opponent, who was feminized by being penetrated in the rear (see "Gallus as Phallus" [1994] for an *extension* of this argument). In light of Dundes's argument (and his naval ref-erences in "As the Crow Flies"), Bronner explored the importance of line crossing as a male transformative ritual (2006a).

Dundes used less cross-cultural analysis in this essay than in others, referring loosely to lineality as an American or Western worldview, although he intimated that it was becom-ing dominant globally as a "modern" mode of thought. Lee, in her classic essay, referred to the non-lineal thinking of Trobiand Islanders ([1950] 1968); in Dundes's essay, he gave a Native American tribe as an example of a group with circular-based cognition. Folklorist Barre Toelken, especially, developed the concept of a circular worldview among the Navajo, as a contrast to non-Native linearity, in his widely circulating textbook *The Dynamics of Folklore*. With regard to Dundes's attention, in the present essay, to architecture as a sym-bol of worldview, Toelken observed that "the [Navajo] hogan, not surprisingly, is made of a combination of plants (trees and branches used for the internal structure), animal substances (like rawhide) used in the lashing of materials together, dirt from the earth covering the outside, corn pollen rubbed along the main beams inside when the hogan is blessed, and the whole combination created for, and lived by, people *whose concept of their position in the world is expressed in terms of circles and interaction with those various aspects of nature*" (1996, 289; emphasis added).

Dundes's example of the American perception of the life course as linear, proceeding from birth to death, rather than being viewed cyclically, with a process of reincarnation, invited comparison to Eastern religious systems and group orientations, which suggest circularity. Hajime Nakamura's seminal text, *Ways of Thinking of Eastern Peoples* (1964), did not describe Eastern thinking as monolithic. Yet it did identify associations of nature with the divine, and the importance of a social nexus in a harmonious group, which was often represented by circular cosmological icons in China, Tibet, Korea, and Japan (e.g., the forces of Ying and Yang incorporated into the circular design of the traditional symbol *taijitu*, or the Poem of Reality in Zen Buddhism, consisting of twenty characters arranged in a circle).

If the distinctiveness of linearity as an American worldview within "Western thinking" was left culturally vague in Dundes's essay, other studies have been more forceful in historically viewing an American embrace of linearity as a sign of material expansion, technological progress, and intellectual novelty, characteristic of "modern" American experience. Historian John Demos traced the American evolution from a traditional, colonial world of natural cycles to the Revolutionary environment of architecture and writing, which made a "liberating" break with the past by having a "forward, future-directed outlook . . . [and] the self firmly situated at its center" (2004). Simon J. Bronner observed a dynamic between the intimate, touch orientation of the community circle, which offered Americans a sense of belonging, and the rising, sight-oriented, expansive horizon of urban technological linearity, which gained prominence since the nineteenth century (1986b). Both works avowed Dundes's line of thought.

As the Crow Flies: A Straightforward Study of Lineal Worldview in American Folk Speech

"WE DO NOT SEE THE lens through which we look." So wrote anthropologist Ruth Benedict (1887–1948) in an essay entitled "The Science of Custom" that appeared in *The Century Magazine* in 1929. Although this essay was later expanded to become the first chapter of her classic *Patterns of Culture*, published in 1934, for some reason, this succinct articulation of the difficulty of perceiving one's own culturally relative cognitive categories was omitted. From a folklore perspective, it suggests that one of the important potential contributions of folklore with respect to identifying the characteristics of that critical lens may be that native categories of perception are clearly delineated in various genres, including those subsumed under the rubric of folk speech.

In 1950, another outstanding anthropologist, Dorothy Demetracopoulou Lee (1905–75) published her insightful paper "Codifications of Reality: Lineal and Non-Lineal" in *Psychosomatic Medicine*. Her main point was to demonstrate that fellow anthropologist Bronislaw Malinowski (1884–1942) had misread some of his famous Trobriand Island ethnographic data by seeing lines where the Trobrianders did not. In other words, Malinowski was guilty of imposing Western lineality upon nonlineal phenomena. While she did speak of anthropologists referring to "unilinear" or "multilinear" courses of development and more generally of Westerners following a "line of thought," she was not particularly concerned with documenting Western lineal worldview. The bulk of her discussion provided instances of Malinowski's misinterpreting Trobriand culture. She did conclude, however, that "much of our present-day thinking, and much of our evaluation are based on the premise of the line and of the line as good" (Lee 1950, 96).

Lee's brilliant essay did not receive all the credit it deserved (see Graves 1957). It is my contention that Dorothy Lee was on the right track and American folk speech amply confirms her assertion that the line is absolutely central, if not sacred, in American worldview. But she did not distinguish between drawing parallel lines and concentric circles as a lecturer's means of making a point. In contrast, I argue it is "straight lines" that are crucial, not curved ones. Moreover, the straight lines are often displayed in the form of a square or box. It is precisely the combination of "line," "straight," and "square," I suggest, that shapes the lens through which Americans (and other Westerners) look. These constituent features that so significantly affect our perception are found repeatedly in dozens of examples from familiar folk speech.

The word "line" or the plural "lines" occurs alone, in combination in various compounds, and often as an affix, e.g., guidelines, deadlines, outlines, bloodlines, hemlines, necklines, hairlines, headlines, bylines, baselines, goal lines, property lines, airlines, ship lines, railroad lines, bus lines, trolley or streetcar lines, chorus lines, battle lines, pipelines, assembly lines, picket lines, time lines, datelines, telephone lines, fishing lines, waterlines, coastlines, shorelines, skylines, and lifelines, among many others.

The *line* functions as a kind of limit. One must "toe the line," not "cross the line," "lay it on the line," or have one's fate be "on the line." One may be asked to "hold the line," meaning to maintain the status quo at any cost to prevent any unfavorable incursion or development. One can think or be "in line" (with the prevailing code or trend) and by the same token, if an individual's behavior or suggestion is inappropriate, he may be admonished that he is "(way) out of line." One may seek to keep a rebellious child "in line," that is, insist that he or she conform to existing social conventions. The son or daughter of a king is said to be "in line" to occupy the throne. Presumably the heir must belong to the appropriate "lineage." To reach the Internet or use e-mail, one must go "online." Runners begin a race at the "starting line" and end at the "finish line."

A line can be an occupation or profession. Upon an initial meeting, one person may ask another, "What's your line?" meaning "What do you do for a living?" If one's vocation is the same as one's father/mother and grandfather/grandmother, one may boast that he or she comes from "a long line" of doctors, lawyers, educators, etc. If a line can reflect the past, it can also represent a trajectory pointing toward the future. One can look forward to success "down the line." In business, one speaks of a line of products with the "top of the line" being the best. The "bottom line" refers to the grand total or final figure on a financial balance sheet but more metaphorically, to the final upshot of a contract or deal. If one seeks information about a product or a person, he is said to be trying to "get a line on" it.

A line is also an insincere formulaic ploy (often a well-rehearsed sales pitch) or tactic intended to sway or seduce an addressee, as in trying to persuade a member of the opposite sex to accept an invitation for a date. These are often termed "pickup lines." Such usage almost certainly relates to the notion of a "line of argument" or "line of reasoning." Political organizations often have specific agendas or platforms which may be referred to as "party lines." It may simply be the influence of print, but one tends to refer to poetry, even purely oral poetry, in terms of lines, and the same goes for "learning one's lines" or "forgetting one's lines" in a stage play. Clothing has "lining," and a metaphor speaks of "lining one's own pockets" (with illegal funds). Even clouds have a "lining," as in the proverb, "Every cloud has a silver lining," which in the best tradition of American optimism urges citizens to "always look for the silver lining."

A line is still a line even if it's narrow. One speaks of a "fine line" or a "thin line" when making a subtle distinction between two different things. A line is no less a feature for its being intermittent, as in a "dotted line" upon which to sign one's name, say, to open a "line of credit" at a bank. With telephones, in former times, one could have a "party line" or indulge in a "private line." A difficult superior may take a "hard line" in dealing with a subordinate, especially if his performance is adjudged "borderline," and consequently "draw the line" in demanding future improvement. A fired employee, without adequate salary or benefits, may well fall below the "poverty line." One can also draw a "line in the sand" to indicate that an opponent can approach no farther. The names of famous borders also include the word line, such as the Mason-Dixon Line or the Maginot Line. Banks and insurance companies often "redline" impoverished urban areas where credit is denied residents. The red line in this instance serves as an unofficial and often illegal demarcation of areas that loan officers use to evaluate requests for funds.

It is not just that one is forced to stay "in line" and not "jump the line" by disregarding the folk principle of "first come, first served" in a "checkout line" at a grocery store, but there is an implicit and sometimes explicit understanding that the line must be straight. Lines, of course, can be either straight or curved, but the straight line provides the norm. "As the crow flies" is a traditional response to an inquiry as to how far away a given objective is. "As the crow flies" means the minimum distance from the present point to the objective as measured in a straight line. There is also the proverb: "The shortest distance between two points is a straight line." Often, however, it is not possible to go directly from point *A* to point *B*. Only crows (and other birds) can do so, flying over obstacles that impede the progress of land-bound creatures.

Straight means direct, honest, and right, among other things. One tries to "get one's facts straight," that is, correct. "Be straight with me" is a request for honesty. "Setting the record straight" is an attempt to eliminate previous errors. "Straight from the horse's mouth" refers to an unimpeachable source of information, presumably deriving from the practice of actually examining a horse's teeth (to determine its age and condition) as opposed to simply taking the word of a horse trader. To speak "straight from the shoulder," a phrase apparently derived from boxing (referring to a direct punch), means being frank and to the point, without exaggeration or embellishment. The "straight dope" is slang for true information. To be a "straight shooter" or a "straight arrow" implies that the individual in question is completely honest and trustworthy. Someone who is not so dependable may be urged to "straighten up and fly right." "Straight talk" is sincere, honest talk. To "see straight" means to discern reality clearly. "To go straight" implies that one may have had a shady past but has now decided to lead a righteous, law-abiding life. If a person "plays it straight," he or she is being totally above board, completely honest.

If a person is successful in a job, he or she may be promoted. The promotion may be gradual, or it may be dramatic so that he goes "straight to the top." In stage comedy, the "straight man" has to keep a "straight face" when he or she delivers a "straight line" to set up the joke's "punch line" uttered by the principal comedian. Straight can also mean unadulterated, as in taking one's whiskey "straight" or "straight up," that is, without any diluting mixer or ice cubes. To do something "straightaway" means doing it right away. A parent may tell a child to "come straight home" after school, meaning to come directly home without meandering or taking any wrong turn or detour. Ideally, one's destination lies "straight ahead." To win seven "straight" games (seven in a row) signifies that one has won an unbroken series or sequence. Straight also designates conventional norms in sexuality. Hence, a "straight" is a heterosexual as opposed to a homosexual, at least in gay slang.

If straight conveys honesty, frankness, forthrightness, then it may be contrasted with "crooked" (cf. the abridged form "crook" for a criminal) or "bent," as in "bent out of shape," or someone who "bends the law" or terms involving circles or the adjective "round." One must not get "out of line" and certainly, as already mentioned, not "cross the line." Incidentally, "cross" implies departing from "straight." An individual may betray another by "crossing up" that person. An even worse betrayal is called a "double cross." In any event, one makes a "beeline" for an objective and does so by going "straight ahead" toward one's goal.

This is very different from taking a "roundabout" way. Someone who "beats around the bush" is not being direct. Someone who gets the "run around" is not being treated in an honest, truthful manner. To "mess (kid, horse) around" is to waste time and not stay on course. Someone who is driven crazy may be said to be "(a)round the bend." There is an old American folk metaphor, "to go 'round Robin Hood's barn," meaning to follow a winding road or be long-winded. "Round Robin Hood's barn makes a tedious yarn" (Whiting 1977, 365; Mieder 1992, 38). The word "around" may also signify inexactness or at best a vague approximation. A friend tells another they should meet "around five o'clock." That is certainly not the same as specifying "five on the dot" (the dot presumably being a point on the line?). Even the use of the Latin "circa" with respect to dates reflects the same indulgence with approximation. A certain person may be said to have been born circa 1900, circa being, of course, cognate with the English word "circle." A similar nuance of around is found in the common leave-taking formula, "See you around," meaning in no particular place at no particular time. To "round off" a number, say an amount of money owed, is a self-conscious admission that one is willing to be inexact just for the sake of keeping things simple.

The negative associations of round and roundness in contrast to straight are occasionally reversed in American proverbs. We know that proverbs are famous for presenting two completely opposite points of view. "He who hesitates is lost" urges immediate action to ensure success while "Look before you leap" recommends caution. There is even a proverb covering this characteristic of the genre: "The devil can quote scripture," meaning that one can always find a proverb to justify one's position. So in contrast to "The shortest distance between two points is a straight line," we have "The longest way round is the shortest way found." But by the same token, we also have "Don't go round the world for a short cut." So the upshot is, "You pays your money, and you takes your choice." Still the general mistrust of round prevails: "Money is round and rolls away" (Mieder 1992, 416).

The epitome of roundness is, of course, the *circle* (Loeffler-Delachaux 1947; de Alvarez de Toledo 1951). "Circular reasoning" is clearly in opposition to "thinking straight." In terms of logic, if one uses a proposition to lead to a conclusion and then purports to prove the proposition by means of the conclusion, one is guilty of "circular reasoning," the idea being that one has completed a circle so there is no starting point. One has argued or reasoned in a circle (see Walton 1991; Rips 2002). A folk belief also states that when one becomes lost, say in a forest, in the course of trying to find one's path to safety, one will wind up "going around in circles." A bit of military doggerel, which is, however, known generally, confirms the association of being frustrated or lost with going in circles: "When in danger, when in doubt; Run in circles, scream and shout." Perhaps analogous to going in circles as a metaphor for working to no purpose may be the expression "spinning your wheels" that signifies "going nowhere fast." A wheel is, conceptually speaking, a kind of circle (Loeffler-Delachaux 1947, 69), and a "wheeler-dealer" or someone who "wheels and deals" is typically a person who is deceptive or even ruthlessly dishonest. Finally, one of the most striking pieces of evidence revealing the folk perception of circles is that a repeated series of actions that lead to an increasingly negative situation may be termed a "vicious circle." The adjective is surely telling!

If the circle (and roundness) connotes an undesirable state of confusion, the *square* does the opposite. The square is obviously an expanded form of straight lines. "To square" accounts is to settle matters equitably. One tries to treat others "fair and square," for example, by giving them a "square deal." Meals that are substantial and satisfactory are called "square meals." One tries to get "squared away," meaning to get things in order, to be prepared for whatever the future may hold. A "square shooter" is synonymous with "straight shooter," referring to someone who is scrupulously honest. To face an issue "squarely" means to confront it head-on and directly. To stand behind someone or something "four-square" implies being steady, unswerving, and without equivocation. Two opponents will "square off" or "square up," that is, face one another directly, for a fight.

The literal centrality of square in American (and very likely Western) thought is also present in dwellings and city planning. It is no coincidence that major cities typically express their identities in open areas commonly called "squares." This is so even if the shape of the area is not actually a square. Such is the case, for example, with Times Square in New

York City. Some city squares are in that quadrangular shape, but many are not. Other venues such as arenas may reflect the penchant for squares, e.g., Madison Square Garden, also in New York City.

Since the area of a geometric square is the length of one side multiplied by itself—if a side is represented by *s*, then the area of that square is said to be *s* "squared"—this principle has been extended so that any number *n* multiplied by itself is said to be *n* squared. This leads further to the term "square root." The square root of nine is therefore three. But there is nothing literally square about either the number nine or threes. Mathematics has other connections with lines and squares. For centuries, mathematicians interested in number theory have been fascinated by what is called the "magic square." This consists of an arrangement of numbers in the form of a square so that every column, every row, and each of the two diagonals adds up to the same sum, this total being called the "constant" (Meister 1952). A branch of geometry is called "lineal geometry," and there are "linear algebras." In addition, there are "linear equations," and in physics there are "lines of force," not to mention the "linear accelerator" by means of which particles are propelled in straight paths.

The contrast between the square and the circle is not just a matter of there not being any vicious squares. The fundamental opposition between these two basic metaphors is signaled by the expression about attempting to "put a square peg in a round hole" or the equally apt but perhaps less well known variant "to put a round peg in a square hole." The phrase may be used to label a misfit, someone deemed not qualified or fit to carry out a particular task. In the present context, the expression states that squareness and circularity are incompatible; they are mutually exclusive. Another traditional articulation of this incompatibility is the mathematical fool's errand of trying to "square the circle." The idea of trying to find a circle and square with equal areas is allegedly an insoluble problem, a mathematical impossibility (Hobson 1913; Jesseph 1999; but see Ruthen 1989). Hence, the idiom is a way of suggesting the futility of a given action. Speaking of futility, when some project comes to naught, one may well exclaim that it is "back to square one," that is, one must return to the very beginning of the enterprise to start all over again (possibly an allusion to a game such as hopscotch). A wastepaper basket may be referred to as "the circular file," that is, the place to deposit unneeded correspondence. It may be worth noting that both of the binary oppositions straight/crooked and square/round are reported in a single catchphrase once popular in England. Evidently, a humorous hyperbolic way of "setting a man on his word" was to say, "Straight down the crooked lane and all round the square" (Partridge 1961, 818).

Because square signals fairness and honesty, one should not be surprised to see just how much squareness permeates society. Perhaps the most popular traditional folk dance in American culture is called the "Square Dance." This may be contrasted with round dances such as the waltz, where dancers move or whirl in circular fashion. But for that matter, in social dancing, beginners are frequently taught to do the "box step." *Boxes,* like squares, are linear in nature. One is obliged to remain in a box in the same sense as toeing the line and not crossing it.

In baseball, for example, the batter steps into the "batter's box," where a pitcher from the opposing team throws the ball into what is called the "strike zone," an imaginary rectangular area above home plate through which a pitch must pass for the umpire behind the plate to call it a strike. If he misses the strike zone (and the batter doesn't swing), the pitch is labeled a ball, much as a ball hit outside the left- or right-field lines (also called "foul lines") is called a foul (as opposed to fair) ball. The place where the pitcher stands is sometimes called the "pitcher's box," and if too many batters are successful, thus forcing him to leave (to be replaced by another pitcher), it is said he has been "knocked out of the box." The final results of a baseball game, often appearing in newspapers and giving the statistics (e.g., runs, hits, errors, etc.), are called the "box score."

Baseball, America's national pastime, is just one instance of the way boxes and lines permeate the culture. A "line drive" or "liner" is a sharply hit ball with little or no arc. One of a pitcher's most effective pitches is a "curve" or "curveball," that is, a ball that does not go in a straight line toward home plate but rather bends or curves in its flight, the aim being to fool the batter so he fails to hit it. In American slang, to "throw someone a curve," taken from baseball, means to ask an unfair question or make an unreasonable demand. Again, "curve" like circle and round implies a departure from the "straight and narrow," from directness and honesty.

Many sports and games have lines. For example, in basketball, one shoots foul shots from a position immediately behind "the foul line" aka "the free-throw line." In football, there is an "offensive line," consisting of players who protect their quarterback when the team is on offense, or a "defensive line," consisting of players who attack the opposing quarterback. When a team is on defense, there may be several of eleven players who are positioned slightly behind the defensive line to shore up the defense, e.g., protect against a short pass by the opposing offense. These players are called "linebackers." In football, the playing field is divided into ten ten-yard strips. Position on the field is accordingly measured by "yard lines."

No one likes to "boxed in," but the fact is that Americans are always "behind enemy lines," so to speak. Lines are everywhere, it seems, and when they meet, they frequently form rectangles and squares. (One need look no further than to the shape of most windows and window panes, bricks and boards, picture frames, postage stamps, rugs, and hundreds of other mundane objects.) Though businessmen may look for an "angle," there is always a danger of being "cornered." It is one thing to be boxed in but even worse to be forced into a small corner of a quadrilateral enclosure. At sporting events or theaters, would-be spectators go to the "box office" to purchase tickets. Typically, the best seats in the house are the "box seats." At sporting events, spectators are not allowed to enter the actual playing area, e.g., the "boxing ring" (despite its name, a square) or the baseball or football field. They are obliged to remain on the "sidelines." An injured player may have to be "sidelined" for a period of time. In ice hockey, a player who commits an infraction is punished by being sent to a particular area on the sidelines termed the "penalty box."

Houses and rooms therein may resemble boxes, and in the bedroom, one sleeps on a rectangular mattress that sits squarely on a "box spring." Office workers may be forced to occupy small spaces called "cubicles." (Why are pieces of ice used to chill drinks in the shape of cubes? Round bits of ice surely function equally well.) Early on, children are socialized by such rhymes as "Step on a line, break your father's (mother's) spine." The variant uses terms other than line, but the message is the same: "Step on a crack, break your father's (mother's) back." A line is a limit that must be respected, that is, not stepped on. In tick-tack-toe, the winner is the person who can draw a straight line through either three *x*'s or three *o*'s. In hopscotch, one must step carefully so as not to go outside any of the series of boxes.

Whether it's the military or show business, individuals are constantly asked to "line up." Suspected criminals are frequently asked to participate in a "lineup" (to see if eyewitnesses can identify them as perpetrators of a crime). One also speaks of an outstanding "lineup" of talent, either on a sports team or a theatrical stage. Drunk drivers, when stopped by police officers, may be asked to "walk a straight line" (as a sobriety test to prove that they are sufficiently sober to be permitted to continue driving their vehicles).

It should be noted that despite the ubiquity of lines and squares in American worldview, the semantic associations are not always positive. A square in slang terms is a "strait-laced" person, someone who is excessively conventional and law abiding. There have even been a few proverbial attempts to denigrate squareness, for example, "Be there or be square." In other words, show up for the event in question unless you are too inhibited or fearful to do so. Other traditional verbal efforts to escape the vise of linearity include the notion of "reading between the lines" and the exhortation to "think outside the box." But it can be said that these very attempts to escape the boundaries imposed by lines and boxes confirm the existence of such cultural restraints.

If a person is terminally ill in the hospital and the EEG monitor suddenly shows that he or she has "flatlined," one can safely say that person has reached "the end of the line" and, unless cremated, is very likely to be shortly thereafter buried in a box (coffin).

What can we conclude from this brief demonstration of the apparent American penchant for straight lines and squares as well as a complementary mistrust of round curves and circles? Do we, in fact, have a window on a facet of American worldview? Anthropologist Aidan Southall suggests in a provocative, if admittedly speculative, essay devoted to an evolutionary approach to architecture that original "circularity" has given way to "rectangularity" (1993, 378). Citing the discovery of a dome-shaped construction of arched branches, unearthed in the Ukraine and said to be fifteen thousand years old, perhaps one of the oldest-known examples of human architecture, Southall wonders if this structure in any way symbolized the "dome of heaven." He might well have also considered such examples as the shape of the Eskimo igloo or the curious beehive-shaped *trulli* in the village of Alberobello in southern Italy. In any event, he remarks that whereas "sticks and stones are naturally round," they tend to be replaced as building materials by the cultural invention or borrowing of "rectangular bricks and square stones." He notes further, "Round stools precede square thrones and chairs" and that "humankind as a whole has clearly moved from the universal occupation of the round to an almost universal occupation of the rectangular" (1993, 379).

Here is Southall's thesis in his own words:

> It is more natural (though I use this adjective with great caution), to live in the round than in the square, whether it is a question of dwelling or village, settlement or city. For virtually nothing in nature appears in rectangular form, whereas round, spherical and curved phenomena, both stationary and in motion are both ubiquitous and so impressive as to imprint themselves on the human imagination and consciousness. Is the rectangular city, then, a symbolic statement of human culture triumphing over nature by making an opposite statement? Surprisingly, in all the literature on nature and culture I have not noticed the question raised. With the other pair lurking behind, it becomes a question of whether the rectangular city is a male statement as well." (1993, 380)

Southall is not the first to suggest an evolutionary sequence from circular to rectangular structures. Robbins, for instance, suggested that dwelling shapes and settlement patterns were related to whether people were nomadic or sedentary: "Considerable archaeological data also indicate that as cultures have moved from shifting to more settled subsistence patterns temporally, there has been a corresponding trend from circular to predominantly rectangular dwellings," and he hypothesized "that circular ground plans will tend to be associated with relatively impermanent or mobile settlement patterns, and that rectangular house ground plans will tend to be associated with more permanent or sedentary community settlement patterns" (1966, 7; see also Flannery 1972, 29–30).

One emerging controversial issue is not so much whether there are round or square dwellings, but rather whether or not specific social organizational constellations are associated with either one (see Saidel 1993 and Flannery's response). Of interest in the present context is the possibility there may be a common observable pattern in both house type and the configuration or grouping of multiple dwellings. Whiting and Ayres claim (1968, 126) that societies that build rectangular houses tend to arrange them in a line or square. If this is the case, it indicates that the pattern of circularity or squareness may apply equally to house or dwelling shape and the overall settlement plan. Moreover, the charter, so to speak, for such a pattern may well extend to the cosmos. One explanation for the priority of the circle is that the sun (and moon) are perceived as celestial circles (Peet 1888; Loeffler-Delachaux 1947; Lurker 1966, 523), not to mention the perception of the horizon. Hence, architectural plans might have been intended to mirror the celestial model. One thinks of the circular form of Stonehenge, for example, as a prime example of a likely sacred construction connected with sun worship.

Lest the reader think that the idea that circularity may be manifested in dwelling construction or other social forms is just pure speculation on the part of academics, one should ponder the following testimony given by a talented professional Oglala Sioux storyteller in the early twentieth century:

> The Oglala believe the circle to be sacred because the Great Spirit caused everything in nature to be round except stone. . . . The sun and the sky, the earth and the moon are round like a shield. . . . Everything that breathes is round like the body of a man. Everything that grows from the ground is round like the stem of a tree. Since the Great Spirit has caused everything to be round, mankind should look upon the circle as sacred for it is the symbol of all things in nature except stone. It is also the symbol of the circle that marks the edge of the world. . . . The day, the night, and the moon go in a circle above the sky. . . . *For these reasons the Oglala make their tipis circular, their camp circle circular and sit in a circle for all ceremonies.* The circle is also the symbol of the tipi and of the shelter." (Walker 1917, 160; italics added)

It may well be that the distinction between nature and culture is not so much matched by one between the circle and the square as by the presence or absence of the line. Nature does not necessarily come in lines. Rather, humans attempt to impose order by perceiving or drawing lines. In terms of folk speech, there is a desire to "connect the dots," but the connected dots may form circles as well as squares. Lines of latitude and longitude follow the shape of the earth. Still, Southall may be correct in identifying a preference for rectangles, though I suggest that it would be more accurate to say a preference for straight as opposed to curved lines. It is a desideratum to "get all one's ducks in a row," and it is surely no coincidence that one tends to plant crops in straight rows, or that the military obliges soldiers to march in precise line formations, or that seniority and rank are indicated by the number of stripes, which are essentially glorified lines. In the navy, there is a distinction between "line officers" as opposed to staff or supply officers, referring to an old label assigned to warships or "ships of the line." All military units, not just the navy, insist on performing prescribed tasks "in the line of duty."

While the evidence adduced from American folk speech cannot necessarily support the evolutionary aspects of Southall's argument, it seems to corroborate his "delineation" of a critical distinction between the circle and the square. If one accepts and expands upon his suggestion that the "rectangular city" is male—and one can easily cite numerous examples of penile architecture, for example, the Washington Monument or the Empire State Building—then one may go on to propose that roundness and circles belong to the realm of the feminine. In evolutionary terms, the (linear?) progression from circle to square then corresponds to the alleged schema whereby original matriarchy was in time replaced by patriarchy. Certainly in American folk speech, "curvaceous" refers to a woman's well-shaped figure, signifying voluptuousness. It would not be used to refer to a man's physique. Moreover, it is women, according to American male stereotypes, who are accused of not being able to think logically, that is, lineally.

In Shakespeare's day, we have indisputable evidence that circle referred to the female pudendum. In *Romeo and Juliet* (2.1.23–26), we find Mercutio's bawdy remark: "'Twould anger him to raise a spirit in his mistress' circle of some strange nature, letting it there stand till she had laid it, and conjured it down." In more recent times, women of easy virtue were called "round heels," presumably because they spent so much time on their backs that their heels became increasingly rounded. (The term is also applied to inferior boxers, who were so frequently knocked out that they consequently suffered a similar fate.) So perhaps one can make a justifiable case that women are round while men are square. It is, after all, women who by nature have menstrual "cycles"; men do not. The stereotypical association of women with roundness and men with squareness (and hence women with vagueness, dissemblance, and dishonesty, as opposed to men with precision, directness, and candor) can easily be construed as part of the larger paradigm that "aligns" women with nature and men with culture (Ortner 1974). For that matter, the proposal that "rectilinear represents the male body image and curvilinear the female" is not new (see Whiting and Ayres 1968, 128).

However, I would argue that both men and women in American culture think in lineal terms. This may be why there is resistance to the notion of reincarnation. Reincarnation implies that a person's being or soul, after death, is recycled. A person is reborn and begins life anew. In some religions, the recycling is repeated ad infinitum. In American worldview, in contrast, the progression from birth through life to death is an irreversible path or line. One may choose to believe (in a culturally sanctioned denial of human mortality) that one continues to live on in heaven, but that belief does not include the possibility of being reborn on earth as a new baby. Americans do observe a certain cyclicity of seasons: spring, summer, fall, winter, a sequence from birth to death and then rebirth, as well as the recurrent series of the days of the week and months of the year, and Eliade credits the phases of the moon: "appearance, increase, wane, disappearance, followed by reappearance after three nights of darkness" as contributing significantly to the belief in cyclical concepts of time (1954, 86). Nevertheless, years, the larger temporal units, are counted serially in an irreversible sequence. One can go back in time only through fiction and fantasy. The point is that Americans, males and females alike, perceive both time and space in lineal terms. It is of some interest that a native Aleut environmentalist from Alaska claims that it is precisely the lineal bias of Western society that causes problems in the repeated failure to understand the cyclical worldview systems of many aboriginal societies (Merculieff 1994).

We may conclude, therefore, that Dorothy Lee was right when she alluded to the American (and Western) propensity toward codifying reality in lineal terms. In fact, the straight/circular dichotomy is of some antiquity; it existed in classical Greek literature and philosophy (Bellew 1979). However, we may wish to modify slightly Ruth Benedict's pessimistic dictum that "we do not see the lens through which we look." Inasmuch as folklore does encapsulate native cognitive categories, we may through its analysis indeed be able to see at least some small portion of that lens, as I hope these few lines have succeeded in demonstrating. On the other hand, perhaps I simply assumed what I planned to prove, in which case I am undoubtedly guilty of *circulus probandi.*

References

Bellew, Lynne. 1979. *Straight and circular: A study of imagery in Greek philosophy.* Assen: Van Gorcum.

Benedict, Ruth. 1929. The science of custom. *The Century Magazine* 117:641–49.

———. 1934. *Patterns of culture.* Boston: Houghton Mifflin.

de Alvarez de Toledo, Luisa G. 1951. Contribucion al conocimiento del significado del circulo. *Revista de Psicoanalisis* 8:465–77.

Eliade, Mircea. 1954. *The myth of the eternal return.* Princeton: Princeton University Press.

Flannery, Kent V. 1972. The origins of the village as a settlement type in Mesoamerica and the Near East: A comparative study. In *Man, settlement, and urbanism,* edited by Peter J. Ucko, Ruth Tringham, and G.W. Dimbleby, 23–53. London: Duckworth.

———. 1993. Will the real model please stand up: Comments on Saidel's "Round house or square?" *Journal of Mediterranean Archaeology* 6:109–17.

Graves, Robert. 1957. Comments on lineal and non-lineal codifications. *Explorations* 7: 46–51.

Hobson, Ernest William. 1913. *"Squaring the circle": A history of the problem.* Cambridge: Cambridge University Press.

Jesseph, Douglas Michael. 1999. *Squaring the circle: The war between Hobbes and Wallis.* Chicago: University of Chicago Press.

Lee, Dorothy Demetracopoulou. 1950. Codifications of reality: Lineal and non-lineal. *Psychosomatic Medicine* 12:89–97.

Loeffler-Delachaux, Marguerite. 1947. *Le cercle, un symbole.* Geneva: Aux Éditions du Mont-Blanc.

Lurker, Manfred. 1966. Der Kreis als symbolische Ausdruck der kosmichen Harmonie. *Studium Generale* 19:523–33.

Meister, Friedrich. 1952. *Magische Quadrate.* Zürich: Ernst Wurzel.

Merculieff, Harion (Larry). 1994. Western society's linear systems and Aboriginal cultures: The need for two-way exchanges for the sake of survival. In *Key issues in hunter-gatherer research,* edited by Ernest S. Burch, Jr. and Linda J. Ellana, 405–15. Oxford: Berg.

Mieder, Wolfgang, Stewart A. Kingsbury, and Kelsie B. Harder, eds. 1992. *A dictionary of American proverbs.* New York: Oxford University Press.

Ortner, Sherry B. 1974. Is female to male as nature is to culture? In *Women, culture & society,* edited by Michelle Zimbalist Rosaldo and Louise Lamphere, 67–87. Stanford: Stanford University Press.

Partridge, Eric. 1961. *A dictionary of slang and unconventional English.* New York: The Macmillan Group.

Peet, Stephen D. 1888. The circle as a sun symbol. *American Antiquarian* 10:135–53.

Rips, Lance J. 2002. Circular reasoning. *Cognitive Science* 26:767–95.

Robbins, Michael C. 1966. House types and settlement patterns. *Minnesota Archeologist* 28: 2–35.

Ruthen, Russell. 1989. Squaring the circle. *Scientific American* 261 (1): 22–23.

Saidel, Benjamin Adam. 1993. Round house or square? Architectural form and socio-economic organization in the PPNB. *Journal of Mediterranean Archaeology* 6:65–108.

Southall, Aidan. 1993. The circle and the square: Symbolic form and process in the city. In *Urban Symbolism,* edited by Peter J.M. Nas, 378–93. Leiden: E. J. Brill.

Walker, J.R. 1917. The sun dance and other ceremonies of the Oglala division of the Teton Dakota. *Anthropological Papers of the American Museum of Natural History* 16 (2): 53–221.

Walton, Douglas N. 1991. *Begging the question: Circular reasoning as a tactic of argumentation.* New York: Greenwood Press.

Whiting, B.J. 1977. *Early American proverbs and proverbial phrases.* Cambridge, Mass.: Harvard University Press.

Whiting, John W.M., and Barbara Ayres. 1968. Inferences from the shape of dwellings. In *Settlement archaeology,* edited by K.C. Chang, 117–33. Palo Alto: National Book Press.

11

MUCH ADO ABOUT "SWEET BUGGER ALL": GETTING TO THE BOTTOM OF A PUZZLE IN BRITISH FOLK SPEECH

Introduction

Dundes's frequent reference to folklore's homoerotic symbolism, which is missed by scholars who are narrowly focused on genre studies, supported Freud's view that homosexuality was "constitutional," or innate, in humans, but was socially suppressed. Freudian theory holds that society inhibits same-sex affection, especially for males, and individuals deal with the restraint by expressing their desires, as well as frustrations, in symbols found in dreams—and folk customs and narratives. For instance, in "Infantile Sexuality" (his second of Three Contributions to the Theory of Sex), Freud noted that the "anal zone" is significantly "erogenous" at an early age. He wrote, "Through psychoanalysis, one finds, not without surprise, the many transformations that normally take place in the sexual excitations emanating from here, and that this zone often retains for life a considerable fragment of genital irritability" ([1905] 1995).

Another of Dundes's concerns, drawn from Freud, was the relation of folklore to human development and gender identity. Following sexual development through the life course, Freud understood puberty as a special period when conflicting desires—affective ties to the mother and father, a combination of homoerotic and heterosexual impulses, simultaneous longing for past childhood and future adulthood—produced anxieties that were projected in an abundance of rituals, jokes, and customs. Freudian theory further holds that a common response to extra societal pressure on the male is for him to separate from his feminine attachments by symbolically repudiating his mother, so as to fit the expectation of acquiring the manly traits of independence, aggression, and strength. The boy shifted his attachments to other males, Freud observed, and dealt with ambivalent feelings of embracing, and replacing, the father. Of consequence to the nature of male initiatory rituals, male bonding invites the risk of homophobic prejudice, and males often compensate with ritualized displays of aggressive, hypermasculine, and homophobic behavior, or so the theory goes.

To Dundes, it appeared odd that, according to this theory, homosexuality was an integral part of the social and psychological dynamic of male development evident in the symbolism of folklore, but that cultural scholars had been relatively silent on the matter.

Dundes surmised that despite the paths of folklore investigation opened by the Freudian revolution, cultural scholars, particularly folklorists, resisted taking this interpretative route, both on an external level, because of a socially instilled homophobia, and internally, because of their proclivity toward anal eroticism—evident in an "obsession" with collection and classification of piles of texts (see his essay on the "Psychology of Collecting" at the end of this volume). Texts with homosexual themes were defined as "obscene," and not analyzed, even though risqué material in jokes, customs, and speech are prevalent in oral tradition. This, to Dundes, epitomized the folkloristic dilemma of keeping an open mind while probing the folk mind. Stated as a question, can scholars free themselves from cultural biases so as to render the meaning of traditions in culture—especially when there is a suppression of liberated, critical inquiry? Notable exceptions to the prevalent suppression of scholarly inquiry into erotica, frequently cited by Dundes as Freudian analyses of humor, were Gershon Legman's *Rationale of the Dirty Joke*, which included a long section on homosexuality (1975, 55–183), and Martha Wolfenstein's *Children's Humor* (1978), with a foreword by Alan Dundes. Elliott Oring is a prominent folklorist who often disputed Dundes's interpretations of humor as projections of sexual and aggressive tendencies. Instead, Oring proposed the contextual concept of "appropriate incongruity" as an alternative to psychoanalytic interpretation (2003, 1992). Dundes emphasized humor as societal constructs, but there are also a variety of essays on individual humor (e.g., Oring 1984b; Davies 1998).

As a folklorist, Dundes strove to view the relation of folklore to homosexuality as one more problem to be explicated. In examining the acquisition of gender identity during adolescence, manly displays invited analysis because of their function in repudiating the feminine by enacting homosexual activities. To Dundes, the prevalence of homoerotic content in folkloric performance also suggested the constant emergence and enactment of folklore as expressions of wish fulfillment, and as projective processes. In addition to viewing folklore as a *consequence* of anxiety and ambiguity, a fictive plane or social outlet in which conflicts could be mediated, Freudian theory raised questions of the psychological *source* of folklore for Dundes, particularly in the symbolic models of dreams. Although his interpretive logic is rooted in Freudian theory (i.e., the discernment of symbols as signifiers in the outward, disguised expression of repressed thoughts which are moving from unconscious to conscious levels), Dundes applied the interdisciplinary concepts of cultural relativism, textual and contextual comparison, and linguistic structuralism to depathologize homosexuality, and place it in a cross-cultural perspective. He unshackled homosexuality from the biological determinism of "constitution" and reproductive function, and located it culturally in the issues of societal worldview, and of gender, age, and national identity.

In this essay concerning the folk speech complex of "bugger," representing a sodomite, Dundes went beyond the usual facile comparison of linguistic difference between British and American English (e.g., a "lift" in Britain is an "elevator" in the United States). He addressed the symbolic and cognitive significance of distinguishing active from passive sexual roles in the British mindset. This led to questioning the meaning of replacing bugger in America with words that did not differentiate between these roles. Characteristically, Dundes used a play on words in the title of "Much Ado About 'Sweet Bugger All.'" Readers may think of Shakespeare's play "Much Ado About Nothing," and wonder whether cultural impact can be shown from an analysis of a single word. The "nothing," though, refers to the idiomatic meaning of "bugger all," and Dundes showed that there is indeed much ado about it. He demonstrated the national obsession with rhetoric and its negation in the

United States, and raised the question of the relationship of language to culture. The rationale for this analysis was that rhetoric was a socially constructed vehicle for self-knowledge, while language was the primary expression, from early on in people's lives, of the workings of a mind responding to social and historical conditions. Folk speech told scholars about deep-seated values conveyed, through tradition, into everyday life. Similarly, Dundes argued that what made people laugh was often what they took most seriously, or was what they had difficultly in broaching in everyday speech, and in their consciousness. Humor therefore deserved analysis, to understand anxieties in the course of life and the contexts of different cultures.

Although Dundes presented the divide across the Atlantic vis-à-vis the word bugger in either/or terms, readers can consider whether the shared American and British fondness for "boogie" and "bogey" men in children's folklore may be related conceptually, if not etymologically, to bugger. Boogie and bogey are usually traced to a specter or goblin, but they are frequently reported as applying to a dreadful character (consistently male), an old, ugly, or black man. The "bug" root is found, in fact, in various figures scaring children, such as buggie, bugaboo, and bugbear. Linguist John Widdowson observed that the complex of boo, bug, boggart, pooh, and poop all have "unpleasant or frightening connotations" because of the use of labial sounds in the initial positions of these words. According to oral tradition, scary "boogie" figures often lurk in closets and under the bed. Narrations involving these figures exert social control over children. But is this because of an unconscious fear of molestation, as well as the more conscious fear of the dark? Or is the tradition connected to Freud's idea of anal sexuality early in human development, by suggesting the risk of assault on a child's erogenous zone while that child is sleeping in the dark? Is there sexual significance in the common rhetoric of the boogie man "having," "getting," "grabbing," "gobbling," "pouncing on," and "bagging" children, especially as a metaphor for the consequences of "immoral or undesirable behavior," to quote Widdowson (1977)?

Boogie men in both America and Britain are connected by being less often ghosts and goblins than scary men, and they are often connected racially to dark or diabolical figures. Yet Dundes has a credible point that in America, the sexual object may be male or female, and the binary collapses between receiver and giver. The American jazz dance of boogie-woogie (perhaps a play on the erotic "oriental" dance of "hoochie-coochie" at late-nineteenth-century world fairs) is usually visualized as a gyration of the hips and buttocks, and is especially sexually suggestive in the frequent call to "boogie my woogie" or "boogie on down!" The genre—a musical performance with energetic key pounding and a host of double entendre lyrics—can also be viewed as sexual, with animated variations on the upper keys overlaying a steady bass beat. An example of a traditional verse in African-American boogie music, with its sexual bravado and verbal dueling, is: "I like your mama, I like your sister too, I did like your daddy, but your daddy wouldn't do, I met your daddy on the corner the other day, You know about that he was funny that way." (For more on homosexual themes in blues and boogie music, see chapter four in Paul Oliver's *The Meaning of the Blues* [1960]). Even if readers accept or deny that there are more cognates of bugger in American usage than Dundes allowed, they should heed Dundes's central proposition that the cultural context, and folkloric expression, of related tendencies toward homophobia and homoeroticism vary according to historical and social conditions.

Prior to writing this essay, Dundes had inquired into differences of worldview between Americans and Brits in "Misunderstanding Humor: An American Stereotype of the Englishman" (1982; reprinted in his *Cracking Jokes* [1987]). In this study, he examined jokes concerning the symbolism of national differences in the English language. Often distinctions between English and American usage (such as the British use of "tin" for what Americans call a "can") became the basis of humor, underscoring the stereotype that Americans were inferior while the Brits were superior. Linguistically, Dundes observed, Brits viewed the Americans as exaggeration-prone, and the Americans viewed Brits as favoring understatement. Perhaps inspiring the later study on "bugger," Dundes reported "one of the very best examples of the marred anecdote tradition" was a misinterpretation of a limerick by an Englishman on an American practice of sex.

For other interpretations by Dundes of homoeroticism in different cultural traditions, see Dundes, Leach, and Özkö 1970; Dundes 1979b (reprinted in *Interpreting Folklore* [1980b]); Dundes and Pagter 1991; Dundes and L. Dundes 2002; and Dundes 2002a, 2004c. For examples of folklorists applying Dundes's explanations for homoeroticism in folklore, see Mechling 1980; Newall 1986; Dresser 1994; and Bronner 2006a.

Much Ado About "Sweet Bugger All": Getting to the Bottom of a Puzzle in British Folk Speech

Introduction

There is a well-known quotation enjoying near proverbial status claiming that "England and America are two nations (countries) divided by a common language." According to the *Oxford Dictionary of Quotations*, this bit of oxymoronic wisdom is usually attributed to George Bernard Shaw (Partington 1992, 638) despite the fact that it does not seem to appear in the playwright's published writings. It is not listed, for example, in Bryan and Mieder's comprehensive *The Proverbial Bernard Shaw: An Index to Proverbs in the Works of George Bernard Shaw* (1994).

On a purely lexical *level,* it is easy enough to demonstrate the "divide" and there have been quite a number of semi-popular books containing lists of many of the distinctive vocabulary differences (de Funiak 1967; Bickerton 1973; Moss 1978; Schur 1987; Walmsley 1987; Davies 1997). I am not speaking of variations in spelling, for example, American "flavor" versus British "flavour," nor am I concerned with differences in pronunciation, for example, of the word "tomato" (Americans pronounce the second vowel like the one in "may" while the English pronounce the second vowel like the one in the abbreviated form of "mamma," that is, "ma") but of actual clear-cut lexical distinctions. Examples would include the following:

British English	American English
Biscuit (sweet)	Cookie
Braces	Suspenders
Bum	Butt(ocks)
Chemist	Druggist
Crisps	Potato chips
Dustbin	Garbage can
Estate agent	Realtor
Flat	Apartment
Fortnight	Two weeks
Lift	Elevator
Lorry	Truck
Nappy	Diaper
Pram	Baby carriage

An example of the sort of sexual terminology that is the subject of this article would be wank off (British) and jerk off (American).

215

This brief list is meant only to give a few representative examples of definite differences between British and American English (cf. Zviadadze 1983 and Davies 1997). These lexical pairs tend to be in complementary distribution. No American would feel comfortable referring to a lorry carrying a load of crisps. Nor would s/he be likely to refer to a "jerk" as a "wanker" even though both terms derive similarly from slang idioms for masturbation. And few Americans are even aware of the large number of British slang expressions involving the term "bugger."

Bugger and Buggery

Bugger in its original and literal sense refers to an act of sodomy; that is, an act of anal penetration. Bugger as a noun signifies the active agent in such an act while bugger as a verb refers to the act itself. Legman (1975, 75) offers several folk definitions of buggery: Queen Victoria asks her chamberlain, "What is a bugger?" "A bugger, Your Majesty," replies the courtier imperturbably, "is a man who does another man an injury behind his back." This text comes from England c. 1927. In a variant, it is a butler who replies, "A bugger is an individual who enlarges the circle of his acquaintances." Another folk definition of buggery cited by Legman is: "Buggery: The right man in the wrong place," which he points out is undoubtedly intended as a spin-off of the folk definition of adultery as "The wrong man in the right place" (Legman 1968, 791).

Buggery in Limericks

The popularity of buggery as a folk theme is nowhere more evident than in limericks. Among the dozens referring to buggery reported in Legman's canonical collections, the first published originally in Paris in 1953 (1974, 92–108) and the second compilation some years later (1977, 187–218), is the following:

> Then spoke the headmaster of Rugger,
> A most accomplished old bugger:
> "I spend half each night
> With a smooth catamite.
> My wife? I don't even hug'er" (Legman 1977, 212, no. 1051).

Although some buggers are thus depicted as women-hating homosexuals, there are also limericks indicating that females may provide appropriate fodder for such appetites (cf. Legman 1974, 110, no. 534), or the object of a bugger's action in the world of limericks may frequently be an animal rather than a human. Legman includes numerous examples under "Zoophily" (1974, 118–36; 1977, 238–71) and La Barre in his pioneering survey of limerick content notes that "Male bestiality occurs with an ape, hog, cat, parrot, mule, porcupine, bear, swans, owls, a duck and a bug" (1939, 208). One representative example, a truly classic limerick, should suffice:

> There was a young man of St John's
> Who wanted to bugger the swans,
> But the loyal hall-porter
> Said, "Pray take my daughter!
> Them birds are reserved for the dons" (Legman 1974, 130, no. 637).

The limerick is a fixed-phrase folkloristic genre, meaning that the reciter performs a given text exactly verbatim each time s/he narrates it. (Free-phrase genres, in contrast, allow for improvisation and the wording may vary.) The precise and invariable generic restrictions with respect to meter and rhyme make it an ideal form for obscene content (for discussion of some of the more formal characteristics of limericks, see Matthews 1911, 144–45; Bouissac 1977; Bibby 1978, 69–75). The underlying rationale is to manage to compress as much content as possible within severely limiting textual constraints, so the limerick embodies the more or less successful insertion of sexual content in a narrowly defined restrictive poetic container. If artfully constructed, the last line of the limerick may well serve as a fitting climax to a purported sexual intrigue.

In any case, the abundant limerick tradition clearly demonstrates that buggery unquestionably refers to anal intercourse, and can refer to male or female sexual objects, human or animal. It is also noteworthy, as Legman points out, that the limerick is part of the folklore of the educated classes (1964, 439; cf. La Barre 1939, 204; Belknap 1981, 28) rather than the uneducated, and since buggery is such a frequent subject of limericks, one can logically assume that the popularity of "bugger" idioms in England cannot be explained away as simply being a vulgar practice of lower-class speech. There is even a classic anecdote that attributes the use of the word to none other than King George V. Supposedly, on his deathbed in 1936, his last words were said to be "How goes [or "is"] the Empire?" But a much more famous and well-known tradition offers an alternative version. According to this bit of apocrypha, his physician to cheer him up suggested he would soon be well enough to visit his favorite resort, Bognor Regis, at which point the King allegedly responded: "Bugger Bognor!" (Guthke 1992, 207 note 4; Green 1999, 20).

Although there has been some debate about where and when the limerick form may have originated (Baring-Gould 1967, 29; Belknap 1981), a few authorities have claimed an English origin for it. Brander Matthews remarked, "The humble limerick has the distinction of being the only fixed form which is actually indigenous to English" (1911, 145). Similarly, Norman Douglas, in his delightfully witty 1928 compilation, *Some Limericks,* insisted that limericks are "English to the core" and "are as English as roast beef" (1928, 24 and 25). Others, including Legman (1974, lxxii), concur with respect to the theory that the limerick seems to be an original English creation. Whether or not the theory is correct, it is safe to say that whatever the origin of the limerick may have been, the frequency of occurrence of "buggery" in English limericks is irrefutable. Moreover, it is also to be found repeatedly in "rugby songs," a staple of the English bawdy folk song tradition (Morgan 1967; 1968). Here is just one stanza from the classic "The Good Ship Venus," which in fact is in limerick format:

> The captain's name was Slugger
> He was a dirty bugger
> He wasn't fit
> To shovel shit
> On any bugger's lugger (Morgan 1967, 68).

"Bugger" in British Folk Speech

A survey of entries in various English dictionaries does reveal that "bugger" is "chiefly British" (Aman 1986–87, 238–41). This is confirmed by entries in American slang dictionaries stating that "The standard English sense 'sodomite' is no longer commonly understood in the U.S." (Lighter 1994, 293). Writing in the first half of the twentieth century, Mencken claimed that "bugger" was "not generally considered obscene in the United States." Mencken also recalled that as a small boy, he heard his father use "bugger" often "as an affectionate term for any young male," adding that "if it shows any flavor of impropriety today the fact must be due to English influence" (1938, 314). An authoritative dictionary of American regional English cites a 1945 discussion of New England sailor slang that observed that "to bugger is to confuse or perplex," such that "I'll be buggered" is an expression of mild astonishment. The discussion cited includes:

> That seamen—at least fifty years back—had not the remotest idea of the real meaning of the word is amply proved . . . by the fact that they used it freely in the presence of respectable women. (Cassidy 1985, 437)

Along the same lines, we find that "bugger all," which means "nothing," is labelled as "Rare in the United States" (Lighter 1994, 294). What we have, then, is "bugger" as a very common slang item in Great Britain (and Australia) that is virtually absent in American slang. Moreover, it is "a wholly innocent word in America" but "not at all welcome in polite conversation in Britain" (Bryson 1990, 224). Hughes, in his *Swearing: A Social History of Foul Language, Oaths and Profanity in English,* ranks "buggery" as the most flexible term of all English obscenities (1992, 31), claiming it is even more flexible than "fuck" though Sheidlower's remarkable compilation (1995) of phraseological constructions based on the F word might challenge that assertion. (It is curious that the field known as "Phraseologie" [cf. Pilz 1981] in Germany and Europe generally, a field which treats traditional idioms ranging between single lexical items of folk speech and sentential proverbs, appears not to be often identified by that label in the Anglo-American academic world.)

Perhaps the most common phraseological construction involving "bugger" is "bugger off," demanding that the addressee depart, leave immediately, get lost, or cease bothering the speaker. We find "bug off" in American slang, meaning "Get out!" or "Go away!" (Cassidy 1985, 434; Lighter 1994, 295; Spears 1997, 51), but with absolutely not the slightest connotation of "hugger." The likely original English phrase in question, "bugger off," is deemed equivalent to "piss off" (Phythian 1986, 135) or "sod off" (ibid., 164), which is another expression totally absent from American folk speech. It is noteworthy that the exhortation to "piss off" in this context is also not common in American folk speech although the expression "pissed off," meaning angry, disgusted or fed up, is widespread in the United States (Wentworth and Flexner 1967, 393), albeit sometimes euphemised as "to be P.O.'d" (Burke 1993, 9). The popularity of the "Piss off" idiom in England is suggested by the dismissive acronymic POETS, standing for "Piss Off Early, Tomorrow's Saturday."

"Sod" is clearly short for "sodomite" (Schur 1987, 338). According to one authority, "Sod all" is an intensification of "bugger all," which is, in turn, an intensification of "damn all, and means 'not a goddamned thing'" (ibid.). Another comparable locution meaning "nothing" is "fuck all" (Sheidlower 1995, 123), which also seems to be largely in British usage. What this suggests is that "bugger" equals "sod" equals "fuck." The only difference is that "bugger" and "sod" have homosexual connotations whereas "fuck" can in theory refer to either sex.

A verbal technique of emphasising the absoluteness of the state of "nothing," especially with reference to the alleged degree of knowledge held by an individual, consists of inserting the adjective "sweet" before the idiom. Accordingly, while "bugger all" does mean "nothing," "sweet bugger all" means "absolutely nothing." In similar fashion, "Sweet Fanny Adams" or

"Sweet Fanny" or "Miss Adams" (Brophy and Partridge 1931, 364), or "sweet eff-all" or "Sweet F.A." (Ayto and Simpson 1993, 253) are slightly disguised ways of saying "Sweet fucking all" meaning "not a goddamned thing" (Schur 1987, 358). I do not believe that "Sweet Fanny Adams" and its variations are known to any extent in the United States. Both "bugger" and "fanny" are listed as offensive and vulgar words "to be avoided by an American in Britain" (Davies 1997, 95). "Bugger all" is also found in Australia where it is defined as meaning "Very little" (Hudson and Pickering 1987, 25). Doing "bugger all" therefore means "doing nothing whatsoever" (Jonsen 1988, 73). Brophy and Partridge, in their extended discussion of World War I British soldiers' slang, report an Australian soldier's description of a desert as "miles and miles and bloody miles of b—r all" (1931, 289; cf. Schur 1987, 36). The continued traditionality of the expression in Australia is attested by the title of a pamphlet protesting the plight of the aborigines: *We Have Bugger All!: The Kulaluk Story* (Buchanan 1974). Incidentally, Brophy and Partridge indicate that "Bill Adams" served as a euphemism for "Bugger all" much as "Fanny Adams" did for "Fuck All" (1931, 282).

Lest any American reader still be sceptical about the prevalence of bugger idioms in British folk speech, let me cite a small sample of some of the more colourful examples. "Go to buggery" (Go away), "Oh bugger" (damn), "Oh bugger me" (frustration), "I'm buggered if I know" (I haven't a clue), "Well, bugger me" (I'm surprised or Well, I never did hear the like), "Bugger me sideways" (even more surprised), "Bugger me with a wire brush" (extremely surprised), "It's buggered" (it's messed up), "Bugger it" (damn or fuck it), "It's a bugger" (that's a really taxing situation or a tiresome problem to be dealt with), "A bugger's muddle" (an absolute mess), "What a bugger!" (Something's gone wrong or not turned out as expected), "I don't give a bugger" (I care not a jot or I don't give a damn), "Bugger this/that for a lark" (I'm having none of it or I don't want to continue doing this annoying or boring activity), and "Bugger this (Stuff that) for a game of soldiers" (I'm fed up and not happy with the plans for the further conduct of this operation, reminiscent of a futile military exercise) and "Blown (Gone, all) to buggery" (vanished, usually with a nuance of having been totally demolished). The great variety of buggery idioms lends credence to the comment made in a popular primer on Australian slang that "bugger" seems to function as a "utility word" that, at least in Australia, has lost its original offensive connotation and can be used whenever one can't think of the "right word" to employ in a given situation (Bowles 1986, 18; for an enlightening discussion of the semantics of "bugger" in Australia, see Wierzbicka 1997, 223–27).

There are many other derivative expressions. For example, "to play silly buggers" means to get up to mischievous tricks, or to pay insufficient attention to an issue or to behave in an inappropriate and foolish manner (Phythian 1986, 136). Australian sources define "Silly buggers" as "People who waste time on trivial things" or "play the fool" (Hudson and Pickering 1987, 25 and 99) or "who badly mismanage a situation" (Bowles 1986, 18). Australian prime minister Bob Hawke, during a visit to Japan in the 1980s, used a variant form when he said, "We are not going to play funny buggers," an expression that his interpreter was unable to render in Japanese (Wierzbicka 1997, 224). "Sillybuggers" is described as "A mythical game supposedly played by a person trying to avoid work or be deceptive" (Hudson and Pickering 1987, 115). "Buggeration" means utter ruin and confusion: "This word is often used as an exclamation of impatience by middle-class and upper-class speakers" (Thorne 1990, 68). A New Zealand slang glossary lists "buggerama" as an "exclamation of mock disgust or distress" (McGill 1988, 22). An "embuggerance factor" is something unforeseen that unexpectedly delays or impedes the execution of a plan (Jolly and Wilson 1989, 97). A vivid idiom dating from World War I evidently referring to being given an irritating and lengthy runaround is "buggered about from arse-hole to breakfast time" (Partridge 1985, 39). "Bugger's grips" or "buggery grips" or "bugladders" (James 1999, 23) refers to sideburns or side-whiskers (mutton chops). According to one source, "The phrase invokes the idea of any unorthodox protuberance inviting homosexual attention" (Thorne 1990, 69). Specifically, the active member of the homosexual pair might grasp his companion's sideburns from behind to facilitate anal intercourse. Bugger's grips would thus be roughly analogous to "love handles" in American folk speech, a term that refers to rolls of fat around the waist that can be held on to during lovemaking (Spears 1997, 239). An alternative Royal Navy slang term for "bugger's grips" is "muff diver's depth marks" (Jolly and Wilson 1989, 189), but this refers to the heterosexual act of performing cunnilingus (Rodgers 1972, 139; Richter 1995, 147).

While "bugger" has a primary meaning of "sodomite," it is also true that the word can be employed in a totally non-sexual sense to refer to a guy, a chap, a fellow (Partridge 1972, 124). "Silly old bugger" can be used affectionately to someone who has done something either stupid or touching. In the latter case, for instance, if the person had gone out of his way to help or reward the speaker, the phrase would be appropriate. Similarly, "Poor (little) bugger" could serve as a means of expressing pity for someone who has suffered some kind of misfortune or disaster. The addition of "little" would be used if the referent were a small child (usually male). "Little bugger" or "cute little bugger" by itself can function as a term of affection (typically to a small male child). On the other hand, the basic taboo nature of "bugger" probably accounts for why "beggar" is sometimes substituted instead. There is even the euphemistic "I'll be beggared" in place of "I'll be buggered" (Partridge 1972, 60). Such euphemisms are unmistakable markers of taboo words, comparable in American English to "By golly" (for By God), "gosh darn" (for God damn), "Dagnabbit" or "Doggone it" (for God damn it), "my gosh" or "my goodness" (for my God), "Oh my" (for Oh my God), "egad" (for Oh God), "Oh shoot" or "Oh sugar" or "Aw shucks" (for Oh shit), "Oh fudge" (for Oh fuck), "Phooey" (for fuck), "Jeez" or "Jeez Louise" or "Gee whiz" or "Gee Whillikers" (for Jesus), "By Jimmy" (for By Jesus), "Cripes" or "Crikey" (for Christ), "Jeepers Creepers" or "Jimmy Cricket" (for Jesus Christ), "for crying out loud" (for Christ's sake), "Holy Cow" (for Holy Christ) and *"Sacrébleu"* in French (for *"Sacré Dieu"*) (cf. Allan and Burridge 1991, 38–9; Hughes 1992, 13–14; Burke 1993; Green 1997, 137–46).

The taboo nature of "bugger" is also signalled by the fact that Brophy and Partridge felt it necessary to dash the word in their 1931 compilation of military slang. In fairness, it should be noted that up until 1934, one could be fined or imprisoned for saying or writing "bugger" (Bryson 1990, 224). "Bugger" has even been called "one of the most unprintable words in British English" (Pyles 1952, 151). In 1954, the BBC broadcast Dylan Thomas's play *Under Milk Wood,* apparently unaware of the fact that the name of the fictional Welsh town Llareggub described in the play was an ingenious literary back-slang creation, namely, "bugger all" spelled backwards (Moss 1978, 128; Richter 1995, 32). Sometimes, establishment institutions are more alert to detect possible verbal transgressions. According to one anecdote, which may or may not be apocryphal, Oxford University Press once considered entitling the *Shorter Oxford English Dictionary* as simply "Shorter Oxford Dictionary" but upon reflection decided that the resultant acronymic abbreviation might prove to be an embarrassment (Schur 1987, 338).

Origin of the Term

The alleged origin of "bugger" seems not to be in dispute. Most authorities accept the theory that the word derives from the French "Bougre," meaning "a Bulgarian," with the idea that Bulgarians were thought to indulge in anal intercourse (Hyde 1970, 36–7; Hughes 1992, 129; Williams 1994, 164). In twelfth-century France, "bogre," meaning heretic, evolved into "bougre" in the thirteenth century, meaning sodomite (Coward 1980, 239). A pamphlet entitled *Dom-Bougre*, published at the time of the French Revolution, indicates that buggery served as a recognised form of birth control (Bretonne 1789, 15). In England, the initial meaning of heretic (1340) evolved into sodomite (1555) before becoming a general term for "chap, fellow or customer" (1719) according to another summary (Hughes 1992, 254). Supposedly, the medieval Latin "Bulgarus" for Bulgarian was the source of the French term (Aman 1986–87, 238–41). Certainly, it is common xenophobic practice to attribute sexual perversity or illness to another nation or people. So the English call syphilis "the French disease" (Roback 1979, 33; Green 1997, 236), just as the Germans do, calling the same malady "französische Krankheit" (Roback 1979, 104). The French, however, call syphilis "the disease of Naples" (ibid., 99; Allan and Burridge 1991, 174) or "le vice italien" (Hyde 1970, 6; Coward 1980, 234). Sodomy is described by similar *blason populaire* traditions. For example, in modern Greek folk speech, sodomy is called "ala toúrka," that is, "in the Turkish way" (Koukoules 1983, 148). In American folklore, however, the same activity is associated with modern Greeks. The "Greek way" refers to anal copulation (Thampson 1988, 184; Green 1997, 231).

Despite the overwhelming consensus and conventional wisdom pointing to a "Bulgarian" origin of "bugger," there is another possibility that has hitherto not, to my knowledge, been considered by scholars. In ancient Greece, a critical distinction was made between active and passive male homosexuals. It is no disgrace to be the active member of a homosexual pair, but it was considered to be dishonorable to be the submissive "female" individual. The English utilitarian philosopher Jeremy Bentham (1748–1832) commented on this in an essay recommending the decriminalisation of sodomy written c. 1785: "According to the notion of the antients there was something degrading in the passive part which was not in the active . . . it was playing the woman's part: it was therefore unmanly" (1978, 395). Even, apparently, in ancient Assyrian law where it is mandated that "If a man has lain with his neighbour . . . he shall be lain with and be made a eunuch," the punishment for the "active" participant, as David Daube astutely remarks, is that "he is to suffer first the despicable passive role, then castration—in a way, a double unmanning" (Daube 1986, 447–48).

A similar differentiation was articulated in Old Norse culture. The condition of anal submission was called *argr* (Vanggaard 1972, 118; cf. Weisweiler 1923, 16–27). As one scholar puts it, "The man who is *argr* is willing or inclined to play or is interested in playing the female part in sexual relations" (Sorensen 1983, 18). There is also a synonymous word, *ragr*, created by metathesis which even occurs in a more overt form also produced by metathesis, *rassragr*, with the initial morpheme derived from anus or "arse" (Weisweiler 1923, 27–9; Strom 1974, 6). But what is significant in the Norse case is that there is a word, *baugr*, that means anus (Pipping 1930; Ross 1973, 82). (The word literally refers to "ring" but then so does the Latin word "anus.") Inasmuch as buggery specifically refers to anal intercourse (whether with male or female partners), the phonetic and semantic similarity is quite striking. One might speculate that it was the Old Norse word *"baugr"* in the sense of anus that is the true root of English "bugger" and that the anti-Bulgarian *blason populaire* merely provided a convenient later verbal foil and support for the folk speech. In the Old Norse tradition, just offering a male a ring evidently constituted a highly offensive insult as it implied that the male had submitted to or would submit to anal intercourse (Ross 1973). In English slang, "ring" means anus but can also signify vagina (Phythian 1986, 147; Thorne 1990, 426; Richter 1995, 186).

Explaining "Bugger's" Presence in England and Absence in the United States

Questions of origins are almost always problematic, however, and the obvious issue, with respect to "bugger," is not so much where and when it began as why is it so prevalent in British oral and written tradition? And secondly, why is it essentially absent in the United States? The answer to the first question may lie in part in legal and moral attitudes towards homosexuality and the specific act of buggery in England. Whether or not pederasty was ever an Indo-European adolescent rite of passage, as has been suggested (Bremmer 1980; cf. Tarnowsky 1967; Bleibtreu-Ehrenberg 1990), there is plenty of documentation of the fact that male homosexual acts including buggery were fairly common in sex-segregated institutions in England for many centuries. These institutions include the military, prisons, boarding schools, and universities among others. Henry VIII's Act of 1533 proclaimed that "the detestable and abominable Vice of Buggery" was a felony, punishable with death by hanging (Hyde 1970, 39; Vanggaard 1972, 167), and buggery remained in theory a capital offence in England until 1861 and "conviction from that date until 1967 was punishable by life imprisonment" (Gilbert 1976, 72). The 1967 Sexual Offences Act did legalize homosexual acts between consenting adults (age twenty-one) in private, but no mere legislative act could possibly succeed in overturning centuries of stigmatized behaviour with one stroke of the pen. There is surely no need to rehearse the various trials, for example famous ones like that of Oscar Wilde, to prove that buggery was, and continues to be, a very serious moral issue in England (Bloch 1934; Bailey 1975, 145–52). Indeed, part of the hubbub arising from the publication of D. H. Lawrence's *Lady Chatterley's Lover* and the trial held at the Old Bailey was caused by his graphic descriptions of anal intercourse, though in this case involving a male and a female (Sparrow 1962). Some definitions of buggery include anal intercourse with women as well as with animals though the term for the latter is more often referred to as "bestiality" (Hyde 1970, 37 note 1; Aman 1986–7, 229).

C. S. Lewis, remembering his days at Wyvern College, downplays the pederasty that occurred. "I cannot give pederasty anything like a first place among the evils of the Coll" (1955, 108). Older boys "would have preferred girls to boys if they could have come by them" but "we should have to say that pederasty, however great an evil in itself, was, in that time and place, the only foothold or cranny left for certain good things . . . A perversion was the only chink left through which something spontaneous and uncalculating could creep in" (1955, 109–10). Leaving aside the rather explicit metaphorical language consisting of "cranny left for good things" and "only chink which something . . . could creep in," we have the testimony of what anthropologists would label a "participant observer" confirming the existence of "buggery" in a representative upper-class English educational institution. Similar personal accounts refer to practices at other elite schools, for example, Harrow and Eton (Hyde 1970, 110–12). Supposedly, British schoolboys once spoke of the three B's of single-sex public boarding school life: "birching, boredom and buggery" (Paros 1984, 161). A diary entry written in the 1960s by a sixteen-year-old boy muses, "the thought of actually buggering a little boy is repulsive to me but they're just a substitute, something pretty to look at when there are no girls around" (Lambert and Millham 1974, 23). Knowler comments, "Generations of public-school boys have reported sodomy" but confirms that "Girls would be best, but as the sailor says in *Fanny Hill,* 'any port in a storm'" (Knowler 1974, 112 and 113), quoting a proverb seemingly appropriate as a justification for buggery (Legman 1977, 197 no. 979). Knowler adds that poet Rupert Brooke, acting as temporary housemaster at Rugby, said, "What is the whole duty of a house-master? To prepare boys for Confirmation, and turn a blind eye on sodomy" (Knowler 1974, 113). One angry letter written after the Oscar Wilde trial in 1895 asked indignantly, "Why does not the Crown prosecute every boy at a public or private school or half the men in the Universities?" (Hyde 1970, 170).

Iwan Bloch, in his book *Sex Life in England*, in speaking of homosexuality but almost certainly referring to buggery in particular makes this strong statement: "No other people has looked upon this act with so much disgust or judged those participating in it as harshly" (1934, 124). Knowler makes a more restrained comment: "I know of no evidence that the British are more inclined to homosexual practice than other nations. We certainly view it with less tolerance than some" (1974, 111). If there is any truth to this judgment, one can well understand why the accusation of having indulged in pederasty could carry so much emotional freight. No one would want to be called a "bugger" in such a climate of prejudice. So, I would maintain that it was not just the threat of legal punishment that brought buggery to the forefront of public consciousness, but rather, the general attitude towards male homosexual acts, an attitude which was no doubt responsible for the enactment of the legislation pertaining to sodomy in the first place.

The question then arises as to what were the causes of this abhorrence of pederasty. A simplistic answer might refer to the biblical charter prohibiting homosexual acts. *Leviticus* 20:13: "If a man also lie with mankind, as he lieth with a woman, both of them have committed an abomination: they shall surely be put to death" (cf. *Leviticus* 18:22) and the sad saga of Sodom and Gomorrah provide ample charters for both Jewish and. Christian homophobia (Bailey 1975; Goodich 1974–76). One intriguing, if somewhat speculative, argument suggests that God is not really homophobic but, rather, simply opposed to the misuse or wasting of precious male semen (Cohen 1990, 7 and 14), which would also account for the prohibition against acts of bestiality and masturbation. While the Bible tends to treat both active and passive participants in a homosexual act as equally guilty, Derek Bailey has suggested that patriarchal and androcentric bias may be a factor in placing a particular stigma on the male who takes or assumes the female role. The logic runs along the following lines: if God created man superior to woman, then a man who acts as a woman "has betrayed not only himself but his whole sex" (1975, 162).

Whether or not the biblical tradition is responsible for the European tradition of attaching particular disgrace to the passive homosexual, there can be no question that, as observed previously, the "female" participant who submits to anal intercourse is considered to be especially disgraced. Legman phrases the distinction succinctly: "The insert*or* is male, the insert*ee* homosexual" (1975, 150). Once again, the relevant Scandinavian data is typical. *Argr* signifies "what a man *must* not be, since in that case he is no man" (Sorensen 1983, 24). Calling a man *argr* constitutes a serious insult. In Norse terms, "The man attacked must show that he is fit to remain in the community . . . that is to say, he must challenge his adversary to battle" (Sorensen 1983, 32). The word *argr* is not dissimilar in sound to "bugger" and, has been noted, *"baugr"* means anus. Extrapolating from this, we might propose that "bugger off" is a verbal attempt to resist any attempt to be put in the humiliating position of serving as a "female" homosexual victim of a predatory male. Moreover, since in European practice (as opposed to the letter of the biblical law), the active participant in a homosexual relationship is not considered to be shameful—he is, after all, still functioning as a male, as the penetrator, not the penetrated—he can assert his masculinity by offering to "bugger" anything and everything. In American folk speech, the same function is achieved by the word "fuck." Though referring to what is basically a heterosexual act, a male typically uses the word in addressing a fellow male. But whereas an American male uses "fuck" in such instances, an Englishman uses "bugger" or "sod" instead.

This may help explain the frequent use of "bugger" in British folk speech. It can be seen as a kind of hyper-masculinity marker serving as a total repudiation of any implication that the speaker would consider playing a female role in a sexual act. Of course, women, at least in modern times, may also employ the term, but perhaps only as a means of aping male speech. On the other hand, the British male's underlying concern with "covering one's back(side)" for fear of being attacked literally or figuratively by an "arse-bandit" (Thorne 1990, 13; Ayto and Simpson 1993, 6) or "bum bandit" (Jolly and Wilson 1989, 46) or "bumjumper" (Bowles 1986, 85) might conceivably be related to what has been termed the "backside fixation" of the English (Knowler 1974, 105) reflected in English music hall humour centred on the buttocks (Gorer 1955, 192). Knowler observes that the mere mention of the word "bum" can "raise a giggle" (1974, 105). As for the fear, real or imagined, of being attacked from the rear, a remark from a fifteen-year-old public school boy tells the tale as well as anything: "Congreve's queer. *We* don't like them here. Whenever he comes down the corridor, people stand aside and go 'Eeeuggh!' and say 'Backs to the wall chaps, here comes Congers!'" (Lambert and Millham 1974, 258).

There is yet another possible factor involved in the repugnance felt for the act of buggery and that is its animalistic associations. Again, the folk speech is telling. One of the most common slang adjectival terms for ventro-dorsal intercourse is dog-style or doggie-fashion (Thorne 1990, 141; Lighter 1994, 620, Richter 1995, 68). Accordingly, men who participate in sexual acts entailing penetration from the rear are deemed to be no better than savage brutes.

In addition, it has been suggested that anal intercourse is unclean because of the likelihood of the sodomiser being contaminated by contact with "dirty" fecal material (Gilbert 1981, 65–6). In case the reader finds this suggestion far-fetched, s/he might take note of the folk metaphor "to be up the creek (without a paddle)" that means being hopelessly stuck in a situation without being able to extricate oneself. Regardless of whether or not the lack of a paddle has castratory overtones, the fact is that the original full form of the expression is "to be up shit creek," referring to the dangers of being engaged (or discovered) in an act of homosexual anal intercourse (Wentworth and Flexner 1967, 562). The twentieth-century marginally euphemistic folk metaphors "to stir fudge" or "to stir chocolate" for anal intercourse (Richter 1995, 209) would seem to offer additional evidence for the contamination argument. Similarly, such British slang terms for predatory sodomites as "chocolate bandit," "fudgepacker," "brownie-hound," and "turd burglar" (Thorne 1990) would seem to further corroborate the thesis.

But why is "bugger" not to be found to any great extent in American folk speech? The answer may come from the fact that Americans do not tend to distinguish active from passive homosexuals. For prudish Americans, *both* participants in a homosexual act are equally abhorrent (as the Bible states). Consequently, no American male wants anything to do with "bugger." Instead, "fuck," which carries no obvious homosexual connotation, is used to "put down" a male opponent. Since American males do use "fuck" to insult a rival or enemy, they are in effect threatening to carry out a homosexual act. But the use of "fuck" (rather than "bugger") tends to conceal the homosexual implications of the threat. This may explain why "bugger" and its many colorful idioms have remained in England and have failed to cross the Atlantic. The differences in British and American folk speech are significant. Most Americans telling a "jerk" to "bug off" would not know that the terms in question referred originally to masturbation and anal intercourse. There seems little doubt that "bug off" is an abridged version of "bugger off" (Hughes 1992, 169). I suspect most Englishmen, or English males, at any rate, telling a "wanker" to "bugger/sod off" would be well aware of these terms' sexual connotations. In marked contrast, Americans, for their part, know "sweet bugger all" about "sweet bugger all."

And to illustrate this, let me conclude by citing a joke, which would be easily intelligible anywhere in the English-speaking world except for the United States. A judge in a London court addresses the defendant and says, "Is there anything you would like to say before I pass sentence?" The defendant mutters, "Bugger all!" The judge, somewhat hard of hearing, leans over and asks the bailiff, "What did he say?" "He said 'Bugger all,' my Lord." "That's strange, I distinctly saw his lips move."

Acknowledgement

I wish to thank my dear friend, famed Oxford anthropologist Rodney Needham, for his kindness in sending me countless newspaper and magazine clippings illustrating the pervasive popularity of the term "bugger" and its derivatives. I am grateful also to my colleague, Professor Emeritus Burton Benedict, to educator Martin Scarratt, and to my former students, June Anderson and Di Beach, for providing illustrative examples of "bugger" idioms. None of these individuals, however, should be held responsible for the use I have chosen to make of their invaluable data.

References

Allan, Keith, and Kate Burridge. *Euphemism and Dysphemism: Language Used as Shield and Weapon.* New York: Oxford University Press, 1991.

Aman, Reinhold. "Offensive Words in Dictionaries III: Sodomy, Bestiality, Buggery, Bugger, Pederasty." *Maledicta* 9 (1986–7): 227–46.

Avto, John, and John Simpson. *The Oxford Dictionary of Modern Slang.* Oxford:Oxford University Press, 1993.

Bailey, Derrick Sherwin. *Homosexuality and the Western Christian Tradition.* Hamden: Archon Books, 1975.

Baring-Gould, William S. *The Lure of the Limerick.* New York: Clarkson S. Potter, 1967.

Belknap, George N. "History of the Limerick." *The Papers of the Bibliographical Society of America* 75 (1981): 1–32.

Bentham, Jeremy. "Offences Against One's Self: Paederasty." *Journal of Homosexuality* 3 (1978): 389–405; 4:91–107.

Bibby, Cyril. *The Art of the Limerick.* Hamden: Archon Books, 1978.

Bickerton, Anthea. *American English, English American: A Two-Way Glossary of Words in Daily Use on Both Sides of the Atlantic.* 2nd ed. Bristol: Abson Books, 1973.

Bleibtreu-Ehrenberg, Gisela. "Pederasty Among Primitives: Institutionalized Initiation and Cultic Prostitution." *Journal of Homosexuality* 20 (1990): 13–30.

Bloch, Iwan. *Sex Life in England.* New York: The Panurge Press, 1934.

Bouissac, Paul. "Decoding Limericks: A Structuralist Approach." *Semiotica* 19 (1977): 1–2.

Bowles, Colin. *G'Day: Teach Yourself Australian in 20 Easy Lessons.* North Ryde: Angus and Robertson, 1986.

Bremmer, Jan. "An Enigmatic Indo-European Rite: Paederasty." *Arethusa* 13 (1980): 279–98.

Bretonne, Restif de la. *Dom-Bougre aux États-Généraux.* Foutropolis: Braquemart, 1789.

Brophy, John, and Eric Partridge. *Songs and Slang of the British Soldiers: 1914–1918.* 3rd ed. London: Scholartis Press, 1931.

Bryan, George B., and Wolfgang Mieder. *The Proverbial Bernard Shaw: An Index to Proverbs in the Works of George Bernard Sha.* Westport: Greenwood Press, 1994.

Bryson, Bill. *The Mother Tongue: English and How It Got That Way.* New York: William Morrow, 1990.

Buchanan, Cheryl. *We Have Bugger All!: The Kulaluk Story.* Carlton, Victoria: Australian Union of Students, 1974.

Burke, David. *Bleep! A Guide to Popular American Obscenities.* Los Angeles: Optima Books,1993.

Cassidy, Frederic G. *Dictionary of American Regional English.* vol. I. Cambridge: Harvard University Press, 1985.

Cohen, Martin Samuel. "The Biblical Prohibition of Homosexual Intercourse." *Journal of Homosexuality* 19.4 (1990): 3–20.

Coward, D. A. "Attitudes to Homosexuality in Eighteenth-Century France." *Journal of European Studies* 10 (1980): 231–55.

Daube, David. "The Old Testament Prohibitions of Homosexuality." *Zeitschrift der Savigny-Stiftung* 103 (1986): 447–48.

Davies, Christopher. *Divided by a Common Language: A British/American Dictionary PLUS.* Sarasota: Mayflower Press, 1997.

deFuniak, William Q. *American-British Dictionary.* San Francisco: Orbit Graphic Arts, 1967.

Douglas, Norman. *Some Limericks.* Florence: Orioli, 1928.

Gilbert, Arthur N. "Buggery and the British Navy, 1700–1861." *Journal of Social History* 10 (1976): 12–98.

———. "Conceptions of Homosexuality and Sodomy in Western History." *Journal of Homosexuality* 6 (1981): 57–68.

Goodich, Michael. "Sodomy in Ecclesiastical Law and Theory." *Journal of Homosexuality* 1 (1974–6): 427–34.

Gorer, Geoffrey. *Exploring English Character.* New York: Criterion Books, 1955.

Green, Jonathon. *Slang Through the Ages.* Chicago: NTC Publishing Group, 1997.

———. *Famous Last Words.* Enderby: Silverdale Books, 1999.

Guthke, Karl S. *Last Words: Variations on a Theme in Cultural History.* Princeton: Princeton University Press, 1992.

Hudson, Bob, and Larry Pickering. *First Australian Dictionary of Vulgarities and Obscenities.* Newton Abbot: David and Charles, 1987.

Hughes, Geoffrey. *Swearing: A Social History of Foul Language, Oaths and Profanity in English.* Oxford: Blackwell, 1992.

Hyde, H. Montgomery. *The Love That Dared Not Speak Its Name.* Boston: Little, Brown, 1970.

James, Ewart. *Contemporary British Slang.* Chicago: NTC Publishing Group, 1999.

Jolly, Rick, and Tugg Wilson. *Jackspeak: The Passer's Rum: Guide to Royal Navy Slanguage.* Torpoint: Palamando Publishing, 1989.

Jonsen, Helen. *Kangaroo's Comments and Wallaby's Words: The Aussie Word Book.* New York: Hippocrene Books, 1988.

Knowler, John. *Trust an Englishman.* Frogmore: Paladin, 1974.

Koukoules, Mary. *Loose-Tongued Greeks: A Miscellany of Neo Hellenic Folklore.* Paris: Digamma, 1983.

La Barre, Weston. "The Psychopathology of Drinking Songs." *Psychiatry* 2 (1939): 203–12.

Lambert, Royston, and Spencer Millham. *The Hothouse Society.* Harmondsworth: Penguin, 1974.

Legman, Gershon. "The Limerick: A History in Brief." In *The Horn Book: Studies in Erotic Folklore and Bibliography.* 427–53. New Hyde Park: University Books, 1964.

———. *Rationale of the Dirty Joke.* New York: Grove Press, 1968.

———. *The Limerick.* New York: Bell, 1974.

———. *No Laughing Matter.* New York: Breaking Point, 1975.

———. *The New Limerick.* New York: Crown, 1977.

Lewis, C. S. *Surprised by Joy: The Shape of My Early Life.* New York: Harcourt, Brace and World, 1955.

Lighter, J. E. *Random House Historical Dictionary of American Slang.* Vol. I. New York: Random House, 1994.

Matthews, Brander. *A Study of Versification.* Boston: Houghton Mifflin, 1911.

McGill, David. *Up the Boohai Shooting Pukakas: A Dictionary of Kiwi Slang.* Lower Hutt, New Zealand: Mills Publications, 1988.

Mencken, H. L. *The American Language.* 4th ed. New York: Alfred A. Knopf. 1938.

Morgan, Harry. *Why Was He Born So Beautiful and Other Rugby Songs.* London: Sphere Books,1967.

———. *More Rugby Songs.* London: Sphere Books, 1968.

Moss, Norman. *What's The Difference: An American-British/British-American Dictionary.* London: Arrow Books, 1978.

Paros, Lawrence. *The Erotic Tongue: A Sexual Lexicon.* New York: Henry Holt, 1984.

Partington, Angela, ed. *The Oxford Dictionary of Quotations.* 4th ed. Oxford: Oxford University Press, 1992.

Partridge, Eric. *A Dictionary of Historical Slang.* Harmondsworth: Penguin, 1972.

———. *A Dictionary of Catch Phrases.* Revised ed. New York: Stein and Day, 1985.

Phythian, B. A. *A Concise Dictionary of English Slang and Colloquialisms.* 3rd ed. London: Hodder and Stoughton. 1986.

Pilz, Klaus Dieter. *Phraseologie.* Stuttgart: Metzler, 1981.

Pipping, Hugo. "Havamal 136." In *Studies in Honor of Hermann Collitz.* 155–8. Baltimore: Johns Hopkins Press, 1930.

Pyles, Thomas. *Words and Ways of American English.* New York: Random House, 1952.

Richter, Alan. *Sexual Slang.* New York: HarperCollins, 1995.

Roback, Abraham. *A Dictionary of International Slurs.* Waukesha: Maledicta Press, 1979.

Rodgers, Bruce. *The Queens' Vernacular: A Gay Lexicon.* San Francisco: Straight Arrow Press, 1972.

Ross, Margaret Clunies. "Hildr's Ring: A Problem in the Ragnarsdrápa, Strophes 8–12." *Mediaeval Scandinavia* 6 (1973): 75–92.

Schur, Norman W. *British English A to Zed.* New York: Facts on File Publications, 1987.

Sheidlower, Jesse. *The F Word.* New York: Random House, 1995.

Sørensen, Preben Meulengracht. *The Unmanly Man: Concepts of Sexual Defamation in Early Northern Society.* Odense: Odense University Press, 1983.

Sparrow, John. "Regina *v.* Penguin Books Ltd.: An Undisclosed Element in the Case." *Encounter* 101 (1962): 35–43.

Spears, Richard A. *A Dictionary of 10,000 American Slang Expressions Hip and Hot.* New York: Gramercy Books, 1997.

Ström, Folke. *Níd, Ergi and Old Norse Moral Attitudes.* London: Viking Society for Northern Research, 1974.

Tarnowsky, Benjamin Michael. *Anthropological, Legal and Medical Studies on Pederasty in Europe.* North Hollywood: Brandon House, 1967.

Thampson, Walter. *Dictionary of Slang and Unconventional English.* Delhi: GOYLSaab, 1988.

Thorne, Tony. *The Dictionary of Contemporary Slang.* New York: Pantheon Books, 1990.

Vanggaard, Thorkil. *Phallos: A Symbol and Its History in the Male World*. New York: International Universities Press, 1972.

Walmsley, Jane. *Brit-Think, Ameri-Think*. New York: Penguin, 1987.

Weisweiler, Josef. "Beiträge zur Bedeutungsentwicklung Germanischer Wörter für sittliche Begriffe. Erster Teil." *Indogertnanische Forschungen* 41 (1923): 13–77.

Wentworth, Harold, and Stuart Berg Flexner. *Dictionary of American Slang*. New York: Thomas Y. Crowell, 1967.

Wierzbicka, Anna. *Understanding Cultures through their Key Words*. New York: Oxford University Press, 1997.

Williams, Gordon. *A Dictionary of Sexual Language and Imagery in Shakespearean and Stuart Literature*. 3 vols. London: Athlone Press, 1994.

Zviadadze, Givi. *Dictionary of Contemporary American English Contrasted with British English*. New Delhi: Arnold-Heinemann, 1983.

12

Grouping Lore:
Scientists and Musicians

(*A*) Science in Folklore? Folklore in Science?

(*B*) Viola Jokes: A Study of Second String Humor

Introduction

Addressing the question "Who are the folk?" at the American Association for the Advancement of Science (AAAS) in 1977, Dundes told the group identifying themselves as scientists that he understood the popular perception that "folklore is precisely what science has advanced from" (see Bascom 1977). Dundes declared that the notion that science displaces folklore was false. One reason this fallacy arose, he explained, was the European intellectual construction of several hierarchical dichotomies, in response to nineteenth-century industrialization. He set up the following table to highlight the European equivalence of folk with peasantry, and civilization with the elite, who were associated with so-called rational science.

Folk or Peasant	Civilized or Elite
Illiterate	Literate
Rural	Urban
Lower Stratum	Upper Stratum

Instead of a linear table contrasting upper and lower strata, Dundes's model was one of folk encircling human existence. Dundes bemoaned the fact that the concept of folk "as an old fashioned segment living on the margins of civilization" persisted into the "modern" era despite ample evidence from field collections of folklore among the literate, urban, upper crust. He proposed to show that these dichotomies were logically, indeed scientifically, false by demonstrating that "one essential part of the science of folklore includes the study of the folklore of science (and scientists)." If such an elite group could be shown to be "folk," then folklore could arguably be viewed as a fundamental, cultural, identity-forming

229

process in socializing people as part of groups. It was a strategy Dundes frequently employed in his research, and one he also applied to other "elite" groups, including symphony musicians, mathematicians, physicians (see the essays in the next chapter), computer programmers, and college students.

Dundes proposed a "modern conception of folk" as "*any group of people whatsoever* who share at least one common factor." He added that "it does not matter what the linking factor is—it could be a common occupation, language, or religion—but what is important is that a group formed for whatever reason will have some traditions which it calls its own. In theory a group must consist of at least two persons, but generally most groups consist of many individuals. A member of the group may not know all other members, but he or she will probably know the common core of traditions belonging to the group, traditions which help the group have a sense of group identity." In this definition, it is possible to have "part-time folk" who engage in traditions temporarily, such as at summer camp or military bases, and it is common in modern life to have many overlapping groups and, therefore, traditions and identities that one possesses. Another implication of this definition is that people can take on identities and customs of their own choosing and creation, in addition to inheriting identities and following traditions. Besides working with the usual identity categories of ethnicity, religion, nationality, region, and occupation, one could observe folklore emerging from the formation of a family, group of friends, or people who share an interest (e.g., motorcyclists, surfers, and music fans), and from an organization (e.g., the Navy, Boy Scouts, or a volunteer association). It should be pointed out that some folklorists building on this definition have proposed a host of dyadic traditions (traditions emerging from a couple), such as between a person and a pet, and even one with oneself (e.g., talking to yourself with ritualized expressions such as "you idiot!") (see Oring 1984a, 1986; Mechling 1989b, 2006).

In this chapter, Dundes used a rhetorical device that can be read in other writings, differentiating between the folklore of a group and a group's folklore. The first essay, for example, had texts that demonstrated popular, "exoteric" beliefs *about* lab-coat clad scientists, which were differentiated from the "esoteric," insider lore of scientists. (Dundes included the classic statement on "The Esoteric-Exoteric Factor in Folklore" by William Hugh Jansen in his textbook *The Study of Folklore* [1965], in which a definition of folk group figured prominently.) The identification of folk ideas, therefore, was not limited to oral stories, but could also be seen in the mass media. Dundes carried this message—presented as a speech in the first essay—directly to scientists in the magazine *New Scientist*, in an article published the same year as his address to the AAAS. Dundes applied the thesis that professions constitute a folk, and, indeed, "the folklore of a group . . . defines that group," to mathematicians. Thought of as people dealing with numbers rather than expressive narrative and customs, Dundes (with his physicist son-in-law Paul Renteln) instead showed that mathematicians as a group shared slang, proverbs, limericks, and jokes (Dundes and Renteln 2005). Nonetheless, scientists, purportedly devoted to impersonal objectivity, still have the image of being acultural, although a few studies following Dundes's contributions have explored the scientific realm (Gilkey 1990; Jackson 1972; and Shapiro 1987).

Dundes, as a concert musician (he composed for and performed on the clarinet), was also aware of the lore of orchestral musicians, popularly thought of as an elite group. The orchestra provided an apt metaphor for the social dynamics of expressive lore defining overlapping groups. Orchestra members shared an identity as a musical organization, but within the body, humor and speech *about* "sections" of the orchestra expressed hierarchies within the unit. Instrumental players within the sections had "esoteric" lore that they shared among themselves as well. Dundes, the analyst, teamed up with Meegan Brown, a musician in the San Diego area, to collect the material in the second essay. In keeping with his psychological-outlet theory of humor, he interpreted the material as projecting the anxiety connected with performing in a musical group before a live audience. For other perspectives on folklore in the esoteric and exoteric lore of musicians, see Groce 1996; Rahkonen 2000; and Adler 1982. Beyond musicians and scientists, a host of modern groups have been investigated, with Dundes's definition of the folk group and process of identity-formation in mind. For instance, among the entries in the *Encyclopedia of American Folklife* (Bronner 2006b) are nurses, soldiers, sports teams, students, taxi drivers, trial lawyers, twelve-step groups, skateboarders, steelworkers, bodybuilders, Boy Scouts, automobile racing fans, martial artists, youth gangs, truck drivers, unions, firefighters, and folklorists. That is in addition to the familiar folk groups of cowboys, loggers, miners, railroaders, and sailors. So what was Dundes's answer to the question of "who are the folk?" He exclaimed, "among others, *we* are!"

A

Science in Folklore? Folklore in Science?

IN AUGUST 1846, ENGLISHMAN WILLIAM Thoms, using the nom de plume Ambrose Merton, wrote a letter to the Athenaeum in which he proposed the term "Folklore" as an appropriate Anglo-Saxon term to refer to "manners, customs, observances, superstitions, ballads, proverbs, etc. of the olden time." This neologism was well received and it has achieved virtual world-wide currency. In 1878, the English Folklore Society was created, later serving as a model for the American Folklore Society, which began in 1888. As the English Folklore Society approaches its centenary, folklorists from many countries may take pride in the growth of folkloristics from what was originally an amateurish antiquarian hobby of gentlemen and gentlewomen, who collected quaint customs and beliefs from rural parishes to a full fledged academic discipline with its own panoply of theories and methods.

Professional folklorists are concerned with how the folklore of a given group reflects the ideology and worldview of that group. Folklore, i.e., the myths, epics, folktales, legends, riddles, proverbs, curses, charms, songs, dances, games, gestures, costumes, festivals, etc. of a group, provides a unique type of expressive material in which that group's cognitive categories and anxieties are unselfconsciously set forth. Typically, folklore provides a socially sanctioned framework within which members of the folk in question feel free to probe critical issues and problems. One can say in jest or song what one may be ashamed or embarrassed to say without the safety of a folkloric form.

In the beginning of the 19th century, the conception of "folk" was limited to the illiterate in a literate society, that is, people who could not read or write in a society which had a written language. So the Grimm brothers in Germany and their counterparts in other countries collected folklore exclusively from the local illiterates or peasants. Only recently in the 20th century have folklorists realized that the original definition of folk was too narrow. A folk in modern parlance is any group of people who share at least one common linking factor. The common linking factor may be nationality, ethnicity, religion or occupation. Thus one could speak of French folklore (as opposed to German folklore), of the folklore of Jews or Mormons, and of the folklore of coal miners or cowboys. A flexible definition of folk would include an entity as large as a nation or as small as a family. From this definition, it is clear that folklore is not restricted to rural areas. Cities are full of folklore whether it is the folklore of particular city districts or the folklore of such groups as labor unions or militant political organizations. Individuals may belong to a number of different and distinct folk groups, and as they move from family or ethnic groups to professional or occupational groups, they often are expected to "code-switch." Family folklore would be inappropriate at the office, just as office folklore might be equally inappropriate at home.

Scientific tongues

From this discussion, it should come as no surprise to learn that scientists qualify as folk. For that matter, each subgroup of scientists surely has its own folklore. The folklore of biologists is not the same as the folklore of chemists. Some of the folklore of science or scientists is rather esoteric and might be virtually unintelligible to anyone outside the in-group. However, some of the folklore of science is understandable to outsiders. (Indeed some of the folklore about science circulates primarily among non-scientists.) In jokes, one of the most common forms of folklore in the modern world, stereotypes of scientists, may be found.

A physicist, a statistician, and a mathematician were in an aircraft flying over Montana. They looked out and saw below a herd of sheep all of which were white, except one which was black. The physicist began calculating the number of black sheep in the universe, based on the sample. The statistician began calculating the probability of a black sheep occurring in any given herd. The mathematician, on the other hand, knew that there exists at least one sheep that is black, ON TOP!

The role of empiricism is a frequent theme in the folklore of science. In the following example, it is a social scientist who is non-empirical.

A chemist, a physicist and an economist are marooned on a desert island without food. Suddenly they discover a cache of canned goods but there is no opener. The chemist begins looking about for chemicals in their natural state so he can make up a solution which will dissolve the tops of the cans. The physicist picks up a rock and begins calculating what angle, what force, what velocity he will need to strike the can with the rock in order to force it open. The economist merely picks up a can and says, "Let us assume this can is open." (In a variant, "Let us assume we have a can opener.")

Scientific method lampooned

If the need for some form of the experimental method is the hallmark of the natural scientist, that too can be the subject of the folklore of science. In a classic story existing in many variant forms—all folklore manifests multiple existence, typically with variation—we find the experimental method in a *reductio ad absurdum* form.

A researcher is studying a unique six-legged caterpillar (in some versions a flea). Through extraordinary conditioning, the researcher has trained the caterpillar to jump over a little barrier upon command, namely the word "jump." A true scientist, he wonders what it is that is making the caterpillar jump. It must be the front legs. The researcher tears off the front legs and gives the command to jump. The caterpillar jumps over the barrier. The researcher then pulls off the middle two legs. Again he says "Jump," and again the caterpillar jumps over the barrier. Finally, the researcher pulls off the two hind legs and gives the command. This time the caterpillar remains immobile and does not jump the barrier. The researcher therefore draws the conclusion that pulling off the two hind legs has made the caterpillar deaf.

Not only does this text lampoon the "logic" of drawing faulty conclusions from experimental data, it also expresses the stereotype of the cold and cruel scientist for whom scientific truth is more important than ethical questions of cruelty to animals. Caterpillars may not be of the same order as white mice, guinea-pigs, or monkeys, but the apparently callous behavior of the researcher is relevant. The phrase "to be a guinea-pig" has become part of the folklore of Western nations precisely because of the extended use of guinea-pigs as hapless participants (victims) of various scientific laboratory experimentation.

If one were asked to select the single most common piece of the folklore of science, one might well think of Murphy's Law. In theory, scientists are seeking to describe the nature of objective reality with such descriptions embodying such ideal criteria as predictability. The codification of a particular principle frequently bears the name of the scientist who discovered or formulated it. So presumably Murphy's Law was first articulated by a man named Murphy. Carrying scientific worldview to its extreme form, Murphy's Law and analogous "laws" suggest that even failure is acceptable so long as it can be codified and rendered predictable. Here is a representative list of "Basic precepts of science" which includes Murphy's Law:

Murphy's Law: If anything can go wrong, it will.

Patrick's Theorem: If the experiment works, you must be using the wrong equipment.

Skinner's Constant: That quantity which, when multiplied by, divided into, added to, or subtracted from the answer you got, gives the answer you should have obtained.

Horner's Five Thumb Postulate: Experience varies directly with the equipment ruined.

Flagle's Law of the Perversity of Inanimate Objects: Any inanimate object, regardless of its composition or configuration, may be expected to perform at any time in a totally unexpected manner for reasons that are either totally obscure or completely mysterious.

Allen's Axiom: When all else fails, read the instructions.

The Spare Parts Principle: The accessibility, during recovery, of small parts which fall from the work bench, varies directly with the size of the part . . . and inversely with its importance to the completion of the work underway.

The Compensation Corollary: The experiment may be considered a success if no more than 50 per cent of the observed measurements must be discarded to obtain a correspondence with theory.

Gumperson's Law: The probability of a given event occurring is inversely proportional to its desirability.

The Ordering Principle: Those supplies necessary for yesterday's experiment must be ordered no later than tomorrow noon.

The Ultimate Principle: By definition, when you are investigating the unknown, you do not know what you will find.

The Futility Factor: No experiment is ever a complete failure . . . it can always serve as a bad example.

One of the characteristics of folklore is that authors are rarely if ever known. We do not know who was the first to tell the story of the six-legged caterpillar or who invented the list of "Basic precepts of science." This puts folklore, which is transmitted from person to person, in contrast with mass or popular culture, in which the authors of comic strips, television series, or movies are known. Popular culture, like folklore, is frequently deemed to be unworthy of serious study by the literary Brahmins of the academy, but this is a mistake. For popular culture also affects the public's perception of science and scientists. Certainly the stereotype of the mad scientist as depicted in so many horror films is a reflection of the image of the scientist not unlike the one delineated in the caterpillar story.

I want to consider briefly one television series and one motion picture to illustrate how and what science fiction as found in popular culture communicates. Typically in *Star Trek,* a space ship makes an *uninvited* visit to some alien culture which somehow threatens the existence or safety of the ship. Often the progress of the ship is imperiled or stopped temporarily. The USS initials supposedly stand for United Star Ship and not United States Ship, but a clue as to the identity of the ship is suggested by its name *Enterprise.* The captain of the ship is named Kirk, an English word meaning church. The rest of the leadership bears similar names, e.g., Spock, Scotty, McCoy, but when commands are issued, they are carried out by an assorted set of ethnic underlings (Asian, African American, etc). If the alien culture does not respond to suggestions of reform (along the lines of democracy and Christianity), the crew has no choice but to destroy it. The reform or destruction of the alien culture usually frees the ship which thus becomes once again a "free *Enterprise,*" a fantasy-form justification of free-floating American influence and intervention all over the world. Science fiction, like science itself, may not be as free of political implications as "pure" scientists might think or wish. In the motion picture *Star Wars*, we find an interesting combination of folklore and science fiction. The plot is basic fairytale with a hero falling in love with an image of a princess whom he attempts to rescue. His parents dead, Luke Skywalker is raised by foster parents as is required by the heroic formula. From a wise old man, who functions as the traditional donor figure of fairy tales, the hero obtains the inevitable magic sword (the life force) which belonged to his father. The hero is accompanied on his quest by an assortment of helpers with unique abilities. However, superimposed upon the underlying fairy tale plot is a fairly standard Second World War film scenario. The enemy consists of "stormtroopers," who dress and act like Germans as depicted in World War films. The little creature who in the memorable bar scene tries to collect an outstanding debt owed by the mercenary pilot Han Solo speaks a foreign tongue which is accompanied by English subtitles. The language is not identified but if it were to be Japanese, it would support the Second World War pattern in which the Japanese and Germans were part of an axis. In this context, the somewhat effete robot C-3PO, who has great polyglot linguistic expertise and who speaks with an English accent, might well represent the British ally of the American hero attacking the German stronghold. If fairy tale and Second World War adventure film were not enough, there is a phallic component in which a boy learns to handle his life force well enough to fly through a long slot and drop a bomb down a virtually inaccessible and closely guarded tube leading to the one weak spot or Achilles' heel of the enemy. It may or may not be relevant that the archvillain's name is Darth Vader which strongly suggests death and father. As a concession to modern taste, the hero is taught to close his eyes and trust his (life force) feelings while the heroine, something of a liberated woman, refuses to play the conventional passive female part found in fairy tales. Her irreverent attitude seems to delight not one but two heroes: Luke Skywalker and Han Solo, who compete for her attentions.

Science fiction is not science any more than the folklore of science is science. What is important is that one measure of the impact science has had on the modern world lies in the artistic efforts it has inspired. Scientists themselves are influenced by folklore. Why, for example, was the lunar mission labelled Apollo? With presumably an infinity of names to choose from, why was the name Apollo selected? Selecting the name Apollo consciously or unconsciously invoked mythology. In Greek mythology, Apollo the Sun is the brother of Artemis or Diana the Moon. After achieving enough "thrust" to lift off and overcome the gravitational pull of the (mother) Earth, Apollo the Sun/son rises and is able to land on the Moon, his sister, where astronaut Armstrong (whose name means powerful body extremity) was the very first to step on the virgin soil of the Moon and to erect a flag. The astronauts brought back pieces of Moon to show off to peers back home. Who remembers the names of the second set of astronauts to land on the Moon? Very few. The point might be that the Moon could be "violated" only once. This is, of course, not an analysis of heavenly bodies but of earthly ones. But that is precisely the issue. Scientists are folk too and as such they are bound by folklore. That is why it is imperative that the science of folklore include the study of the folklore of science.

B

Viola Jokes: A Study of Second String Humor

THERE IS A SUBSTANTIAL SCHOLARLY literature devoted to the study of musical humor. Most of it tends to deal with individual composers and specific compositions,
for example, Haydn's musical jokes.[1] Much less studied are the numerous jokes told by
and about musicians. Anyone who performs regularly in bands or orchestras is likely to be
familiar with these traditional jibes. Whether the jokes stem from the anxiety connected
with performing on one's instrument (in front of peers or an audience) or the competitive
aspect of seeking to move from third chair up to second or first chair, there can be no question of the jokes' continued popularity.

As with ethnic humor, there is usually a scapegoat to serve as the butt of the jokes. So
the English tell jokes about the Irish, the French about the Belgians, the Germans about
the East Frisians, and so on.[2] Almost every cultural group has some other group or subgroup to beat up on, so to speak. No doubt one of the psychological benefits of telling
such jokes is to bolster feelings of inadequacy. If A says B is inferior, then that automatically makes A feel superior.

In musical joking traditions, different instruments or instrumentalists fill the role of
scapegoat. There are jokes about conductors or prima donnas, mostly about their highfly-
ing egos. One of the chestnuts about conductors is: *What's the difference between a bull and
a symphony orchestra? The bull has the horns in front and the asshole in back.*[3] Another series
involves drummers and the fact that their musicianship is said to be minimal or lacking
altogether. *What do you call someone who hangs out with musicians? A drummer.* But surely
the leading figures in music joke cycles are banjo players and violists.

Viola jokes have been noticed. A brief article by Martin Boyd on the subject appeared
in *The Strad* in 1995. The following year, Nancy Groce's "Knowing the Score: The
Transmission of Musician Jokes among Professional and Semi-Professional Musicians" was
published in *New York Folklore* as well as her more complete compilation *The Musician's
Joke Book*. In 1997, Dave Marsh and Kathi Kamen Goldmark completed *The Great Rock
'n' Roll Joke Book*. In 2001, we find a newspaper essay by Olin Chism entitled "Violins
Get the Glory, While Viola Is Butt of Jokes" in the *Dallas Morning News*. But by far the
most comprehensive consideration of the viola jokes is violist and ethnomusicologist
Carl Rahkonen's "No Laughing Matter: The Viola Joke Cycle as Musicians' Folklore" in
Western Folklore in 2000.[4]

Groce speculates as to why violists have been singled out for jocular disparagement.
According to Groce, "Violists are widely believed to be intellectually dull, musically timid,
and to have boring personalities."[5] She also remarks that violists have a much more limited
solo repertoire than do violins and that generally speaking, viola parts tend to be less technically exacting than those of other instruments, often playing harmony rather than mel-
ody. Violist Rahkonen says much the same: "Orchestral viola parts are easier than violin

parts and they tend to be the less important, non-melodic parts. If viola players do get difficult parts, as they do from time to time, violists in amateur orchestras tend to struggle while trying to play them.[6] Groce even goes so far as to suggest that the majority of violists are failed violinists who may have been encouraged early on by their teachers to switch to the less demanding viola. Whether or not this is nothing more than a standard stereotype of violists, the fact remains that there is an impressive spate of viola jokes. The stereotype of a violist as a violinist manqué is clearly indicated in the following definition of a string quartet: *A good violinist, a bad violinist, a would-be violinist, and someone who hates violins getting together to complain about composers.* Here is another version of the same joke. *What makes up a string quartet? A person who can play violin, a person who can't play violin, a person who used to play violin, and a person who hates violins.*

For the benefit of readers who may not be familiar with this joke cycle, we shall present a generous sampling of representative texts.[7] One should keep in mind that viola jokes, like all traditional jokes, in fact like all folklore, demonstrate multiple existence and variation. That means that an individual joke will usually exist in more than one time and place. Moreover, the transmission process is such that no two versions will be verbatim identical. In some instances, the same basic joke may be told about various instruments. Such parallels to some, though by no means all, of the viola jokes will be noted.

The first examples have to do with the alleged poor musicianship of violists.

> *What's the difference between the first stand and the last stand in the viola section? About two bars.* In other versions, the answer is *A semi-tone* or *Half a measure* or *About a measure and a half.*[8]
>
> *How do you get a violist to play a passage pianissimo tremolano? Mark it solo.* The implication is that violists are so unused to playing solos that their nervousness makes them shake their bow uncontrollably resulting in a pianissimo tremolando.
>
> *How do you get a viola section to play spiccato? Write a whole note with "solo" above it.*[9]
>
> Another version of this joke involves vibrato: *How can you make a violist play with vibrato? Write a fermata over a whole note and mark it solo.*[10]
>
> Vibrato also figures in other viola jokes: *What's the difference between a viola and scraping your nails on a blackboard? Vibrato.*[11]
>
> The sound made by violas is a common leitmotif in the joke cycle: *What's the difference between a violist and a dog? The dog knows when to stop scratching.*[12]
>
> *What's the most common viola tuning system for Western music? Bad-tempered.*
>
> *Why can't you hear a viola on a digital recording? Because technology has reached such an advanced level of development that all extraneous noise is eliminated.*
>
> *What kind of microphone works best for viola in a live band? A cordless mini condenser with a dead battery.*
>
> *Who makes the best viola mutes? Smith & Wesson.*
>
> *How do you make a violin sound like a viola? Sit in the back and don't play* or *Play in the low register with a lot of wrong notes.*
>
> *How do you get a beautiful sound out of a viola? Sell it and buy a violin.*[13]

The majority of viola jokes, however, are variations on the theme of sloppy technique on the part of violists: *What's the difference between a viola player and a dressmaker? The dressmaker gets paid to tuck up the frills; A viola player . . . never mind.*

Why are violists' fingers like lightning? They never strike the same place twice.

Why do violists get antsy when they see the words "Kama Sutra"? All those positions!

What's the difference between a violist and a prostitute? 1. A prostitute knows more than two positions. 2. Prostitutes have a better sense of rhythm.

A German text involving positions suggests that the viola jokes are also to be found in Germany: *Was sind die drei Lagen auf der Bratsche? Erste Loge, Notlage, und Niederlage.* (What are the three positions of the viola? First position, emergency, and defeat.) An American variant: *How many positions does a violist use? First, third, and emergency.*[14]

Why are viola parts written in Alto Clef? Harder to prove that wrong notes weren't copying errors.

Where did Alto Clef originate? Bach took a bribe from a wealthy viola player.

How is a violist like a terrorist? They both mess up bowings [Boeings].

How can you tell if a violist is making mistakes? His bow is moving.[15] The same answer is found with a different question: *How can you tell if a viola is out of tune? The bow is moving.*

What's the difference between a viola and a lawnmower? You can tune a lawnmower. There is also *Why isn't a viola like a lawn mower? Nobody minds if you borrow their viola.*[16]

How do you get two viola players to play in tune (or in unison)? Shoot one of them.[17]

What's the definition of a minor 2nd? Two violas playing in unison.

What's the definition of atonal music? A violist playing Bach.[18]

What's the definition of a cluster chord? A viola section playing on the C string.

How was the canon invented? Two violists were trying to play the same passage together.

Why do violists stand for long periods outside people's houses? They can't find the key and they don't know when to come in.[19]

Sometimes it is the viola rather than the violist that is subjected to ridicule: *What's the useless woody material around the F holes? A viola.*[20]

What is the range of a viola? As far as you can kick it. In another version, the answer is: *About 35 yards if you have a strong arm.*[21]

What is the definition of "perfect pitch"? Throwing a viola into a dumpster without hitting the rim. In several variants, perfect pitch is defined as throwing a viola or banjo into a toilet without hitting the rim[22]; in another, perfect pitch consists of lobbing an oboist into a garbage can without hitting the rim.[23]

What's the difference between a viola and an onion? People cry when they chop an onion to pieces[24] or *Nobody cries when they chop up a viola.*

What's the difference between a viola and a trampoline? You should take your shoes off before you jump on a trampoline.

What's the difference between a viola and a TV dinner? The viola doesn't fit in a microwave oven (unless you break the neck off).

What's the difference between a viola and cello? You can fit more violas into a trash compactor.[25]

What's the difference between a violin and a viola? The viola burns longer.[26]

This joke has inspired a follow-up text: *Now we all know that a viola is better than a violin because it burns longer. But why does it burn longer? It's usually still in the case.*[27] The implication here is that one reason violists play so poorly is that they never practice. Hence their violas remain in their cases at all times. The violist's supposed reluctance to practice is also reflected in the following texts: *After his retirement, the violist arrived home carrying his viola case. His wife saw the case and asked, "What's that?"* In Germany, for example, it is a standing joke that some players leave their instruments in their lockers, removing them only for rehearsals and performances. In other words, they don't bring their instruments home to practice.

Why is a viola the perfect murder weapon? It is a classic blunt weapon and it never has any fingerprints on it.[28]

How is a violist similar to a lawyer? Everyone is happiest when the case is closed. In a variant: *How its a viola like a jury trial? Everyone breathes a sign of relief when the case is closed.*[29]

How do you keep your violin from getting stolen? Put it in a viola case.[30]

Why do viola players keep their cases on their car dashboards? So they can park in handicapped spaces.

Why does the violin player keep a spare viola in his trunk? So that he can park in the handicapped zone. In a variant: *Why did the musician hang a small viola from his rear view mirror? So he could park in "handicapped" zones.*[31] The implication is that violists by definition are considered to be physically less gifted than other musicians. Accordingly, the viola or a representation thereof is a telltale sign of such a limitation. It may or may not be relevant that several of the most famous violists were noticeably short in stature (for example, Lionel Tertis[32] and Lillian Fuchs), for they may possibly have felt lesser in some sense, a feeling that might have unconsciously led them to choose to play the viola, a "second string" instrument, so to speak. The jokes, however, indicate that although the violist may be handicapped, he has turned his handicap into an advantage. It enables him to find a parking space, that is, a place in the orchestra that others cannot occupy.

Why are violas bigger than violins? They're really not. It just looks that way because violists' heads are smaller. Here is another version of that joke: *Why are violas so large? It's an optical illusion. It's not that violas are large, just that the viola players' heads are so small.* In yet another version, the joke is at the expense of violinists rather than violists: *Why are violins smaller than violas? They're actually the same size—it's the violinists' heads which are larger.*[33] Here the allusion is to the perceived conceit of violinists.

One notable joke about the purported lack of intelligence of violists is the following: *What's the most challenging requirement for finalists in the International Viola Competition? A finalist must be able to hold his viola from memory.*[34]

Some jokes concern the lack of employment opportunities for violists: *What's the difference between a viola player driving into town and a plumber driving into town? The plumber is going to a gig.*

What's the difference between a dead viola player lying in the road and a dead Country Singer lying in the road? The Country Singer was going to a record date.

Why do violin players double on viola? So they can get less work.

Definition of an optimist: A viola player with a beeper.

A few jokes hint at the relative lack of importance of the viola in the overall orchestral setting:

What's unique about viola concertos? They're the only concertos in which the soloist plays the harmony.[35]

Why don't violists play hide and seek? Because no one will look for them.

Why shouldn't violists take up mountaineering? Because f they get lost, it takes ages before anyone notices that they're missing.

If you're lost in the desert, what do you aim for? A good viola player, a bad viola player, or an oasis? The bad viola player. The other two are only figments of your imagination.

A number of viola jokes portray the violist as dead:

What do you do with a dead violist? Move him back one stand.[36]

What's the difference between a viola and a coffin? The coffin has the stiff on the inside.

Why is the viola section like the Beatles? 25% of them are dead, and the other 75% haven't played together for years.[37]

If you see a violist and a conductor in the road, which do you hit first? The violist— business before pleasure.[38]

The basic message of viola jokes is that the viola (its solos and sounds) and the violist should be avoided if at all possible:

Why do most people take an instant dislike to violists? Saves time.

Why is a viola solo like premature ejaculation? Because even when you know it's coming, there's nothing you can do about it.

Why do people tremble with fear when someone comes into a bank carrying a violin case? They think he's carrying a machine gun and might be about to use it. Why do people tremble with fear when someone comes into a bank carrying a viola case? They think he's carrying a viola and might be about to use it.

What is the most popular recording of the "William Walton Viola Concerto?"

Music Minus One. In this joke, which refers to recordings made with the accompaniment only so that would-be instrumentalists can practice with a full orchestra or other members of an ensemble, the implication is that the Walton concerto, featuring the viola as soloist, would sound better without the viola solo part.

Why is playing a viola solo like wetting your pants? Both give you a nice warm feeling while everybody moves away from you.[39]

What's the definition of a perfect gentleman? Someone who can play the viola but chooses not to.[40]

Why did the chicken cross the road? To get away from a viola recital.[41]

The recognition of the viola joke cycle is attested by the fact that there is even a text referring to such jokes: *What is the longest viola joke?* "*Harold in Italy.*"[42] This is a reference to the composition composed by Hector Berlioz expressly for the viola and orchestra.

What is one to make of this spate of viola jokes? And to what extent, if any, does it reflect actual attitudes towards violists or, for that matter, violists' attitudes towards themselves and their chosen instrument? An examination of several prominent violists' autobiographies clearly reveals that the traditional disdain held by so many towards the viola is keenly felt by violists. Consider the following statement made by famed violist Lionel Tertis (1876–1975) writing about his experience at the beginning of the twentieth century: "When I first began to play the viola as a solo instrument, prejudice and storms of abuse were my lot. The consensus of opinion then was that the viola had no right to be heard in solos, indeed the consideration of its place in the string family was of the scantiest. It was not only a despised instrument, but its cause was far from helped by the down-and-out violinists who usually played it. The executants in those days were violinists too inferior to gain a position in orchestras as such. A wretchedly low standard of viola-playing was in fact accepted simply and solely because there was no alternative."

It turns out that Tertis's own professional trajectory lends credence to some portions of the stereotype. He started out as a violinist and took up the viola on a whim. Henry Wood of the Henry Wood's Queen's Hall orchestra learned of Tertis's interest in the viola and asked to hear him play. At the time, Tertis was "the last player at the last desk of the second violins." After the audition, Terns "jumped from last violinist to principal viola in the orchestra.[44] Curiously enough, there is a joke which reverses this *cursus honorum* from lowly violinist to high-ranking violist. Moreover, the joke departs from the joking question format of most of the viola jokes. Instead, it employs a folktale framework and is in fact a variant of a well-known tale of three wishes.[45]

The last chair violist of the Minot North Dakota Symphony found a magic lamp, and after rubbing it, a genie appeared and granted him three wishes. His first wish was to be an 80% better player than he was now. The genie granted his wish and—poof—he became the principal violist of the Minot North Dakota Symphony. Soon he wasn't satisfied with this so he made his second wish—again to become an 80% better player than he was and—poof—he became the principal violist of the Philadelphia Orchestra. Well, he still had one wish to go and— you guessed it—he asked once more to become an 80% better player than he had been. So—poof—he became the last chair second violin of the Minot North Dakota Symphony Orchestra.[46]

Violist Lillian Fuchs (1902–1995) had an instrument-changing experience somewhat parallel to that of Tertis. She began on the piano, but influenced by the example of her successful older brother Joseph, a talented violinist, she too took up the violin. However, at one point, her violin teacher urged her to switch from violin to viola. Her father was adamantly opposed to this and she herself thought her decision might be "the catastrophe of her life."[47] In 1992, when she received a Medallion Award for Distinguished Artistry from the New York Viola Society, she was asked how she came to play the viola instead of the violin. Her answer given in the third person: "Lillian didn't intend to play the viola. She was talked into learning it by her teacher, Franz Kneisel."[48]

Violist William Primrose (1904–1982) also reports starting out on the violin and that eventually his teacher Eugène Ysaÿe suggested that he switch to viola.[49] Like Fuchs' father, Primrose's father firmly opposed the shift, becoming "deeply despondent" at his son's decision.[50] Primrose's father, despite being a violin teacher who himself "doubled" on the viola, felt that "anyone who was confined to play out his musical life on what he regarded as the secondary instrument did but confess his failure as a violinist."[51] At the time, a highly respected orchestra player told Primrose, "you're making the biggest mistake of your life. You will regret this as you've regretted no other thing." Late in life at the outset of a lengthy interview, Primrose claimed that he would rather accept as a pupil someone who had come to the viola via the violin rather than someone who started from the beginning on the viola.[53] Rahkonen claims that "one of the first assumptions in junior high school orchestras is that the director will switch the poor violinists over to viola, where they will do less harm. and perhaps even contribute."[54]

Primrose was certainly well aware of the violist stereotype. In describing the make-up of a string quartet, he said that "the violist was usually, as we know to our sorrow, a disappointed violinist" and this was one reason why he so admired Lionel Tertis for his many years of advocacy of the lightly regarded member of the string family. As Primrose phrased it, "after he championed the cause of the instrument. those who followed no longer felt ashamed to be playing the viola."[56]

In his autobiography, Tertis repeatedly referred to the viola in such demeaning folk verbiage as a "Cinderella" or "Ugly Duckling."' He spoke of the viola's reputation "as a nasty, growling, and grunting instrument."[58] What this suggests is that violists have internalized the stereotype so that it functioned as a self-stereotype. Regardless of whether violists are truly inferior musicians or whether the viola is truly an inferior string instrument, the fact is that violists are well aware of the stereotype and feel obliged to do their best to overcome the stigma attached to their choice of musical vocation.

We should stress that not all the jokes pick on the viola. There are other instruments that come in for ribbing. The French Horn, for example, is featured in such texts as: *How do you make a trombone sound like a French Horn? Put your hand in the bell and miss a lot of notes*[59] or *How can you tell you are kissing a French Horn player? Because he has his hands up your ass.* Bagpipes may also be victimized: *Why do bagpipers walk when they play? To get away from the noise.* Other musicians are also featured in traditional jokes. Besides conductors, singers are famous for their prima donna personalities. *What's the definition of a male quartet? Three men and a tenor*[60] and *What's the difference between a soprano and a terrorist? You can reason (negotiate) with a terrorist.*[61] Still, it is the viola, among orchestral instruments, that takes the most jocular punishment.

Unanswered remains the question of why these jokes should exist at all. We know that states of anxiety are often relieved by humor, but is it sufficient to say that the anxiety or nervousness resulting from a form of stage fright, exacerbated when one has to perform a solo in front of one's peers or in front of an audience, explains the existence of viola and other musical jokes? We believe an examination of the content of the jokes, the themes and variations so to speak, provide an illuminating clue as to the function and meaning of viola jokes. One must keep in mind that viola jokes are told by many musicians, not just string players or violists. So whatever the significance of the joke cycle might be, it is likely that it is relevant to the act of musical performance.

It is our contention that musical groups, whether large (orchestras or bands) or small (string quartets or other small ensembles), are microcosms of the larger European (and American) societies that produced them. The social organization of orchestras and bands is extremely hierarchical. Not all musical groups in other cultures have a dictatorial conductor to "govern" and control the group. In fact a Martian might find it strange that the conductor holds only a small stick (baton) and does not actually play one of the orchestral or band instruments. The social organization includes a second in command, the concertmaster, typically the first violinist. The various instrumental sections are ranked such that one can be first chair, second chair, third chair, etc. Even at an early age, young musicians are encouraged to compete in order to move up the ladder, say from second clarinet to first clarinet in a high school band. The emphasis upon regimentation and order in bands is usually marked by a form of folk costume. Military bands obviously have members in uniforms, but even high school and college marching bands typically wear some kind of uniform dress. Members of orchestras do not wear such uniforms, but on the other hand, formal dress, for example, tuxedos or coat and tails for piano soloists, surely can be construed as a sort of uniform, again underlining the formality of such performance events.

The rigorous nature of performance constraints is by no means limited to the social organization of the orchestra or band or even string quartet. The very nature of musical performance is such that strict demands are made in terms of time and place. Members of musical groups are required to play together. One must know one's place and one must stay in it. An individual cannot simply play whenever he or she feels like it. There is a score. One must begin at a particular time and even more important, one must end at a particular time. Nothing is more embarrassing for an instrumentalist to be heard playing after all his fellow group members have stopped. Similarly, one of the greatest fears for a musician is that he or she has lost his or her place during a performance. (It is worth noting that several of the viola jokes specifically refer to being lost, for example, "lost" in the desert or "lost" as a result of mountaineering.) Upon realization that he or she is lost, the befuddled musician may cease playing, hoping that he or she will be able to recognize an opportune (and correct) moment to start playing again in the right place. There is even a joke, usually told of a trombonist, that expresses this fear: *The town's brass band had just finished a loud but not very coordinated selection. The musicians had just sunk down to their seats after bowing to the applause when the trombonist asked: "What are we playing next?" The band director replied, "The Stars and Stripes Forever." "Oh my gosh!" exploded the trombonist. "I just got through playing that!"*[62]

If we consider the themes of the viola jokes, we can easily see that they concern playing in unison or in tune or the lack thereof. Another theme concerns time rather than tone. The difference between the first and last section of violas is said to involve two bars or a measure and a half. Such jokes are all about not playing together properly, that is, being either ahead or behind one's fellow musicians. What these jokes seem to do is to provide a socially sanctioned vehicle for the expression of rebellion against the various forms of restraint and order inherent in group musical performances. So it is not only violists who are afraid of not playing in unison or finishing a half measure ahead or behind their comrades. In this connection, it is of interest that in Mozart's *Ein musikalischer Spass* KV 522 [A Musical Joke] composed in 1787, part of the humorous scoring by Mozart included having an instrument enter one beat too late in both the third and fourth movements.[63] What is perhaps even more striking in the present context is the fact that the instrument in question was a viola! This may suggest that Mozart as well was aware of the tradition of making the viola the butt of the string section of the orchestra.

It is not just instrumentalists playing harmony who are concerned with losing their place. Soloists also worry about playing in concert with their accompanists or the orchestra. Group musical performance by its very nature demands conformity of the highest order. Moreover, one mistake, one missed entrance, one false note, can ruin an entire performance for an audience and for the orchestra or band. No matter how seasoned a musician may be, no matter how many times he or she may have performed a given composition, there is always the possibility of making a mistake. It is one matter to make a mistake in the privacy of one's practice room at home; it is quite another to make it in front of a live audience and one's peers. We believe it is this constant pressure to perform at the highest level, the worry about meeting the expectations of a sophisticated audience or one's fellow musicians that has generated the viola jokes which in effect list all the things that could possibly go wrong—playing out of tune, missing one's cue, and the like. What this means is that viola jokes fulfill a valuable function in articulating the traditional anxieties of musicians. Telling a viola joke to a fellow musician is a tacit admission that one knows full well what pitfalls lie in performing a piece of music. The listener laughs because he or she recognizes the point of the joke, albeit unconsciously. Non-musicians would probably not find most of the jokes very amusing and for that matter might not even understand some of the more technical musical terminology. In that sense, some of the viola jokes tend to be somewhat esoteric, intelligible only to true *cognoscenti.* That special knowledge is required only makes such jokes more enjoyable as it is clear that only real musicians can fully appreciate their nuances. In that sense, the telling and re-telling of viola jokes helps create a bond among musicians. They not only share the jokes; they share the anxieties that produced the jokes in the first place.

As to why the viola joke cycle flourished in the 1990s, it is difficult to say. Rahkonen, who claims that the cycle began in 1991, admits that he "could find nothing specific to point to a cause for the beginning of the cycle."[64] Presumably, the tensions articulated in the jokes have existed for centuries. It is always difficult to pinpoint the actual moment of the onset of a joke cycle and just as hard to explain why the cycle started at that particular time. In this instance, we might speculate that the popularity of the viola joke cycle seems to have coincided with the emergence of a censorious perspective known as "political correctness." According to the guidelines of PC, it was no longer permissible to poke fun at minority cultures. Racist and sexist jokes were, in theory, no longer acceptable.[65] Dumb "Pollack" or dumb "blonde" jokes were considered offensive and definitely not PC. In that context, it became necessary to find some other group that could be depicted as "dumb" or otherwise undesirable or inferior.[66] As violists already had a stereotyped reputation as second class citizens, it was a simple enough matter to abuse them verbally as a group that few would feel obliged to defend. Of course, assuming there is any causal connection between "political correctness" and the emergence of viola jokes in the early 1990s, the question of why political correctness should have emerged at that particular time remains.

In any event, the empirical reality of the viola jokes is irrefutable. As we have suggested, much of the content of the jokes expresses fundamental sources of abiding concern among musicians. There will probably always be anxiety connected with performing in a musical group before a live audience. The nervousness and the excessive flow of adrenalin may even be considered positive factors in helping to make a musician perform at his or her very best. But the inescapable presence of anxiety also means that musicians will need an escape valve to relieve the pressure. And that is why we believe that viola jokes or their successors in the future will continue to circulate among both professional and amateur musicians.

Notes

The jokes reported in this article were collected by Meegan M. Brown in 1996 from several fellow musicians in the San Diego area, from members of the Ying Quartet, and mostly from nationwide alumni of the Interlochen Arts Camp in Michigan. We are indebted to famed opera staging director Jonathan Miller who was kind enough to send us several pages of musicians' jokes.

1. For representative studies of Haydn's humor, see Gretchen A. Wheelock, *Haydn's Ingenious Jesting with Art: Contexts of Musical Wit and Humor* (New York: Schirmer Books, 1992) and Andreas Ballstaedt, "'Humor' and 'Witz' in Joseph Haydn's Musik," *Archiv für Musikwissenschaft* 55 (1998): 195–219. For musical humor in general, see Laurie-Jeanne Lister, *Humor as a Concept in Music* (Frankfurt: Peter Lang, 1994) and James E. Myers, ed., *A Treasury of Musical Humor* (Springfield: Lincoln-Herndon Press, 1998).

2. For an excellent introduction to ethnic humor, see Christie Davies, *Ethnic Humor Around the World: A Comparative Analysis* (Bloomington: Indiana University Press, 1990).

3. For other versions of this joke, see Nancy Groce, "Knowing the Score: The Transmission of Musician Jokes among Professional and Semi-Professional Musicians." *New York Folklore* 22 (1996): 44; Myers, 199; and Carl Rahkonen, "No Laughing Matter: The Viola Joke Cycle as Musicians' Folklore," *Western Folklore* 59 (2000): 58.

4. Martin Boyd, "Alter Ego: A Brief History of the Viola," *The Strad* 106 (1995): 818–819; Nancy Groce, "Knowing the Score: The Transmission of Musician Jokes among Professional and Semi-Professional Musicians," *New York Folklore* 22(1996): 37–47; Groce, *The Musician's Joke Book* (New York: Schirmer Books, 1996); Dave Marsh and Kathi Kamen Goldmark, *The Great Rock 'n' Roll Joke Book* (New York: St. Martin's Griffin, 1997); Olin Chism, "Violins Get the Glory, While Viola Is Butt of Jokes," *San Francisco Chronicle*, Thursday, January 4, 2001, p. D7; Carl Rahkonen, "No Laughing Matter: The Viola Joke Cycle as Musicians' Folklore," *Western Folklore* 59 (2000): 59–63. The fact that viola jokes have begun to be included in general anthologies of modern humor suggests that the jokes are by no means confined to musical circles. See, for example, Geoff Tibballs, ed., *The Mammoth Book of Humor* (New York: Carroll & Graf Publishers, 2000), 218–221.

5. Groce, "Knowing the Score," 41.

6. Rahkonen, 55.

7. Many of the jokes included in this essay or variants thereof were reported by Rahkonen who collected them during the period 1991–1995 from a cellist and violist in the Pittsburgh Symphony.

8. Groce, *The Musician's Joke Book*, 24.

9. For a variant, *How do you get a viola player to play flying staccato? Write a semibreve with the word "solo" beside it*, see Boyd, "Alter ego," 818.

10. Groce, "Knowing the Score," 41.

11. For a text in which adding vibrato is supposedly the way to make a bass saxophone sound like a chainsaw, see Myers, *A Treasury*, 220.

12. Groce, *The Musician's Jokebook*, 20; for a version with an oboe player in place of a violist, see Myers, 213.

13. Groce, "Knowing the Score." 42.
14. Groce, *The Musician's Jokebook*, 24.
15. Groce, "Knowing the Score," 41.
16. Groce, *The Musician's Jokebook*, 19; for texts substituting a kettledrum or a tenor sax for the viola, see Myers, 161, 215.
17. This joke is often told about piccolos. For a version recommending the shooting of three of four oboe players to accomplish the same end, see Myers, 216.
18. Groce, *The Musician's Jokebook*, 26.
19. The version reported by Rahkonen makes no mention of the key: *How do you know it is a violist who knocked at your door? He won't come in,* See Rahkonen, 52. For a version about a lead singer that does include a reference to a key, see Groce, *The Musician's Jokebook*, 41.
20. Groce, *The Musician's Jokebook*, 26.
21. Chism, D7; for an unlikely version involving a tuba rather than a viola, see Groce, *The Musician's Jokebook*, 36.
22. Groce, "Knowing the Score," 41; Marsh and Goldmark, 23.
23. Myers, 224. This is one of the very few viola jokes not contained in Rahkonen's comprehensive collection.
24. Chism, D7.
25. Groce, *The Musican's Jokebook*, 21.
26. For a version about a bass instead of a viola, see Marsh and Goldmark.
27. Rahkonen, 50.
28. Groce, "Knowing the Score," 42; for a version with a pianist instead of a violist, see Myers,53.
29. Groce, *The Musician's Jokebook*, 20.
30. Ibid., Myers, 2.
31. Rahkonen, 51.
32. David Dalton, *Playing the Viola: Conversations with William Primrose* (Oxford: Oxford University Press, 1988), 10.
33. Rahkonen, 53.
34. Groce, *The Musician's Jokebook*, 21.
35. Ibid.
36. Groce, "Knowing the Score." 42.
37. Ibid.
38. For a version with a trombone player and a conductor, see Groce, *A Musician's Jokebook*, 34; for a version turning on the question of whether to push a bass player or a conductor off a pier first, see Myers, 179.
39. For a version referring to playing a tuba, see Myers, 242.
40. Boyd, 819. For versions involving a banjo or a bassoon, see Myers 22, 215; for a version with bagpipes, see Tibballs, 218.
41. For versions involving a violin solo or an oboe recital, see Myers, 22, 214; for a cello recital, see Tibballs, 219.
42. Cf. Groce, *The Musician's Jokebook*, 21.
43. Lionel Terti, *My Viola and I* (Boston, Crescendo Publishing Company, 1974), 16.
44. Tertis, 19.
45. See tale type 750A, The Wishes, in Antti Aarne and Stith Thompson, *The Types of the Folktale,* FF Communications No. 184 (Helsinki: Academia Scientiarum Fennica, 1961), 254–255.
46. Rahkonen, 54.
47. Amedee Daryl Williams, *Lillian Fuchs, First Lady of the Viola* (Lewiston: The Edwin MellenPress, 1994), 16.
48. Williams, 129.
49. William Primrose, *Walk on the North Side: Memoirs of a Violist* (Provo: Brigham Young University Press. 1978), 59.
50. Ibid., 45.

51. Ibid., 19.
52. Ibid., 46
53. Dalton, 5.
54. Rahkonen, 56.
55. Primrose, 69; Dalton 226.
56. Primrose, 165.
57. Tertis, 86–87, 138, 162.
58. Dalton, 197.
59. Cf. Groce, *The Musician's Jokebook*, 37.
60. Ibid., 44.
61. Ibid., 41.
62. Myers, 241, 213.
63. Lister, 126.
64. Rahkonen, 59.
65. For an interesting extended roundtable discussion of the impact of political correctness on traditional humor, see Paul Lewis, ed. "Humor and Political Correctness," *Humor* 10 (1997): 453–513.
66. There are a few viola jokes that portray the violist as truly dimwitted. For example, *During a concert, a fight broke out between the oboe player and the viola player. At the interval, the orchestra went to investigate. "He broke my reed," said the oboe player. "He undid two of my strings," countered the viola player, "but he won't tell me which ones!"* See Tibballs, 220.

13

MEDICAL SPEECH AND
PROFESSIONAL IDENTITY

(*A*) The Gomer: A Figure of American Hospital Folk Speech

(*B*) "When You Hear Hoofbeats, Think Horses, Not Zebras":
A Folk Medical Diagnostic Proverb

Introduction

Showing that medical professionals constituted a folk group, with a complex of subgroups (physicians by specialty and school background, residents at different stages of development, and nurses assigned to different units), fit into Dundes's general goal of demonstrating that elite scientific groups defined their group identity through folklore. Their communication is replete with slang and story that express their relation to one another, and to patients. One approach to identifying and interpreting the material heard from medical professionals, therefore, was to gauge folklore's capacity to convey values within the group, and to express attitudes toward those outside the group. In other words, it not only defined the group, but also marked the boundaries and hierarchies within a sociocultural system of which patients were generally unaware.

The hospital setting separated Dundes's analysis of medical professionals from others he did of elite groups. Scholarship often distinguished folklore by cultures of region, religion, ethnicity, age, and gender, Dundes saw the medical professional in a distinct institutional context, one that differed, inside its doors, in its visual appearance and social world. It was a world of emergency and stress, with life and death at stake, and therefore provided an excellent test of folklore's function to express and mediate anxiety. Indeed, as the first essay shows, different types of hospitals (Dundes discussed the distinction of Veterans Administration hospitals) had their own lore, reflecting their institutional culture. Dundes hypothesized that the more stress a group faced, dealing with life and death issues in the hospital complex, the more likely it was that folklore, often of a morbidly humorous nature, would arise or would be needed.

An early indication of Dundes's interest in the subject was in his interpretation of several legends in *American Folk Legend* (Hand 1971). There, he reinterpreted the legend, known as "The Cadaver Arm," circulating in medical schools. In this legend, medical students put a coin in a cadaver's hand and drive through a toll booth. The attendant is startled when the driver leaves that arm behind as the medical students speed away. Dundes pointed out that the story was one of many about cadavers among medical students. He concluded that among professional groups, this unusual concentration of narratives around the theme of dead bodies provided "an outlet for the anxiety initially felt about treating a dead human body, as a mere 'nonhuman' object." One of the story's lessons is that doctors cannot get too attached to their patients' ailments. In addition to separating the would-be doctors in the narrative from their previous identities as part of the public, offering the cadaverous arm with a coin attached reversed the normal roles of patient and doctor. This, according to Dundes, functioned as a way to deal with the anxiety of taking money from sick or dying people. (See Dundes's summary of this interpretation in "Getting the Folk and the Lore Together" [1976a], presented in the next chapter).

In the first essay, Dundes collaborated with a nurse, Victoria George, to collect materials—printed in the form of photocopied sheets as well as communicated orally—by questionnaire and interview. Dundes compared the stereotypes patients had of doctors and nurses with the lore devised by hospital staff for patients. According to Dundes, the "gomer" was a prime example of staff slang. It referred to a chronic problem patient, offering a safety valve for ritual reversal—turning human tragedy into comedy. In addition, Dundes extended the interpretation of the socioeconomic gap between the figure of the gomer (as the "dregs of society") with the affluent doctor (begun with his treatment of the "Cadaver Arm") to one of "critical differences in class and values." Here, the stress is the ethical responsibility of the doctor to treat all patients equally, despite his or her class biases.

The second essay is about a proverb—"If you hear hoofbeats think horses, not zebras"—used in hospital instruction. Published twenty-one years after the Gomer piece, it was also written with health professionals. One was his daughter Lauren Dundes, a medical sociologist at Western Maryland College, and the other was Michael Streiff, a physician with the Johns Hopkins University School of Medicine. Indicating the divide between the proverb, as part of "esoteric" hospital lore, and the public, the senior Dundes explained to the editor, "I don't think the majority of proverb scholars know the proverb despite its widespread popularity among doctors" (Mieder 2006a, 153). Of interest in interpreting the proverb is the fact that it can hold multiple meanings, in changing socioeconomic contexts, for the professional medical community.

An advertising campaign by the Carcinoid Cancer Foundation, begun at the start of the twenty-first century, may change the esoteric nature of the proverb, although the campaign is primarily aimed at healthcare professionals. Using the zebra and its stripes as logos, the advertisement gives "The Story Behind the Zebra": "Physicians are taught 'If you hear hoof beats think horses, not zebras.' Zebras, like Carcinoid Cancer, are less common. Therefore we want to remind the medical community to also 'think zebras.'" Following the custom of displaying different colored ribbons for various causes (pink for breast cancer, yellow for soldiers abroad), carcinoid cancer advocacy groups brandish black-and-white striped ribbon pins, stuffed zebra dolls, and car magnets. Fundraisers include "The Zebra Ball: Stars for the Stripes," and a book, *Carcinoid Cancers, Zebras and Stardust* (Girsch-Bock 2006). Audiences of the hit television show *CSI: Las Vegas* (featuring scientific details of forensic science) may have wondered about the zebra proverb, used in a segment ("Pirates of the Third Reich" in 2006) to refer to an apparently outrageous theory by the lead medical investigator, which of course turned out to be right. It also remains to be seen whether another proverb suggested by the Carcinoid Foundation takes hold in the medical community: "You must suspect it to detect it."

For further folkloristic work with the culture of healthcare professionals, see Tangherlini 1998; Hufford 1989; Berkman 1978; Burson 1982; Burson-Tolpin 1989; Winick 2004: and Meehan and Bronner 2006.

A

The Gomer: A Figure of American Hospital Folk Speech

ONE OF THE GROUPS LEAST studied by folklorists is the medical profession. To be sure, there has been a long-standing scholarly interest in folk medicine, but this refers primarily to medicine practiced by patients themselves or by healers not usually considered to be part of the "scientific" medical establishment. Folk medicine, in fact, is often contrasted with so-called scientific medicine. This has perhaps tended to suggest that scientific medicine is devoid of any folkloristic content. Yet doctors and nurses not only constitute an important occupational folk group, they constitute one which by its very nature involves an unusually great amount of anxiety. It is to be expected that matters of health care which are literally concerned with life and death create nervous tension—not just for the patient but also for the dedicated medical personnel who are charged with the responsibility of treating the patient. In most hospitals, a rich albeit esoteric folklore flourishes providing a much needed outlet for doctors and nurses who are under almost continual round-the-clock pressure.

Unless readers have had professional training in medicine, they will probably not be familiar with in-group hospital folk speech. In some instances, the terminology is specifically designed to conceal information from patients. "Code Blue," for example, is used in some California hospitals to alert personnel that someone is *in extremis* and that emergency assistance is needed immediately. If "Code Blue 123" is announced on the public address system, it creates far less anxiety for the general patient population than would an announcement that the patient in room 123 is suffering cardiac arrest. Similarly "Dr. Red" (or in some versions Mr. Firestone) is paged to indicate that a fire has broken out. "Mr. Strong, Mr. Strong, 456" means that help is needed in room 456 to subdue an unruly or difficult patient. By using this "secret" code language, hospital staff members can communicate effectively and at the same time they can reduce the chances of causing widespread panic and alarm among patients.

Acronymic initials used by doctors in the admission process are also a part of hospital folklore. FLK, for instance, means "Funny Looking Kid." This might be put on the record to indicate that the admitting doctor noticed something odd about the appearance of a child but also that he was unable to pinpoint exactly what it is. (It would not necessarily be written on the permanent record but rather on a temporary card in the Kardex file which is commonly used for quick reference by the staff to determine at a glance a patient's condition, diagnosis, prescribed medication, etc.) FLK is not really derogatory; it suggests rather that the diagnosis is incomplete. Such a label on the admitting card would alarm neither the patient nor the patient's parents.

Similar to FLK is the code acronym TSTSH which stands for "Too Sick To Send Home." This could also be used by a doctor in the admitting process when he finds himself unable to diagnose accurately the patient's condition. The code initials indicate only that the patient appeared to be too ill to be released and that the lack of a proper full-fledged diagnosis should not be construed by a doctor entering the scene later to be grounds for assuming there was nothing wrong with the patient. Some of the acronymic folklore is never written. For example, there is ECU, Eternal Care Unit, which is a euphemism for death or the afterlife. Among hospital personnel, the question "Where is patient so-and-so?" might be answered, "He went to the ECU." Another example of a traditional acronym is the triple H. HHH, at least in the past when enemas were quite commonly prescribed, stood for "high, hot, and a hell of a lot." This term, in contrast to the preceding ones, could be revealed to patients.

Among the most interesting examples of hospital folk speech are those items which refer to patients, especially those patients who are incapacitated or who present particular problems for the hospital staff. A patient who has suffered extensive brain damage, for example, as the result of a severe stroke, may be termed a "vegetable." The term suggests that although the patient is technically alive, he or she may be totally unable to speak and perhaps even unable to think. This term may be known by some members of the general public, but the term "gork" which means much the same thing is probably not. Thus a "gork ward" is a "vegetable garden." Neither "vegetable" nor "gork" would ever be used in front of a patient or his family. According to one apocryphal story, a doctor visiting such a patient would daily ask the nurse, "Did you water the gork today?" and he did so in front of the patient. As it happened, the patient's speech was impaired but there was nothing wrong with his mind. Eventually he recovered his speech faculties, and he brought suit against the doctor for having subjected him to unnecessary mental anguish, namely being termed a gork. This cautionary tale not only warns medical staff members about using in-group folklore in front of patients but it also expresses the increasing concern of doctors with the dangers of being named in malpractice or negligence suits filed by disgruntled patients. Clearly the term "gork" would never be put on a patient's medical chart—unlike some of the acronyms discussed above.

Of all the terms used by hospital staff members to refer to patients, one of the most fascinating is "gomer." The gomer is a stereotyped patient character known reluctantly by most doctors and nurses who work in what are called "high stress areas." High stress areas are those units in a hospital where severely ill patients are found. Such areas include the intensive and coronary care units and, of course, the emergency room. Nowhere in the hospital are the energies and skills of the medical staff more in demand, and this is why there is great resentment among the staff if they feel their talents and dedication are being wasted on individuals whom they consider to be malingerers and hypochondriacs.

What precisely is a "gomer?" He is typically an older man who is both dirty and debilitated. He has extremely poor personal hygiene and he is often a chronic alcoholic. A derelict or down-and-outer, the gomer is normally on welfare. He has an extensive history of multiple admissions to the hospital. From the gomer's standpoint, life inside the hospital is so much better than the miserable existence he endures outside that he exerts every effort to gain admission, or rather readmission to the hospital. Moreover, once admitted, the gomer attempts to remain there as long as possible. Because of the gomer's desire to stay in the hospital, he frequently pretends to be ill or he lacks interest in getting well on those occasions when he really is sick. Often he appears to be confused and hostile—though he may be genuinely grateful for the care and attention he does receive. One must remember that most patients look forward to the day when they are able to leave the hospital. In contrast, the gomer looks forward to the day when he is readmitted to the hospital and dreads the day he may have to leave. This presents a frustrating problem for the hospital staff, and it is no doubt this frustration which has encouraged the development of the folk figure of the gomer.

The gomer is reported in hospitals all over the United States.[1] Since the gomer is familiar primarily to doctors and nurses who work in high stress areas, he is found mostly in large county hospitals, Veterans Administration hospitals, and university teaching hospitals. The gomer is rarely encountered in private hospitals, which usually screen their patients very carefully before admitting them. Because of the gomer's inevitable lack of adequate financial resources, he is customarily rejected by private hospitals and sent to charity or public hospitals.

Informants were unsure about the origin of the term "gomer." Some mentioned Gomer Pyle, the name of the central character of a popular television series in the 1960s still shown on reruns in the 1970s. According to the *Dictionary of American Slang, gomer* or *gomar* is an Air Force slang term meaning "A first-year or naive Air Force cadet."[2] In the television series, Gomer Pyle was portrayed as a bumpkin and a loser (although sympathetically). The loser connotation would be akin to the gomer as he appears in hospital folklore. Other informants suggested a biblical source for the gomer (see Genesis 10:2–3; 1 Chronicles 1:5–6; Ezekiel 38:6; and Hosea 1:3), but this seems unlikely.[3] It is possible though by no means demonstrable that the term derives from an older English slang abbreviation GOM meaning Grand Old Man. It is also conceivable that "gomer" is a modern derivative of such older words as Scottish *gomerel* meaning fool or simpleton or Anglo-Irish *gomus* meaning fool.[4] There is also a word *gome* which may be cognate with Latin *homo* meaning man. A second word *gome* has a dialect meaning (listed as obsolete) referring to heed, attention, notice, or care. "To take *gome*" would thus mean to give heed or to pay attention to, or to take care of. If this is relevant, then a gomer might logically be an individual who needed attention and care, a meaning quite close to the current usage in American hospital folklore.

Several folk etymologies have been proposed for "gomer." Differing interpretations of the word as an acronym seem to fall roughly along geographical lines. On the east coast of the United States, gomer is explained as an acronym for "Get Out of My Emergency Room." On the west coast, the interpretation more usually advanced is "Grand Old Man of the Emergency Room."[5] There is agreement, however, that gomer always refers to a man. (One informant claimed that the female version of a gomer was a "gomerette.")

It is difficult to determine just how long "gomer" has been a part of American hospital folklore. One report took it back at least to 1964 when it was used by medical students at the University of Washington in Seattle.[6] Several informants thought they remembered its being used in the 1950s. Some doctors and nurses suggested "gomer" might be of recent coinage because until the advent of Medicare and comparable state programs, a "gomer" would not have been able to afford extensive and expensive medical treatment. Presumably as socialized medicine increases, the folklore of individuals perceived to be abusers of the system will develop. To the extent that a form of subsidized medicine has existed for some time, as in Veterans Administration hospitals (not to mention the venerable tradition of charity wards in major public hospitals), it is quite likely that "gomer" or some analogous folk expression has had a much longer life in tradition than we are able to document.

Although "gomer" appears to be the most common term in hospital argot for an unkempt, unsavory, chronic problem patient, there are others. Among the near synonyms are: "turkey," "crock," "trainwreck," "lizard," and "reeker."[7] Three informants, all staff members of San Francisco General Hospital's Emergency Room, mentioned "grume" defining it as a filthy "gomer," in other words, an individual whose condition was even worse than the average "gomer." "Grume" which comes from the Latin *grumus* meaning "little heap" can in medical parlance refer to a clot (as in blood). Folklorists may know the term from the phrase *grumus merdae* referring to the curious custom of some burglars leaving a "calling card" or pile of feces behind at the scene of the crime.[8]

Gomer's pre-eminence as a term is attested to by its occasional occurrence in song[9] as well as by its serving as the inspiration for derivative expressions. For example, one informant, a doctor who had worked in the emergency room at San Francisco General, reported that he had seen nurses there make what are called "gomersicles." A gomersicle, an obvious popsicle oikotype, is made by freezing the patients' orange juice on tongue depressors (which results in something resembling the various frozen desserts on a stick available commercially). These improvised snacks are then eaten by the doctors and nurses while they make rounds on patients they consider to be gomers. Normally doctors and nurses wouldn't eat in front of patients, so the eating of gomersicles suggests a certain lack of respect toward gomers.

Generally speaking, "gomer" is a term used more by younger staff members. As a matter of fact, older hospital staff members and senior administrators tend to resent the use of the term. For example, a forty-one year old head nurse from the Yale-New Haven Hospital said, "The use of the term says more about the user than about the patient. It would be nice to think that it is only used by professionals when they are *very* tired and discouraged." Older informants understood the reason for the term gomer, but they considered its use to be unprofessional and excessively cruel.

The resistance to the term—as well as to letting the outside world know about the existence of the term—created definite obstacles to the conduct of fieldwork. After Victoria George distributed questionnaires at a Veterans Administration hospital in the Bay Area, she received an irate telephone call from the Chief Nurse of the hospital, demanding to know who she was—she is in fact a Licensed Vocational Nurse although not at that hospital and what she was doing circulating such a disgusting questionnaire in *her* hospital. The Chief Nurse contended that the questionnaire and the proposed study were distasteful because "gomer" had such negative connotations. When Miss George suggested the possibility that the gomer may have originated in Veterans Administration hospitals, the Chief Nurse replied, "I've worked in hospitals in the midwest where I tried to stop people from talking about 'gomers' and having just arrived here [the San Francisco Bay Area] I have found that everyone talks about 'gomers' in the west too." She continued, "It is the university doctors who bring the expression 'gomer' to the Veterans Administration hospitals, and I wouldn't think my staff would say such things. It must have come from the University!" (This sentiment could, of course, have been partly a reaction to the fact that we were individuals from the University of California, Berkeley, who were making the inquiry about the gomer. In terms of projection, this makes perfect sense. Rather than have the University point an accusing finger at members of the medical profession for using such a calloused concept, a member of the profession was suggesting that it was the university community which was responsible for the term.) After the questionnaires—most of which were blank—were retrieved from this Chief Nurse, an interesting additional one was received through the mail from a nurse in the very same hospital. This nurse elected to answer the question "Where do you work?" by writing, "The V.A., home of the gomer."

The particular association of the gomer with V.A. hospitals was confirmed by an expression elicited from a female intern who had been a medical student at a Veterans

Administration hospital in Omaha, Nebraska, in 1974. The expression "gomer patrol" referred to a group of rehabilitated gomers who came back to the V.A. hospital to take volunteer jobs sweeping the floors and the like because they very much wanted to be around the hospital and to be with their gomer friends. Other informants who knew the phrase "gomer patrol" indicated they had not heard the expression anywhere except in V.A. hospitals. The point is that even if the gomer did not originate in V.A. hospitals, there can be no question that the term is in common use in these hospitals. Administrators in such hospitals may do their best to stamp out such folklore (on the grounds that it is not in the best interest of projecting and protecting a favorable public image of doctors and nurses) but the gomer lives on—in fact and in folklore!

By a strange coincidence, it was in the same San Francisco Bay Area V.A. hospital where most of the questionnaires were returned blank that a "gomer assessment sheet" had been collected several years earlier in 1974.[10] This assessment sheet was circulated to doctors and medical students on Sunday morning rounds which are often especially long and tedious. The gomer point list is a prime example of in-group xerographic folklore. Through humor, a feeling of in-group solidarity is achieved. The humor is at the expense of the patient and it is for this reason that many doctors and nurses would prefer the gomer point list to remain strictly within the group.

The gomer point list surely functions for medical students as a remarkable enumeration of many of the things which can go wrong in patient care or rather things that patients can do to make life difficult or unpleasant for the hospital staff. The list also reassures the medical student or intern that he is not the only one who has to contend with the array of problems and frustrations caused by gomers. The premise of the gomer point lists is that the examining doctor is supposed to grade the patient as to his degree of gomerism. No doubt this parody also provides a form of revenge for all the required charts and records that conscientious medical personnel are constantly filling out for gomers and other patients. There are many gomer point lists; no two are identical. Some have special rules; for example, point values may double after midnight. The following 1974 version is representative. Many of the abbreviations and terms will not be familiar to the lay person, but some, like "Pt." for patient, or "dx" for diagnosis, will probably be intelligible enough without further explanation.

Gomer Assessment

Characteristic	*Assessed point value*
1. Transferred to another service on day of admission[11]	2
2. Stool found under dressing at first post op dressing changer[12]	10
with no B.M.'s recorded	14
3. Chart weighs over two pounds[13]	2
4. No known address other than other V.A. hospitals	6
5. Develops new complaint on evening of discharge[14]	4
6. Returns from leave with hematoma beneath incision[15]	4
7. Attempt at discharge by resident fails	6
each additional failure	2
8. Pt. has seizure or hematemesis while checking out clothing for discharge[16]	5
9. Pt. sent to ward by admitting physician with dx which pertains to organ system actually involved	-3

10. If diagnosis by admitting physician is correct — -5
11. Unemployed because of low back pain since:[17]
    Korean War — 1
    WW II — 3
    WW I — 8
    Spanish American War — 15
    Civil War — 25
    If due to arrow wound — 50
12. Pulls I.V. out[18] — 6
    If in full restraints with teeth — 15
    If edentulous — 20
13. Removes Foley catheter with bag inflated[19] — 9
    5 cc bag — 10
    30 cc bag — 30
    In full restraints — additional 10
14. Urinates on physician — 10
    on nurse — 8
    on orderly — 6
    on medical student — 4
15. Defecates in doctor's bag — with honors 23
16. Patient visited by American Legion — 1
    each additional visit — 1
    visited by VFW — 1/2
    by VFW auxiliary — 3
17. Pt. writes irate letter to American Legion on discharge — 8
    to Congressman — 10
18. Pt. gets Foley drainage tube tied into pajama tie — 10
19. Pt. has tracheotomy performed because of inability to trigger IPPB[20] — 12
20. Past history reads "See old chart"[21] — 1
21. Concentration of Airwick required in patient's room causes conjunctivitis among visiting personnel[22] — 4
22. Patient answers all questions asked to any other patient on open ward — 11
23. Patient drinks from urinal — 12
    from another patient's urinal — 14
24. Resident irately calls admitting when patient arrives on ward[23] — 6
25. Pt. fractures hip while leaving hospital — 8
26. Remains in hospital through entire resident rotation[24] — 10
    each additional rotation — 15
27. Service connected syphilis contracted before 1935 — 13
28. Unable to do B.E.; pt. returned to ward[25] — 7
29. Films have to be repeated more than twice — 2
    each additional repeat — 2
30. Films acceptable on first try — -5
31. Admitted with diagnosis of ataxia manifested by scratch marks on forehead secondary to attempts at nose picking[26] — 13
32. Refused admission at another VA hospital before being admitted — 2
    each additional hospital — 2

33. If Foley catheter is under more than 10 lbs. of traction without complaints
    from patient   11
34. Toenails cannot be cut with clippers, chisel or drill   7
35. Semiformed guaiac positive stool found more than 7 1/2 ft. from bed
    of source[27]   9
      each additional foot, add   1
      each wall or window, add   3
      on sidewalk below window near bed   14
36. Any two of the following: beard, lice, jaundice, disorientation, dacubiti,
    fecal impaction, ETOH on breath[28]   4
37. Regulates his own I.V.   4
      other patients' I.V.'s   4
38. Bites bulb off of oral thermometer   3
      rectal thermometer   4
      another pt.'s rectal thermometer   11
39. Found in another patient's bed[29]   3
      each additional pt. in bed   3
40. Drinks after shave lotion purchased in canteen   5
      each additional bottle   3
41. Pt.'s status prompts investigation by American Legion   6
42. Frequently overlooked on rounds[30]   3
43. Asks for schedule of American Legion movies on initial workup[31]   1
44. Source of admitting history is patient's mistress   4
      patient's mother   7
45. Admitting orders include, "Bath, STAT"[32]   5
46. Patient eats pajamas   11
      another patient's pajamas   13
47. Found in hallway without pajama bottoms   10
48. Loses more than 20 lbs. of adm. weight when put on diuretics[33]   14
49. Found with dentures in upside down   7
50. Develops chemical tracheitis secondary to aspiration of a fly[34]   11
51. Decubitus on occipital protuberance[35]   11
52. Defecates in or on bed of another pt.   14
      if while in bed with another pt.   19
53. Pt. irately asks "on what grounds" when told that he is going
    to be discharged[36]   10
54. Pt. states "I'm a disabled American Veteran" when irate resident, intern or
    medical student is called at 3 AM to restart I.V. pt. has pulled out while hav-
    ing the DTs[37]   17

Gomer point lists circulate in typewritten or xerographic form. It would be truly astonishing to find any individual who had committed to memory any of the more extensive versions. At Presbyterian Hospital in San Francisco in 1976, informants in the absence of a written list could remember only the following gomer items (which one can easily see are much less detailed than are the analogous offenses in the preceding text).[38]

1.   Drinking own urine   2

2.	Drinking roommate's urine	4
3.	Drinking from urinal while restrained	6
4.	Having a seizure without dropping a cigarette[39]	10
5.	Admitting note ends with "sorry"	10
6.	Climbing out of bed	2
7.	Climbing out of roommate's bed	4
8.	Biting through intravenous tubing	8
9.	Long yellow fingernails	6
10.	Toenails that curl under	6
11.	Covered with feces that is five or more days old	10
12.	Attempting to eat plastic silverware	8
13.	Admitted to nursing home before the age of 40	10
14.	Wearing patient gown backwards	4
15.	Positive O sign[40]	6
16.	Positive Q sign[41]	8
17.	Pulling out Foley catheter	5
18.	Pulling out Foley catheter with balloon up	7
19.	Defecates in medical student's bag	15
20.	BUN higher than IQ[42]	10
21.	Drinks out of toilet when NPO[43]	10
22.	Lice on patient survive 5 Kwellings[44]	12

These gomer point lists provide a very vivid and graphic portrait of the gomer. Several informants mentioned "gomer Olympics" with awards (medals) for patients who vomited the farthest or for patients who made the greatest number of suicide attempts in one week. This may be sick humor, but it is, after all, humor which is literally a response to sickness. Doctors and nurses are humans like everyone else and they need folkloristic outlets for the expression of their anxieties just as the members of any folk group do.

It is not hard to understand why medical practitioners might feel anger and hostility toward individuals who demand and often receive a disproportionate amount of the precious time and energy of the hospital staff. Why should doctors and nurses have to care for someone who evidently cares little or nothing about himself? No matter what is done for such patients, they will only return again and again to the hospital admitting room in the same miserable, unfortunate condition. In fact, the logic could easily be: the better the care in the hospital, the sooner the gomer will return to plague the staff once more. In contrast, there is presumably an incentive to cure a normal pesty or pesky patient. The sooner he or she is cured, the sooner he or she can be released from the hospital. This is decidedly not the case with the gomer. There seems to be no way of escaping permanently from such patients. Creation of the gomer figure and compiling gomer point lists is one of the few available defenses against this deplorable situation.

Other possible factors contributing to the tension existing between hospital staff members and gomers include critical differences in class and values. On the whole, doctors tend to come from affluent families, and they may not be accustomed to seeing or interacting with the "dregs of society" on a regular basis. Like other members of the middle or upper class, doctors may resent the gomer in part because he is perceived to be a creature or product of the welfare state. The gomer is considered to be a Medicare abuser, and it is the tax monies paid by doctors themselves, among others, that presumably pay for the care of such patients.

Gomers create stress in the hospital setting. In theory, doctors and nurses are pledged to offer the finest medical care they can to patients regardless of these patients' ethnic, religious, social and personal characteristics. Yet in practice, the personal hygiene and habits of the gomer are so repugnant and distasteful as to prove offensive even to the most hardened and dispassionate staff member. The inevitable stress in any doctor-patient relationship resulting from the anxiety which accompanies illness and its treatment is greatly exacerbated by the wretched and foul condition of the gomer. As folklorists we know that the greater the stress, the greater the need for folklore to relieve the pressures caused by that stress. The gomer as a figure of American hospital folk speech provides an esoteric socially sanctioned outlet for such pressures. The gomer as a shared folk concept tends to unite the hospital staff. Any in-group is likely to be strengthened by concentrating upon creating a stereotype of the out-group. So doctors and nurses need to have stereotypes of patients. It has long been known that patients need to resort to stereotypes about doctors and nurses. For example, it has been observed that patients' jokes such as the story of the nurse who wakes you up to give you a sleeping pill are not new, but are part of hospital folklore.[45] The point is that it is just as necessary and normal for medical practitioners to have folklore about patients.

Although the expression "gomer" would never be used directly to a patient or even in front of him or members of his family, it is possible notwithstanding that at times the gomer does sense the attitude of the staff toward him. In any case, the idealized stereotypes of doctors and nurses held by most patients and to some extent the doctors' and nurses' own professional behavioral code requires the suppression of emotion. Doctors and nurses are supposed to be cool and calm no matter what the medical crisis may be. The patient known as a gomer severely tests this professional facade with its requisite politeness and "bedside manner." As long as such patients exist, the gomer and other forms of American hospital folklore will continue to thrive. Like so much of folklore, the gomer and specifically the gomer assessment point list offer a safety valve opportunity for ritual reversal. The more disastrous and disgusting the behavior, the more points are assigned. Unrewarding activities are rewarded through the magic mirror of folklore, and for a much needed moment in the unremitting strain of hospital routine, human tragedy is miraculously translated into human comedy.

Notes

1.   Information was obtained by sending questionnaires to eight hospitals in five major American cities. Sixty-three questionnaires were filled out and returned by personnel from Yale-New Haven Hospital, Albany Medical Center, Millard Fillmore Hospital in Buffalo, University of Utah Medical Center in Salt Lake City, and from the following four hospitals in San Francisco: University of California Medical Center, Veterans Administration Hospital, San Francisco General Hospital, and Presbyterian Hospital of the Pacific Medical Center. We wish to thank all of the individuals who were kind enough to take the time to complete the gomer questionnaire. It should be noted that the geographical range of the data collected is much greater than that suggested by the list of hospitals above inasmuch as doctors and nurses move relatively freely from one part of the country to another. Responses to the question where the informant had first heard of the gomer elicited no less than thirty-six different places.

2. Harold Wentworth and Stuart Berg Flexner, *Dictionary of American Slang* (New York: Thomas Y. Crowell, 1967), p. 687.
3. Nevertheless, it is interesting that Andrew Borde in 1552 in The *breviary of healthe* claimed that "gomer passion," by which he apparently meant such supposed sexual anomalies as masturbation and nocturnal emissions, was derived from the earlier sin of the people of Gomorrah. See Robert H. MacDonald, "The Frightful Consequences of Onanism: Notes on the History of a Delusion," *Journal of the History of Ideas,* 28 (1967), 431. The more general connotations of "self-abuse," a conventional euphemism for masturbation, might well apply to the modern gomer who makes little effort to take care of himself.
4. We have relied upon the *Oxford English Dictionary* (1933) for our discussion of *gomerel* and *gome.* For *gomus,* see also J. S. Farmer and W. E. Henley, *Slang and Its Analogues* (New York: Arno Press, 1970).
5. This might seem to suggest that the west is a bit more tolerant and hospitable than the east! One informant could recall only a portion of what she remembered of a different acronymic referent: "Goes Out _____ _____ Repeatedly." The variation in alleged referents of course confirms the overall traditionality of the word "gomer."
6. This information was collected in December 1964, by M. Patricia Miller from Susan Halverson who was at that time a Registered Nurse in Oakland, California.
7. A turkey is a patient who is feigning illness and/or has an obnoxious personality. A crock is also a patient pretending to be sick. Crock implies lie, as in the more general idiom "a crock of shit." A trainwreck is someone who is *very* sick. He has several medical problems simultaneously and he is usually comatose. A lizard is a physically dirty patient with scaly skin. A reeker is a dirty patient with a strong disagreeable body odor.
8. See Albert B. Friedman, "The Scatological Rites of Burglars," *Western Folklore,* 27 (1968), 171–179; and Theodor Reik, *The Unknown Murderer* (New York: International Universities Press, 1945), pp. 76–81.
9. The following parody of the "Twelve Days of Christmas" was collected by Victoria George from the San Francisco General Hospital Emergency Room in 1977. Written by nurses Lauren Lockridge and Philis Harding, it contains a number of examples of hospital folk speech:

> On the twelfth day of Christmas
> Central sent to M.E.H.
> Twelve 'terns a'flailing
> Eleven blades a'cutting
> Ten grumes a'scratching
> Nine turkeys seizing
> Eight pelvics waiting
> Seven psychs a'screaming
> Six stabs a'swearing
> Five P.I.D.s
> Four D.O.A.s
> Three flail chests
> Two "H" O.D.s
> and a gomer in the D.T.s

For the benefit of readers unfamiliar with medical argot, Central Emergency has sent the following to Mission Emergency Hospital: Twelve interns are flailing about, that is, acting in a frantic way to no useful purpose. Eleven surgeons are performing with scalpels. Ten grumes (extra filthy gomers) are scratching to relieve their itching. Nine turkeys are having or are pretending to have seizures. Eight women are waiting to have pelvic examinations. Seven psychotic patients are screaming. Six victims of stabbing are cursing. Five women have pelvic inflammatory disease. Four individuals are brought in "Dead on Arrival." Three individuals are brought in with flail chests, that is, with crushed rib cages. Two drug users who overdosed with Heroin are admitted. A gomer suffering from delerium tremens is the first to enter the emergency room, a fact which signals the importance of the gomer in hospital life.

10. This excellent text was collected in March 1974, by Jo Anne Morrow from William Cory who was then a medical student in San Francisco.

11. Rather than burden those readers who may already be acquainted with hospital routine by repeatedly interrupting the text with bracketed explanations, we have chosen instead to place brief explanatory remarks in footnotes for those who desire further information about abbreviations and medical procedures. The transferral to another service means that the patient upon admission presented a complaint, but the doctor later found something entirely different. (Or it could refer to the fact that when an examining doctor investigated an initial complaint he found it to be groundless, whereupon the patient registered a new complaint requiring a transfer to another service and a different examiner.)

12. This means that the patient somehow managed to place feces under his sterile dressing after surgery and before the doctors changed it a few hours later. Such a patient would probably be in a confused state.

13. The excessive weight of the chart implies that the patient has been in the hospital a long time, long enough to have accumulated a very extensive chart.

14. When the patient discovers he is scheduled to be released, he finds another symptom so that he can stay longer in the hospital.

15. A hematoma is a tumor containing effused blood or what in lay terms is called a bruise or swelling. The implication is clearly that the patient didn't take very good care of himself.

16. Hematemesis means vomiting blood. This and seizures are considered serious medical problems, and either would require additional hospitalization.

17. Many doctors and nurses tend to consider low back pain as an attention-getting device rather than a legitimate complaint.

18. I.V. means intravenous.

19. A Foley catheter is a tube inserted into the urethra extending into the bladder for the purpose of draining the bladder of urine. A balloon is attached to the end of the tube that is in the bladder to hold it in place. It is quite painful to pull out.

20. A tracheotomy is the surgical creation of an opening into the trachea (windpipe through the neck. Through a tube which is inserted in this opening, the patient breathes. IPPB is an abbreviation for the Intermittent Positive Pressure Breathing machine which is started by the patient taking a deep breath through a mouthpiece. If a patient were unable to do this, doctors might well perform a tracheotomy.

21. Old chart is a record of past hospitalizations. If a patient came in with the same problem repeatedly, a doctor might make this notation. The implication is also that the patient has a very extensive past history. In theory, a doctor should always make a new examination and record a current history, but when confronted with a gomer, a doctor might be sorely tempted not to bother.

22. Conjunctivitis is an irritation of the mucous membrane of the eyes. Airwick is a commercial brand-name air freshener designed to remove or conceal unpleasant odors. A strong deodorizing agent, Airwick in *very* concentrated form could cause eye irritation. The reference is, of course, to the foul smell of the gomer caused by his poor personal hygiene.

23. The doctor is angry because he feels that this patient has been admitted unnecessarily.

24. A resident's rotation is usually of six weeks duration which would mean a fairly protracted hospital stay for the patient.

25. B.E. refers to a barium enema. Barium sulfate is used in a standard X-ray procedure to visualize the digestive tract including the colon. In order for a clear X-ray picture to be taken, the colon must be free of fecal matter. Most patients are easily prepared for this through diet and/or laxatives. Some gomer types, however, are very full of stool and the test has to be repeated again and again. Not until the gomers have evacuated their colons completely are there likely to be successful X-ray films. (The reference in the next entry to repeated films has to do with the same problem.) The time required for the gomer to prepare himself sufficiently for the barium enema

may thereby entail an extra day or two in the hospital.

26. Ataxia is a failure of muscular coordination resulting in irregular muscular action. Presumably a patient with this condition desiring to pick his nose might miss, causing scratches on his forehead. The image evoked is similar to the Polack joke: How did the Polack get 35 holes in his head? Trying to learn to eat with a fork. See Alan Dundes, "A Study of Ethnic Slurs: The Jew and the Polack in the United States," *Journal of American Folklore,* 84 (1971), 201.

27. Guaiac is a test to determine whether there is blood in the feces. Guaiac positive means that blood is present. Most gomers are alcoholics and bleeding problems are common enough among severe alcoholics.

28. A decubitus ulcer is a bed sore. It is caused by prolonged pressure resulting from a patient's confinement to bed for a long period of time. ETOH means alcohol.

29. This refers to a patient's being disoriented or confused.

30. This suggests the patient has been there so long that the doctors have nothing more to say about him and see little point in checking him.

31. The implication is that if a patient is well enough to want to know what movies are playing, he is probably not sick enough to warrant being admitted, and he is simply using the hospital as a recreation center.

32. STAT means immediately if not sooner—from the Latin *statim.* The patient is so dirty that the admitting doctor is unable to examine him thoroughly.

33. While it is likely that a gomer might be suffering from fluid buildup, losing twenty pounds through diuretics is probably a facetious allusion to the gomer's having been on a liquid diet before coming to the hospital, the liquid being some form of alcohol!

34. The patient has an infected trachea (windpipe) as a result of having inhaled a fly.

35. This is a bed sore on the back of the head. It implies that the patient has been lying down in bed absolutely supine for an extended period of time.

36. The patient does not want to be released from the hospital.

37. D.T.s means delirium tremens, a condition marked by sweating, trembling, hallucinations, etc., caused by excessive drinking of alcohol.

38. This gomer list was collected orally by Victoria George from her colleagues. The various details were elicited individually from different informants.

39. If an individual were really having a seizure, it would be impossible for him to hold on to a cigarette. The description means that the patient is only pretending to have a seizure.

40. This refers to the mouth positioning of a sleeping or comatose patient. Specifically, the mouth is slightly open and more or less in the shape of an O. In some versions, it signifies that the patient is totally unresponsive and that he may be about to die.

41. This is a variant of the previous sign. The patient's mouth hangs open in the shape of an O but in this case his tongue is hanging out, suggesting an overall configuration of Q. The Q sign indicates a more serious condition than the O sign inasmuch as the protrusion of the tongue may signify the loss of muscular coordination.

42. BUN, an abbreviation for blood urea nitrogen, is a test which provides an index of renal function. Since many gomers have poor renal function, their BUN would be high. Normal results are 18–22 so that even a high BUN figure would be far less than the average IQ of 100. An IQ lower than a BUN would be low indeed.

43. NPO means nothing by mouth *(nihil per ōs),* that is, the patient is to have nothing to eat or drink.

44. Kwell is a commercial brand of lindane, a preparation used in treatment of scabies and pediculosis (lice infestation). It is a fairly strong agent which normally kills lice with one application.

45. Rose Laub Coser, "Some Social Functions of Laughter: A Study of Humor in a Hospital Setting," *Human Relations,* 12 (1959), 176. For more examples of hospital folklore see Lois A. Monteiro, "Nursing-Lore," *New York Folklore Quarterly,* 29 (1973), 97–110.

B

"When You Hear Hoofbeats, Think Horses, Not Zebras": A Folk Medical Diagnostic Proverb

IN 1995, A CASE HISTORY was reported in the *Journal of Clinical Endocrinology and Metabolism* entitled "Sometimes the Hooves Do Belong to Zebras! An Unusual Case of Hypopituitarism." In 1993, a guest editorial "Horses and Zebras" in *Regional Immunology* offered alternative explanations for immune regulation in lungs. In 1992, Drs. Stephen G. Pauker and Richard I. Kopelman published a case history in the *New England Journal of Medicine* "Interpreting Hoofbeats: Can Bayes Help Clear the Haze?" They recommended the use of "Bayes' rule" which refers to the likelihood of disease in a patient with a given set of findings being estimated as the proportion of patients with the same findings who also have the disease, and this inspired a letter to the editor by Dr. Otto Kuchel. This letter, accompanied by a response from the authors, appeared a year later in the same journal. In none of these three instances is the reference to hoofbeats, horses and zebras in any way explained. The clear implication is that readers of these technical case histories, that is, members of the medical profession, are thoroughly familiar with a traditional metaphor involving hoofbeats, and that therefore no explanation of the metaphor is necessary.

In 1993, a case history contained originally in Kenneth Klein's *Getting Better: A Medical Student's Story* (1981:93, 95–96) was reprinted in *Health* but with a new title: "When You Hear Hoofbeats, Think Horses, Not Zebras: Case No. 1478." The title is not explained, but the case well illustrates the sense of the expression. It involved a woman who hadn't had a period for over three months. At the time Klein was a young inexperienced medical student who tried to impress his supervisor by rattling off a series of possible diagnoses along with various tests that might be run in order to confirm or disconfirm them. His supervisor's response: "Whew! That's a very nice differential diagnosis, but you forgot an important cause of secondary amenorrhea, in fact the most common one. Remember, in medicine common things are common. What's the first test to do before you get all those fancy hormone assays?" Klein racked his brains but could not think of anything else. His supervisor had to tell him which test to run. "Half an hour later, the pregnancy test came back positive." The moral is clear: Klein had proposed zebras when he should have been thinking horses!

In 1996, Kathryn Hunter in an essay in *Theoretical Medicine* devoted entirely to a discussion of the proverb claims that "When you hear hoofbeats, don't think zebras" is clinical medicine's most frequently heard maxim (1996:225). But she astutely points out that the aphorism paradoxically contains the seeds of its own negation. There wouldn't be any point in attempting to dissuade doctors from thinking zebras if there were not an obvious tendency to do so. It is rather analogous to understanding that the Ten Commandments plainly refer to wishful thinking on the part of all those who adhere to the religious faiths based on the Decalogue. There would be little point in forbidding behavior for which there was no desire to indulge. Hunter describes the paradoxicality of the maxim very well indeed: ". . . the zebras are there, unforgotten, unforgettable, right in the aphorism. Not only does the advice generate its own contradiction among the young, but as a reminder to forget, it is paradoxical in itself. As long as the injunction not to think zebras comes to mind, zebras cannot be unthought. Physicians think zebras as they think not to think them" (1996:2128). And certainly the vast majority of the various communications in medical journals referring to "zebras" would tend to support Hunter's argument.

In 1995, in a chapter of his book, *The Man Who Grew Two Breasts* which bears the title "The Hoofbeats of a Zebra," Berton Roueché describes the sad case of a young woman whose myasthenia gravis went undiagnosed for some years until one doctor finally recognized her symptoms. The doctor who had had a long-standing special interest in the disease explained his success: "There is a saying about diagnosis—about why doctors often fail to recognize one of the less-common diseases. It goes: When you hear hoofbeats, you don't necessarily think of a zebra. I recognized the hoofbeats of a zebra. That was my only magic" (1995:175).

In 1996, Dr. Charles Davant in an article in *Medical Economics* entitled "When You Hear Hoofbeats, Sniff the Air," referred to "the old saw—think horses, not zebras, when you hear hoofbats (1996: 107). But after presenting several case histories encountered as a family physician in Blowing Rock, North Carolina, Davant takes issue with the advice articulated in the "old saw" when he concludes "As I've always maintained hoofbeats sometimes *do* belong to zebras" (1996:114). In 1997, virologist C. J. Peters chose to title the prologue to his fascinating autobiographical account of his lifetime of tracking virally caused infectious diseases "The Hoofbeats of Zebras." Peters begins his book "There's an old adage in medicine that goes something like this: *Common things occur commonly. Uncommon things don't. Therefore, when you hear hoofbeats, think horses, not zebras* (1997:1). Hunter offers another version of the first portion of the adage: "Uncommon presentations of common diseases are more common than common presentations of uncommon diseases" (1996:227). But Peters as a medical specialist, tends to be more concerned with zebras than horses. In his words, "I didn't want to be overly alarmist, because I knew very well that most hoofbeats in our neck of the woods come from horses . . . But what if the hoofbeats we were hearing weren't from the proverbial horses? What if it was zebras after all?" (1997:261, 19). Pauker and Kopelman end their 1992 communication with a stronger warning: "Hoofbeats usually signal the presence of horses, but the judicious application of Bayes' rule can help prevent clinicians from being trampled by a stampeding herd that occasionally includes a zebra" (1992:1013). Similar caution is urged by Dr. Alan J. Waldman of the Department of Psychiatry at the College of Medicine at the University of Florida. His 1992 letter to the *Journal of Neuropsychiatry,* starts with "A classic axiom taught to virtually all medical students, especially during their internal medicine rotation is 'When you hear hoofbeats, think of horses and not zebras.'" But Waldman continues, "Yet in the practice of neuropsychiatry one must be continually aware that the hoofbeats may in fact not be horses" (19923:113). He then proceeds to demonstrate the validity of his caveat by reporting two case histories where what appeared initially to be psychiatric symptoms proved to be the results of relatively rare metabolic disorders.

In yet another attempt to counter the alleged wisdom of the proverb, this time from the area of dermatology, Dr. Richard W. Sagebiel, writing an editorial in the *Journal of the American Academy of Dermatology* in 1995 entitled "Who needs zebras?," begins by claiming that few medical students avoid the obligatory saying, "When you hear hoofbeats,

think horses, not zebras." He calls it a "perpetuated cliché" which encourages "sloppy thinking." He is particularly concerned with a medical "zebra" called desmoplastic neurotrophic
melanoma (DNM). Admitting that it is "uncommon, perhaps rare, and difficult to diagnose," Sagebiel nevertheless urges his colleagues to be on the lookout for it. In his words,
"Few among us look at a nonpigmented 'scar' and think DNM. And yet if we do not begin
to pay attention to the 'zebras' of diagnosis, then as consultants we will be replaced by generalists who will think 'horses'" (1995:800). Specialists' fear that they might be replaced
by generalists who are deemed incapable of distinguishing the more exotic zebras from
the commonplace horses seems to be quite widespread, judging from the number of communications found in so many medical journals, especially those serving as the principal
forums of specialized medical practitioners, urging that one cannot ignore the serious-
ness of failing to recognize life-threatening zebras. Indeed, it would appear that the original medical school aphorism advising newly educated doctors to think horses rather than
zebras has been virtually repudiated insofar as the conventional wisdom seems rather to
propose the opposite: think zebras, not horses!

It is difficult to ascertain just how old the hoofbeats proverb is. Samuel Shem in his best-
seller *The House of God,* a fast-paced novel describing the rigors and horrors of being an intern
after completion of medical school first published in 1978, refers disparagingly to a typical
medical student when he "hears hoofbeats outside his window, the first thing he thinks of
is a zebra" (1998:46). There can be no question about the meaning of "zebra" in this context as Shem provides a helpful glossary of terms as an appendix to his novel where zebra is
defined as "an obscure diagnosis" (1998:429). Elsewhere in the novel, the protagonist doctor reports that he learned more about functioning in the intensive care unit from the experienced night nurse than he had in his "four rarefied" medical school years which were filled
with details of "zebraic diseases" (1998: 335). Yet this term "zebra" most often heard initially
in the course of a medical school internship or residency, that is, during the early stages of
training, not surprisingly is older than 1978. A retired cardiologist in Berkeley, California,
reported in 1998 that he had learned the following dictum at Cincinnati General Hospital
circa 1960: "If you hear hoofbeats behind you, don't turn around and expect to see zebras."
Hematologists at Johns Hopkins Hospital confirmed this approximate dating of the dictum, and it is very likely that the expression is considerably older than 1960.

Although the proverb seems to be largely confined to the medical community and is
not widely known to the general population, there is some slight evidence that it may
have diffused outside the world of medical practice. For instance, Shems Friedlander's
book *When You Hear Hoofbeats Think of a Zebra* first published in 1987 contains no
reference whatsoever to anything remotely related to medicine. The book is a literary
polemic advocating Sufism and the title is meant merely to encourage the reader to stop
thinking in old tradition-bound ways and to start trying to gain knowledge of Allah
through Islam and Sufism (Friedlander 1987:1). On the other hand, the fact that the
proverb seems to be largely restricted to members of the medical profession may explain
why it is not to be found in Charles Clay Doyle's valuable 1996 listing of "new" proverbs
of the twentieth century.

The ostensible meaning of the proverb in its more familiar medical context is to warn
medical students about the dangers of looking too hard for esoteric rare diseases, thereby
perhaps resulting in the overlooking of the most obvious and common diagnosis indicated
by the symptoms manifested by the patient. There is another proverb employed by physicians which conveys the same message: "It's always darkest at the foot of the lighthouse."

The proverb's meaning is that things that are common and should be easy to see are often overlooked in favor of the remote. This proverb which is found in general usage, not just in a medical context, exhibits various forms, as does all folklore, e.g., "It is always dark just under a lamp" or "It is always darkest under the lantern" (Mieder 1992:134) and it is also known in Japan "The base of a lighthouse is dark" (Mieder 1986: 278).

The advice is also reminiscent of that offered by "Occam's razor." William of Occam, an early fourteenth century English philosopher, (c. 1285–1349), is credited with articulating the principle *Entia non sunt multiplicando praeter necessitatem* which literally translates roughly as "Entities should not be multiplied without necessity." However, the general agreed-upon meaning, according to the *Oxford Dictionary of English Proverbs,* is that: "for purposes of explanation, things not known to exist should not, unless it is absolutely necessary, be postulated as existing." In other words, the simpler explanation is always to be preferred over a more complex one.

The problem with Occam's razor is that simple solutions to complex problems do not always suffice. And the same holds for the hoofbeats proverb. Sometimes, it does turn out that the hoofbeats were made by zebras, not the more common horses. Some doctors have even had their own very personal experience in the fallacy of always assuming horses rather than zebras. For example, Dr. John H. Frierson writing in the *Virginia Medical Quarterly* in 1995 provides a telling illustration. "It started out," he says, "as a sore right shoulder which I attributed to a combination of golf practice and yard work." At the suggestion of a physiatrist who made a provisional diagnosis which included bursitis, he tried physical therapy which did afford some temporary relief, but soon thereafter the symptoms moved to his left shoulder and then down to both legs. "At its peak," Frierson reports, "I was a virtual cripple." Finally, a neurologist helped make the correct diagnosis of polymyalgia rheumatica (PMR), and a rheumatologist then prescribed prednisone and a single dose completely relieved all the soreness and stiffness. Frierson's conclusion: the initial diagnosis of a quite common ailment such as bursitis had been a mistake. "No consideration was given to the rarer 'zebra' diseases, i.e., PMR. As a result time was lost in making the diagnosis" (1995:79). Frierson's final advice: "So watch out for the 'zebras.' They're out there and they'll getcha!"

How the dilemma in choosing the proper diagnosis on the basis of just hoofbeats can be exacerbated is illustrated in the following narrative:

> Late at night in an institution—presumably a famous teaching hospital—an internist and a family practitioner are sitting in the on-call room and hear the unmistakable sound of hoofbeats in the hallway. They both look up at each other, and the family practitioner says, "My God! Horses?" And the internist cocks his head, listens for a second more and says, "No, Zebras" (Prasad 1998:19).

In this text, there is a clear opposition between the generalist and the specialist. The generalist interprets the hoofbeats as being those made by horses. This is the obvious, more common inference to be drawn. However, the generalist does not simply assert his conclusion. Rather he puts his remark in the form of a question, as if asking for confirmation from the specialist. The internist, the specialist in this instance, listens further apparently utilizing his greater knowledge of such phenomena before correcting his generalist colleague by pronouncing the hoofbeats as those made by zebras. The explosion of medical knowledge has made it more and more difficult for general practitioners to keep pace with all the new advances made in all branches of medical research. The corresponding increase in the number of specializations in medicine has created an even larger gap between members of such specializations and the old-fashioned general practitioner. A zebra belongs to the *equus* family, but it is rather a distinctive example with its striking black and white stripes. Presumably it takes a highly experienced ear to be able to distinguish the sound of exotic zebra hoofbeats from those made by ordinary garden-variety horses. And that is precisely why the metaphor is so apt. Of course, the very idea of being able to make any kind of an educated guess as to the identity of an animal solely on the basis of the sound of hoofbeats is itself a bit of folkloric fantasy attesting to the very real difficulties faced by physicians who are often asked to diagnose illnesses without very much in the way of defining symptoms.

So what can we conclude about the dictum, aphorism, adage, proverb: When you hear hoofbeats, think horses, not zebras? Is it true folk wisdom, in this instance, true folk medical wisdom with respect to the difficult task of making diagnoses from limited data? The answer to this question turns on the very nature of the proverb genre. Proverbs contain relative, not absolute wisdom. The wisdom is always contingent on time and place, in short, on context. The very existence of contradictory proverbs in many languages and cultures demonstrates the relativity of proverbial wisdom. "Look before you leap" recommends caution before action; "He who hesitates is lost" advocates an opposite course. "Absence makes the heart grow fonder" is poor solace for the cynical "Out of sight; out of mind." Hunter reminds us: "They say you can't teach an old dog new tricks" and "You're never to old to learn" (1996:239). With the understanding that proverbial wisdom is always bounded by contextual considerations, we can see that "Think horses" might be good advice for young doctors who have just completed medical school and inevitably have been introduced to a plethora of rare and esoteric diseases. On the other hand, more experienced medical practitioners who are well aware of the greater statistical frequency of "common" diseases should remain vigilant for the possibility of a zebra occurring on occasion among herds of horses.

The importance of context also is apparent in consideration of two co-existing yet contradictory modern phenomena: defensive medicine and managed care. In the case of the former, physicians may conduct tests or procedures to investigate the possibility of a zebra which, if overlooked, could result in a lawsuit. The other force, managed care, which controls spending by closely monitoring physicians' treatment of patients, encourages the interpretation of hoofbeats as horses to avoid unnecessary spending with a low probability of finding a zebra. Thus, doctors must consider the adage amidst constraints which include the threats of malpractice if zebras are ignored and refused reimbursement if zebras are sought.

The issue of general practitioner or generalist versus specialist is not so easy to resolve. Clearly, patients need both kinds of physicians. The rapidly expanding universe of information relevant to a particular disease is such that only a specialist can possibly keep up. No one physician can possibly be expected to have total knowledge of all areas of medical practice. So by definition, a generalist's competence in any one area cannot match that of the qualified specialist. On the other hand, the whole is always greater than the sum of its parts. Partial knowledge, no matter how great, may not necessarily lead to the optimum treatment. If one asks a surgeon for advice, the recommendation is very likely to be for surgery! A general practitioner who can synthesize the sometimes contradictory counsel of specialists remains critical for ideal patient care. So in that sense, when one hears hoofbeats, one should not really choose between assuming either horses or zebras, but one should rather in the best interest of the patient consider both alternatives.

References

Davant, Charles. 1996. When You Hear Hoofbeats, Sniff the Air. *Medical Economics* 73 (19):107,111–112, 114.

Doyle, Charles Clay. 1996. On "New" Proverbs and the Conservativeness of Proverb Dictionaries *Proverbium* 13:69–84.

Friedlander, Shems. 1987. *When You Hear Hoofbeats, Think of a Zebra: Talks on Sufism.* New York: Harper & Row.

Frierson, John H., Jr. 1995. Watch Out for the "Zebras." *Virginia Medical Quarterly* 122:79.

Hunter, Kathryn. 1996. "Don't Think Zebras": Uncertainty, Interpretation, and the Place of Paradox in Clinical Education. *Theoretical Medicine* 17:225–241.

Klein, Kenneth. 1981. *Getting Better: A Medical Student's Story.* Boston: Little, Brown.

———. 1993. When You Hear Hoofbeats, Think Horses, Not Zebras: Case No. 1478. *Health* 7(3):100–101.

Kuchel, Otto. 1993. Clinical Problem-Solving: Interpreting Hoofbeats: Can Bayes Help Clear the Haze? *The New England Journal of Medicine* 328:290.

Mieder, Wolfgang. 1986. *The Prentice-Hall Encyclopedia of World Proverbs.* Englewood Cliffs: Prentice-Hall.

Mieder, Wolfgang, Stewart A. Kingsbury, and Kelsie B. Harder. 1992. *A Dictionary of American Proverbs.* New York: Oxford University Press.

Pauker, Stephen G., and Richard I. Kopelman. 1992. Interpreting Hoofbeats: Can Bayes Help Clear the Haze? *The New England Journal of Medicine* 327:1009–1013.

Peters, C. J., and Mark Olshaker. 1997. *Virus Hunter: Thirty Years of Battling Hot Viruses Around the World.* New York: Anchor Books.

Prasad, Che. 1998. *Physician Humor Thyself: An Analysis of Doctor Jokes.* Winston-Salem: Harbinger Medical Press.

Rou-ché, Berton. 1995. *The Man Who Grew Two Breasts and Other True Tales of Medical Detection.* New York: Truman Talley Books.

Sagebiel, Richard W. 1995. Who Needs Zebras? Comments on Desmoplastic Melanoma. *Journal of the American Academy of Dermatology* 32:800–802.

Shem, Samuel. 1998. *The House of God.* New York: Dell.

Stein-Streilein, Joan, and Richard P. Phipps. 1993. Horses and Zebras. *Regional Immunology* 5:127–133.

Waldman, Alan J. 1992. Sometimes When You Hear Hoofbeats. . . . Two Cases of Inherited Metabolic Diseases With Initial Presentation of Psychiatric Symptoms. *Journal of Neuropsychiatry* 4:113–114.

Wilson, R. P., ed. 1970. *The Oxford Dictionary of English Proverbs.* Third Edition. Oxford: Clarendon Press.

Part III

Symbol and Mind

14

GETTING THE FOLK AND THE LORE TOGETHER

Introduction

This essay addresses the connection of Dundes's folkloristic perspective with semiotics, concisely defined as the study of signs. The ideas in it became central to his symbolist approach in "Projection in Folklore" (1976a), which was incorporated in *Interpreting Folklore* (1980b), and it stood as a manifesto for a psychoanalytic enterprise within folkloristics. Dundes originally wrote it in 1975 as a presentation to the Charles Sanders Peirce Symposium on Semiotics and the Arts at Johns Hopkins University. The goal of semiotics, to understand how meaning is made and understood, was of special importance to Dundes, evident in his opening verbal salvo: "Folklore *means* something." What it meant, he announced, was often not obvious from a literal reading of folkloric texts; it was indeed often something about something else. The source of that meaning in something else involved anxiety, ambivalence, or ambiguity, contextualized in sociohistorical conditions as well as in psychological development. The title of the essay referred to the polarization between those scholars emphasizing the social basis of the folk, and the predominantly literary approach to the texts of lore. Dundes proposed to bring the two together in the discipline of folklore study, by drawing attention to the mind as a source of projective expression that reflects and creates social organization and interaction.

As a structuralist influenced by Ferdinand de Saussure's ideas of signs (the basic unit of language) and signification (the separation of the signified object from the signifier), and the distinction between *langue* (the systematic dimension of natural language) and *parole* (speaking, or manifestations of *langue*), Dundes also related folkloristics to semiotics, interpreting expressive culture as symbolic systems. Dundes's contribution was to suggest applying psychoanalytic concepts of the unconscious, and projection, to the study of meaning in a cultural context. "There is patterning and system in folklore," Dundes asserted, "so that the symbol employed in any one given folkloristic (con)text may be related to a general system of symbols." In folkloristic analysis, his preference for the rhetoric of symbol over signs derived from the psychological view that meanings resided not only in language, but also in the entire domain of culture. This view was the background for his statement that "what I am saying is that within a cultural relative system of symbols, the use of a particular symbol may be remarkably consistent. I also hasten to add that symbols may carry multiple meanings."

Dundes presented folkloric examples (jump rope rhymes and wedding rituals) that he interpreted earlier as an anthropological "mirror of culture," but which, in this essay, he couched as symbolic readings in "projective" processes. He revised the Freudian theory of projection by distinguishing projection that transfers feelings and desires to an external object, so that, for example, male sexual impulses might be viewed in phallic references. Dundes called this projective process one of "more or less direct translations of reality into fantasy." Projective inversion, on the other hand, described a sublimation or avoidance, where an undesirable wish toward someone else was reversed, so that the statement "I hate him" became "He hates me." Dundes argued that the projective inversion in the Oedipal plot inverted the son's wishful thinking to kill the father into the father killing the son. From the viewpoint of the son, blame is placed on the victim (the father), and guilt is avoided. Dundes used this concept of projective inversion to explain narrative details involving incest, murder, cannibalism, and homosexuality, all of which appear out of place if seen as a true mirror of culture (see, for example, "Madness in Method Plus a Plea for Projective Inversion in Myth" in the present volume; also 1989e, 1976b, 1991b).

In the present essay, Dundes referred to Henry Nash Smith's theory of "virgin land," which deserves some elaboration because of its use of symbolist approaches in the interpretation of American culture. Smith had argued that even before America was settled, an image of the New World had been developed in narrative and art, comparing it to a biblical garden paradise and mythical wilderness. Europeans imagined the lure of America as a bounty of fertile, untrampled land. The natives did not deserve this plenty, European thinking went, because, using the rhetoric of reproduction, they supposedly did not make the land productive or cultivable. Smith saw a new national identity emerging even among a panoply of settlers, as a result of communicating shared values through the symbolic lessons of folklore, literature, and art. Settlers may not have been aware of the fusion of these values into cognitively held "myths" or folk ideas, but their expressions and actions revealed collectively shared beliefs that were distinct from those in Europe ([1950] 2005). Smith's theory, then, related to Dundes's, in representing the importance of folklore in identity-building, at a national as well as a local level, and in positing that the meaning of these expressions and actions had sources in unconsciously held ideas. Dundes made more of the sexual symbolism of the land's "virginity" than Smith, and related the national mission to penetrate the untouched frontier to updated ideas, such as America's space program, science fiction, and commercial advertising. (For a connection of Dundes's ideas to American Studies, see Gürel 2006).

Along with the virgin land of the frontier, race is another constructed American image, Dundes viewed it as one more anxiety-producing problem which was expressed in folkloric form. He pointed out that the constructed binary of white/black in American culture favored the superiority of whiteness. Even celebrated black folk heroes, such as John Henry, drew his critical inquiry into unconscious racism. Dundes contended that in social movements such as the Civil Rights movement, this troubling binary produced humorous responses that testified to the adjustments needed for social change. From a symbolist approach, the elephant jokes which arose during the period combined sexual imagery with the social symbolism of the elephant (representing African Americans). Simon Bronner made the argument that there was a symbolic shift of the elephant to women's independence, as the feminist movement advanced during the 1970s (Bronner 1988, 125–27). For more discussions of racial (and racist) folklore, see Dundes and Abrahams 1987; and Dundes [1973] 1990. For an alternative reading of the elephant joke, see Oring 1975b.

Getting the Folk and
the Lore Together

FOLKLORE *MEANS* SOMETHING—TO THE TALE teller, to the song singer, to the riddler, and to the audience or addressees. A given item of folklore may mean different things to different tale tellers or to different audiences. It may mean different things to different members of the same audience; it may mean different things to a single tale teller at different times in his life. So much seems obvious. But despite the assiduous collection of scores and scores of folklore texts, there has been precious little attention paid to what these texts mean—which is sad and curious, for folkloristics, with semiotics, must ultimately be concerned with meaning.

One difficulty impeding the study of folklore's meaning stems from the fact that a goodly portion of folklore is fantasy, collective or collectivized fantasy. I do not refer here to any Jungian sense of a collective unconscious. When I speak of folklore being collective, I mean that a myth or a folksong is known by more than a single individual—usually many individuals—and it is transmitted from person to person, often over the course of generations. Collective folklore also differs from individual dreams. Dreams appear to be similar to narratives, in part because they are related in words. But folktales, unlike individual dreams, must appeal to the psyches of many, many individuals if they are to survive.

It is my contention that much of the meaning of folkloric fantasy is unconscious. Indeed, it would have to be unconscious—in the Freudian sense—for folklore to function as it does. For among its functions, folklore provides a socially sanctioned outlet for the expression of what cannot be articulated in more usual ways. It is precisely in jokes, folktales, folksongs, proverbs, children's games, gestures, etc. that anxieties can be vented. If people knew exactly what they were doing when they told a joke to their boss or to their spouse (or if the boss or spouse knew what they were doing), the joke would probably cease to be an escape mechanism. People need such mechanisms, which is why there will always be folklore, and also incidentally why there is always new folklore being created to take care of new anxieties—I refer, for example, to the folklore of bureaucracy transmitted so effectively by the office-copier machine.

The unconscious nature of so much of folklore makes the study of meaning difficult, but not impossible. Fortunately, there is patterning and system in folklore, so that the symbol employed in any one given folkloric (con)text may be related to a general system of symbols. This does not mean that I think any one symbol is necessarily universal. In fact, I know of no symbol which is reported from all peoples, just as I know of no myth which has universal distribution. What I am saying is that within a culturally relative system of symbols, the use of a particular symbol may be remarkably consistent. I also hasten to add that symbols may carry multiple meanings.

I intend to illustrate the above by referring to several specific examples of folklore, but before I do so I should like to mention briefly the crucial device of projection. In psychology, projection refers to the tendency to attribute to another person or to the environment

275

what is actually within oneself. What is attributed is usually some internal impulse or feeling which is painful, unacceptable, or taboo. The individual is not consciously aware of that; he or she perceives the external object as possessing the taboo tendencies, without recognizing their source in himself or herself.

Most of the examples of folklore I shall discuss will be familiar ones, to allow readers to confirm or reject my ideas out of their own knowledge of the culture.

Let us begin with a standard jump rope rhyme.

> Fudge, fudge, tell the judge
> Mama's got a newborn baby.
> It ain't no girl, it ain't no boy
> Just a newborn (or "common" or "plain ol'," or "ordinary") baby
> Wrap it up in tissue paper
> Throw (send) it down the elevator.
> First floor, miss
> Second floor, miss, etc. (until jumper misses)

What does this rhyme mean? Were we to ask little girls jumping rope to it to give us a full *explication du texte*, what would we elicit? What does "fudge" mean? Why is there a judge? Is it merely, as some might say, a matter of "judge" rhyming with "fudge" or "fudge" rhyming with "judge?"

I think not. Folklore is admirably concise, and I am persuaded that whatever is contained in a folkloric text is meaningful—even if we do not always have full insight into that meaning. Why would individuals bother to remember something and repeat it with such gusto if it had no meaning? It seems clear that if an item remains in tradition, it must have meaning for the carriers of the tradition.

We can see that the jump rope rhyme reflects sibling rivalry. A newborn baby is a threat to the older children, who may resent all the attention paid to it. We know that there is often a wish on the part of older children to dispose of the new baby. Wishful thinking and wish fulfillment, of course, are widely found in folklore. There is more than a hint that Mama has committed a crime in producing a sibling rival. The crime is signaled in the first line, insofar as a judge is to be informed. (And possibly the punishment for the "crime" of throwing the baby away is projected to the judge.)

But why fudge? If one thinks of the color and texture of fudge, *and* is also familiar with infantile sexual theory, one can arrive at a possible explanation. In the days before sex education was taught in elementary school, young children in our culture did not always fully grasp the nature of childbirth. After having been told by a parent that a baby brother or sister was present in mother's obviously expanding abdomen and that it would soon come out to join the family, the bewildered child frequently assumed that this new baby would come out of the stomach area in the same way that material exited from the child's own stomach, namely, via the anus. The equation of feces with babies is reported extensively in psychoanalytic literature, although I doubt that any little girl jumping rope would offer any such interpretation of the possible meaning of "fudge."

Yet there is additional evidence, for cultural symbols rarely occur in unique single texts. Another children's rhyme, though not one used for jumping rope, goes as follows:

> Milk, milk, lemonade
> Around the corner, fudge is made.

Gestures accompanying this rhyme point in turn to several areas of female anatomy (breast, breast, genitals, and anus). However distasteful or crude one may find the rhyme, one cannot very well deny the explicit equation of fudge and feces.

Returning to our original jump rope rhyme, we can now better understand the action taken. Wrap it up in tissue (toilet) paper, throw it down the elevator. The new baby is "gift-wrapped to go," namely, to be flushed down the toilet-elevator. Notice also that the more skillful the jumper, the greater the number of floors, the farther away, the baby is sent. The rhyme thereby provides a most effective way of "passing" judgment or "wasting" a sibling rival, in a symbolic and socially acceptable way—a healthy release of a normal tension.

Children's projections of parents occur more commonly in narrative form than in rhymes. Fairy tales, for instance, are essentially stories about children and their relationships to siblings and parents. The "step" relationship is a convenient device to allow full-fledged hatred; a girl can hate wicked stepsisters or stepmothers with a clear conscience. Fairy tales with girl protagonists may include not only wicked siblings rivals but also a wicked mother in form of a stepmother or witch. Fairy tales with boy heroes may include the same kind of wicked brothers, plus a male antagonist in the form of a monster (such as a dragon) or a giant. Let me select one fairy tale found primarily in England and the United States to illustrate the nature of such symbolic projection.

Once upon a time, a boy named Jack lived *alone with his mother!* That very opening should give pause to anyone with a psychological bias. In boy-centered fairy tales, the father is often missing or dead—which allows the boy to be "alone with his mother." (In girl-centered fairy tales, the mother is similarly missing or deceased which allows the girl to be alone with her father.)

As most will remember, Jack trades his milk-giving cow to an old man who gives him some beans in exchange. At the sight of Jack's beans, his mother insists he throw them out the window. (I shall refrain from commenting on each any every symbol.) The next day, a huge beanstalk is discovered. Jack's mother begs him not to climb it, but he disobeys. Up in the beanstalk world, there is a cannibalistic giant who often in some vague way is linked to Jack's father—e.g., the giant allegedly stole Jack's father treasures. Fortunately, someone up there helps Jack: It is Mrs. Giant. Did it ever strike you as somewhat peculiar that Mrs. Giant would help a total stranger, a young boy, taking sides against her own husband? (In this Oedipal projection, the upper world is an extension of the lower one.) And it may also be worth recalling where Mrs. Giant hides Jack—it is in her oven. (The symbolism of ovens in European folklore is generally quite consistent.)

In any event, the stupid old giant fails to see Jack hiding in his wife's oven. Finally, Jack rushes down the stalk with the giant close in pursuit. As it happens, down at the bottom of the beanstalk, waiting with a hatchet in hand, is Jack's mother. Taking the hatchet, Jack cuts down the stalk, which causes the death of the giant, and the story ends with Jack living happily ever after—*with his mother.*

Surely the maternal aid in both the upper and lower world can be understood as a projection of the young boy's point of view, in terms of an Oedipal struggle against the villainous giant.

From Jack and the beanstalk, I should like to turn to another example of projection. This example is not folklore, but is dependent on folklore and folkloristic associations. Further, it demonstrates the importance of projection, which in my view is such an important device that it may utilize even historical events. The example of projection I have in mind is the first lunar landing. I must insist that nothing of what I am about to present in any way demeans the real and splendid achievement of landing on the moon. My sole purpose is to demonstrate, if I may, the power of folkloric projection in all of our lives—whether we are aware of it or not.

First of all, we have the name of the lunar mission. It was Apollo. I should stress that it is precisely in the selection of names and symbols that those interested in psychoanalytic semiotics are afforded prime data. It might be erroneous to interpret a detail which is integral to the scientific apparatus, but the choice of the name Apollo is not such a detail. In theory, the mission might have had any one of a hundred names.

The name Apollo is a conscious or perhaps unconscious invocation of traditional mythology, in which Apollo the sun is the brother of Diana the moon. Thus mythologically speaking we have a brother trying to reach or land on his sister. And what are the semantic associations of Diana? One of the most obvious is virginity; Diana is traditionally associated with chastity.

Once the projective metaphor has been pointed out, it is easy enough to see its consistency. Among the principal problems to be overcome in the Apollo missions was gaining enough power to escape the gravitational pull of the earth. The standard term for this power was "thrust." Keeping in mind that the mythological associations of the earth include "mother," we have the astronauts trying to get up enough thrust to escape the gravitational pull of mother earth. (I shall not dwell on the symbolism of rockets other than to recall that "to have a rocket in my pocket" can be a euphemistic phrase for masturbation. Cf. "pocket pool.")

And what were the names of the three astronauts, and who was chosen to be the first man on the moon? Neil Armstrong. Why was Armstrong the first? Was it mere alphabetical order? No, it was not, because in that event, Aldrin would have been first, not Armstrong or Collins. Could it have been the association of Jack Armstrong, the all-American boy, hero of radio adventure serials of several decades past? And could it have been that the name Armstrong was deemed appropriate because it literally refers to a strong body extremity? A well placed television camera allowed all other earthlings to voyeuristically watch as Armstrong's leg emerged from the capsule and stepped upon the surface of the moon. Certainly it made symbolic sense for the name of the first man to stand on the moon to begin with the first letter of the alphabet. Who can remember the names of any of the men who made the second lunar landing? The point is that the moon could only be violated once. No one cares who the other violators were. It is, after all, only on a maiden voyage that a bottle of champagne is broken over a ship's hull.

Once on the moon, the astronauts put up an American flag, a common symbolic ritual act for claiming virgin land for one's mother country (or fatherland). We may have here the same projection which led earlier generations of American explorers into what Henry Nash Smith has so aptly termed the "Virgin Land." What did the astronauts bring back as souvenirs of their conquest? Pieces of rock. In this context, the whole mission involved going out to get a piece of virgin moon to show off to one's peers back home —a super masculinity dream come true! Americans surely wanted to get to the moon before the Russians did.

The fantasy I have just delineated is not a universal one; in some cultures the moon is considered masculine. But in American culture the moon is definitely feminine. It even has the maternal associations of a cow jumping over it or being made of green cheese. The maternal associations of the moon hint at an Oedipal projection; and in English the choice of the name Apollo at least permits the possibility of a homonymic pun on sun/son.

So the sun/son who leaves mother earth to be the first to violate the virgin moon (sister, mother) may well be related to American fantasy—regardless of the purely scientific features of the mission.

The lunar mission brings to mind the interweaving of folklore and history. The point is that historical events and personages may serve as anchors for flights of projective fantasy. I believe many historians err seriously in dismissing or ignoring elements which they label as spurious or apocryphal. Folklore, as an item of folk speech—think of the phrase "that's (just) folklore"—means error, that is, something to be carefully weeded out of otherwise accurate historical source material. As a folklorist, I have learned to respect what the folk say and think about history regardless of the historicity of their words and thoughts. What happened is important, but no less important is what people think happened or what people wished had happened. Folk history may tell us more about folk than about history, but surely that is worth knowing.

The folk history of George Washington, for example, includes his famous confrontation with his father over the chopping down, not of a beanstalk, but of a cherry tree. Actually George, a son in that anecdote, is more celebrated for his paternal role. Why is it, for instance, that George Washington is reputed to have slept in so many beds on the east coast of the United States? Signs proclaim that George Washington slept here, not ate, drank, or visited here. Of course, if he is considered to be the father of our country then the verb choice is apt—as is the particular style of monument erected to honor him.

But can there be any validity to the projections discussed thus far? I can anticipate the most obvious objection: Readers may have watched the lunar landing, and they did not think of any associations of Apollo-Diana, brother-sister incest, etc. They did not think of the lunar landing as a violation of the moon. Any tension they may have felt was strictly due to their genuine concern for the safety of the astronauts.

But sometimes the tension was excessive. Some individuals refused to believe that the lunar landing actually occurred. Rather they assumed that the whole event was simply a fictionalized television program. Several individuals suffered breakdowns evidently precipitated by the successful lunar landing. And here one must reiterate the important point that folkloric projection is often, though not always, unconscious. Rarely is the nature of the projection consciously recognized. I am always amused by would-be critics of the Oedipal reading of the Oedipus story when they claim that the Freudian interpretation is invalid because Oedipus didn't know that he was killing his father and marrying his mother. That is precisely the point. It is the bringing of the unconscious into the purview of the conscious which is difficult and painful for the psyche. Projection is one of a number of psychological defense mechanisms which provide an unconscious screen or arena for the display of the causes of anxiety; it is for this reason that folkloric projections are so indispensable as tools in the human arsenal for mental health.

One helpful aspect of the study of folkloric projections is the possible play of "literal versus metaphorical." Sometimes seeing projections as literal versions of metaphors—or, if one prefers, as metaphorical transformations of literal statements—can greatly aid in deciphering the unconscious content of folklore.

Let me illustrate this by briefly considering an important detail of American wedding ritual, the bride's casting her floral bouquet to the females in attendance. What is the meaning of this act? (I wish to reiterate my firm conviction that semiotics must ultimately be concerned with meaning.) In terms of the literalization of metaphor, the bride, through the ritual act of throwing away her floral bouquet, is signifying her willingness or intention of being deflowered. Interestingly enough, the flowers once separated from the bride furnish an example of contagious magic—which is analogous to simile, by the way—as the lucky girl who catches the bouquet is said to be the next to marry.

An even better example of the literalization of metaphor in folkloric projections may be found in another genre, namely nursery rhymes. "There was an old woman who lived in a shoe; she had so many children she didn't know what to do." Now, what possible connection could there be between a woman living in a shoe and her having a superabundance of children?

Upon reflection, we may recall that there is a traditional connection between shoes and marriage. Not only does Cinderella find her prince charming through the perfect fit between her foot and a glass slipper, but in American culture we continue to tie old shoes on the bumpers of cars carrying newlyweds off on their honeymoon.

The mystery of the precise nature of the connection is solved by another version of the Mother Goose rhyme, reported from the Ozarks from the 1890s. "There was another old woman who lived in a shoe. She didn't have any children, she knew what to do." (One could easily cite additional illustrations, such as "Cock a doodle doo / My dame has lost her shoe [a real challenge for transplant surgeons] / Her master's lost his fiddling stick / They don't know what to do.") At any rate, the consistency of the symbolism should be apparent. In nursery rhymes, in fairy tales, in post-wedding customs, the same symbolic equation is found. This supports the idea that symbol patterns are culturewide.

I fear I may have done a serious disservice to my thesis by using so many examples of sexual symbolism. Some may think that I have misconstrued the term "semiotics" as being the scientific study of the "seamy." So I must stress that projection in folklore is not limited to sexuality. Any anxiety producing topic can find expression in projective form. For example, there is projection in the modern urban legend in which a family is obliged to take its old grandmother along on a vacation trip. In a remote area, grandmother dies and the family is forced to curtail its vacation. Strapping the body to the roof of the Volkswagen, the family starts for home. Enroute the family stops for lunch, during which time the car plus grandmother's corpse is stolen. Sometimes the absence of the body causes delay in probating grandmother's will.

I have argued that this legend reflects American attitudes toward the older generation and toward death. In terms of wishful thinking, there is the wish that grandmother should die and that someone else should dispose of the body. In terms of the literalization of metaphor, grandmother is "taken for a ride." The normally unutterable mercenary interest in grandmother's demise also finds expression in the concern about the delay in probate.

Similarly, there is projection in the standard legend of the medical school prank in which a group of medical students crossing a toll bridge leave a cadaver's arm holding the coin in the surprised and shocked grasp of the tollbooth attendant. Medical students have anxiety—at least initially—about handling cadavers and probably also about paying their way through life at the expense of the health of their patients. After all, the families of patients are charged for operations whether the operations are successful or not. Doctors have to learn to be dispassionate, objective practitioners, able to leave their patients' medical problems behind them (e.g., anatomical parts such as an arm), even as these problems literally hold the lucrative financial rewards of medical practice. Notice that in this projection, the fear and shock of taking money from a dead man's hand is displaced from the medical students to the outside world, the tollbooth attendant.

Racism is another anxiety-producing problem which is expressed in folkloric form. Let us briefly consider the folksong "John Henry." A popular folksong, this ballad tells the sad story of a black steel-driver who wages a valiant struggle against the steam drill. He wins the battle but the victory is Pyrrhic, for in the end John Henry dies. I have had white middle class school teachers tell me they use this folksong in the classroom as an example of African-American folklore. They like the ballad's depiction of the increasingly important issue of man versus machine. This is all well and good, but as a projection, John Henry is little more than the white stereotype of what black men should be. John Henry is strong, doggedly loyal to the white boss, and he dies doing the white man's work. He is, in short, a projection of the ideal "good nigger," completely removed from the rough, aggressive, militant stance of the "bad nigger." He even dies with his hammer in his hand—no threat there to the white womanhood of the south. The ballad of John Henry is thus more part of white folklore about blacks than of African-American folklore, and its continued use in schools promotes the image of the strong, docile, Uncle Tom figure of the black male.

The unconscious aspects of folkloristic projection make its use all the more insidious—and perhaps dangerous—inasmuch as few individuals are aware of the semiotic implications of the projection. Racism is nonetheless virulent for its being unconscious. Many whites may not see the racism in an advertisement for "flesh-colored bandaids" but it is there all the same. A terse bit of African-American folklore conveys a unique indictment of the use of white folklore in classrooms containing black students. There's the young black girl who asks a question of the mirror on the wall. "Mirror, mirror on the wall, who's the fairest one of all?" And the mirror answers, "Snow White, you black bitch, and don't you forget it!" Americans inherited from Europe an entire semiotic of color in which black was evil and white was good. Even a lie, if it's white, is all right. "Black is beautiful" is a conscious attempt by the black community to fight the semantic set of countless words (blackmail, blackguard, blackball, black-list, etc.) which assert the contrary.

Projections are to be found in all types of literature including comics, television, and motion pictures. My discussion today is based primarily upon folklore only because I am most familiar with folkloric data. But popular culture too can and must be understood as projective material. One thinks of the generic "western" with its rugged individual hero, who often has to take the law into his own hands vigilante style, in order to prevail over the "bad guys" and to establish law and order.

Similarly, we might look at *Star Trek*, a popular television program which relates the adventures of an eternally floating bastion of American values in the context of popular science fiction. Typically the space ship makes an uninvited visit to some alien culture which somehow threatens the existence or safety of the ship, (Or the ship itself is invaded by the alien culture.) Often the progress of the space ship is imperiled or stopped. Its leader heroes, of obvious Anglo-Saxon ancestry (Kirk, Spock, Scotty, McCoy), assisted by various assorted ethnic underlings, take whatever action they deem necessary to free the ship. Since the ship's name is "Enterprise," we have an all too thinly disguised projection of what Americans will do in the name of free enterprise. And what does the crew of the Enterprise do? The usual solution consists of converting or destroying the alien cultures. Only after such justifiable homicide can the United Star Ship (= U.S.S. = U.S.) Enterprise return to its set course—in accordance with its "manifest destiny."

Projection can involve placement in the far distant past or the far distant future, which is why one can study projection in myth (the far distant past), or projection in science fiction (the far distant future). The plots and dramatis personae are strikingly similar in myth and science fiction. In sum it is the projection which is crucial, not so much the time or place or local coloring. It is the removal from reality to fantasy which allows the human spirit free rein to portray its spiritual struggles and to play out its moments of anguish.

Sometimes, however, even fantasy does not afford sufficient disguise for such struggles, not without recourse to what I would call projective inversion. Most of the projections discussed thus far have been more or less direct translations of reality into fantasy. But there are some human problems that evidently require more elaborate disguise.

One of the finest examples of projective inversion in folklore is the one first analyzed by Otto Rank in his brilliant monograph, *The Myth of the Birth of the Hero*, first published in 1909. In this classic study, Rank attempts to explain why the Indo-European hero should so often be born of a virgin mother and why he should be abandoned to die immediately after birth. According to Rank, it is an Oedipal plot from the son's point of view. A virgin mother represents a complete repudiation of the father and especially of his necessary role in procreation. In Oedipal theory, it is supposedly the son who would like to get rid of his father, which would thereby reserve his mother for his exclusive use. But a narrative in which a son deposed or disposed of his father would produce considerable guilt. Thus, according to Rank, the child's wish to get rid of the father is neatly transposed in the myth to the father's getting rid of the child.

Rank called this projection, but I would like to call it projective inversion. The son's wishful thinking is projected in inverted form so that the father does everything he can to kill the son. One obvious advantage of such projective inversion is the avoidance of guilt. The son need not feel guilt for wanting to get rid of his father; to the contrary, the traditional fantasy projects the "crime" and the presumed responsibility for the crime upon the victim. Projective inversion thus permits one to blame the victim. Rather than feeling guilt, the son-hero can justifiably take Oedipal style revenge and kill the villainous father figure.

Let me give an example of projective inversion from modern American legend. The gist of the legend is a report that black youths have castrated a young white boy in a public bathroom. Like all legends, it is told as true, and in fact several years ago (1969) it was reported repeatedly by telephone to various police stations in San Francisco. The legend's sudden popularity was almost certainly related to the discussion of the bussing of school children in San Francisco to achieve desegregation. But historically, one may ask which race has castrated which race? It is surely whites who castrated blacks as punishment for actual or imagined crimes. But in this exemplar of urban folklore, through projective inversion, the whites have metamorphosed their own fears of the stereotyped super-phallic black male into a form where their victim becomes the aggressor. The wish to castrate black males is projected to those males who are depicted as castrating a white boy. This makes it possible to blame the black victim for the crime the white would like to commit.

This raises once again the question of the interrelationship of historical event to folkloristic projective fantasy. Some scholars tend to feel that historical and psychological approaches are mutually exclusive, but I believe this to be a serious error. Frequently a historical event may rekindle an old projection or inspire a new one.

It has been suggested, for example, that the elephant joke cycle of the early 1960s might be related to the rise of the Civil Rights movement of the same period. Elephants, like blacks, are associated by whites with African origins. In the joke cycle, elephants were typically described in terms of color—"Do you know why elephants are gray? So you can tell them from bluebirds"—and in terms of making phallic leaps down from trees upon unsuspecting victims. "Why do elephants climb trees? To rape squirrels." The Civil Rights movement aroused longstanding fears among whites that the superphallic militant black male might assert himself with respect to former white oppressors. As mentioned in the analysis of the previous legend, castration, symbolic or literal, is one solution. "How do you keep an elephant from charging? Take away his credit card." "How do you keep an elephant from stampeding? Cut his 'tam peter off."

In the same way, I believe it is possible to show historical roots for other recent American folkloric phenomena. For example, the spate of "dead baby" jokes in the early 1970s provides a challenging instance. "What's red and hangs from the ceiling? A baby on a meathook." "What's red and sits in the corner? A baby chewing on a razor blade." It is never easy to make sense of nonsense, but that does not mean that nonsense has no meaning. These jokes, told by post-pubertal adolescents, may reflect simple sibling rivalry; but that would not explain why this particular cycle became so popular in the early 1970s. Sibling rivalry, after all, has presumably always existed. I would hazard a guess that new techniques of contraception (including the pill), and especially the liberalized laws governing abortion, have generated an increased discussion (and guilt) concerning the "murder" of babies.

Whether not a particular joke cycle or legend derives from a historical impetus is not crucial for the present argument. The issue is whether or not there is a projective aspect to the collectivized forms of fantasy we call folklore. If so, as I believe, then there are important implications for semiotic studies, in which the projective aspect has thus far been almost totally ignored. For example, one of the finest examples, in my opinion, of semiotic analysis is Paul Bouissac's insightful descriptions of various circus acts. In his essay "Poetics in the Lion's Den: The Circus Act as a Text," Bouissac analyzes the constituent elements of a lion act performance. He even describes some of the standard tricks as metaphorical, e.g., the lion walks in the center of the ring to be ridden by the man, or the lion straddles two stools to allow the man to bend under him and carry the lion on his shoulders. Bouissac's analysis is fine as far as it goes. My point is that semiotics seems to stop with description, classification, and typology, whereas description, classification and typology ought to be beginnings not ends.

Circus acts, like zoological gardens, involve human attitudes toward animals and toward animality—including human animality. Part of the thrill and pleasure in circus and zoo is the implicit struggle of man versus animal. The animals are caged and kept in check, as man's own animal nature is supposed to be. Yet there is always the possibility, the danger, or the risk one could call it, that the animal will escape the bonds of man, or to put it metaphorically that emotion and passion will escape the bonds of reason. One technique used to keep the animal or animality in check consists of requiring the animal, in this case a lion, to perform human acts. In terms of projective inversion, one is tempted to suggest that although people would like to yield to "animal" desires and to perform animal acts, this is not a guilt-free wish. Hence, through inversion, it is pretended that animals would like to be like humans. The more human the behavior performed by the animal, the more complete the projective inversion. The inversion is hinted at by such sequences as those in which the animal first carries the man, and later the man carries the animal. The latter trick would appear to reverse the normal roles of man and beast.

Whether or not my particular analysis of a lion's act in terms of projection is valid, the issue, it seems to me, is the necessity of adding a consideration of projection to conventional semiotic analysis. For in my view, psychoanalytic semiotics could be applied to a wide variety of phenomena, folkloric and otherwise. One could, for example, imagine a projective study of the bullfight. In addition to studying the structure of the bullring or the social hierarchy of the participants, one could also perceive the matador versus the bull as a projection. It is not just man versus animal, culture versus nature, but a projection of traditional male rivalry in Spanish (and other Mediterranean) cultures. In a homosexual battle of masculinity, it is critical just who penetrates whom. If the matador penetrates the bull properly, then the bull becomes feminized (as symbolized by having one or more of his extremities—tail, hoofs—cut off as trophies). As a projective drama, the bullfight is a ritualized cognate of ordinary verbal dueling as found among adolescent youths.

There is great variety in the projective dimensions of even a single item of folklore. Each age and each individual in an age is free to interpret art, music, and literature anew. And so it is with folklore. Each individual who tells a tale or who hears a tale cannot help but project his or her own personality into that tale, which is why the study of projection in folklore cannot be limited to the text alone; the process of projection also occurs in the very act of communicating an item of folklore.

As one example, let us take a text related to me in 1964 by a black male informant from Alabama. "Governor Wallace of Alabama died and went to heaven. After entering the pearly gates, he walked up to the door of a splendid mansion and knocked. A voice inside exclaimed, 'Who dat?' Wallace shook his head sadly and said, 'Never mind, I'll go the other way.'"

First of all, the item is older than 1964; a similar joke was told during World War II with Adolf Hitler as the protagonist, confronted by a heavenly voice with a pronounced Jewish accent. In the present version, the projective aspects include wishful thinking (for Wallace's death) and Wallace's being sent to hell by his own prejudice. The historical fact of Governor Wallace's having stood dramatically at the door of the University of Alabama to deny admission to black students is also relevant—as is no doubt the context of a black informant telling the joke to a white folklorist.

But the joke may function as a projective text for whites as well as blacks. What is understood by individual whites when they hear the stereotyped dialect "Who dat?" Clearly the implication is that a black man is inside the mansion. But individuals differ markedly as to the identity of the black voice. Some think it is God; others think it might be Saint Peter. A few assume it is a doorman or gatekeeper or other menial. The joke itself does not say, and I would argue that it is projection on the part of the interpreter that governs the identity made. Similarly, some whites claim they understood from "Who dat?" that heaven is now integrated, while others assumed that heaven has been completely "taken over" by African Americans. None of this is articulated in the joke proper, but it is part of the joke as semiotic text.

Thus folklore is not only projective material, but it allows if not encourages projection on the part of the participants as the lore is communicated. In fact, I would go so far as to argue that if folklore did not provide a socially sanctioned outlet for projection, it would almost certainly cease to exist. The problem in folkloristics is that while we have literally thousands upon thousands of folklore texts recorded, the projective part of the semiotic text has not been recorded. So it is that we continue to have lore without reference to folk, and that we miss an important tool for the study and enjoyment of some of the marvels of the human mind.

15

GALLUS AS PHALLUS:
A PSYCHOANALYTIC
CROSS-CULTURAL CONSIDERATION
OF THE COCKFIGHT AS FOWL PLAY

Introduction

A year before Dundes died, he reflected on his tremendous output of essays in over forty years of publishing and told me that the present essay could be his "most important and significant," although he noted that others probably have received more attention. His regard for this study, originally published in 1993, was due to the way it integrated several important positions he took through his career. First, it exemplified a folkloristic methodology of working with cross-cultural variants and identifying the structural underpinnings of texts, leading to a symbolist, psychoanalytic interpretation. Second, it provided explanations about gender identity, by postulating that men engaged in combat games to prove their manhood. The symbolic system in the text of the event was apparent—seeing the cockfight, in its various cultural contexts, as "mutual masturbation or a phallic brag duel." A victor displayed his manhood by emasculating an opponent, in an all-male setting, through the threat of castration, or symbolically transforming him into a female. The participants might not have been aware of the symbolism, and that, in Dundes's logic of explanation, demonstrated the function of folklore, as a frame of play or fantasy in order to deal with anxieties and conflicts. Dundes offered the general statement that "the whole point of folklore in general, and the cockfight as an instance of folklore, is to allow individuals to do or say things they could not otherwise do or say. If people actually knew what they were doing, e.g., in telling a joke, they could not participate in that activity, e.g., tell that joke" (1994, 241). Third, it illustrated the unconscious content of folklore, which allows it to function as it does, that is, as a socially sanctioned outlet for the expression of taboo thoughts and acts. Fourth, it set forth the implications such studies had regarding scholars' cultural biases against psychoanalytic interpretation. A frequent theme for Dundes was that, because of these biases, scholars tended to negate his prevalent call for "depth" of analysis, and read cultural events as texts of social relations.

The motivation for writing "Gallus as Phallus" came from re-evaluating Clifford Geertz's seminal essay "Deep Play: Notes on the Balinese Cockfight" (1972), which later became the anchor for the widely used book *The Interpretation of Cultures* (1973). In light of Dundes's essays such as "The Study of Folklore in Literature and Culture: Identification and Interpretation" (1965c, and chapter 2 in the present volume), one could understand his attraction to Geertz's analytical work on a folk custom, with its rhetorical emphasis on "interpretation." Geertz, like Dundes, also used the metaphor of depth to describe latent meanings, although Dundes referred to Freudian depth psychology, while Geertz's "deep play" had its roots in philosopher Jeremy Bentham's term, and in the sociological tradition of Max Weber. Dundes, like many other professors, assigned Geertz's essay in seminars as a prime example of the ethnographic analysis of events as "texts" that could be symbolically read. For Geertz, the cockfight was a text, because it constituted "a Balinese reading of Balinese experience; a story they tell themselves about themselves."

Yet Dundes became dissatisfied with Geertz's reductionist argument that cultural texts of "deep play" stood, ultimately, for relations of social status in a single culture, especially when Dundes recognized cross-cultural patterns and the hard-to-miss literalization of "cock" references, thereby suggesting homoerotic phallic symbolism. From this analysis, Dundes asked, could generalizations be made from the cockfight to other male competitive contests, shedding light on gender identity? In one of Dundes's last essays, in *Manly Traditions* (Bronner 2005), he located the cockfight in a continuum running from competitive games to actual warfare because in these activities males "demonstrate their masculinity at the expense of male opponents whom they feminize." Dundes speculated that there were a number of contributing factors to the concept that men had a greater need to prove their masculinity than women did to reaffirm their femininity. One was the infantile conditioning of boys growing up in a "strongly female-centered world." Therefore, boys later broke away from the world of women and joined the world of men, by engaging in all-male puberty rites. He also hypothesized that in adolescence, the time when male sexuality peaked, the only sexual objects immediately available were other males. As a result, Dundes surmised, all-male competitive sport teams, and the military, were organizations where sexual energies could be expended on other males within a group, or on males construed as opponents. Dundes also proposed a biological factor, the male phallic erection. Because an erection is a temporary state, he thought that males felt the need for proving, repeatedly, that they were able to achieve this "indisputable demonstration of masculinity." Dundes claimed that winning one match or one game probably was not enough: "One has to prove one's ability to feminize or emasculate one's opponent again and again" (2005a).

For other case studies by Dundes testing these hypotheses on gender identity, see 2002a, 1987h, and 1997b; and Dundes and Falassi 1975. For examples of folkloristic gender studies of ritual and festival that cite Dundes's ideas, see Mechling 2001; Bronner 2006a, 2005a, 2004; and Suárez-Orozco 1993.

Gallus as Phallus: A Psychoanalytic Cross-Cultural Consideration of the Cockfight as Fowl Play

THE COCKFIGHT IS ONE OF the oldest, most documented and most widely distributed traditional sports known to man.* It has been reported in ancient India (Sarma 1964; Bhide 1967; Chattopadhyay 1973), ancient China (Cutter 1989a, b), ancient Iran (Modi 1911), and ancient Greece (Witte 1868). From Greece, cockfighting moved to Rome, as mosaics attest (Magaldi 1929). The earliest recorded cockfight in China dates from 517 B.C. (Cutter 1989a, p. 632; 1989b, p. 10), which would make cockfighting at least 2500 years old. (See also Danaë 1989, p. 34, who suggests that cockfighting existed before 2000 B.C.) The antiquity of cockfighting in India is attested by a specific reference in the *Kama Sutra* (3d century A.D.), Chapter 2 of Part 1, where young women are advised to study some sixty-four arts, of which number 41 includes "The rules of cockfighting," the clear implication being that a woman would be more pleasing to men who are vitally interested in such activities (Vatsyayana 1963, p. 14).

There is some consensus that the cock itself (and perhaps the cockfight) may have originated in southeast Asia (Peters 1913, p. 395; Tudela 1959, p. 14), where it diffused to China, India, and eventually Iran and on to classical Greece and Rome before moving to Western Europe and thence to the Caribbean. The cock may have come to the New World as early as the second voyage of Christopher Columbus in 1493 (Tudela 1959, p. 15). From Asia, the cockfight spread eventually nearly throughout the Americas. The cockfight, however, is by no means universal, as it seems never to have spread to any great extent to native North and South America or to sub-Saharan Africa.

Once popular in much of western Europe, including England (Pegge 1773; Egan 1832; Boulton 1901), Scotland (Beattie 1937); Ireland (Beacey 1945; O'Gormon 1983), and Wales (Peate 1970), cockfighting is still to be found in the north of France (Demulder 1934; Cegarra, 1987, 1988, 1989), in Belgium (Desrousseaux 1886, 1889, pp. 115–124; Delannoy 1948; Remouchamps and Remade 1949), and in Spain (Justo 1969; Marvin 1984). Nowhere is cockfighting enjoyed more than in southeast Asia, as is confirmed by reports from Borneo (Barclay 1980), Celebes (Kaudern 1929, pp. 337–348), and Java (Serière, 1873, pp. 92–100; Kreemer 1893; Soeroto 1916–1917), Malaysia (Wilkinson 1925), the Philippines (Bailey 1909; Lee 1921; Lansang 1966; Guggenheim 1982), Sarawak (Sandhi 1959), Sumatra (Scheltema 1919), and, of course, Bali (Eck 1879; Knight 1940; Bateson and Mead 1942; Geertz 1972; Picard 1983). Cockfighting is equally popular in the Caribbean (Challes 1972), for example, in Martinique (Champagnac 1970; Affergan 1986), in Haiti (Paul 1952; Marcelin 1955a, h), in Cuba (Wurdemann 1844, pp. 87–93; Hazard 1871, pp. 191–195), and in Puerto Rico (Alonso 1849, pp. 77–93; Dinwiddie 1899; Cadilla de Martinez 1941; Calderin 1970; Feijoo 1990). There are cockfight enthusiasts throughout Latin America, for example, in Argentina (Mantegazza 1916, pp. 69–71; Saubidet 1952, pp. 345–356), Brazil (Leal 1989), Colombia (León Rey 1953), Mexico (Mendoza 1943);

and Venezuela (Armas Chitty 1953–1954; Acosta Saignes 1954; Marquez 1954; Perez 1984; Cook 1991, pp. 79–94).

In the United States, cockfighting is technically banned in most states. Nevertheless, we have published accounts of cockfights from California (Beagle 1968), Connecticut (Liebling 1950), Florida (Vogeler 1942), Georgia (Hawley 1987), Louisiana (Del Sesto 1975; Hawley 1982; Donlon 1991), New York (Hyman 1950), North Carolina (Roberts 1965; Herzog 1985), Tennessee (Cobb 1978; Gunter 1978), Texas (Braddy 1961; Tippette 1978), Utah (Walker 1986), Vermont (Mosher 1989, pp. 96–102), and Virginia (Anderson 1933; Carson 1965, pp. 151–164), among others.

Some of the abundant literature devoted to cockfighting includes detailed discussions of the various "rules" that prevail in different locales (cf. Eck 1879; Nugent 1929; Saubidet 1952, pp. 354–356; Marquez 1954; Champagnac 1970, pp. 58–65; Herzog 1985; Harris 1987). Other writings are concerned with the elaborate intricacies of breeding and caring for fighting cocks—one source noted 253 different names of breeds and cross-breeds, and this list included only English-language designations (Nugent 1929, p. 79; see also Jull, 1927; Finsterbusch 1980). A number of how-to manuals are incredibly specific and include the minutiae of recommended regimen right down to the details of diet (see, e.g., Phillott 1910; Feijoo 1990).

The cockfight has been a source of inspiration for a host of poems and short stories (Fraser 1981; Cutter 1989h) as well as paintings (Tegetmeier 1896; Bryden 1931; Gilbey 1957; Marçal 1967, pp. 350–351; Cadet 1971, pp. 159–165). There is, for example, an entire Irish novel based on cockfighting (O'Gormon 1983; for an American novel, see Willeford 1972). Cockfighting has its own folk speech, which has led to the compilation of cockfight slang glossaries (Jaquemotte and Lejeune 1904; Mendoza 1943; Saubidet 1952, pp. 345–354; León Rey 1953; Marcelin 1955b; Perez 1984, pp. 17–78). In English, too, the cockfight has provided a rich set of metaphors for everyday life. The phrases "to turn tail," "to raise one's hackle(s)," and "to show the white feather" are some of the most familiar (Scott 1957, pp. 118–119). Similarly, to be "cocky" or "cocksure," or to be "cock of the walk" (Gilbey 1957, p. 24), and perhaps "to pit" (someone against another) presumably derive ultimately from the lexicon of cockfighting. There is one etymology, possibly a folk etymology, for the word "cocktail," that supposedly comes from "cock ale" or a liquid concoction designed to serve as a tonic to strengthen fighting cocks (Nugent 1929, p. 80). It is also tempting to ponder the possible metaphorical associations of the "cock" found in guns (as in "Don't go off half-cocked") or in pipes where cocks regulate the flow of liquids (or gases). Among the more esoteric cockfighting traditions that have been studied are the names of fighting cocks in Brazil (Teixeira 1992) and the folk art motifs used to decorate the carrying boxes used in northern Utah (Walker 1986, pp. 39–41).

Most considerations of cockfighting invariably cite the classical instance of Themistocles, who was leading his Athenian army against the Persians in the fifth century B.C. when he chanced to see some cocks fighting. His alleged, but oft-quoted, remarks were: "These animals fight not for the gods of their country, nor for the monuments of their ancestors, nor for glory, nor for freedom, nor for their children, but for the sake of victory, and that one may not yield to the other" (Pegge 1773, p. 137). This impromptu speech supposedly inspired and rallied the troops of Themistocles. (The standard source is Aelian, *Varia Historia* 2: 28; cf. Bruneau 1965, p. 107.)

Particular techniques are found in specific local cockfighting traditions. Some of these seem to be quite ancient. For example, there is an arcane system of cockfighting lore in the

Philippines that suggests that there are definite times of the day that favor cocks of a particular color (Guggenheim 1982, p. 11). This set of associations of calendar and cock color is almost certainly related to a complex "cock almanac" reported in south India (Saltore 1926–1927, pp. 319–324).

The most common form of cockfight involves a one-on-one confrontation between two equally matched cocks, a battle that may be interspersed with standard periods of respite. Yet there is considerable variation within the one-to-one scenario. For example, a nineteenth-century account of cockfighting in Cuba summarizes some of the alternatives:

> There are various modes of fighting: *Al cotejo*—that is, in measuring, at sight, the size or spurs of both chickens. *Al peso*—or by weight, and seeing if the spurs are equal. *Tapados*—where they settle the match without seeing the chickens, or, in fact, "go it blind." *De cuchilla*—when they put on the artificial spurs, in order to make the fight sharper, quicker, and more fatal. *Al pico*—when they fight without any spurs. (Hazard 1871, pp. 192–193)

There were other, more elaborate forms of cockfighting. These include the battle royal and the Welsh main, once popular in England. We may cite an eighteenth-century description of these special forms of cockfighting:

> What aggravates the reproach and the disgrace upon us Englishmen, is those species of fighting which are called the Battle-royal, and the Welsh-main, known nowhere in the world, as I think, but here; neither in China, nor in Persia, nor in Malacca, nor amongst the savage tribes of America. These are scenes so bloody as almost to be too shocking to relate; and yet, as many may not be acquainted with the horrible nature of them, it may be proper, for the excitement of our aversion and detestation, to describe them in a few words. In the former an unlimited number of fowls are pitted; and when they have slaughtered one another for the diversion, dii boni! of the otherwise generous and humane Englishman, the single surviving bird is to be esteemed the victor, and carries away the prize. The Welsh-main consists, we will suppose, of sixteen pair of cocks; of these the sixteen conquerors are pitted a second time; the eight conquerors of these are pitted a third time; so that, incredible barbarity! thirty one cocks are sure to be most inhumanly murdered for the sport and pleasure, the noise and nonsense, nay, I must say, the profane cursing and swearing, of those who have the effrontery to call themselves, with all these bloody doings, and with all this impiety about them, *Christians*. (Pegge 1773, pp. 148–149; see also Boulton 1901, pp. 189–190)

As the unmistakable tone of the preceding passage reminds us, a large part of the mass of writings devoted to the cockfight concerns the question of whether the sport should be banned on the grounds of excessive cruelty to animals. According to one source (Powel 1937, p. 191), the Society for the Prevention of Cruelty to Animals insists that the cockfight "is a blot on civilization's fair escutcheon." The typical strategy of the humane protest against cockfighting consists of simply describing cockfights in gory detail:

> In almost every fight at least one cock is seriously multilated or killed. In about half of the fights, more or less, both birds are maimed beyond further use if not killed. Eyes are gouged out, abdomens slit and slashed until the birds are

anguished monstrosities, legs and wings are broken. But so long as a bird can and will keep facing towards the opposing cock he is left in the pit and cheered for his "courage." (Anon. 1952, p. 11; cf. Hawley 1989)

Of course, the cockfighting community has fought back. One of their common arguments is that cockfighting is much less cruel than other sports, less cruel, for example, than boxing, in which men may be maimed or even killed. In England, cockfighting, which is illegal, is compared to foxhunting, which is legal, by one cocker as follows: "Cockfighting isn't as unfair as foxhunting, you see. One of my cocks has a 50–50 chance of winning. What chance has a fox got when there are fifty hounds chasing him? A million to one shot of getting away" (Penrose 1976, p. 236). Another standard argument is that cocks are naturally inclined to fight, and that man is only facilitating or expanding on what occurs by itself in nature. Even the use of gaffs or blades is defended on the grounds that they are "used solely to end a fight quickly, and the winner will then return to his harem to propagate his species whilst the loser will die the death he has chosen" (Jarvis 1939, p. 378). Incidentally, there are many different types of gaffs, for instance "brike special, skeleton, split socket, bayonet, jagger, regulation, and hoisters" (Jones 1980, p. 144; cf. Worden and Darden 1992).

Another argument put forth by cockfighters is "that it is impossible to make a cock fight an adversary if the bird does not wish to fight . . . if at the particular moment the joy of battle is not in him, neither skill by the 'setter' nor insult by the adversary will make him fight. The game-cock is never an unwilling gladiator" (James 1928, p. 140). Yet another popular argument is that people raise chickens to be slaughtered for food— think of all the fried chicken franchises in the United States alone. Is that more cruel to the species than cockfighting? Cockfighters are wont to point out that chickens raised for market may be slaughtered when they are anywhere from eight to ten weeks of age. In contrast, a gamecock

> will not even be fought before he's one year old and during that one year, he will receive excellent care. . . . Many are retired to stud after only three or four wins. The question seems to be whether it is less cruel for the cock to be killed by a man rather than by another cock. (Tippette 1978, p. 274; see also Allred and Carver 1979, p. 59)

Despite continuing efforts to ban the cockfight, there are places where cockfighting is legalized. In the north of France near the Belgian border, there are thirty-two authorized "gallodromes" (Cegarra 1989, p. 671). In Puerto Rico, there are reportedly six hundred cockpits with 100,000 fights annually, attended by two million spectators. Promoted by the island's official Department of Recreation, cockfights are even broadcast on television (Bryant 1991, p. 20). Even in places where cockfighting is officially illegal, it thrives.

While the vast majority of the written reports of cockfighting tend to be purely descriptive and not the least bit analytic, there is a small body of literature that seeks to interpret the cockfight. Of these, unquestionably the most famous is Clifford Geertz's (1972) "Deep Play: Notes on the Balinese Cockfight." This essay marks a turning point in the history of cockfight scholarship. All modern writing on the subject is directly or indirectly derived from Geertz's discussion of the Balinese material. Geertz argued in his interpretation of the cockfight "the general thesis is that the cockfight, and especially the deep cockfight, is fundamentally a dramatization of status concerns" (p. 18). According to Geertz,

What sets the cockfight apart from the ordinary course of life . . . [is] that it provides a metasocial commentary upon the whole matter of assorting human beings into fixed hierarchical ranks and then organizing the major part of collective existence around that assortment. (p. 26)

Geertz thus interpreted the cockfight exclusively in terms of Balinese social organization or social structure.

Geertz's reading of the Balinese cockfight has attained the status of a modern classic in anthropology (Watson 1989) although it has received some criticism (Roseberry 1982; Parker 1985; Schneider 1987). Anthropologist James A. Boon (1977), an expert on Balinese ethnography who is understandably reluctant to criticize one of his former mentors, remarked that "Geertz does not survey the range of Balinese cockfights; rather he telescopes repeated observations into an ideal-typical description of a choice elaboration of the form in one village area" (p. 33). More severe is Vincent Crapanzano (1986), who, although very admiring of Geertz's "interpretive virtuosity" (pp. 53, 75), contends that Geertz offered his own subjective interpretation of the Balinese cockfight. Moreover, Crapanzano argues, Geertz presented little or no empirical evidence in support of *his* interpretation (pp. 72–75). Crapanzano concludes there is "no understanding of the native from the native's point of view. There is only the constructed understanding of the constructed native's constructed point of view," and Geertz's "interpretation is simply not convincing" (p. 74; cf. Fine 1992, p. 248).

Crapanzano's critique is echoed by Jacobson (1991), who maintains that Geertz made assertions unsupported by ethnographic data.

Yet no evidence presented warrants conclusions about how Balinese think or feel about themselves or their society. Whereas the language and rules of the cockfight are described in detail, perceptions are simply attributed to Balinese. In short, Geertz develops his interpretation of the interpretive function of the Balinese cockfight by stating and restating his claims without providing data that substantiate them. He presents no evidence for accepting his reading of the "text." (pp. 52–53)

Unlike Crapanzano and Jacobson, anthropologist Scott Guggenheim (1982) has himself made an ethnographic study of a cockfight, in this case in the Philippines. Guggenheim agrees with Geertz that cockfighting is a "cultural performance" (p. 29), but he disagrees that the cockfight provides an indigenous or native model of social structure or status hierarchy. In some ways, Guggenheim argues, the cockfight in the Philippines is "strikingly blind to social reality" and the cockfight as folk model "skews social reality" (p. 29). In this context,

There is, for example, no mention of women, despite women's prominent role not only in household management, but in marketing agriculture, wage-earning labor, professional occupations, and politics. Nor does it say very much about what all those high ranking people do to deserve their positions, besides buying expensive chickens. (p. 29)

The theoretical issue here, with respect to the role and function of folklore in culture— and the cockfight is an example of folklore: it is a traditional game or sport—is that the old-fashioned Boasian notion of "folklore as culture reflector," which wrongly assumed a one-to-one relationship between folklore and culture, is inadequate. Folklore, to be sure, does articulate and sometimes enforces the norms of a culture, but it also, often at the same time, offers a socially sanctioned *escape* from those norms. This is what Bascom (1954) called the paradoxical double function of folklore (p. 349). To the extent that folklore involves fantasy, and I believe that it does to a very great extent, the literal one-to-one relationship posited between folklore and culture automatically assumed by a majority of anthropologists and folklorists is doomed to failure as a methodological principle designed to illuminate the content of folkloristic phenomena. Just as anthropologists inevitably assume that myths provide a "charter" for belief in social organization, á la Malinowski's literal, anti-symbolic theory of myth, so Geertz and others wrongly interpret the cockfight as a charter or articulation of social structure, status hierarchy in particular. Guggenheim (1982) is on the right track in pointing out that the cockfight in the Philippines hardly qualifies as a model of normal Filipino social structure—why are women left out of the cockfight, he asks? But like other anthropologists who have considered the cockfight, he fails to appreciate its obvious and overt symbolism.

Although Guggenheim pays the usual social anthropological lip service to symbolism, his conclusions show that he too has missed the basic underlying significance of the cockfight: "Taken as a symbolic system, cockfighting successfully couples individual self-identity and self-esteem, social and political loyalties, and even aesthetic satisfaction to an elegant and exciting event" (p. 30). How do Geertz's and Guggenheim's interpretations of the cockfight compare with other anthropological analyses of the same event? Del Sesto (1980) sees the cockfight as "a symbolic representation of man's continual struggle for survival, as displays of courage and bravado in the face of adversity, and as attempts to understand the meaning and suffering of death" (p. 275). Parker (1986) claims that "the cockfight can be seen as a contest that is totally concerned with violence, competition, and aggression" (p. 26). Several ethnographers have sensed the importance of the masculine elements inherent in the cockfight. Marvin (1984), in his study of the Andalusian cockfight, sees it as a confirmation of male values:

> In all conversations concerning the cockfight those involved with the event emphasized that it was *una cosa de hombres* (a men's thing). It is a totally male-oriented event, the audience is almost totally male, the birds which fight are male and the virtues which are extolled are male virtues. (p. 641)

Marvin concludes, "The cockfight, though, is a celebration in that it is an event which extols certain aspects of masculinity" (p. 68).

This view is echoed by Leal (1989), one of the few women to analyze the cockfight. In a superb ethnographic account, she also suggests that "cockfighting is a celebration of masculinity where men, through their cocks, dispute, win, lose, and reinforce certain attributes chosen as male essence" (p. 210). This report from Brazil reaches conclusions similar to those of another female ethnographer who investigated cockfighting in northern France near the Belgian border. The latter confirms the masculinity aspect: "cockfights represent only one exclusive part of human society, that of the virile element" (Cegarra 1988, p. 55). Similarly, Danaë, in his magisterial survey of cockfighting worldwide, concludes with a discussion of cockfighters as an esoteric masculine society (1989, pp. 227–247). Affergan, in his study of cockfighting in Martinique, claims it is an outlet for male identity and aggression by male members of an oppressed group (1986, p. 120), while Kimberley Cook, in her analysis of cockfighting in Venezuela, sees it as a "ritualistic firm of aggression" where men vie to gain public recognition of their virility (1991, pp. 89–90).

All these interpretations of the cockfight, in my opinion, are flawed to some extent. Perhaps the most obvious methodological weakness is the failure to employ a comparative, cross-cultural perspective. The quintessential anthropological credo of cultural relativism notwithstanding, it is always a mistake to study data from one particular culture as if it were peculiar to that culture if comparable, if not cognate, data exist in other cultures. The cockfight is found outside of Bali, the Philippines, Louisiana, Tennessee, Brazil, northern France, Martinique, and Venezuela. Hence any would-be interpretation of the cockfight based on data from just one of these locations is bound to be inadequate. Let us assume, strictly for the sake of argument, that Geertz's interpretation of the Balinese cockfight as a "native" representation of Balinese status concerns is correct. If so, what, if anything, does this tell us about about the possible significance of the cockfight in all of the other many cultures in which the cockfight occurs? Balinese social structure is not to be found in Puerto Rico or Belgium. The point is that if an item of folklore has cross-cultural distribution, it must be studied from a cross-cultural perspective, especially if one is interested in possible symbolic aspects. This does not mean that the cockfight necessarily means the same thing in all of its cultural contexts—although this cannot be ruled out a priori. The study of a cross-cultural phenomenon in just one cultural context is clearly a limited, partial one. In that sense, all previous studies of the cockfight have been limited and partial.

Along with the plea for a larger comparative perspective to view the cockfight, I suggest that the cockfight itself cannot be understood without being seen as an exemplar of a more comprehensive paradigm involving male gladiatorial combat. There are many forms of male battle, running the gamut from simple children's games to all-out war. It is my contention that the cockfight can best be analyzed as part and parcel of that paradigm.

Accordingly, let us begin our consideration of the cockfight as an instance of the broad category of male competitive games and sports. I believe one can discern a common underlying symbolic structure shared by most if not all such activities. It might be useful to distinguish three basic variants with respect to the nature of the participants. The first would be human male versus human male. This category includes fencing, boxing, wrestling, tennis, badminton, ping-pong, and such board games as chess and checkers. By extension, it could also subsume male team sports such as football, soccer, hockey, lacrosse, basketball, and so on. The second category would be human male versus male animal. Perhaps the classic illustration of this category is the bullfight. The third category would be male animal versus male animal. Here the obvious example is the cockfight.

It is my contention that all of those games and sports are essentially variations on one theme. The theme involves an all-male preserve in which one male demonstrates his virility, his masculinity, *at the expense of a male opponent.* One proves one's maleness by feminizing one's opponent. Typically, the victory entails (no pun intended!) penetration. In American football, the winning group of males get into their opponents' "end zones" more times than their opponents get into their end zones (see Dundes 1987, pp. 178–194). In the bullfight, the battle of man against bull is to determine whether the matador penetrates the bull or whether the bull's horns penetrate the matador. The penetrator comes away triumphant and with his masculinity intact; the one *penetrated* loses his masculinity. In the case of the bullfight, the expertise and skill of the matador can be rewarded with different degrees of symbolic castration of the bull. The bull, if penetrated cleanly and dextrously, may have his hooves, ears, or tail cut off to be "presented" to the successful matador.

The cockfight, despite its great antiquity and its continued popularity into the twentieth century, has never been properly understood as male phallic combat. Despite an enormous literature devoted to the cockfight ranging from vivid descriptions to purported analyses, there is to my knowledge no single discussion that takes adequate account of the symbolic nature of the contest. I should like to test my hypothesis that the cockfight is a thinly disguised symbolic homoerotic masturbatory phallic duel, with the winner emasculating the loser through castration or feminization. I believe that the evidence for this interpretation is overwhelmingly abundant and cross-cultural in nature. Nevertheless, it seems to me that the symbolic meaning of the cockfight is not consciously recognized either by those who participate in the event or those who have written about it. The sole exception occurs in Cook's chapter on cockfighting on the island of Margarita off the coast of Venezuela in her 1991 doctoral dissertation, when she remarks "that when two individual men fight cocks and one loses, the loser assumes a feminine role" (1991, p. 98; see also Affergan 1986, p. 119). Baird (1981–1982, p. 83) claims that among the ancient Greeks the cockfight symbolized homosexual rape.

Let us first consider the gallus as phallus. In all of the many essays and monographs devoted to cockfighting, only a few actually comment on the phallic nature of the cocks. Scott (1941) in a paragraph in his survey volume *Phallic Worship* does mention the phallic significance of the cock (p. 262), but in his full-length history of cockfighting (Scott 1957), he drew no inferences from this. In Geertz's (1972) essay, which was first presented at a conference held in Paris in October of 1970, we are told:

> To anyone who has been in Bali any length of time, the deep psychological identification of Balinese men with their cocks is unmistakable. The double entendre here is deliberate. It works in exactly the same way in Balinese as it does in English, even to producing the same tired jokes, strained puns, and uninventive obscenities. (p. 5)

It is a pity that Geertz was not a bit more ethnographically specific here, inasmuch as he failed to give even a single example of the "tired jokes" and "uninventive obscenities." Tired jokes and uninventive obscenities constitute valuable folkloric data that any journeyman folklorist fluent in the language would have almost certainly recorded. Geertz (1972) does cite Bateson and Mead's (1942) contention that the Balinese conception of the body "as a set of separately animated parts" allows them to view cocks as "detachable, self-operating penises, ambulant genitals with a life of their own" (p. 5), but then claims that he does "not have the kind of unconscious material either to confirm or disconfirm this intriguing notion." Again, one regrets his failure to collect the jokes, puns, and obscenities available to him. So, although Geertz did nominally acknowledge that cocks "are masculine symbols *par excellence*" among the Balinese, this fact did not play a major part in his interpretation of the cockfight as a whole.

The English word "cock," meaning both rooster and phallus, is the subject of wit among cockfighters in the United States. According to Hawley (1982), "One Florida informant was heard to say 'My cock may not be the biggest, but it's the best in this county.'" Apparently such double meanings were so common as to make older cockers use the term "rooster" in mixed company (p. 105; see also Baird 1981).

Among the various surveys of the folklore of cocks (e.g., Gittée 1891; Fehrle 1912; Raseh 1930; and Coluccio 1970), only a few bother to mention the cock as a symbol of virility (Castillo de Lucas 1970, pp. 363–364; Cadet 1971, p. 109). The phallic associations of the rooster, even apart from its apparent potential for magical resuscitation in cockfighting, explains why the cock was a logical, if not psychologically obvious, choice

as a symbol for resurrection (Modi 1911, p. 112). Resurrection, if understood as reerec-
tion, or even in the narrow Christian sense of rising miraculously from the dead, is perfectly understandable in cockfight terms. There are numerous reports in the cockfight literature of a cock, apparently totally vanquished and lying motionless, somehow managing
to recover sufficiently to arise and earn a victory over its opponent. This phallic symbolism would help explain why the cock is so often found atop penile Christian architectural
constructions such as church towers, often in the form of weather vanes which pointedly
mark wind direction (see Callisen 1939; Kretzenbacher 1958; Cadet 1971, pp. 166–168,
199–204; see also Forsyth 1978 and Baird, 1981–1982). The same rationale would illuminate the occurrence of a cockfight motif on sarcophagi and other funerary monuments
(Bruneau 1965, p. 115; Forsyth 1978, pp. 262–264). It would also elucidate the frequent
occurrence of the "Coq gaulois" as an emblem mounted on the prows of French warships
(Vichot 1970).

Occasional comments indicate that cockfighting is analogous to sexuality. In a Filipino
cockfighting manual we are told, "An ideal cock must be able to top a hen several times before
letting her get up, because sex and gameness complement each other. . . . Indeed, no other
sport has as much connection with sex as cockfighting" (Lansang 1966, pp. 41, 59, 139).
The explicit anthropomorphic projection upon roosters and chickens in the Philippines
is such that a strict double standard is maintained. Cocks are expected to indulge themselves, but hens are considered to be "sexually promiscuous" (p. 151), and breeders must
keep watch over hens in the barnyard "because the hen is a natural whore" (p. 140).

Similar male chauvinism is found in other descriptions of chickens and roosters:

> Females are strongly sexual and thus impulsive. Their actions are instinctively
> generated by feelings, and they need the presence of a male. They are amorous.
> Nature made them so and provided that their actions be governed by their sexual
> impulses. Males are cooler in disposition and have developed a different brain.
> They act according to logic. Females act impulsively. (Finsterbusch 1980, p. 166)

Hard to believe that these are descriptions of chickens and roosters, and not humans!

It is likely that the symbolic equation of cock and human phallus exists regardless of
whether or not the term for "rooster" in a given culture refers explicitly to the male organ.
In Spanish and Portuguese, for example, we are told that this verbal equation does not
exist. However, in Brazil, a "tea of cock's spurs is recommended for sexual potency" (Leal
1989, p. 241). In an Arabic tract from the thirteenth century we learn, "If you take a cock's
blood and mix it with honey, and place it on the fire, and apply the mixture to the penis
of a man, it will increase his virile power as well as his sexual enjoyment" (Phillott 1910, p.
91). Moreover, if a woman ate a cock's testicles after intercourse, she greatly increased her
chances of becoming pregnant (Smith and Daniel 1975, p. 54; Hawley 1982, p. 106). In
other words, customs and belief systems make the connection between rooster and phallus perfectly clear. There are also numerous winged phallic amulets in the shape of cocks
(Baird 1981–1982, p. 84).

The sexual component is alluded to only en passant by most writers on cockfights, if
it is mentioned at all. In an essay in *Esquire,* Crews (1977) remarked that when a man's
cock quits in the pit, he suffers profound humiliation. *When a man's cock quits!* Yes, that's
part of the ritual, too. Perhaps the biggest part. A capon—a rooster that has been castrated
to improve the taste of the meat—seldom crows, never notices hens, and will hit nothing
with spur or beak. But a game fowl is the ultimate blend of balls and skill, all of which is

inextricably bound up with the man who bred it and fed it and handles it in the pit (p. 8). Attributing "balls" to cocks is not all that unusual. In Andalusia, for example, according to Marvin (1984, p. 66), men may say admiringly of an especially aggressive cock "tienes los cojones de ganar bien" ("it has the balls to win well") (p. 65). The same idiom is found in Nathanael West's account of a cockfight in *The Day of the Locust,* when the Mexican cocker Miguel praises a red rooster: "That's a bird with lots of cojones" (West 1950, p. 123). One difficulty in "proving" the sexual component of the cockfight lies in the fact that such a component is largely unconscious. Consequently, it is not easy to obtain informant confirmation of the symbolism through interviews. Wollan (1980) phrased the problem as follows:

> How much of this symbolism is present in modern cockfighting, and how much of it would be understood by cockers themselves, is difficult to say. How to research the topic is equally puzzling. Conversation promises to yield little information about cockfighting as a symbol, and certainly nothing about its sexual dimensions. Hence, interpretation of a sort not commonly done, certainly not in fashion in the social sciences, would seem indispensable. (p. 28)

Hawley, whose 1982 Florida State doctoral dissertation in criminology sought to define cockfighters as a deviant subculture, claimed that in his field experience "sexual entendre was encountered infrequently. . . . However, the implicit sexual nature of the activity was omnipresent" (p. 104). Still, he admitted, "Sexual animism was definitely the most difficult cultural theme to study in any fashion systematically or haphazardly . . . [and] a ticklish subject to study in the field under the best of conditions" (pp. 107, 147). Hawley himself does not doubt "the significance of the cock as a symbol of aggressive, male-oriented sexual behavior." In his words, "The cock is, to all appearances, a walking unselfconscious set of eager genitals . . . the cock represents male sexuality raised (or lowered) to the most primitive extremity." But, Hawley remarks, "the obvious sexual significance of the cock is characteristically ignored by the cocking fraternity in all but the most casual and relaxed settings" (p. 121). Hawley might have added the anthropological and folkloristic fraternities as well. A far too typical comment contained in one of several essays devoted to a twenty-year retrospective view of Geertz's 1972 essay exemplifies the "meaningless" school of interpretation. One of the co-authors, a Louisiana native who wrote his Master's thesis on Louisiana cockfights, claimed he "found many, if not most, of the same metaphors in cockfights in southern Louisiana that Geertz observed in Bali," but his "reading was that cockfights there had no deep meaning but were just for fun" (Chick and Donlon 1992, p. 239).

Yet the sexual symbolic significance of the "cock" is attested by countless bawdy jokes. One exemplar can stand for many: Q. What is the difference between a rooster and Marilyn Monroe? A. A rooster says "Cock-a-doodle-do." Marilyn Monroe says "Any cock'll do." It may or may not be relevant that St. Augustine in his interesting fourth-century discussion of cockfights discusses them in a paragraph that begins with a consideration of the sexual organs of animals which one cannot bear to look at (Russell 1942, p. 95).

If we accept the premise that the gallus can symbolically be a phallus, and if we provisionally accept the possibility that there is an underlying sexual component in the cockfight, we must next emphasize that the cockfight is an all-male event. Women do not usually attend cockfights. An early eighteenth-century account of cockfighting in England specifically remarks that "ladies never assist at these sports" (Saussure 1902, p. 282). Geertz (1972) even bothers to comment that "the cockfight is unusual within Balinese culture in being a single-sex public activity from which the other sex is totally and expressly excluded"

(p. 30*n*). Even in those cultures where women arc permitted to observe cockfights, they are not active participants and do not handle the cocks. Some women resent their virtual exclusion from the world of cockfighting, and they resent as well the extraordinary amount of time their male companions devote to that world. From northern France we have a report of a female reproach that carries an overt sexual connotation: "He holds his cocks more often than he holds me" (Cegarra 1988, p. 58). Also from northern France, we find a distinction between women who may kill chickens as part of preparing food and men who are involved in cockfights. The fighting cock is a wild animal whose death, necessarily violent, is symbolic. The arming of cocks for battle is an affair of men, not women, and should not be confused with the domestic household requirement of killing chickens for food (p. 59).

The separation from women in cockfights is also signaled by the fact that the roosters themselves are not permitted access to hens during the period immediately preceding a cockfight. This form of quarantine is surely analogous to the modern-day football coach's forbidding his players to spend the night before a game with their wives or girlfriends, or to a bullfighter's sexual abstinence the night before a bullfight. Here is an account of the training of roosters in the Texas-Mexico area:

> The most important experience of the young stag commences when his trainer moves him from his solitary cage and places him in a hennery. There he bosses his harem of hens, living and learning the meaning of his cockhood. Later, when the trainer takes him away from the pullets, the cockerel turns into a bird of Mars. Now he has a lust to fight, his lust arising from his strong sex drive. (Braddy 1961, p. 103)

In another account from Texas, we are informed, "They have had no food this morning, and for two weeks have been penned up and deprived of female company" (Gard, 1936, p. 66).

In the Philippines, "it is a mistake to release your stag in a place where too many hens are kept, for so many hens make him tread often, and much treading greatly debilitates a bird and makes him feeble when he comes to fight" (Lansang 1966, p. 61). We learn that in Martinique sexual abstinence during the cocks' training is strict and that one makes a concerted effort to keep hens away from the cages in which the cocks are contained the evening before or the day of the cockfight for fear the cocks will dissipate their energies (Affergan 1986, p. 114). In the north of France, too, keeping the cock in isolation away from females is suppose to increase his aggressivity tenfold (Cegarra 1989, p. 673).

In Brazil, cocks

> are not permitted sexual intercourse for long periods before fighting. . . . It is believed that sexual abstinence will give [them] the strength and will to fight, and that decreased sexual activity will create better quality semen. The underlying assumption is that sexual intercourse or even contact with a female will turn the male into a weaker being. (Leal 1989, p. 238)

In some traditions, the handler as well as the cock must abstain from heterosexual intercourse. In the Philippines, "sex should be avoided before going to the cockpit; the man stupid enough to have sex before a match will be ignominiously humiliated when his bird runs away." However, "Sex is heartily recommended for after the fight, when men no longer need conserve their vital energies" (Guggenheim 1982, p. 10).

The renunciation of heterosexuality in conjunction with the cockfight seems to support the idea that the cockfight is an all-male, or homosexual, affair. Thus, if the gallus is a phallus and if there is a sexual component to the cockfight, it is a matter played out between two sets of males: roosters and men. In this sexual battle, one begins with *two* males, but ends with *one* male and *one* female. Is there any evidence to support this contention? In Malaysia, the term used for matching two roosters for a forthcoming fight may be relevant. "The stakes are all deposited with a stake-holder (who receives a percentage for his good services); and the cocks are plighted or 'betrothed' to one another by the simple ceremony of allowing each bird one single peck at its rival" (Wilkinson 1925, p. 65). The curious idiomatic usage of the word "betrothal"—the author does not provide the Malay native term—for the matching of two male cocks is significant. They are mates, analogous to heterosexual humans, but the fight is to determine which one will be the male and which the "female." In Bali, according to Bateson and Mead (1942), "In speaking of real courtship, the Balinese liken the behavior of boy and girl to that of two cocks straining toward each other with their heads down and their hackle feathers up" (p. 172). That the Malay term and Balinese image are not flukes is corroborated by a parallel custom in Martinique in which the two cocks to be paired in combat are said to be joined in "marriage" (Champagnac 1970, p. 72; Affergan 1986, p. 115). Of possible relevance to the matrimonial metaphor is the Anglo-American usage of the term "flirt" to refer to the initial contact of the two cocks (Egan 1832, p. 152; Worden and Darden 1992, p. 277).

In one of the finest ethnographic accounts of the cockfight to date, Leal (1989) describes the crowd's cheers during a typical Brazilian bout.

> During a fight every movement of the cock is followed by the crowd's cheers of "go ahead! Mount him! (*monta nele! trepa nele!*)." Inasmuch as "to mount" or "to climb" (*trepar*) are also expressions commonly used to refer to sexual intercourse, usually implying the man's position in the sexual act, the crowd's cheers are not only metaphorical. (pp. 217–218)

Here is certainly incontrovertible evidence supporting the equation of "gallus as phallus." Leal even recorded a folk poem that confirms the already explicit erotic significance of "mounting":

Quien tuviera la suerte	Who would have the luck
que tiene el gallo	that the cock has,
clue en medio de la juria	that in the middle of the fight
monta a caballo.	to be mounted on a horse. (p. 218)

The allusions to courtship, marriage, and mounting do underscore the sexual nuances of the cockfight, but what evidence is there to support the proposition that the loser in a cockfight is deemed a female?

In a cockfight, sometimes a cock will freeze in the face of a feared opponent. This so-called tonic immobility (Herzog 1978) might simply be a desperate defense mechanism, that is, playing dead to prevent the dominant cock from attacking further. More commonly, a cock that loses its nerve may choose to flee. In an account from Texas, we are told:

> When a beaten gamebird decides to withdraw from the battle, he lifts his hackle, showing to the spectators the white feathers underlying his ruff. This act gave rise to the famous expression "showing the white feather," which symbolizes cowardice. (Braddy 1961, pp. 103–104)

In the north of France, a cock that flees, crying, is immediately declared to have lost if his opponent is standing (Demulder 1934, p. 13). Such flight and such crying are deemed cowardly acts. In Belgium, too, a cock that starts crying is declared vanquished (Jaquemotte and Lejeune 1904, p. 226). In the mid-nineteenth century, the pioneering Italian anthropologist and sexologist Paulo Mantegazza, perhaps best known for his Frazerian survey, *The Sexual Relations of Mankind* (1916), visited Argentina, where he described a cockfight. He remarked on the different ways the fight could end. One way involved an exit from the arena "siempre abierta para los cobardes" (always open for cowards) in which a bloody and beaten rooster might sing, calling for aid from the hens of his harem (p. 69).

There is even better evidence that winning in a cockfight is associated with masculinity, whereas losing is considered to belong to the realm of the feminine. In Venezuela, one may hear a spectator yell, "Vamos, como tu padre!" ("Let's go, like your father!") to exhort a cock to do better (Marquez 1954, p. 45); in Brazil, during a cockfight, one may hear comments referring to the losing cock along the lines of "the mother's blood is showing" (Leal 1989, p. 216).

In Colombia, a cock that runs away is thought to cry like a chicken (León Rey 1953, p. 93). In Mexico, to be a "gallo-gallina," a rooster-hen, is to be a coward or homosexual (Mendoza 1943, p. 123). In Venezuela, there is a general folk belief that a rooster who "clucks" like a chicken is a sure sign of an imminent disgrace (Acosta Saignes 1954, p. 39). In Andalusia, too, a cock may lose a fight by fleeing from its opponent while making a low clucking sound. This is called "canta la gallina," which may be translated as "the hen sings" (Marvin 1984). Anthropologist Marvin astutely observes, "What should be noted here is not only does the bird flee but it also makes what is perceived to be the sound of a hen, a female. This behavior is regarded as reprehensible, for the cock is not acting as a true male" (p. 64). Here is prima facie evidence that the loser in the Andalusian cockfight is considered to be a chicken rather than a rooster, a female rather than a male. In Borneo, we find a possible parallel; we are told that "occasionally the bird was "chicken," and ran after the first scuffle (Barclay 1980, p. 18), although it is not altogether certain whether "chicken" is a native-language term in Borneo or not. The placing of it in single quotes suggests, however, that it might be. Of course, in American folk speech, to be "chicken" is to be cowardly, especially among a group of male peers.

The feminization of the loser in a cockfight cannot really be disputed. In Martinique, there is a proverb "Kavalie vol a dam," which presumably has a literal meaning of "a cavalier flies to a lady [dame]." The proverb refers to the fact that there must always be an adversary for a cock, but, more important in the present context, that a good cock never hesitates to fly toward his opponent (as does a man toward a woman). The winning cock affirms his maleness, his virility, while the loser is forced to take the female role with a strongly negative connotation. It is clearly preferable to be a true female than a false (effeminate) male (Affergan 1986, p. 119). Also in Martinique we find the idiom "faire la poule" (to be chicken) applied to a cock who cowers in front of an opponent, refusing to fight (Champagnac 1970, p. 35). Leal (1989) reports that in Brazil, if a losing rooster attempts to run from the pit "crying like a chicken" (cacarejando feito galinha), this would constitute the worst kind of dishonor to the cock's owner and supporters since "symbolically at that moment the cock and the men become females." "Chicken" is a slang term for both "loose woman" and coward (p. 211). Such data support our contention that the losing cock in a cockfight becomes feminized, becomes a chicken.

Other details of the cockfight take on new significance in the light of the argument here proposed. These details include specific techniques designed to stimulate or revive a wounded cock. Prefight preparation sometimes involved inserting stimulants in prescribed orifices. For example, in Bali, according to Geertz (1972), red pepper might be stuffed down a cock's beak or up its anus to give it spirit (p. 6). Guggenheim (1982) reported that in the Philippines "sticking chili up the anus" (p. 10) was thought to increase the cock's "natural ferocity." In Belgium, just before a fight a cock might be given a piece of sugar soaked in cognac (Remouchamps and Remacle 1949, p. 65).

Another prefight ritual is reported from Haiti. There, in order to convince the judge that no poison has been placed on a particular cock's spurs—poison that would unfairly eliminate the opposing cock if it entered its bloodstream—the cock's handler will suck the spurs of his cock and perhaps also the beak and neck of his bird as well (Marcelin 1955b, p. 59). For the same practice in the Philippines, see Roces (1959, pp. 65–66); for Martinique, see Affergan (1986, p. 115). There also the cock is forced to drink the water in which he is bathed. This is similar to a technique in southern Louisiana where an official uses a wet cotton ball to wipe the metal gaffs after which he squeezes water drops into the cock's mouth (Donlon 1990, 282; 1991, p. 106). In Venezuela, Cook (1991, p. 92) notes the poison is applied at the last minute, right before the fight starts because otherwise the cock with the poisoned spur might accidentally scratch itself.

This practice is reasonable enough, but a similar one used to resuscitate wounded cocks during a fight requires a different rationale. In Bali, during breaks in the fight, handlers are permitted to touch their birds to revive them. The handler "blows in its mouth, putting the whole chicken head in his own mouth and sucking and blowing, fluffs it, stuffs its wounds with various sorts of medicines, and generally tries anything he can think of to arouse the last ounce or spirit which may be hidden somewhere within it" (Geertz 1972, p. 9). An earlier account of cockfighting in Bali confirms that the handlers try to revive their cocks' "ardour by petting, massage or by blowing into their beaks" (Knight 1940, p. 81), This means of "sucking the wounds of an injured cock is one of the oldest prescriptions for healing a bird" (Smith and Daniel 1975, p. 86). A physician traveling in Cuba in the mid-nineteenth century confirmed the practice as he reported seeing owners "sucking the whole bleeding head repeatedly" (Wurdemann 1844, p. 92). The technique continues to be popular and is reported from Tennessee (Gunter 1978, p. 166; Cobb 1978, p. 92) and Texas (Braddy 1961, p. 105) among other places. Literary critic Stanley Edgar Hyman (1950), describing a cockfight he attended in Saratoga Springs, New York, in the summer of 1949, noted the following:

> For centuries, it has been the custom for the handler during the breaks in the
> fighting, to wipe the blood out of his chicken's eyes on his mouth—a procedure
> that undoubtedly goes back to the ancient ritualistic origins of the sport, which
> are to be found in cock sacrifice and blood-drinking. (p. 101)

Hyman, of course, presented not one shred of documentary evidence for his hypothetical ritual origin of the practice. He was well known for his ardent advocacy of "myth-ritual" theory, according to which all folklore was supposedly a survival from an original ritual of some kind (see Bascom 1957). In some versions of the practice, the handlers blow water on the wounded cock, but some cockfighters preferred the licking system "because of the supposed healing power of human saliva" (Cobb 1978, p. 92). An informant at a New York state cockfight claimed that cold water is dangerous for the birds' systems but that "human saliva not only is just the right temperature but is well known to have effective germicidal properties (Hyman 1950, p. 101).

After a fight is over, a handler may attempt to apply a more conventional disinfectant to the cock's wounds such as tincture of iodine, but one old tradition (in Belgium and in England) insists that it is preferable to urinate on the wounds immediately after the combat on the grounds that urine is the best of disinfectants (Remouchamps and Remacle 1949, pp. 75–76; Scott 1957, p. 49). There are also reports that a cock should be fed urine. Scott (1957) remarked, "I well remember a famous exhibitor telling me some thirty years ago that the secret of getting birds into perfect show condition was to feed them on wheat which had been steeped in urine" (p. 42). In Brazil a handler "will put the cock's entire head inside his mouth in a desperate attempt to revive the cock for the coming round" (Leal 1989, pp. 237–238). Leal has offered an ingenious interpretation of the exchange of bodily fluids between man and cock (p. 244). The man gives his body fluids saliva and urine to the cock while the cock gives his blood to the man: "Man's fluids (food, saliva, urine) become cock's fluids (semen and blood)" (p. 246). Still, the act of sucking the cock's whole head seems to require further explanation. In Venezuela, for instance, the practice is called "mamar el gallo" (Olivares Figeroa 1949, p. 186), which might be translated as "sucking the cock"—"mamar" being the same word used for babies' nursing; mamar as in mammary gland, and ultimately the term "mama."

Hawley (1987), in his description of cockfights in the southern United States writes, "The handlers try to revive the weakened birds by various seemingly bizarre methods: taking the bleeding bird's head into his mouth to warm it and drain blood from its lungs" (pp. 22–23). Hawley (1982) mused about this practice in his unpublished doctoral dissertation, not in print.

> Occasionally the seemingly bizarre resuscitative behavior in which handlers indulge during cockfighting has been observed to be the source of some coarse, jocular, and sometimes disapproving commentary from spectators and informants. As one might expect, when a handler puts a wounded cock's head in his mouth to suck out the blood, he is indeed engaging in behavior that some would find highly fraught with sexual implications. Since, according to informants, this maneuver is highly efficacious in reviving fatigued birds, perhaps the sexual entendre is unwarranted. It is, nonetheless, a disconcerting sight for the uninitiated to behold. (p. 106)

There is another curious technique sometimes employed to revive a wounded cock. A Georgia informant, for example, after remarking, "I've seen guys put a whole chicken's head in their mouth," went on to describe another practice, "And one trick I've seen . . . they will blow that chicken in his vent, you know, if he's about dead or about cut down or something. They'll blow him back there to try to help him get a little air and get him cooled off" (Anon. 1984, p. 483). A striking parallel to this practice is reported from south India. Among the people of Tuluva, we learn that

> sometimes, the beaten cock will again be encouraged to fight, by its owner, who, after taking it to a place near by, will pour cold water over its head or will air it through the anus. . . . The method of airing through the anus is a very curious one, and they say cocks, once beaten, if they survive this process of resuscitation, generally strike down cock after cock in the combat, much to the pride of their owners. (Saltore 1926–1927, p. 326)

According to anthropologist Peter Claus (1992, personal communication), who has carried out extensive fieldwork among the Tulu, the Tulu handlers still engage in this technique of reviving an injured or fatigued cock. In fact, blowing in the cock's anus is even used jokingly as a metaphor in everyday life. For example, if a student were tired and nervous about a forthcoming examination, a friend might facetiously volunteer to blow in his anus to inspire him to put forth greater effort in studying for the exam. There is apparently an analogous procedure employed with cattle in India. Gandhi (1929) in his autobiography spoke against "the wicked processes . . . adopted to extract the last drop of milk from . . . cows and buffaloes" and even went so far as to claim that it was this very process of "phooka" ("blowing") that had led him to give up drinking milk altogether (pp. 245, 474).

In our attempt to demonstrate that the cockfight is a homoerotic male battle with masturbatory nuances, another important facet of the event must be considered. As Guggenheim (1982) put it, "Whatever the social, psychological, or political reasons why people attend cockfights, any cocker will say the main reason he goes is to bet" (p. 19). In the Celebes, "Cock-fights are always connected with betting" (Kaudern 1929, p. 340). Geertz (1972), after an initial overview of the generic Balinese cockfight, gave considerable detail of the intricate betting system employed by the participants and observers of the cockfight. Geertz failed to note that betting accompanies cockfights in almost all parts of the world where cockfighting occurs. This omission is one consequence of his failure to consult other ethnographic reports of the cockfight, even those concerned with the phenomenon in Bali (Eck 1879; Knight 1940) or nearby Java (Kreemer 1893; Soeroto 1916–1917), another area studied by Geertz. Usually the betting is one-to-one, that is, one person will call out a bet and another person will accept it (Parker 1986, p. 24). In this way, the betting scenario mirrors the one-on-one action of the fighting cocks. A cocker turned academic describes betting in his thesis as follows: "Betting at cockfights is an overt expression of machismo. The larger the bet the bigger the man. . . . In a cockfight the betting opponents are in a face-to-face confrontation, a man-against-man contest so to speak" (Walker 1986, p. 49).

While one may well applaud Geertz's (1972) poetic insight that the cockfight's "function, if you want to call it that, is interpretive: It is a Balinese reading of Balinese experience; a story they tell themselves about themselves" (p. 26), one may not agree with Geertz about what that story is. Is the Balinese cockfight simply an extended metaphor for the Balinese social status hierarchy? And what is the connection between the gambling behavior of the Balinese (and others) and the cockfight proper? Had Geertz or other anthropologists been at all familiar with the psychoanalytic theory of gambling, he might have been better able to relate the two sections of his essay: the cockfight and the betting on the cockfight.

Ever since Freud's brilliant (1928) paper on "Dostoevsky and Parricide," the psychoanalytic community has been aware of the possibility that gambling is a symbolic substitute for masturbation. "The passion for play is an equivalent of the old compulsion to masturbate; 'playing' is the actual word used in the nursery to describe the activity of the hands upon the genitals" (p. 193). Actually, Ernst Simmel (1920) had previously suggested that "the passion for gambling thus serves auto-erotic gratification, whereby the playing is fore-pleasure, the gaining orgasm, and the loss ejaculation, defecation and castration" (p. 353). Lindner (1953) discussed the gambling-masturbation equation with clarity:

> Now gambling and masturbation present a wide variety of parallels—Both are repetitive acts, both are compulsively driven, and the nervous and mental states

accompanying the crucial stages in the performance of each are almost impossible to differentiate. (p. 212)

A characteristic of gambling that is perhaps most reminiscent of masturbatory activity is the "inability of the gambler to stop" (Fuller 1977, p. 28), even when winning. Here we cannot help but be reminded of the Filipino manual on cockfighting that warns against "holding-handling" the cock in public, as "handling is habit-forming and once acquired, it is hard to get rid of" (pp. 97–98). As we shall seek to demonstrate, both the cockfight itself and the gambling that accompanies it are symbolic expressions of masturbatory behavior.

It should be noted that not all psychiatrists agree with the Freudian hypothesis of a masturbatory underpinning to compulsive gambling. However, for every psychiatrist who says, "In my experience with compulsive gamblers I find no support for Freud's formulation that compulsive gambling is a replacement for compulsive masturbation" there is one who reports, "What I had found, in my one patient (a gambler), to be the core of the psychopathology—the struggle against masturbation the content of his unconscious masturbation fantasies" (Niederland et al. 1967, pp. 180, 182). Fuller (1977), in the most extensive survey of the psychoanalytic study of gambling to date, concurs that masturbation may underlie it, but he argues that there is an anal component as well (to the extent that gamblers play with money—a fecal symbolic substitute).

The somewhat eccentric Wilhelm Stekel (1924) regarded sexuality as the most important component of gambling, and he used a bit of folkloristic evidence, a proverb, to support his contention. The proverb "Glück in Spiel, Unglück in der Liebe" (p. 240; see also Greenson 1947, p. 74), unquestionably a cognate of the English proverb "Lucky at cards, unlucky in love," does suggest a kind of limited good. There is only so much luck (= sexual energy). If one uses it up in gambling, for example, playing cards, then there will be insufficient for heterosexual lovemaking. There is some clinical evidence to support this conclusion. It involves a compulsive gambler who fell in love. "He had abandoned gambling during the 18 months of his involvement, and resumed it when "the love" was discarded (Galdston 1960, p. 555). This view that there is a finite amount of sexual capacity, or perhaps of sexual fluid, is reminiscent of old-fashioned views of masturbation. The idea was that all the ejaculations resulting from masturbation decreased the amount of sexual fluids available for heterosexual acts. The connotations of the German word "Spiel" in the proverb, analogous to the English word "play," do include explicit allusions to masturbation (see Borneman 1971). The proverb might then he rendered, "Lucky in masturbation, unlucky in (heterosexual) love." (This discussion of the proverb is mine, not Stekel's.) The proverbial equation might also be relevant to the alleged connection between gambling and impotence. The argument is essentially that the "excitement of gambling and the symbolic equivalents for sexual release built into many games serve as a substitute for sexual relationships" (Olmsted 1962, pp. 104–105, 120).

According to Bolen and Boyd (1968), "Latent homosexual manifestations are present in the antifeminine aspect of the gambling hall where there is relative exclusion of women and 'antifeminine vocabulary' (i.e., queens [in card games] are referred to as 'whores')" (p. 622; see also Greenson 1947, pp. 64–65). Greenson (1947) had this to say about the homosexual component of gambling:

> The fellow gamblers are cohorts in homosexual activities. Gambling with other men was equivalent, in the unconscious, to comparing penises with other men;

winning meant having the largest penis or being the most potent. Excitement together often represented masturbation. (p. 74)

Greenson was speaking in general about gambling and not with reference to the cockfight, but his comments do seem applicable to the cockfight. The allusion to penis comparison cannot help but remind us of the care with which cocks are weighed—in the United States, the cocks are matched on the basis of weight down to ounce distinctions. Bateson and Mead (1942) note that in Bali "before the fight each man holds the other man's cock so that he can feel the enemy cock's strength and make sure that it is not much stronger than his own (p. 140). In this context, the cockfight might be construed as a metaphorical performance of a phallic brag session: "My cock is stronger than yours" or "My cock can outlast yours." This view is confirmed by a statement made by a cocker who wrote a thesis on cockfighting in Utah: "As a man's own penis or cock is the staff of his manhood so by extension is his fighting cock an extension of himself. The man whose cock lasts the longest and thus wins the fight is judged the better man. A man's own sexual prowess is largely judged by how long he can maintain an erection. The obverse helps prove this statement. A man who is plagued with premature ejaculation is someone to be pitied and given professional counseling. Thus by association a man who has a battle cock with staying power [and] pride and [which] fights to the end is macho indeed" (Walker 1986, pp. 59–60).

Bergler (1957), expanding on Freud's analysis of gambling, argued that "the unconscious wish to lose becomes . . . an integral part of the gambler's inner motivation" (p. 24; see also 1943, pp. 379, 381; Fuller 1977, p. 88). The logic, in part, is that if gambling is really symbolic masturbation, then the participant should feel guilt for this act and should expect to be punished by a parent or parental surrogate. Bergler (1943) even goes so far as to speak of the gambler as a "naughty" child who expects punishment after performing his forbidden act (p. 386). According to this logic, the gambler is obliged to play until he loses because losing constitutes a form of punishment by an external authority, that is, fate.

The question is: to what extent, if any, is it legitimate to interpret the cockfight (and the gambling that accompanies it) as a symbolic form of male masturbation? Here we may turn to the relevant ethnography to find an answer to this question. Time and time again, we read reports of how much time a cock handler devoted to grooming and stroking his bird. In the Philippines, we learn, "the cock is handled and petted daily by his master" (Lansang 1966, p. 140). Bailey (1909) described a cock tied on a wagon in the Philippines as being "unremittingly fondled" (p. 253). Again from the Philippines, a how-to primer for cock handlers warns against excessive handling or stroking of the cock, especially in public: "You can do the holding-handling at home as much as you desire." But the prospective cock handler is told in no uncertain terms that "handling" is habit-forming and, once acquired, hard to get rid of (Lansang 1966, pp. 97–98). The grooming behavior found in the Philippines is by no means unique. In Martinique, "the cock is the object of a veritable loving passion on the part of its master, who caresses, fondles, kisses it and tells it sweet words" (Affergan 1986, p. 119).

What about Bali? Knight (1940) reported, "You may be sure to find any [male] member of the village community from the age of fifteen up to eighty using any leisure moments toying with and fondling their birds" (p. 77). Bateson and Mead (1942) described Balinese behavior in similar detail:

> The average Balinese man can find no pleasanter way to pass the time than to walk about with a cock, testing it out against the cocks of other men whom he

meets on the road. . . . Ruffling it up, smoothing it down, ruffling it up again, sitting among other men who are engaged in similar toying with their cocks—this passes many hours of the long hot afternoons. (pp. 24–25)

Long before Geertz (1972) described the Balinese cockfight, Bateson and Mead (1942) had remarked, "The evidence for regarding the fighting cock as a genital symbol comes from the postures of men holding cocks, the sex slang and sex jingles, and from Balinese carvings of men with fighting cocks" (p. 140). Yet, despite this insight and such commentaries accompanying photographs as "Many men spend hours sitting, playing with their cocks" (p. 140), Bateson and Mead stop short of calling the cockfight itself a form of mutual symbolic masturbation. On the other hand, according to Olmsted (1962), "Bateson and Mead have remarked on the fact that in Bali, cocks are first taken to, and held and petted and fondled at just about the time that masturbation must be given up as 'babyish' . . ." (p. 181). This observation (which unfortunately is not documented by Olmsted) clearly suggests that cock grooming is a direct substitute for masturbation. In a fascinating gestural comparison, Bateson and Mead (1942) claim that a mother "may ruffle the penis [of a baby] upward with repeated little flicks, using almost the exact gesture that a man uses when he ruffles up the hackle feathers of his fighting cock to make it angry" (p. 131).

Even Geertz (1972) could hardly avoid the overt behavior of the Balinese:

Whenever you see a group of Balinese men squatting idly in the council shed or along the road in their hips down, shoulders forward, knees up fashion, half or more of them will have a rooster in his hands, holding it between his thighs, bouncing it gently up and down to strengthen its legs, ruffling its feathers with abstract sensuality, pushing it out against a neighbor's rooster to rouse its spirit, withdrawing it towards his loins to calm it again. (p. 6)

Geertz never once mentioned the word "masturbation," nor do any of the other post-Geertzian analysts of the cockfight except for Cook, in her 1991 doctoral dissertation, who calls "the careful cleaning, stroking, bouncing and constant handling that fighting cocks receive from their owners" a form of "symbolic masturbation" (1991, p. 98).

For those skeptics who may not be able to see the possible symbolic meaning of a handler's massaging the neck of his cock, I call their attention to the fact that in American slang "to choke the chicken" is a standard euphemism for masturbation and that a "chicken-choker" is a male masturbator (Spears 1990, p. 33).

Once the masturbatory underpinnings of the cockfight are recognized, many of the details of the cockfight can be much better understood. For example, there is a common rule that the handler can touch his own bird, but should at no time touch the opponent bird. In Tennessee, for example, "when a cock hangs a gaff in its opponent, the informant stated 'never touch another guy's bird'" (Cobb 1978, p. 93). Ostensibly the rule is to prevent someone unethical from harming the opponent bird, but symbolically it suggests that one is expected to handle only one's own phallus. The same rule is reported in the Philippines. When cocks are being matched, we are told, "don't let anyone hold your cock to avoid regrets later" (Lansang 1966, pp. 96, 179). Filipinos in California adhered to the same code: "You never do that, touch someone else's bird" (Beagle 1968, p. 29).

Typically, cocks are kept in covered baskets right up until the time they are scheduled to enter the pit. The cock is *exposed* at the last minute for everyone to admire (and to encourage betting). After the exposure, the opposing cocks are juxtaposed so that they are in striking or pecking distance of one another (so as to stimulate them to want to fight). We can now more fully appreciate the possibly symbolic significance of the particular means handlers use to resuscitate flaccid cocks. By taking the cock's head into their mouths and sucking on it and blowing on it, we would seemingly have an obvious case of fellatio. Normally, it is considered demeaning for a male to indulge in such behavior—at least in public. It is worth recalling that the term of choice in Anglo-American slang for someone who performs such an act is "cock sucker." (The reference to "blowing" may carry a similar symbolic association. It is interesting that an Irish description refers to a handler who "put his bird's head into his own mouth to revive it. It used to work all right but whether he was sucking or blowing, I could not decide" (Crannlaighe 1945, p. 512). Also relevant may be the gambler's custom of "blowing" on dice before throwing them.)

Additional ethnographic evidence alludes to oral-genital acts. In Brazil, the cockpit may have a bar or restaurant adjacent where drinks and barbecued beef are available. Leal (1989) reports that men may joke along the lines of "We are eating your cock," even though chicken is not served there (p. 232). Such specifics of joking behavior (of the sort Geertz, 1972, mentioned but failed to record) is absolutely critical for a full understanding of the symbolic significance of the cockfight. According to Leal (1989), "Jokes are made about 'mounting' *(trepar)* or 'eating' *(comer)* 'someone's cock' (that is to say, the cock's owner) in the cockfight situation. Both words, *trepar* and *comer,* in Brazilian Portuguese are used for coitus while *cock* can stand for man, although not for a man's genitals" (p. 241).

Another piece of ethnographic data from Brazil bears on the connection between cockfighting and masturbation.

> When a good quality cock leaves the pit badly hurt there is a general commotion and his owner or handler carefully examines his wounds. As soon as the cock is better, the handler checks the cock's sexual organs to see if they have been affected: with the cock supine the man gently rubs behind the cock's leg in the direction of its testicles. If the cock ejaculates and the sperm contains blood, it is considered that the cock is seriously hurt and will not be able to fight again. (Leal 1989, pp. 239–240; see also Finsterbusch 1980, p. 245)

In a novelistic account of a cockfight set in northern Florida, massaging a cock's testicles is deemed a foul disqualifying that cock. The explanation: "You rub a cock's balls and you take every speck of fight right out of him. It's a deliberate way of throwing a fight" (Willeford 1972, pp. 180–181).

Usually, the masturbatory aspects of the cockfight are not quite so overt. An 1832 account of a cockfight in England describes one individual attending a cockfight:

> He was trying to look demure and unmoved . . . but I was told that he was a clergyman, and that he would be "quite up in the stirrups" when the cocks were brought in. He forced himself to be at ease; but I saw his small, hungry, hazel eyes quite in a fever—and his hot, thin, vein-embossed hand, rubbing the unconscious nob of his umbrella in a way to awaken it from the dead—and yet all the time he was affecting the uninterested, incurious man! (Egan 1832, p. 151)

Fuller (1977) remarked that sometimes, especially in fictional accounts of gambling, "the masturbatory element erupts through its defenses" (p. 101), which seems to apply to the abstemious clergyman attending a cockfight and rubbing the nob of his umbrella.

The present argument also illuminates the fact that cockfights are illegal in many coun-tries. No doubt being outside the law makes cockfights more exciting for those participat-ing. In other words, it is illegal to play with cocks in public; hence, one must do it *sub rosa,* in secret. That authorities ban cockfighting but then allow it to take place in secret loca-tions seems to confirm its symbolic value. Masturbation is typically proscribed by parents, but masturbation occurs nonetheless. We can now better appreciate Geertz's description of a Balinese cockfight. "This process ... is conducted in a very subdued, oblique, and even dissembling manner. Those not immediately involved give it at best but disguised, sidelong attention; those who, *embarrassedly,* are involved, attempt to pretend somehow that the whole thing is not really happening (Geertz 1972, p. 8, my emphasis).

Other symbolic inferences can be drawn from the notion that the cockfight may be a sublimated form of public masturbation. Harris (1964, p. 515) quoted earlier psychoana-lysts who suggested that orgasm and death might be symbolically equivalent. We know that even in Shakespeare's day not only did "cock" mean "penis" (Partridge, 1960, p. 88), but "to die" meant to experience orgasm (p. 101). So, metaphorically speaking, if one's cock dies, one achieves orgasm. In the cockfight, if one's cock dies and the opponent's does not, one loses money as well; that is, one is punished for reaching orgasm in an all-male environment in a mutual-masturbation duel. The bleeding of the losing cock fur-ther strengthens the image insofar as there is a visually empirical loss of fluid for all the world to see. Of course, the winning cock may bleed as well. Presumably both masturba-tors lose fluid at the end of the cockfight, the difference being that the winner is not pun-ished, but rather is rewarded for outlasting his opponent, the loser. He has masturbated but remains alive perhaps to masturbate on another occasion. That a particularly strong cock may fight again and again demonstrates the "repetition compulsion" aspect of cock-fighting (and masturbation).

If the cockfight does represent symbolic masturbation with grown men playing with their cocks in public, all the details from the grooming behavior to the gambling make sense. The grooming, involving the heavy use of the *hands* is analogous to shaking dice, shuffling cards, or pulling the handles on slot machines (one-armed bandits). Although Geertz (1972) made passing reference to "a large number of mindless, sheer-chance type gambling games (roulette, dice throw, coin-spin, pea-under-the-shell)" (p. 17), it was actu-ally Bateson and Mead (1942) who reminded us that the dice thrown at a cockfight are "spun with the hand" (p. 143). The cockfight involves not only the risk of injury to or the loss of one's cock, but also the loss of money wagered on the fight. Losing would constitute "punishment" for indulging in symbolic masturbation while winning would permit great elation as having masturbated and gotten away with it. The Balinese say "Fighting cocks ... is like playing with fire only not getting burned" (Geertz, 1972, p. 21). As Lindner (1953) put it, winning confirms the gambler-masturbator's feelings of omnipotence (p. 216). To be rewarded for masturbating is surely flying in the face of convention. In most cockfights, however, there are more losers than winners.

If a gambler's losing is a form of symbolic castration, as Freudians suggest (Fuller 1977, p. 102), then betting in a cockfight would exactly parallel the symbolic infrastructure of the cockfight itself. If one's cock loses by being put out of commission or by being killed, this would be a symbolic instance of castration. (One is reminded of Cicero's quip in *Pro Murena* when, in trying to ridicule Zeno's Stoic teachings such as the idea that all misdeeds are equal, he remarked "'The casual killing of a cock is no less a crime than strangling one's father" [Cicero 1977, p. 263].) If one had bet on one's cock and lost, the castration would be corroborated and confirmed. If, on the other hand, one's cock prevails, one avoids the immediate threat of castration, and if one wins the bet on one's cock, one does the same thing symbolically speaking.

From the foregoing analysis, one can see that the link between the cockfight and the betting associated with it is much less obscure. *Both* the cockfight *and* the betting are related to male masturbation. We can, then, also better understand why women are not welcome at cockfights. Geertz (1972) noted that the cockfight was unusual in Balinese culture "in being a single-sex public activity from which the other sex is totally and expressly excluded" (p. 30*n*). But he offered no explanation whatsoever for this. If men are competing in public with their cocks, one can easily appreciate why they prefer to do so without women present. In terms of the thesis of this essay, the whole point of the phallic competition is to "feminize" one's opponent. This symbolic feminization becomes less meaningful in the presence of actual women.

We may now have insight into some of the first reports of cockfighting in England and western Europe. According to most histories of cockfighting, the sport seems to have emerged among adolescent schoolboys, a custom that goes back to the middle ages (Anon. 1888, p. 812; Demulder 1934, p. 13; Vandereuse 1951). This schoolboy tradition of cockfighting continued into the early twentieth century (Cegarra 1988, p. 56). Often there would be a series of elimination bouts, with the schoolboy owner of the winning cock called "Roi du Coq" ("King of the Cocks") (Vandereuse 1951, p. 183). There were related customs in which a rooster was beheaded (Vandereuse 1951, p. 197; see also Coluccio 1970, pp. 75–76) or a group of boys threw sticks at a rooster suspended between two trees. The boy whose stick delivered the death blow was proclaimed king (Vandereuse 1951, p. 199). Given the symbolic analysis of the cockfight proposed here, it seems perfectly reasonable for it to be popular in all-male secondary schools.

One more element in the totality of cockfighting is, I believe, worthy of mention. It concerns the breeding of roosters. Many of the treatises on cockfighting offer advice about how best to produce a "game" cock. One old Georgia informant reported:

> Those chickens were raised—most of 'em came from one hen and one rooster.
> They single mated 'em. They'd take the offspring from that and test 'em in the pit
> to see whether they suited them or not. If they did, then they'd take six full sisters
> and the sisters' father or grandfather and they'd breed all those hens. That's what
> they call inbreeding and line breeding. (Allred and Carver, 1979, p. 52)

In one of the many books devoted to cockfighting, we find an alternative term: "Full blood" mating. "'Full blood' mating was approved; father with daughter, mother with son, brother with sister" (Gilbey 1912, p. 8). The oedipal implications of such breeding practices are obvious enough. "You can only try your hens single breeding them and keeping exact records of their sons' performances, and when you come across a true-blooded hen, do not hesitate to breed the choicest son back to his mother" (Finsterbusch 1980, p. 165). According to this same source, "when fowls are bred in, it can be done in two forms: (1) in a vertical sense, i.e., from parents to offspring and grandparents to grandchildren; or (2) in a horizontal sense, i.e., from sister to brother or inter-cousins" (p. 140).

In a cockfighting novel, we are told that a cock bred from a father and a daughter "usually runs every time," whereas "those bred from mother and son have the biggest heart for fighting to the death" (Willeford 1972, p. 39). Breeders may well argue for the genetic efficacy of such inbreeding, but from a psychoanalytic perspective—in which breeders might be said to identify with their cocks (and their behavior), such breeding might constitute wishful thinking as well as fantastic acting out. The point is that such fantasies would not be at all inconsistent with masturbation.

With all of the rich ethnographic detail available in print concerning the cockfight, it is surprising to read what anthropologists have written about it. The refusal to acknowledge the existence of clear-cut symbolic data can only be attributed to what might generally be characterized as an anti-symbolic stance among social and cultural anthropologists. So-called symbolic anthropologists are among the chief examples of those espousing what I would term an anti-symbolic stance. Symbolic anthropologists unfortunately define symbolism very narrowly, typically limiting it to matters of social structure.

Although some authors (e.g., Hawley 1989) have observed a "sexual subtext" in the cockfight, they are quick to say that "sometimes a cockfight is just a cockfight or a gaining opportunity, and not an implicit homoerotic struggle" (p. 131). Hawley, for example, differs with "animal rights activists, who see cockfighters (and hunters and gun owners) as 'insecure about their masculinity' " (p. 131). (For attempts to disprove the negative stereotypes of cockfighters see Bryant [1991]; and Bryant and Li [1991].) A cocker who temporarily turned academic to write a thesis about cockfighting in northern Utah remarked: "Most leave a cockfight as emotionally and physically spent as if they had engaged in extreme sexual activity. I am not saying the release is sexual, but the physical and emotional release is very similar" (Walker 1986, p. 28). Geertz (1972), after dutifully noting phallic elements, totally ignored them in his analysis of the Balinese cockfight as being a metaphor for concerns about status and hierarchy.

Leal (1989), notwithstanding her splendid ethnographic documentation of the phallic nature of the Brazilian cockfight, declines to interpret it along such lines. Says Leal:

> We can see the cockfight as a play of images where ultimately what is at stake is masculinity, not cocks, not even "ambulant penises" as Bateson, Mead or Geertz suggested. . . . I wonder if the equation cocks = penises is not an oversimplification, specific to English-speaking people. . . . In my understanding, phallus itself is a sign invested with the meaning of manliness and power: androcentric cultures ascribe power to the ones who have penises. In contrast to Bateson and Mead, Geertz does not limit his analysis to the cock as a phallic symbol; masculinity and status concern are his main points. (p. 220)

Thus Leal falls back to a nonphallic reading when she says, "Without doubt cockfighting is a dramatization of male identity" (p. 227). Her position is stated clearly enough:

> The association men/cocks, which seems to be self-evident in cultures that have the word cock as a signifier for penis, is not an obvious one in gaucho culture. I am not denying the semantical association man/cock; rather I am suggesting that in cockfighting situations, the meaning of cock imagery cannot be reduced to the notion of male genitals. . . . (p. 240)

For Leal, if a man is able to "perform the tasks and rites which assure masculinity he becomes a man; he acquires the phallus, which means he gains prestige and power" (p. 240). It should be noted that in northeast Brazil far from where Leal carried out her fieldwork—little boys' genitals can be called "pintinho" ("little chick"), in contrast to adult men's, which are often called "galo" ("rooster") (Linda-Anne Rebhun 1992, personal communication). Still, Leal's view is echoed by Marvin (1984), who in his ethnographic account of cockfights in Andalusia noted, "Unlike Bali, in Spain there is no identification of men as individuals with their cocks" (p. 63). Certainly the data from English is more explicit. One thinks of the slang term "pecker" for penis, for example. In a cockfight where both cocks are wounded, it is the one who is still able to "peck" his opponent who is declared the winner. The pecker wins!

My own view is that it is not an oversimplification found exclusively among English-speaking people to equate cocks and penises, especially in view of the ample evidence of that equation available wherever cockfighting exists. The data from Bali and from Brazil are exceptionally explicit, even though both Geertz (1972) and Leal (1989) tend to dismiss the obvious phallic implications of their data in favor of interpretations that favor emphases on "status" and "prestige and power." Indeed, it is my opinion that it is an oversimplification of the cockfight to claim that it is only about status hierarchy and prestige.

The predictable tendency of social anthropologists to interpret virtually all aspects of culture solely in terms of social structure and social organization is easily discernible in previous readings of the cockfight. The combination of the bias toward social structure and the bias against psychoanalytic symbolic interpretation has prevented anthropologists from understanding the explicit implications of their own ethnographic data. It is ironic and paradoxical that social anthropologists—as well as conventional folklorists—invariably condemn Freudian interpretations as *reductionistic,* whereas in fact it is social anthropologists who are reductionists. They reduce all folkloristic phenomena (such as myths and cockfights) to reflections of social structure.

Geertz (1972) and those anthropologists who have followed his basic approach to the cockfight have erred in not being comparative in perspective, in failing to see the cockfight as a form of mutual masturbation or a phallic brag duel, in not offering a plausible explanation as to why women are unwelcome at cockfights, and, above all, in misreading the overall symbolic import of the cockfight with its paradigmatic aim of feminizing a male opponent either through the threat of castration (via the gaff or spur) or by making the losing cock turn tail to be labeled a female "chicken."

Psychoanalysts, to my knowledge, have not considered the cockfight. Ferenczi (1913) did discuss the case of a five-year-old boy who very much identified with roosters (to the extent of crowing and cackling) but who was also at the same time very much afraid of roosters. Ferenczi suggested that the boys morbid dread of cocks "was ultimately to be traced to the threat of castration for onanism" (p. 212).

Is there any evidence of symbolic castration in the traditional cockfight? I argue that all those versions of the cockfight which involve the attachment of sharp metal spurs (also called "heels" or "slashers") to the cock's feet add a castrative element to the sport. Some cultures forbid the use of such armor, in which case the natural spurs of the rooster may serve a similar purpose. Placing spurs on one's cock essentially entails arming a phallus. It is, in my view, symbolically equivalent to competitive kite-fighting in southeast Asia and elsewhere, where a young man will attach pieces of broken glass to his kite string. He does so with the hope that his kite-string will sever that of his opponent. In kite-fighting, the initial action is get one's kite up (a symbolic erection), but this is quickly followed by the battle to cut one's opponent's kite off. Bateson and Mead (1942, p. 135) noted that kite-fighting is a form of "vicarious conflict" analogous to cockfighting, but did not explicitly mention castration. In cockfighting, one puts sharp blades on one's cocks to cut down one's opponents' cocks. If the gallus is a phallus, then cutting a cock could properly be construed as symbolic castration. There is an anecdote about a Javanese official who was employed by the Dutch government which lends credence to this interpretation. When asked by the Dutch authorities to take action against illegal cockfights, he did not want to betray his own people and refused to do so. Instead, he proposed to castrate the cocks so that they would not wish to fight. No one paid any attention to the new rule because the men felt that if they castrated their cocks, they themselves would be castrated as well (Serière 1873, p. 101).

If my analysis of the cockfight as a symbolic, public masturbatory, phallic duel is sound, one should be able to understand why participants might be reluctant or unable to articulate consciously this symbolic structure. In effect, the cockfight is like most folklore fantasy: its content is largely unconscious. If the participants consciously realized what they were doing, they would in all probability not be willing to participate. It is precisely the symbolic facade that makes it possible for people to participate in an activity without consciously understanding the significance of that participation.

Less forgivable and understandable is the utter failure of anthropologists and folklorists to decipher the symbolic significance of the cockfight. Anthropologists can presumptuously label their superficial ethnographic descriptions of the cockfight as "deep," but calling "shallow" deep does not make it so. Perhaps psychoanalytic anthropologists and folklorists should not really complain. If conventional anthropologists and folklorists actually understood the unconscious symbolic dimensions of human behavior—such as that consistently demonstrated in the cockfight—there would be far fewer challenges for psychoanalytic anthropologists and folklorists to take up.

Note

*I am indebted to Rafaela Castro Belcher and Margot Winer for their bibliographical surveys of cockfighting compiled in my folklore theory seminars in 1976 and 1986 respectively. For additional references, I am grateful to Jim Anderson, Caroline McCullagh, Judy McCulloh, Dan Melia, and Herb Phillips. I thank folklore archivist Almudena Ortiz for her assistance in translating several Spanish idioms, and my student Mariella Jurg for translating several passages from Dutch to English.

References

Acosta Saignes, M. 1954. "Introduction al estudio de la gallina en el folklore de Venezuela." *Tradición* 6.15:29–46.
Affergan, F. 1986. "Zooanthropologie du combat de coqs à la Martinique." *Cahiers Internationaux de Sociologie* 80:109–126.
Allred, K. and Carver, J. 1979. "Cockfighting." *Foxfire* 13:50–61, 151–172.
Alonso, M. A. 1849. *El Gibaro: cuadro de costumbres de la Isla de Puerto-Rico.* Barcelona: D. Juan Oliveres.
Anderson, R. L. 1933. "Chicken-fight." *Amer. Mercury* 30:111–115.
Anon. 1888. "Fighting-cocks in Schools." *Chamber's J.* 65:812–814.
Anon. 1952. "Your Taxes Support Cockfights." *National Humane Rev.* 40.11:10–11, 25.
Anon. 1984. "Cockfighting." *Foxfire* 8:385–487.
Armas Chitty, J. A. De 1953–1954. "Las rinas de gallo en el Oriente del Guárico *Archivos Venezolanos de Folklore* 2–3:149–158.
Axon, W. E. A. 1899. "Cock-fighting in the Eighteenth Century." *Notes & Queries,* 9th Series, 4: 62–64.
Bailey, G. H. 1909. "'The Cockpit and the Filipino." *Overland Monthly* 54:253–256.

Baird, L. Y. 1981. "O.E.D. Cock 20: The Limits of Lexicography of Slang." *Maledicta* 5: 213–225.

———. 1981–1982. "Priapus gallinaceus: 'The Role of the Cock in Fertility and Eroticism in Classical Antiquity and the Middle Ages.'" *Stud. Iconogr.* 7–8: 81–111.

Barclay, J. 1980. *A Stroll Through Borneo.* London: Hodder & Soughton.

Bascom, W. R. 1954. "Four Functions of Folklore." *J. Amer. Folklore* 67:333–349.

———. 1957. "The Myth-ritual Theory." *J. Amer. Folklore* 70:103–114.

Bateson, G. and Mead, M. 1942. *Balinese Character: A Photographic Analysis.* New York: New York Academy of Sciences.

Beacey, P. 1945. "Prelude to a cockfight." *The Bell* 11:574–576.

Beagle, P. S. 1968. "Cockfight." *Saturday Evening Post* 241.17:28–29, 76–77.

Beattie, G. 1937. "The Scottish Miner and his Game-cock." *The Scots Magazine* 14:213–217.

Bergler, F. 1943. "The Gambler: A Misunderstood Neurotic." *J. Criminal Psychopathol.* 4:379–393.

Bergler, L. 1957. *The Psychology of Gambling.* New York: Hill & Wang.

Bhide, V. V. 1967. "Cock in Vedic Literature." *Bharatiya Vidya* 27:1–6.

Bolen, D. W. and Boyd, W. H. 1968. "Gambling and the Gambler: A Review and Preliminary Findings." *Arch. Gen Psychiat.* 18:617–630.

Boon, J. A. 1977. *The Anthropological Romance of Bali 1597–1972.* Cambridge: Cambridge University Press.

Borneman, E. 1971. *Sex im Volksmund.* Reinbek bei Hamburg: Rowohlt Verlag.

Boulton, B. 1901. *The Amusements of Old London,* vol. 1. London: John C. Nimmo.

Braddy, H. 1961. "Feathered Duelists." In M. C. Boatright, W. M. Hudson and A. Maxwell, eds., *Singers and Storytellers,* pp. 98–106. Dallas: Southern Methodist University Press.

Bruneau, F. 1965. "Le motif des coqs affrontés dans l'imagerie antique." *Bulletin de correspondance hellénique* 89:90–121.

Bryant, C. D. 1991. "Deviant Leisure and Clandestine Lifestyle: Cockfighting as a Socially Disvalued Sport." *World Leisure and Recreation* 33:17–21.

Bryant, C. D. and L. Li. 1991. "A Statistical value profile of cockfighters." *Sociology and Social Research* 75:199–209.

Bryden, A. 1931. "Cock-fighting and its Illustrations." *The Print Collector's Quart.* 18:351–373.

Cadet, A. 1971. "Le Coq." *Société d'Etudes folkloriques du Centre-Ouest: Revue de recherches ethnographiques* 5:99–112; 144–168, 199–210, 292–308.

Cadilla De Martinez, M. 1941. "De los gallos y sus peleas." In *Raices de la Tierra,* pp. 145–146. Arecibo, PR: Tipografia Hernandez.

Calderin, G. G. 1970. "El gallo de pelea." *Isla Literaria* 10–11:16–18.

Callisen, S. A. 1939. "The Iconography of the Cock on the Column." *Art Bull.* 21:160–178.

Carson, J. 1965. *Colonial Virginians at Play.* Williamsburg: University Press of Virginia.

Castillo De Lucas, A. 1970. "El gallo: Simbolismo refraneado de su preferente figura en la alfareria popular." *Revista de Etnografia* 14:361–367.

Cegarra, M. 1987. *Le Cercle, le plume, le sang: étude anthropologique des combats de coqs dans le Norde de la France.* Paris: Mission du Patrimonic ethnologique.

———. 1988. "Les coqs combattants." *Terrain* 10:51–62. 276.

———. 1989. "Les combats de coqs dans le nord de la France." In M. Segalen, ed., *Anthropologie Sociale et Ethnologie de la France,* pp. 671–676. Bibliothèque des Cahiers de l'Institut de Linguistique de Louvain 44, vol. 2. Louvain-La Neuve: Peeters.

Challes, M. De 1972. "Cockfighting in the 19th Century Caribbean." *Caribbean Rev.* 4.4:12–14.

Champagnac, A. 1970. *Coqs de combat et combats de coqs à la Martinique.* Alfort: Maisons-Alfort.

Chattopadhyay, A. 1973. "Cocks in Ancient Indian Life." *J. Oriental Instit.* 23:197–201.

Chick, G. and Donlon, J. 1992. "Going out on a Limn: Geertz's 'Deep Play: Notes on the Balinese Cockfight' and the Anthropological Study of Play." *Play & Culture* 5:233–245.

Cicero, 1977, "Pro Murena." In *Cicero in Twenty-Eight Volumes,* vol. 10, pp. 167–299.Cambridge: Harvard University Press.

Cobb, J. E. 1978. "Cockfighting in East Tennessee." In C. H. Faulkner and C. K. Buckles, ed.,

Glimpses of Southern Appalachian Folk Culture, misc. paper no. 3, pp. 175–196. Tennessee Anthropological Association.

Colluccio, M. I. 1970. "El gallo." *Revista de Ethnografia* 14:59–81.

Cook, H. B. K. 1991. "Small Town, Big Hell: An Ethnographic Study of Aggression in A Margariteno Community." Ph.D. dissertation, University of California, Los Angeles.

Crannlaighe, P. O. 1945. "Cock Fighting." *The Bell* 19:510–513.

Crapanzano, V. 1986. "Hermes' Dilemma: The Masking of Subversion in Ethnographic Description." In J. Clifford and G. E. Marcus, ed., *Writing Culture,* pp. 51–76. Berkeley: University of California Press.

Crews, H. 1977. "Cockfighting: An Unfashionable View." *Esquire* 87.3:8, 12, 14.

Cutter, R. J. 1989a. "Brocade and Blood: The Cockfight in Chinese and English Poetry." *Tamkang Rev.* 19:631–661.

Cutter, R. J. 1989b. *The Brush and the Spur: Chinese Culture and the Cockfight.* Hong Kong: Chinese University Press.

Danaë O. 1989. *Combats de coqs: Histoire el actualité de l'oiseau guerrier:* Paris: Editions L'Harmattan.

Del Sesto, S. L. 1975. "Roles, Rules, and Organization: A Descriptive Account of Cockfighting in Rural Louisiana." *Southern Folklore Quart.* 39:1–14.

———.1980. "Dancing and Cockfighting at Jay's Lounge and Cockpit: The Preservation of Folk Practices in Cajun Louisiana." In R. B. Browne, ed., *Rituals and Ceremonies in Popular Culture,* pp. 270–281. Bowling Green, OH: Bowling Green University Popular Press.

Delannoy, R. 1948. *Coqs de combat et combats de coqs dans le nord le Pas-de-Calais.* Paris: R. Foulon.

Demulder, R. 1934. "Coqueleux et combats de coqs dans le nord de la France." *Revue de Folklore Français* 5:8–14.

Desrousseaux, A. 1886. "Les combats de coqs en Flandre." *Revue des Traditions Populaires* 1:338–339.

———. 1889. *Moeurs Populaires de la Flandre Française,* vol. 2. Lille: L. Quarre.

Dinwiddie, W. 1899. *Puerto Rico: Its Conditions and Possibilities.* New York: Harper & Brothers.

Donlon, J. 1990. "Fighting Cocks, Feathered Warriors, and Little Heroes." *Play & Culture* 3:273–285.

Donlon, J. G. 1991. "Leisure Most Fowl: Cock Fighting in a Cultural and Historic Milieu." Master's thesis, University of Illinois.

Dundes, A. 1987. *Parsing Through Customs: Essays by a Freudian Folklorist.* Madison: University of Wisconsin Press.

Eck, R. V. 1879. "Schetsen uit het Volksleven (I. Hanengevecht)." *De Indische Gids* 1:102–18.

Egan, P. 1832. *Book of Sports and Mirror of Life.* London: T. T. & J. Tegg.

Fehrle, E. 1912. "Der Hahn im Aberglauben." *Schweizerisches Archiv für Volkskunde* 16:65–75.

Feijoo, L. J. R. 1990. *Apuntes sobre el arte de castor gallos de pelea.* Puerto Rico: Taller Gráfico Gongoli.

Ferenczi, S. 1913. "A Little Chanticleer." In *First Contributions to Psycho Analysis,* 204–213. London: Karnac Books, 1980.

Fine, G. A. 1992. "The Depths of Deep Play: The Rhetoric and Resources of Morally Controversial Leisure." *Play & Culture* 5:246–251.

Finsterbusch, C. A. 1980. *Cock Fighting All Over the World.* Hindhead, U.K.: Saiga.

Forsyth, I. H. 1978. The Theme of Cockfighting in Burgundian Romanesque Architecture. *Speculum* 53:252–282.

Fraser, H. M. 1981. "The Cockfight Motif in Spanish American Literature." *Inter-Amer. Rev. Bibliog.* 31:514–523.

Freud, S. 1928. "Dostoevsky and Parricide." *Standard Edition* 21:173–194. London: Hogarth Press, 1961.

Fuller, P. 1977, "Introduction." In J. Halliday & P. Fuller, ed., *The Psychology of Gambling,* pp. 1–4. New York: Penguin.

Galdston, I. 1951. "The Psychodynamics of the Triad, Alcoholism, Gambling and Superstition."
    Mental Hyg. 35: 589–598.
———. 1960. "The Gambler and his Love." *Amer. J. Psychiat.* 117:553–555.
Gandhi, M. K. 1929. *The Story of My Experiments with Truth,* 2 vols. Ahmedabad: Navajivan Press.
Gard, W. 1936. "Rooster Fight." *Southwest Rev.* 22:65–70.
Geertz, C. 1972. "Deep Play: Notes on the Balinese Cockfight." *Daedalus* 101.1:1–37.
Gilbey, J. 1957. "Cockfighting in Art." *Apollo* 65:22–24.
Gilbey, W. 1912. *Sport in the Olden Time,* London: Vinton.
Gittée, A. 1891. "De I Haan in de Volksverbeelding." *Volkskunde* 4:154–166.
Greenson, R. R. 1947. "On Gambling." *Amer. Imago* 4.2:61–77.
Guggenheim, S. 1982. "Cock or Bull: Cockfighting, Social Structure, and Political Commentary in
    the Philippines." *Filipinas* 3.1:1–35.
Gunter, C. R., Jr. 1978. "Cockfighting in East Tennessee and Western North Carolina." *Tennessee
    Folklore Soc. Bull.* 44:160–169.
Harris, H. I. 1964. "Gambling Addiction in an Adolescent Male." *Psychoanal. Quart.* 33:513–525.
Harris, J. 1987. "The Rules of Cockfighting." In F. E. Abernethy, ed. *Hoein' The Short Rows,* pp.
    101–111. Dallas: Southern Methodist University Press.
Hawley, F. F. 1982. "Organized Cockfighting: A Deviant Recreational Subculture." Ph.D. disserta-
    tion, Florida State University.
———. 1987. "Cockfighting in the Pine Woods: Gameness in the New South." *Sport Place*
    1.2:18–26.
———. 1989. "Cockfight in the Cotton: A Moral Crusade in Microcosm." *Contemp. Crises*
    13:129–144.
Hazard, S. 1871. *Cuba with Pen and Pencil.* Hartford, CT: Hartford Publishing Company.
Herzog, H. A., Jr. 1978. "Immobility in Intraspecific Encounters: Cockfights and the Evolution of
    'Animal Hypnosis.'" *Psycholog. Record* 28:543–548.
———. 1985. "Hackfights and Derbies." *Appalachian J.* 12:114–126.
Herzog, H. A., Jr. and Cheek, P. B. 1979. "Grit and Steel: The Anatomy of Cockfighting." *Southern
    Exposure* 7.2:36–40.
Hyman, S. E. 1950. "Department of Amplification." *The New Yorker* 26.11:100–101.
Jacobson, D. 1991. *Reading Ethnography.* Albany: State University of New York Press.
James, L. 1928. "The Ancient Sport of 'Cocking.'" *Natl. Rev.* 92:138–143.
Jaquemone, E. and Lejeune, J. 1904. "Vocabulaire du coqueli." *Société liegeoise de literature wallonne*
    45:225–230.
Jarvis, C. S. 1939. "Blood-sports and Hypocrisy." *Cornhill Mag.* 159:368–378.
Jones, R. 1980. "Chicken Fighting is a Hobby." *Foxfire* 14:143–150.
Jull, M. A. 1927. "The Races of Domestic Fowl." *Nat. Geogr. Mag.* 51:379–452.
Justo, E. 1969. "Las peleas de gallos." *Revista de Dialectologia y Tradiciones Populares* 25:317–323.
Kaudern, W. 1929. *Ethnographical Studies in Celebes,* vol. 4. The Hague: Martinus Nijhoff.
Knight, F. C. E. 1940. "Cockfighting in Bali." *Discovery,* 2nd series. 3.23:77–81.
Kreemer, J. 1893. "De Javaan en zijne hoenders." *Mededeelingen van wege het Nederlandsche
    Zendelinggenootschap* 37:213–225.
Kretzenbacher, L. 1958. "Der Hahn auf dem Kirchturm." *Rheinisches Jahrbuch für Volkskunde*
    9:194–206.
Lansang, A. J. 1966. *Cockfighting in the Philippines (Our Genuine National Sport).* Atlag,Malolos,
    Bulacan: Enrian Press.
Leal, O. F. 1989. "The Gauchos: Male Culture and Identity in the Pampas." Ph.D. dissertation,
    University of California, Berkeley.
Lee, F 1921. "Filipinos' favorite Sport." *Overland Monthly* 77:20–22.
León Rey, J. A. 1953. "Rinas de gallos y vocabulario de gallistica." *Revista Columbiana de Folklore*
    2:79–96.
Liebling, A. J. 1950. "Dead Game." *The New Yorker* 26.6:35–45.

Lindner, R. 1953. "The Psychodynamics of Gambling." In R. Lindner, ed., *Explorations in Psychoanalysis*, pp. 197–217. New York: Julian Press.

Magaldi, E. 1929. "I 'Ludi Gallinarii' a Pompei." *Historia* 3:471–485.

Mantegazza, P. 1916. *Viajes por el Río de la Plata*. Buenos Aires: Universidad de Tucumán.

———. 1935. *The Sexual Relations of Mankind*. New York: Eugenics Pub.

Marçal, H. 1967. "O Galo na Tradiçáo Popular." *Revista de Etnografia* 9:345–408.

Marcelin, M. 1955a. "Jeu de coqs." *Optique* 13:35–41.

———. 1955b. "Termes de gagaire ou de combat de coqs." *Optique* 20:51–59.

Marquez, L. G. 1954. *Reglameto del Club Gallistico de Caracas*. Caracas: Tip. Londres.

Marvin, G. 1984. "The Cockfight in Andalusia, Spain: Images of the Truly Male." *Anthropolog. Quart.* 57:60–70.

McCaghy, C. H. and Neal, A. G. 1974. "The Fraternity of Cockfighters: Ethical Embellishments of an Illegal Sport." *J. Pop. Cult.* 8:557–569.

Mendoza, V. T. 1943. "Folklore de los gallos." *Anuario de la Sociedad Folklorica de Mexico* 4:115–125.

Modi, J. J. 1911. "The Cock as a Sacred Bird in Ancient Iran." In *Anthropological Papers*, pp. 104–121. Bombay: British Indian Press.

Mosher, H. F. 1989. A *Stranger in the Kingdom*. New York: Doubleday.

Niederland, W. G. et al. 1967. "A Contribution to the Psychology of Gambling." *Psychoanal. Forum* 2:175–185.

Nugent, W. H. 1929. "Cock Fighting Today." *Amer. Mercury* 17:75–82.

O'Gormon, M. 1983, *Clancy's Bulba*. London: Hutchinson.

Olivares Figueroa, R. 1949. "Gallos y galleros." In *Diversiones Pascuales en Oriente y Otros Ensayos*, pp. 179–191. Caracas: Ardor.

Olmsted, C. 1962. *Heads I Win, Tails You Lose*. New York: Macmillan.

Parker, G. L. 1986. "An Outlet for Male Aggression: The Secret Fraternity of the Southern Cockfighter." *Tenn. Anthropolog.* 11:21–28.

Parker, R. 1985. "From Symbolism to Interpretation: Reflections on the Work of Clifford Geertz." *Anthropol. & Humanism Quart.* 10:62–67.

Parsons, G. E., Jr. 1969. "Cockfighting: A Potential Field of Research." *N.Y. Folklore Quart.* 25:265–288.

Partridge, E. 1960. *Shakespeare's Bawdy*. New York: Dutton.

Paul, E. C. 1952. *"La gaguère" ou le combat de coqs*. Port-au-Prince: Imprimerie de l'Etat.

Peate, I. C. 1970. "The Denbigh Cockpit and Cockfighting in Wales." *Trans. Denbigshire Historical Soc.* 19:125–132.

Pegge, S. 1773. "A Memoir on Cock-fighting." *Archaeologia* 3:132–150.

Penrose, B. 1976. "Blood in the Suburbs." *The Listener* 95:236.

Perez, O. A. 1984. *La Pelea de Gallos en Venezuela: Léxico, Historia y Literatura*. Caracas: Ediciones Espada Rota.

Peters, J. P. 1913. "The Cock." *J. Amer. Oriental Soc.* 33:363–396.

Phillott, D. C. 1910. "Murgh-Nama." *J. Asiatic Soc. Bengal* 6:73–91.

Picard, M. 1983. "En Feuilletant le 'Bali Post': A propos de l'interdiction des combats de coqs à Bali" *Archipel.* 25:171–180.

Powel, H. 1937. "The Game Cock." *Amer. Mercury* 41:185–191.

Rasch, J. 1930. "De Haan in het volksgeloof" *Eigen Volk* 2:216–221.

Remouchamps, E. and Remacle, L. 1949. "Les combats de coqs." *Eitquêtes du Musée de la Vie Wallonee* 4:40–80.

Roberts, B. S. C. 1965. "Cockfighting: An Early Entertainment in North Carolina." *N. C. Hist. Rev.* 42:306–314.

Roces, A. R. 1959. *Of Cocks and Kites*. Manila: Regal.

Roseberry, W. 1982. "Balinese Cockfights and the Seduction of Anthropology." *Soc. Res.* 49: 1013–1028.

Russell, R. P. 1942. *Divine Providence and the Problem of Evil: A Translation of St. Augustine's De Ordine*. New York: Cosmopolitan Science and Art Service.

Saltore, B. A. 1926–1927. "Cock-fighting in Tuluva." *Quart. J. Mythic Soc.* 17:316–327.

Sandin, B. 1959. "Cock-fighting: The Dayak National Game." *Sarawak Museum J.* 9:25–32.

Sarabia Viejo, M. J. 1972. *El juego de gallos en Nueva Espaná*. Sevilla: Escuela de Estudios Hispanoamericanos de Sevilla.

Sarma, I. K. 1964. "The Ancient Game of Cock-fight in India." *Quart. J. Mythic Soc.* 54: 113–120.

Saubidet, T. 1952. *Vocabulario y refranero criollo*. Buenos Aires: Editorial Guillermo Kraft.

Saussure, C. De 1902. A *Foreign View of England in the Reigns of George I & George II*. London: Murray.

Scheltema, J. F. 1919. "Roostam, the Game-Cock." *J. Amer. Folklore* 32:306–323.

Schneider, M. A. 1987. "Culture-as-Text in the Work of Clifford Geertz." *Theory and Soc.* 16:809–839

Scott, G. R. 1941. *Phallic Worship*. London: Laurie.

———. 1957. *The History of Cockfighting*. London: Skilton.

Serière, V. De 1873. "Javasche volksspelen en vermaken." *Tijdschrift voor Nederlandsch Indië*, 4th series, 2.1:81–101.

Simmel E. 1920. "Psycho-Analysis of the Gambler." *Internat. J. Psycho-Anal.* 1:352–353.

Smith, P. and Daniel, C. 1975. *The Chicken Book*. Boston: Little, Brown.

Soeroto, N. 1916–1917. "Hanengevechten op Java." *Nederlandsch-Indië Oud & Nieuw* 1:126–32.

Spears, R. A. 1990. *Forbidden American English*. Lincolnwood, IL: Passport Books.

Stekel, W. 1924. *Peculiarities of Behavior*, vol. 2. New York: Liveright.

Tegetmeier, W. B. 1896. "Sport in Art: Cockfighting." *Magazine of Art* 19:408–412.

Teixeira, S. A. 1992. A *Sementica Simbolica dos Nomes de Gatos de Briga, Bois, Prostitutas, Prostitutos e Travestis*. Cadernos de Anthropologia, no. 8., Porto Alegre: PPGAS.

Tippette, G. 1978. "The Birds of Death." *Texas Monthly* 6:163–165, 271–277.

Tudela, J. 1959. "Los gallos de dos mundos." *Amerikanistische Miszellen. Mitteilungen aus dem Museum für Völkerkunde in Hamburg* 25:14–20.

Vandereuse. 1951. "Le coq et les ecoliers (anciennes coutumes scolaires)." *Folklore Brabançon* 23:182–208.

Vatsyayana, 1963. *Kama Sutra: The Hindu Ritual of Love*. New York: Castle.

Vichot, J. 1970. "La Symbolique du coq." *Neptunia* 98:2–13.

Vogeler, E. J. 1942. "Cock Fighting in Florida." *Amer. Mercury* 54:422–428.

Walker, J. L. 1986. "Feathers and Steel: A Folkloric Study of Cockfighting in Northern Utah." Master's thesis, Utah State University.

Watson, R. J. 1989. "Definitive Geertz." *Ethnos* 54:23–30.

West, N. 1950. *The Day of the Locust*. New York: New Directions Books.

Wilkinson, R. J. 1925. *Papers on Malay Subjects: Life and Customs, Part III. Malay Amusements*. Kuala Lumpur: F. M. S. Government Press.

Willeford, C. 1972. *Cockfighter*. New York: Crown.

Witte, J. De 1868. "Le Génie des combats de coqs." *Revue Archéologique, n.s.* 17: 372–381.

Wollan, L. A., Jr. 1980. "Questions from a Study of Cockfighting." *Bull. Center Study of Southern Culture & Religion* 4.2:26–32.

Worden, S. and Darden, D. 1992. "Knives and Gaffs: Definitions in the Deviant World of Cockfighting." *Deviant Behavior* 13:271–289.

Wurdemann, J, G. 1844. *Notes on Cuba*. Boston: Munroe.

16

The Symbolic Equivalence of Allomotifs: Towards a Method of Analyzing Folktales

Introduction

Having argued for changing the units of folk narrative analysis from etic elements of motifs and types to emic ones of motifemes and allomotifs, Dundes contemplated how to integrate these units into a consistent method (see "From Etic to Emic Units in the Structural Study of Folktales" [1962g], chapter 4 in this volume). He was aware of the criticism that his interpretations were speculative and could not be proven empirically. Indeed, Dundes disarmed critics by rebuking Freudian theory, with which he was associated, for universalistic assumptions. His contribution as a folklorist, he announced, was to make interpretation culturally situated and relative. He thus elaborated on an objective method that could provide reproducible results, take into account contextual concerns, and still incorporate psychoanalytic principles of the mind's symbol-making capacity.

Dundes used the outline of "identification and interpretation," which he had earlier established as a framework for folkloristic investigation (see "The Study of Folklore in Literature and Culture" [1965c], chapter 2 in this volume), and focused particularly on establishing "symbolic equivalence" as the key analytical outcome leading to interpretation. After all, most of the questions in his interpretations of folklore revolved around various symbolic readings of folkloric texts within their cultural contexts (e.g., the hook in hookman parking legends as a phallus, money in gambling activities related to cockfights as masturbation, fudge in children's jump-rope rhymes as feces). "Where did he come up with that?" skeptics asked. Besides doubting the theoretical premise of symbols in folklore disguising wishes and desires in response to repressed anxieties, they objected on procedural grounds: "How could these symbolic equivalencies possibly be confirmed and validated as anything but the analyst's perception, unrelated to the meaning intended by the tradition-bearer?"

As an answer, Dundes proposed a way to "decipher" the symbolic code in folktales, but he also suggested that the method could be applied to all folklore genres. Folktales were a focus because of the issue of units of analysis. Since the emic units were based on the "syntagmatic" structural model of narration proposed by Russian formalist Vladimir Propp (involving the positioning of narrative functions in their sequence within a plot, as opposed to the paridigmatic approach of Claude Lévi-Strauss, arranging thematic binary relations in a story), they facilitated an identification step, geared toward the interpretation of meaning (see chapter 6, "Structuralism and Folklore," in this volume). Dundes argued that emic structural units empirically represented stories as they are told. The motifemes or functions within the narrative sequence are predictably stable, but different allomotifs or symbols could be inserted into those functional slots. Dundes surmised that those symbols consistently placed in the same motifemic slot are equivalent, and this could be verified by a comparison of many field-collected texts. He found this especially convincing when a single teller used different allomotifs in the composition of the story, suggesting their congruence mentally. Dundes represented the logic of explanation mathematically, as "If A = B and B = C, then A = C." Having established a symbolic equivalence (e.g., money/feces, womb/tomb, decapitation/castration), then psychoanalytic and cross-cultural analyses could determine the signification of the expression in a social context. He was careful to note that symbols can have multiple meanings, depending on the situation or culture in which they are used, such as his discussion of the equivalencies, in different traditions, of eyes to testicles, breasts, or buttocks.

Dundes applied this method to the story of the "Rabbit-Herd" (AT 570), in which he sought to prove the symbolic equivalence of head and phallus, evident in the congruent actions of decapitation and castration (see chapter 6 of *Parsing Through Customs* [1987h]). In one of his last publications, he used this equivalence to explain the ritual beheadings of American civilians by Iraqi captors, which had shocked American viewers. In answer to the question of why the civilians were decapitated rather than shot, strangled, or beaten, Dundes answered that capturing the head of a male opponent was symbolically possessing his masculinity, and simultaneously acquiring a trophy of victory, much as bullfighters claim an extremity of a conquered bull (2005a). For other applications of Dundes's method, see Carroll 1992a, 1992b; Holbek 1993; and S. S. Jones 1990.

The Symbolic Equivalence of Allomotifs: Towards a Method of Analyzing Folktales

FOLKTALES CONTAIN FANTASY AND MORE often than not, the fantasy is expressed through symbols. Folktale plots are filled with a wide variety of incredible magical transformations, objects and powers (cf. the D or Magic motifs in the *Motif-Index of Folk-Literature*), and since no one has ever offered solid evidence of the actual existence of a self-grinding salt-mill (D 1601.21.1) or a magic object which answers for a fugitive (D 1611) and the like, it is not unreasonable to assume that such fictional creations might be symbols of some kind. Indeed, except for a few remaining fanatic literalists who might insist that folktales are ultimately historical and factual with respect to their portrayal of reality, most folk-tale scholars would presumably accept the notion that the content of folktales includes symbols. The important question is not really whether folktales are symbolic, but rather what are they symbolic of, and is there any rigorous and reliable methodology available to folklorists interested in investigating the symbolism of folktales. In sum, if there is a symbolic code in folktales, how can folklorists decipher this code?

In theory, it ought to be possible to devise a method which could be utilized to unlock the secrets of symbolism in folklore, and moreover unlock them in a way that is replicable. Two or more scholars should be able to apply the same methodology and produce the same results. The problem with nineteenth century solar mythologists and twentieth century Freudians is that typically the symbolic readings of folktales presented give the appearance of being arbitrary, subjective, and unsubstantiated. For a Freudian psychoanalyst, it is sometimes deemed sufficient if a single patient has offered a free association to a symbol or if some authority figure of the past (preferably Freud himself) has previously articulated a particular symbolic equation.

Freud well knew the dangers of interpreting symbols, and in the present context, it is significant that he specifically recognized the value of folkloristic data for the serious study of symbols. In a remarkable paper written in 1911 with the collaboration of David Ernst Oppenheim, a professor of classics interested in mythology, Freud examined a number of folktales in which dreams occurred. The tales for the most part were taken from the periodical *Anthropophyteia* (1904–1931) edited by folklorist F. S. Krauss which provided an important outlet for the obscene folklore collected by eminent folklorists around the turn of the century (and which could not be published in the conventional folklore journals). The dreams in these tales were "interpreted" either by characters in the tales or by the denouements of the plots. Freud was obviously delighted to discover that the penis and feces symbolism found in the folktale dreams corresponded almost exactly to his understandings of the symbolism found in the dreams of his patients. The congruence of folk and analytic dream symbol interpretations does not necessarily "prove" the validity of the interpretations. Both the folk and psychoanalysts could simply be in error. Still, the congruence noted by Freud and Oppenheim does require some explanation. The folk make their interpretations of symbols with no help from psychoanalytic theory and without any

319

favorite theory they are predisposed to champion. (It is more likely that psychoanalytic theory found inspiration and help from the folk. For example, the possible connection between toilet training and adult anal characteristics such as a concern for order and cleanliness was made in German and Austrian folklore long before Freud suggested the connection in 1908—cf. Dundes, 1981.)

The study by Freud and Oppenheim is a promising one, but it must be pointed out that the vast majority of folktales do not have explicit interpretations of the symbols presented in the tales. And so the question remains just how can folklorists decode the symbolic structure of folktales as well as other genres of folklore?

Most of the conventional approaches to the study of folktales are not concerned with the possible symbolic meanings of the tales. The comparative method, for example, seeks to assemble as many versions of a particular tale type as possible in order to make an educated guess at the tale's original form, age, and place of origin. The hypothetical construction of an archetype of each individual trait of the tale as well as the entire tale itself can be accomplished without paying any attention whatsoever to the symbolism of the traits. Similarly, the application of syntagmatic (Propp) or paradigmatic (Lévi-Strauss) structural analysis to a folktale can be carried out without regard for symbolic implications. Propp delineated a thirty-one function schemata for Aarne-Thompson tale types 300–749 without worrying the least little bit about the possible symbolism of individual functions or motifs. As the comparative folktale scholar desires to show the distribution of a tale through space and time, so the structuralist folktale scholar attempts to describe the underlying structure of a tale.

Students of the folktale have become accustomed to distinguishing the various different theoretical approaches to folktale, e.g., the Finnish (comparative) historic-geographic method, structural analysis, psychoanalysis, etc. One could easily get the mistaken notion that these approaches or methods are totally separate and distinct, and that they cannot be used together to attack a common problem. In fact, it sometimes appears that the practitioners of one theoretical approach are downright hostile to the others, as if the methods were somehow mutually exclusive. Thus if one is a good comparativist, he or she might see little value in structural or psychoanalytic studies. Similarly, a good structuralist might demean the painstaking work of the comparativist who carefully locates and compiles hundreds of versions of a given tale. Both comparativists and structuralists tend to dismiss the psychoanalytic readings of folktales—if they bother to comment on them at all—as being merely the doctrinaire applications of a Procrustean a priori theory. While it is unlikely that any scholar would object to the idea of synthesizing these and other approaches, it seems that intellectual synthesis is more an ideal than a common practice.

I should like to propose a method for the analysis of folktale symbolism which depends upon a combination of the comparative method and structuralist theory with implications for psychoanalytic theory. I believe the methodology, if valid, can be employed anywhere in the world—though my particular examples shall be drawn from the European folktale tradition. And I further suggest that the method can be applied to any genre of folklore, not just folktales.

First of all, what is needed is a large number of versions of a tale type. A single version of a tale is insufficient to carry out the methodology set forth here. In fact, the more versions of a tale available, the more reliable the results of the methodology are likely to be. Since we have a substantial number of completed comparative studies of folktales (cf. the tale types in the Aarne-Thompson tale type index which have double asterisked bibliographical references), we have ample materials with which to test the method.

Secondly, we need to take (Proppian) structural analysis into account. We understand from Propp that folktales consist of sequential sets of functions (which I have relabelled motifemes). Although Propp was not concerned to name the various motifs which could fulfill a given function (motifeme) slot, I have suggested (1962) that such motifs be termed allomotifs. Thus for any given motifemic slot in a folk-tale, there would presumably be two or more alternative motifs, that is, allomotifs, which might occur. If we have a full-fledged comparative study of a tale available, we probably have a good idea of what the range of allomotifs are for any one motifeme. Please note again that the concept of allomotif cannot be applied if one has just a single version of a tale type. One would need at least two versions to demonstrate the variation within a motifeme and probably a great many more than two versions to ascertain the full gamut of allomotific variation.

Now what has this to do with the analysis of folktale symbolism? Propp in his 1928 *Morphology* was only interested in the functional (or structural) equivalence of what I have termed allomotifs. But I submit that the equivalence may be symbolic as well as functional. So if motif A and motif B both fulfill the same motifeme in a tale type, I think we are justified in assuming that in some sense the folk consider them mutually substitutable. A may be used in place of B and B may be used in place of A. This is so even if any individual storyteller knows only one of the alternatives. In a study (1980B) of Aarne-Thompson tale type 570, the Rabbit-Herd, I have pointed out that if the hero fails to herd the rabbits, the king may punish him in a number of ways including throwing the hero into a snake pit, cutting off his head, or cutting off the hero's male organ. These alternatives occur in different versions of the tale. The point is that they are allomotifs. The plot is advanced equally well with any of them. What this suggests, among other things, however, is that cutting off the hero's head is regarded as the equivalent of cutting off the hero's phallus. One of Vance Randolph's Ozark informants actually knew both allomotifs, using decapitation for mixed audiences of males and females while reserving emasculation for audiences of males only (cf. Randolph, 1977:47).

From a theoretical point of view, if A and B are allomotifs of a given motifeme, it is true that we do not necessarily know whether A is a symbol of B or B is a symbol of A. The combination of comparative materials with structuralism tells us only that A = B or B = A. On the other hand, the folklorist is perfectly free to investigate the allomotifs in his or her sample in cultural context to determine if one or more are taboo or sensitive in nature. The fact that an informant uses one motif for an audience of men and women, and another for an audience of men only would argue that the latter was the tabooed alternative. It would thus be perfectly logical to assume—on the basis of the allomotif evidence from Aarne-Thompson tale type 570—that decapitation was a symbolic form of cutting off the phallus. Please note that this equation comes from folklore data, from the folk so to speak, not from some folklorist blindly committed to psychoanalytic theory. It may be that both the folk and psychoanalysis are wrong, that decapitation is not symbolic emasculation, but the fact that folklore contains the symbolic equation independent of and apart from psychoanalytic interpretations remains to be explained.

A symbolic equation having once been established through allomotific comparison in folktales may well be manifested in other folklore genres. For example, if cutting off a head = cutting off a phallus, one might reasonably expect to find other instances of a head-phallus equation. One thinks of the pretended obscene riddle: What sticks out of a man's pajamas so far that one can hang a hat on it. Answer: his head. The same equation is found in traditional custom. Among the gamut of apotropaic methods employed to ward off the evil eye are: displaying overtly phallic amulets, making the fica gesture, touching one's genitals, and spitting (Dundes, 1980A:99, 111). How can we explain why the act of spitting should be a part of this paradigm? Well, if head equals phallus, then spitting equals ejaculation, and saliva equals semen. Not only does the initial consonant cluster "sp" occur in both sputum and sperm, but there is the further corroborative metaphorical evidence from the idiom "spitten image" (or "spit and image" or "spitting image") used in English to refer to a child who greatly resembles his father. The symbolic equivalence is also attested in such jokes as the two twins conversing in the womb. One asks the other, "Who's that bald-headed guy that comes in here every night and spits in my eye?" (Legman, 1968:584).

From the same methodological viewpoint, we can see that eyes and breasts are equivalent allomotifs in Aarne-Thompson tale type 706B, Present to the Lover. Maiden sends to her lecherous lover (brother) her eyes (hands, breasts) which he has admired (cf. Dundes, 1980A:113). It should be emphasized that eyes may symbolize referents other than breasts. For example, in Aarne-Thompson tale type 1331, The Covetous and the Envious, the plot summary is as follows: Of two envious men one is given the power of fulfilling any wish, on condition that the other shall receive double. He wishes he may lose an eye. In a version of the tale type reported from New York City in 1936 (Legman 1975:611), we find "A Jew in heaven is told that whatever he asks for, Hitler will get double. He asks that one of his testicles be removed." So eyes and testicles can be equivalent allomotifs—which may explain why in Irish mythology there is motif J 229.12, Prisoners given choice between emasculation and blinding, and also why Oedipus blinds himself as self-imposed punishment for the sexual crime of incest (cf. Dundes, 1962:102). Some students of symbolism in folklore have wrongly assumed that a given object always had one, fixed, standard symbolic meaning. The data suggest otherwise. One of the methodological points of this exercise is precisely to indicate that there may be different sets of allomotific equivalences for a given item or image, even in the same culture. The eye, for instance, can also be metaphorically understood as an anus (cf. Dundes, 1980A:127). If we apply the same method proposed here for folktales to traditional idioms, we can easily document this symbolic equation. In Anglo-American folk speech, one can express an emphatic negative response to a proposition by saying either "In a pig's eye" or "In a pig's ass" (Cohen and Germano 1980:65). Since the alternatives are equivalent, eye = ass. Again, it is important to keep in mind that it is not a question of applying some a priori rigid theory to unlock the symbolic code of folklore. It is rather the folklore itself which provides the necessary key. By assembling many versions of an item of folklore (the comparative method) and by examining the variation occurring within the structure of the item (structuralism), one can determine sets of allomotific equivalents. The folklore data suggest then that in the Euro-American cultures in which the above tales or idioms occur, eyes may be symbols of breasts or testicles and a single eye may be a symbol of the anus.

The method briefly proposed here can be applied within a single culture assuming that variation within a given motifemic slot occurs. In such a context, one has the possibility of delineating a culture-specific or culturally relative set of symbolic equations. On the other hand, to the extent that a particular tale type is found in more than one culture—and few folktales are limited in distribution to one culture—one may employ the method to investigate the difficult question of cross-cultural symbolic equivalents. Please keep in mind that cross-cultural symbolic equivalents are not the same thing as universal symbols. For one thing, if few tales are found in just one culture, even fewer may be said to have worldwide distribution. Most folktales have very definite limited distribution patterns.

Thus there are Indo-European (and Semitic) folktales, African/African-American folktales, Asian-American Indian tales, etc. Accordingly, a listing of all the allomotifs occuring in a motifemic slot in an Indo-European folktale would yield only symbolic equivalences for Indo-European cultures. From such data, it would be methodologically incorrect to assume the universality of such equivalences. One cannot assert that eyes = breasts in all cultures without presenting specific evidence of the existence of such an equation in all cultures, not an easy task.

The methodology does permit, however, the application of the comparative method to the question of the distribution of symbolic equations. One could identify equations from allomotific sets in one cultural context and then compare these results with symbolic equations derived from allomotif sets in other cultures. By such comparisons, one could address the longstanding issue of the distribution of symbols with some data rather than sheer speculation.

There is a final methodological technique which is made possible through the identification of symbolic equivalences. In terms of our mathematical metaphor, if we establish that A = B and we already know that B = C, then we might be able to suggest that A = C. In Genesis (2:21–23), God "caused a deep sleep to fall upon Adam, and he slept; and he took one of his ribs, and closed up the flesh instead thereof." From this rib, God fashioned Eve. The creation of the first woman from Man's rib, Motif A 1275.1, is not a very widespread myth, though it is a puzzling one. What is the significance of God's removing one of Adam's bones to create Eve? Is there a symbolic element here? I believe it is the "bonelessness" of a portion of a man's anatomy which is critical. For one thing, the human phallus, unlike the phalluses of man's primate relatives, does not have a bone. Man is missing the *os baculum*. Early man could easily have noticed the human male lacked a bone in an area of his body in contrast to many of the animals he slaughtered for food. Yet how can we prove that the phallus was ever perceived as a boneless object? An answer comes from riddles and traditional metaphors. A Rigveda text begins: "His stout one appeared in front hanging down as a boneless shank" while an Exeter Book riddle text reads "I have heard of something which increases in a corner, swelling and rising, lifting the covers. A proud-minded maid seized that boneless thing with her hands; with a garment the prince's daughter covered the swelling thing" (Watkins, 1978). Thus both literally and figuratively, the missing bone in man clearly refers to his phallus. Having identified this symbolic equation (A = B), we may look at the account in Genesis (B = C) in a new light. In a male chauvinist creation myth in which biological reality is reversed so that man creates woman from his body, it is perfectly appropriate for man to use his genital organ (Just as woman uses hers in giving birth). The "rib" translation of "Bone of my bones, and flesh of my flesh" is very likely a euphemistic one.

I am convinced that the methodological combination of the comparative method and structuralism can be applied in any culture. Unfortunately, there have been relatively few full-fledged comparative studies of Australian aboriginal tale types or African tale types undertaken. Hence it is not easy to determine the allomotific variation for tales in these areas. On the other hand, once such comparative investigations have been carried out, one could apply the method set forth here. Similarly, I believe the method can be applied to genres other than folktale. Once such studies have been completed, it may be possible to either validate or reject symbolic equations proposed in the past by psychoanalysts and others. It is time that folklorists themselves made an attempt to better understand the symbolic nature of the materials they have collected and classified for so long.

References

Arewa, Erastus Ojo. 1980. *A Classification of the Folktales of the Northern East African Cattle Area by Types*. New York, Arno Press: 297p.

Cohen, G. L. and Germano, E. 1980. "In a Pig's Eye and Related Expressions," *Maledicta*, 4:65–70.

Dundes, Alan. 1962. "From Etic to Emic Units in the Structural Study of Folktales," *Journal of American Folklore*, 75:95–105.

———. 1980A. *Interpreting Folklore*. Bloomington, Indiana University Press: 304p.

———. 1980B. "The Symbolic Equivalence of Allomotifs in the Rabbit-Herd (AT 570)," *Arv*, 36: 91–98.

———. 1981. "Life is like a chicken coop ladder: A study of German national character through folklore," *Journal of Psychoanalytic Anthropology*, 4:265–364.

Freud, S. and Oppenheim, D. E. 1958. *Dreams in Folklore*. New York, International Universities Press: 111p.

Lambrecht, W. 1967. "A Tale Type Index for Central Africa" unpublished doctoral dissertation in Anthropology, University of California, Berkeley: 368p.

Legman, G. 1968. *Rationale of the Dirty Joke. An Analysis of Sexual Humor*. New York, Grove Press: 810p.

———. 1975. *No Laughing Matter. Rationale of the Dirty Joke, 2nd Series*, New York, Breaking Point: 992p.

Propp, Vladimir. 1968. *Morphology of the Folktale*. Austin, University of Texas: 158p.

Randolph, Vance. 1976. *Pissing in the Snow and Other Ozark Folktales*. Urbana: University of Illinois Press: 153p.

Waterman, Patricia Panyity. "A Tale-Type Index of Australian Aboriginal Oral Narratives," unpublished doctoral dissertation in Anthropology, University of California, Berkeley: 342p.

Watkins, Calvert. 1978. "ΑΝΟΣΤΕΟΣ ΟΝ ΠΟΔΑ ΤΕΝΔΕΙ," *Études et Commentaires*, 91:231–235.

17

EARTH-DIVER:
CREATION OF THE MYTHOPOEIC MALE

(*Postscript*) Madness in Method
Plus a Plea for Projective Inversion in Myth

Introduction

Dundes's 1962 interpretation of the widespread "earth-diver" myth (motif A 812) as an example of the projection, in fantasy, of male "pregnancy envy" and anal birth, set the stage for several other applications of this post-Freudian idea to folklore, religion, and media. The essay was also significant for its critical survey of previous anthropological, and Freudian and Jungian, approaches to myth. He found that psychoanalytical approaches tended to overstate the universality of symbols, while most anthropological approaches were too literal in reading myths or too culturally specific in their contextual accounts. Both approaches were guilty of confusing genres (between folktales and myths, particularly) and overlooking variants that folklorists had identified. Dundes proposed a modern folkloristic approach, focusing on symbolic patterning in cross-cultural variants while questioning, for the purposes of interpretation, the particular symbols and specific projections that were culturally relative. As Dundes stated, "insofar as conditions of early childhood may vary from culture to culture, so adult projective systems, including myth, may also vary." The key psychoanalytic premise he applied was developmental and gendered: "There is a relationship, perhaps causal, perhaps only correlational, between the initial conditions of infancy and early childhood (with respect to parent-child relations, sibling relations, etc.) and adult projective systems, which include myth" (1984b).

The story of this essay's writing reveals the challenges that Dundes faced in proposing psychoanalytic approaches. In *Bloody Mary in the Mirror*, he recalled a class on South American Indian folklore at Indiana University, led by professor Erminie Wheeler-Voegelin. In response to a report by a fellow student on the plot—involving a series of animals diving into primeval floodwaters to scoop up mud, which then expands magically to form the earth—Dundes commented that "it was a classic case of male anal-erotic creativity (in which males attempt to compete with females by creating from a substance produced by their bodies)" (2002a). Dundes remembered being ridiculed by his classmates, but he persisted nonetheless, and prepared the present paper, which was originally published in the premier flagship journal of the American Anthropological Association (1962b). The essay has not been without its critics, but it has stood, through the years, as an exemplary post-Freudian interpretation of myth.

The criticisms came first from anthropological circles. From a qualitative viewpoint, they questioned his cross-cultural comparisons (scorned as a "shreds and patches" approach) without field experience in the cultures. Quantitatively, they critiqued Dundes for drawing conclusions without a broader statistical inventory of variants (see Parker 1963). Dundes responded that for a hypothetical symbolic interpretation of a myth, having hundreds more examples would not make the interpretation any more correct. Regarding the particularistic cultural test, Dundes's argument was "that since in *all* cultures, there are *some* restrictions governing the infant's handling of his faeces, there may well be symbolic substitutes for faeces" (1963). Since Dundes's application of pregnancy envy is often viewed as a feminist psychoanalytic interpretation, it may seem surprising that another criticism applied to Dundes's work was the tendency of male ethnographers to "talk about creation through excrement and other effluvia as well as to enact elaborate male rites of couvade and not to address childbirth" (Weigle 1987). Dundes's answer was that ethnographers generally, and male ethnographers particularly, were resistant to psychoanalytic ideas of compensatory creativity as a result of mental blocks against this symbolism.

Dundes was still commenting on issues of method thirty-seven years after his "earthdiver" essay came out. In "Madness in Method" (1996a), given as a postscript to this chapter, Dundes summarized much of his mythological analysis, using the concept of projective systems (particularly inversions), as well as male birth-envy. He continued his line of thinking about womb envy in an examination of the biblical myths of Genesis, and editorialized that they caused "social damage and mental anguish of Western women." Public intellectuals, such as Joseph Campbell, popularized finding Jungian archetypes in myth. Dundes countered by addressing the differences between Jungian and Freudian interpretations, and criticized the Jungian assumption of the existence of precultural, pan-human archetypes, which are manifested in myths. (For more critical comment on the Campbellian craze, see Dundes 2005c). In the "Madness in Method" essay, Dundes echoed his early concern that myths (which he defined as "sacred narratives explaining how the world and mankind came to be in their present form" that are told as true and set in the postcreation era) were confused with folktales ("narratives understood to be fictional). "Mythologists," unlike folklorists, narrowly considered their material without reference to variants and comparable genres. Thus the present essays are significant not only for their definition of myth and an interpretative approach to it, but also for describing the disciplinary distinction of a folklorist.

Earth-Diver: Creation of the Mythopoeic Male

FEW ANTHROPOLOGISTS ARE SATISFIED WITH the present state of scholarship with respect to primitive mythology. While not everyone shares Lévi-Strauss's extreme pessimistic opinion that from a theoretical point of view the study of myth is "very much the same as it was fifty years ago, namely a picture of chaos" (1958:50), still there is general agreement that much remains to be done in elucidating the processes of the formation, transmission, and functioning of myth in culture.

One possible explanation for the failure of anthropologists to make any notable advances in myth studies is the rigid adherence to two fundamental principles: a literal reading of myth and a study of myth in monocultural context. The insistence of most anthropologists upon the literal as opposed to the symbolic interpretation, in terms of cultural relativism as opposed to transcultural universalism, is in part a continuation of the reaction against 19th century thought in which universal symbolism in myth was often argued and in part a direct result of the influence of two dominant figures in the history of anthropology, Boas and Malinowski. Both these pioneers favored studying one culture at a time in depth and both contended that myth was essentially nonsymbolic. Boas often spoke of mythology reflecting culture, implying something of a one-to-one relationship. With this view, purely descriptive ethnographic data could be easily culled from the mythological material of a particular culture. Malinowski argued along similar lines: "Studied alive, myth, as we shall see, is not symbolic, but a direct expression of its subject matter" (1954:101). Certainly, there is much validity in the notion of mythology as a cultural reflector, as the well documented researches of Boas and Malinowski demonstrate. However, as in the case of most all-or-nothing approaches, it does not account for all the data. Later students in the Boas tradition, for example, noted that a comparison between the usual descriptive ethnography and the ethnographical picture obtained from mythology revealed numerous discrepancies. Ruth Benedict (1935) in her important Introduction to *Zuni Mythology* spoke of the tendency to idealize and compensate in folklore. More recently, Katherine Spencer has contrasted the correspondences and discrepancies between the ethnographical and mythological accounts. She also suggests that the occurrence of folkloristic material which contradicts the ethnographic data "may be better explained in psychological than in historical terms" (1947:130). However, anthropologists have tended to mistrust psychological terms, and consequently the pendulum has not yet begun to swing away from the literal to the symbolic reading of myth. Yet it is precisely the insights afforded by advances in human psychology which open up vast vistas for the student of myth. When anthropologists learn that to study the products of the human mind (e.g., myths) one must know something of the mechanics of the human mind, they may well push the pendulum towards not only the symbolic interpretation of myth but also towards the discovery of universals in myth.

Freud himself was very excited at the possibility of applying psychology to mythology. In a letter to D. E. Oppenheim in 1909, he said, "I have long been haunted by the idea that our studies on the content of the neuroses might be destined to solve the riddle of the formation of myths . . ." (Freud and Oppenheim 1958:13). However, though Freud was pleased at the work of his disciples, Karl Abraham and Otto Rank, in this area, he realized that he and his students were amateurs in mythology. In the same letter to Oppenheim he commented: "We are lacking in academic training and familiarity with the material." Unfortunately, those not lacking in these respects had little interest in psychoanalytic theory. To give just one example out of many, Lewis Spence in his preface to *An Introduction to Mythology* stated: "The theories of Freud and his followers as to religion and the origin of myth have not been considered, since, in the writer's opinion, they are scarcely to be taken seriously." What was this theory which was not to be taken seriously? Freud wrote the following: "As a matter of fact, I believe that a large portion of the mythological conception of the world which reaches far into the most modern religions, is *nothing but psychology projected to the outer world.* The dim perception (the endopsychic perception, as it were) of psychic factors and relations of the unconscious was taken as a model in the construction of a *transcendental reality,* which is destined to be changed again by science into *psychology of the unconscious"* (1938:164). It is this insight perhaps more than any other that is of value to the anthropologist interested in primitive myth.

There is, however, an important theoretical difficulty with respect to the psychoanalytic interpretation of myth. This difficulty stems from the fact that there are basically two ways in which psychoanalytic theory may be applied. A myth may be analyzed *with* a knowledge of a particular myth-maker, or a myth may be analyzed *without* such knowledge. There is some doubt as to whether the two methods are equally valid and, more specifically, whether the second is as valid as the first. The question is, to employ an analogy, can a dream be analyzed without a knowledge of the specific dreamer who dreamed it? In an anthropological context, the question is: can a myth be interpreted without a knowledge of the culture which produced it? Of course, it is obvious that any psychoanalyst would prefer to analyze the dreamer or myth-maker in order to interpret more accurately a dream or myth. Similarly, those anthropologists who are inclined to employ psychoanalysis in interpreting myths prefer to relate the manifest and latent content of myths to specific cultural contexts. However, this raises another important question. Do myths reflect the present, the past, or both? There are some anthropologists who conceive of myths almost exclusively in terms of the present. While tacitly recognizing that traditional myths are of considerable antiquity, such anthropologists, nevertheless, proceed to analyze a present-day culture in terms of its myths. Kardiner's theory of folklore, for instance, reveals this bias. Speaking of the myths of women in Marquesan folklore, Kardiner observes, "These myths are the products of the fantasy of some individual, communicated and probably changed many times before we get them. The uniformity of the stories points to some common experience of all individuals in this culture, not remembered from the remote past, but currently experienced." According to Kardiner, then, myths are responses to current realities (1939:417, 214). Róheim summarizes Kardiner's position before taking issue with it. "According to Kardiner, myths and folklore always reflect the unconscious conflicts of the present generation as they are formed by the pressure brought to bear on them by existing social conditions. In sharp contrast to Freud, Reik, and myself, a myth represents not the dim past but the present" (1940:540).

The evidence available from folklore scholarship suggests that there is remarkable stability in oral narratives. Myths and tales re-collected from the same culture show considerable similarity in structural pattern and detail despite the fact that the myths and tales are from different informants who are perhaps separated by many generations. Excluding consideration of modern myths (for the myth-making process is an ongoing one), one can see that cosmogonic myths, to take one example, have not changed materially for hundreds of years. In view of this, it is clearly not necessarily valid to analyze a *present-day* culture in terms of that culture's traditional cosmogonic myths, which in all likelihood date from the prehistoric *past*. An example of the disregard of the time element occurs in an interesting HRAF-inspired cross-cultural attempt to relate child-training practices to folk tale content. Although the tales were gathered at various times between 1890 and 1940, it was assumed that "a folk tale represents a kind of summation of the common thought patterns of a number of individuals . . . "(McClelland and Friedman 1952:245). Apparently common thought patterns are supposed to be quite stable and not subject to cultural change during a 50 year period. Thus just one version of a widely diffused North American Indian tale type like the Eye Juggler is deemed sufficient to "diagnose the modal motivations" of the members of a culture. Nevertheless, Kardiner's theoretical perspective is not entirely without merit. Changes in myth do occur and a careful examination of a number of variants of a particular myth may show that these changes tend to cluster around certain points in time or space. Even if such changes are comparatively minor in contrast to the over-all structural stability of a myth, they may well serve as meaningful signals of definite cultural changes. Thus, Martha Wolfenstein's comparison of English and American versions of Jack and the Beanstalk (1955) showed a number of interesting differences in detail, although the basic plot remained the same. She suggested that the more phallic details in the American versions were in accord with other cultural differences between England and America. Whether or not one agrees with Wolfenstein's conclusions, one can appreciate the soundness of her method. The same myth or folktale can be profitably compared using versions from two or more separate cultures, and the differences in detail may well illustrate significant differences in culture. One thinks of Nadel's (1937) adaptation of Bartlett's experiment in giving an artificial folk tale to two neighboring tribes in Africa and his discovery that the variations fell along clear-cut cultural lines, rather than along individualistic lines. However, the basic theoretical problem remains unresolved. Can the myth as a whole be analyzed meaningfully? Margaret Mead in commenting briefly on Wolfenstein's study begs the entire question. She states: "What is important here is that Jack and the Beanstalk, when it was first made up, might have had a precise and beautiful correspondence to the theme of a given culture at a given time. It then traveled and took on all sorts of forms, which you study and correlate with the contemporary cultural usage" (Tax 1953:282). The unfortunate truth is that rarely is the anthropologist in a position to know when and where a myth is "first made up." Consequently, the precise and beautiful correspondence is virtually unattainable or rather unreconstructible. The situation is further complicated by the fact that many, indeed, the majority of myths are found widely distributed throughout the world. The historical record, alas, only goes back so far. In other words, it is, practically speaking, impossible to ascertain the place and date of the first appearance(s) of a given myth. For this reason, anthropologists like Mead despair of finding any correspondence between over-all myth structure and culture. Unfortunately, some naive scholars manifest a profound ignorance of the nature of folklore by their insistent attempts to analyze a specific culture by analyzing myths which are found in a great many cultures. For example, the subject of a recent doctoral dissertation was an analysis of 19th century German culture on the basis of an analysis of the content of various Grimm tales (Mann 1958). Although the analyses of the tales were ingenious and psychologically sound, the fact that the Grimm tales are by no means limited to the confines of Germany, and furthermore are undoubtedly much older than the 19th century, completely vitiates the theoretical premise underlying the thesis. Assuming the validity of the analyses of the tales, these analyses would presumably be equally valid wherever the tales appeared in the same form. Barnouw (1955) commits exactly the same error when he analyzes Chippewa personality on the basis of a Chippewa "origin legend" which, in fact, contains many standard North American Indian tale types (Wycoco). It is clearly a fallacy to analyze an international tale or widely diffused myth *as if* it belonged to only one culture. Only if a myth is known to be unique, that is, peculiar to a given culture, is this kind of analysis warranted. It is, however, perfectly good procedure to analyze the differences which occur as a myth enters another culture. Certainly, one can gain considerable insight into the mechanics of acculturation by studying a Zuni version of a European cumulative tale or a native's retelling of the story of Beowulf. Kardiner is at his best when he shows how a cultural element is adapted to fit the basic personality structure of the borrowing culture. His account of the Comanche's alteration of the Sun Dance from a masochistic and self-destructive ritual to a demonstration of feats of strength is very convincing (1945:93).

The question is now raised: if it is theoretically only permissible to analyze the differentiae of widely diffused myths or the entire structure of myths peculiar to a particular culture, does this mean that the entire structure of widely diffused myths (which are often the most interesting) cannot be meaningfully analyzed? This is, in essence, the question of whether a dream can be analyzed without knowledge of the dreamer. One answer may be that to the extent that there are human universals, such myths may be analyzed. From this vantage point, while it may be a fallacy to analyze a world-wide myth as if it belonged to only one culture, it is not a fallacy to analyze the myth as if it belonged to all cultures in which it appears. This does not preclude the possibility that one myth found in many cultures may have as many meanings as there are cultural contexts (Boas 1910b:383). Nevertheless, the hypothesis of a limited number of organic human universals suggests some sort of similar, if not identical, meaning. It should not be necessary to observe that, to the extent that anthropologists are scientists, they need not fear anathematic reductionism and the discovery of empirically observable universals. The formula $e = mc^2$ is nonetheless valid for its being reductionistic.

A prime example of an anthropologist interested in universals is Kluckhohn. In his paper, "Universal Categories of Culture," Kluckhohn contends that "The inescapable fact of cultural relativism does not justify the conclusion that cultures are in all respects utterly disparate monads and hence strictly noncomparable entities" and "Valid cross-cultural comparison could best proceed from the invariant points of reference supplied by the biological, psychological, and socio-situational 'givens' of human life" (1953:520, 521). Of even more interest is Kluckhohn's conviction that these "givens" are manifested in myth. In "Recurrent Themes in Myths and Mythmaking," he discusses "certain features of mythology that are apparently universal or that have such wide distribution in space and time that their generality may be presumed to result from recurrent reactions of the human psyche to situations and stimuli of the same general order" (1959:268). Kluckhohn's recurrent themes appear somewhat similar to Freud's typical dreams. Although Freud specifically warned against codifying symbolic translations of dream content and, although he did clearly state his belief that the same dream content could conceal a different meaning in the case of different persons or contexts, he did consider that there are such things as typical dreams, "dreams which almost every one has dreamed in the same manner, and of which we are accustomed to assume that they have the same significance in the case of every dreamer" (1938:292, 39). While there are not many anthropologists who would support the view that recurrent myths have similar meaning irrespective of specific cultural context, that does not mean that the view is false. For those who deny universal meanings, it might be mentioned that the reasons why a particular myth has widespread distribution have yet to be given. The most ardent diffusionist, as opposed to an advocate of polygenesis or convergence, can do little more than show how a myth spreads. The how rarely includes the why. In order to show the plausibility of a symbolic and universal approach to myth, a concrete example will be analyzed in some detail.

One of the most fascinating myths in North American Indian mythology is that of the earth-diver. Anna Birgitta Rooth in her study of approximately 300 North American Indian creation myths found that, of her eight different types, earth-diver had the widest distribution. Earl W. Count who has studied the myth for a number of years considers the notion of a diver fetching material for making dry land "easily among the most widespread single concepts held by man" (1952:55). Earth-diver has recently been studied quite extensively by the folklorist Elli Kaija Köngäs (1960) who has skillfully surveyed the mass of previous pertinent scholarship. The myth as summarized by Erminie Wheeler-Voegelin is:

> In North American Indian myths of the origin of the world, the culture hero has a succession of animals dive into the primeval waters, or flood of waters, to secure bits of mud or sand from which the earth is to be formed. Various animals, birds, and aquatic creatures are sent down into the waters that cover the earth. One after another animal fails; the last one succeeds, however, and floats to the surface half dead, with a little sand or dirt in his claws. Sometimes it is Muskrat, sometimes Beaver, Hell-diver, Crawfish, Mink who succeeds, after various other animals have failed, in bringing up the tiny bit of mud which is then put on the surface of the water and magically expands to become the world of the present time (1949:334).

Among the interesting features of this myth is the creation from mud or dirt. It is especially curious in view of the widespread myth of the creation of man from a similar substance (Frazer 1935:4–15). Another striking characteristic is the magical expansion of the bit of mud. Moreover, how did the idea of creating the earth from a particle of dirt small enough to be contained beneath a claw or fingernail develop, and what is there in this cosmogonic myth that has caused it to thrive so in a variety of cultures, not only in aboriginal North America but in the rest of the world as well?

Freud's suggestion that mythology is psychology projected upon the external world does not at a first glance seem applicable in the case of the earth-diver myth. The Freudian hypothesis is more obvious in other American Indian cosmogonic conceptions, such as the culture hero's Oedipal separation of Father Sky and Mother Earth (Róheim 1921:163) or the emergence myth, which appears to be a projection of the phenomenon of human birth. This notion of the origin of the emergence myth was clearly stated as early as 1902 by Washington Matthews with apparently no help from psychoanalysis. At that time Matthews proposed the idea that the emergence myth was basically a "myth of gestation and of birth." A more recent study of the emergence myth by Wheeler-Voegelin and Moore makes a similar suggestion en passant, but no supporting details are given (1957:73–74). Róheim, however, had previously extended Matthews' thesis by suggesting that primitive man's conception of the world originated in the pre-natal perception of space in the womb (1921:163). In any event, no matter how close the emergence of man from a hole in Mother Earth might appear to be to actual human birth, it does not appear to help in determining the psychological prototype for the earth-diver myth. Is there really any "endo-psychic" perception which could have served as the model for the construction of a cosmogonic creation from mud?

The hypothesis here proposed depends upon two key assumptions. The two assumptions (and they are admittedly only assumptions) are: (1) the existence of a cloacal theory of birth; and (2) the existence of pregnancy envy on the part of males. With regard to the first assumption, it was Freud himself who included the cloacal theory as one of the common sexual theories of children. The theory, in essence, states that since the child is ignorant of the vagina and is rarely permitted to watch childbirth, he assumes that the lump in the pregnant woman's abdomen leaves her body in the only way he can imagine material leaving the body, namely via the anus. In Freud's words: "Children are all united from the outset in the belief that the birth of a child takes place by the bowel; that is to say, that the baby is produced like a piece of faeces" (1953:328). The second assumption concerns man's envy of woman's childbearing role. Whether it is called "parturition envy" (Boehm) or "pregnancy envy" (Fromm), the basic idea is that men would like to be able to produce or create valuable material from within their bodies as women do. Incidentally, it is this second assumption which is the basis of Bruno Bettelheim's explanation of puberty initiation rites and the custom of couvade. His thesis is that puberty rites consist of a rebirth ritual of a special kind to the effect that the initiate is born anew *from males*. The denial of women's part in giving birth is evidenced by the banning of women from the ceremonies. Couvade is similarly explained as the male's desire to imitate female behavior in childbirth. A number of psychoanalysts have suggested that man's desire for mental and artistic creativity stems in part from the wish to conceive or produce on a par with women (Jones 1957:40; Fromm 1951:233; Huckel 1953:44). What is even more significant from the point of view of mythology is the large number of clinical cases in which men seek to have babies in the form of feces, or cases in which men imagine themselves excreting the world. Felix Boehm makes a rather sweeping generalization when he says: "In all analyses of men we meet with phantasies of anal birth, and we know how common it is for men to treat their faeces as a child" (1930:455; see also Silberer 1925:393). However, there is a good deal of clinical evidence supporting the existence of this phantasy. Stekel (1959:45), for example, mentions a child who called the feces "Baby." The possible relevance of this notion to the myth of the origin of man occurred to Abraham (1948:320), Jung (1916:214), and Rank (1922:54). Jung's comment is: "The first people were made from excrement, potter's earth and clay." (Cf. Schwarzbaum 1960:48). In fact, Jung rather ingeniously suggests that the idea of anal birth is the basis of the motif of creating by "throwing behind oneself" as in the case of Deucalion and Pyrrha. Nevertheless, neither Abraham, Jung, nor Rank emphasized the fact that anal birth is especially employed by men. It is true that little girls also have this phantasy, but presumably the need for the phantasy disappears upon the giving of birth to a child. (There may well be some connection between this phantasy and the widespread occurrence of geophagy among pregnant women [Elwin 1949:292, n. 1].)

Both of the assumptions underlying the hypothesis attempting to explain the earth-diver myth are found in Genesis. As Fromm points out (1951:234), the woman's creative role is denied. It is man who creates and, in fact, it is man who gives birth to woman. Eve is created from substance taken from the body of Adam. Moreover, if one were inclined to see the Noah story as a gestation myth, it would be noteworthy that it is the man who builds the womb-ark. It would also be interesting that the flood waters abate only after a period roughly corresponding to the length of human pregnancy. Incidentally, it is quite likely that the Noah story is a modified earth-diver myth. The male figure sends a raven once and a dove twice to brave the primordial waters seeking traces of earth. (Cf. Schwarzbaum 1960:52, n. 15a.) In one apocryphal account, the raven disobeys instructions by stopping to feast on a dead man, and in another he is punished by having his feathers change color from white to black (Ginzberg 1925:39, 164). Both of these incidents are found in American Indian earth-diver myths (Rooth 1957:498). In any case, one can see that there are male myths of creation in Genesis, although Fromm does not describe them all. Just as Abraham, Jung, and Rank had anal birth without pregnancy envy, Fromm has pregnancy envy without anal birth. He neglects to mention that man was created from dust. One is tempted to speculate as to whether male creation myths might be in any way correlated with highly patriarchal social organization.

Of especial pertinence to the present thesis is the clinical data on phantasies of excreting the universe. Lombroso, for example, describes two artists, each of whom had the delusion that they were lords of the world which they had excreted from their bodies. One of them painted a full-length picture of himself, naked, among women, ejecting worlds (1895:201). In this phantasy world, the artist flaunting his anal creativity depicts himself as superior to the women who surround him. Both Freud and Stekel have reported cases in which men fancied defecating upon the world, and Abraham cites a dream of a patient in which the patient dreamed he expelled the universe out of his anus (Freud 1949b:407; Stekel 1959:44; Abraham 1948:320). Of course, the important question for the present study is whether or not such phantasies ever occur in mythical form. Undoubtedly, the majority of anthropologists would be somewhat loath to interpret the earth-diver myth as an anal birth fantasy on the basis of a few clinical examples drawn exclusively from Western civilization. However, the dearth of mythological data results partly from the traditional prudery of some ethnographers and many folklorists. Few myths dealing with excretory processes find their way into print. Nevertheless, there are several examples, primarily of the creation of man from excrement. John G. Bourke (1891: 266) cites an Australian myth of such a creation of man. In India, the elephant-headed god Ganesh is derived from the excrement of his mother (Berkeley-Hill 1921: 330). In modern India, the indefatigable Elwin has collected quite a few myths in which the earth is excreted. For instance, a Lanjhia Saora version describes how Bhimo defecates on Rama's head. The feces is thrown into the water which immediately dries up and the earth is formed (1949:44). In a Gadaba myth, Larang the great Dano devoured the world, but Mahaprabhu "caught hold of him and squeezed him so hard that he excreted the earth he had devoured. . . . From the earth that Larang excreted, the world was formed again" (1949:37). In other versions, a worm excretes the earth, or the world is formed from the excreta of ants (1949:47; 1954:9). An example closer to continental North America is reported by Bogoras. In this Chukchee creation myth, Raven's wife tells Raven to go and try to create the earth, but Raven protests that he cannot. Raven's wife then announces that she will try to create a "spleen-companion" and goes to sleep. Raven "looks at his wife. Her abdomen has enlarged. In her sleep she creates without effort. He is frightened, and turns his face away." After Raven's wife gives birth to twins, Raven says, "There, you have created men! Now I shall go and try to create the earth." Then "Raven flies and defecates. Every piece of excrement falls upon water, grows quickly, and becomes land." In this fashion, Raven succeeds in creating the whole earth (Bogoras 1913:152). Here there can be no doubt of the connection between pregnancy envy and anal creation. Unfortunately, there are few examples which are as clear as the Chukchee account. One of the only excremental creation myths reported in North America proper was collected by Boas. He relates (1895:159) a Kwakiutl tale of Mink making a youth from his excrement. However, the paucity of American Indian versions does not necessarily reflect the nonexistence of the myth in North America. The combination of puritanical publishing standards in the United States with similar collecting standards may well explain in part the lack of data. In this connection it is noteworthy that whereas the earlier German translation of Boas' Kwakiutl version refers specifically to excrement, the later English translation speaks of a musk-bag (1910a:159). Most probably ethnographers and editors alike share Andrew Lang's sentiments when he alludes to a myth of the Encounter Bay people, "which might have been attributed by Dean Swift to the Yahoos, so foul an origin does it allot to mankind" (1899:166). Despite the lack of a great number of actual excremental myths, the existence of any at all would appear to lend support to the hypothesis that men do think of creativity in anal terms, and further that this conception is projected into mythical cosmogonic terms.

There is, of course, another possible reason for the lack of overtly excremental creation myths and this is the process of sublimation. Ferenczi in his essay, "The Ontogenesis of the Interest in Money" (1956), has given the most explicit account of this process as he traces the weaning of the child's interest from its feces through a whole graduated series of socially sanctioned substitutes ranging from moist mud, sand, clay, and stones to gold or money. Anthropologists will object that Ferenczi's ontogenetic pattern is at best only applicable to Viennese type culture. But, to the extent that any culture has toilet training (and this includes any culture in which the child is not permitted to play indiscriminately with his feces), there is some degree of sublimation. As a matter of fact, so-called anal personality characteristics have been noted among the Yurok (Posinsky), Mohave (Devereux), and Chippewa (Barnouw, Hallowell). Devereux (1951:412) specifically comments upon the use of mud as a fecal substitute among the Mohave. Moreover, it may well be that the widespread practices of smearing the body with paint or daubing it with clay in preparation for aggressive activities have some anal basis. As for the gold-feces equation, anthropologists have yet to explain the curious linguistic fact that in Nahuatl the word for gold is *leocuitlatl*, which is a compound of *teoll*, "god," and *cuitlatl*, "excrement." Gold is thus "excrement of the gods" or "divine excrement" (Saville 1920:118). This extraordinary confirmation of Freudian symbolism which was pointed out by Reik as early as 1915 has had apparently little impact upon anthropologists blindly committed to cultural relativism. (See also Róheim 1923:387. However, for an example of money/feces symbolism in the dream of a Salteaux Indian, see Hallowell 1938.) While the gold-feces symbolism is hardly likely in cultures where gold was unknown, there is reason for assuming that some sort of sublimation does occur in most cultures. (For American Indian instances of "jewels from excrements" see Thompson 1929:329, n. 190a. In this connection, it might be pointed out that in Oceanic versions of the creation of earth from an object thrown on the primeval waters, as found in Lessa's recent comprehensive study [1961], the items thrown include, in addition to sand, such materials as rice chaff, betel nut husks, and ashes, which would appear to be waste products.) If this is so, then it may be seen that a portion of Ferenczi's account of the evolutionary course of anal sublimation is of no mean importance to the analysis of the earth-diver myth. Ferenczi states: "Even the interest for the specific odour of excrement does not cease at once, but is only displaced on to other odours that in any way resemble this. The children continue to show a liking for the smell of sticky materials with a characteristic odour, especially the strongly smelling degenerated produce of cast off epidermis cells which collects between the toes, nasal secretion, ear-wax, and the dirt of the nails, while many children do not content themselves with the moulding and sniffing of these substances, but also take them into the mouth" (1956:273). Anyone who is familiar with American Indian creation myths will immediately think of examples of the creation of man from the rubbings of skin (Thompson 1955:Motif A 1263.3), birth from mucus from the nose (Motif T 541.8.3), etc. The empirical fact is that these myths do exist! With respect to the earth-diver myth, the common detail of the successful diver's returning with a little dirt under his fingernail is entirely in accord with Ferenzci's analysis. The fecal nature of the particle is also suggested by its magical expansion. One could imagine that as one defecates one is thereby creating an ever-increasing amount of earth. (Incidentally, the notion of creating land masses through defecation has the corollary idea of creating bodies of water such as oceans through micturition [Motif A 923.1]. For example, in the previously mentioned Chukchee myth, Raven, after producing the earth, began to pass water. A drop became a lake, while a jet formed a river.)

The present hypothesis may also serve to elucidate the reasons why Christian dualism is so frequently found in Eurasian earth-diver versions. Earl Count considers the question of the dualistic nature of earth-diver as one of the main problems connected with the study of the myth (1952:56). Count is not willing to commit himself as to whether the earth-diver is older than a possible dualistic overlay, but Köngäs agrees with earlier scholars that the dualism is a later development (Count 1952:61; Köngäs 1960:168). The dualism usually takes the form of a contest between God and the devil. As might be expected from the tradition of philosophical dualism, the devil is associated with the body, while God is concerned with the spiritual element. Thus it is the devil who dives for the literally lowly dirt and returns with some under his nails. An interesting incident in view of Ferenczi's account of anal sublimation is the devil's attempt to save a bit of earth by putting it in his mouth. However, when God expands the earth, the stolen bit also expands, forcing the devil to spit it out, whereupon mountains or rocks are formed (Köngäs 1960:160–61). In this connection, another dualistic creation myth is quite informative. God is unable to stop the earth from growing and sends the bee to spy on the devil to find a way to accomplish this. When the bee buzzes, in leaving the devil to report back to God, the devil exclaims, "Let him eat your excrement, whoever sent you!" God did this and the earth stopped growing (Dragomanov 1961:3). Since the eating of excrement prevented the further growth of the earth, one can see the fecal nature of the substance forming the earth. In still another dualistic creation myth, there is even an attempt made to explain why feces exists at all in man. In this narrative, God creates a pure body for man but has to leave it briefly in order to obtain a soul. In God's absence, the devil defiles the body. God, upon returning, has no alternative but to turn his creation inside out, which is the reason why man has impurities in his intestines (Campbell 1956:294). These few examples should be sufficient to show that the dualism is primarily a matter of separating the dross of matter from the essence of spirit. The devil is clearly identified with matter and in particular with defecation. In a phrase, it is the devil who does the dirty work. Thus Köngäs is quite right in seeing a psycho-physical dualism, that is, the concept of the soul as being separable from the body, as the basis for the Christian traditional dualism. However, she errs in assuming that both the creator and his "doppelgänger" are spiritual or concerned with the spiritual (1960:169). Dualism includes one material entity and, specifically in earth-diver dualism, one element deals with dirt while the other creates beauty and valuable substance from the dirt.

It should be noted that earth-diver has been previously studied from a psychoanalytic perspective. Géza Róheim, the first psychoanalytic anthropologist, made a great number of studies of the folklore and mythology of primitive peoples. In his earlier writings, Róheim tended to follow along the lines suggested by Freud, Abraham, and Rank in seeing folk tales as analogous to dreams (1922:182), but later, after he discovered, for example, that the Aranda word *altjira* meant both dream and folk tale (1941:267), he began to speculate as to a more genetic relationship between dream and folk tale or myth. In a posthumously published paper, "Fairy Tale and Dream" (1953a), this new theory of mythology and the folk tale is explained. "To put this theory briefly: It seems that dreams and myths are not merely similar but that a large part of mythology is actually derived from dreams. In other words, we can not only apply the standard technique of dream interpretation in analyzing a fairy tale but can actually think of tales and myths as having arisen from a dream, which a person dreamed and then told to others, who retold it again, perhaps elaborated in accord with their own dreams" (1953a:394; for a sample of Róheim's exegesis of what he terms a dream-derived folk tale, see 1953b). The obvious criticism of this theory has been made by E. K. Schwartz in noting that "one can accept the same psychoanalytic approach and techniques for the understanding of the fairy tale and the dream, without having to accept the hypothesis that the fairy tale is nothing else but an elaboration of a dream" (1956: 747–48). Thus Schwartz, although he lists 12 characteristics of fairy tales which he also finds in dreams, including such features as condensation, displacement, symbolism, etc., does conclude that it is not necessary to assume that fairy tales are dreams. Róheim, in *The Gates of the Dream*, a brilliant if somewhat erratic full-length treatment of primitive myth and dream, had already addressed himself to this very criticism. He phrases the criticism rhetorically: "Then why assume the dream stage, since the unconscious would contain the same elements, even without dreams?" His answer is that the dream theory would explain not only the identity in content but also the striking similarity in structure and plot sequence (1951:348). Actually, the fundamental criticism is not completely explained away. There is no reason why both dream and myth cannot be derived from the human mind without making the myth only indirectly derived via the dream.

Róheim's theory comes to the fore in his analysis of earth-diver. In fact, he even states that the earth-diver myth is "a striking illustration of the dream origin of mythology" (1951:423). Róheim has assumed the existence of what he calls a basic dream in which the dreamer falls into something, such as a lake or a hole. According to Róheim, this dream is characterized by a "double vector" movement consisting both of a regression to the womb and the idea of the body as penis entering the vagina. In interpreting the earth-diver as an example of this basic dream, Róheim considers the diving into the primeval waters of the womb as an erection. Of considerable theoretical interest is Róheim's apparent postulation of a monogenetic origin of earth-diver: *"The core of the myth is a dream actually dreamed once upon a time by one person. Told and retold it became a myth . . ."* (1951:428). Actually, Róheim's over-all theory of the dream origin of myth is not at all necessarily a matter of monogenesis. In fact, he states that it is hardly likely as a general rule that an original dream was dreamed by one person in a definite locality, from which the story spread by migration. Rather, "many have dreamed such dreams, they shaped the narrative form in many centers, became traditional, then merged and influenced each other in the course of history" (1951:348).

The validity of Róheim's interpretation of earth-diver depends a great deal on, first of all, his theory of the dream origin of myth and, secondly, the specific nature of his so-called basic dream. One could say, without going so far as to deny categorically Róheim's theoretical contentions, that neither the dream origin of myth nor the existence of the "basic dream" is necessary for an understanding of the latent content of the earth-diver myth. Curiously enough, Róheim himself anticipates in part the present hypothesis in the course of making some additional comments on earth-diver. In discussing the characteristic trait of the gradual growth of the earth, Róheim cites an Onondaga version in which he points out the parallelism between a pregnant woman and the growing earth. From the point of view of the present hypothesis, the parallelism is quite logically attributable to the male creator's desire to achieve something like female procreativity. Thus the substance produced from his body, his baby so to speak, must gradually increase in size, just as the process of female creativity entails a gradually increasing expansion. (Here again, the observation of the apparently magically expanding belly of a pregnant woman is clearly a human universal.) Róheim goes on to mention what he considers to be a parallel myth, namely that of "the egg-born earth or cloacal creation." As will be shown later, Róheim is quite correct in drawing attention to the egg myth. Then following his discussion of the Eurasian dualistic version in which the devil tries to keep a piece of swelling earth in his mouth, Róheim makes the following analysis: "If we substitute the rectum for the mouth the myth makes sense as an awakening dream conditioned by excremental pressure" (1951: 429). In other words, Róheim does recognize the excremental aspects of earth-diver and in accordance with his theory of the dream origin of myth, he considers the myth as initially a dream caused by the purely organic stimulus of the need to defecate. Róheim also follows Rank (1912, 1922:89) in interpreting deluge myths as transformations of vesical dreams (1951:439–65). Certainly, one could make a good case for the idea that some folk tales and myths are based upon excremental pressures, perhaps originally occurring during sleep. In European folklore, there are numerous examples, as Freud and Oppenheim have amply demonstrated, of folk tales which relate how individuals attempt to mark buried treasure only to awake to find they have defecated on themselves or on their sleeping partners. It is quite possible that there is a similar basis for the Winnebago story reported by Radin (1956:26–27) in which Trickster, after eating a laxative bulb, begins to defecate endlessly. In order to escape the rising level of excrement, Trickster climbs a tree, but he is forced to go higher and higher until he finally falls down right into the rising tide. Another version of this Trickster adventure is found in Barnouw's account of a Chippewa cycle (1955:82). The idea of the movement being impossible to stop once it has started is also suggested in the previously cited Eurasian account of God's inability to stop the earth's growth. That God must eat excrement to stop the movement is thematically similar to another Trickster version in which Trickster's own excrement, rising with flood waters, comes perilously close to his mouth and nose. However, the fact that there may be "excremental pressure myths" with or without a dream origin does not mean that excremental pressure is the sole underlying motivation of such a myth as earth-diver. To call earth-diver simply a dream-like myth resulting from a call of nature without reference to the notions of male pregnancy envy and anal birth theory is vastly to oversimplify the psychological etiology of the myth. Róheim, by the way, never does reconcile the rather phallic interpretation of his basic dream with the excremental awakening dream interpretation of earth-diver. A multi-causal hypothesis is, of course, perfectly possible, but Róheim's two interpretations seem rather to conflict. In any event, Róheim sees creation myths as prime examples of his dream-myth thesis. He says, "It seems very probable that creation myths, wherever they exist, are ultimately based on dreams" (1951:430).

The idea of anal creation myths spurred by male pregnancy envy is not tied to the dream origin of myth theory. That is not to say that the dream theory is not entirely possible but only to affirm the independence of the two hypotheses. In order to document further the psychological explanation of earth-diver, several other creation myths will be very briefly discussed. As already mentioned, Róheim drew attention to the cosmic egg myths. There is clinical evidence suggesting that men who have pregnancy phantasies often evince a special interest in the activities of hens, particularly with regard to their laying of eggs (Eisler 1921:260, 285). The hens appear to defecate the eggs. Freud's famous "Little Hans" in addition to formulating a "lumf" baby theory also imagined that he laid an egg (1949b:227–28). Lombroso (1895:182) mentions a demented pseudo-artist who painted himself as excreting eggs which symbolized worlds. Ferenczi, moreover, specifically comments upon what he calls the "symbolic identity of the egg with faeces and child." He suggests that excessive fondness for eggs "approximates much more closely to primitive coprophilia than does the more abstract love of money" (1950:328). Certainly the egg-creation myth is common enough throughout the world (Lukas 1894), despite its absence in North America. It is noteworthy that there are creations of men from eggs (Motifs T 542 or A 1222) and creation of the world from a cosmic egg (Motif A 641). As in the case of feces (or mud, clay, or dirt), the cloacal creation is capable of producing either men or worlds or both.

Another anal creation myth which does occur in aboriginal North America has the spider as creator. The Spider myth, which is one of Rooth's eight creation myth types found in North America, is reported primarily in California and the Southwest. The spider as creator is also found in Asia and Africa. Empirical observation of spiders would quite easily give rise to the notion of the spider as a self-sufficient creator who appeared to excrete his own world, and a beautiful and artistic world at that. Although psychoanalysts have generally tended to interpret the spider as a mother symbol (Abraham 1948: 326–32; cf. Spider Woman in the Southwest), Freud noted at least one instance in folklore where the thread spun by a spider was a symbol for evacuated feces. In a Prussian-Silesian tale, a peasant wishing to return to earth from heaven is turned into a spider by Peter. As a spider, the peasant spins a long thread by which he descends, but he is horrified to discover as he arrives just over his home that he could spin no more. He squeezes and squeezes to make the thread longer and then suddenly wakes up from his dream to discover that "something very human had happened to him while he slept" (Freud and Oppenheim 1958:45). The spider as the perfect symbol of male artistic creativity is described in a poem by Whitman entitled "The Spider." In the poem, the spider is compared to the soul of the poet as it stands detached and alone in "measureless oceans of space" launching forth filament out of itself (Wilbur and Muensterberger 1951:405). Without going into primitive Spider creation myths in great detail, it should suffice to note that, as in other types of male myths of creation, the creator is able to create without any reference to women. Whether a male creator spins material, molds clay, lays an egg, fabricates from mucus or epidermal tissue, or dives for fecal mud, the psychological motivation is much the same.

Other cosmogonic depictions of anal birth have been barely touched upon. As Ernest Jones has shown in some detail (1951:266–357), some of the other aspects of defecation such as the sound (creation by thunder or the spoken word), or the passage of air (creation by wind or breath), are also of considerable importance in the study of mythology. With respect to the latter characteristic, there is the obvious Vedic example of Pragapati who created mankind by means of "downward breathings" from the "back part" cited by Jones (1951:279). One account of Pragapati's creation of the earth relates the passing of air with the earth-diver story. "Prajapati first becomes a wind and stirs up the primeval ocean; he sees the earth in the depths of the ocean; he turns himself into a boar and draws the earth up" (Dragomanov 1961:28). Another ancient male anal wind myth is found in the Babylonian account of Marduk. Marduk conquers Tiamat by the following means: "The evil wind which followed him, he loosed it in her face. . . . He drove in the evil wind so that she could not close her lips. The terrible winds filled her belly" (Guirand 1959:51). Marduk then pierces Tiamat's belly and kills her. The passage of wind by the male Marduk leads to the destruction of the female Tiamat. Marduk rips open the rival creator, the belly of woman, which had given birth to the world. There is also the Biblical instance of the divine (af)flatus moving on the face of the waters. Köngäs (1960:169) made a very astute intuitive observation when she suggested that there was a basic similarity between the spirit of God moving upon the primeval water and the earth-diver myth. The common denominator is the male myth of creation whereby the male creator uses various aspects of the only means available, namely the creative power of the anus.

Undoubtedly anthropologists will be sceptical of any presentation in which evidence is marshalled á la Frazer and where the only criteria for the evidence appears to be the grist-worthiness for the mill. Nevertheless, what is important is the possibility of a theory of universal symbolism which can be verified by empirical observation in the field in decades to come. Kluckhohn, despite a deep-seated mistrust of pan-human symbolism, confesses that his own field work as well as that of his collaborators has forced him to the con-clusion that "Freud and other psychoanalysts have depicted with astonishing correctness many central themes in motivational life which are universal. The styles of expression of these themes and much of the manifest content are culturally determined but the under-lying psychological drama transcends cultural difference" (Wilbur and Muensterberger 1951:120). Kluckhohn bases his assumptions on the notion of a limited number of human "givens," such as human anatomy and physiology. While it is true that thoughts about the "givens" are not "given" in the same sense, it may be that their arising is inevitable. In other words, man is not born with the idea of pregnancy envy. It is acquired through experi-ence, that is, through the mediation of culture. But if certain experiences are universal, such as the observation of female pregnancy, then there may be said to be secondary or derived "givens," using the term in an admittedly idiosyncratic sense. This is very impor-tant for the study of myth. It has already been pointed out that from a cultural relativis-tic perspective, the only portion of mythology which can be profitably studied is limited to those myths which are peculiar to a particular culture or those differences in the details of a widely diffused myth. Similarly, the literal approach can glean only so much ethno-graphic data from reflector myths. Without the assumption of symbolism and universals in myth, a vast amount of mythology remains of little use to the anthropologist. It should also be noted that there is, in theory, no conflict between accepting the idea of universals and advocating cultural relativism. It is not an "either/or" proposition. Some myths may be universal and others not. It is the all-or-nothing approach which appears to be errone-ous. The same is true for the polygenesis-diffusion controversy; they also are by no means mutually exclusive. In the same way, there is no inconsistency in the statement that myths can either reflect or refract culture. (The phrase was suggested by A. K. Ramanujan.) Lévi-Strauss (1958:51) criticizes psychoanalytic interpretations of myth because, as he puts it, if there's an evil grandmother in the myths, "it will be claimed that in such a society grand-mothers are actually evil and that mythology reflects the social structure and the social relations; but should the actual data be conflicting, it would be readily claimed that the purpose of mythology is to provide an outlet for repressed feelings. Whatever the situation may be, a clever dialectic will always find a way to pretend that a meaning has been unravelled." Although Lévi-Strauss may be justified insofar as he is attacking the "Have you stopped beating your wife?" antics of some psychoanalysts, there is not necessarily any inconsistency stemming from data showing that in culture A evil grandmothers in fact are also found in myth, while in culture B conscious norms of pleasant grandmothers disguise unconscious hatred for "evil" grandmothers, a situation which may be expressed in myth. In other words, myths can and usually do contain both conscious and unconscious cultural materials. To the extent that conscious and unconscious motivation may vary or be contradictory, so likewise can myth differ from or contradict ethnographic data. There is no safe monolithic theory of myth except that of judicious eclecticism as championed by E. B. Tylor. Mythology must be studied in cultural context in order to determine which individual mythological elements reflect and which refract the culture. But, more than this, the cultural relative approach must not preclude the recognition and identification of transcultural similarities and potential universals. As Kluckhohn said, ". . . the anthropologist for two generations has been obsessed with the differences between peoples, neglecting the equally real similarities—upon which the 'universal culture pattern' as well as the psychological uniformities are clearly built (Wilbur and Muensterberger 1951:121)." The theoretical implications for practical field work of seeking psychological uniformities are implicit. Ethnographers must remove the traditional blinders and must be willing to collect *all* pertinent material even if it borders on what is obscene by the ethnographer's ethnocentric standards. The ideal ethnographer must not be afraid of diving deep and coming up with a little dirt; for, as the myth relates, such a particle may prove immensely valuable and may expand so as to form an entirely new world for the students of man.

References

Abraham, Karl. 1948. *Selected papers on psycho-analysis*. The International Psycho-Analytical Library No. 13. London, Hogarth.

Barnouw, Victor. 1955. A psychological interpretation of a Chippewa origin legend. *Journal of American Folklore* 68:73–85, 211–23, 341–55.

Benedict, Ruth. 1935. *Zuni mythology*. Columbia University Contributions to Anthropology 21.

Bettelheim, Bruno. 1955. *Symbolic wounds*. London, Thames and Hudson.

Berkeley-Hill, Owen. 1921. The anal-erotic factor in the religion, philosophy and character of the Hindus. *International Journal of Psycho-Analysis* 2:306–38.

Bozs, Franz. 1895. *Indianische sagen von der nord-pacifischen küste Amerikas*. Berlin.

———. 1910a. *Kwakiutl tales*. Columbia University Contributions to Anthropology 2.

———. 1910b. Psychological problems in anthropology. *American Journal of Psychology* 21:371–84.

Boehm, Felix. 1930. The femininity-complex in men. *International Journal of Psycho-Analysis* 11:444–69.

Bogoras, Waldemar. 1913. *Chuckchee mythology*. Jesup North Pacific Expedition Publications 8.

Bourke, John G. 1891. *Scatalogic rites of all nations*. Washington, W. H. Lowdermilk & Co.

Campbell, Joseph. 1956. *The hero with a thousand faces*. New York, Meridian.

Count, Earl W. 1952. The earth-diver and the rival twins: a clue to time correlation in North-Eurasiatic and North American mythology. In *Indian tribes of aboriginal America*, Sol Tax, ed. Selected Papers of the 19th International Congress of Americanists. Chicago, University of Chicago Press.

Devereux, George. 1951. Cultural and characterological traits of the Mohave related to the anal stage of psychosexual development. *Psychoanalytic Quarterly* 20:398–422.

Dragomanov, Mixailo Petrovic. 1961. *Notes on the Slavic religio-ethical legends: the dualistic creation of the world*. Russian and East European Series Vol. 23. Bloomington, Indiana University Publications.

Eisler, Michael Joseph. 1921. A man's unconscious phantasy of pregnancy in the guise of traumatic hysteria: a clinical contribution to anal erotism. *International Journal of Psycho-Analysis* 2:255–86.

Elwin, Verrier. 1949. *Myths of middle India*. Madras, Oxford University Press.

———.1954. *Tribal myths of Orissa*. Bombay, Oxford University Press.

Ferenczi, Sandor. 1950. *Further contributions to the theory and technique of psycho-analysis*. International Psycho-Analytical Library No. 11. London, Hogarth.

———. 1956. *Sex in psycho-analysis*. New York, Dover.

Frazer, James George. 1935. *Creation and evolution in primitive cosmogonies*. London, Macmillan.

Freud, Sigmund. 1938. *The basic writings of Sigmund Freud*. New York, Modern Library.

———. 1949a. *Collected papers II*. London, Hogarth.

———. 1949b. *Collected papers III*. London, Hogarth.

———. 1953. *A general introduction to psycho-analysis*. New York, Permabooks.

Freud, Sigmund, and D. E. Oppenheim. 1958. *Dreams in folklore*. New York, International Universities Press.

Fromm, Erich. 1951. *The forgotten language*. New York, Grove Press.

Ginzberg, Louis. 1925. *The legends of the Jews*. Vol. I. Philadelphia, Jewish Publication Society of America.

Guirand, Felix. 1959. Assyro-Babylonian mythology. In *Larousse Encyclopedia of Mythology*. New York, Prometheus Press.

Hallowell, A. Irving. 1938. Freudian symbolism in the dream of a Salteaux Indian. *Man* 38:47–48.

———. 1947. Myth, culture and personality. *American Anthropologist* 49:544–56.

Huckel, Helen. 1953. Vicarious creativity. *Psychoanalysis* 2: (2) :44–50.

Jones, Ernest. 1951. *Essays in applied psycho-analysis*, Vol. II. International Psycho-Analytical Library No. 41. London, Hogarth.

———. 1957. How to tell your friends from geniuses. *Saturday Review* 40 (August 10):9–10, 39–40.

Jung, Carl Gustav. 1916. *Psychology of the unconscious*. New York, Moffat, Yard and Company.

Kardiner, Abram. 1939. *The individual and his society*. New York, Columbia University Press.

———. 1945. *The psychological frontiers of society*. New York, Columbia University Press.

Kluckhohn, Clyde. 1953. Universal categories of culture. In *Anthropology Today*, A. L. Kroeber, ed. Chicago, University of Chicago Press.

———. 1959. Recurrent themes in myths and mythmaking. *Proceedings of the American Academy of Arts and Sciences* 88:268–79.

Köngäs, Elli Kaija. 1960. The earth-diver (Th. A 812). *Ethnohistory* 7:151–80.

Lang, Andrew. 1899. *Myth, ritual and religion*. Vol. I. London, Longmans, Green, and Co.

Lessa, William A. 1961. *Tales from Ulithi Atoll: a comparative study in Oceanic folklore*. University of California Publications Folklore Studies 13. Berkeley and Los Angeles, University of California Press.

Lévi-Strauss, Claude. 1958. The structural study of myth. In *Myth: a symposium*, Thomas A. Sebeok, ed. Bloomington, Indiana University Press.

Lombroso, Cesare. 1895. *The man of genius*. London, Walter Scott.

Lukas, Franz. 1894 Das ei als kosmogonische vorstellung. *Zeitschrift des Vereins für Volkskunde* 4: 227–43.

Malinowski, Bronislaw. 1954. *Magic, science and religion and other essays*. New York, Doubleday Anchor.

Mann, John. 1958. The folktale as a reflector of individual and social structure (Unpublished doctoral dissertation, Columbia University.)

Matthews, Washington.

———.1902. Myths of gestation and parturition. *American Anthropologist* 4:737–42.

McClelland, David C. and G. A. Friedman. 1952. A cross-cultural study of the relationship between child-training practices and achievement motivation appearing in folk tales. In *Readings in social psychology*, G. E. Swanson, T. M. Newcomb, and E. L. Hartley, eds. New York, Henry Holt and Company.

Nadel, S. F. 1937. A field experiment in racial psychology. *British Journal of Psychology* 28:195–211.

Posinsky, S. H. 1957. The problem of Yurok anality. *American Imago* 14:3–31.

Radin, Paul. 1956. *The trickster*. New York, Philosophical Library.

Rank, Otto. 1912. Die symbolschichtung im wecktraum und ihre wiederkehr im mythischen den-ken. *Jarhbuch für psychoanalytische Forschungen* 4:51–115.

———. 1922. *Psychoanalytische beiträge zur mythenforschung*. Leipzig, Internationaler Psycho-analytischer Verlag. (Second edition.)

Reik, Theodor. 1951. Gold und kot. *International Zeitschrift für Psychoanalyse* 3:183.

Róheim, Géza. 1921. Primitive man and environment. *International Journal of Psycho-Analysis* 2:15778.

———. 1922. Psycho-analysis and the folk-tale. *International Journal of Psycho-Analysis* 3:180–86.

———. 1923. Heiliges geld in Melanesien. *Internationale Zeitschrift für Psychoanalyse* 9:384–401.

———. 1940. Society and the individual. *Psychoanalytic Quarterly* 9:526–45.

———. 1941. Myth and folk-tale. *American Imago* 2:266–79.

———. 1951. *The gates of the dream*. New York, International Universities Press.

———. 1953a. Fairy tale and dream. *The Psychoanalytic Study of the Child* 8:394–403.

———. 1953b. Dame Holle: dream and folk tale (Grimm No. 24). In *Explorations in psychoanaly-sis*, Robert Lindner, ed. New York, Julian Press.

Rooth, Anna Birgitta. 1957. The creation myths of the North American Indians. *Anthropos* 52:497–508.

Saville, Marshall H. 1920. *The goldsmith's art in ancient Mexico*. Indian Notes and Monographs. New York, Heye Foundation.

Schwartz, Emanuel K. 1956. A psychoanalytic study of the fairy tale. *American Journal of Psychotherapy* 10: 740–62.

Schwarzbaum, Haim. 1960. Jewish and Moslem sources of a Falasha creation myth. In *Studies in Biblical and Jewish folklore*, Raphael Patai, Francis Lee Utley, Dov Noy, eds. American Folklore Society Memoir 51. Bloomington, Indiana University Press.

Silberer, Herbert. 1925. A pregnancy phantasy in a man. *Psychoanalytic Review* 12:377–96.

Spence, Lewis. [1921]. *An introduction to mythology*. New York, Farrar & Rinehart.

Spencer, Katherine. 1947. *Reflection of social life in the Navaho origin myth*. University of New Mexico Publications in Anthropology 3.

Stekel, Wilhelm. 1959. *Patterns of psychosexual infantilism*. New York, Grove Press.

Tax, Sol et al. (Eds.). 1953. *An appraisal of anthropology today*. Chicago, University of Chicago Press.

Thompson, Stith. 1929. *Tales of the North American Indians*. Cambridge, Harvard University Press.

———.1955. *Motif-index of folk-literature*. Bloomington, Indiana University Press.

Wheeler-Voegelin, Erminie. 1949. Earth diver. In *Standard Dictionary of Folklore, Mythology and Legend*, Vol. I, Maria Leach, ed. New York, Funk and Wagnalls.

Wheeler-Voegelin, Erminie and Remedios W. Moore. 1957. The emergence myth in native North America. In *Studies in folklore*, W. Edson Richmond, ed. Bloomington, Indiana University Press.

Wilbur, George B. and Warner Muensterberger (Eds.). 1951 *Psychoanalysis and culture*. New York, International Universities Press.

Wolfenstein, Martha. 1955. "Jack and the beanstalk": an American version. In *Childhood in con-temporary cultures*, Margaret Mead and Martha Wolfenstein, eds. Chicago, University of Chicago Press.

Wycoco (Moore), Remedios. 1951. The types of North-American Indian tales (Unpublished doc-toral dissertation, Indiana University.)

Postscript

Madness in Method
Plus a Plea for Projective Inversion in Myth

MYTH AS A FORM OF folk narrative has long fascinated scholars from a variety of academic disciplines including anthropology, classics, literature, philosophy, religion, among others. Yet the study of myth by folklorists tends to be virtually ignored by these would-be mythologists. Consequently, from a folkloristic perspective, most of these academic discussions of "myth" have little or nothing to do with myth in the strict and technical sense of the term. Even in volumes purportedly treating "myth and method" one will find essays treating folktales and legends, rather than myths. There is, of course, nothing inherently wrong with analyzing folktales and legends, or short stories or poems for that matter, but it is truly dismaying to folklorists to see such analyses wantonly labeled discussions of "myth."

The generic distinctions between myth, folktale, and legend have been standard among folklorists for at least two centuries, going back to the publications of the brothers Grimm, who published separate works on each of these genres.[1] For the folklorist, a myth is a sacred narrative explaining how the world and mankind came to be in their present form. Myths and legends (narratives told as true and set in the postcreation era) are different from folktales, which are narratives understood to be fictional, often introduced as such by an opening formula such as "Once upon a time." These generic distinctions are independent of dramatic personae. Thus it is possible to have a myth of the creation of Adam and Eve, but once these individuals are created, one can tell legends of these same individuals. Moreover, it is also possible to have folktales involving Adam and Eve.[2]

If we agree that a myth must minimumly involve a narrative, then we can dismiss all the references to "myth" as a synonym for error or fallacy. In popular as opposed to academic parlance, myth, like the word "folklore," is frequently used in this sense. The phrase "That's just folklore" or "That's a myth" means typically that the previously mentioned subject is an erroneous belief. Such usage is certainly worth noting, but it has nothing to do with the formal definition of myth as employed by folklorists.

Members of other academic disciplines may complain about what they perceive to be the narrowness and specificity of the folkloristic concept of myth. They claim the right to interpret the term "myth" any way they wish, even at the risk of inventing idiosyncratic definitions of the term. This is just fine as an illustration of free speech or poetic license, but such a practice has little to do with scholarship and intellectual rigor. Let me cite one or two examples of what I mean.

Little Red Riding Hood is a standard folktale. It is Aarne-Thompson tale-type 333, The Glutton (Red Riding Hood), and it is almost certainly related to Aarne-Thompson tale-type 123, The Wolf and the Kids, which is the same tale using exclusively animal characters.[3]

It has been the subject of numerous analyses as it is quite a fascinating tale. In no way can the story be considered a sacred explanation of how the world or mankind came to be in their present form. Hence it is not a myth. Nor is it told as true. It is a fictional story set in no particular place and time—"Once upon a time" partly signals the timelessness of the plot. As it falls under the rubric of tales of magic (Aarne-Thompson tales 300 to 749), it is a particular kind of folktale, namely, a tale of magic, or fairy tale. *(Fairy tale,* the term of choice in English, is a misnomer inasmuch as fairies rarely if ever appear in fairy tales. Stories involving fairies—and other supernatural creatures—are usually told as true and are consequently legends.) No folklorist would call Little Red Riding Hood a "myth" any more than he or she would call Cinderella a myth. (Cinderella is Aarne-Thompson tale-type 510A, Cinderella.)[4]

Another all too common mislabeling occurs with respect to the story of Oedipus. Classicists, psychoanalysts, and others adamantly insist upon calling the Oedipus story a myth. Yet the, story is *not* a sacred narrative offering an explanation of how the world and humankind came to be in their present form. It is the standard folktale, namely, Aarne-Thompson tale-type 931, Oedipus.[5]

One unfortunate result of the sloppiness of literary critics and anthropologists and others in claiming almost any narrative as a "myth" is that folklorists simply cannot trust the titles of books and articles allegedly concerned with the subject of myth. For example, if one examines *Recent Studies in Myths and Literature 1970–1990,* one finds that more than half the entries have nothing whatever to do with myth in the folkloristic sense.[6] Most of these tend to refer to either themes or patterns, but definitely not myths.

In the absence of a proper myth-type index, folklorists usually refer to myths by motif number. The six volume *Motif-Index of Folk-Literature,* first published in 1932–1936 (second revised edition, 1955–58) employs letter prefixes to indicate motif categories. A motifs are mythological motifs, B motifs are animal motifs, C motifs are taboo motifs, and so on. The system is not airtight and there is obviously overlap, as in the case of a myth involving an animal that breaks a taboo! Nevertheless, the A section of the *Motif-Index* does in effect constitute an inventory of the world's myths. Thus A 710, Creation of the sun, and A 740, Creation of the moon, would refer to narratives treating the origins of those celestial bodies. Folklorists expect fellow professionals to use motif designations when appropriate, and they deem writings amateurish that fail to do so.

Unlike the tale-type index, wherein all references following a tale-type number are assumed to be cognate—that is, historically or genetically related—the references grouped under a motif rubric may or may not be cognate. Any myth of the origin of death, for example, could in theory be labeled A 1335, Origin of death. Still, one can often get some sense of the geographic distribution of a particular myth (motif) from the *Motif-Index.* While on the subject of geographic distribution of myths, let me point out that even the most cursory examination of the various A motifs clearly demonstrates that *no motif is universal.* To my knowledge, there is not one single myth that is universal, "universal" meaning that it is found among every single people on the face of the earth, past and present. Indeed, myth scholarship clearly and conclusively proves that individual myths have their own particular circumscribed areas of geographical or cultural provenience.

Accordingly, there are Indo-European myths that are *not* found among native North or South American Indians; there are Asian-Amerind myths that are not found in Europe or Africa. So it is one thing to say that all peoples may have some myth allegedly explaining how death came into the world, but *it is not the same myth*. In Africa, for example, the most popular origin-of-death myth, according to Abrahamsson's superb 1951 monograph is "The Message that Failed."[8] This is motif A 1335.1 Origin of death from falsified message. The gist of this myth is that "God sends the chameleon to mankind with the message that they should have eternal life, and the lizard with the message that they must die. The chameleon dawdled on the way, and the lizard arrived first. When she had delivered her message, the matter was settled. The chameleon's message was no longer valid, and death had entered the world."[9]

This is quite different from the standard myth of the origin of death in Oceania. According to Anell's excellent survey, the most common story refers to how "primitive man in a bygone age could rejuvenate himself by changing his skin like a snake. In the usual version it is an old woman who is rejuvenated in this matter and subsequently reappears before her young children (grandchildren). They fail to recognize her in this young woman, however, and cry for their mother (grandmother) until she is forced to resume her old skin. This act, alas, leads to death for all mankind."[10] This is motif A 1335.4 Origin of death when early people put on new skins.

Neither the African perverted-message myth nor the Oceanic skin-renewal myths are to be found among the large corpus of native North American Indian origin-of-death myths.[11] The important theoretical point is that no one origin-of-death myth is found among all peoples. Different peoples have different myths!

The implications of the limited distribution of any of the world's inventory of myths should give pause to all those mythologists who espouse universalist or psychic unity theories. If there really were panhuman Jungian archetypes, then all peoples should in theory have the same myths. They do not! So how is it that dozens of literary scholars find credible the mystical and nonrational concept of Jungian archetypes? Without empirical evidence to support the notion of archetype, it is astounding to folklorists that so many writers on myth continue to advocate such an implausible theory.

It would take too long to demonstrate all the logical (not to say psychological) flaws in the Jungian archetype, but let me cite just a few of Jung's own words on the subject. Consider his double talk on the issue of whether archetypes are "inherited." In a statement made in August 1957, he said, "It is important to bear in mind that my concept of the 'archetypes' has been frequently misunderstood as denoting inherited patterns of thought." Note his clarification: "In reality they belong to the realm of the activities of the instincts and in that sense they represent inherited forms of psychic behavior."[12] Actually, in his famous essay "The Psychology of the Child Archetype," Jung's view is less garbled. Speaking of "impersonal fantasies" "which cannot be reduced to experiences in the individual's past," Jung maintains that "they correspond to certain *collective* (and not personal) structural elements of the human psyche in general, and like the morphological elements of the human body, are inherited."[13]

I shall forebear commenting on the blatant ethnocentrism of Jungian myth theory with its claim that Jesus Christ is an archetype![14] Keep in mind that archetypes are supposed to be pan-human, and as Jung says, "For the archetype, of course, exists a priori."[15] Since archetypes are panhuman, and since Jesus Christ is an archetype, then Jesus Christ is presumably part of *all* people's collective unconscious. What hubris and arrogance in such an assumption!

The real problem for mythologists comes from the difficulty in applying Jungian theory to myth texts. The problem stems from the fact that, according to Jung, archetypes are unknowable: "Contents of an archetypal character are manifestations of processes in the collective unconscious. Hence they do not refer to anything that is or has been conscious, but to something essentially unconscious. In the last analysis, therefore, it is impossible to say what they refer to."[16] If the master of archetypes admits that it is impossible to ascertain the referents of archetypes, then how can lesser critics presume to do so? Jung continues, "If, then, we proceed in accordance with the above principle, there is no longer any question whether a myth refers to the sun or the moon, the father or the mother. . . . The ultimate meaning of this nucleus was never conscious and never will be."[17] I cannot improve on this pessimistic statement. What amazes me is how serious scholars could possibly take this kind of vague approach as a bona fide means of studying myth. It is vastly different from Freud's approach to myth, which is utterly opposed to mysticism and a know-nothing attitude. Freud believes that the unconscious content of myth (and other forms of folklore) is knowable, and it is precisely the task of the mythologist to decipher that content.

Most folklorists refuse to consider either Jung or Freud when analyzing myth texts. They prefer to avoid dealing with the unconscious content of myths; instead they employ every means possible to avoid confronting that content. Whether it is motifing the texts, or mapping a myth's geographical distribution and guessing at possible paths of diffusion, or deconstructing a text into its structural constituents, any method of myth analysis is preferable to coming to grips with the highly human content of myths.

One reason why Freudian theory can be used in myth analysis (whereas Jungian theory cannot) is that it is possible to reconcile some Freudian theory with cultural relativism. With Jungian pan-human archetypes (Jung refers as follows to them: "the archetype—let us never forget this—is a psychic organ present in all of us")[18] there is no place for the intervention of culture and cultural differences. Archetypes are basically precultural givens. In contrast to the Freudian notions of symbolism, displacement, condensation, and projection, one can add the dimension of culture.

If we assume, for example, that there may be a correlation between patterns of infantile conditioning in a culture with adult-projective systems in that same culture (including folklore, film, literature, and the like), then to the extent that infantile conditioning differs from culture to culture, there could and should be different adult-projective systems. And that is precisely what the empirical data suggest. Different cultures have different myths; and different cultures have different norms of infantile conditioning (with respect to weaning, toilet training, etc.). In any case, a possible correlation between infantile conditioning and adult-projective systems in a given culture is certainly knowable. One can examine infantile conditioning and the adult-projective systems in a culture, and either there is a demonstrable correlation or there is not. It is not a question of dealing with something that "was never conscious and never will be."

I should like to indicate very briefly the utility of Freudian theory to the analysis of myth by distinguishing projection from what I call projective inversion. Simple projection, in my view, consists of displacing an individual psychological configuration directly onto another plane or into a different arena. It is roughly analogous to shining a light behind shadow puppets (or the fingers of a hand) to "project" an image or shadow on a wall or screen or other surface. Stellar constellations in the heavens, if perceived as mythological gestalt figures (often involving myths) would be an illustration of simple projection. A human drama is projected to the heavens such that heavenly bodies enact or play out the problems of human bodies here on earth. (Is it just a coincidence that in Western cosmology the earth is situated between the planets Venus [love] and Mars [war]?) Sex and violence are surely earthly or earthy matters.

Perhaps a more striking example of projection in myth is found in the World parents myth. The basic myth is motif A 625 World parents: sky-father and earth-mother as parents of the universe. The sky-father descends upon the earth-mother and begets the world. This is a widespread myth, but it is not universal. Consider motif A 625.1 Heaven-mother–earth-father. The World-parents myth would appear to be a celestial projection of one of the more common forms of human sexual intercourse, a form that also reflects male dominance: man on top, woman on the bottom. But the more interesting projection occurs in motif A 625.2 Raising of the sky. In this widespread myth, a male culture hero (= son) pushes the sky-father upward, off the earth-mother to make room for mankind. Even a non-Freudian ought to be able to see the possible Oedipal implications of that myth.

What I term *projective inversion* differs from straightforward projection inasmuch as a reversal or inversion takes place. The terminology difficulty arises from the fact that it is this latter psychological process that Freud and his followers called "projection." In Freud's terms, the "proposition 'I hate him' becomes transformed by *projection* into another one: 'He *hates* (persecutes) me,' which will justify me in hating him."[19] An individual's view of hate or dislike, for example, is supposedly projected outward onto the object of hate or dislike. In this way, subject and object exchange places. I think this transformational principle was a brilliant insight and further that it has enormous relevance to the study of myth content. Otto Rank illustrated it beautifully in his classic *The Myth of the Birth of the Hero.*[20] Using Oedipal theory, Rank argues convincingly that sons want to get rid of their fathers (in order to marry their mothers) but as this is a taboo thought, the narrative projection transforms this wish into the invariable attempt by the fathers to get rid of their sons.[21] Inasmuch as the majority of Rank's narrative illustrations come from folktales (such as Oedipus) or legends (such as Romulus and Siegfried), it is clear that the device of projection, or what I prefer to call projective inversion, occurs in narrative genres other than myth. Curiously enough, Rank fails to interpret the detail of the father's refusal to give his daughter to any of her suitors in the same way, instead understanding it literally from the father's perspective (as wishing to retain his daughter for himself). If Rank were consistent (keep in mind that most of the early Freudians did *not* understand women as well as they understood men), he might have realized that the father's keeping his daughter for himself could have been a projective inversion of the daughter's (Electral) wish to keep her father for herself![22] The point here is that I do think there is a critical distinction between straightforward one-to-one projection, as to the heavens, and projective inversion, a distinction that is in many ways analogous to the literal-versus-symbolic approaches to myth. Simple projection would be parallel to a literal approach while projective inversion would be parallel to a symbolic approach.

In a previous study I have sought to utilize projective inversion as a means of explaining the puzzling blood-libel legend in which the Jews were said to murder Christian infants so as to extract their blood to use in making matzohs. Jews are forbidden to eat blood whereas Christians are encouraged to do so, especially via partaking of the Eucharist.[23] I have argued that Christians have displaced any guilt arising from their cannibalistic eating of the blood and body of Jesus Christ through a legend involving projective inversion: by means of this inversion it is no longer Christians eating the blood-body of a Jew (Jesus) but Jews eating the blood-body of a Christian sacrificial victim![24] Let me add that without invoking the transformational principle of projective inversion, the blood-libel legend remains an enigmatic, bizarre, and virtually incomprehensible plot in terms of normal logic. These examples suggest that projective inversion can indeed be applied to the content of tales and legends. The question is, Can projective inversion also illuminate myths?

In the Old Testament there are two distinct creation myths that recount the origin of man. In the first chapter of the Book of Genesis, we find what might be termed the *simultaneous* creation of man and woman. Genesis 1:27 reads: "So God created man in his own image, in the image of God created he him; male and female created he them." Less egalitarian is the myth found in the second chapter of Genesis. First in 2:7 we are told "And the Lord God formed man of the dust of the ground, and breathed into his nostrils the breath of life; and man became a living soul." And then after God planted a garden in Eden, placed man there, instructed man not to eat of the tree of the knowledge of good and evil, and after the man, Adam, named all the animals, then and only then did God begin a totally separate creation of woman. According to Genesis 2:21 and 22; "And the Lord God caused a deep sleep to fall upon Adam, and he slept; and he took one of his ribs, and closed up the flesh instead thereof. And the rib, which the Lord God had taken from man, made he a woman, and brought her unto the man."

The first part of the second myth is a version of motif A 1241. Man made from clay (earth) while the second part is motif A 1275.1 Creation of first woman from man's rib. The second myth clearly implies a *sequential* (as opposed to *simultaneous)* creation inasmuch as man has to be created prior to woman if his rib is to be used in that creative act. Both second-creation myths reflect a strong undeniable male bias. In the first portion we have a typical male creation myth involving the creation of the world or man from feces or fecal substitute (clay earth, dust). Men trying to compete with women who are apparently magically able to create new life from their bodies have to resort to cloacal creation in order to create new life from *their* inadequate bodies. In the second portion the very order of creation implies social priority man first, woman second! This male bias is entirely consistent with the notion of a *male* god as creator, and a male savior figure, Noah, who in a re-creation myth builds a male womb (ark) that floats for approximately nine months. (It is noteworthy in this context that Mrs. Noah doesn't even merit having a name!) in Noahian Arkcology, we have an echo or reverberation of the male creation myths of Genesis 1:27, and 2:7, 21–22. All this may be persuasive in the light of feminist ideology, but what about projective inversion? Can it be applied to these two myths of creation or not?

In the second myth, we see an articulation of the male wish to procreate like females. How do females procreate? From their bodies. In biological reality man comes from woman's body. In the fantasy world of mythical reality, biology is reversed. It is woman who comes from man's body. Moreover, inasmuch as biology dictates that man comes specifically from the woman's genital area, the reversal would logically have woman coming from man's genital area. That is why it is almost certainly the missing bone in man, the *os baculum* that is the likely *fons et origo* of woman. The penis bone is found among a number of animals, a fact no doubt observed by early hunters who slaughtered such animals for food. The first recorders of the biblical narratives would not easily include narratives involving a penis bone and so the euphemistic dodge of substituting a rib bone instead was doubtless employed.[25] There are few texts in print from any culture exemplifying motif A 1263.6 Man created from culture hero's genitals (but the very existence of the motif at all makes this hypothetical interpretation plausible). The inevitable censorship difficulties involved in translating oral tradition into writing or print could account for the dearth of such texts. In the Bible, we know that euphemisms were frequently employed. When Abraham asks his eldest servant to swear an oath, he instructs that servant "Put, I pray thee, thy hand under my thigh" (Genesis 24:2). If one swears by something holy, then it was very likely the male genitals, not the thigh, on which the oath was sworn through placement of the hands. This is signaled even in contemporary times by the words "testify" and "testimony" (from *testes)* and even the word *Testament* itself. In any event, it is the principle of projective inversion that allows us to propose such a hypothetical reading of the second myth of the creation of woman.

Returning now to the first myth, we recall "So God created man in his own image," which would strongly suggest a very anthropomorphic deity fully equipped with ears, eyes, nose, mouth, and so on. If man were created in God's image, then one could logically assume that God must look very much like man does. However, armed with the principle of projective inversion, we can understand that it was not God who created man in his image, but rather man who created God in *his* image! So just as a patriarchal society demanded that normal biology be contravened through myth—by creating a male myth whereby woman was said to come from man's body, so the male invention of a male deity (to justify and fortify a male-oriented society) can be denied or concealed by constructing a male myth whereby it is a male deity who creates males in his image. Myth once created and accepted as dogma or truth is not easily overturned.

The long-term effects of these two instances of male-inspired projective inversions in the form of two separate creation myths in Genesis are indisputable. They constitute in large measure the "sociological charters for belief" (in Malinowski's words) in a male-dominated society.[26] The belief in such a society is bolstered by the assumed existence of a male deity as well as a myth which claims that woman was created secondarily, almost as an afterthought. When fantasy is elevated to the level of myth, it becomes a force to be reckoned with. Thus the principle of projective inversion can add a new dimension to the burgeoning feminist literature on myth. The power and deleterious impact of these two myths in Genesis continue unabated, and it is hard to gauge just how long it will take to undo the social damage and mental anguish of Western women caused directly or indirectly by these two fundamental myths in Genesis.

Notes

1. For a useful delineation of these three genres, see William Bascom, "The Forms of Folklore," 3–20. For further definitions of these genres as well as numerous subgenres, see Laurits Bødker, *Folk Literature (Germanic).*
2. All tale-type numbers cited come from Aarne and Thompson, *The Types of the Folktale.* For this tale in particular, see Geddes, *Various Children of Eve.*
3. For details, see Dundes, *Little Red Riding Hood: A Casebook.*
4. Dundes, *Cinderella: A Casebook.*
5. Edmunds and Dundes, *Oedipus: A Folklore Casebook.*
6. Accardi et al. *Recent Studies in Myths and Literature 1970–1990.*
7. Thompson, *Motif-Index of Folk-Literature.*
8. Abrahamson, *The Origin of Death: Studies in African Mythology,* 4–34.
9. Ibid., 4.
10. Anell, *The Origin of Death According to the Traditions in Oceania,* 1.
11. For surveys of native American origin-of-death myths, see Boas, "The Origin of Death," 486–91, and Dangel, "Mythen vom Ursprung des Todes bei dun Indianern Nordamelikas," 341–74.
12. Jung, Preface, in de Laszlo, *Psyche & Symbol,* xvi.
13. Jung, "The Psychology of the Child Archetype," in Jung and Kerényi, *Essays on a Science of Mythology,* 74.
14. Jung, "Aion," in *Psyche & Symbol,* 36.
15. Ibid., 15.

16. Jung, "The Psychology of the Child Archetype," 75.
17. Ibid.
18. Ibid., 79.
19. Freud, "Psycho-Analytic Notes upon an Autobiographical Account of a Case of Paranoia," 449. For representative discussions of "projection," see Bellak,"On the Problems of the Concept of Projection," in Abt and Bellak, *Projective Psychology*, 7–32; and Lindzey, *Projective Techniques and Cross Cultural Research*, 25–31. Rycroft in his *A Critical Dictionary of Psychoanalysis* 125–26, includes both types of projection under the same rubric noting only that "reversal" occurs more frequently.
20. Rank, *The Myth of the Birth of the Hero* was first published in 1909.
21. Ibid., 78.
22. Ibid., 80. For an Electral interpretation, see Dundes, "To Love My Father All: A Psychoanalytical Study of the Folktale Source of *King Lear*," in Dundes, *Interpreting Folklore*, 211–22.
23. Dundes, "The Ritual Murder or Blood Libel Legend," in Dundes, *The Blood Libel Legend: A Casebook in Anti-Semitic Folklore*, 336–76.
24. Ibid., 354–59.
25. Dundes, "Couvade in Genesis," in Dundes, *Parsing through Customs*, 145–66.
26. Malinowski, *Magic, Science and Religion*, 144.

References

Aarne, Antti, and Stith Thompson. *The Types of the Folktale*. 2nd rev. FF ommunications no. 184. Helsinki: Academia Scientiarum Fennica, 1961.

Abrahamsson, Hans. *The Origin of Death: Studies in African Mythology, Studia Ethnographica Upsaliensia* 3. Uppsala: Almqvist and Wiksells, 1951.

Abt, Lawrence Edwin, and Leopold Bellak, eds. *Projective Psychology*. New York: Alfred A. Knopf, 1950.

Accardi, Bernard, David J. Charlson, Frank A. Doden, Richard E Hardin, Sung Ryol Kim, Sonya J. Lancaster, and Michael H. Shaw, comps. *Recent Studies in Myths and Literature, 1970–1990: An Annotated Bibliography*. New York: Greenwood Press, 1991.

Anell, Bengt. "The Origin of Death according to the Traditions in Oceania." *Studio Ethnographica Upsaliensia* 20 (1964): 1–32.

Bascom, William. "The Forms of Folklore: Prose Narratives." *Journal of American Folklore* 78 (1965): 3–20.

Boas, Franz. "The Origin of Death." *Journal of American Folklore* 30 (1917): 489–91.

Bødker, Lamits. *Folk Literature (Germanic)*. Copenhagen: Rosenkilde and Bagger, 1965.

Dangel, R. "Mythen vom Ursprung des Todes bei den Indianern Nordamerikas." *Mitteilungen der Anthropologischen Gesellschaft in Wien* 58 (1928): 341–74.

De Laszlo, Violet S., ed. *Psyche and Symbol: A Selection from the Writings of C. G. Jung*. Garden City: Doubleday Anchor Books, 1958.

Dundes, Alan, ed. *The Blood Libel Legend: A Casebook in Anti-Semitic Folklore*. Madison: University of Wisconsin Press, 1991.

———. *Cinderella: A Casebook*. Madison: University of Wisconsin Press, 1988.

———. *Interpreting Folklore*. Bloomington: Indiana University Press, 1980.

———. *Little Red Riding Hood: A Casebook*. Madison: University of Wisconsin Press, 1989.

———. *Parsing through Customs: Essays by a Freudian Folklorist*. Madison: University of Wisconsin Press, 1987.

Edmunds, Lowell, and Alan Dundes, eds. *Oedipus: A Folklore Casebook*. New York: Garland, 1983.

Freud, Sigmund. "Psycho-Analytic Notes upon an Autobiographical Account of a Case of Paranoia (Dementia Paranoides)." In Sigmund Freud, *Collected Papers*, vol. 3. New York: Basic Books, 1959, 387–470.

Geddes, Virginia G. *"Various Children of Eve" (AT 758): Cultural Variants and Antifeminine Images.* Uppsala: Etnolugiska Institutionen, 1986.

Jung, C. G., and C. Kerényi. *Essays on a Science of Mythology.* New York:Harper Torchbooks, 1963.

Lindzey, Gardner. *Projective Techniques and Cross-Cultural Research.* New York: Appleton-Century-Crofts, 1961.

Malinowski, Bronislaw. *Magic, Science and Religion.* Garden City: Doubleday Anchor Books, 1954.

Rank, Otto. *The Myth of the Birth of the Hero.* New York: Vintage Books,1959.

Rycroft, Charles. *A Critical Dictionary* of *Psycho-Analysis.* New York: Basic Books, 1968.

Thompson, Stith. *Motif-Index of Folk-Literature.* 6 vols. 2d rev. ed. Bloomington: Indiana University Press, 1955–58.

18

THESES ON FECES:
SCATOLOGICAL ANALYSIS

(*A*) The Folklore of Wishing Wells

(*B*) Here I Sit: A Study of American Latrinalia

(*C*) The Kushmaker

Introduction

I should advise readers that the present rubric of "Theses on Feces," along with the previous headings of "Grouping Lore" and "Medical Speech and Professional Identity," are mine. They thematize sets of exemplary essays that Dundes wrote. In the present case, my title denotes his frequent references to scatological themes in folklore. The significance of this feculent topic is more than the taboo or censorship commonly surrounding its frank, if disquieting discussion. As a central image rendered in folk speech, humor, and ritual, it has raised, precisely because it is socially and psychologically unsettling, crucial cultural questions about symbolic and functional ties to human development, religion, sexuality, gender, and cognition. In his work on folkloristic uses of fecal symbolism and traditions, Dundes often cited a cross-cultural classic by John G. Bourke, entitled *Scatologic Rites of All Nations* (1891). It was bold for its open treatment of the begrimed subject, although its scientific subtitle downplayed its sensational contents: A Dissertation upon the Employment of Excrementitious Remedial Agents in Religion, Therapeutics, Divination, Witchcraft, Love-Philters, etc., in all Parts of the Globe. Dundes was also drawn to Freud's foreword to Bourke's volume (1913), in which Freud summarized the importance of feces in human development. He described an infantile state of interest in bodily secretions and the pleasure derived from excretion. He observed that not only are children proud of their defecations, but they also "make use of them in asserting themselves against adults." Dundes used Freud's thesis—that children view feces as symbolic, assertive "gifts" to adults. He expanded on Freud's signification of feces in human thought and folk expression in relation to male appropriation of procreation ("womb envy"), symbolic functions of defilement and toilet training, and the anal-erotic cultural personality (see book-length analyses in Dundes 1984a, 1997d, and 2002c).

As children grow, Freud theorized, their fascinations with feces are repressed. The child, according to Freud, "learns to keep them secret, to be ashamed of them and to feel disgust at their objects." Referring to the use of projective systems to deal with this repression, Freud proposed that "the interest which has hitherto been attached to excrement is carried over on to other objects—for instance, from faeces to money, which is, of course, late in acquiring significance for children. Important constituents in the formation of character are developed, or strengthened, from the repression of coprophilic inclinations." Freud made a connection between excremental and sexual instincts in children, a link which is later "divorced" and "remains incomplete." Another scatological/sexual tie that Freud postulated is the existence of an anal erogenous zone, which is associated with the infantile stage, and remains with a person, but is repressed later in life. In Freudian theory, this repression of a created anxiety is sublimated through symbols that are embedded in fantasies, such as folklore. Dundes avowed more than Freud the sublimatory function of scatological imagery in folklore.

Freud commented on folklore not only as material, but as a "method of research" and found in Bourke's tome that folklore study, although different from psychoanalysis, "has reached the same results as psychoanalysis." Freud declared that folklore "demonstrates the persistent and indeed ineradicable nature of coprophilic interests, by displaying to our astonished gaze the multiplicity of applications—in magical ritual, in tribal custom, in observances of religious cults and in the art of healing—by which the old esteem for human excretions has found new expression." For Dundes, the symbolic equivalences of money, mud, and the color brown to feces, and of smearing and dropping to excretion—all apparent in folklore—opened up interpretative possibilities. (See his use of the mud/feces equation in the last chapter on the earth diver myth.) These projections were, he proclaimed, "keys" to solving "puzzles" of meaning in the content of folklore. He recognized that not all readers would agree, especially early on in his career, but as he found repeated examples of fecal symbolism in rituals, beliefs, and narrative, he became more assertive.

An example is "The Folklore of Wishing Wells" (1962f), one of Dundes's first publications. It appeared, not in a folkloristic journal, but in the psychoanalytic outlet of *American Imago*, which was friendlier to his interpretative stance. Unlike Bourke, whom he cited as being preoccupied with exotic "primitive" examples, Dundes examined the ritual of dropping pennies in wishing wells, one of the most prevalent modern folk practices. It had primarily been interpreted literally, as giving money in exchange for a wish, but Dundes asked, as he often did, why the offering should take the forms it does. Having established a symbolic equivalence of money to feces, he linked "dropping in water" to developmental concerns for maternal attention. A *key* detail, to borrow Dundes's rhetoric, is the tradition of children throwing the coin in the well. Navy lore, in contrast, has the fictional story of a fecal "kush" being thrown overboard by an adult. That developmental shift led Dundes to interpret telling stories of the "kush" as a subversive act, in defiance of strict military (paternal) discipline (1980c). As a former Navy man, Dundes related this to the formal context of the ship, and the role of folklore as a social outlet. (See his recollection of joketelling during his tour of duty in *Cracking Jokes* [1987c]).

"Here I Sit" also dealt with one of his experiences—going to bathrooms in Berkeley, where his folkloristic antennae picked up an abundance of written lore. He noted that they were much more common in facilities for men, rather than women, raising gender questions about the praxis of writing verses and sayings he called "latrinalia," to distinguish it from the more general term "graffiti" for any wall markings. The *key*, in this essay, is the behavioral correlation of latrinalia to fecal "smearing," within the context of male bathroom inscriptions (1966b). In a rejoinder (Dundes 1963) to an article by Parker (1963), Dundes presaged this interpretation by commenting on that critic's "facetious parenthetical admission that he has repressed desires to play with faeces" (note the rhetorical equivalence of play, facetious, and faeces). "This could well explain," Dundes quipped, "his pleasure in mudslinging, which for a member of Western culture, at any rate, is very probably a derivative of a general infantile impulse to smear" (Dundes 1963).

Ever since Dundes's latrinalia essay was originally published, it has been cited as a benchmark interpretation of bathroom graffiti. See Gonos, Mulkern, and Poushinsky 1976; Stocker et al. 1972; Birney 1973; and Longenecker 1977. While the above citations are mostly of men's facilities, for an exemplary look at a woman's bathroom as "community," see Gordon 2003. For other interpretative essays on folklore using Dundes's scatological theses, see Fleisher 1981; Mechling 1984a and 1984b; Carroll 1987; Klein 1993; and Bronner 2007.

A

The Folklore of Wishing Wells

ALTHOUGH THERE HAVE BEEN SEVERAL noteworthy attempts to apply psychoanalytic theory to myth, there are other areas of folklore which have thus far not been
much studied psychoanalytically. One of these areas is that of superstition. This is somewhat surprising in view of the fact that Freud himself suggested the possible origins of
such superstitions as bad luck ensuing from the groom's forgetting the ring (i.e., the groom
does not really want to marry) or bad luck augured by one's stumbling across a threshold.[1]
However, aside from studies such as Ernest Jones' "The Symbolic Significance of Salt in
Folklore and Superstition," there are comparatively few extended analyses of superstitious
beliefs and customs.

One superstition which appears to lend itself to psychoanalytical treatment is the one
involving wishing wells. According to the modern version of this belief, a person is assured
of good luck if he drops a small coin, usually a penny, into a well.[2] An English film (1945)
entitled: "Wishing Well Inn" was based upon this popular practice and the film and song
"Three Coins in a Fountain" are familiar to most Americans. Actually the custom is of
considerable antiquity, dating back at least to Roman times.[3] In many instances, objects
other than coins were deposited. These objects included stones, pebbles, shells, broken
plaster, glass beads, buttons, needles, pins, and nails.[4] Nevertheless, in spite of the variety
of objects, the idea of making an offering to obtain good luck was apparently the same.
Often the good luck desired was in the nature of a cure of a disease. The wishing well custom is widespread in continental Europe[5] and in the British Isles.[6] Curiously enough, it is
even reported among North American Indians and for example, the basin of an Arapaho
spring is supposed to have contained beads and wampum.[7] Whether the Indian instances
are attributable to acculturated diffusion or to polygenesis is difficult to determine. In any
event, it suffices for present purposes to say that the practice of throwing a penny into a
well in order to ensure good luck or to make a wish is well established in American and
European folklore.

The question is now raised, why do people part with something of value, albeit only a
penny, in the hope of being granted a wish? There are superstitions whereby one may make
a wish without making an offering, e.g. after seeing a shooting star or passing a loaded hay
wagon. But in the case of the wishing well custom, the offering must be made in order for
the wish to come true. Many persons, otherwise extremely economical will forsake reality
by discarding perfectly good money. Some of these persons are not particularly superstitious; it is almost as if there were some form of pleasure involved in the simple act of throwing a penny into a well. Despite the supposed present-day scientific mindedness, the fact
that some charity fund raisers have constructed wishing wells in order to collect contributions attests to the extraordinary appeal of the custom. Perhaps the etiology of this custom
can be revealed through psychological analysis.

There have been a number of attempts to explain the custom. The eminent English folklorist Edwin Sidney Hartland noted that the custom has interested students of folklore ever since folklore came to be studied.[8] However, statements like that made by Robert Charles Hope in which he says that wishing wells are a curious survival and that their origin must be looked for in remote antiquity are of little value since historical origins are by no means necessarily identical with ultimate origins.[9] As a matter of fact, most folklorists have tended to explain the custom on the basis of animism. According to this view, there was early the belief that each well had a guardian spirit. Mackinlay, who held this view, claimed that "From a belief in guardian spirits to a belief in the necessity of offering gifts to them is an easy transition."[10] These gifts or offerings were thus an expression of good will and an obvious attempt to propitiate the spirit of the well. Lewis Spence considered that the ancient practice of throwing coins into wells "must be interpreted as an act of placation or sacrifice to the spirit residing in the well."[11] Apparently although the guardian spirit is to be feared, this fearful spirit will accord good luck or the granting of a wish to the ritual participant. With regard to those wells renowned for curative powers, a difficulty arises which was noted by Hartland. On the one hand, there are articles left as offerings to the presiding spirit and on the other hand, these articles contain the disease of which the participant desires to be rid. Hartland comments that these two explanations appear to be mutually exclusive.[12] It seems unlikely that so undesirable an object would be well received as a propitiatory offering by an intelligent spirit. The weakness in all previous explanations is that the origin is not ultimate (Hartland suggested that the custom was an act of ceremonial union with the spirit but he gave no motive for such an act) and that the specific use of money is not made especially relevant. An explanation seeking the ultimate origin of the custom would have to explain the presence of the spirit and also the reason for the pecuniary offering. There may indeed be an "easy transition" from a belief in spirits to the necessity of offering gifts to these spirits as Mackinlay contended but the transition remains to be seen.

Essentially there are two material objects involved in the action of an individual engaging in the custom: the well and the offering, which is usually a penny. Part of the key to the puzzle is provided by the very materials of folklore. The well is a frequent womb or maternal symbol. To employ the bowdlerized language of folklorists, there is a motif[13] T 589.6.4, "Children laid to come from a well." There are sufficient examples of Kinderbrunnen[14] in European folklore to discourage the common criticism leveled against psychoanalytic interpretations, namely of cleverly selecting and stacking evidence. Interestingly enough, one well in Lancashire is described as having been constructed in the form of a horseshoe.[15] The significance of the horseshoe as a female genital symbol is discussed in Jones' important essay on folklore.[16] If the well does represent the womb, it requires no great imagination to identify the guardian spirit of the well as the mother. However, there is still the question of the nature of the offering.

There is general agreement that money is a symbolic equivalent of faeces.[17] Although one might disagree with Ferenczi when he claims that folklore confirms the "phylogenetic origin of symbols"[18]—a cultural relativist would settle for repeated ontogenetic symbolism encouraged by consistent transmission of traditional symbols contained in each generation's cultural legacy—his account of the ontogenesis of the symbolism of money is both clear and convincing. There is additional contemporary evidence of this symbolism. A modern slang expression popular among federal employees including servicemen emphasizes the symbolic equation. The employees refer to the activity of payday as "the eagle shits." One is also tempted to conjecture that the passion of some children (and adults) for the parlor game Monopoly and similar games springs from the same source. In any event, there is some reason for assuming that the penny is odorless, dehydrated fecal material. It is also noteworthy that Ferenczi's progression from faeces proper to money passes through intermediate stages of stones, pebbles, glass marbles, buttons, and so on. This variety of objects is strikingly similar to the various offerings deposited in wells. Assuming the symbolic validity of the two material objects involved in the wishing well custom, that is, the well and the offering, one can from the latent level elucidate the manifest content of the superstition.

The Freudian reconstruction of infantile life includes a consideration of toilet-training. It has been noted that the child is encouraged by the parents, usually the mother, to part with the precious excrement. As Reik said, "we owe to Freud the discovery that the child regards faeces as a present, a mark of affection to be offered to a beloved person."[19] The pleasure in defecation is depreciated or denied and the child is persuaded to yield his "savings"[20] or treasure to his mother either for promised rewards or under threats of punishment. The pattern of making a fecal offering in return for either the good will of the mother or the avoidance of punishment is thus established quite definitely in the lives of most children in Western civilization. If the child-parent relationship is the prototype of man's relation to deity, then one would expect to find the gift of faeces to the parent reflected in the adult's offering to deity. Actually, Bourke reported a number of instances in which a devotee defecated on the altar of a deity. For example, the Assyrian Venus supposedly had offerings of dung placed upon her altars.[21] The fact that fecal material is originally conceived as being an efficacious means of ensuring the attention and love of the mother, makes it reasonable that human ordure would be an important ingredient in love philters. As a matter of record, excrement has historically been used in the preparation of such philters.[22] If this same infantile pattern does underlie the wishing well superstition, then it is understandable that some well spirits are regarded ambivalently. On the one hand the spirit of the well must be given the penny in order for the participant to avoid the spirit's punishment and on the other hand, the spirit of the well may reward the individual who is willing to sacrifice something valuable. Hartland's point is also clarified in that it is now comprehensible how something disagreeable, to be gotten rid of, could still be a proper type of offering. Incidentally, one reason why the superstition has continued to flourish in modern times may be the ever-increasing number of standard plumbing fixtures. In most American homes, for example, the child is taught to put his treasure in a half-filled "white well." The etiology does not, however, depend upon comparatively recent innovations in household plumbing facilities. The custom definitely antedates flush toilets.

The psychoanalytic perspective would appear to illuminate some of the details of the wishing well practice and related practices. For instance, it is significant that in several cases, it is stipulated that the coin offering must be dropped by a child.[23] In a curious Shropshire wishing well custom, the votary must throw a handful of water at a particular stone in the back of the well. If all the water lands upon the stone without touching any other spot, the votary's wish will be fulfilled.[24] This action may represent the parental reward for the exact control of the excretory process, in this case, urination. Another interesting detail is the frequent occurrence of rag-bushes with wishing wells. The rags were presumably part of the clothing of the votary. It is possible, although by no means demonstrable, that the rag-bushes stem from the same source as the coin offering. When a very young child produces his gift for his mother, more often than not, the mother accepts the offering with a soiled garment. Thus, in this light, it is reasonable that a more complete propitiatory ritual would include both a fecal and cloth offering. The fact that in later childhood only the former offering is welcomed (provided it is properly placed) whereas the latter is not, might account for the comparative rarity of the rag-bushes. The reason why the faeces undergoes symbolic transformation while the cloth does not might be the societal prohibitions against anything relating to excrement.

While it is doubtful that many folklorists will accept the above etiological hypothesis, perhaps some psychoanalysts may. In any case, regardless of the validity of this particular study, it is to be hoped that both folklorists and psychoanalysts will devote some of their professional energies towards revealing the rationales underlying one of humanity's most fascinating mental products, superstitions.

Notes

1. Freud, Sigmund. *A General Introduction to Psychoanalysis*. New York: Permabooks, 1953, p. 61.
    Freud. *The Basic Writings* of *Sigmund Freud*. New York: The Modern Library, 1938, p. 165.
2. Ferm, Vergilius. *A Brief Dictionary of American Superstitions*. New York: Philosophical Library,
    1959, p. 52.
3. Hope, Robert Charles. *The Legendary Lore of the Holy Wells of England*. London: Elliot Stock,
    1893, p. xvi. Lubbock, John. *The Origin of Civilisation and the Primitive Condition of Man*.
    New York: D. Appleton and Co., 1882, p. 294.
4. Brand, John. *Observations on the Popular Antiquities of Great Britain*. Vol. II, London: G. Bell
    and Sons, 1882, p. 382. Westropp, Thomas J. "A Folklore Survey of County Clare (XV)" *Folk-
    Lore* XXII (1911),p. 213.
5. Schmidt, August F. *Danmarks Helligkilder,* Danmarks Folkeminder Nr.33. Copenhagen: Det
    Sehonbergske Forlag, 1926, pp. 75–76.
6. Gomme, George Laurence. *Ethnology in Folklore*. New York: D. Appleton and Co., 1892, pp.
    79–80.
7. Dorman, Rushton M. *The Origin of Primitive Superstitions*. Philadelphia: J. B. Lippincott &
    Co., 1881, p. 314. Cf. A. S. G. "Wexford Folk-Lore" *Folk-lore Journal* VII (1889), p. 40.
8. Hartland, Edwin Sidney. "Pin-Wells and Rag-Bushes" *Folk-Lore* IV (1893), p.451.
9. Op, cit., p.xviii.
10. Mackinlay, James M. *Folklore of Scottish Lochs and Springs*. Glasgow: W. Hodge & Co., 1893, p.
    331.
11. Spence, Lewis. *The Fairy Tradition in Britain*. London: Rider, 1948, p.322.
12. Op. cit., p. 469.
13. Thompson, Stith. *Motif-Index of Folk-Literature*. 6 vols. Bloomington:Indiana University Press,
    1955–1958.
14. M'Kenzie, Dan. "Children and Wells" *Folk-Lore* XVIII (1907), p. 267. Rank, Otto. *The Myth
    of the Birth of the Hero*. New York: Vintage, 1959, p. 73, n. 7.
15. Taylor, Henry. *The Ancient Crosses and Holy Wells of Lancashire*. Manchester: Sheratt & Hughes,
    1906, p. 262.
16. Jones, Ernest. " Psycho-Analysis and Folklore" *Essays in Applied Psycho-Analysis*, Vol. II, The
    International Psycho-Analytical Library No. 41. London : The Hogarth Press, 1951, p. 12,
17. Freud. "Character and Anal Erotism" *Collected Papers*, Vol. II, The International Psycho-
    Analytical Library No. 8. London: The Hogarth Press, 1949, p. 49. Freud and D. E. Oppenheim.
    Dreams in Folklore. New York: International Universities Press, 1958, p. 37. Jones, Ernest.
    "Anal-Erotic Character Traits" *Papers on Psycho-Analysis*, Fifth ed. London: Bailliere, Tindall
    and Cox, 1950, p. 426. Ferenczi, Sandor. "The Ontogenesis of the Interest in Money" *Sex in
    Psycho-Analysis*. New York: Dover, 1956, p. 270.
18. p. 269.

19. *The Unknown Murderer.* New York: International Universities Press, p. 78.
20. Ferenczi, p. 271.
21. Bourke, John G. *Compilation of Notes and Memoranda Bearing Upon the Use of Human Ordure and Human Urine in Rites of a Religious or Semi Religious Character among Various Nations.* Washington, D. C., 1888, p. 32. Cf. pp. 36–37.
22. Walton, Alan Hull. *Aurodisiacs: From Legend to Prescription.* Westport: Associated Booksellers, 1958, p 95.
23. Mackinlay, p. 15.
24. Burne, Charlotte Sophia, ed. *Shropshire Folk-Lore.* London: Trübner & Co., 1883, p. 428.

B

Here I Sit: A Study of American Latrinalia

ANY AMERICAN MALE WHO HAS ever had an occasion to enter a public bathroom such as one found in a railroad or bus terminal has surely observed at one time or another one of the many traditional inscriptions found on the walls of the facilities.[1] In some quarters, e.g. in the rest rooms of some bars and cafés, one finds the custom has been institutionalized in that a small slate and an accompanying piece of chalk are hanging on the wall. This allows individuals to write freely and at the same time it saves the establishment the expense of continually repainting walls.

Despite the widespread distribution of these inscriptions and despite the fact that many of them are demonstrably traditional, one looks in vain for extended collections of published texts and for any rational discussion of them or the practice of writing them. Most histories of the water closet (e.g. Pudney, Reynolds, Wright) do little more than recognize that such traditions exist. Typical is the remark made by poet John Pudney, author of *The Smallest Room*, who bothers to say (1954:130), "I must here resist the temptation urged on me by several men of letters to quote more freely from this poetry of the smallest room." Certainly there can be no doubt as to the antiquity of the genre. In the chapter devoted to latrines of John G. Bourke's classic *Scatalogic Rites of All Nations*, one finds references to the obscene poetry written in Roman latrines (1891:136). What little evidence is available in print does attest to the age and international spread of this popular form of written folklore. Gershon Legman, an authority on erotic folklore bibliography, mentions (1964:254, 451) *The Merry-Thought or The Glass-Window and Bog-House Miscellany* of 1731 with the only known complete copy at Oxford. In the important journal of obscene folklore, *Anthropophyteia*, one finds a handful of brief collectanea, e.g. one entitled "Skatologische Inschriften" or ones by Fischer and von Waldheim, which indicates the presence of the form in modern Europe. A fair sampling of Mexican examples appeared in a chapter "Grafitos en Los Comunes" in Jiménez' best-selling *Picardia Mexicana*. The classic study of the form in America was made by Allen Walker Read who privately published it in 1935 under the euphemistic title, *Lexical Evidence from Folk Epigraphy in Western North America: A Glossarial Study of the Low Element in the English Vocabulary*. The title page of this eighty-three page monograph announced that the circulation was restricted to students of linguistics, folklore, abnormal psychology, and allied branches of the social sciences. Professor Read's term "folk epigraphy" raises the question of what to call bathroom wall writings.

The term graffiti is too broad in that it includes all kinds of inscriptions and marks placed on walls. Moreover, the walls may be any walls, not just bathroom walls. Professor Read included in his compilation everything he saw on walls during an extensive sight-seeing trip made in the western United States and Canada in the summer of 1928. Much of his material is traditional in form only, but not content. The various homosexual

360

rendezvous requests with listings of dimensions and telephone numbers are clearly the traditional in form and are surely worth studying as indicators of one of the obvious functions of men's rooms in a culture which forbids homosexual activities. However, the specific content of these assignation attempts is often idiosyncratic. The folklorist is primarily interested in those mural inscriptions which are traditional in both form and content. Thus while he or she may record the *hapax logomena* or one-time occurrences, he or she is more concerned with those which have multiple-existence, that is, those which are found with almost exactly the same form and wording in many different places. Obviously, a one-time occurrence may become traditional in time, but the vast majority of the nontraditional graffiti are much too localized to diffuse easily. For the traditional inscriptions, I propose the term *latrinalia*. This is preferable, I think, to the closest thing to a folk term, "shithouse poetry" inasmuch as not all latrinalia is in verse or poetic form.

Before examining the nature of latrinalia in America and discussing its significance, I should like to comment briefly on the failure of American social scientists to study this kind of material. It is curious that it is perfectly permissible to investigate the graffiti of the past, say the graffiti of classical cultures, but it is not equally acceptable, academically speaking, to study the graffiti of our own culture. The rationale is apparently that it is safe to study the "once removed" whether once removed in space or time, but not so safe to study what is all too readily available in one's immediate environment. Perhaps one of the reasons why individuals are attracted to the discipline of anthropology is that the "once removed" framework is provided. Archaeologists, practicing "dirt archaeology," are free to dig into the bowels of the earth searching for buried treasures among the remains of what men of the past produced. In this connection, archaeologists have even begun to indulge in the analysis of coprolites. Physical anthropologists are free to examine every part of the human body in great detail. Ethnographers can perfectly properly go into the "field" and voyeuristically observe exotic customs, the analogues of which they might be embarrassed to watch at home in their own culture. (One is reminded of the folk definition of anthropology: the study of man . . . embracing woman!) Even the unusually great concern with the finer points of kinship may reflect an abiding and fundamental curiosity about basic family relationships. That ethnographies reflect the culture of the ethnographers as much as the people described cannot be doubted. Germane to the present study is the lack of data in standard ethnographies on defecation and urination. When, where, and how are these acts performed? When and how precisely is toilet training for infants introduced? One can read an entire ethnography without ever coming upon any reference to these daily necessities. The study of humainty must include *all* aspects of human activity.

Since ethnography, like charity, should begin at home (how can we possibly perceive the bias of our accounts without fully understanding our own culture?), the study of latrinalia is clearly a legitimate area of inquiry. One must not forget that it is humans who write on bathroom walls and humans who read these writings. As one writer has put it (Reynolds 1943:171–172), "Stereotyped and crude, our lavatory inscriptions are the measure of our social fixations; and that enterprising anthropologist who is said to be collecting photographs of them in all parts of the world should reveal more of the truth than all of the bombastic historians who will so soon be clothing our grotesque society with dignified phrases and political stercorations, representing its present antics as studied movements, to be explained in terms of high principles and rational conduct." So then let us proceed with our essay in hard core ethnography!

In American culture, anything which leaves the body from one of its various apertures is by definition dirty. The transition is immediate. Saliva is not defiling until it leaves the mouth. Similarly, nasal, ear, or eye secretions (with the possible exception of tears) are not offensive until they are removed from the body. The emitted materials are frequently as disgusting to the emitter as to others. Few Americans would be able to drink a glass of water into which they or someone else had just expectorated or even drooled. It is true that French or soul kissing allows for swapping spits, but in this case, the saliva is encountered while still inside the mouth and it is presumably not deemed dirty. A more mundane example would be the removal of partly masticated food from the mouth. Since by definition anything which emerges from the body is dirty and disgusting, an unchewed morsel may presents a social problem. Does one grasp it with the fingers or with an eating utensil? Is there any sense of embarrassment at removing the morsel in front of others and realizing the removal is being observed? How does one dispose of the chewed bit of gristle? Is it placed surreptitiously on one's plate and perhaps concealed with a convenient lettuce leaf? Of course, there is nothing inherently dirty. Humans, not nature, make dirt and one can say that dirt, like beauty, lies in the eyes of the beholder. The concept of dirt is part of culture and as such it falls into the province of the cultural anthropologist.

One of the few places where dirt may be displayed and discussed in American culture is the bathroom, private and public. Bathrooms, generally speaking, are status symbols and not infrequently houses are measured in part by the number of bathrooms they possess. It is in the home bathroom that the boy is taught to deposit his feces and urine. Here is one place where he is allowed to manipulate his genitals and expose them to view, either his own view or the view of others. Not only are the genitals and buttocks exposed, but the products of micturition and defecation may also be observed. Later, in public rest rooms, the child soon learns that he must make public what has hitherto been private. He must urinate alongside strangers and in the course of so doing, he may observe the organs of others in the act just as these other individuals may observe him.

Despite the overt behavior, the culturally prescribed pretense that such activities do not exist, as manifested in the taboo against referring directly to them, continues. The large number of euphemisms attest to that. The private family idioms of the home, e.g. to go potty, to do number one (urination) or number two (defecation), to wee wee, to make a poo, etc., cannot be used in the public context. Children in school are taught to "excuse" themselves. (Note that to "excuse oneself" may carry the sense of apologizing!) The ironic part is that the child must go through the public confessional act of raising his hand to tell the teacher and all of his peers that he wishes to answer a "call of nature." The child soon learns the gamut of farfetched euphemisms ranging from "washing" or "freshening" up to "seeing a man about a dog," going to "shake hands with the head of the family," or trying to do something about the fact that one's "back teeth are floating." (For an extended discussion of such euphemisms, see Pudney 1954:20–37 and Sagarin 1962:69–74.) Note that the term lavatory literally refers to cleaning and thus to sinks, not toilets. Yet the word lavatory has become almost taboo and is now substituted for by newer euphemisms (Reynolds 1943:179). Once in the school bathroom, however, the behavior cannot be anything other than to the point. It is in the public school bathroom (termed boys' and girls' "basement" at my secondary school in Pawling, New York, though the rooms were not located in the basement) that important social interactions take place. Boys meet there to discuss the problems of the day while girls similarly go there to gossip. It is in many ways a place of comparative freedom from the normal restraints imposed by the adult world. The necessity of some sexual exposure no doubt contributes to the bathroom's role as a place of sanctioned license. It is in public bathrooms, particularly men's rooms, that one finds latrinalia.

The variety of latrinalia forms includes: (1) advertisements or solicitations, normally of a sexual nature; (2) requests or commands, often concerning the mechanics of defecating or urinating; (3) directions, which consist of false or facetious instructions; (4) commentaries, either by the establishment or by clients; and (5) personal laments or introspective musings. These categories are not hard and fast and they are not necessarily mutually exclusive. A sampling of each of the categories should serve to illustrate the nature of American latrinalia.

The majority of advertisements are probably not traditional in that individuals simply write their own names and telephone numbers. Furthermore, in view of the paucity of published materials, it is difficult to ascertain whether or not a number of items have appeared elsewhere. Typical "want ads," which may or may not be traditional, include:

1. For a good blow job, call 777 2024
    Bill, don't call, it's me, Bob.
2. I'm big. 9" long, 3" round, and ready to go.
    (In another hand) How big is your prick?

In view of the nontraditional content of most latrinalia advertisements, I will proceed to the more common traditional category of requests or commands. The following are usually placed near men's urinals:

3. Don't throw cigarette butts in the urinal—
    It makes them soggy and hard to light.
4. Please do not throw butts in the urinal.
    Do we piss in your ash trays?

This is strikingly similar in style to the private swimming pool sign which reads:

1. We don't swim in your toilet
    Please don't piss in our pool.

The pool sign reflects, of course, the fact that Americans do in fact urinate in swimming pools (just as American infants urinate in their baths)!

A large number of urinal latrinalia specifically ask for care in aiming the stream of urine. Typical examples of this "toilet training" tradition include:

5. We aim to please
    you aim too please
6. It is our aim to keep this place clean.
    Your aim will help.

These are often written by the management. A common request urges men to stand close to the urinal to reduce the chances of spillage.

7.   Stand up close. The next man might have holes in his shoes.

8.   Stand close, the next person may be barefooted.

9.   Stand up close. The next fellow may be a Southerner
      And be barefooted. (Camp Maxey, Paris, Texas, 1945)

10.   If your hose is short
      And your pump is weak
      You better stand close
      Or you'll pee on your feet.

11.   Old rams with short horns please stand up close. (Fort Lewis, Tacoma,
      Washington, circa 1945; cf. Read 1935:20)

An appropriately localized version from New England is as follows:

12.   Puritans with short muskets step up to the firing line. (Damiscotta,
      Maine, circa 1950)

Another example of latrinalia which is posted by the management rather than the customers is one found in diners' restrooms:

13.   If you shit here, eat here.
      We don't want just the tail end of your business.

Occasionally, there are *blason populaire* latrinalia:

14.   Shake well. Texas needs the water.

For the special case when a man urinates into a toilet rather than into a urinal, special instructions may be found:

15.   Be like brother
      Not like Sis
      Lift the seat
      When you take a piss. (New York City, 1924)

16.   Be like Dad and not like Sis
      Pull your lid before you piss. (Camp Maxey, Paris, Texas, 1945)

Some commands are concerned with toilet flushing.

17.   Flush your toilets for Wichita's sake. (Hutchinson, Kansas, circa 1958;
      cf. Read 935:20)

18.   Flush twice: L.A. needs water.

19.   Flush hard. It's a long way to the kitchen.

This insult to the chef is a reversal of the conception that man is a dirt-making machine which transforms food into feces. This conception is illustrated by a latrinalia verse in French which was found in Oxford, England, in 1947: "Ici tombent en ruines les merveilles de la cuisine." In the above text and the following, the "natural" procedure is reversed as feces becomes food.

20. Don't flush the toilet. The next man might be hungry. (Chicago, 1960)
21. Please flush the toilet. We want the niggers to starve to death. (A Missouri café, 1965)

There is also some instruction designed to keep the toilet seat clean.

22. Here is the place we all must come
    To do the work that must be done
    Do it quick and do it neat
    But please don't do it on the seat.
23. Boys we all must use this throne
    Please keep it clean and neat
    Shit down the hole God damn your soul
    And not upon the seat. (Camp Maxey, Paris, Texas, 1945)

The reference to "throne" recalls the euphemisms in other cultures which speak of going to the place where the king goes on foot or alone (Pudney 1954:97). A common American fantasy technique designed to minimize one's awe of a great personage is to imagine that individual at stool.

24. For those in a hurry
    With no time to sit
    Please lift the lid
    For a more direct hit. (Women's restroom, Berkeley, 1963)

This may refer also to the practice of many women of not actually sitting on a toilet seat but of squatting over it.

One commentary complains about the nature of men's clothing as opposed to women's clothing with special reference to defecation.

25. Women women what a blessing
    You can shit without undressing
    But we poor men we sons of bitches
    We must strip or shit in our britches. (Camp Maxey, Paris, Texas, 1945)

The influence of television programs and such contemporary events as demonstrations by civil rights groups (e.g. the Congress of Racial Equality) is evident in some commands.

26. Smile, You're on Candid Camera.

This is usually written on the inside of the door of the toilet stall.

27. Stay seated. This is a Core shit-in. (University library, Berkeley campus, April, 1964)

Some commands or requests are bitter parodies:

28. Support mental health or I'll kill you.

In the "directions" category, one finds mostly parodies. In the following text, the accuracy of the first line and of the order of the remaining lines was questioned by the informant. It is, however, an excellent example of a latrinalia verse of the "how-to-do-it-yourself" variety.

29. If you want to shit at ease
     Place your elbows on your knees
     Place your hands upon your chin
     Work your asshole out and in. (cf. Read 1935:51, 73)

30. Directions to get to Texas: Go west until you smell shit, that's Oklahoma. Then, go south until you step in it—that's Texas. (Manchester, New Hampshire, circa 1953)

31. In case of atomic attack . . .
     1. Put your hands over your ears
     2. Put your head between your legs
     3. Kiss your ass goodbye. You've had it.

32. In case of attack, hide under this urinal.
     Nobody ever hits it. (Great Lakes, Illinois, 1951)

There are also false directions which are really a form of what folklorists sometimes call a catch. Repeated many times, each time in smaller writing is the line: "If you can read this come closer." Then at the bottom right below a miniscule version appears the line: "You are now shitting at a 45° angle." In similar vein is the sign on the ceiling over the urinal which says, "While you're reading this, you're peeing on your shoes."

The content of the latrinalia commentaries varies. Some are unexpectedly intellectual.

33. "God is dead." Nietzsche
     "Nietzsche is dead." God

However, not many commentaries have this kind of sophistication. Few American latrinalia verses are as philosophical, for example, as the following latrinalia verse popular in Spain:

> En este lugar cerrado
> donde viene tanta gente
> hace fuerza el más cobarde
> y se cagy el más valiente. (cf. Jiménez 1960:124)

The majority of American commentaries stay close to home. An "x" marked high over the wall of a men 's urinal is accompanied by the explanatory line:

34. Anyone who can piss this high ought to be a fireman.

One wonders if there is any insight here into the psychological rationale underlying the motivation to become a fireman. (Note the slang term "hose" for penis and see text 10 in this paper.) One recalls the desire of many small boys to grow up to be firemen and the custom of adolescent boys of urinating on campfires to extinguish them (cf. Bettelheim 1962:166–167).

35.   You are holding the future of America in your hands.

Here is a reminder during the act of urination that the same organ is one used for reproduction. Note the pseudo-patriotic responsibility to procreate.

One common commentary deals with the very real problem of those last drops of urine which all too often drip down into one's pants or down one's leg.

36.   You can wiggle, jiggle, jump or dance
          But the last three drops go down your pants.

37.   No matter how you dance and prance
          The last two drops go down your pants.

38.   You can shake and shake as much as you please
          But there'll still be a drop for your B.V.D.'s.

An English version has a different rhyme for the same message:

39.   However hard you shake your peg
          At least one drop runs down your leg.

The "shaking" is also found in other latrinalia.

40.   You are now shaking your best friend
          And he stood up for you on your wedding night. (Camp Maxey, Paris, Texas, 1945)

However, the shaking act can be suspicious if carried on too long. Excessive manipulation of the genitals could be construed as masturbatory activity:

41.   If you shake it more than three times, you're cheating. (cf. Read 1935:68)

There are other anti-masturbation verses.

42.   Be a man, not a fool
          Pull the chain, not your tool.

43.   This is a teepee
          For you to peepee
          Not a wigwam
          To beat your tomtom.

Another topic of commentaries is the cleanliness of toilets.

44.   No need to stand on the toilet seat
          For the crabs in this place jump forty feet. (cf. Read 1935: 40, 44)

45.   It does no good to line the seat
          The crabs here jump fifteen feet.

The last verse reveals the practice of putting sheets of toilet paper on the top of toilet seats as a means of avoiding contact with the seat. This folk custom has recently become formalized by the presence of paper seat cover dispensers.

There are occasional political latrinalia. Here are several demeaning presidential candidate Barry Goldwater:

46.   When I look down, I see Goldwater.

47.   Urine is goldwater; the only benefit is derived from the comfort of its removal.

Mathematics, the language of science, has exerted some influence:

48.   The heat of the meat is inversely proportional to angle of the dangle.

The heat of the meat, that is, the state of sexual excitement, is directly proportional to the degree of erection. The greater the erection, the less the "angle of dangle." The internal rhyme in this last verse shows the poetic quality of latrinalia. (Poetic features are found in other obscenity. One thinks of the alliterative folk alternatives for saying "I've been screwed," to wit: to be "fucked by the fickle finger of fate" or to be "dangled by the diddling digit of doom.")

Another latrinalia comment on sexuality occurs in the folkloristic form of a toast:

49.   Here's to the hole that never heals
      The more you rub it the better it feels
      All the water this side of hell
      Can't wash away the codfish smell. (Camp Maxey, Paris, Texas, 1945)

The language of advertising can be found too. A borrowing from a Ban deodorant advertisement was found in November, 1965, on a prophylactic dispenser in a Shafter, Nevada, restroom:

50.   It takes the worry out of being close.

By far the best poetry is to be found in the personal laments or introspective musings category. One of the most popular of these is:

51.   Here I sit broken hearted
      Tried (Came) to shit and only farted. (cf. Read 1935:50)

The sadness is actually economic inasmuch as one ordinarily pays to use many public toilets. One must make a small deposit before entering the toilet stall. The "failure to get one's money's worth," an important theme in American culture, is explicit in some versions.

52.   Here I sit broken-hearted
      Paid a nickel and only farted.

This last verse has a traditional response:

53.   Don't cry brother
      You had your chance

> I didn't have a nickel
> And shit (in) my pants.

There is also a combination of both verses:

54. Here I sit broken hearted
    Tried to shit and only farted.
    But think of the man who took the chance
    Tried to fart and shit his pants.

There are other examples of American latrinalia with the introductory opening formula "Here I sit."

55. Here I sit in stinking vapor
    Some sonuvabitch stole the toilet paper.
56. Here I sit in silent bliss
    Listening to the trickling piss
    Now and then a fart is heard
    Calling to the coming turd. (Los Angeles, 1918; cf. Read 1935:51, 81)
57. Here I sit in solemn bliss
    Listening to the dribble of piss
    And now and then a fart is heard
    Then followed by a thundering turd. (Camp Maxey, Paris, Texas, 1945)

These last two verses are obviously cognates and are related to the versions from Lake Tahoe and Visalia, California, reported by Read (1935:51).

Noteworthy is the sound aspect of the process of elimination. Most people are ashamed of anyone's hearing the sound of their urinating or defecating. Even the sound of a toilet flush is embarrassing to some. The whole philosophy of pretending that the activity doesn't exist is of course threatened by the possibility of someone's hearing the unavoidable telltale sound. The listener, as opposed to the voyeur, is depicted in the following verse:

58. Sam, Sam, the janitor man
    Chief superintendent of the crapping can.
    He washes out the bowls and picks up the towels
    And listens to the roar of other men's bowels. (cf. Read 1935: 39)

The sound is also involved in some of the onomatopoeic euphemisms, e.g. "tinkle" meaning to urinate.

Some latrinalia explore the motivations for visiting bathrooms.

59. Some come here to sit and think
    But I come here to shit and stink. (Camp Maxey, Paris, Texas, 1945; cf. Read 1935:21, 49, 74)

60.   Some come here to sit and think
       And some come here to wonder
       But I come here to shit and stink
       And fart away like thunder.

A comparison of the last two reveals how a two-line verse may be expanded into a four-line verse. In the following verse, the expansion utilizes a different rhyme scheme:

61.   Some people come to sit and think
       Others come to shit and stink.
       But I just come to scratch my balls
       And read the bullshit on the walls.

All these latrinalia texts are representative and they should serve to illustrate the nature of this on-going mural tradition. However, these materials raise a number of questions. Probably the most intriguing questions about latrinalia are psychological. Why are they written at all and why in bathrooms? Why are they so much more common in men's rest rooms than in women's rest rooms?

There has been little theorizing about the psychological functions of latrinalia. Reynolds (1943:170) has stated that generations of lavatory wall writers simply write for the pleasure of breaking a taboo, presumably the taboo of referring to body elimination activities. Allen Walker Read suggests that latrinalia probably results from many different motivations. Nevertheless, he notes (1935:17) that, "A principal reason is the well-known human yearning to leave a record of one's presence or one's existence." If this is correct, the question remains, what is the psychological significance of a yearning to leave a record of one's presence?

Allen Walker Read has also observed (1935:17) that writing latrinalia was the same order of activity as the carving of initials or names on trees. Interestingly enough, psychoanalyst Ernest Jones tried to explain the latter custom in his famous paper on "Anal-Erotic Character Traits." Jones hypothesizes (1961:432) that it may possibly be a derived and sublimated form of what he terms a "primitive smearing impulse," the desire that infants allegedly have to handle and manipulate their feces, a desire whose fulfillment is invariably forbidden by toilet-training conscious parents. People who carve or write their names are leaving a memento of themselves which may injure and spoil something beautiful (1961:432). Although Jones makes no mention of latrinalia, I suggest that it may well stem from the same impulse to smear feces or dirt on walls. Dirty words are dirt by themselves, independent of the dirtiness of their referents. Certainly this theory would explain why the writing was placed on bathroom walls in particular. The fact that much of the content of latrinalia does refer to defecation and urination would tend to support the assertion that there is some relationship between the acts of writing on walls and playing with feces. Farfetched as this may sound to some, *it is precisely the explanation given by the folk*! In one of the best known latrinalia verses, the rationale for writing latrinalia is as follows:

62.   Those who write on shithouse walls
       Roll their shit in little balls
       Those who read these words of wit
       Eat the little balls of shit.

Here is an explicit equation of the act of writing on walls with the manipulation of one's own feces. It could not be said any more plainly than "Those who write on shithouse walls roll their shit in little balls!"

From earliest childhood, the American is taught to deny his anus and its activities. The smearing impulse is redirected to suitable substitute activities: working with modeling clay, finger paints, or throwing mud pies (cf. Ferenczi). Using words, dirty words, some individuals finally do give vent to the impulse to sully walls. Since "dirt" is supposed to be deposited in the clean white receptacles found in bathrooms, what more flagrant act of rebellion than to place symbolic dirt on the very walls surrounding the receptacles!

While Freudian explanations are not popular in anthropological and folkloristic circles, the fact that the folk confirm the Freudian explanation must be taken into account and explained by anti-Freudians. The independent congruence of analytic and folk or native theories does, it seems to me, present a reasonably convincing argument. Noteworthy also in this connection is the fact that the second couplet of the above mentioned metafolkloristic text corroborates another psychoanalytic insight into toilet ritual. It has been suggested (Abraham 1948:385; Fenichel 1953:374) that the popular practice of reading while at stool is essentially an act of incorporation designed to balance the material which is lost through defecation. (The common rationale for such reading is the desire not to waste time. By reading in the bathroom, one can save time and make it more productive. Additionally the reading also permits and encourages the prolongation of the defecation act.) Thus "eating" the dirty words compensates for the evacuated fecal dirt. Once again, the folk apparently agree with the explanation: "Those who read these words of wit eat the little balls of shit."

A more recent localized bit of latrinalia appearing in Berkeley supports the writing-feces equation:

63. Don't write on our walls
     We don't shit in your notebooks.
     The Regents
     What's found in our notebooks is shit anyway
     The Students
     (Main Library, U.C. Berkeley, 1965)

The equation of defecation and writing is not limited to American culture. Apparently in parts of Bulgaria, one who has gone to the "thinking place" is described as "thinking" or "writing" (Pudney 1954:25). The writing-defecation equation suggests that the academic motto "publish or perish," an oicotypal example of what might be termed the alternative structure proverb (cf. "do or die," "put up or shut up," "fish or cut bait," etc.), may be "shit or get off the pot" in symbolic disguise. One might remember that scholars are first supposed to amass great quantities of data from which they are expected to "get stuff out regularly" (Dundes 1962c). (Cf. the notion of weighing the output on the scales at the end of the year.)

The suggested anal erotic basis of writing may also explain why men rather than women write latrinalia. According to current theory, men the world over suffer from pregnancy envy (Bettelheim, Dundes 1962a:1038). In essence, men are envious of women's ability to bear children and they seek to find various substitute gratifications, e.g. couvade behavior, having an intellectual "brainchild," calling their pet project their "baby," etc. Bettelheim has assembled a good deal of convincing anthropological evidence to document the pregnancy envy hypothesis. However, although Bettelheim does cite (1962:128) the instance of the Chaga men's practice of stopping up their rectums as a form of symbolic pregnancy, he does not see that males commonly use their anuses to provide substitutes for parturition. Feces, like babies, are produced by the body. When a man defecates, he is a creator, a *prime mover*. Women produce feces too, but since they *can* produce babies from within, there is less need for women to emphasize this type of body product. That women have less need of fecal substitute activities is suggested by the fact that few women indulge in sculpture, painting, blowing wind instruments, etc. (cf. Jones 1961:435, n. 4). Certainly in American culture, it is men who are more concerned than women with creative feces metaphors. It is usually men, not women, who are "full of it," who are "BS *artists*," who tell "cock and bull stories."

In American culture, the emphasis is on productivity and the male must *make* much more than feces. He must *make* something of himself and he must *make* a living. The word "*make*" is itself indicative of the productive component of defecation. An infant may be told to *make water, make weewee, make B.M.*, or just plain *make* (Sagarin 1962:47, 52). As an adult in a "man's world," he tries to *make* money or *make* time. Once he is successful, he may be told that he's *got it made*. "Time is money," the proverb says, but both time and money are symbolic fecal substitutes (Brown 1959:277; Carvalho Neto 1956:125–148; Ferenczi; Dundes 1962a, 1962b; Jones 1961:425–427) as folk speech and other folklore so abundantly attests (cf. to be filthy rich, to be rolling in it, to have money up the ass, to make one's pile, to have time on one's hands, to *pass* time or *piddle* the time away, etc.). Time and money can be saved or hoarded; time and money can be spent or wasted. In American ideal culture, saving is valued. Think of all the money and time *saving* devices enjoyed by Americans. Yet in American real culture, prestige accrues to those who spend or waste time and money. If a man wants to *make it big* or *make a splash*, he has to produce, to put out. He can't *sit tight*; he can't *sit on his material*. Even God, a masculine figure, is termed a *maker*, which is entirely appropriate in view of the anal nature of man's creation, that is, man's being molded from dust or dirt (Dundes 1962a:1046). (Note also that the "fart-thunder" linkage so patent in the latrinalia hints at an infantile origin of thunder gods as Róheim [1952:515] almost says.)

The *make* metaphor also applies to genital matters. A man is expected to *make* out, to *make* a woman and to *make* love. The couching of genital affairs in anal terms is paralleled by the whole concept of dirty words in American culture. Dirty jokes, for example, are largely genital, not anal in content. Yet jokes about sex are called "dirty jokes." The word on the sign at Berkeley was an obscene word which no false acrostic, "Freedom Under Clark Kerr," could disguise, but it was thought of as a dirty word (cf. the filthy speech movement—no pun on movement intended!). One reason why genitality is considered to be "dirty" may be guilt by association. The organs concerned are recognized and identified first as producers of urine, that is, as producers of dirt. Later it is discovered that the sexual act is performed by the same dirt-producing instrument. This situation has been summed up by Yeats in his poem "Crazy Jane Talks With the Bishop" when he wrote: "But Love has pitched his mansion in the place of excrement." Here is dirt by association.

The desire to make one's mark or to leave something *behind* for posterity is also very likely involved in the writing of latrinalia. Defecation as a technique to mark a place for identification is found not only in folk tales (Freud and Oppenheim 1958:38) but among other forms of primate life who apparently demarcate territorial boundaries through urination and defecation (Harrisson). The goal is also perhaps to achieve notice and immortality by producing dirt. A final example of latrinalia bears on this:

64. To the shithouse poet
    In honor of his wit
    May they build far and wide
    Great monuments of shit.

One wonders about the significance of leaving great stone memorials. Many great men have taken an active part in designing and building that which was to remain after they had departed. There is the obvious phallic significance of some monuments. The Washington monument is certainly appropriate for the father of our country. But the majority are massive pieces of stone, often in the shape of little rooms or houses. (Writing on these walls involves epitaphs rather than latrinalia.) The psychology of making one's mark, of leaving some memorial behind, may be related to American males' desire to successfully compete with females who can "make" children as their form of immortality.

For those who may be skeptical of the theory that the psychological motivation for writing latrinalia is related to an infantile desire to play with feces and to artistically smear it around, I would ask only that they offer an alternative theory. For those who doubt that the greater interest on the part of males in latrinalia *is* related to anal creativity stemming from pregnancy envy, I would ask the same. It is all too easy to elicit destructive criticism. We know that latrinalia exists. What we want to know is why it exists and what function it serves. One day when we have more information about the writers of latrinalia (and perhaps psychological projective tests administered to such writers) and when we have better cross-cultural data, we may be better able to confirm or revise the present attempt to answer the questions.

Note

1. This paper was presented at the 1966 meeting of the California Folklore Society at Davis, California. I am indebted to many of my students and colleagues for contributing examples of latrinalia. Unless otherwise indicated, all materials were collected from men's rooms in Berkeley and the surrounding Bay Area in 1964. I am especially grateful to psychologist Nathan Hurvitz who provided all of the items from Paris, Texas. My thanks also to Sam Hinton for his suggestion that the paper be entitled "Ars(e) Poetica." Explanations of the meaning of most of the slang terms appearing in the latrinalia may be found in the works by Read and Sagarin cited in the list of references for this paper.

References

Abraham, Karl. 1948. Contributions to the theory of the anal character. In *Selected Papers of Karl Abraham*. London, Hogarth, pp. 370–397.
Anonymous. 1912. Skatologische inschriften. *Anthropophyteia* 9:503–510.
Bettelheim, Bruno. 1962. *Symbolic Wounds*. New York, Collier Books.
Brown, Norman O. 1959. *Life Against Death*. New York, Random House.
Carvalho Neto, Paulo De. 1956. *Folklore y psicoanalisis*. Buenos Aires, editorial psique.
Dundes, Alan. 1962a. Earth-Diver: Creation of the Mythopoeic Male. *American Anthropologist* 64:1032–1051.
———. 1962b. The Folklore of Wishing Wells. *American Imago* 19:27–34.
———. 1962c. On the Psychology of Collecting Folklore. *Tennessee Folklore Society Bulletin* 28:65–74.
Fenichel, Otto. 1953. The Scotophilic Instinct and Identificaton. *In The Collected Papers of Otto Fenichel: First Series*. New York, W. W. Norton, pp. 373–397.

Ferenczi, Sandor. 1956. The Ontogenesis of the Interest in Money. In *Sex in Psychoanalysis*. New York, Dover, pp. 269–279.

Fischer, Heinrich. 1909. Abortspruch aus Rumänien. *Anthropophyteia* 6:439.

Freud, Sigmund and D. E. Oppenheim, 1958. *Dreams in Folklore*. New York, International Universities Press.

Harrisson, Barbara. 1963. Dundes Continued. *American Anthropologist* 65: 921–922.

Jiménez, A. 1960. *Picardía Mexicana*. Mexico City, Libro Mex.

Jones, Ernest. 1961. Anal-erotic character traits. In *Papers on Psycho-analysis*. Boston, Beacon Press, pp. 413–437.

Legman, Gershon.1964. *The Horn Book: Studies in Erotic Folklore and Bibliography*. New Hyde Park, University Books.

Pudney, John.1954. *The Smallest Room*. London, Michael Joseph.

Read, Allen Walker.1935. *Lexical Evidence from Folk Epigraphy in Western North America*. Paris, privately printed.

Reynolds, Reginald.1943. *Cleanliness and Godliness*. London, George Allen & Unwin.

Róheim, Géza. 1952. *The Gates of the Dream*. New York, International Universities Press.

Sagarin, Edward. 1962.*The Anatomy of Dirty Words*. New York, Lyle Stuart.

Von Waldheim, Dr. 1909. Breslauer locus-inschriften. *Anthropophyteia* 6:433–435.

Wright, Lawrence. 1960. *Clean and Decent*. New York, Viking Press.

C

The Kushmaker

IF FOLKLORISTICS IS EVER TO become an academic field of inquiry truly respected by members of other disciplines, folklorists must do far more than simply collect and classify data. Yet despite the growing number of folklorists trained at university graduate centers offering advanced degrees including the doctorate in folklore, the vast majority of published articles in professional periodicals (and *Festschriften*!) continue to consist of little more than pure descriptions with occasional forays into classification and typology. The essential question of what a given item of folklore might *mean* is typically ignored. I am convinced that unless or until questions of *meaning* are addressed by folklorists, they will inevitably remain second-class citizens in the world community of scholars. Field collection and the construction of classificatory schemes may well be necessary means to the end of interpreting possible meanings of folklore, but if that end is not achieved, folklorists cannot claim to have progressed much beyond the nineteenth-century antiquarian mentality, according to which the primary goal was to record vestigial exotica surviving from earlier ages.

The plight of folkloristics is exemplified by the state of current knowledge of the tale of the kushmaker, Richard M. Dorson devotes a paragraph in his *American Folklore* (1959) to the tale:

> One of the most popular folktales of the last war dealt with the "Kush-Maker." A draftee in the Navy states his occupation as a "kush-maker"—or kletch, splooch, kaplush, gleek, ka-swish, kloosch, squish; the designation varies in every telling. Not wishing to show ignorance, the CD assigned the man to duties in the hold, where he remained until the admiral came to inspect the ship. Running down the ship's roster, he spied the kush-maker, and demanded an explanation. The kush-maker is summoned forth, and makes elaborate preparations for the display of his special skill; in the end a complicated steel sphere is hoisted over the ship's side, or even lowered from an airplane, into the water below, making the sound of "kush," or its equivalent. Curiously, a comparable tale, attached to a blacksmith, is credited both to Davy Crockett and Abraham Lincoln.[1]

Although Dorson gives us a useful synopsis of the tale's plot, he offers no explanation whatsoever of the tale's function or meaning. If it was truly "one of the most popular folk tales" of World War II, the obvious question is why? What is the point of the story? What is the meaning, if any, of the tale?

Dorson was not the first to report the tale. Agnes Noland Underwood in her 1947 article "Folklore from G.I. Joe" ends her essay with a fine account of Murgatroyd the Kluge Maker.[2] No commentary on or analysis of the story is provided by Underwood. Similarly, William Hugh Jansen in his brief 1948 note entitled "The Klesh-Maker" does little more than report texts, although to his credit he did discover an apparent parallel to a tale attributed to Davy Crockett.[3] Supposedly Davy Crockett was in the Tennessee legislature opposing a bill designed to create a county. Near the end of the debate, he rose to make the following speech:

> Mr. Speaker,—Do you know what that man's bill reminds me of? Well, I 'spose you don't, so I'll tell you. Well, Mr. Speaker, when I first come to this country, a blacksmith was a rare thing; but there happened to be one in my neighbourhood; he had no striker, and whenever one of the neighbours wanted any work done, he had to go over and strike till his work was finished. These were hard times, Mr. Speaker, but we had to do the best we could. It happened that one of my neighbours wanted an axe, so he took along with him a piece of iron, and went over to the blacksmith's to strike till his axe was done. The iron was heated, and my neighbour fell to work, and was striking there nearly all day; when the blacksmith concluded the iron wouldn't make an axe, but 'twould make a fine mattock; so my neighbour wanting a mattock, concluded he would go over and strike till his mattock was done; accordingly, he went over the next day, and worked faithfully; but towards night the blacksmith concluded his iron wouldn't make a mattock, but 'twould make a fine ploughshare; so my neighbour wanting a ploughshare, agreed that he would go over the next day and strike till that was done; accordingly, he again went over, and fell hard to work; but towards night the blacksmith concluded his iron wouldn't make a ploughshare. but 'twould make a fine *skow*; so my neighbour, tired of working, cried, a *skow* let it be—and the blacksmith taking up the red hot iron, threw it into a trough of water near him, and as it fell in, it sung out *skow*. And this, Mr. Speaker, will be the way with that man's bill for a county; he'll keep you all here doing nothing, and finally his bill will turn out a *skow*, now mind if it don't.[4]

Whether or not Davy Crockett actually told the story, we do know that the tale goes back to at least 1833 and that it illustrates "much ado about nothing." The version attributed to Abraham Lincoln makes use of a different sound-word in the punchline:

> I was not more successful than the blacksmith in our town, in my boyhood days, when he tried to put to a useful purpose a big piece of wrought-iron that was in the shop. He heated it, put it on the anvil, and said: "I'm going to make a sledge-hammer out of you." After a while he stopped hammering it, looked at it, and remarked: "Guess I've drawed you out a little too fine for a sledge-hammer; reckon I'd better make a clevis of you." He stuck it in the fire, blew the bellows, got up a good heat, then began shaping the iron again on the anvil. Pretty soon he stopped, sized it up with his eye, and said: "Guess I've drawed you out too thin for a clevis; suppose I better make a clevis-bolt of you." He put it in the fire, bore down still harder on the bellows, drew out the iron, and went to work at it once more on the anvil. In a few minutes he stopped, took a look, and exclaimed: "Well, now I've got you down a leetle too thin even to make a clevis-bolt out of you." Then he rammed it in the fire again, threw his whole weight on the bellows, got up a white heat on the iron, jerked it out, carried it in the tongs to the water-barrel, held it over the barrel, and cried: "I've tried to make a sledge-hammer of you, and failed; I've tried to make a clevis of you, and failed; I've tried to

make a clevis-bolt of you, and failed; now, darn you, I'm going to make a fizzle of you"; and with that he soused it in the water and let it fizz.[5]

So we have a twentieth-century tale with possible if not probable nineteenth-century analogues. What else has folkloristic research achieved with respect to the kushmaker? In 1963, Jan Brunvand included the tale in his comprehensive shaggy dog story classification scheme published in the *Journal of American Folklore*. In this scheme, we find:

> D500. *The Kush-Maker.* A Navy man says he is a specialist. a "Kush-Maker" (also Klesh, Gluck, Gleek, Ka-Swish, Kloosch, Squish, Glug, Spleoch, Blook, Kaplush, and Ding-Dong.) A great deal of time and many tools and materials are used up until he announces that he has made one. A large fantastically-shaped box is dropped overboard and it goes "Kush!"[6]

Thanks to Brunvand, the kushmaker can be neatly filed in folklore archives under D500 in the Shaggy Dog Story section. But texts, nineteenth-century analogues, and classificatory designations are no substitute for content analysis. That seems obvious enough. Yet what I have surveyed for the kushmaker is not unlike what folklorists have achieved with respect to the vast majority of folk-tales and legends. If one examines the Aarne-Thompson tale type index, for example, one can easily see that relatively few of the tales have double asterisked references following the plot summaries. (Double asterisked bibliographical references indicate that a substantial monograph or article has been devoted to a particular tale[7]) This fact confirms the paucity of analytic studies devoted to the meaning of tales.

Before suggesting a possible interpretation of the kushmaker, let us present a typical version of the story rather than relying upon composite or synoptic summaries. The following text was collected in 1975 from a Chief Petty Officer in the U. S. Navy, stationed in San Diego, California.

> Well, sure I've heard about a cushmaker. It goes back God knows how many years when a new crew of a ship were reporting. One by one they would walk up the gangplank, salute the American flag, and report to the OOD [Officer of the Deck] for duty. You know, the same way it's done today. Well, the first man walked up the plank, saluted the flag, and reported, "Chief Boatswainmate Smith reporting for duty, sir." The second I think was quartermaster. This went on and on until a man came up, saluted, and reported, "Third Class cushmaker Jones reporting for duty, sir." Well, the OOD was really surprised and couldn't think what the hell a cushmaker was, but decided not to show his ignorance so he passed him on board. Each man then had to report to the Executive Officer with his orders and then be assigned his station. Well, old Jones reported to the XO as a cushmaker, and that XO, just like the OOD, thought he just might have forgotten what a cushmaker was so he just told him to get to work. So every day Jones would go into one of the forward compartments, close the door, and go to work. Most of the officers eventually knew there was a cushmaker on board, but none of them wanted to admit they couldn't remember what a cushmaker was and ask him what he was up to; they all left him alone. Well, this went on till his two year tour on the ship was about up. Finally the Captain decided that he couldn't stand it any more and sent for Jones. "Well, Jones," said the Captain, "you're a cush-maker." "Yes sir," said ol' Jones. "You've been on board almost two years now; so what the hell have you been doing for two years as a cushmaker!!"

"Making a cush, sir." "A cush!! WHAT IS A CUSH!!" "I'll show you, sir," said Jones and he took off. In a couple of minutes he came back topside with the strange contraption. He said, "Look sir," and dropped it overboard. It hit the water, "CUSH!!!"[8]

This version is representative. In other Navy versions, it is the annual inspection of the ship by the admiral which provides the occasions for the kushmaker to demonstrate his skills. Typically the kushmaker has insisted upon obtaining tons of scrap metal which he claims are needed to do the job. The enormous mass of scrap is deposited on deck and then attached to a boom. At the magic moment when all hands are assembled to pay homage to the visiting admiral, the signal is given, the boom swung out over the side of the ship, and the mass of scrap is let go into the water where it produces the sound "kush" or some such sound.

Clearly on one level, the story involves a parody of military life. The whole military chain of command is lampooned. No one is willing to admit that he does not understand something and everyone passes the responsibility to his immediate superior. This "buck-passing" behavior is common enough in military, government, and other large institutional establishments. In addition, the kushmaker plot provides a social commentary on the large amount of waste motion found in so many military maneuvers. Anyone who has spent any time in the military knows full well how much effort and energy is devoted to doing things for show, to impress admirals and inspecting officers. "Spit and polish" has long been a tra- ditional part of military life—though not always in time of war! But I believe there is more to the story than a comical, literal reflection of military hierarchy and values. There is, after all, an element of fantasy in the story. Besides the unrealistic acceptance of the kushmaker's statement of his specialty, there is the elaborate playing out of the whole long process of making a kush. What then is the significance, if any, of kushmaking?

I suspect that the story is an anal erotic fantasy. Specifically, the plot revolves around a projection of an infant or small child defecating in front of a parent or parent surrogate. This explanation would provide a reason why a simple act of dropping a useless object into water could be part of an attempt to please an authoritarian figure such as a captain or admiral. An infant is taught to part with a valueless body product, his feces. At the same time, the very process of toilet training tends to give value to the feces. The infant soon learns that releasing its feces pleases his parents in some way. So the valueless material seems to have great value.

The words used in the punch lines of the story tend to support this interpretation. The expression to "make a gush" or "kush" is reminiscent of parent-baby talk for the act of def- ecation. In households where such a term is used, an infant might well be told to "make a gush" and he might well receive lavish praise from a parent or authority figure for hav- ing successfully made a gush. Certainly there are numerous onomatopoeic words found among the various folk circumlocutions for urinating and defecating. A female term for urinating, for example, is to "go tinkle." In this context, the use of "make" in kushmaker may also be relevant. The verb "make" frequently has a definite anal association as in such idioms as to "make a B. M." [bowel movement], "make a poo," or just plain "make."[9] The initial phoneme /k/ in "kush," or the phonemic cluster /kl/ in "klesh" or "kluge" is not so strange in the light of such Latin terms as cacare and cloaca and their derivatives in related languages (cf. "cul," meaning end or backside). In 1978, a word "kludge" or "kloodge" was used to refer to an unlikely conglomeration of items intended to fix something in an unusual way. Chewing gum, rubber bands, or clothes hangers might be employed as a means of temporary repair. The finished product works, but it is called a "kloodge." In computer science, a kludge is a program which is four or five times as long as it should be. The word thus implies waste products or waste motion. Something useless has been made useful (in the case of the repair idiom) or a computer program contains material which could have or should have been eliminated! The word "gush" in English means to issue with force, to have a copious flow of something—for example, blood or tears. It conveys a connotation of emitting suddenly, forcibly, or copiously. The adjective "gushy" connotes something messy.

The word "cush" in American slang means money. According to the *Dictionary of American Slang*, "cushy" means money easy to obtain.[10] The money-feces equation is well established: consider, for example, such American idioms as "filthy rich," "to have money up the ass," or the reference to payday in the military as "the day the eagle shits."[11] A cushy job supposedly refers to a kind of sinecure where one has comfort and is left alone, free from cares and responsibilities. (The kushmaker would appear to have a "cushy" job.[12]) Making money is therefore symbolically equivalent to making feces. In fact, one does not literally make money, but rather earns money. The use of "make" in connection with money is therefore a metaphor and hence susceptible to interpretation (cf. the discussion of "make" above).

If there is any validity to the hypothesis that making a kush is a symbolic equivalent of defecating, what does this add to our understanding of the kushmaker story? First of all, there is the initial detail that no one seems to know what a kush is. In American society, one finds a strong tendency to deny one's body, and specifically to deny one's need to eliminate waste products. A host of euphemisms is employed to refer even to bathrooms. Even "bathroom" seems crude in some circles despite the fact that the reference to "bath" is already circumlocutory, just as "lavatory" literally refers to cleaning rather than urinating or defecating. Most of one's visits to a bathroom or restroom are not concerned with either bathing or resting. At parties, one often tries to slip off unobserved to urinate or defecate. When one returns, one hopes that his absence has not been noticed or at least that his reason for being temporarily absent has not been guessed. It may also be of interest that some individuals are particularly embarrassed by the sounds made by urinating or defecating. Such individuals have been known to turn on water faucets in a bathroom sink so as to "drown" the sounds made by urination or defecation (or perhaps also to pretend that the reason for going to the bathroom was only to "wash" or "freshen up") The importance of the sound "kush" in the punchline of the kushmaker tale makes sense in this context. In the version of the kushmaker presented here, it may be significant that the Executive Officer and other officers "might just have forgotten what a cushmaker was." This implies that they knew once, but have forgotten (or repressed) this information. Adults have all experienced toilet training, that is, making kush, but they have probably forgotten all about it inasmuch as it occurred early in their lives. The point is really that in American culture one does not admit that one urinates and defecates. Thus when the new recruit tells the interviewer that he is a kushmaker, the interviewer does not know what to make of this. Even if the interviewer did recognize the activity, he presumably would not admit it. It is ultimately only to please the captain or admiral, the highest-ranking figures in the local military power structure, which forces the kushmaker to make a kush. Normally one can deny the activity and others can overlook the activity, but a powerful father figure can demand anything, even that a kushmaker make a kush.

In the light of the present argument, we can better understand why the kushmaker seeks privacy. In Dorson's summary, the kushmaker is assigned to the ship's hold, that is, to the veritable bowels of the ship. Wherever the kushmaker is sent, he normally works in private. At the end, the kushmaker is obliged to do in public what he has hitherto done only in private. Certainly the living quarters in the military force individuals to urinate and defecate more or less in public. What an individual may have done in the privacy of his bathroom at home before entering the military, he must now do in mass bathrooms, perhaps under the uncomfortable scrutiny of fellow sailors.

We can also appreciate those versions of the tale in which the kushmaker specifically sends for s(crap). It is significant, symbolically speaking, that waste materials often form the mass which is to be dropped in the water, On older Navy ships in the 1940s and 1950s (when the kushmaker story was told), one did not always have flush toilets. Rather one sat on one of several wooden seats set upon a long trough. A stream of flowing water ran along the bottom of the trough to carry off the feces. For that matter, even with modern flush toilets, one can still hear the splashing noise of feces entering the water (cf. the range of sounds used in the kushmaker tale: splooch, kaplush, and so on).

The elaborate making of a kush at the request of a captain or admiral also fits well into the general set of fecal metaphors found in military usage. Strict military discipline is often referred to as chickenshit (cf. a chicken colonel used in the army). Enlisted men in the Navy (as in other armed forces) are sometimes treated like children. They are told when and what to eat, when to go to bed, what to wear, and just about when to urinate and defecate. Whether they are "shit on" by higher ranking individuals or forced to suffer because of being on someone's "shit list," or just stuck eating "shit on a shingle" (chipped beef on toast) for breakfast, enlisted men usually have to take it rather than dish it out. If the enlisted man is treated like a child, then why would it not make perfect sense for him to combat the system by using a childish device—such as making a great big kush for the admiral-father figure? Since so much of what the admiral or power structure asks the enlisted man to do seems to the enlisted man to be pointless and a complete waste of time and effort, it is only fair that the admiral be duped into watching a lowly enlisted man make a huge kush, thereby forcing the admiral in turn to be stuck wasting his time and effort. In addition, there seems to be a common tradition of imagining authority figures in the act of defecation. Even presidents and popes cannot ignore calls of nature. Thus an old idiom in French for going to the bathroom is "*aller où le roi va pied*" (to go where the king goes on foot)[13] has analogues in many European languages; for example, in German, "*Ich gehe dahin wo der König zu Fuss hingeht.*" The kushmaker story could represent the individual's revenge on the whole military system. The waste motion involved in accumulating a huge mass of material to be dropped over the side is very likely a metaphorical expression to the effect that Navy ritual (including inspections) is a bunch of shit. The strict military rank hierarchy is reversed. It is the admiral or captain who carries out the kushmaker's orders (for example, by obtaining the necessary materials). There may even be a hint that any admiral who does not know what a kush is—that is, doesn't know "shit from Shinola" (a brand of shoe polish)—richly deserves being made a fool of.

Regardless of whether or not one finds the above speculative interpretation of the meaning of the kushmaker at all plausible, one should at least realize that there are details of the story which require explanation. Kushmakers do not exist in fact, only in fiction. Fiction in the form of folkloric fantasy can and should be interpreted. Why should we laugh at the image of a captain or admiral watching a mass of material fall into water?

What is the point of a story whose punchline consists of a nonsense sound such as "kush?" These are precisely the kinds of questions that must be addressed if one wishes to try to understand the kushmaker. And these are the kinds of questions that folklorists must seek to answer if folkloristics is to progress beyond data gathering and classification.

Notes

1. Richard M. Dorson, *American Folklore* (Chicago: University of Chicago Press, 1959), p. 271.
2. Agnes Nolan Underwood, "Folklore from G.I. Joe," *New York Folklore Quarterly* 3 (1947): 285–97. Murgatroyd the Kluge Maker is found on pp. 295–97.
3. William Hugh Jansen, "The Flesh-Maker," *Hoosier Folklore* 7 (1948): 47–50.
4. *Sketches and Eccentricities of Col. David Crockett of West Tennessee* (New York: J. and J. Harper, 1833), 79–80. Dorson points out that the story does not appear in Crockett's autobiography. See Richard M. Dorson, "Oral Styles of American Folk Narrators," in *Style in Language*, ed. Thomas A. Sebeok (New York: John Wiley, 1960), p. 47, no. 10.
5. Carl Sandburg, *Abraham Lincoln: The War Years*, vol. 4 (New York: Harcourt, Brace & Company, 1939), p. 150. Sandburg cites two texts. The first version, included here, was collected by Horace Porter. See General Horace Porter, *Campaigning with Grant* (New York: The Century Co., 1906), 414–15. A second version reported by U. S. Grant ends with the exasperated blacksmith acting as follows: "Then with his tongs he lifted it from the bed of coals, and thrusting it into a tub of water near by, exclaimed with an oath, 'Well, if I can't make anything else of you, I will make a fizzle anyhow.'" Fizzle is a slang term meaning failure still in current use. In the context of the argument to be advanced in this paper, it may be noteworthy that "fizzles" can be a slang term for flatus. See G. Legman, *No Laughing Matter: Rationale of the Dirty Joke*, 2nd Series (Wharton, New Jersey: Breaking Point, 1975), p. 863.
6. Jan Harold Brunvand, "A Classification for Shaggy Dog Stories," *JAF* 76 (1963): 67.
7. Stith Thompson neglected to discuss this convention in his "Preface" to the Second Revision of Antti Aarne and Stith Thompson, *The Types of the Folktale* (FFC no. 184; Helsinki, 1961). In his introduction to the *Motif-Index*, however, he does note that "Special studies are indicated by two asterisks; valuable lists of variants by a single star." See Stith Thompson, *Motif-Index of Folk-Literature*, vol. 1 (Bloomington: Indiana University Press, 1955), p. 23.
8. This text was collected from Chief Petty Officer George T. Green on 30 November 1975 by Johnny Green and Pamela Yazman, two undergraduate folklore students at the University of California, Berkeley. Chief Green had served in the Navy for twenty-two years and he said that he had heard the kushmaker story many times over the years and had himself told it on numerous occasions. He also indicated that sometimes a man on a ship is called a cushmaker if he has rather clever ways of getting out of work. The word in such cases is definitely not a compliment.
9. Edward Sagarin, *The Anatomy of Dirty Words* (New York: Lyle Stuart, 1962), pp. 47, 52. See also Alan Dundes, "Here I Sit—A Study of American Latrinalia," in *Analytic Essays in Folklore* (The Hague: Mouton, 1975), p. 190.
10. Harold Wentworth and Stuart Berg Flexner, comps., *Dictionary of American Slang* (New York: Thomas Y. Crowell, 1967), p. 135.
11. For an anthology of essays on this subject plus an excellent introductory essay entitled "On the Psychoanalysis of Money," see Ernest Borneman, *The Psychoanalysis of Money* (New York: Urizen Books, 1976). Included are classic studies by Freud, Ferenczi, Abraham, and others.
12. See the discussion of the connotations of "kushmaker" in note 8 above.
13. A French text is cited, for example, in *Bibliotheca Scatologica* (Leipzig: Zentral-antiquariat der Deutschen Demokratischen Republik, 1970), p. 111. (This is a facsimile of a book published originally in 1849.)

19

THE RITUAL MURDER OR
BLOOD LIBEL LEGEND:
A STUDY OF ANTI-SEMITIC VICTIMIZATION
THROUGH PROJECTIVE INVERSION

Introduction

This essay brings out an important principle in Alan Dundes's work—that folkloristic analysis can help combat bigotry by illuminating the cause and content of material used to maintain prejudice from generation to generation. One problem he encountered was that collectors avoided or repressed offensive texts, because they did not fit into their preconceived image of folklore as charming and quaint. Dundes countered that the collectors' selectivity, driven by an urge to romanticize cultural expression, rendered folklore sterile and inconsequential. He wanted to show that folklore was a powerful cultural force, and could be used by scholars as evidence to objectively assess social divisions, as well as bonds. He maintained that folklore could have dire consequences, and necessitated serious attention as a source of social biases, beliefs, and actions. If a better world was to be constructed, he argued, then the folk processes by which attitudes were formed and spread needed to be uncovered—and understood.

Dundes used the terms evil, horrible, insidious, and dastardly to describe the subject of blood libel. It was, in his words, "one of the most bizarre and dangerous legends ever created by the human imagination." He blamed the narrative for causing Jews psychological pain and physical injury, and frequently death. Rather than suppressing awareness of the lore, Dundes called for holding it "up to the light of reason with the hope of nullifying its pernicious influence." To him, this appeal to reason meant doing more than showing that the accusation was untrue. Many scholars had already established its falsehood, but that had not stopped its regeneration. As his contribution, Dundes sought to provide a psychological rationale to explain the content and persistence of the narrative that had apparently irrationally spread through several continents for many centuries.

Blood libel is the allegation that around Easter, Jews murder Christian children to obtain blood for rituals. A key motif of the narrative, in Dundes's interpretation, was the accusation that Jews mixed the blood into the Passover ceremonial food of matzoh, an unleavened bread. Other ritual murder charges included taking blood for Purim pastries, medicinal remedies, and sorcery. Despite the fact that Jewish law expressly forbids blood sacrifices, the legend created an image of Jews as bloodthirsty, demonic, and depraved. Another questionable detail is the function of the blood in the end product, since matzoh is white, but the implication was that Jews, as an ancient people with mystical powers, retained profane magical practices—represented by using blood as a magical ingredient— that stood in contrast to sacred Christian norms.

The blood libel legend is characterized by the narrative's localized setting, and a temporal reference to a contemporary moment or the recent past. As a legend, the narrative drew attention to itself because of its bizarre content, frequently thought to be true when it was circulated orally in song and story, in print and image, and even in courts of law. Or else its legendary context raised questions, if not doubts, about a central belief in blood sacrifice, conveyed in the actions of the text. Structurally, its ending invited commentary on the unusual feature of murder-lust, resulting from inhuman or un-Christian ritual uses of blood. The blood libel legend drew listeners from members of the dominant group and possessed symbolic characteristics because Jews, as a marginalized group, often conveyed a degree of mystery. It was as if a secret was revealed about their true nature, encapsulated in key actions and objects within a narrative.

From the viewpoint of Christians, the legend confirmed the "othering" of Jews (or other minorities) as profanely despicable, and therefore socially intolerable. From the Christian perspective, the theological implication of the legend's message was that the Jews were inconvertible and incorrigible. This conclusion was significant, in that it obviated the need to convert Jews (since Christians, particularly during the medieval period, believed that conversion was a prerequisite for the Second Coming of Christ). The danger of the blood libel legend was that it encouraged mobs to spill Jewish blood in retribution, whereas the Christian theology of the New Testament would have called for preservation of the Jewish presence, as the precursor people of the "old" testament (Jewish terminology prefers the Torah or Hebrew Bible), until conversion was successful. Dundes viewed this background as a crucial context for the inclusion of converted or apostate Jews in the plots of blood libel variants. Extending the example of Jews to other victimized minorities, Dundes's essay stated: "When Jews resisted acting out their assigned part in this overt Christian fantasy [that the guilty Jew should accept his punishment and be converted to Christianity], Christians became angry, very angry—just as whites become angry if blacks don't conform to the white stereotype of blacks and just as men become angry if women won't conform to the men's stereotype of women."

Jewish chronicles and conversations refer to blood libel to epitomize an extremely virulent strain of anti-Semitism in a region, evident in a metafolkloric statement: "Scratch a (national identity), and you get an anti-Semite; they even had a blood libel case there." Dundes mentioned several medieval examples in England, a concentration of blood libel trials in Eastern Europe during the nineteenth century, the revival of the legend by Nazis during the Holocaust, and several American examples in the early twentieth century. Since Dundes's essay was written, a number of twenty-first century blood libel accusations have been identified in Islamic countries (Israeli 2002, 2003). In speeches and in the media, Islamist demagogues demonized Jews as drinkers of Muslim children's blood and enemies of humanity. At first glance, this development of a non-Christian victim negates Dundes's thesis that blood libel projects Christian guilt (over the cannibalism implicit in the Eucharist) to Jewish blood-lust. Yet many sources claim that the Islamic manifestation of blood libel came from Christian influence and was adapted to the Islamist goal of eliminating Jews; it contained the projective inversion of turning the wish fulfillment of "I want to rid the world of them" to "They want to get rid of me." Thus, contemporary legends associated with blood libel include Jews poisoning Muslim wells, spreading plagues among Arabs in Jewish-prepared foods, and surreptitiously sterilizing Muslim men through various products (Wistrich 2002; and Karsh 2006).

Dundes was concerned with what associated texts revealed about blood libel in the Christian world. The primary example he gave in this essay was the "Wandering Jew," but he did not gloss it in detail, perhaps because he treated it separately in *The Wandering Jew: Essays in the Interpretation of a Christian Legend* (Hasan-Rokem and Dundes 1986). The central motif (Thompson Q502.1, The Wandering Jew. Ceaseless wandering with inability to die as punishment for blasphemy) is that, because of not helping Jesus on his way to crucifixion, a Jew is punished by being doomed to remain homeless, roaming the land on foot, unable to die. The most common legendary plot is of a modern sighting of an aged man of strange appearance, usually bearded and carrying a walking stick. The unusual figure is introduced as a shoemaker named Ahasuerus, the Wandering Jew, who, when Jesus leaned against his house, drove him away. Jesus then is reported to have said, "I will stay and rest, but you shall go." Thus the story accounts for why Ahasuerus had to give up his home and his family, and roam the world. Along with blood libel, the Wandering Jew legend was used in Nazi propaganda and other anti-Semitic campaigns. Another connection between the two legends is in the Christian interpretation of the Jewish characters as Christ-killers. In the Wandering Jew, Ahasuerus (or Ahasver) is blamed for Christ's demise, and punished. Set in the context of Christian ambivalence toward Jews as both the theological parents of Christians and their enemies, an Oedipal theory, familiar to Dundes, claimed that the Christian son (Jesus) is opposed to the Jewish father (Ahasuerus). A result of their separation is that Jesus is the father one can love, while the Wandering Jew is the father one can despise and abuse (Isaac-Edersheim 1986). The Jewish character thus becomes transformed into a symbol for all Jews. In blood libel, vengeance is exacted because the bleeding innocent child is viewed as a Christ figure, in contrast to the demonic, predatory, older Jew. Jews were pictured as doing in reality what the Christian worshiper was doing in fantasy: killing a child (son of God) and ritually drinking its blood. (Dundes's source is Hyam Maccoby's *The Sacred Executioner: Human Sacrifice and the Legacy of Guilt* [1982], which he excerpted in *The Wandering Jew*). In a casebook he compiled about blood libel, Dundes included the psychoanalytical reading of blood libel as a reflection of the Christian need to reenact the crucifixion of Christ (see Rappaport 1991, excerpted from Rappaport 1975). According to Dundes, Christians directed against others the calumny once directed against themselves. A cognate text that Dundes cited in support of this symbolism—one that led him to an interpretation through projective inversion—was the anti-Semitic belief that Jews profaned the host by piercing the wafer and making it bleed (Strack 1909).

Dundes's use of projective inversion in the blood libel legend has been applied, in contemporary life, to groups other than Jews. Folklorist Bill Ellis pointed out the way that, beginning in the late twentieth century, rumor-panics about the threat of satanic cults and brainwashed devil-worshipers in America and Great Britain related to Christian Charismatic views of teenagers as social menaces, all of which symbolized dissatisfaction with the decline of religious authority. He observed that the projective inversion suggested by Dundes revealed the "inner stresses" of the persecuting group. Documenting examples of legends involving the blood sacrifices of children among occultists who are mainstreamed into society, Ellis discerned an othering function of the narratives by Christian Charismatics, to show that ordinary people, undetectable in everyday encounters, can be diabolical, waiting for a chance to satisfy their blood-lust. He concluded that the Charismatic agenda was to scapegoat a "*hidden* source of social evil," reminiscent of the demonization of Jews, that would explain the world's economic, social, and moral prob-lems, and rally citizens to the Charismatic cause. Ellis's interpretation was that "recogniz-ing the existence of this evil would then encourage people to adopt Charismatic religion in spite of its internal problems" (2000). Surveying African legends of sorcerers who were accused of eating souls, and of killing and devouring young children to acquire their vital force, folklorist Véronique Campion-Vincent extended Dundes's use of blood libel as a Christian anti-Semitic legend to the Western ruling-class fears of minorities and deviants. She examined texts of conspiracy theories that were often linked to blood libel. To her, leg-endary accusations of plots to deliberately infect populations (legends of a conspiracy to spread AIDS among Africans through Western food products) and to undermine sexual restrictions (Muslim beliefs in an aphrodisiac-laced gum given to women to undermine their chastity) took the role of the oppressed against outsiders (2005).

Anti-Semitism was a frequent topic of Dundes's research. Although not religious, Dundes had come from a Jewish lineage. Becoming aware of the Holocaust after World War II, he often related his horror at the Nazi legacy of hate and genocide against Jews. Essays he wrote that deal with anti-Semitism and Holocaust themes included Dundes and Hauschild 1987; Dundes 1987f, 1987e, 1997f, and 1984a; and Banc and Dundes 1990.

For essays on bigotry expressed in folklore against various ethnic groups and women, see Dundes and Abrahams 1987; Dundes 1987d (both of these essays interpret the symbolism of African Americans in joke cycles told by whites); as well as Dundes 1980a, 1997d. See also Dundes's comments on the educational uses of folklore to build tolerance in the first chapter of this volume, "Folklore as a Mirror of Culture."

The Ritual Murder or Blood Libel Legend: A Study of Anti-Semitic Victimization through Projective Inversion

IF ONE WERE TO POLL most folklorists as to whether or not folklore was on the whole a positive force in human culture, I suspect there would be considerable consensus that indeed it was. A tale well told, a song well sung ordinarily give pleasure to the performers themselves and almost certainly to those in the performer's audience. Esthetically speaking, it would appear to be a safe generalization that life is more pleasant because of the charm of folk costume and the delight in participating in a favorite calendrical festival. Shorn of its folkloric dress, daily life would be ever so much more drab and dull than it otherwise is. Yet it is important to keep in mind that there is some folklore which is highly pernicious and even life-threatening. I am thinking of various forms of racist and sexist folklore. Social scientists are normally reluctant to attach value judgments to the data they study, but it is my contention that one can make a convincing case for the label "evil folklore" for selected individual items of tradition.[1]

Among the prime candidates for placement under the rubric of the folklore of evil, I would rank at or very near the top of the list the so-called blood libel legend. Other phrases designating this vicious legend include *blood accusation* and *ritual murder (accusation)*. These terms are used almost interchangeably but there are several scholars who have sought to distinguish between ritual murder and blood libel, arguing that ritual murder refers to a sacrificial murder in general whereas the blood libel entails specific use of the blood of the victim.[2] In the case of alleged Jewish ritual murder, the blood motivation is nearly always present which presumably accounts for the equally common occurrence of both ritual murder and blood libel as labels.

The relevant motif is V361, Christian child killed to furnish blood for Jewish rite. The typical gist of the story line is that one or more Jews murder an innocent Christian infant or child, supposedly to obtain blood required for ritual purposes, e.g., to mix with unleavened bread or to make matzah. The legend has been in constant circulation in oral and written tradition from the twelfth to the twentieth centuries, often leading to deadly consequences for Jews accused of the crime. Like all legends, the blood libel story is traditionally told as true, that is, as an actual historical happening.

Joshua Trachtenberg begins his chapter of *The Devil and the Jews* devoted to a discussion of ritual murder as follows: "Of all the bizarre charges against the Jewish people the one that has enjoyed the hardiest tenacity and the utmost notoriety and has produced the direst consequences, is the so called ritual-murder accusation. In its popular version, it foists upon Jewish ritual the need for Christian blood at the Passover. The subject of much study and infinitely more polemics, its absurdity has been conclusively established, but the true nature of the accusation has never been made sufficiently clear."[3] Salomon Reinach made a similar comment: "Of all the accusations which fanaticism and ignorance have used as a weapon against Judaism, there is none which can be compared in terms of improbability and absurdity to that of ritual murder."[4] Max Grunwald, the pioneer of Jewish folklore studies, had this to say: "Of all the attacks on Jews, there could scarcely be one capable of inflicting a deeper or more painful injury than the blood-lie."[5] Another major figure in Jewish folkloristics, Moses Gaster, in a strong letter to the London *Times* of 2 October 1888 remarked: "Baseless and without foundation as these legends are, they are dangerous even in normal times; how much more in abnormal? Who can foresee to what terrible consequences such a superstition might lead, when the people fanatic with rage and terror, get hold of it and wreak their vengeance on innocent men?"[6] Finally, American ballad scholar Francis James Child used the following language: "And these pretended child-murders, with their horrible consequences, are only a part of a persecution which, with all moderation, may be rubricated as the most disgraceful chapter in the history of the human race."[7]

Anglo-American folklorists are reasonably familiar with the plot, in part because it occurs in ballad form, namely as "Sir Hugh, or, The Jew's Daughter," Child Ballad 155. It has many titles in oral tradition, e.g., "Hugh of Lincoln" or "Little Sir Hugh" among others. In the ballad, a Jewish temptress induces a young Christian boy to enter her garden where she brutally murders him, often taking special care to catch the blood in a basin or cup.[8]

The narrative is also well known because it is one of Chaucer's celebrated *Canterbury Tales*: the Prioress's Tale. The murder of Hugh of Lincoln supposedly occurred in 1255; Chaucer's tale was written near the end of the fourteenth century. The earliest subtype of the legend, according to the standard typology, goes back to before the year 1200 and contains the following elements:

1. A boy sings the responsorium "Gaude Maria" as he passes daily along a street in which Jews dwell, thereby provoking their resentment.

2. He is slain (either by a single Jew or by a group of them in conspiracy), and his body is buried under the earth in the Jew's house, in his garden, in a trench beside the door, in a stable under the manure, etc.

3. The boy's mother, in her search for him, passing by the Jew's door, hears the voice of her child, and with the assistance of friends, a crowd of citizens, forces an entrance.

4. The boy is dug up from the earth alive and unharmed.

5. In consequence of this miracle, the Jew (or Jews) according to most versions is converted.[9]

In other versions of the legend, the boy's body is thrown into a latrine. When the body is recovered, it miraculously continues to sing praise to the Virgin Mary, typically until a Christian priest removes a seed from under the child's tongue whereupon the singing stops (cf. motif V254.7, Murdered boy still sings "Ave" after his death).

It would be one thing if this classic bit of anti-Semitic folklore existed only in ballad or legend form, but the sad truth is that what has been so often described in legend and literature is also alleged to have occurred in life. There have not been tens, but hundreds of actual cases of blood libel tried in various courts in various countries. The map of Western and Eastern Europe and the Near East is profusely dotted with sites where ritual murders were said to have occurred.[10] Moreover, one must keep in mind that many of these allegations led to lengthy trials (often involving torture to extract "confessions" from the accused Jews) and eventual executions: "In 1171 at Blois, after due trial, thirty-eight Jews were burned at the stake; in 1191, at Bray-sur-Seine, the number of victims reached one hundred."[11] Trials occurred in England, France, Czechoslovakia, Germany, Hungary, Italy, Poland, Russia, Spain, and elsewhere. There is no comprehensive or definitive list of all the alleged instances of ritual murder, despite the fact that many of the numerous books devoted to the subject consist of little more than synopses of reported instances. For example, Frank (1901) reviews 172 cases. Monniot (1914) in a chapter entitled "The Facts" discusses more than 100 separate purported eases. Manzini (1930) lists 137 examples. Folklorist Peuckert (1935–36) gives some 175 examples in chronological order while Lyutostanskii (1934) summarizes 144 instances. Trachtenberg gives a round number of 150 charges of ritual murder but suggests these are not more than a "fraction" of the whole.[12]

Although one might have logically assumed that this strange medieval legend might have died out over time and that the number of recorded eases might have declined over the centuries, this does not appear to be the case at all. One observer noted that there seem to have been almost as many blood accusations in the nineteenth century as in all the previous centuries combined and that, for example, between 1887 and 1891, there were twenty-two indictments in Europe alone with some fifty cases of blood libel reported between 1870 and 1935.[13] It should also be remarked that compared to the large number of Jews actually brought to trial on the basis of blood libel or ritual murder charges, only a tiny percentage of the anti-Semitic accusers were ever themselves brought to trial.[14]

Some readers may find it hard to believe that Jews were dragged in front of tribunals accused of having performed ritual murder, often having been first tortured on several occasions so as to elicit a confession of guilt from them. But a considerable number of monographic studies have detailed these heinous trials which have sometimes ended with condemning the "guilty" Jew(s) to death. Some of the trials, especially those which took place in the nineteenth and early twentieth centuries attracted international notice.

One of the earliest trials was in Norwich, England, in 1144. Some even go so far as to claim that it was in England that the ritual murder charge first appeared,[15] and that it was with this account that "the continuous history of the Ritual Murder libel begins."[16] In fifteenth-century Spain, we find "El Santo Nino de la Guardia."[17] It was said that a group of Jews and Catholic converts (from Judaism) had ritually murdered a child at La Guardia, near Avila, in imitation of the Passion of Jesus. This version of the blood libel legend, incidentally, was apparently used as part of the pretext to expel Jews from Spain in 1492.[18] (The infant was supposedly murdered in 1488 with the trial held in 1490 and 1491.) If this is so, then it would demonstrate the extraordinary power of folklore in general and legend in particular to effect political events. An annual ten-day holiday in La Guardia is said to continue to the present day and local clergy are not anxious to close down the La Guardia festival because it is the major village holiday and it brings in valuable income from tourist-pilgrims.[19]) This instance of a festival springing up from a legend shows that the blood libel story remains alive and that it is even celebrated annually in the twentieth century. Unfortunately, this is not an isolated instance. For example, the Domingo del Val cult is widespread in Spain. According to tradition, little Domingo was a choir boy whose singing hymns so enraged Saragossa Jews in the 1250s that they secretly crucified him and buried his body. However, his body began to glow mysteriously, and in the twentieth century he is known as the patron saint of choir boys in Spain; in the Seo Cathedral in Saragossa, there is a brightly lighted chapel devoted to him, a chapel which actually serves as a site of destination for modern pilgrimages.[20]

The blood libel legend is not only the basis of ongoing festivals, but it has also been memorialized in church decoration. Legends proclaiming the Jewish "ritual murder" of Christian children or the profanation or desecration of holy wafers are celebrated in various European towns in such artistic form as tapestries or stained glass church windows. For example, there are such windows or pictures or tapestries ornamenting the choir of the Saint Michael-Saint Gudule Cathedral in Brussels, a ceiling fresco in the small Tyrol village of Judenstein, paintings in a church sanctuary in the Vienna suburb of Korneuberg, and a stained glass window in a Paris church chapel.[21] These artistic renderings of the legend provide daily reminders in such locales of the existence (and by extension presumably the truth or historicity) of the story.

One might think that in modern times there would have been protests against festivals or stained glass representations of the legend, but that is not the case. In only a few instances have campaigns waged against this blatantly anti-Semitic folklore had any success. In the Judenstein case, we have perhaps a typical situation. A French Jew, Jean Hauser, whose brother died at Auschwitz, tells of a vacation trip in 1952 in Austria not far from Innsbruck when he took an unexpected detour to an apparently idyllic hamlet of Judenstein (the name meaning, of course, the stone of Jews).[22] Entering the village church, he found in the nave, near the altar, in front of a tapestry, three figures made of wood or wax in a menacing pose with knives in hand surrounding a stone upon which was stretched out a supplicating infant garbed in white. The scene purportedly commemorated the ritual murder of Andrew of Rinn at Judenstein, as Hauser soon discovered when he purchased souvenir postcards in the shop located conveniently and immediately across from the church. He later learned that for nearly two centuries, Judenstein had been a place of pilgrimage where children led by their parents could see for themselves the reconstruction of the assassination by three Jews of a small child of about their own age.[23]

Interestingly enough, the Judenstein site had been noted a year earlier in 1951 by famed Nazi-hunter Simon Wiesenthal who wrote a short essay "Tiroler Ritualmord Märchen" in protest. In that report, Wiesenthal voices his dismay at seeing full cars and busloads of school children making annual pilgrimages to Rinn under the tutelage of their religious instructors to see the ritual murder lie depicted as a historical event. Wiesenthal was sufficiently concerned to bother to write a letter of protest about these pilgrimages to Cardinal Innitzer via Innsbruck Bishop Rusch, but he was rebuffed by the latter when he replied that ". . . the Jewish writer goes much too far if he meant to claim that Jews had never done such things."![24] Prejudice and bigotry die hard if at all. Part of the problem is clearly that of trying to disprove the negative. As one report of Bishop Rusch's response to a protest from the Jewish community of Linz reads: "The Jews have not up to the present time ever proved that they never committed a parallel crime [of ritual murder]."[25]

After several repeated unsuccessful attempts to halt the pilgrimages, a plaque was finally put up in 1961 in the Judenstein church by a secret order of Pope John XXIII. The plaque stated that the case of Andrew of Rinn was nothing other than a legend and that "it is clear that the event had nothing to do with the Jewish people." Pope John also directed that the cult of Andrew be suppressed and that the various tableaux, statues, and frescoes be removed from the church. But the villagers of Rinn became incensed. If the statue of the martyred Andrew were removed, they would openly revolt against the church. So despite the papal order, the statue was left intact, and a large fresco on the ceiling of the church showing a group of Jews in the act of burying little Andrew was similarly left alone. Moreover, the pilgrimages continued with the statue of the infant martyr surrounded by flowers and candles left by those who came to pray from near and far.[26] It may be concluded from this that it is not easy to legislate folklore out of existence. Since the Austrian authorities decided not to suppress the artwork celebrating the legend or to remove the statue of the martyr,[27] it remains to be seen if the installation of the plaque can succeed in defusing a legend which has circulated and flourished for centuries. (Andreas Oxner of Rinn was said to have been killed by Jewish merchants on the "Jew-stone" in 1462 and although he was never officially beatified or canonized by the Catholic church, a plenary indulgence for pilgrims to Rinn was granted on 15 January 1754.)[28] All this attests to the remarkable staying power of folklore. While folklore's resistance to censorship may be deemed a positive thing, e.g., when folklore opposes political repression or social injustice, this very same strength of tradition also means that dangerous and pernicious racist folklore cannot really be checked or halted either.

There have been so many famous cases and trials involving ritual murder that it is simply not possible to recount them all in a brief overview. In 1840, the Jews of Damascus were accused of the ritual murder of a Capuchin friar, Father Tommaso. To obtain "evidence" that it was a case of ritual murder, some seventy Jews were tortured to secure the necessary confessions.[29] There was a concerted surge of international protest and it did have some effect.[30] The Sultan Abdul Mejid issued a firman or proclamation which said in part:

> An ancient prejudice prevailed against the Jews. The ignorant believed that the Jews were accustomed to sacrifice a human being, to make use of his blood at their feast of Passover. . . . the religious books of the Hebrews have been examined by learned men, well versed in their religious literature, the result of which examination is that it is found that Jews are strongly prohibited not only from using human blood but even that of animals. It therefore follows that the charges made against them and their religion are nothing but pure calumnies. . . . we cannot permit the Jewish nation whose innocence of the crime alleged against them is evident) to be vexed and tormented upon accusations which have not the least foundation in truth.[31]

The sultan's words—like the words uttered by various popes—proved to be insufficient to put the legend to rest.

It should be noted that there were a number of papal bulls on the subject of ritual murder, e.g., in 1247, 1259, 1272, 1422, 1540, as well as Cardinal Ganganelli's famous investigative report of 1759.[32] Although a number of popes did honestly seek to repudiate and deny the blood libel legend, it is also true that the semi-official Vatican periodical, the *Civiltà Cattolica* from 1881 to 1914 promoted and systematically "documented" the legend,"[33] and this was the case as well with other nominally Catholic periodicals, e.g., *La Croix,* in the late nineteenth century.[34] In some instances, Catholic priests cleverly used the ritual murder accusation as a weapon against Jews.[35]

In his oft-cited report of 1759, Cardinal Ganganelli, the future Clement XIV (1769–74), reviewed a large number of the alleged ritual murder cases and rejected them all with the exception of Andrew of Rinn (1462) and Simon of Trent (1475). In Ganganelli's words, "I admit, then, as true the fact of the Blessed Simon, a boy three years old, killed by the Jews in Trent in the 1475 in hatred of the faith of Jesus Christ. . . . I also admit the truth of another fact, which happened in the year 1462 in the village of Rinn . . . in the person of the Blessed Andreas, a boy barbarously murdered by the Jews in hatred of the Faith of Jesus Christ."[36] Ganganelli generously adjudged his own findings as being generally an exculpation of the Jews. In his own words, "It should then be concluded that, among so many infanticides imputed by writers to the Jews in hatred of our Holy Faith, only two can be said to be true, since these two only can be said to be proved by authentic proofs after much diligent search and a considerable lapse of time. . . . I do not believe, then, that by admitting the truth of the two facts . . . one can reasonably deduce that this is a maxim, either theoretical or practical, of the Jewish nation; for two isolated events are not enough to establish a certain and common axiom."[37] Vacandard plausibly suggests that Ganganelli's views of these two cases was very probably influenced by the political fact that there had been previous papal decisions authorizing the cults of Simon and Andrew and the miracles attributed to these martyrs.[38]

Among the more famous cases of the late nineteenth and early twentieth centuries are that of Tisza-Eslar, Hungary (1882);[39] the murder of a nineteen-year-old Christian girl, Agnes Hruza, on 29 March 1899, in the Grzina Forest near Polna in Czechoslovakia,[40] a case which fortunately was influenced by the critical intervention of T. G. Masaryk, then a professor at the Czech university in Prague, who would later (1918) be elected as the first president of Czechoslovakia;[41] the ritual murder case in Kiev in 1911 involving a twelve-year-old boy, also known as the Beilis case, which came to trial in 1913;[42] and a case in Massena, New York, in 1928.[43] Many of these and other cases are discussed at length in detailed essays and book-length monographs, many of which reprint actual trial transcripts.[44]

Even in those instances where the accused was eventually found innocent, the very fact that a trial took place in which the basis of the accusation was essentially the existence of the legend demonstrates the undeniable tenacity of the story. Some well-known individuals went on record to state their conviction that the ritual murder story was true. The celebrated traveler and amateur anthropologist-folklorist Sir Richard Burton in his book, *The Jew, the Gypsy and El Islam*, published posthumously in 1898, ends his supposedly objective ethnographic description of the Jews with a list of "what *history* [my emphasis] tells us concerning the Jews, their crimes, and their condemnations,"[45] a list which includes numerous alleged instances of ritual murder. The editor of this curious volume claims he elected to suppress Burton's special "Appendix on Human Sacrifice among the Sephardim or Eastern Jews," the data for which Burton was said to have gathered during the period from 1869 to 1871 when he served as British Consul in Damascus, although one anti-Semitic source claimed that the appendix in question had been suppressed through pressure from influential Jews.[46] The important point is that Burton evidently considered blood libel legends as "history," not fiction.

Unfortunately, the research of folklorists has on occasion been utilized to "prove" the existence and veracity of ritual murder. Toward the middle of the nineteenth century, the Russian Ministry of Foreign Affairs set up a special secret commission to investigate the supposed "use by Jews of the blood of Christian children" and this commission enlisted the aid of folklorist V. I. Dal. He wrote a book in 1844 on ritual murder based upon fieldwork carried out among the so-called Old Believers.[47] Apparently, Dal was himself persuaded by his informants of the truth of the custom and his research was cited in the Kiev trial of Beilis in 1913.[48] It may or may not be a total coincidence that Dal's book was reprinted in 1913.[49]

In similar fashion, Sir James George Frazer's writings were also cited in the Kiev trial. When Frazer learned of this, he immediately wrote a letter to the London *Times* protesting the citation of his research in such a trial. The particular passage from "The Scapegoat" volume of *The Golden Bough* which had been quoted in the trial was actually published in the *Times* of the day preceding, that is, 10 November 1913. However, a close reading of both the passage itself and Frazer's letter of protest of November 11 reveals considerable equivocality on Frazer's part. The upshot is that he does not really deny the possibility of Jewish ritual murder. His position is rather that if ignorant lower-class Jews did commit such crimes on occasion, that was no reason to hate all Jews. In other words, Frazer's anti-Semitism was tempered by typical British class consciousness: It wasn't Jews who committed the crime, but lower-class Jews. "If all the charges of ritual murder which have been brought against the Jews in modern times are not, as seems most probably, mere idle calumnies . . . the extraordinary tenacity of life exhibited by the lowest forms of superstition in the minds of ignorant people, whether they are Jews or Gentiles, would suffice to account for an occasional recrudescence of primitive barbarity among the most degraded part of the Jewish community.[50] Frazer acknowledges the debate about the issue of historicity, but he hedges by saying, "Into this troubled area I prefer not to enter; I will only observe that, so far as I have looked into the alleged cases, and these are reported in sufficient detail, the majority of the victims are said to have been children and to have met their fate in spring, often in the week before Easter." [51] That statement could hardly be taken as any kind of a repudiation of the truth value of the ritual murder legend! Shortly thereafter, he again fails to take a stand: "If deeds of the sort alleged have been really done by Jews—a question on which I must decline to pronounce an opinion—they would then interest the student of custom as isolated instances of reversion to an old and barbarous ritual which once flourished commonly enough among the ancestors both of Jews and Gentiles. . . . Such customs die hard."[52]

In his letter to the *Times,* Frazer does not alter his position: ". . . while I discuss hypothetically the possibility of an occasional crime instigated by superstition among the dregs of the Jewish as of the Christian population, I stigmatize such accusations against the Jewish people as 'a monstrous injustice,' and speak of all the charges of ritual murder as *'most probably'* mere idle calumnies, the baneful fruit of bigotry, ignorance, and malice" [emphasis mine].[53] The continued and insistent use of such words as "occasional" crime and "probably" certainly strongly suggest that Frazer may have harbored some personal conviction that Jewish ritual murder was in part a historical reality.

Some twentieth-century folklorists apparently believe in the historicity of the blood libel legend, e.g., Caro Baroja of Spain[54] and Peuckert of Germany. The latter called for a scientific study to determine which cases were false and which were fact. After having compiled a considerable chronological list of cases, Peuckert comments, "There remains only one question to be answered in connection with this shocking list: For what purpose did the Jews use the blood?"[55] Moses Gaster, in his review of the volume of the *Handwörterbuch des Deutschen Aberglaubens* in which Peuckert's extensive entry on "Ritualmord" appeared, remarked scathingly, "It is unfortunate that this volume should be disfigured by a disgraceful article on the foul blood-libel accusation of which author, publisher, and editors ought to be thoroughly ashamed."[56]

If folklorists considered the blood libel legend credible, then it is no wonder that various folk groups did so as well. It is, however, disheartening to realize that the legend has continued to exert its maleficent influence well into the twentieth century. A book published in Russia in 1917 recapitulating the Beilis trial in Kiev in 1913 made the following shameful statement: "The fanatic murder committed by the *Zhidi* [Yids] in order to obtain Christian blood is not a legend even in the twentieth century; it is not a blood libel; it is a terrible reality."[57] The lie and legend also surfaced in the United States. Besides the

Massena incident of 1928, among others, there was also a pamphlet which claimed that the 1932 kidnapping of Charles A. Lindbergh's baby was an instance of Jewish ritual murder.[58]

The striking revival or perpetuation of the blood libel legend in the twentieth century was very much nurtured by Nazi Germany. The legend was obviously made to order for anti-Semitic propaganda efforts. Leaflets circulated in Berlin and Dresden in 1933 telling of ritual murder accusations and calling for the prosecution of Jews.[59] A special ritual murder of *Der Stürmer* was published in May of 1934. The campaign of hate continued throughout World War II. Nazi researcher Hellmut Schramm compiled a massive 475-page collection of blood libel legends entitled *Der jüdische Ritualmord*. Published in 1943, the book struck a responsive chord. Here is part of a letter dated 19 May 1943, and addressed to SS Gruppenführer Dr. Kaltenbrunner, chief of police in Berlin:[60]

> Dear Kaltenbrunner,
>
> I have ordered a large number of copies of the book *Jewish Ritual Murder* and I have distributed them to individuals up to the rank of *Standartenführer* [SS colonel]. . . . We should proceed to investigate ritual murders among the Jews with respect to those who have not yet been evacuated. Every case discovered should be submitted to me. We will organize then several trials for this category of crime. The problem of ritual murder ought to be treated by experts in such countries as Rumania, Hungary, and Bulgaria. I have the idea that we could pass on these ritual murder cases to the press in order to facilitate the evacuation of Jews from these countries . . . .
>
> [The letter concludes:] In short, I am of the opinion that we could give anti-Semitism an incredible virulence with the help of anti-Semitic propaganda in English and perhaps even in Russian by giving huge publicity to ritual murders.
>
> [Signed) Heil Hitler!
> Heinrich Himmler

But the blood libel legend did not end with the end of World War II either in Germany or anywhere else where anti-Semitism flourishes. In November of 1960, Golda Meir, addressing Israel's Knesset specifically protested against blood libel charges appearing in the official newspaper of the Soviet Republic of Daghestan, which accused Jews of using the blood of Moslem children for ritual purposes—Moslems being the predominant group in Daghestan. Soviet authorities apparently ignored a delegation sent to Moscow seeking a retraction.[61] The legend may have been Christian in origin but it also can function in a Moslem context. In 1985, Mustafa Tlas, then Defense Minister and Deputy Prime Minister of Syria, holder of a law degree and at one time a doctoral candidate at the Sorbonne, published a book in Arabic entitled *The Matza of Zion,* a two-hundred-page book which revives the 1840 Damascus legend. A quote from the book provided by the Simon Wiesenthal Center in Los Angeles, which sought to alert people about the existence of this updated version of the legend, reads: "From that moment on every mother warned her child: Do not stray far from home. The Jew may come by and put you in his sack to kill you and suck your blood for the Matza of Zion."

It is not my purpose in this essay to document all the countless cases of blood libel which have occurred or even to demonstrate how the legend may have encouraged prostitutes or unwed Christian mothers to practice infanticide and then blame Jews for the crime. There is evidence that the victims of child abuse or child murder may have been "planted" on Jewish property.[62]

My interest lies in other questions. Why did such a legend arise in the first place? Why has it continued to be popular? Why should it have been believed to be true for at least eight centuries? There isn't a shred of evidence whatsoever to indicate that Jews ever killed Christian children to obtain blood for sacrificial or ritual purposes. We are dealing here not with fact but with fiction, not with history but with folklore, not with life but with legend. But how could such a bizarre legend have come into existence to be used as a continuing basis for cruel prejudice and as a charter for anti-Semitic sentiments?

Psychology is necessary, I submit, for the analysis of fantasy material. Most of the writers who have studied the blood libel legend have tried to treat it historically or rather have tried to show that the legend lacks historicity. I have no quarrel with those of a historical turn of mind, but I remain convinced that historical analysis alone cannot fully explicate the content of fantasy. The question can then be phrased: Why should Christians think that Jews murder innocent children to obtain blood to mix with their matzah?

Some scholars have recognized the need for psychological interpretation in connection with the challenge of illuminating the blood libel legend. Isidore Loeb writing in 1889 remarked that savants searching for a historical origin of the blood accusation would search in vain. "The problem is not one of history, but one of psychology."[63] Among the earliest psychoanalytic interpretations of the blood libel legend was that proposed by Theodor Reik in 1923.[64] According to Reik, the legend represented a displacement of the reproach that the Jews had killed and eaten Christ who was substituting for the father god. The reproach "derives from an unconscious feeling of guilt accomplished by projection. Mankind insofar as it has turned Christian confesses in this legend without any disguise the old tendency to deicide."[65] It is equivalent to the argument between two brothers who have together murdered the father and now want to shift the guilt to each other. But it is not immediately obvious—at least to me—why we are obliged to interpret the legend as an example of killing a father figure, especially keeping in mind that in the vast majority of reported instances, it is specifically a child or infant who is ostensibly murdered.

In a later (1967) psychoanalytic reading of the legend, Seiden argues along similar Oedipal lines to explain ritual murder by suggesting that Christian sons want to kill Jewish fathers—Judaism did historically give rise/birth to Christianity—claiming that this is why the Jew is "the monstruous father who threatens or destroys the lives of his innocent primordial children. He is the guilt-ridden father who must be punished by his imaginary Christian son."[67] In a further articulation of the Oedipal model, Seiden claims, "As a ritual murderer of little children, the medieval Jew thus personifies and reflects the unconscious fear of 'the primordial male child': the child's fear that his father, whose rival he is for the latter's wife (and consequently for his own mother), may one day castrate him."[68] One difficulty here is that the "plot" of the blood libel legend rarely involves a battle for a female mother-wife figure. Moreover, the hypothetical suggestion that Christians want to kill their father-figure Jews would *not* seemingly elucidate such details of the blood libel legend as the Jews requiring Christian infant blood to make matzah.

Rappaport argues in 1975, in yet another psychoanalytic reading of the legend, that "by committing the ritual murder the Jews are to act out the doctrine of the transubstantiation by mixing the blood into the host. . . . By the reference to Passover . . . the ritual murder is acknowledged as infanticide whose repetition is desired for the acquisition of the unlimited life expectancy of the . . . eternal infant on the eternal lap of the eternal virgin.[69] But it is by no means clear why ritual infanticide committed by Jews would ensure eternal life for the infant Jesus.

Finally in 1982, Rosenman suggests that the blood libel legend gives "expression to the adult's desire to destroy enviable youth."[70] Adults thus do to infants what they think infants will want to do to adults. According to this formula, adults believe that infants want to devour their (adult) blood and so to forestall that, the adults devour the infants' blood. Supposedly this parental hatred for their children is projected onto Jews. In addition Rosenman contends, "Also projected upon the Jew in the blood libel is envy of the young sibling who drains all the mother's nuturant fluids, leaving the mother too depleted to succor the subject." Here we find the standard psychoanalytic arguments based upon the familiar parent-child as well as sibling rivalries. Yet the semantic fit, if any, between conventional psychoanalytic theory and the actual details of the blood libel legend seems a bit contrived or forced. A Jungian as opposed to a Freudian reading of the legend offers even fewer specifics insofar as a Jungian might simply label the legend as a reflection of the dark or shadow side of man.[71]

I am persuaded that a more appropriate and revealing approach to the legend lies in the Christian need for a Jewish scapegoat and in the psychological process I have termed "projective inversion."[72] In a brilliant analysis of the legend of the Wandering Jew, Hyam Maccoby has proposed that Christians needed a dead Jesus to worship, but that they also needed someone to kill Jesus, to take the blame or bear the guilt for committing the crime.[73] Although Jews did not kill Jesus (who, of course, was himself a Jew—the Romans did), Christian folklore insists that the Jews were Christ-killers. In this context, the blood libel is simply another example of the same kind of Christian folklore. Christians blame Jews for something which the Christians needed to have happen, a thing which the Jews never did.

Projective inversion refers to a psychological process in which A accuses B of carrying out an action which A really wishes to carry out him or herself. Otto Rank described this process (but without calling it projective inversion) in his path-breaking *The Myth of the Birth of the Hero* in 1909. In standard Indo-European biographies, the father tries to kill his own son. According to Rank, it is the son who wishes to kill his own father (along Oedipal wish-fulfillment lines), but since this is a taboo thought, it is expressed in folklore the other way round, namely that the father wishes to kill his son.

This psychological process of "blaming the victim" is also found in female terms. A girl would like to remove or kill her own mother (so as to have her father for herself), but this is a taboo thought. So in fairy tales, it is invariably the mother who tries to remove or kill her own daughter. In the tale of Hansel and Gretel (Aarne-Thompson tale type 327), it is really Gretel's story. It is a girl-centered tale and therefore it is about a girl's struggle with her mother. In the original *oral* tale, it is actually Gretel's *mother* who sends the children out to the forest to die, but the Grimms altered the tale and changed "mother" to "stepmother."[74] The fight for nourishment involves Gretel and the witch (an evil mother imago) who seduces the children with the orally attractive gingerbread house so that she can eat the children. The struggle ends when Gretel dupes the witch/mother into being burned up in her own oven—a symbol which suggests both the production of food and the production of infants—to have "a bun in the oven" is a conventional euphemism for pregnancy. Or in other fairy tales, the girl's taboo wish to marry her own father is transformed through projective inversion into a father who wishes to marry his own daughter.

In the case of majority-minority group relations, it is typically the minority group which is victimized by the majority group's stereotype or image of the minority group. Blacks are victimized by having to conform to white stereotypes of blacks; women are victimized by having to conform to men's stereotypes of women; and in the present instance, Jews are victimized by having to conform to Christian stereotypes of Jews.

Let us be absolutely clear about this. I am saying that it is Christians, *not* Jews, who would like to commit the blood libel and in a way they do. It is, after all, Romans, not Jews, who killed a savior and it is Christians who use his blood in *their* ritual. The Eucharist is one of the central rituals of Christianity and this is so whether one believes that the bread and wine actually turn into the body of Jesus Christ or simply commemorate Jesus' last supper. Either way, it is an act of patent cannibalism. To incorporate the blood and body of one's savior is at the very least symbolic cannibalism. The doctrine of transubstantiation as found in Roman Catholicism and the Orthodox Eastern churches would seemingly entail literal rather than figurative cannibalism.

The Eucharist is a fairly complex symbolic ritual for it entails not only cannibalism, but also the male usurpation of the female nurturant role. It is men who give their body and blood (no milk is available from males) to nurture their followers. That is presumably why women are not permitted to give the Eucharist. It is a purely male ritual involving the imitation of female nurturance.[75]

For the commission of an aggressively cannibalistic act, participants in the Eucharist would normally feel guilt,[76] but so far as I am aware, no one has ever suggested that a Catholic should ever feel any guilt for partaking of the Host. Where is the guilt for such an act displaced? I submit it is projected wholesale to another group, an ideal group for scapegoating. By means of this projective inversion, it is not we Christians who are guilty of murdering an individual in order to use his blood for ritual religious purposes (the Eucharist), but rather it is you Jews who are guilty of murdering an individual in order to use his or her blood for ritual religious purposes, making matzah. The fact that Jesus was Jewish makes the projective inversion all the more appropriate. It is a perfect transformation: Instead of Christians killing a Jew, we have Jews killing a Christian![77]

Another indication that projective inversion underlies the blood libel legend comes from the supposed motivation for Jews to commit ritual murder. Almost invariably, the anti-Semitic tract will proclaim that the Jews killed the innocent Christian infant because Jews hate Christians.[78] In the language of the 1759 report of Cardinal Ganganelli, infants Simon and Andrew were killed by the Jews "in hatred of the faith of Jesus Christ."[79] We know that in standard projective inversion, "I hate you" becomes transformed into "You hate me." By transposing subject and object, the initial party is left free to hate his or her enemy and furthermore to be totally absolved of feelings of guilt therefore. So the Christian hatred of Jews is neatly transformed into Jews' hatred of Christians. (Another modern example of this kind of projective inversion occurs when men accused of raping women claim that the women victims actually wanted sexual activity. The undoubted power of this projective inversion is such that rape victims are sometimes made to feel that they, not the rapists, are on trial.)

Projective inversion also serves to illuminate the curious detail in which Jews are alleged to need Christian blood to make matzah. First of all, Jews are not supposed to consume blood. Genesis 9:4: "Only you shall not eat flesh with its life, that is, its blood." Leviticus 3:17: "It shall be a perpetual statute throughout your generations, in all your dwelling places, that you eat neither fat nor blood." Leviticus 17:12: "There I have said to the people of Israel, No person among you shall eat blood." As many authors have pointed out, Jews are expressly forbidden to incorporate blood and this is why Kosher butchers take great care to drain blood from any animal to be eaten.[80] English folklorist

Venetia Newall goes so far as to suggest that it may have been the non-Jew's misunderstanding of such ritual rules of blood-letting that led to the formation of the blood libel legend in the first place![81]

The consistency of the Old Testament rule prohibiting the eating of blood may perhaps be usefully contrasted with the New Testament words of Jesus (John 6:53–56): "Truly, truly, I say to you, unless you eat the flesh of the Son of man and drink his blood, you have no life in you; he who eats my flesh and drinks my blood has eternal life, and I will raise him up at the last day. For my flesh is food indeed, and my blood is drink indeed. He who eats my flesh and drinks my blood abides in me, and I in him." The point is obvious: Whereas Jews are specifically forbidden to drink blood, Christians are specifically ordered to do so. This is why Rappaport is correct when he says, "The paradox of the blood accusation is that the Jews are accused by the Christians of consuming blood which is in accordance with Christian ritual tradition, but is trespassing the Mosaic law."[82] But now thanks to the device of projective inversion, we can understand this paradox. In a *Christian* projection, the Jews operate under Christian, *not* Jewish, terms. One has only to compare the highly *negative* image of evil Jews standing with basins waiting to collect the blood from the slain innocent child with the very *positive* image in Christian iconography of Joseph of Arimathea who used a chalice (the Holy Grail) to collect the precious blood from the body of Jesus![83]

The fundamentally Christian aspect of the projection also explains why, as Maccoby reminds us, "the accusation is associated with the Christian festival of Easter, *not* with the Jewish festival of Passover; it was at Easter-time that these alleged crimes took place."[84] Since Easter is the time of crucifixion (as well as resurrection), this might be a period of maximum or intensified guilt feelings on the part of Christians for eating the body and blood of their god. Other evidence that projective inversion is involved comes from the celebrated case of Simon of Trent in 1475 when Jews were alleged to have admitted that they required "fresh Christian blood" because it was a "jubilee year," but as Trachtenberg astutely observes, it was a jubilee in the *Catholic* calendar, but not in the Jewish calendar.[85] The Jews under duress and torture had to confess their "crime" in strictly Christian terms.

What about the blood being used or needed to make matzah? If the story needed a functional equivalent for the Christian Eucharist which involved wine (blood) and a wafer, then obviously the nearest thing in Jewish ritual to the Eucharistic wafer is the matzah. The obvious parallels between the Eucharist and the ritual murder/blood libel were pointed out by earlier writers, but were explained solely from a Christian perspective in terms of the Jews intentionally seeking to mock the Passion.[86] Maccoby puts it this way: "The Jews . . . were pictured as doing in reality what the Christian worshipper was doing in fantasy, i.e., killing a child and drinking its blood."[87]

We can now better understand why the blood libel legend so often gets mixed up with related legends of profaning the host."[88] Using blood to make matzah is in symbolic terms not all that different from making the host bleed. The belief that Jews pierced the wafers making them bleed apparently goes back at least to the end of the thirteenth century.[89] Reports indicate that Jews were persecuted and burned as punishment for this alleged miraculous crime.

Again in terms of projective inversion, it is Christians who profane the Passover meal by claiming that Jews use blood to make matzah. The Last Supper was in all probability a Passover meal, but that historical fact has little to do with the projective fantasy. The Jews did not and do not profane Christian Eucharistic ritual. It is the underlying Christian guilt for orally incorporating the blood and flesh of their god, commonly perceived as the Christ *child,* which makes them project that guilt to the convenient Jewish scapegoat.

As Maccoby observes in his analysis of the Wandering Jew, Christians want Jews to accept the role assigned to them by Christian fantasy, e.g., as killers of Christ.[90] Recall that in the summary of the major subtype of the Prioress's Tale, the story ends with the Jews being converted. This is straight, unadulterated wishful thinking on Christians' part. The guilty Jew should accept his punishment and be converted to Christianity. This is perhaps why so many blood libel legends involve converted or apostate Jews in their plots. When Jews resisted acting out their assigned part in this overt Christian fantasy, Christians became angry, very angry—just as whites become angry if blacks don't conform to the white stereotype of blacks and just as men become angry if women won't conform to the men's stereotype of women.

The blood libel legend is clearly *not* a significant part of Jewish folklore any more than the legend of the Wandering Jew is part of Jewish folklore.[91] The blood libel legend and the legend of the Wandering Jew are part of the Christian folklore about Jews. Unfortunately, because of the very nature of the legend genre—that is, a story set in the modern, post-creation world and told as true—the blood libel legend has had a devastating effect upon Christian-Jewish relations in Europe and elsewhere.

There is yet one more piece of evidence to be adduced in support of the interpretation of the blood libel legend proposed here. To what extent is it reasonable to assume that the Christian celebration of the Eucharist is perceived as a form of ritual cannibalism or murder? Has this perception existed in a documentable form? Relevant here is the fact that it was the Christians themselves who in the earliest years of Christianity were accused of killing infants to obtain their blood to be used for sacrificial purposes.[92] Presumably, the accusation was made by non-Christians who recognized the bloody cannibalistic underpinnings of the Eucharist, although not everyone agrees with this explanation.[93] These charges were leveled very early in the history of Christianity. Pliny the Younger writing the Emperor Trajan circa A.D. 110 commented that he had interrogated Christian prisoners who adamantly denied that they had murdered children and drunk the blood.[94] Tertullian, born in the middle of the second century, who became one of the most important early Christian writers, referred to Pliny's letter in his famous *Apologeticus,* written near the end of the second century, before articulating the charges in somewhat gory detail. He begins his seventh chapter: "We are called abominable from the sacrament of infanticide and the feeding thereon." Then after directing some well-chosen criticisms at rumor, which is what he aptly labels the blood accusation, he tries in the next chapter to show the absurdity of the rumor by recounting it: "Come, plunge the sword into an infant who is no one's enemy, guilty of no crime, the child of all: or if such bloodshed is another's duty, do you merely stand by a human dying before he has really lived; wait for the flight of the new life; catch the scarce-formed blood; with it soak your bread, and enjoy your meal." Tertullian even imagines someone in charge of the ritual murder giving verbal instructions: "You have need of a little child, still soft, with no knowledge of death, who will smile under your knife; also bread, in which to gather the blood sauce."[95] This enables us to understand a wave of persecutions of Christians in southern France in A.D. 177 in which mobs accused Christians of cannibalism. Reports of the Eucharist led to rumors that Christians had consumed someone's blood and flesh.[96]

Anyone the least bit familiar with the simplistic attempts of small children to counter insults by turning the very same insults back upon the initial insulters ought to be able to see how Christians might try to deflect the blood libel accusations aimed at them by claiming that it was instead another group which was guilty of performing ritual murder. In one scholar's words, "Unfortunately Christians, after the Christian religion became dominant, directed against others the calumny once directed against themselves."[97] As we have noted, through projective inversion, it was not Christians who were guilty of murdering the Jewish son of a Jewish father god, but it was Jews who were guilty of murdering a Christian innocent (usually a boy).

Before the advent of psychoanalytic theory and the identification or formulation of such concepts as projective inversion, as defined here, some scholars did intuitively understand the basic psychodynamics of the blood libel legend. The Dutch jurist and philosopher Hugo Grotius, in a letter dated 12 December 1636, suggested that the ritual murder accusation derived simply from the Christian hatred of the Jews and that the accusation was strangely similar to comparable accusations made against the early Christians themselves.[98] Isidore Loeb who was one of the first to recognize that the problem was one of psychology, not history, spoke astutely about the popular obsession with the mystical idea of blood. "Those who accuse the Jews accuse or betray themselves. The Jew is there only to put into action the dream [nightmare] they carry within themselves. They burden them [the Jews] with playing in their place the drama which simultaneously attracts and terrifies them."[99] Loeb appears to have understood that the blood libel legend is a Christian fantasy in which Jews were forced to act against their will.

In much the same way, twentieth-century scholars have understood the issue even if they fail to utilize such psychoanalytic concepts as projective inversion. For example, René Girard in his provocative 1987 essay "Generative Scapegoating" does not make specific mention of the blood libel legend, but he speaks eloquently of the "imaginary crimes and real punishments" of victims, and more to the point, he draws attention to the role reversal of victimizer and victim: "The victimizers see themselves as the passive victims of their own victim, and they see their victim as supremely active, eminently capable of destroying them."[100] So many Christians saw and for that matter still see the Jews.

The sad truth about the blood libel legend is not so much that it was created—the need for such a psychological projection on the part of Christians is evident enough—but that it was believed to be true and accepted as such and that the lives of many individual Jews were adversely affected by some bloodthirsty Christians who believed or pretended to believe in the historicity of the blood libel legend.

Let me end as I began by remarking once again that not all folklore constitutes a positive and constructive force in human society. Folklore is powerful fantasy material and it unfortunately has the capacity to act as a dangerous and all too potent force for evil. I wish I could be sanguine about the blood libel legend's eventually dying out. But the undeniable persistence of this pernicious legend for the past eight centuries must give one pause. Louis Ginzberg, the celebrated student of Jewish legends, probably summed up the problem best in the first sentence of his unpublished 24-page "A Reply to Mr. Pranaitis," inspired by the Beilis case in Kiev: "August Dillmann, the famous oriental scholar and Professor of Hebrew at the Berlin University, once remarked, 'I do not see any use in refuting the Blood-Accusation; those who spread it do not believe it, and the fanatical who believe it do not read the refutation, nor would it have any weight with them if they would read it."[101]

Notes

1. See Rysan 1955.
2. Cf. Cohen 1982:244; Cohen 1983: ln.2. Trachtenberg also devotes separate chapters to ritual murder (1966:124–39) and to the blood accusation (1966:140–5).
3. Trachtenberg 1966:124.
4. Reinach 1892:161.
5. Grunwald 1906:5.
6. Gaster's letter is cited in full in Newall 1975:198–200.
7. Child 1962:240–41.
8. There is considerable scholarship devoted to this ballad. See Michel 1834a and 1834b; Halliwell-Philips 1849 (drawn largely from Michel); Hume 1849; Jacobs 1893–94; Gresham 1934; Beckwith 1951; Woodall 1955; Ridley 1967; Hippensteel 1969; Bebbington 1971; and Langmuir 1972. It should be noted that the blood libel was the subject of folksongs in other countries as well, e.g.,Germany. See Lewin 1906 and Hsia 1988:59–60. For a general account of the image of the Jew in German folksong, see Kynass 1934.
9. This summary follows the research of Brown 1906. For a further consideration of Crown's typology, see Statler 1950. For an entrée into the scholarship on the Prioress's Tale, see Morris 1985. Chaucerians have argued to what degree Chaucer himself was anti-Semitic as opposed to poking fun at anti-Semitism (cf. Friedman 1974; Archer 1984; Rex 1984; and Boyd 1987:43–50).
10. For such a map, see Ben Sasson 1971:1125–26.
11. Poliakov 1974:60. There is some question about the exact number of victims in the Blois incident. See Chazan 1968:15n.4 who mentions thirty-one or thirty-two martyrs.
12. Trachtenberg 1966:125.
13. Kubovy 1964:23–24.
14. Cf. Bloch 1973:121, 353.
15. Roth 1933:523; cf. Schultz 1986:6. For discussions of William of Norwich, see Berger1897; Anderson, 1964; Langmuir 1984.
16. Maccoby 1936.
17. See Loeb 1887; Lea 1889; and Baer 1966:398–423.
18. Trachtenberg 1966:134; Baer 1966:423; and Shepard 1968:78.
19. Anon. 1975:284.
20. Ibid., 283–84; cf. Bishop 1974:105.
21. Anon. 1975:283.
22. Hauser 1969: 120–22; Anon. 1975:284.
23. Hauser 1969:123.
24. Wiesenthal 1951.
25. Despina 1971a:22.
26. Ibid., 26–27. The plaque at Judenstein is reminiscent of similar plaques installed at other sites of martyrs allegedly the victims of Jewish ritual murder. For example, a notice at the shrine of Little Saint Hugh in the Cathedral Church of Saint Mary in Lincoln reads: "Trumped-up stories of 'Ritual Murders' of Christian Boys by Jewish communities were common knowledge throughout Europe during the Middle Ages and even much later. These fictions cost many innocent Jews their lives. Lincoln had its own legend, and the alleged victim was buried in the cathedral in the year 1255.

    Such stories do not redound to the credit of Christendom, and so we pray: Remember not, Lord, our offenses, nor the offenses of our Forefathers." See Boyd 1987:vii.
27. Braun 1973. The importance of such artwork is also attested by Mary Anderson's account of how her curiosity was piqued by a damaged painting she noticed on the roodscreen of an East Anglian church in the village of Loddon and how it led her to write a book on the "Strange Death of William of Norwich." Again the scene depicted three Jews murdering a child. One has pierced the child's side with a knife and is holding a basin to catch the blood. See Anderson

1964:14. For a striking series of illustrations of the martyrdom of Simon of Trent evidently printed in 1475, the same year of his death, see Tessadri 1974:164–65. Similar illustrations appear in children's textbooks. For example, one popular booklet in Spain designed to prepare children for their first communion contains the story of Saint Domingo de Val accompanied by a picture of four Jews and a child. Two Jews are nailing the child to a wall while the other two catch his blood in wineglasses. See Shepard 1968: 74 n.8. See also Bishop 1974 for comparable materials in Italian and French teaching materials.

28. Despina 1971a:17. One may compare this case with that of the cult of Simon of Trent (1475) which was not officially abrogated until October of 1965 when the Archbishop of Trent relayed such a notification from the Vatican Commission for Religious Customs and Observances. See Z. 1967. Cf. the removal of the Werner relief from the Werner chapel in Oberwesel in 1968— the relief celebrated the ritual murder of "Good Werner of Bacharach" in 1287. See Petzoldt 1986:41. For other accounts of Andrew of Rinn, see Hruby 1960–62; and Hauer 1985.

29. Hyamson 1952:49. The Damascus incident of 1840 inspired J. B. Levinsohn to compose a fictional dialogue between a Greek Orthodox Priest and a Rabbi in which the blood libel is discussed at length. See Levinsohn 1841.

30. Ezekiel 1900; Jacobs 1902; Meisl 1930; and Helfand 1980.

31. Hyamson 1952:70, 71.

32. For the papal bulls, see Anon. 1900; Strack 1909:250–59; for an English language text of Cardinal Ganganelli's 1759 report, see Roth 1934; for additional references to Ganganelli's findings, see Szajkowski 1963: 207n.33.

33. Klein 1974.

34. Sorlin 1967: 296n.114.

35. Cohen 1982:43–44; cf. Burbage 1916.

36. Roth 1934:83.

37. Ibid., 85.

38. Vacandard 1912:353, 359; cf. Poliakov 1974:272.

39. Wright 1883; Handler 1980.

40. Nussbaum 1947; Rychnovsky 1949.

41. For details of Masaryk's involvement, see Rychnovsky 1949.

42. This is one of the best-known cases of ritual murder in the twentieth century. The best account is to be found in Tager 1935. For other discussions, see Polak 1949; Szajkowski 1963; Rogger 1966; Samuel 1966; Zeitlin 1968; and Giffin 1980. The case was the inspiration for Malamud's novel *The Fixer* (1966), which in turn was the basis for an American (MGM) film with the same title released in 1968. There is a long history of ritual murder trials being the source of poems, novels, and dramas. The Endingen incident of 1470, for example, evolved into a full-fledged folk drama. Trachtenberg 1966:149 claims that the Endingen *Judenspiel* was one of the most popular German dramas of the seventeenth century. See also Hsia 1988:36–40 for more detail. In the same way, the La Guardia incident in Spain in 1490 inspired a drama by Lope de Vega. For a discussion of this 1605 play, see Shepard 1968:71.

43. See Friedman 1978; Jacobs 1979. For other American instances of blood libel, see Duker 1980.

44. There are simply too many individual case studies to list. See, for example, Chazan 1968 for Blois (1171); Molinier 1883 for Valréas (1247); André-Michel 1914 for a case in 1297; Esposito 1938 for Savoy (1329); Kracauer 1888 and Hsia 1988:14–41 for Endingen (1470); and Menestrina 1903; Eckert 1964; and Tessadri 1974 for the case of Simon of Trent (1475), etc. For a sample of the enormous bibliography devoted to the subject, see Chwolson 1901 and Hayn 1906, who lists 121 separate items, mostly from German sources. For later German references, see Lehr 1974 and Hsia 1988. For Russian cases, see Lintostanskii 1934; Wolpe 1961; and Slutsky 1972.

45. Burton 1898:120; for the list, see 120–29.

46. Ibid., xv; Monniot 1914:315; see also Holmes 1979:49–62; and Holmes 1981:269–70.

47. Slutsky 1972: 1129; Baer 1972:26.
48. Polak 1949: 265.
49. Baer 1972:26.
50. Frazer 1913b:395–96.
51. Ibid., 395.
52. Ibid., 396.
53. Frazer 1913a; cf. Holmes 1981:282n.27.
54. Shepard 1968:74.
55. Peuckert 1935–36:734.
56. Caster 1937:324.
57. Tager 1935:225.
58. Anon. 1938:8; Jacobson 1948:127–28.
59. Tager 1935:xviii.
60. For the full text of the letter, see Poliakov and Wulf 1959:292.
61. Wolpe 1961:22; Newall 1973:113.
62. Anderson 1964:97; Rappaport 1975:109. For a consideration of the blood libel legend from the perspective of parental treatment or mistreatment of children, see Schultz 1986 (pp. 273–303 in this volume). For discussion of how "evidence" can be trumped up, see Strack's "The Pretended Evidence of History for Jewish Ritual Murder" 1909:169–235; or Bloch's "Attempts at Fabricating 'Ritual Murder'" 1973:365–73; or the intricate details of the effort to frame Beilis in Tager 1935.
63. Loeb 1889:184.
64. Reik 1923:128–129.
65. Ibid., 129; cf. Rappaport 1975:113; Rosenman 1977:21.
66. Reik 1923:129; cf. Rappaport 1975:113–14.
67. Seiden 1967:78.
68. Ibid., 145–46.
69. Rappaport 1975:115.
70. Rosenman 1982:243.
71. Liefmann 1951:494.
72. Dundes 1976.
73. Maccoby 1982:167; cf. Hasan-Rokem and Dundes 1986:245–46.
74. Ellis 1983:73.
75. This feature of the Eucharist was overlooked by Schuster 1970 in his psychoanalytic consideration of the ritual.
76. Rosenman 1977:19 mentions "the discomfiture that the Mass, so close to the parricidal crime, calls forth in its celebrants" in connection with the legend of the Jewish desecration of the consecrated wafer, but not with the blood libel legend.
77. Schultz 1986:13 does rightly insist that the blood libel is the product of projection, but she does not explain the legend in terms of projective inversion.
78. For a typical statement, see Desportes 1889:277–85.
79. Roth 1934:83.
80. Cf. Strack 1909:124 for additional biblical citations regarding the prohibition against consuming blood. The lack of Old Testament or talmudic sanctions for Jews requiring Christian blood posed no problem for the true anti-Semite. The sanctions came, supposedly, by means of a secret oral tradition passed on from generation to generation. Cf. Desportes 1889:252–53.
81. Newall 1973: 114. This speculation is somewhat analogous to Roth's conjecture that the blood accusation arose from Christian misunderstanding of the Jewish feast of Purim. See Roth 1933.
82. Rappaport 1975:103.
83. Cf. Bebbington 1971:33.
84. Maccoby 1982:153.

85. Trachtenberg 1966: 137.
86. Roth 1933:525; Trachtenberg 1966:131.
87. Maccoby 1982:159, 155.
88. Cf. Browe 1926; Despina 1971b.
89. Strack 1909:59.
90. Maccoby 1982:167; Cohen 1983.
91. But see Noy 1967 and Alexander 1987 for Jewish texts of the blood libel legend. There is also the curious figure of the Golem (Motif D1635), a clay anthropoid mannikin which in Prague was thought to have been created by a rabbi who employed it to expose ritual murder accusations against Jews and to apprehend the instigators of these blood libels. Cf. Bloch 1925:37; Goldsmith 1981; and Sherwin 1985. I am indebted to Professor Dan Ben-Amos of the University of Pennsylvania for these references.
92. Levinsohn 1841:171; Labriolle 1913; Schultze 1953–54; Cohn 1977:1–9.
93. Cf. Harris 1914:200. Cohn 1977:8, however, is confident of this interpretation when he says, "As it happened, there was one feature of Christian ritual which could easily be interpreted as cannibalistic: the Eucharist." In the light of the argument of the present essay, I am very tempted to see a possible correlation between the point in time when the doctrine of transubstantiation first arose and the initial flourishing of the blood libel legend in the twelfth century. The basic idea of transubstantiation apparently existed as early as the ninth century but it was not fully adopted until the Fourth Lateran council in 1215. Strack (1909:59) suggests a connection between the doctrine and the legends of Jews desecrating the host, but not the blood libel legend itself.
94. Pliny 1925:168 (letter XCIV).
95. Tertullian 1917:25, 29.
96. Schuster 1970:231.
97. Strack 1909:283.
98. Balaban 1930:88.
99. Loeb 1889:184–85.
100. Girard 1987:87, 91.
101. Pranaitis was an obscure Catholic priest who had written a pamphlet purporting to prove that the practice of ritual murder was advocated by Jewish religion and he had been called as an expert witness in the trial of Beilis in 1913. For details, see Tager 1935:199–212; Polak 1949:266; and Samuel 1966:87. A copy of Louis Ginzberg's unpublished essay is located at the Jewish Theological Seminary of America in New York City.

References

Alexander, Tamar. 1987. "A Legend of the Blood Libel in Jerusalem: A Study of a Process of Folk-Tale Adaptation." *International Folklore Review* 5:60–74.

Anderson, M. D. 1964. *A Saint at Stake: The Strange Death of William of Norwich, 1144.* London: Faber and Faber.

André-Michel, R. 1914. "Une accusation de meurtre rituel contre les Juifs d'Uzès en 1297." *Bibliothèque de l'Ecole des Chartes* 75:59–66.

Anon. 1882. *Christliche Zeugnisse gegen die Blutbeschuldigung der Juden.* Berlin: Walther & Apolant.

Anon. 1883. *The 'Blood Accusation,' Its Origin and Occurrence in the Middle Ages: An Historical Commentary on the Tisz Eszlar Trial.* London: Jewish Chronicle.

Anon. 1900. *Die Päpstlichen Bullen über die Blutbeschuldigung.* Munich: August Schupp.

Anon. 1913. *Der Fall lustschinski: Offizielle Dokumente und private Gutachten.* Berlin: R. Boll.

Anon. 1934. *Zur Ritualmordbeschuldigung.* Berlin: Philo Verlag und Buchhandlung.

Anon. 1938. *The Ritual Murder Accusation.* Chicago: Fireside Discussion Group of the Anti-Defamation League B'nai B'rith.

Anon. 1967. "Arab Antisemitism—Blood Libel Revived." *Wiener Library Bulletin* 21, no. 3:46–7.

Anon. 1975. "Persistence of Ritual Libel Charges." *Intellect* 103:283–84.

Apple, Raymond. 1972. "Pesach and the Blood Libel." *Common Ground* 26, no. 1:12–15.

Archer, J. 1984. "The Structure of Anti-Semitism in the 'Prioress Tale.'" *Chaucer Review* 19:46–54.

Baer, Joachim T. 1972. *Vladimir Ivanovič Dal' as a Belletrist*. The Hague: Mouton.

Baer, Yitzhak. 1966. A *History of the Jews in Christian Spain*. Vol. 2. Philadelphia: Jewish Publication Society of America.

Balaban, Majer. 1930. "Hugo Grotius und die Ritualmordprozessc in Lublin (1636)." In *Festschrift zu Simon Dubnows siegzigstem Geburtstag*, ed. Ismar Elbogen, Josef Meisl and Mark Wischnitzer, pp. 87–112. Berlin: Jüdischer Verlag.

Bebbington, Brian. 1971. "Little Sir Hugh: An Analysis." *Unisa English Studies* 9:30–36.

Beckwith, Martha W. 1951. "The Jew's Garden." *Journal of American Folklore* 64:224–25.

Beilis, Mendel. 1926. *The Story of My Sufferings*. New York: Mendel Beilis Publishing Co.

Ben-Sasson, Haim Hillel. 1972. "Blood Libel." *Encyclopedia Judaica*. vol. 4, pp. 1120–28. Jerusalem: Keter Publishing House.

Berger, S. 1897. "Le prétendu meurtre rituel de la Pâque juive (II)." *Mélusine* 8:169–174.

Bischoff, Erich. 1929. *Das Blut im jüdischen Schriftum und Brauch: Eine Untersuchung*. Leipzig: L. Beust.

Bishop, Claire Huchet. 1974. *How Catholics Look at Jews: Inquiries into Italian, Spanish and French Teaching Materials*. New York: Paulist Press.

Bitton-Jackson, Livia. 1982. *Madonna or Courtesan? The Jewish Woman in Christian Literature*. New York: Seabury Press.

Bloch, Chayim. 1925. *The Golem: Legends of the Ghetto of Prague*. Vienna: The Golem.

Bloch, Joseph S. 1973. *My Reminiscences*. 2 vols. New York: Arno Press.

Boyd, Beverly. 1987. A *Variorum Edition of the Works of Geoffrey Chaucer*, Vol. 11, *The Canterbury Tales*, pt. 20, *The Prioress's Tale*. Norman: University of Oklahoma Press.

Braun, Roger. 1973. "La fin d'une legende de crime rituel: Une plaque à Judenstein." *Rencontre: Chrètiens et Juifs* 8:34–36.

Browe, Peter. 1926. "Die Hostienschändungen der Juden im Mittelalter." *Römische Quartalschrift für christlische Altertumskunde und für Kirchengeschichte* 34:167–97.

Brown, Carleton. 1906. "Chaucer's Prioress' Tale and Its Analogues." *Publications of the Modern Language Association* 21:485–518.

Burbage, Thomas H. 1916. "Ritual Murder Among the Jews." *Catholic Bulletin* 6:309–14, 354–60, 434–41.

Burton, Sir Richard F. 1898. *The Jew, The Gypsy and El Islam*. London: Hutchinson & Co.

Chazan, Robert. 1968. The Blois Incident of 1171. *Proceedings of the American Academy for Jewish Research* 36:13–31.

Child, Francis James. 1962. *The English and Scottish Popular Ballads*. Vol. 3. New York: Cooper Square Publishers.

Chwolson, D. 1901. *Die Blutanklage und sonstige mittelalterliche Beschuldigungen der Juden: Eine historische Untersuchung nach den Quellen*. Frankfurt: T. Kauffmann.

Cohen, Jeremy. 1982. *The Friars and the Jews: The Evolution of Medieval Anti-Judaism*. Ithaca: Cornell University Press.

Cohen, Jeremy. 1983. "The Jews as the Killers of Christ in the Latin Tradition, From Augustine to the Friars." *Traditio* 39:1–27.

Cohn, Norman. 1977. *Europe's Inner Demons*. New York: NAL Penguin.

Corve, Karl Ignaz. 1840. *Ueber den Ursprung der wider die Juden erhobenen Beschuldigung bei der Feier ihrer Ostern sich des Blutes zu bedienen*. Berlin: L. Fernbach.

Dal', V. I. 1844. *Ob ubivanii evreiami khristianskikh mladentsev*. Moscow.

Despina, Soeur Marie. 1971a. "Le Culte d'Andreas de Rinn historique et situation actuelle." *Rencontre: Chrétiens et Juifs* 5: 8–27.

Despina, Soeur Marie. 1971b. "Les accusations de profanation d'hosties portees contre les Juifs." *Rencontre: Chretiens et Juifs*:150–70, 179–91.

Desportes, Henri. 1889. *Le Mystère du sang chez les Juifs de tous les temps.* Paris: Albert Savine.

Duker, Abraham G. 1980. "Twentieth-Century Blood Libels in the United States." In *Rabbi Joseph H. Lookstein Memorial Volume,* ed. Leo Landman, pp. 85–109. New York: KTAV Publishing House.

Dundes, Alan. 1976. "Projection in Folklore: A Plea for Psychoanalytic Semiotics." *Modern Language Notes* 91:1500–1533.

Eckert, Willehad Paul. 1964. "Beatus Simoninus—Aus den Akten des Trienter Judenprozesses." In *Judenhass-Schuld der Christen!!* ed. W. P. Eckert and E. L. Ehrlich, 329–58. Essen: Hans Driewer Verlag.

Ehrman, Albert. 1976. "The Origins of the Ritual Murder Accusation and Blood Libel." *Tradition* 15, no. 4:83–89.

Ellis, John M. 1983. *One Fairy Story Too Many.* Chicago: University of Chicago Press.

Esposito, Mario. 1938. "Un Procès contre les Juifs de la Savoie en 1329." *Revue d'Histoire Ecclésiastique* 34:785–801.

Ezekiel, Jacob. 1900. Persecution of the Jews in 1840. *Publications of the American Jewish Historical Society* 8:141–45.

Frank, Friedrich. 1901. *Der Ritualmord vor den Gerichtshofen der Wahrheit and Gerechtigkeit.* Regensburg: G. J. Manz.

Frazer, Sir James George. 1913a. "Dr. Frazer's Disclaimer." *Times,* 11 November, p. 8.

———. 1913b. *The Scapegoat. The Golden Bough: A Study in Magic and Religion.* 3d ed. Vol. 9. London: Macmillan.

Freimut, Bernardin. 1895. *Die jüdischen Blutmorde von ihreniersten Erscheinen in der Geschichte bis auf unsere Zeit.* Munster: Adolph Russel's Verlag.

Friedman, Albert B. 1974. "The *Prioress's Tale* and Chaucer's Anti-Semitism." *Chaucer Review* 9:118–29.

Friedman, Saul S. 1978. *The Incident at Massena: The Blood Libel in America.* New York: Stein and Day.

G[aidoz], H[enri]. 1892–93. "Le prétendu meurtre rituel de la Pâgue juive (I)." *Mélusine* 6:169–71.

Gaster, Moses. 1937. Review of *Handwörterbuch des Deutschen Aberglaubens.* Vol. 7. *Folklore* 48:322–24.

Giffin, Frederick C. 1980. "American Reactions to the Beilis Case." *Social Science* 55:89–93.

Girard, Rene. 1987. "Generative Scapegoating." In *Violent Origins,* ed. Robert G. Hamerton-Kelly, pp. 73–105. Stanford: Stanford University Press.

Goldsmith, Arnold L. 1981. *The Golem Remembered, 1909–1980: Variations of a Jewish Legend.* Detroit: Wayne State University Press.

Gresham, Foster B. 1934. "The Jew's Daughter: An Example of Ballad Variation." *Journal of American Folklore* 47:358–61.

Grunwald, Max. 1906. *Zur Psychologie und Geschichte des Blutritualwahnes.* Vienna: L. Beck & Sohn.

Halliwell-Phillips, James Orchard. 1849. *Ballads and Poems Respecting Hugh of Lincoln, A Boy Alleged to have been Murdered by the Jews in the Year MCCLV.* Brixton Hill: for private circulation only.

Handler, Andrew. 1980. *Blood Libel at Tiszaeszlar.* East European Monographs no. 68. Boulder, Colo.

Harris, J. Rendel. 1914. "The Blood-Accusations against the Jews in Southern Russia." *Expository Times* 25:199–200.

Hasan-Rokem, Galit, and Alan Dundes, eds. 1986. *The Wandering Jew: Essays in the Interpretation of a Christian Legend.* Bloomington: Indiana University Press.

Hauer, Nadine. 1985. *Judenstein: Legende ohne Ende.* Vienna.

Hauser, Jean. 1969. "A propos de Paccusation de meurtres rituels: La legende d'Andre de Rinn." *Rencontre: Chrétiens et Juifs* 3:117–27.

————. 1973. "Les Legendes ont la vie dure." *Rencontre: Chrétiens et Juifs* 8:37–40.

Hayn, Hugo. 1906. *Uebersicht der (meist in Deutschland erschienen) Litteratur übe die angeblich von Juden verübten Ritualmorde und Hostienfrevel*. Jena: H. W. Schmidt's Verlagsbuchhandlung.

Helfand, Jonathan I. 1980. "A *Megillah* for the Damascus Affair." In *Rabbi Joseph H. Lookstein Memorial Volume*, ed. Leo Landman, pp. 175–84. New York: KTAV Publishing House.

Hellwig, Albert. 1914. *Ritualmord und Blutaberglaube*. Minden: J. C. C. Bruns.

Hippensteel, Faith. 1969. "'Sir Hugh': The Hoosier Contribution to the Ballad." *Indiana Folklore* 2:75–140.

Holmes, Colin. 1979. *Anti-Semitism in British Society, 1876–1939*. London: Edward Arnold.

Holmes, Colin. 1981. "The Ritual Murder Accusation in Britain." *Ethnic and Racial Studies* 4:265–88.

Hruby, Kurt. 1960–62. "Der Ritualmord von Rinn—Zusammenhänge und Hintergründe." *Der Judenchrist* 7, no. 3:6–16; 8, no. 2:10–12; 8, no. 2:10–14; 9, no. 1:12–15; 9, no. 2:10–14.

————. 1964. "Verhängnisvolle Legenden und ihre Bekämpfung." In *Judenhass—Schuld der Christen!!* ed. W. P. Eckert and E. L. Ehrlich, pp. 281–308. Essen: Hans Driewer Verlag.

Hsia, R. Po-chia. 1988. *The Myth of Ritual Murder: Jews and Magic in Reformation Germany*. New Haven: Yale University Press.

Hume, Abraham. 1849. *Sir Hugh of Lincoln; or, An Examination of a Curious Tradition respecting the Jews, with a notice of the Popular Poetry connected with it*. London: John Russell Smith.

Hyamson, Albert M. 1952. "The Damascus Affair—1840." *Transactions of the Jewish Historical Society of England* 16:47–71.

Jab. 1889. *Le Sang Chrétien dans les rites de la synagogue moderne*. Paris: Henri Gautier.

Jacobs, Joseph. 1894. "Little St. Hugh of Lincoln: Researches in History, Archaeology and Legend." *Transactions of the Jewish Historical Society of England* 1: 89–135.

————. 1902. "The Damascus Affair and the Jews of America." *Publications of the American Jewish Historical Society* 10:119–28.

Jacobs, Samuel. 1979. "The Blood Libel Case at Massena—A Reminiscence and a Review." *Judaism* 28:465–74.

Jacobson, David J. 1948. *The Affairs of Dame Rumor*. New York: Rinehart and Company.

Kennan, George. 1913. "The 'Ritual Murder' Case in Kiev." *Outlook* 105:529–35.

Klein, Charlotte. 1974. "Damascus to Kiev: *Civiltà Cattolica* on Ritual Murder." *Wiener Library Bulletin* 27:18–25.

Kracauer, Isidor. 1887. "Accusation de meurtre rituel portée contre les Juifs de Francfort au XVIᵉ siècle." *Revue des études juives* 14:282–89.

————. 1888. "L'Affaire des Juifs d'Endingen de 1470: Prétendu meurtre de chrétiens par des juifs." *Revue des études juives* 16:236–45.

Kubbovy, Myriam. 1964. "Matzoh, Red Wine and the Eucharist." *Jewish Spectator* 29 (November):21–25.

Kurrein, Adolf. 1900. *Brauchen die Juden Christenblut?* Prague: J. Brandeis.

Kynass, Fritz. 1934. *Der Jude in deutschen Volkslied*. Greifswald: E. Panzig & Co.

Labriolle, Pierre de. 1913. "Le meurtre rituel." *Bulletin d'ancienne littérature et d'archéologie chrétiennes* 3:199–203.

Landau, Jacob. M. 1973. "Ritual Murder Accusations in Nineteenth-Century Egypt." In Jacob M. Landau, *Middle Eastern Themes: Papers in History and Politics*, 99–142. London: Frank Cass.

Langmuir, Gavin I. 1972. "The Knight's Tale of Young Hugh of Lincoln." *Speculum* 47:459–82.

————. 1977. "L'absence d'accusation de meurtre rituel a l'ouest du Rhône." In *Juifs et Judaisme de Languedoc*, Cahiers de Fanjeaux 12, pp. 235–49.

————. "Thomas of Monmouth: Detector of Ritual Murder." *Speculum* 59:820–46.

Lea, Henry Charles. 1889. "El Santo Niño de la Guardia." *English Historical Review* 4:229–50.

Lehr, Stefan. 1974. *Antisemitismus-religiöse Motive im sozialen Vorurteil: Aus der Fruhgeschichte des Antisemitismus in Deutschland 1870–1914*. Munich: Chr. Kaiser Verlag.

Levinsohn, J. B. 1841. *Éfés Dammim: A Series of Conversations at Jerusalem Between a Patriarch* of *the Greek Church and a Chief Rabbi of the Jews, Concerning the Malicious Charge against the Jews of using Christian Blood.* London: Longman, Brown, Green, and Longmans.

Lewin, Adolf. 1906. "Die Blutbeschuldigung in oberbadischen Liedem aus dem 15. und 16. Jahrhundert." *Monatsschrift für Gesehichte and Wissenschaft des Judentums* 50:316–33.

Liefmann, Else. 1951. "Mittelalterliche Überlieferungen und Antisemitismus: Ein tiefenpsychologischer Beitrag zu seinem Verständnis." *Psyche* (Stuttgart) 5:481–96.

Loeb, Isidore. 1887. "Le Saint Enfant de la Guardia." *Revue des études juives* 15:203–32.

———. 1889. Un Mémoire de Laurent Ganganelli sur La Calornnie due Meurtre Rituel. *Revue des études juives* 18:179–211.

Loge, Christian. 1934. *Gibt es jüdische ritual-morde? Eine sichtung und psychologische klärung des geschlichtlichen materials.* Graz: Ulrich Moser.

Lyutostanskii, Ippolit Iosifovich. 1934. *Die Juden in Russlund.* Vol. 2, *Jüdische Ritual morde in Russland.* Berlin: Deutsche Kultur-Wacht.

Maccoby, Hyam. 1982. *The Sacred Executioner: Human Sacrifice and the Legacy of Guilt.* London: Thames and Hudson.

Maccoby, S. 1936. "Ritual Murder: The Growth of an Anti-Jewish Legend." *Jewish Chronicle Supplement* 168 (April):vii–viii.

Malamud, Bernard. 1966. *The Fixer.* New York: Farrar, Straus and Giroux.

Manzini, Vincenzo. 1930. *La Superstizione Omicida e i Sacrifici Umani con particolare riguardo alle accuse contro gli ebrei.* 2d ed. Padua: CEDAM.

Marcus, Jules. 1900. *Étude medico-legale du meurtre rituel.* Paris.

McCaul, Alex. 1840. *Reasons for Believing That the Charge Lately Revived Against the Jewish People Is a Baseless Falsehood.* London: B. Wertheim.

Meisl, Josef. 1930. "Beiträge zur Damaskus-Affäre (1840)." In *Festschrift zu Simon Dubnows siebzigstem Geburtstag,* ed. Ismar Elbogen, Josef Meisl, and Mark Wischnitzer, pp. 226–36. Berlin: Jüdischer Verlag.

Menestrina, Giuseppe. 1903. "Gli Ebrei a Trento." *Tridentum* 6:304–16; 348–74; 385–411.

Michel, Francisque. 1834a. "Ballade Anglo-Normande sur le meurtre commis par les Juifs sur un enfant de Lincoln." *Mémoires de la Société Royale des Antiquaires de France* 10:358–92.

———. 1834b. "Hugues de Lincoln: Recueil de Ballades anglo-normades et écossaises relatives au meurtre de cet enfant commis par les Juifs en MCCLV." Paris: Sylvestre.

Molinier, Auguste. 1883. "Enquète sur un meurtre imputé aux Juifs de Valréas (1247)." *Cabinet historique* 29:121–33.

Monniot, Albert. 1914. *Le crime rituel chez les Juifs.* Paris: Pierre Téqui.

Morris, Lynn King. 1985. *Chaucer Source and Analogue Criticism: A Cross-Referenced Guide.* New York: Garland.

Newall, Venetia. 1973. "The Jew as a Witch Figure." In *The Witch Figure,* ed. Venetia Newall, pp. 94–124. London: Routledge & Kegan Paul.

———. 1975. "The English Folklore Society Under the Presidency of Haham Dr. Moses Gaster." In *Studies in the Cultural Life of the Jews in England,* ed. Dov Noy and Issachar Ben-Ami, pp. 197–225. Folklore Research Center Studies 5. Jerusalem: Magnes Press.

Noy, Dov. 1967. "Alilot Dam b'sipurei Ha'eidot." *Mahanayim* 110:32–51.

Nussbaum, Arthur. 1947. "The 'Ritual-Murder' Trial of Polna." *Historia judaica* 9:57–74.

Petzoldt, Leander. 1986. "The Eternal Loser: The Jew as Depicted in German Folk Literature." *International Folklore Review* 4: 28–48.

Peuckert, Will-Erich. 1935–36. "Ritualmord." *Handwörterbuch des deutschen Aberglaubens* 7:727–39. Berlin: Walter de Gruyter.

Pliny. 1925. *The Epistles of Pliny.* Trans. William Melmoth, ed. Clifford H. Moore. Boston: Bibliophile Society.

Polak, I. R. 1949. "Mendl Bejlis." In *Thomas G. Masaryk and the Jews: A Collection of Essays,* pp. 257–68. New York: B. Pollak.

Poliakov, Leon. 1974. *The History of Anti-Semitism.* New York: Schocken Books.

Poliakov, L. and Wulf J. 1959. *Le IIIe Reich et les Juifs.* 3d ed. Pans: Gallimard.

Rank, Otto. 1959. *The Myth of the Birth of the Hero.* New York: Vintage Books.

Rappaport, Ernest A. 1975. *Anti-Judaism: A Psychohistory.* Chicago: Perspective Press.

Reik, Theodor. 1923. *Der Eigene and der Fremde Gott: Zur Psychoanalyse der Religiosen Entwicklung.* Leipzig: Internationaler Psychoanalytischer Verlag.

Reinach, Salomon. 1892. "L'accusation du meutre rituel." *Revue des études juives* 25:161–80.

Rex, Richard. 1984. "Chaucer and the Jews." *Modern Language Quarterly* 45 :107–22.

Ridley Florence H. 1967. "A Tale Told Too Often." *Western Folklore* 26: 153–56.

Rogger, Hans. 1966. "The Beilis Case: Anti-Semitism and Politics in the Reign of Nicholas II." *Slavic Review* 25:615–29.

Rokonitz, Heinrich. 1913. "Die Analyse des Ritualmordglaubens." *Der Wage* 16, no. 47:1088–1093.

Rosenman, Stanley. 1977. "Psychoanalytic Reflections on Anti-Semitism." *Journal of Psychology and Judaism* 1, no. 2:3–23.

———. 1982. "Psychoanalytic Knowledge, Jewish Identity, and Germanic Anti-Semitic Legends." *American Journal of Psychoanalysis* 42:239–48.

Roth, Cecil. 1933. "The Feast of Purim and the Origins of the Blood Accusation." *Speculum* 8:520–26.

———. 1934. *The Ritual Murder Libel and the Jew: The Report by Cardinal Lorenzo Ganganelli (Pope Clement XIV).* London: Woburn Press.

Rowan, Steven. 1985. "Luther, Bucer and Eck on the Jews." *Sixteenth Century Journal* 16:79–90.

Rychnovsky, Ernst. 1949. "The Struggle Against the Ritual Murder Superstition." In *Thomas G. Masaryk and the Jews: A Collection of Essays,* pp. 154–243. New York: B. Pollak.

Rysan, Josef. 1955. "Defamation in Folklore." *Southern Folklore Quarterly* 19:143–49.

Samuel, Maurice. 1966. *Blood Accusation: The Strange History of the Beiliss Case.* New York: Alfred A. Knopf.

Schramm, Hellmut. 1943. *Der Jüdische Ritualmord: Eine historische Untersuchung.* Berlin: T. Fritsch.

Schultz, Magdalene. 1986. "The Blood Libel: A Motif in the History of Childhood." *Journal of Psychohistory* 14:1–24.

Schultze, W. 1953–54. "Der Vorwurf des Ritualmordes gegen die Christen im Altertum und in der Neuzeit." *Zeitschrift für Kirchengeschichte* 65:304–6.

Schuster, Daniel B. 1970. "The Holy Communion: An Historical and Psychoanalytical Study." *Bulletin of the Philadelphia Association for Psychoanalysis* 20:223–35.

Seiden, Morton Irving. 1967. *The Paradox of Hate: A Study in Ritual Murder.* New York: Thomas Yoseloff.

Shepard, Sanford. 1968. "The Present State of the Ritual Crime in Spain." *Judaism* 17:68–78.

Sherwin, Byron L. 1985. *The Golem Legend: Origins and Implications.* Lanham, Md.: University Press of America.

Slutsky, Yehuda. 1972. "Blood Libel in Russia." *Encyclopedia Judaica,* Vol. 4, pp. 1128–31. Jerusalem: Keter Publishing House.

Sorlin, Pierre. 1967. *La Croix et les Juifs (1880–1899).* Paris: Éditions Bernard Grasset.

Statler, Margaret H. 1950. "The Analogues of Chaucer's *Prioress Tale:* The Relation of Group C to Group A." *Publications of the Modern Language Association* 65:896–910.

Stauf von der March, Ottokar. 1933. *Der Ritualmord: Beitrage zur Untersuchung.* Vienna: Hammer Verlag.

Strack, Hermann L. 1909. *The Jew and Human Sacrifice [Human Blood and Jewish Ritual].* New York: Bloch Publishing Co.

Tager, Alexander B. 1935. *The Decay of Czarism: The Beiliss Trial.* Philadelphia: Jewish Publication Society of America.

Tertullian, Q. Septimi Florentis. 1917. *Apologeticus.* Cambridge: Cambridge University Press.

Tessadri, Elena. 1974. *L'arpa di David: Storia di Simone e del processo di Trento contro gli ebrei accusati di omicidio rituale, 1475–1476.* Milan: Campironi.

Thompson, Stith. 1955–58. *Motif-Index of Folk-Literature.* 6 vols. Bloomington: Indiana University Press.

Trachtenberg, Joshua. 1966. *The Devil and the Jews.* New York: Harper Torchbooks.

Tugendhold, Jakob. 1858. *Der alte Wahn vom Blutgebrauch der Israeliten am Osterfeste.* Berlin:Weit & Co.

Utikal, Gerhard. 1943. *Der jüdische Ritualmord: Eine nichtjüdische Klarstellung.* Berlin: Widukind-Verlag.

Vacandard, Abbé Elphège. 1912. "La Question du Meurtre Rituel Chez les Juifs." In *Études de Critique et d'Histoire Religieuse,* 3d ser., 2d ed., pp. 311–77. Paris: Librairie Victor Lecoffre.

Wiesenthal, Simon. 1951. "Tiroler Ritualmord-Marchen." *Aufbau* (New York) 17, no. 19 (May 11):40.

Wolpe, Gerald I. 1961. "Russia and the Blood Libel." *Jewish Spectator* 26 (April):20–22.

Woodall, James R. 1955. "'Sir Hugh': A Study in Balladry." *Southern Folklore Quarterly* 19:77–84.

Wright, Charles H. H. 1883. "The Jews and the Malicious Charge of Human Sacrifice." *Nineteenth Century* 14:753–78.

Z., G. 1967. "End of a Blood Libel." *Jewish Observer and Middle East Review* 16, no. 5:17.

Zeitlin, Solomon. 1968. "The Blood Accusation." *Jewish Quarterly Review* 59:76–80.

20

ON THE PSYCHOLOGY OF COLLECTING FOLKLORE

(*Postscript*) Chain Letter: A Folk Geometric Progression

Introduction

The question that drives this provocative essay is from Dundes's senior mentor at Indiana University, Richard Dorson: "Why does the collector gather and publish tales?" Known for being a productive writer, Dorson answered the question with three motivating goals: Money, Art, and Truth. Dorson coined the term "fakelore"—used by Dundes in the present essay to negatively describe commercial, cleverly packaged, uncritical, and random collections of stories presented as genuine folklore—and he accused compilers of folklore anthologies, often titled "treasuries" (e.g., the American best-seller *Treasury of American Folklore* by B. A. Botkin in 1944), of being pseudo-collectors. Dorson implied that the gratification they provided was short lived or deceiving, and the money they made was tainted, drawing Dundes's attention to a money/feces equivalence.

Dorson credited some highly regarded collectors, such as Vance Randolph from the Ozarks or Zora Neale Hurston in the African-American South, for using their artistic skills to render the work of folk narrators as literature to a reading public. While satisfying to their readers, Art, in Dorson's view, concealed the raw power of the original source. He favored the natural material in its original context, which, aesthetically, raised images of folkloristic fascination with its "rough," tactile-like stimulation. The true, "pure" folklorist, Dorson declared, was after Truth, in his or her protection of the sanctity of the text performed in the style of the narrator. According to Dorson, this goal offered a spiritual reward, the intellectual honesty of preserving a natural state. His concluding comment about a model folkloristic publication probably drew Dundes's psychoanalytic attention: "The electric *excitement* of fieldwork and chance encounters with memorable folk can enliven the work, and save it from being a *lifeless* parade of texts. Such an ideal book will employ enough Art to make Truth more visible, and perhaps even a little Money will follow" (Dorson 1957). I have added emphasis to underscore the binary of life and death as the equivalent of varied, liberated stimulation (encounters) and uniform discipline (parade). Besides the priority of the vital natural body—apparent in his statement of folkloristic practice in which money, a fecal substitute, "follows" in excretory fashion rather than coming first—Dorson's essay begged the question of how literally to take the identity-forming metaphor of folklorists' "working," indeed "digging," in the field outside the self, and bringing material back to examine and manipulate.

Dorson's answer of "Money, Art, Truth" can be rephrased as collecting, organizing, and publishing data as human products. That instrumental result raised the additional, more probing question that Dundes focused on: "Why collect?" The condensed question has, on its surface, an epistemological implication of the kind of truth gained from the accretion of variants from oral sources. On a psychological level, it provides an appeal to, or motivation of, workers sustaining this kind of effort. Indeed, collecting takes as its root the Latin *collectus*, for "gathering." According to the *Oxford English Dictionary*, it is related to words of pleasure-deriving agency, such as attract, protect, and correct. The collecting praxis is not unique to folklorists, but it has distinguished them, as Dorson's following comment attested: "What the state paper is to the historian and creative work to the literary scholar, the oral traditional text is—or should be—to the student of folklore" (1964). This point has been reaffirmed in folkloristic reference works extending into the twenty-first century (see the entries for "fieldwork" and "ethnography and fieldwork," respectively, in Brunvard 1996 and Bronner 2006b). In previous essays in the present volume, Dundes problematized several assumptions implicit in this statement: the criterion of orality, the separation of literature and folklore, the reliance on text as a unit of analysis, and a historical or devolutionary bias in recovering texts. To turn the analytical lens from the traditional externalized, creative teller to the folklore collector (as a kind of creator who skillfully "draws out" expressions and crafts products from them), Dundes asked for much of the same kind of life-history taking that is called for in contextualizing narrators in modern folkloristics, in order to answer the question "why tell?" (See, for instance, the chapter "Why Do They Tell?" [MacDonald 2006]).

Dundes's essay drew attention to the need for fieldworkers to take a reflexive position, a point later developed in self-reflective studies such as Jackson and Ives 1996; Georges and Jones 1980; and Clifford and Marcus 1986. Since Dundes's essay appeared, there have been fewer psychobiographies of individual folklorists than experiential accounts, but readers can still consult several examples: Bronner 2005b, 2005c; and Mechling 1989b.

Dundes contended that even if more fieldworkers shared more biographical material about themselves in the research process, they probably would not be able to interpret their own motivations, because of repressed desires and anxieties developed early in infancy. The analyst, aware of the personality characteristics of collectors and the symbolic equivalences of the gathering and ordering praxis, might be able to present, in Dundes's words, a "hypothetical framework" for underlying motivations, and, in the process of analysis, bring into consciousness the significance of folklore as allurement and stimulus, in addition to "truth." Dundes viewed folklore as a constructed object in the folklorist's work of rendering oral expression into visible, and usually fixed, readable form. The background for this objectification was Freud's idea of "anal eroticism," based on postulated infantile stages of psychosexual development in which sensuous pleasure was derived from stimulation of the anus. According to this theory, in the anal stage (from about two to three years old), the child builds object-relationships that have meanings associated with what to them are desirable, feces and defecation. Freud suggested, for example, the symbolic equivalences of feces/gifts (A = B) and gifts/money (B = C), leading to the conclusion that money connotes feces (A = C, represented in the phrase "filthy rich").

Other Freudian analysts, such as Karl Abraham and Ernest Jones, elaborated on anal character traits that could develop from the infantile stage, once as the child got older

adults repressed these into coprophilic activities . Dundes, especially, linked anal retention to collectors who "sit on" or "hold back" their accreting material, ordering and classifying it, in order to gain narcissistic pleasure in the act of possession. Another character trait relevant to folklorists, and a hint of Dundes's own attitude, was anal ejection, a
process of molding and manipulating material, equivalent to the professional who "feels
compelled to publish." The anal-ejective personality is more tolerant of dirt, and generally
relaxed and sharing, according to this theory. One of the folkloristic implications was the
methods and materials that attracted the field's workers. Dundes suggested that the anal-
retentive character was drawn to classificatory systems, such as tale-type and motif indexes
(often containing uncontaminated ideal forms and rare specimens), while the anal-ejective
(or expulsive) personality was enticed by the abundance of earthy or "dirty" materials in
jokes (as Dundes was) and possibly in legends, rituals, and speech. The classificatory praxis,
to Dundes, was inward-directed, since it was intended for one's own organization or for
those separating themselves as folklorists, in contradistinction to the anal-ejective personality, who reproduced and expanded the material to share it with others. Dundes made the
anal-ejective argument that folklore is everywhere, and that the folk are us. Rather than
following the convention of separating folk into layers of self and other, literate and nonliterate, and civilized and peasant, Dundes defined folk as "*any group of people whatsoever
who share at least one common factor.*" Hence, in an ejective mode, different *overlapping*
folk identities can be held simultaneously.

Dundes pointed to the popular association of folklore with childhood (e.g., nursery
rhymes, playground games, taunts, and beliefs) as a source of the connection between anality and collecting. Thus, the materials of folklore correlated with the anal stage of development, even though Dundes, the analyst, had made a case for a "modern," expulsive-sound-
ing definition of folklore as something constantly being adapted, and emerging anew, in
all stages and groups of life. Indeed, to establish his symbolist position, Dundes expressed
dissatisfaction for, and the *limitation* of, collection and classification as *an end in itself.*
Collection tended to preserve old materials as precious antiques (he referred to the pre-
modern concept pejoratively as antiquarianism), while his "modern" definition brought
the "folk" and "lore" together as a living, renewable resource.

Dundes understood that readers might be skeptical of his interpretation of the collecting praxis as an expression of anality, or that they might be able to come up with
alternative readings. It could be pointed out, for example, that in the thrill attributed to
fieldwork by Dorson and others, there are frequently hints of intimacy with one's subject and informants. Further, it is possible to sketch an active, perhaps phallocentric,
position of "getting into" communities, finding human "tradition-bearers" through a
process of social intercourse, and using intrusive technology to distinguish folklorists
from the allegedly "passive" historians and literary scholars, who are trapped in the confines of the library with "lifeless" documents and texts (see Jackson 1987 and Goldstein
1964). Folklorists are often in the fertile field (with its generative rhetoric in the literature, such as "harvesting," "gathering," and "hunting" lore), and they may shed the
trappings of the "ivory tower" while engaging in a "hands-on" participant-observation
approach Dorson claimed he did, in his classic account of fieldwork after leaving the
confines of Michigan State University for the "wilds" of Michigan's Upper Peninsula
(1952). However, folklorists share with other scholars the anal-retentive traits of education—as a learned enterprise involving the accretion of books and knowledge—expressed in the lore of a B.S., M.S. (More of the Same), and Ph.D. (Piled Higher and

Deeper). Again, there may be infantilization suggested by the taunt that scholars have never left school! (See Bronner 1995.)

The postscript to "On the Psychology of Collecting Folklore" took a different kind of reflexive strategy, by pointing to the folklore of folklorists as a reflection of their cognition and values (for an elaboration of the idea of the folklore of folklorists, see Reuss 1974). In this essay, Dundes discussed chain letters he received, as they gave him an opportunity to show the stability and change of a folk item. They also attested that folklore, in this case in the form of a printed letter (more recently adapted to e-mails), was not restricted to oral tradition. The chain letter, as a wish-fulfillment fantasy, reflected men's folklore. Related to the previous essay, it also suggested the appeal of accretion, particularly in a capitalistic society, and, arguably, the objectification of women in a phallocentric culture. For discussions after Dundes's essay on chain letters, see Duncan 1976, Boles and Myers 1988, and Fine and Boles 2006.

Lest folklorists think that the folk are always others, Dundes provided a second example of a chain letter as folk letter, this time one transmitted by folklorists. He implied that to be successful, the chain should involve anal-ejective scholars who felt compelled to produce articles. It also represented what Dundes called "literalization of a metaphor," for in setting up the chain, folklorists were linked by their discipline. Receiving scores of reprints, the reward for producing, made one's piles accrete. As a reflection of values, it also expressed folklore's relation, as a productive field, to other "traditional" disciplines. (For a related chain letter in the folklore of folklorists, see Jan Harold Brunvand 1977.) For Dundes, the example of folklorists' folklore underlined essential points about the folk process: it provided a socially sanctioned outlet for desires, feelings, and taboos; and it was renewable, purposeful, and functional, adapting old forms to new or different conditions and transmitting media. Consequently, Dundes asserted, "there will always be folklore." In his exemplification, society needs folklore—and folklorists to make sense of it all.

On the Psychology of Collecting Folklore

Within recent decades, professional folklorists have placed more and more emphasis upon obtaining biographical and other background information about informants. A collector of folklore is expected to do more than merely indicate his or her sources. He or she is encouraged to provide just as much pertinent data describing his or her informants as possible. The purpose is presumably to aid in relating folklore to individual bearers of tradition and more especially to cultural context. In contrast to the previous practice of studying folklore materials in the abstract, the sociological and psychological study of folklore is facilitated by this new interest in particular informants. Nevertheless, one aspect of the collecting situation remains singularly untouched. While folklorists may be coming closer to an answer to the perennial question of why individuals tell tales, sing folksongs, etc., the motivation of folklorists in collecting folklore in the first place is rarely considered. Richard Dorson, however, does ask, in an important article on collecting folktales, "Why does the collector gather and publish tales?"[1]

In order to answer this question satisfactorily, it will probably be necessary to study background information on the collectors of folklore. Unfortunately, most of the famous collectors, although they do occasionally give numerous details about their various informants, fail to give relevant biographical material about themselves. In the absence of such material, the psychology of collecting folklore must of necessity remain largely a matter of conjecture. The following consideration of this question is admittedly speculative, but it is sincerely hoped that the hypothetical framework suggested will be supported or refuted by forthcoming data provided by honest self-critical collectors of the future. No attempt is made here to discuss the scientific value of folkloric materials collected nor are the various uses to which folklore may be put considered. *Only the underlying psychological motivation for the collecting of folklore is the subject of the present inquiry.*

It has long been recognized that collecting folklore is akin to collecting other objects. W. W. Newell in the very first issue of the *Journal of American Folklore* quotes Charles G. Leland on the popular opinion of the collection of folklore, "that it amounts to gathering mere literary bric-a-brac and collecting traditionary postage-stamps and buttons."[2] More recently, Louise Pound expressed a similar view, but with the additional remark that folklore was a more worthwhile object for collection than many other materials diligently collected.

> Teachers, clergymen, attorneys, writers, and others often feel prompted to hunt out the traditions, legends, songs, and tales of their own region. Why not? Such persons are of much the same type as those who search for antique furniture, old glassware, and the like. Some may call them dillettantes, but surely their hobbies are acceptable enough; and often, too, their activities are helpful to specialists. Indeed, popular traditions seem to me more laudable for collection than do many of the objects now often gathered ardently, such as match covers, pictures of ball players and cinema stars, and among children, of back of playing cards and even of colored milk bottle tops.[3]

Dorson, however, suggests that the aimless collection of folklore is really not so different from collecting less laudable materials when he states that "A collector guided by no larger purpose than the desire to accumulate new species of texts might as well collect buttons or butterflies."[4] If collecting folklore is one aspect of the collecting tradition in general, then perhaps the motivation for collecting folklore is related to the motivation for collecting objects in general.

At the beginning of this century, it was assumed that there was a collecting instinct and that this instinct was manifested in the diverse collecting activities of children.[5] Later studies of children's collecting sought to avoid raising the question of the instinctive character of collecting, although by and large the feeling was that the assumption of a collecting instinct was premature and that collecting was attributable not to a hereditary predisposition so much as to environmental conditioning.[6] The collecting instinct, therefore, became the collecting tendency. However, the environmentalists had difficulty in explaining why frequently the object collected was of little apparent value (e.g., bottle tops, match covers, etc.).

Probably the most comprehensive attempt to elucidate the rationale underlying collecting activities is that formulated by psychoanalysts. According to psychoanalytic theory, the etiological basis of collecting was anal eroticism. Briefly, Freud suggested that individuals from infancy onward find genuine physical pleasure in the act of defecation. However, at least in Western society, the individual is soon made aware of adult demands that this activity should be strictly regulated. Toilet training consists largely of conditioning an infant to control his excretory activity. Psychoanalysts further claim that this controlling or holding back becomes in itself a source of pleasure. According to Ferenczi, "The excrementa thus held back are really the first 'savings' of the growing being, and as such remain in a constant, unconscious inter-relationship with every bodily activity or mental striving that has anything to do with collecting, hoarding, and saving."[7] Moreover, from the Freudian point of view, the infant has a natural curiosity concerning the fecal material he or she produces. But the infant's attempts to explore and play with this material are almost inevitably discouraged by adults and the child is gradually introduced to a succession of less undesirable substances ranging from mud pies to sand piles to modeling clay and finger paints.[8] From this perspective, "Collecting is a sublimation of anal-retentive desires, and the collector's pleasure in it is a continuation of his infantile narcissistic pleasure in his own feces."[9] Actually, there appear to be two separate contributing factors to the genesis of collecting activity and Karl Abraham makes an important distinction between, on the one hand, the act of excretion which provides pleasure, and on the other hand, the products of the excretory process in which an individual may find pleasure.[10]

Although Freud in his paper, "Character and Anal Erotism," did speak of three characteristics of anal character: orderliness, parsimony, and obstinacy, he did not mention collecting specifically.[11] Rather it was Ernest Jones who referred to collecting when he developed Freud's insights in greater detail in his paper "Anal-Erotic Character Traits." Jones noted that there were basically two opposing tendencies resulting from anal conditioning: "the tendencies to keep and postpone production and to produce feverishly." He suggested that the two tendencies might be termed the "retaining" and the "ejecting" tendencies.[12] Combining these two contrasting tendencies with the possibilities of sublimation and reaction formation, Jones delineated a fourfold typology of anal characterology. He was, of course, careful to say that these four classifications are by no means mutually exclusive.

The first classification is retaining-sublimation and its two aspects are "the refusal to give and the desire to gather." In discussing this classification, Jones makes the categorical statement that all collectors are anal-erotics. The second classification is retaining-reaction formation. Reaction formation, in contrast to sublimation which consists of selecting a socially acceptable substitute for a tabooed object or activity, is basically a total rejection of the original pleasure-seeking tendency. Thus pleasure is found, not in dirtiness, but in cleanliness. Cleanliness is often extended into orderliness. Individuals of this disposition are prone to systematize and organize so that objects may be neatly placed in their proper place. The third classification is ejection-sublimation. Individuals in this category are generous and apt to "give out" material. Sublimation may be evidenced by the desire to manipulate the material and to mould it or create out of it. The fourth classification, namely ejection-reaction formation is somewhat similar to the second classification in that it is characterized by a denial of an interest in dirt. Individuals of this type take little interest in their material or mental productions and often seek to discard or get rid of them.

Although the Freudian notion of anal character is by no means universally accepted, even critics admit that it is "the most clearly-drawn picture in Freud's album of characterology."[13] The relevance of the Freudian hypothesis to the psychology of collecting folklore is somewhat dependent upon the idea of occupational determinism. Among psychoanalysts, there are those who insist that people choose vocations (usually unconsciously) on the basis of particular individual infantile conditioning. In fact, it has even been suggested that anal erotica would do well in occupations involving collecting and systematic indexing, as in positions as museum curators or archivists.[14] An example of an anally conditioned occupation choice might be found in the life of Benvenuto Cellini who, in addition to collecting pebbles, shells, and eventually gems, decided at the age of fifteen to become a goldsmith. Gold is a common symbolic equivalent of feces as numerous folklore motifs testify, and the aesthetic pleasure obtained from beating and moulding gold is derived from an early activity, namely the infantile real or fantasied play with excrement.

Though most folklorists are skeptical of psychoanalysis, to say the least, perhaps some may see the application of Freudian theory to the psychology of the collecting of folklore as well as to the specific methods employed in the treatment and study of folklore. In addition, considerable light may be shed upon the personalities of various well-known folklorists.

First of all, folklore as an object of collection is often regarded as a useless product of human activity. Just as cancelled stamps, empty beer bottles, etc., in one sense represent waste products, folklore has historically also been regarded in much the same, way. For example, when the indefatigable Danish collector, E. Tang Kristensen, obtained a new teaching position he had sought, a member of the parish council concerned said to him, "We won't have you, you take up so much of your time with rubbish. . . ."[15] In fact, folklorists are still trying to convince both the public and the foundations that folkloric materials are valuable and worth collecting.

Another curious fact is the professional folklore collector's insistence that the material be entirely oral. It must come from the mouths of informants, and preferably not from printed sources. In other words, the collector stands ready to gather the precious material as it falls from a body aperture, namely the oral cavity. In Freudian parlance, this might be construed as displacement from below upward. Strangely enough there is often the feeling that as soon as the material is put on paper, it is somehow less authentic. It is also of interest that if folklore is considered as survivals or if it is remembered that folkloric material is often first encountered in early childhood, then collecting folklore is, in part, collecting materials of the past and possibly in particular the materials of childhood. (No doubt many non-folklorists consider the study of folklore as something of a regression to childhood.)

It is somewhat of a surprise to discover that part of the accepted methodology of folklore scholarship may be related to the psychology of collecting folklore. Collecting usually implies some order, namely that the objects collected are subject to some kind of classification. Bearing in mind Jones' second classification of anal character (retaining-reaction formation) with its emphasis upon orderly, systematic arrangement, one can appreciate the following statement, written not with reference to folklore, but about collecting in general: "The striving for form also manifests itself in the tendency of modern collectors to follow a specific sequence in forming and arranging collections, as well as in the desire to complete definite 'sets' or series of exhibits. The nature of these sequences will vary according to the subject of the collection itself, They may be historical or geographical. . . ."[16] The historical-geographical method is, of course, a highly organized and systematic form of collecting! This may be seen by noting the representational or relational aspects of collections in general. W. N. Durost, in giving a basic definition of a collection stresses this very point. He suggests that the use or the value of the object collected is of secondary importance for purposes of definition. A collection may or may not be of practical use or of culturally recognized value. What is important, according to Durost, are the representational or relational criteria. He points out that if an object or idea is valued chiefly for the relation it bears to some other object or idea, or objects, or ideas, such as being one of a series, part of a whole, a specimen of a class, then it is the subject of a collection.[17] One can see that the historical-geographical method entails collecting specimens of a class: for example, versions of a single tale type. The more specimens or versions one can amass, presumably the better the study. The idea of considering an object in terms of its being one of a series calls to mind the ballad collector who specializes in collecting numbers in Child's closed canon. A ballad collector obtaining a Child ballad is like a stamp collector obtaining an important stamp in a certain series. D. K. Wilgus mentions the penchant of American ballad collectors for collecting Child numbers and refers, for example, to Reed Smith's score sheets showing which collectors in which states had collected the most Child ballads.[18]

Another aspect of folklore scholarship relating to the classificatory aspect of collecting may be seen by recalling the elaborate book classification scheme of Samuel Pepys. Pepys collected books (and also ballads) but later shifted his interest to arranging his collection. In a letter of August 10, 1663, he remarked that his chief delight was in the neatness of everything and that he could not be pleased with anything unless it was very neat, which he admitted was a strange folly. He had all his books bound alike and he arranged them symmetrically according to size. In order still to be able to use his library Pepys devised a complex cataloging system which provided for the numbering and lettering of shelves and books. According to one account of Pepys' system, a key catalogue was prepared and "by consulting this for the title desired one could locate the volume's position on the shelves by number: i.e., the first book on the front row on the shelf fourth from the top in Press One would be marked '1.4a.1'"[19] Had Pepys lived several centuries later, he might have compiled a motif index!

One can now see how Jones' classifications may be used to distinguish different emphases among folklorists. Some folklorists are primarily interested in collecting (retaining-sublimation) while others are specialists in a classificatory kind of collection (retaining-reaction formation). It might be noted that the latter's reaction formation is clearly revealed by their opposition to discussing so-called "dirty" folklore, or even acknowledging its existence. For example, classification schemes might very well simply omit portions which have to do with obscene materials. The anal retentive nature of some collectors is manifested by their putting their manuscripts or tapes in a secret or locked place, often denying others access to their materials. Frequently, they refuse to publish. By a curious verbal coincidence (which is probably no accident), one often hears such collectors described as "sitting on" their material. ("Sitting tight" has somewhat the same connotation. "Tight" commonly means stingy in the sense of being reluctant to part with something.[20]) Here is the significance of Abraham's distinction between the pleasure of the act of excretion and the pleasure in possessing the products of excretion. To illustrate this type of folklorist, i.e., one who loves to collect but who hates to publish, is not difficult. (Cf. the two aspects of Jones' first classification: the desire to gather and refusal to give.) One example should suffice. It should not be necessary to state that no disrespect is intended nor is there any attempt to minimize, the efforts of one of the most important collectors of American folklore in the following consideration of Frank C. Brown.[21]

Frank C. Brown was an enthusiastic and tireless collector, but he simply could not bring himself to publish. Though a volume of folklore was scheduled to appear by Christmas of 1914, the first volume of Brown's material did not appear until 1952, years after his death. Members of the North Carolina Folklore Society, not understanding Brown's personality pattern, began dropping their memberships in protest over Brown's failure to publish his wealth of materials. (Incidentally, one of the purposes of this study is to make folklorists more tolerant of the foibles of some collectors and at same time to urge those who have material to make it available to others.) The anal retentive nature of Brown's behavior is apparent in a statement opposing the suggestions made by members of the Society. He said, "I am quite, sure that I am not going to give up my own materials to anybody." Brown obviously felt that the materials, though *taken from others*, were his personal possessions. He is a prime example of the collector described in the following passage written by a non-Freudian:

> All the desires and interests which contribute toward making any sort of individual into a collector are given focus by the fact of personal possession. From the small boy to the great connoisseur; the joy of standing before one's accumulated pile and being able to say, "This belongs to me!" is the culmination of that feeling which begins with the ownership of the first item.[22]

Newman I. White observes that Brown was "tenacious of his manuscripts" and that "he allowed nothing to stop him," a personality trait in accord with the third of Freud's characteristics of anal character, obstinacy. Brown was especially interested in ballads and he took great pride in building up the number of Child ballads discovered in North Carolina. He was very pleased that he had been able to gather more than fifty numbers of the canonical series. However, his pleasure was confined to collecting. His own statement of his attempts to publish confirm his personality pattern. "When I try to write an article, I almost invariably lose interest in it before I get my notes copied. My interest is at fever heat in making an outline and in making a rough draft, but as soon as this has been made, somehow my interest lags and I almost become sick when I feel that it is necessary to tear the thing to pieces and rewrite it." Apparently Brown could not bear to touch anything that he produced. Here also is clearly indicated his inability to part with or destroy anything he amassed or created. This is in marked contrast to Jones' fourth classification in which individuals take little interest in their materials and, in fact, seek to get rid of them. Brown gave only two papers at the North Carolina Folklore Society meetings and in view of his unmistakable anal character traits, it is noteworthy that one of them was entitled: "Treasure Hunting in North Carolina."[23] Treasure is a common coprophilic symbol, particularly when it is removed from the "bowels" of the earth in buried form.

While the anal retentive folklore collector is loath to publish, the anal ejective collector is, on the contrary, often feels compelled to publish. Frequently the publication is extremely "regular." Ferenczi refers to the latter type of anal personality as "tolerant on the matter of dirt, extravagant, and easy-going."[24] However, sometimes the anal ejective seeks to mould or manipulate his material. Here may be found one possible reason for the production of fakelore.[25] The material is reshaped according to the aesthetic standards of the anal ejective. Consequently, coarse or dirty elements are fastidiously "eliminated." If this kind of reaction formation and sublimation is combined with the general anal ejective tendency, then such individuals would be quite likely to publish regularly "treasuries" of doctored or re-worked texts. This is in contrast to the anal ejective who is tolerant of, if not attracted by "dirty' materials (e.g. jokes). The latter would also publish regularly, but the materials would be left pretty much as collected, that is, with the crude elements remaining.[26] This practice would undoubtedly annoy the fakelorist who goes to great lengths to eliminate such details in his or her attempt to deny any anal basis to the collection and study of oral tradition. One fakelorist, several years ago, wrote a letter to the officers of the American Folklore Society protesting the work of a collector who insisted upon presenting texts as they were related by the folk. The true nature of the anal-oral quarrel was unwittingly suggested when the author of the letter asked indignantly if the officers of the Society wanted a toilet in their dining room. Of course, to anyone who felt impelled to reshape or mould material, nothing could be more shocking than to be confronted with the anal reality so scrupulously avoided.

Although, as has been mentioned previously, biographical data on collectors is rarely available, one might, nevertheless, suggest certain possible personality characteristics of collectors of folklore. For one thing, it is very likely that they collect other items, such as books (some of which may be in languages they cannot really read), musical instruments (some of which they may be unable to play), records, bibliography, stamps, etc. Walter Anderson, for example, is a bibliographer and numismatist. Some folklore collectors may have the habit of reading in the bathroom. (According to psychoanalysts, such reading is an act of incorporation intended to balance the material which is lost through defecation.[28] If they are anal ejective and enjoy seeing their material in print, they may very well have the habit of looking at their feces after producing it. (The relationship between publishing and bowel habits was supported by the case of one collector who, soon after he started publishing scattered articles in various journals, began to suffer from repeated diarrhea. It would be interesting to know whether those folklorists who have difficulty in publishing ever suffer from constipation. Unfortunately, there are no data available on this point and it is doubtful if those in a position to provide data would be self-sacrificing enough to furnish it.) If they are anal retentive, they may have the habit of never being able to throw anything out. It has been noted that "An unwillingness ever to throw anything away, while in itself not enough to make a collector, is certainly a characteristic directly related to collecting."[29] Thus it is no surprise to learn that the celebrated Norwegian collector Asbjørnsen is described as being "virtually incapable of destroying a scrap of paper if anything was written on it."[30]

While this by no means exhausts the possible anal personality characteristics of collectors of folklore, it is at least an indication of some possible ones. It is to be hoped that someday there will be enough data to explain more fully the psychology of collecting folklore as well as numerous other forms of collecting activity. It may well turn out that the reasons why folklorists collect folklore are related to the reasons why certain members of the folk collect folklore, the latter in some cases becoming prize informants for the professional folklorist.[31]

Notes

1. Richard Dorson, "Standards for Collecting and Publishing American Folktales," *Journal of American Folklore*, LXX (1957), 54.
2. W. W. Newell, "Gypsy Lore Society," *Journal of American Folklore*, I (1883), 235.
3. Louise Pound, "The Scholarly Study of Folklore," *Western Folklore*, XI, (1952), 100. Harold Laurence Leisure's autobiographical account of his change from an "incorrigible collector of such bulky objects as books, old glass antiques," to an enthusiastic collector of folklore, also attests to the affinity of various collecting activities. See his "American Legends in the Making," *Southern Literary Messenger*, 2 (1940), 334.
4. Dorson, op. cit., 55.
5. G. Stanley Hall in a short communication, "Children's Collections," *Pedagogical Seminary*, I (1891), 234–37, referred to the collecting instinct as an "almost universal force in human nature." He suggested that this instinct be studied inasmuch as it was the basis of much of scientific research, pointing out that even the gathering of data about collecting depended upon this very instinct. The first important study of children's collections was Caroline Frear Burk's "The Collecting Instinct," *Pedagogical Seminary* VII (1900), 179–207. This study as well as subsequent ones are surveyed by Walter Nelson Durost in his *Children's Collecting Activity Related to Social Factors*, Teachers College, Columbia University Contributions to Education No. 535 (New York, 1932), pp. 1–4.
6. Paul A. Witty and Harvey C. Lehman, "Further Studies of Children's Interest in Collecting," *Journal of Educational Psychology*, XXI (1930), 113, 124. For an enlightening discussion of the interrelationship between instinctual drives and cultural environment with regard to collecting activity, see Otto Fenichel, "The Drive to Amass Wealth," *Psychoanalytic Quarterly*, VII (1938), 69–95.
7. Sandor Ferenczi, "The Ontogenesis of the Interest in Money," in *Sex in Psycho-Analysis* (New York: Dover, 1956), p. 271.
8. Ibid., pp. 272–74.
9. Otto Fenichel, "Trophy and Triumph," in *The Collected Papers of Otto Fenichel*, Second Series (New York, 1954), p. 148.
10. Karl Abraham, "Contributions to the Theory of the Anal Character," in *Selected Papers of Karl Abraham* (London, 1948), p. 373.
11. *Collected Papers*, Vol. II (London, 1949), p. 45.
12. *Papers on Psycho-Analysis*, 5th ed. (London, 1950), p. 428, n. 6.
13. Harold Orlansky, "Infant Care and Personality," *Psychological Bulletin*, XLVI (1949), 17. A survey of the Freudian position may be found in Ben D. Karpman, "Coprophilia: A Collective Review," *Psychoanalytic Review*, XXXV (1948), 243–72. For a lucid account of the limitations involved in the application of even a modified form of Freudian theory to a non-Western society, see S. H. Posinsky, "The Problem of Yurok Anality," *American Imago* XIV (1957), 3–31.
14. Géza Róheim has repeatedly maintained that occupation choice is determined by infantile conditioning. See "The Evolution of Culture," *International Journal of Psychoanalysis*, XV (1934), 394, or *The Origin and Function of Culture*, Nervous and Mental Disease Monograph Series No. 69 (New York, 1943), p. 72. The specific suggestion of vocations ideally suited for anal

erotica is made by William A. White in his article, "Psychoanalysis and Vocational Guidance," *Psychoanalytic Review*, X (1923), 254–55.

15. W. A. Craigie, "Evald Tang Kristensen, A Danish Folklorist," *Folk-Lore*, (1898), 200.

16. Douglas Rigby and Elizabeth Rigby, *Lock, Stock and Barrel: The Story of Collecting* (Philadelphia, New York, London, 1944), pp. 75–76.

17. Nelson Durost, *Children's Collecting Activity Related to Social Factors*, Teachers College, Columbia University Contributions to Education No. 535 (New York, 1932), p. 10.

18. *Anglo-American Folksong Scholarship Since 1898* (New Brunswick, 1859), pp. 247–48. Somewhat analogous to the collecting of Aarne-Thompson tale types by folktale specialists. Archer Taylor in his review of Waldemar Liungman's *Sveriges Samtliga Folksagor i Ord Och Bild*, *Western Folklore*, X (1951), 185–86, mentions Anders Allardt who printed in full one example of each Aarne-Thompson tale type.

19. Rigby and Rigby, op. cit., p. 240.

20. Jones, *Papers on Psycho-Analysis*, p. 429, n. 1.

21. I am endebted to Jan Brunvand for suggesting Frank C . Brown as a possible example of a folk-lore collector with some of the personality traits described in this study. All of the data on Brown cited comes from Newman I. White's "The Frank C. Brown Collection: Its History, Nature, and Growth," in *The Frank C. Brown Collection of North Carolina Folklore*, Vol. I (Durham, 1952), pp. 12–28.

22. Rigby and Rigby, op. cit., p. 35.

23. The identification of folklore and treasure is not uncommon. For example, the first paragraph of T. M. Pearce's "Tracing a New Mexican Folk Play," *New Mexico Folklore Record*, IX (1954–55), 20, makes extensive use of the equation: A folklore hunt is like a search for buried treasure: all the clues are present in both, but the secret is illusive no matter how earnest the pursuit. Perhaps with folk treasure the yield is more often productive. My experience in searching for the author of the Las Palomas-Pastores play had all the elements of a treasure hunt. Unlike many a chase after hidden gold, this mystery was solved, and the solution may open the way to solving other mysteries and uncovering more folklore treasure."

24. Ferenczi, op. cit., p. 277, n. 1. In view of the hypothetical partial anal erotic basis of the preju-dice against African Americans—African Americans are commonly considered as being black, smelly, and dirty—it is noteworthy that the few eminent American folklorists who have recently collected African American material are "tolerant on the matter of dirt" and have even col-lected and published obscene, i.e., "dirty" folklore. For the suggestion that there may be an anal erotic reason for African American prejudice, see Lawrence S. Kubie, "The Fantasy of Dirt," *Psychoanalytic Quarterly*, 6 (1937), 404.

25. See Richard Dorson, "Folklore and Fake Lore," *American Mercury*, LXX (March 1950), 335–43, for a discussion of his term "fakelore."

26. It should, of course, be obvious, that for the scientific study of folklore, it is imperative that texts should not be altered or changed in any way by the professional folklorist for purposes of pub-lication. Even the most careful minimal editing risks destroy potential data.

27. Emma Emily Kiefer, *Albert Wesselski and Recent Folktale Theories*, Indiana University Publications Folklore Series No. 3 (Bloomington, 1947), p. 30.

28. Otto Fenichel, "The Scoptophilic Instinct and Identification," in *The Collected Papers of Otto Fenichel*, First Series (New York, 1953), p. 374; Abraham, p. 385, no. 1.

29. Rigby and Rigby, op. cit., p. 97.

30. Reidar Th. Christiansen, "Knut Liestøl in memoriam," *Norveg*, III (1953), 14.

31. The striking similarity between informants with large repertoires and professional folklore col-lectors has recently been noted by Charles Seeger. See his "Who Owns Folklore?—A Rejoinder," *Western Folklore*, XXI (1962), 97.

Postscript

Chain Letter: A Folk Geometric Progression

THE APPEAL OF GEOMETRIC PROGRESSIONS is at least as old as the tale of the origin of chess (Motif Z 21.1) in which the inventor asks one grain of wheat for the first square, two for the second, four for the third and so forth. Part of the interest undoubtedly stems from the unexpected "magical" change from an insignificant initial number, namely, one, to an astronomical figure in a relatively short space of time. In the folktale, the effect of the magical incremental increase is the overwhelming of the king for whom the game of chess was invented. Another obvious source of pleasure derives from the fact that the inventor of the game and presumably of the clever mathematical stratagem receives an extraordinary amount of material reward. These same characteristics of overwhelming an antagonist and of "getting rich quick" are also found in a more contemporary traditional form based upon a geometric progression: the chain letter.

The chain letter, probably one of the best known types of a number of equally traditional letters, has been noted by several folklorists. Halpert showed that the chain letter is popular in the United States and England while an earlier note by Deonna revealed the form's existence in Europe (e.g., France, Italy, and Switzerland).[1] In chain letters, there is a definite structural pattern, a pattern which appears to prevail regardless of the particular content of any one individual chain letter. First, there is a statement proclaiming that the letter is a chain letter. This enunciation may perhaps be analogous to the opening formula found at the beginning of other forms of folklore: "Once upon a time," "Riddle me, riddle me right," "Ready or not, here I come." The formula serves to indicate either the nature of the traditional form which is to follow or the formal moment at which an example of a traditional form begins or both. The second important feature in chain letters is the injunction or order to send copies of the letter to a specific number of friends or acquaintances, sometimes within a definite period of time. The third item consists of a description, usually detailed, of the desirable consequences which will occur if the receiver of the letter complies with the terms of the injunction. Sometimes, a case history of a previous "winner" is cited, which functions as an explanatory motif sometimes does in the sense of providing the requisite "ocular proof" that the procedure is a bona fide one. The fourth part of the sequential structure is a warning. Typically it is in the form of a statement of the one or more undesirable consequences which will result if the injunction is ignored or disobeyed. This portion of the chain letter is often illustrated by a case history, but whereas the case history for the third segment was a positive one, the case history for the warning is definitely negative. Usually it is related how an unwise individual scorned the injunction and how by so doing he became a "loser." The structural pattern of chain letters is thus not dissimilar to sequential patterns found in other folkloric forms. In superstitions, one can obtain good luck by complying with an injunction just as one can incur bad luck by violating an interdiction.[2]

The following examples of chain letters should serve to illustrate the nature of this form of non-oral tradition and to attest to its continued popularity in American culture. In addition, these examples show how folklore can both reflect cultural values and institutions and offer an outlet or escape from these same values and institutions.

In the first text, which is very similar to one reported by Halpert from Murray, Kentucky, bearing a 1955 date, the case history exemplification of the desirable consequence is appended as a postscript.[3]

I

June 20, 1957

Dear Friend :

This chain letter was started by a man like yourself in the hope it will bring relief to tired business men.

This does not cost you anything. Kindly send a copy of this letter to five of your friends who seem equally tired and discouraged.

Bundle up your wife and send her to the man whose name appears at the top of the list and then add your name to the bottom of it.

When your name comes to the top of the list, you will receive 16,740 women. Some of them will be dandies.

You must always have faith. Do not break this chain. One man broke the chain and he got *HIS OLD LADY* back again.

Sincerely yours,

P.S. At the date of this writing, a friend of mine received 556 women. They buried him yesterday. It took three undertakers 35 hours to get the smile off his face.

The content of the letter is similar to the content of many jokes. The traditional ingredients of male impotence ("tired business men"), dissatisfaction with one's wife, and the common male dream of having an infinite variety and number of women available as sexual partners are present. G. Legman has observed that this dream of being "husband of all the women in the world" is particularly prevalent among those who are of an age when they are least able physically to indulge in repeated or strenuous sexual activities.[4] The final postscript confirms the fact that men too tired to conduct business affairs may be killed by excess. It is noteworthy that the fantasy is externally initiated. Within the chain letter context, one does not necessarily himself decide to send his wife away while he awaits scores of other women. Rather, the receiver of the letter is ordered to send away his wife and he is thus free from the guilt and responsibility of making a decision of this kind. Similarly, he does not himself seek other women. Rather other women are automatically sent to him. Presumably the "logic" is: how can anyone be responsible for what others send him in the mail? This function of the chain letter in projecting individual desires to an impersonal, mechanical process which requires the individual to fulfill his desires is also manifest in the following example.

II

March 19, 1962

Dear Alan,

Please send a reprint of your latest paper on ethnology and/or cultural anthropology, folklore, linguistics, archaeology, etc., to the first named person on the list below, and copies of this letter to four folklorists, anthropologists, etc., whom you know, within three days.

In about 26 days—if you answer promptly—you should receive 272 reprints from some amazing people.

Please don't spoil this game, which has been going since 1956!

In your four letters copy the following list, leaving out the top name, and adding your own name at the bottom.

Yours sincerely,
Butler Waugh
Assistant Professor of English

1. Prof. Wayland D. Hand, University of California, Los Angeles 24, California, U.S.A.

2. Prof. Francis Lee Utley, Dept. of English, Ohio State University, Columbus 14, Ohio, U.S.A.

3. Prof. Holger Olof Nygard, Dept. of English, Duke University, Durham, N.C., U.S.A.

4. Prof. Butler Waugh, Dept. of English, University of Florida, Gainesville, Florida, U.S.A.

This chain letter is one which circulated recently among folklorists.[5] One reason for noting this particular specimen is that it demonstrates that professional folklorists are folk themselves. There is not only the folklore of folklore; there is the folklore of folklorists! Folklorists do not simply study tradition; they enjoy and participate in it as well, an occupational characteristic which does not necessarily put folklorists in a favorable scholarly light—at least when viewed by suspicious colleagues in other disciplines. However, if students of folksong sing folksongs, if students of jokes like to tell jokes, then it should really come as no surprise to learn that folklorists send chain letters. Of greater import is the evidence supporting the notion that a group will shape a particular folkloric form to fit their own peculiar needs. Folklorists, as a folk group, have transmuted the chain letter into a device for advertising their scholarly accomplishments. The folklorists' chain letter like the "publish or perish" oikotype of the "do or die" proverb is a reflector of culture and of values, in this instance the culture and values of American folklorists. By means of the chain letter, folklorists ask their friends to send a reprint of their last paper to colleagues. (Heaven help the poor soul whose "last" reprint is dated several years back and of course breaking the chain might be construed as a tacit admission that one either had no recent reprint at all or had no recent reprint he or she felt worthy of circulating to professional peers.) Appropriately enough, the material reward consists of scores of reprints. One of the principal functions of folklore is the reinforcement of traditional values. Among the folk of academe, one of the unwritten laws is that one must not only publish, but one must let others know that one is publishing. One of the conventional means of accomplishing this is by sending offprints of articles to colleagues and department chairs. One can see then that the folklorists' chain letter makes mandatory what the folklorist wishes, but the motivation is externalized and removed from the individual, just as was the case in the first chain letter example. In folklore, the unpermitted or the unstated is permitted and stated. Heterosexual body contact might be taboo under ordinary circumstances to those performing folk dances, but by participating in folk dances, the order for body contact is dictated from without (e.g., from a "caller"). Thus in the present instance, folklorists as members of an academic community might not like to admit that sending out reprints is a mechanical procedure done for personal and material gain. However, the chain letter, like other forms of folklore, provides a socially sanctioned outlet or excuse for the overt expression of an actual wish. By using the chain letter, the individual folklorist is free to feel that he or she is sending out a reprint, not because he or she wants to, but because he or she has to. Clearly the fact that folklore so often "obliges" us to do what we really want to do is one reason why there will always be folklore. . . .

Notes

1. Herbert Halpert, "Chain Letters," *Western Folklore*, XV (1956), 287–289. Halpert cites texts from Wright's *English Folklore* and Hyatt's *Folklore from Adams County, Illinois,* but neglects to mention W. Deonna's account of the "Chaine de bonheur" in his "Superstitions actuelles," *Revue d'Ethnographic et des Traditions Populaires*, IX (1928), 213–216.
2. For further discussion of this pattern, see my "Structural Typology of North American Indian Folktales," *Southwestern Journal of Anthropology*, XIX (1963), 121–130.
3. I am indebted to Geraldine Gosche of Oakland, California, for this text. She collected it in 1958 in Berkeley, California.
4. G. Legman, *The Horn Book: Studies in Erotic Folklore and Bibliography* (New Hyde Park, New York, 1964), p. 110.
5. In view of the pattern analysis discussed previously, it is of interest that Professor Waugh felt impelled to add the following comment to the typewritten carbon copy he sent me: "This business is absurd—but pass it on under threat of the folklorist's curse." The principal feature lacking in the letter was the warning and thus Professor Waugh was quite right, in terms of structure, to supplement the letter as he did. I received similar letters from folklorists Jan Brunvand and Paula de Carvalho-Neto. The names in the latter's letter: Carmen Roy, Marius Barbeau, and Roger Pinon indicate that the letter had considerable international circulation.

E

F